Talcott Parsons
1902–1979
Dean of American sociology during the mid-1900s promoted a conception of society as a social system with subsystems of human action, in which individuals fulfill the systems needs of the societies of which they are members.

Samuel Delbert Clark
1910–2003
Canadian historical sociologist and educator founded the University of Toronto's Department of Sociology (1963).

Robert K. Merton
1910–2003
American sociologist and educator developed middle-range theory, which sought to bridge the gap between high-level theories and low-level observations.

Guy Rocher
b. 1924
Canadian educator and pioneer in the sociology of education, law, and medical ethics has sat on several commissions and boards of inquiry at the provincial and federal levels and wrote a lucid and highly regarded introduction to the discipline, Introduction à la sociologie *(1968).*

Erving Goffman
1922–1982
Canadian-born sociologist advanced microsociology and studied social roles, deviance, stigma, and 'total institutions'.

Michel Foucault
1926–1984
French thinker, famous for historical studies of madness and civilization, imprisonment and sexuality, portrayed science as an arbitrary instrument for control and power, and constructed a theory of power as actions and relations.

Herbert Blumer
1900–1987
American student of Mead, who coined the term 'symbolic interactionism'.

Theodor Adorno
1903–1969
German Frankfurt School philosopher argued that philosophical authoritarianism is inevitably oppressive.

John Porter
1921–1979
Canadian sociologist examined connections between ethnicity and barriers of opportunity in Canadian society, which he characterized as a 'vertical mosaic'.

Dorothy Smith
b. 1926
English-born Canadian sociologist developed standpoint theory, which sought to frame and understand everyday life from a feminist point of view.

Everett C. Hughes
1897–1983
American sociologist studied economic organization, work and occupations, and ethnic relations, including a key study of the 'ethnic division of labour' in Quebec.

Oswald Hall
1908–2007
Canadian educator researched the sociology of work and medicine and served on the Royal Commission on Health Services and the Royal Commission on Bilingualism and Biculturalism.

C. Wright Mills
1916–1962
American critical sociologist studied power structure in the US and coined the term 'sociological imagination'.

Jean Baudrillard
1929-2007
French cultural theorist influenced postmodernism and showed how capitalist consumer society erases distinctions between reality and reference, leading to a loss of meaning.

Margrit Eichler
b. 1942
Canadian sociologist has studied family sociology, feminist research methods, and gender inequality.

1900 — **1950**
2000

1960
Negroes in Toronto: A Sociological Study of a Minority Group, by US-born Canadian activist and Ontario Human Rights Commissioner Daniel Hill (1923–2003)

1962
The Developing Canadian Community, a study of US influence on Canada's cultural development, by S.D. Clark

1964
'Institutional Completeness of Ethnic Communities and Personal Relations of Immigrants', an examination of why and how some ethnocultural communities survive while others do not, by Canadian sociologist Raymond Breton

1965
Lament for a Nation: The Defeat of Canadian Nationalism, an examination of the dangers of Canadian cultural absorption by the US, by Canadian social philosopher George Grant (1918–1988)

The Vertical Mosaic: An Analysis of Social Class and Power in Canada, a ground-breaking and influential study of Canada's class structure, depicting a complex system of groups organized in hierarchy across lines of ethnicity and class, by John Porter

1968
Introduction to the Mathematics of Population, a landmark contribution to the field of population studies, by Canadian demographer Nathan Keyfitz (b. 1913)

1969
Doctors and Doctrines: The Ideology of Medical Care in Canada, an examination of Canada's healthcare system in terms of role strains, conflict in values, and relations to the public, by Bernard Blishen

1975
The Rise of a Third Party: A Study in Crisis Politics (1975), a sociological analysis of the growth of nationalist politics in Quebec, by Maurice Pinard

The Canadian Corporate Elite: An Analysis of Economic Power, a response to *The Vertical Mosaic* examining corporate elites and their impact on class and social stratification, by Wallace Clement

1978
The Double Ghetto: Canadian Women and their Segregated Work, a study of gender inequality in the labour force and the home, by Pat Armstrong and Hugh Armstrong

1983
Green Gold: The Forest Industry in British Columbia (1983), an early study in the social, political, and economic aspects of a particular staples industry, the BC forest industry, by Patricia Marchak

1986
'The "Wets" and the "Drys": Binary Images of Women and Alcohol in Popular Culture', a study of gender inequalities and mass media, by Thelma McCormack

1987
The Everyday World as Problematic: A Feminist Sociology, an argument that sociology has developed without proper insight into women's experiences, by Dorothy Smith

1988
Quebec Society: Tradition, Modernity, and Nationhood, a study of Quebec's rising middle class and the separatist movement, by Hubert Guindon

Families in Canada Today: Recent Changes and Their Policy Implications, a study of how the way we think and talk about gender roles pre-empts useful changes in family policy, by Margrit Eichler

1989
The Social Significance of Sport, a study of how individuals take control of and participate in society through voluntary association, by James Curtis (1943–2005)

1996
The Barbershop Singer: Inside the Social World of a Musical Hobby, a study of leisure and hobbies in society, by Robert Stebbins

2002
The Impact of Feminism on Canadian Sociology (2002), a study of the rise of sociology as a feminist discipline, by Margrit Eichler

2004
Perspectives de Recherche en Santé des Populations au Moyen de Données Complexes (2004), an analysis of the Quebec healthcare system, by Paul Bernard

▶ Milestones in Canadian Sociology

Principles of
Sociology
Canadian Perspectives

Second Edition

Principles of
Sociology
Canadian Perspectives

Edited by

Lorne Tepperman • James Curtis

OXFORD
UNIVERSITY PRESS

OXFORD

UNIVERSITY PRESS

70 Wynford Drive, Don Mills, Ontario M3C 1J9
www.oupcanada.com

Oxford University Press is a department of the University of Oxford.
It furthers the University's objective of excellence in research, scholarship,
and education by publishing worldwide in

Oxford New York
Auckland Cape Town Dar es Salaam Hong Kong Karachi
Kuala Lumpur Madrid Melbourne Mexico City Nairobi
New Delhi Shanghai Taipei Toronto

With offices in
Argentina Austria Brazil Chile Czech Republic France Greece
Guatemala Hungary Italy Japan Poland Portugal Singapore
South Korea Switzerland Thailand Turkey Ukraine Vietnam

Oxford is a trade mark of Oxford University Press
in the UK and in certain other countries

Published in Canada
by Oxford University Press

Library and Archives Canada Cataloguing in Publication
Principles of sociology : Canadian perspectives / edited by Lorne Tepperman
and James Curtis. — 2nd edn.

Includes bibliographical references and index.
ISBN 978-0-19-542982-4

1. Sociology—Textbooks. 2. Canada—Social conditions—1991– —Textbooks.
3. Canada—Social conditions—Statistics. I. Tepperman, Lorne, 1943– II. Curtis,
James E., 1943–2005

HM586.P75 2009   301   C2009-900243-4

Cover Image: John Glustina / Getty Images

1 2 3 4 – 12 11 10 09
This book is printed on permanent (acid-free) paper ∞.
Printed in the United States of America

Contents •••••••

● **Part III** **Social Institutions** ● ● ● ● ● ●

● Part IV   Canadian Society ● ● ● ● ● ● and the Global Context

Boxed Features

Principles of Sociology features dozens of theme boxes—arranged in four different types and scattered throughout the text—to highlight compelling issues and stories that are at the heart of sociological inquiry.

GLOBAL ISSUES
A Sociological Perspective on Cases from Around the World

HUMAN DIVERSITY
World Views and Ways of Life of Different Cultures and Social Groups

SOCIOLOGY IN ACTION
Research that Helps Us Understand Our World

OPEN FOR DISCUSSION
Contemporary Social Issues and Debates

From the Publisher

In preparing this edition of *Principles of Sociology: Canadian Perspectives*, we have, from the start, kept in mind one paramount goal: to produce the most authoritative, comprehensive, yet accessible and dynamic introduction to sociology available to Canadian students.

In streamlining the material for this publication, we have combined a number of the chapters from the second edition of *Sociology: A Canadian Perspective* to provide a tighter, more concise editorial focus. We think you will find that, for example, William Michelson's chapter on urbanization blends seamlessly with Frank Trovato's work on population and Keith Warriner's writing about the environment. Similarly, merging the contributions of Bruce Arai (research methods), Neil McLaughlin and Antony Puddephatt (sociological theory), and Lorne Tepperman (sociology, the discipline) has created a cohesive and more theoretical introduction to the text as a whole. We have also brought on board several new contributors, whose perspectives on subjects ranging from gender and mass media to religion and globalization give this edition a broader focus and greater depth of coverage.

This revision builds on the strengths of its predecessor and incorporates many features designed to enhance usefulness and interest for students and instructors alike. We hope that as you browse through the pages that follow, you will see why we believe *Principles of Sociology* is the most exciting and informative textbook for Canadian sociology students.

● **A Contributed Text,**   ● ● ● ● ● ●
    A Cohesive Approach

▶ Because the roles and identities we maintain as individuals so closely relate to the groups and organizations that we participate in on a daily basis, Cheryl Albas and Dan Albas's work on statuses, roles, and identities pairs naturally with Lorne Tepperman's study of organizations.

▶ Combining Peter Sinclair's examination of politics and political movements with John Veugelers and Randle Hart's work on social movements has produced a thorough and detailed study of the Canadian political structure and its effect on Canadian sociology.

● Leading Canadian Sociologists ● ● ● ● ●

▶ Canadians have made unique contributions to the study of sociology worldwide. Sociologists like Vincent F. Sacco (deviance), Terry Wotherspoon (education), and Maureen Baker (families), writing in their areas of expertise, go beyond introducing the key concepts and terminology of sociology as an academic subject by using those concepts to shed light on Canadian society and Canada's place in the world.

● New Contributing Authors ● ● ● ● ● ●

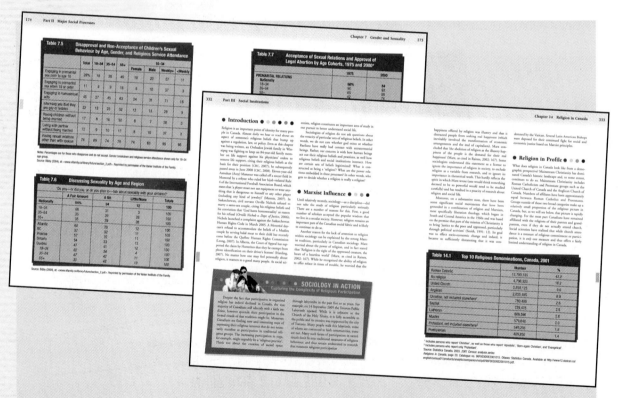

▶ For the second edition, we are delighted to welcome aboard several new contributing authors: Patrizia Albanese (gender and sexuality), Nikolaos Liodakis (ethnic and race relations), David Young (mass media and communication), Lori Beaman (religion), and Satoshi Ikeda (globalization).

● A Global Perspective ● ● ● ● ● ● ●

▶ Although this is a textbook written by and for Canadians, the editors and authors never forget that Canada is but one small part of a vast, diverse, and endlessly fascinating social world. Along with Canadian data, examples, and illustrations, a wealth of information about how humans live and interact with the world around them is presented in every chapter.

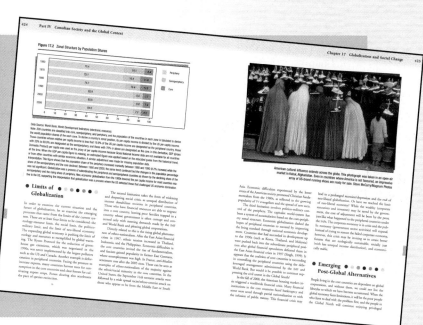

● Contemporary Design ● ● ● ● ● ●

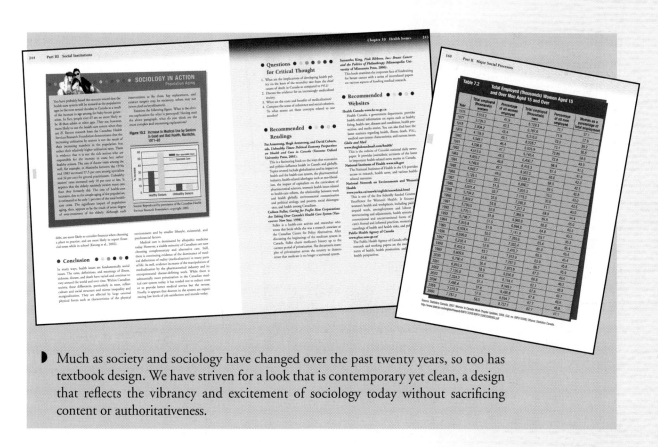

▶ Much as society and sociology have changed over the past twenty years, so too has textbook design. We have striven for a look that is contemporary yet clean, a design that reflects the vibrancy and excitement of sociology today without sacrificing content or authoritativeness.

● **Aids to Student Learning** ● ● ● ● ● ●

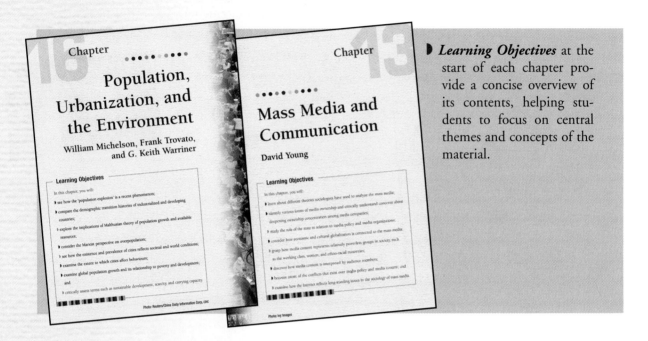

▶ *Learning Objectives* at the start of each chapter provide a concise overview of its contents, helping students to focus on central themes and concepts of the material.

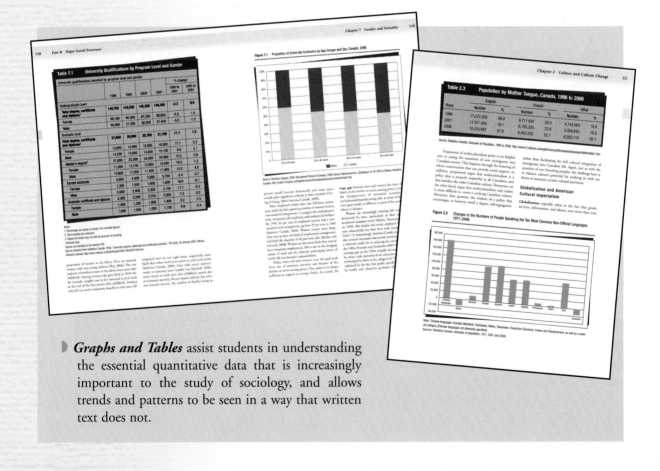

▶ *Graphs and Tables* assist students in understanding the essential quantitative data that is increasingly important to the study of sociology, and allows trends and patterns to be seen in a way that written text does not.

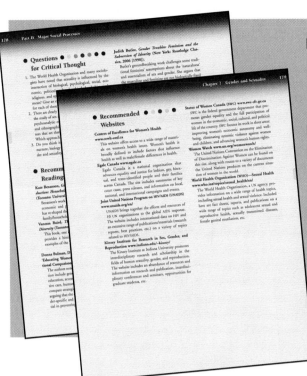

▶ *Questions for Critical Thought*, at the end of each chapter, draw out key issues while encouraging readers to draw their own conclusions about sociological issues.

▶ *Annotated Recommended Readings*, listed at the end of each chapter, point students toward useful sources for further research and study.

▶ *Annotated Recommended Websites* direct readers to additional resources, with useful commentary that will assists students as they navigate through the tremendous volume of information available online.

▶ *Theme Boxes* illustrate important points and provide examples of how sociological research sheds light on the 'real world'.

• *Sociology in Action* boxes show how sociological research can help us better understand the everyday world.

• *Open for Discussion* boxes focus understanding of core concepts through contemporary social issues and debates.

• *Global Issues* boxes show the various opinions and discussions held by sociologists on matters of global importance.

• *Human Diversity* boxes show students how issues of human diversity impact life at local, national, and global levels.

● Aids to Student Learning ● ● ● ● ● ●

▶ New!

A Content Correlation Guide identifies recurring topics and theories, enabling readers to trace key themes of sociological inquiry through different chapters.

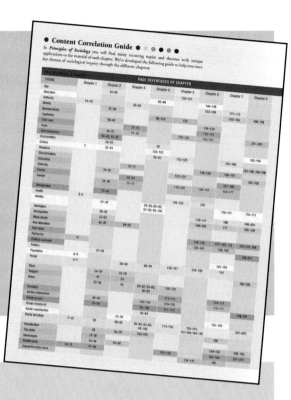

A century ago, schools were often segregated by class and age. Here, young ladies are learning to sketch a live model—a skill that will give them cultural capital when they pass into adult social life.
Courtesy of the Bishop Strachan School Museum & Archives.

▶ New!

Time to Reflect boxes—in every chapter—encourage readers to pause to consider the material they have just read.

● Supplements ● ● ● ● ●

For Instructors

▶ **An Instructor's Manual** includes comprehensive outlines of the text's various parts and chapters, additional questions for encouraging class discussion, and suggestions on how to use videos to enhance classes.

▶ **A Test bank** offers a comprehensive set of multiple-choice, true/false, short-answer, and essay questions, with suggested answers, for every chapter.

▶ **PowerPoint® slides**, summarizing key points from each chapter and incorporating figures and tables from the textbook, are available to adopters of the text. Hundreds of slides are available to download and edit for customized lectures.

Instructors should contact their Oxford University Press sales representative for details on these supplements and for login and password information.

For Students

▶ **The Student Companion Website** offers self-testing study questions, annotated links to useful resources, and much more. Go to **www.oupcanada.com/PrinciplesofSociology** and follow the links!

▶ **MP3 clips of selected CBC Radio One programs** can be downloaded to your MP3 player. Every one of the scores of program clips has been specially chosen to complement the material presented in a related chapter of the textbook.

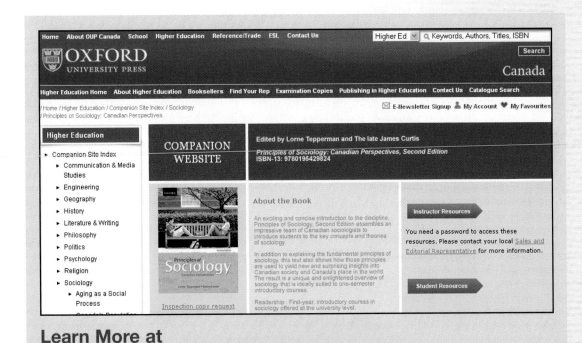

Learn More at
www.oup.com/PrinciplesofSociology

Preface

Is life moving more quickly these days or am I imagining it? Since the first edition of this text, Canada has been jolted (again) by events in our neighbour-state, the USA. The economy has melted down, stoking fears of an economic depression approaching that of the 1930s. But Americans, following a historic election, have a new president, an African-American, fuelling hopes that American might will now be adopting a more peaceful and collegial way than in the recent past. This cannot help but encourage and inspire us all.

These are but hopes and dreams as I write this preface. Yet the reader of Satoshi Ikeda's new chapter on globalization will know that the mere change of personnel, even of presidents, is not likely to alter the institutional structure and fundamental interests of the world's power-brokers. Another enduring reality is that religion will exercise a dominant ideological force. True, American religious fundamentalists were unable to capture the 2008 election for the Republicans, yet for reasons made clear in Lori Beaman's new chapter, religion continues to shape the thoughts, hopes, and actions of people around the world. Religion, as it always has, inspires people both to noble deeds and to violent, foolhardy ones.

Some things haven't changed. Canadians are still governed by a Conservative minority government; the country continues to be fractured by regional differences; and we remain a minor player in the world's political and military dramas. Our everyday lives focused mainly on friends and family, school and work, cyberspace and popular culture, we live in a society widely—and correctly—viewed as moderate, civilized, tolerant, healthy. It makes Canada an attractive destination for immigrants, and with one of the world's highest rates of immigration comes ongoing concern about assimilation—economic, cultural, and social. For all that, Canadian society is relatively safe and peaceful. Sociologists have shown that violent crime is not increasing—not dramatically, at least—but the media continue to fan the fears of older people, small-town citizens, and those who keep indoors and watch a lot of TV. Much of this fear is unfounded, but then high rates of school dropout among young men, who are the prime candidates for violent crime, justify a certain measure of alarm.

Canada, then, is a complicated society: peaceful and violent, calm and fearful, cooperative and conflictual, stable and tempestuous. This new edition of *Principles of Sociology* tries to describe and explain Canadian society today, and I think you will like it. You will find it even more interesting, provocative, and readable than the first edition, although our mission remains the same—namely, to educate Canadians about the society we live in. We have a duty to study and understand this country, and to make it serve our collective needs.

The publisher, Oxford University Press Canada, continues to help our contributors provide the clearest possible portrait of Canadian society. Developmental editor Jennifer Charlton provided valuable guidance during our work to consolidate chapters with multiple authors. Sarah Fox helped to update some of the boxed materials. Jessica Coffey had the final read through the manuscript and took care of the backstage, practical matters at Oxford to make sure that all the pieces came together. Thanks goes also to those talented artists responsible for the photos and illustrations that appear in this great-looking book.

I would also like to thank the following reviewers, whose thoughtful comments and suggestions have helped to shape the first and second editions of this text:

John Bratton, Thompson Rivers University
Michele Byers, Saint Mary's University
Judith Doyle, Mount Allison University
Laurie Forbes, Lakehead University
Jana Grekul, University of Alberta
Morgan Holmes, Wilfrid Laurier University
Kate Krug, Cape Breton University
Diane Naugler, Kwantlen Polytechnic University
Alice Propper, York University
William Ramp, University of Lethbridge
Annette Reynolds, Kwantlen Polytechnic University
Phyllis Rippeyoung, Acadia University
Glenda Wall, Wilfrid Laurier University

Mostly I'd like to thank the authors of the most recent edition of *Sociology: A Canadian Perspective*, whose work forms the basis of this streamlined edition. Without their work, this text would not exist. It has been a privilege working with such a distinguished group of scholars from across the country. Thank you, authors.

In closing, I dedicate this book to our students, who face many challenging decisions. Never in recent times has the economy been so troubled or the future so murky. It will take courage, dedication, and maturity to forge ahead, to make plans and to keep them alive. We wish you well: you are the next generation and our best chance. We hope sociological analysis will prove a useful force in your lives.

Lorne Tepperman
University of Toronto

● Content Correlation Guide ● ● ● ● ● ● ●

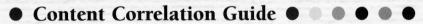

In *Principles of Sociology* you will find many recurring topics and theories with unique applications to the material of each chapter. We've developed the following guide to help you trace key themes of sociological inquiry through the different chapters.

	PAGE REFERENCES BY CHAPTER							
THEME	Chapter 1	Chapter 2	Chapter 3	Chapter 4	Chapter 5	Chapter 6	Chapter 7	Chapter 8
Age		34–36			120–121			
Alienation				86–89		146–148		
Authority	14–16		58–59			134–139	171–173	
Beliefs		32–39					155–156	196–198
Bureaucracies				99–105	125			
Capitalism		39–40				134–139		
Child care			72–75			139–141		
Class		34–37	75–76		122–123	132–151		201–203
Communication		44–45; 45–47						
Communities		52–53		95				
Culture	5	32–54		102–103				192–196
Deviance				82–83	110–129		164–166	
Discrimination								185–188; 196–198
Education			70–71			148–150	156–157	
Ethnicity		34–36			122–123			182–206
Family			62–64				167–168	
Gender		34–36	72–75		119–120	139–141	154–177	
Globalization		53–54						
Health	8–9				124–125	150		
Identity		34–36		82–83; 83–92; 92–93; 93–106			139–141	170–171
Ideologies		39–40				139–141	166	198–201
Immigration		52–53				148–150	177	185–188
Mass media		45–47	64–68					
Neo-liberalism								
Paid work						144–148	157–162; 173	203–205; 206
Patriarchy	14					139–141	156; 165	
Political economy								198–201
Politics		37–38						
Population	8–9						163–164	
Power	6–7		58–59	96–98	126–127	134–139	156	
Race		34–36	75–76					182–206
Religion		47	59					
Roles		37–38	76	82–83; 83–92; 92–93	126–127			
Sexuality					111–113		154–177	
Social construction		44–45		103–104	123–128		170–171	
Social groups		32–39		93–106	111–113			198–201
Social movement				93–94				
Social reproduction			75–76				163–164	
Social structure	7–13	40	60–62	82–83; 83–92; 93–106	114–116	133–141; 141–144; 144–150		201–203
Socialization		33	58–78	102–103			156	
The state		37–38						
Stereotypes		34–36	64–68				154–155	196–198
Stratification	14–16	47–49			123–128		162–164	201–203
Unpaid/domestic work						139–141	162	

PAGE REFERENCES BY CHAPTER

Chapter 9	Chapter 10	Chapter 11	Chapter 12	Chapter 13	Chapter 14	Chapter 15	Chapter 16	Chapter 17
			284–286					422–423
						348–351		
						348–351		
	231–232	257–258	274–277; 280–283					
220–221								
				316–317				
				304–328				
		258–260	291–293					
		248–270						
	232–234							
210–226		264–265						
215–216; 216–225	232–234	258–260	291–293	317–318	342–344	355–356		
				311–314			388; 391–392	410–427
	230–244							
			256–257					
213–214		262–264				348–351		
				304–328				
				310–311				416–421
		264–265	274–300					
213		258–260						
213–214				324–328		354–355		
		262–264				348–376		
							380–406	
		256–257				348; 348–351; 351		
			293–295	318–319		355–356		
					332–344			
215								
			296–299			361–363	401; 402–406	
			282–283					
	231–232							
		248–249						
213–214				310–311		351–352		
216–218								

Sociology: Its Purposes, Theories, and Research Approaches

Bruce Arai, Neil McLaughlin, Antony Puddephatt, and Lorne Tepperman

Learning Objectives

In this chapter, you will:

▶ learn about the purposes of sociology and the types of questions sociologists attempt to understand and answer;

▶ examine the difference in perspective between macrosociology and microsociology;

▶ learn about the development of sociology, its major founders, and their main ideas and contributions;

▶ learn about three major approaches to sociological theory: multivariate, interpretive, and historical-comparative;

▶ identity some of the advantages and disadvantages of each type of theoretical approach and data-gathering method;

▶ review the basic research techniques in sociology; and

▶ learn how to select the best research method.

Figure/ground by Warren Collins, Tasmania, Australia, collage

● Introduction ● ● ● ● ● ●

Why do people become sociologists? There are many answers to this question, and it is likely that everyone at one point or other has been on the brink of becoming a sociologist. We say this because all people experience odd facts of social life that affect their opportunities, and they try to understand them. This is where sociology begins for most people. When people continue from here, there is even more motivation to do sociology. What can be more fascinating, more empowering, and more personal than to begin to understand the society that shapes our lives? For these reasons, sociology is an inherently attractive area of study, and many people do study it.

Maybe as a child you noticed one or more of the following situations:

- Parents sometimes treat their sons differently from their daughters.
- Teachers often treat pretty girls better than plain-looking ones.
- Adults treat well-dressed children better than poorly dressed children.
- Movies typically portray people with 'accents' as strange or ridiculous.

If you noticed these things, you may have wondered why they happen. They may even have affected you, as a daughter or son, a plain-looking or attractive person, a poorly dressed or well-dressed person, or a person with or without an 'accent'. You may have felt ashamed, angry, or pleased, depending on whether you identified with the favourably treated or the unfavourably treated category of people.

Perhaps you grew up in a small town and have moved to a big city, or grew up in a big city and now live in a small town. Since moving, you have noticed that:

- People are not like the media portrayed them.
- The ethnic and racial composition of the people around you is not what you are used to.
- The gap between rich and poor is more pronounced.
- People interact with each other differently than back home.
- They have strange reactions to strangers.
- They talk differently, dress differently, and eat different kinds of foods.

If you noticed these things, you may have wanted to understand them better. These are the kinds of circumstances in which sociological curiosity begins. All sociologists somehow, at sometime or another, got hooked on trying to better understand their own lives and the lives of people around them. They came to understand that common sense gave them only incomplete explanations about what happened to people, about people's behaviour and the society in which they live. They were not satisfied with the incomplete explanations and wanted to know more.

For many people, and for much of what we do, common-sense understanding is just fine. Still, for anyone who wants to understand how society works, it is not good enough. You may already realize there are many questions common sense cannot answer adequately. For example:

- Why are some people so different from you? Why are some so similar?
- Why do apparently similar people lead such different lives?
- How is it possible for different people to get along?
- Why do we treat some people as if they are more 'different' than others?
- Why do we often treat 'different' people much worse than others?
- What do people do to escape from being treated badly?
- Why do some aspects of society change quickly and others hardly at all?
- What can citizens do to make Canadian society a more equitable place?
- What can young people do to make their elders think differently?
- Can we bring about social change by changing the laws of the country?

Sociologists try to answer these questions by studying societies methodically. In fact, their task is to study people's lives—their own and others'—more carefully than anyone else. Sociologists want to understand how societies change and how people's lives change with them. Social changes, inequalities, and conflicts captivate sociologists because such issues—war and peace, wealth and poverty, environmental destruction and technological innovation, for example—are important for people's lives. Sociologists know that 'personal problems' are similar across many individuals. They also know that many of our personal problems are the private side of public issues. American sociologist C. Wright Mills called this knowledge or ability 'the sociological imagination'. With this ability or approach, we know we need to deal with personal problems collectively and, often, politically—with full awareness that we share these problems and their solution with others.

However, solving problems entails clear thinking and careful research. Social theorists and social science researchers have developed concepts, theories, and research methods that help them study the social world more effectively. Our goal as sociologists is to be able to explain social life, critique social inequities, and work towards effecting social change. In this book, you will learn how sociologists go about these tasks, and some of what sociologists have found out about the social world.

Our starting point here is a formal definition of *sociology*. We'll then compare sociology with other related fields of study, and discuss sociology's most basic subject matter.

● A Definition ● ● ● ● ● ● ● of Sociology

Scholars have defined **sociology** in many ways, but most practising sociologists think of their discipline as the systematic study of social behaviour in human societies. Humans are intensely social beings and spend most of their time interacting with other humans. That is why sociologists study the social units people create when they join with others. As we will see in the following chapters, these units range from small groups—comprising as few as two people—to large corporations and even whole societies (see, for example, Chapter 4, on groups, cliques, and bureaucracies). Sociologists are interested in learning about how group membership affects individual behaviour and, reciprocally, how individuals change the groups of which they are members. In most social life, at least in Canadian society, there is a visible tug-of-war between these two forces: the group and the individual.

However, it is impossible for any sociologist to study all social issues or to become an expert in all the sub-areas of sociology. As a result, most sociologists specialize in either macrosociology or microsociology—two related but distinct approaches to studying the social world—and choose problems for study from within these realms.

Macrosociology is the study of large social organizations (for example, the Roman Catholic Church, universities, corporations, or government bureaucracies) and large social categories (for example, ethnic minorities, the elderly, or college students). Sociologists who specialize in the macrosociological approach to the social world focus on the complex social patterns that people form over long periods (see many examples in Parts III and IV of this volume, on social institutions and global society, respectively).

On the other hand, **microsociology** focuses on the typical processes and patterns of face-to-face interaction in small groups. A microsociologist might study a marriage, a clique, a business meeting, an argument between friends, or a first date. In short, he or she would study the common, everyday interactions and negotiations that together produce lasting, secure patterns.

The difference in names—**macro** versus **micro**—refers to the difference in size in the social units of interest. Macrosociologists study large social units—organizations, societies, or even empires—over long periods of time: years, centuries, or millennia. Microsociologists study small social units over short periods of time—for example, what happens during a conversation, a party, a classroom lecture, or a love affair. As in nature, large things move (and change) slowly and small things move more quickly. As a result, macrosociologists are likely to stress how slowly things change and how persistent a social pattern is as it plays itself out in one generation after another. An example is the way society tends to be controlled by its elite groups, decade after decade. The connection between business elites and political elites is persistent. By contrast, microsociologists are likely to stress how quickly things change and how elusive is that thing we call 'social life'. In their eyes, any social unit is constantly being created and reconceived by the members of society. An example is the way one's friendship group changes yearly, if not more often, as one moves through the school system or the world of work. Some people remain our close friends over years, but many are close friends for only a short while.

Combining macro and micro approaches improves our understanding of the social world. Consider a common social phenomenon: the domestic division of labour: Who does what chores around the home? From the micro perspective, who does what is constantly open to negotiation, a result of personal characteristics, the history of the couple, and other unique factors. From a macro perspective, different households tend to have similar divisions of labour, despite differences in personal history. This suggests the answer lies in a society's history, culture, and economy. It is far from accidental that, across millions of households, men enjoy the advantage of a better salary and more social power both in a great many workplaces and at home.

All of this is the subject matter of sociology. We may choose to focus on problems of microsociology or macrosociology because of our preference to understand one or the other, but a proper or full understanding of most problems will need us to consider elements of both, because the two types of processes are closely connected.

Different Styles of Sociological Imagination

While macro and micro approaches are different, they are also connected. After all, both macro- and microsociologists are studying the same people in the same society. All of us are leading unique lives within a common social context, faced by common problems. The question is 'How can sociologists bring these elements together?" As noted above, C. Wright Mills (1959) gave the answer when he introduced the notion of the **sociological imagination** as something that enables us to relate personal biographies—the lives of millions of ordinary people like ourselves—to the broad sweep of human history. The sociological imagination is what we need to use to understand how societies control and change their members and, at the same time, are constantly changed by the actions of their members. It also allows for the creation of general sociological theories to make sense of the complexities of the social world. Too often, sociological theory is considered separately from the empirical research traditions that created it. As a result, we often forget that good sociological theory is based on carefully gathered evidence, and that the most interesting and useful evidence often comes from theoretically-informed research.

There are three major empirical traditions that contribute to sociological theory along different levels of analysis. **Level of analysis** refers to the size and scale of social life under examination. Macro-level theories analyze relations between large numbers of people who may never interact personally, yet who are connected by social factors operating at regional, national, or global levels. In contrast, micro-level theories deal with the social processes and dynamics of small groups, networks, and individuals. Meso-level theories deal with the scale of society in between the macro and the micro levels, for example, organizations and institutions such as businesses, schools, and governments. Sociological theory is designed to examine all three levels of analysis. But what are the major types of sociological theory?

Most textbooks categorize theory into four major camps: (1) **functionalism**, (2) **conflict theory**, (3) **symbolic interactionism**, and (4) **feminism**. Functionalism refers to theories that try to explain the social world in terms of how it fits together and how each part helps the whole to run smoothly. Conflict theory tends to see social life in terms of power and inequality, focusing on the gap between the 'haves' and 'have-nots' in the social world. Symbolic interactionism emphasizes the social meanings

actors give to and take from their own and others' social behaviour and how we need to understand these personal meanings if we are to understand their everyday actions. Finally, feminist theories emphasize how male dominance over women is embedded in institutions and culture, treating gender as a central analytical lens to understand society. These theoretical distinctions are important, yet they also serve to divide theory, rather than unite it around empirical research questions or substantive issues. For example, conflict theorists analyze private schools in terms of how they reinforce class inequality. Functionalists, in contrast, tend to treat private schools as an unquestioned good, stressing how well they function to educate our youth and instill values and norms. Neither camp listens to the other side, since their assumptions about society lead them to view the world in only one way (either in terms of co-operation or conflict). If theorists saw their commonality in a similar topic and level of analysis, they might correct each other's blind spots and gain a more balanced and empirically informed picture of the case at hand. Therefore, it is important to use different kinds of sociological theory together, considering co-operation, conflict, and negotiation as they manifest themselves differentially in particular social contexts.

For these reasons, we will organize our discussion in terms of three distinct empirical traditions of sociological theory: (1) **multivariate theory**, (2) **interpretive theory**, and (3) **historical-comparative theory**. Of course, many theories combine these research methodologies and are applicable at more than one level of analysis. These categories are not always clear-cut, often overlapping in practical research designs (Alford, 1998). Still, different methodological approaches allow for different questions to be asked and give rise to different theoretical claims. We hope that an emphasis on empirical research will help to bridge opposing camps in sociological theory, uniting them in a close dialogue with evidence. Theory is not to be simply admired or adhered to, but applied, tested, and refined in light of ongoing research.

Because of this emphasis on evidence, the best sociologists from the classical era still have valuable things to teach us about contemporary society. Often seen as the 'founders' of modern sociology in nineteenth- and early twentieth-century Europe, Karl Marx, Émile Durkheim, Max Weber, and Georg Simmel each laid out a provocative and original vision for sociological theory in dialogue with empirical research traditions. Although these classical theorists cannot be easily categorized into only one theoretical logic, Durkheim's writings on suicide demonstrate the multivariate logic; Weber and Simmel provide early examples of the interpretive approach; and Marx's writings on capitalism illuminate historical-comparative theory.

Since it will be up to you to decide what theories you find most useful, we will end this chapter by talking about some ways that you, as students, might think critically about the various sociological theories you encounter. What factors help explain why some theories and not others are important and influential among sociologists? How should you go about deciding which theory or combination of theories to use when trying to answer a question of interest to you? After learning about these three theoretical traditions, you will be ready to assess and choose among competing theories, developing your own sociological imagination from a perspective grounded in the Canadian experience.

● What Is ● ● ● ● ● ● Sociological Theory?

Theories in sociology are abstract, general ideas that help organize and make sense of the social world. Theories highlight the place of the individual within larger cultural contexts and social structures. By 'abstract' we do not mean ideas that are out of touch with reality or unconnected to research findings. Theories in sociology must go beyond mere common-sense descriptions of particular people, places, and events. Sociologists instead look for generic concepts and theoretical relationships that are relevant across a wide variety of empirical cases. It is this general nature of sociological theories that makes them so powerful. This is why we still find inspiration in Marx, Durkheim, and Weber today. Indeed, we will demonstrate how the best sociological theories have stood the test of time, and how they can help us to understand and explain the social world around us.

Sociological theories involve systematic efforts to link concepts with empirical evidence, which can then be tested and evaluated by others. Sociological theorists do not always gather evidence themselves. There is value in 'meta-theoretical' work that builds on existing theory and evidence gathered by other researchers to generate original arguments. From our perspective, however, the best sociological theory engages with empirical evidence and systematic data-gathering, which can be categorized into three major types: (1) statistical data, based on measuring large numbers of observable social phenomena; (2) observational data, based on qualitative interviews or notes taken through observing people in their everyday activities; and (3) historical-comparative data, based on written, photographic, and/or oral records of lives,

institutions, and events in different places and times. These three types of empirical data are used in multivariate, interpretive, and historical-comparative theory, respectively.

These different theoretical traditions should *not* be seen as entirely distinct ways of understanding the world, never to be combined in research practice. Sociology, more than any other modern discipline, attempts to combine these different theoretical traditions to provide informed explanations of social phenomena at a number of levels. By doing this, sociologists gain a more comprehensive view of the social world. This is accomplished by combining theoretical strategies to study the interrelationship of social-psychological processes with larger social structures and broad historical traditions. This makes the discipline of sociology relatively unique. These methodological divisions are increasingly breaking down, as scholars are learning the value of using multiple methods to 'triangulate' findings from each theoretical approach in practical research designs.

Each type of theory operates with a different set of assumptions about reality and the social world. Each type of theory also contains its own type of **epistemology**, or 'way of knowing', positing different criteria for how we are able to gain knowledge about the world. In addition, different theorists and schools of thought make use of distinct metaphors or ways of describing reality through the use of language:

- Multivariate theory sees society as being made up of objectively identifiable patterns that we can understand by using the language of hypothesis testing and empirical measurement.
- Interpretive theorists emphasize the unique nature of human behaviour in contrast to the natural world, and argue that studying the conscious and self-aware character of group life requires a method that is sensitive to these features. Reality itself, for most interpretive theorists, is a social product relative to the particular social group in question, and is a product of their own unique perspective.
- Historical-comparative sociologists are less focused on cultural or group definitions of 'meaning' and instead place emphasis on the importance of historical processes and events of particular times and places. From this perspective, societies will be very different from each other today as a result of their evolution from separate and distinct pasts.

Now let us turn to each major type of theoretical logic, beginning with multivariate theory.

HUMAN DIVERSITY
Are Leaders Born or Bred?

Every organization needs leaders. Companies need CEOs to increase profits or to turn around a run of bad years. Churches require strong leaders and universities need visionary presidents to ensure that they remain dynamic and relevant. The Liberal Party of Canada spent months searching its ranks for a new leader, and at the end of its leadership convention in late 2006 the party chose Stéphane Dion over Bob Rae, Michael Ignatieff, and Gerard Kennedy, who had been the other main candidates.

But, are leaders born or bred? Sociologically, this is an important question because if they are born (that is, most of the essential features of a good leader are determined at birth or a young age) then the hundreds of leadership programs available across North American are largely ineffective. If leaders are bred, then a very different story emerges.

This discussion shows how important theory is to the definition of a problem. If leaders are born, we can do little but sit back and hope that the right people end up in the right positions. But if leaders are bred, 'leadership training' as a concept starts to make sense.

The prevailing view at present is that leaders are bred. Perhaps this is because so many organizations are offering leadership training programs, and they all have an interest in this position! But if leaders are bred, then it becomes possible to evaluate the quality or effectiveness of different training programs. A great number of studies attempt to do just that. Sometimes the evidence seems to suggest that these programs work (Mighty and Ashton, 2003; Nichols,

2002) and at other times they don't (Allio, 2005; Fossey and Shoho, 2006).

Methodologically, the interesting point about all of these discussions is that it has proven almost impossible to develop a widespread and consistent theory of leadership. Generally speaking, we have moved past the idea that leaders possess special qualities such as superior intelligence, morality, or motivation to the idea that leadership arises from the relationships among people. Leaders emerge from a group in times of crisis to legitimately move an organization forward. But why has it proven so difficult to identify leaders except after the fact? And consequently, why is it so hard to evaluate these training programs?

At one level, the answer is simple. People are far too diverse in what determines who they will follow and why for anyone to be able to develop a reliable standard measure of either leadership or program success. Some people will follow the head of an organization simply because that person is the head. Others will follow a clerk in the mail room as long as the clerk possesses qualities that inspire them. Others will follow a person of compassion and strong moral character because they find those qualities admirable.

Despite the fact that leadership is critical to the success of virtually all modern organizations, human diversity makes it almost impossible to predict who will follow when. And this in turn makes it extremely difficult to evaluate whether or not these programs are successful.

Multivariate Theory

French scholar Émile Durkheim's *Suicide* (1897) represents an exemplary case of the use of multivariate logic within sociology. In contrast to the psychological approaches of the time, Durkheim wanted to understand human behaviour in terms of what he called **social facts**, as outlined in his *Rules of Sociological Method* (1895). Durkheim considered social facts as large-group patterns explained by forces external to people yet capable of directing people's behaviour. Thus, Durkheim suggested that social behaviour could be explained based on an adequate understanding of the social facts deemed relevant to the case at hand. From this perspective, theories can be seen as clusters of factors that underlie large-scale patterns of behaviour. Durkheim used this multivariate approach to write a pioneering—and still influential—analysis of suicide throughout Europe in the nineteenth century. He provided a *social* explanation of suicide rates, in contrast to individual accounts that ten put forth by psychologists and philosophers. More importantly, this early example of multivariate sociology would set the precedent for later scholars, who would make use of large-scale surveys and increasingly sophisticated statistical analyses.

In political terms, Durkheim's writings on suicide were part of a general trend in late-nineteenth-century social thought. European countries were modernizing rapidly, and were thus trying to come to terms with the social consequences of the changes brought about by the Industrial Revolution. Durkheim used suicide as an indicator of deeper 'pathological' problems of society in ways that other approaches did not. Economists, for example, stressed economic self-interest, arguing that suicides are most common during economic crises. Psychologists stressed individual psychological pathology and mental illness as the major cause of suicide. Durkheim offered a creative *social* explanation of the phenomenon by focusing not on individual cases of suicide, but rather on rates of suicide among different sectors of the population. If such large-scale rates were different and varied by the social facts characterizing the groups, then suicide was not merely an individual problem but a product of larger social forces. For example, Durkheim observed an increase of suicide rates in Western European cities over what was common in earlier feudal and agricultural societies. He also observed that those with more income in large urban centres were more likely to commit suicide and that suicide rates increased during economic booms as well as crises. Thus, a purely economic explanation of group suicide rates was inadequate. Durkheim argued that increased rates of suicide accompanying large-scale economic crises had less to do with poverty than with rapid social change and an accompanying lack of social stability. From Durkheim's perspective, increasing suicide rates were a sign of the pathological aspects of the modernization of society and the erosion of community. Thus, suicide serves as an important indicator of social cohesion in periods of rapid industrial change.

Durkheim examined a great deal of data on suicide rates throughout Europe in the nineteenth century. He compared men and women, married and single men and women, Protestant and Catholic religious affiliations, and even different seasons and times of the day in which suicides were committed. The most important finding was that Protestants had higher rates of suicide than Catholics, while single people were more likely to kill themselves than people who were married with children. Since the Catholic religion emphasizes community cohesion, while Protestantism emphasizes individualism, Catholics have a higher level of social solidarity. Similarly, married people

with children also have a stronger basis for belonging and social solidarity. Thus, Durkheim concluded that the level of social solidarity was the most important factor in determining rates of suicide among different groups.

In addition to drawing our attention to an analysis of a society's health, Durkheim's pioneering work on suicide helped create the multivariate perspective that dominates mainstream sociology today. As a result, contemporary training in the field of sociology requires researchers to be skilled in quantitative data-gathering and statistical variable analysis. More importantly, Durkheim contributed a marvellous study that shows the sociological basis for patterns of individual action. Scholars of the human condition could no longer turn a blind eye to multivariate theoretical analysis.

Interpretive Theory

Interpretive theorizing argues that sociologists should base their research on quantity in sociology based on data in the form of observations and less-structured surveys. This tradition has its roots in two late nineteenth- and early twentieth-century German theorists, Max Weber and Georg Simmel. The interpretive tradition was solidified in America at the University of Chicago, thanks to Robert Park and Everett Hughes, as well as the symbolic interactionist school inspired by George Herbert Mead and formally developed by Herbert Blumer. We will consider the various contributions of these theorists in this section.

Max Weber can be seen as an early exemplar of the interpretive perspective, emphasizing **verstehen**, which refers to understanding the meanings carried by actors that lead them to make decisions. For example, in Weber's *The Protestant Ethic and the Spirit of Capitalism* (1904), he focused on the religious beliefs of Calvinism, which came from John Calvin, the sixteenth-century Swiss Protestant leader in the Reformation, whose influence was broad throughout much of European Protestantism. Calvinists believed in the doctrine of predestination, the idea that one's fate in the afterlife is predestined from birth. As such, there is no way to earn your way to heaven, so Calvinists were desperate to find signs of their potential salvation. Their belief that hard work was a sign that they were among the chosen to get to heaven led them to work hard and resist the temptations of luxury. By living a self-disciplined ascetic lifestyle, they would engage in a sort of 'wishful thinking' that this behaviour was not a result of their own will, but rather a sign of their eternal salvation in heaven. This unique religious culture, Weber believed, fostered the rise

SOCIOLOGY IN ACTION
Émile Durkheim (1858–1917)

Born to a deeply religious Jewish family, Durkheim was an excellent student as a young man and went on to become one of the most influential scholars at the most elite French universities. Initially a professor of education, Durkheim was a widely trusted scholar who helped reform the French national education system. More so than the other major classical theorists we have discussed, Durkheim made the development of a separate discipline of sociology a major life goal. When he died the same year his son was killed fighting for France in World War I, he left a rich legacy of sociology professorships and journals that shaped twentieth-century sociology and anthropology throughout the Western world.

of a related 'spirit of capitalism' associated with economic success. Weber believed this cultural spirit, begun by deep religious beliefs, not merely by technological development, formed the basis of rapid industrialization and the expansion of capitalist societies in Europe and America. This was especially the case because many of the notable early capitalists and industrialists lived in relatively plain personal circumstances, turning their vast profits back into their businesses to make even more profit, rather than enjoying all the trappings their wealth could buy. Not all historians and sociologists agree with the specific argument Weber made about the importance of the 'Protestant ethic' for the development of capitalism (see Hamilton, 1996). Nonetheless, Weber's theoretical argument for the importance of meaning would leave a lasting impact on the interpretive approach.

Another important influence on interpretive theory is Georg Simmel (1950b). Simmel was a controversial German sociologist who had an enormous influence on American sociologists in the early twentieth century. In addition to writing philosophical essays, Simmel wrote sociological pieces on everyday life, including fashion, rumours, the culture of interaction in cities, male and female differences, and even yodelling. Unfortunately, Simmel has become a relatively neglected thinker over the past 40 years. One reason for this is that, as a Jew, Simmel suffered from the anti-Semitism that was common in Europe until well into the twentieth century. Further, his writing and lectures tended to be oriented to popular audiences, and consequently other academics accused him of 'playing to the crowd' rather than engaging in real scholarship. Nonetheless, his influence on later

SOCIOLOGY IN ACTION
Max Weber (1864–1920)

The son of a powerful and authoritarian German politician and a shy and religious Protestant mother, Max Weber dealt with issues of politics and religion in a lifetime of extremely influential scholarly works. Trained in law, history, and economics, Weber became one of the central founders of sociology in Germany. Weber's wife Marianne was an important early feminist in Germany, and Weber helped to educate and support some of the most creative German intellectuals of the time, including his friend Georg Simmel. Weber inherited a large amount of money from his father and thus focused his energies on writing rather than teaching. As a consequence of this and his own natural talent, Weber left an enormous legacy of historical and intepretive sociology that is still being used today. Ever a practical as well as a theoretical intellectual, Weber died in 1920, not long after serving as a hospital administrator in the German war effort in World War I.

theories in symbolic interactionist research is clearly evident and his contributions to sociology have been more widely recognized in recent years. He is now often considered the 'father' of microsociology, especially as it regards the dynamics of small groups and networks.

One of Simmel's foundational theoretical contributions was an emphasis on the *forms of association* in social life (see Simmel, 1950b). That is, he emphasized the patterns and regularities of social interaction over and above their specific content. Thus, the same group dynamics would hold for dyads, as opposed to triads, no matter the content of the communication. Simmel often referred to the law of 'small numbers', emphasizing that the size of an interactive group carries unique patterns of association despite the type of group or activity they engage in. For example, Simmel highlighted the value of external conflicts to unite a group internally against a common threat. Simmel's ideas help us see the similarities in social dynamics across a range of situations. Consider the feelings that are set in motion when an outsider criticizes a member of your family, or how an authoritarian professor creates a cohesive sense of identity among undergraduates who feel

unfairly treated. Simmel's [...]ry also sheds light on why Americans became unite[...] [...]ation, at least for a time, after the terrorist violence [...] [...].

This German traditi[...] [...] [...]retive social theory would have a major influence on the school of symbolic interactionism. The philosopher and social psychologist George Herbert Mead (1934) spent time studying in Germany, where he would encounter much of the social psychology that forms the basis of the contemporary interactionist tradition. Mead's student, Herbert Blumer (1969), would go on to formally define the research tradition of symbolic interactionism and give it its name. Distrusting the reduction of social life to 'objective' social forces in the way of Durkheim, Blumer would argue for the centrality of meaning in the formation of action and decisions. Unlike Weber, however, Blumer would incorporate the influence of the ethnographic methods used by Robert Park to emphasize the importance of up-close observation to gain an 'intimate familiarity' with the social group under study. For Blumer, only by participating and spending time with the group, and forming concepts based on the meanings the members carry, can one

→ patterns more important than content.

Rituals and symbolic objects all around let us communicate to one another the values we hold above all others. Often, they identify the heroes and villains who (we believe) shape our world. The Canadian Press/Erik C. Pendzich/Rex Features

achieve [...] rate understanding of group life. This
general [...] laid the basis for the development of modern ethnographic research and qualitative analysis.

The Historical-Comparative Tradition

Researchers also make use of the historical-comparative approach in contemporary sociology. The historical-comparative tradition explores specific processes that explain a sequence of contingent events that occurred across time (Alford, 1998: 45). Historical theorizing usually relies on empirical evidence in the form of texts, documents, artifacts, and oral histories, and is often sought in historical archives, library collections, and museums. This evidence is then organized using theoretical inferences to judge their significance and their relation to the events of the time. This process of moving back and forth between theory and evidence allows for the creation of empirically-based sociological theory in relation to either specific or broadly sweeping historical events.

The origins of historical-comparative sociology can be traced to the nineteenth century and the works of the French thinker Alexis de Tocqueville and the German émigré intellectual and political radical Karl Marx. Tocqueville authored the famous two-volume *Democracy in America* (1835, 1840). He also pioneered the comparison of different national histories in order to explain differences in culture, political structures, and individual behaviour. Tocqueville was a member of the French aristocracy, a group of people who owned massive amounts of land and ruled France along with King and the Catholic Church before the Revolution of 1789.

Tocqueville had originally visited the United States because he wanted to observe the prison system, which was widely regarded as more humane and well-run than the prisons of France. In the course of his travels in America, he made the case for the value of this New World democracy against the elitist politics of France. Many elites at that time felt that the elimination of the rule by King, Church, and aristocracy brought about by the French Revolution had led to cultural chaos, political anarchy, and the creation of the 'tyranny of the majority'. As a member of the elite himself, Tocqueville shared some of these concerns about the levelling of cultural standards in democracy. But he made a compelling case that the decentralization of the American Republic, the tendency of Americans to join voluntary associations and organizations, and the checks and balances of the new system would lead to an attractive new democratic culture. He predicted this system would soon spread to the 'Old World' of Europe. Tocqueville's analysis still has much to offer the contemporary study of the political system of the United States and the culture of democracy in general.

Writing in the second half of the nineteenth century, Karl Marx became one of the most influential theorists in sociology, developing a 'historical materialist' analysis of contemporary capitalism in Europe (Marx, 1887). Specifically, Marx linked the rise of the textile industry in Great Britain to the 'enclosure movement' that forcibly removed the peasantry from their means of subsistence on [...] lands. Since these peasants were removed from their land to make room for the expanding wool industry, they were forced into cities where they were exploited for cheap labour in factories. Thus, the material relations of production surrounding the textile industry in England gave rise to separate classes of bourgeois owners and proletariat workers. Marx provided an historical account

SOCIOLOGY IN ACTION
Georg Simmel (1858–1918)

As much an artist as a scientist, Simmel lived his life on the margins of the German university system. Initially trained as a philosopher, Simmel made the case for a micro approach in sociology in a series of essays and entertaining public lectures. He died from cancer right before the end of World War I. Because he was both Jewish and an unconventional thinker, Simmel was excluded from good jobs in the German university system until just a few years before his death. Simmel was active in German intellectual life, often associating more with artists, journalists, and writers than with other sociologists. An example of how ideas from the margins can often have enormous influence on scholarship, Simmel is widely regarded as one of the key founders of sociological interpretive theory and the school of symbolic interactionism.

Born in Trier, Germany, to a Jewish couple with a long tradition of rabbis on both sides of the family, Marx inherited a moral approach to politics and scholarship. Forced to drop out of academic philosophy and then made to leave his native Germany as a consequence of persecution for his political views and his defence of freedom of the press, Marx settled in Belgium, France, and eventually England, where he died within two years of his wife and the same year as his oldest daughter (both named Jenny). More of an activist than a scholar, Marx was not himself a sociologist *per se* but his focus on class conflict played a central role in the development of both historical-comparative and conflict theories in our discipline. Marx was relatively poor most of his life and was supported by his long-time friend and collaborator, Friedrich Engels, the wealthy German-born son of an English factory owner.

of how the modern-day class structure arose, which was associated with the shift from feudal to capitalist society in England under the changing market pressures on lords and landowners and the restriction of the means of production for peasants, who were transformed from self-subsistent workers to a new proletariat class. Marx's theorizing has been central to the development of the conflict paradigm in sociology, which focuses our attention on social class and power relations, and seeks to bring about egalitarian social change.

● The Case for Theoretical Diversity

Sociology uniquely contributes to social science because it effectively combines these three types of social analysis in productive ways. Even the best works of social science within one of the three major theoretical paradigms tend to be blind to the challenge posed by competing modes of theorizing. Combining multivariate, historical, and interpretive logics of analysis offers a very powerful approach. For example, Durkheim's classic work *Suicide* tells us much about the systematic patterning of suicide rates that can be predicted by such sociological variables as religion, marital status, and gender. However, his commitment to multivariate analysis blinds him to the symbolic meanings central to suicidal behaviour at the micro level (Alford, 1998). Suicide is a profoundly social-psychological act as well as being a part of larger social trends.

Donna Gaines's (1991) ethnographic analysis of teen suicides in New Jersey, for example, suggests the value of

theorizing based on close qualitative observations rather than the more remote quantitative analysis of variables. Identifying structural correlations alone does not, as Gaines's study suggests, provide more precise explanations of the specific social processes that operate within these larger relationships. The interpretive approach helps to connect structural patterns to the real, lived experiences and interpretations that actually cause suicide. Durkheim's use of aggregate statistical data, moreover, leads him to implicitly suggest that suicidal acts can be understood without an account of the historically specific contexts that influence human action. The historical-comparative perspective might suggest that the same level of social solidarity may have different effects on suicide across different national contexts and historical periods.

It would be a mistake to dismiss too easily the contributions of statistical approaches to the study of social life, something that can be seen when looking at Lipset's work on Canadian–American differences. There is enormous value in taking a historical perspective on Canadian society, revolutions in France, China, or Russia, and gender relations in the Middle East. At the same time, grand generalizations that attempt to explain Canadian character, the success of different revolutionary movements, or the human rights situations of women should also be tested by the kind of careful empirical statistical analysis at the core of the multivariate approach. Social science is best served by trying to combine the three types of theorizing outlined above in order to overcome the specific shortcomings of each of the approaches when used alone. We will now illustrate this point about the value of methodological diversity with three examples from important theorists who combine these three logics of inquiry.

■■ **Time to Reflect** ■■■■■■■■■■■■■■■■■■■■■■■■■■■■■■■■■■■■■■

What makes sociological theory different from our common-sense understandings of the world? Try to think of at least two major differences.

Dorothy Smith's Feminist Ethnography

Few feminist scholars have had as much influence as the Canadian theorist Dorothy Smith. Trained by Erving Goffman at the University of California at Berkeley, she was also influenced by Harold Garfinkel, the founder of an important approach to sociology known as **ethnomethodology**. Ethnomethodologists stress the value of studying the methods and routines of everyday life that people must use to make sense of and establish order in their everyday lives (Garfinkel, 1967). Smith's involvement in the feminist movement in the 1960s and 1970s suggested to her the importance of looking at this everyday world from the perspective of women. The world looks different, Smith (1987) argues, according to where you are placed within the hierarchies established by traditional forms of male dominance. Smith's advocacy of 'standpoint theory' challenged the dominance of the male perspective in sociology. Scholars influenced by Smith's theory do research using an approach known as 'institutional ethnography'. This method examines how social life and traditional 'relations of ruling' by men are created and reinforced in the context of activities both in public workplace organizations and in the private spaces of the family. Further, by focusing on the specific standpoints of those who struggle under relations of power, Smith has argued that an understanding of these structures comes into clearer focus. This has created an exciting new tradition of scholarship that studies power relations in society that is informed by the strategy of qualitative research methods. This theoretical approach is designed to understand the power relations linked to institutions and organizations by exploring the firsthand perspectives of those negatively affected by these traditional arrangements.

The innovative nature of Smith's (1987) contributions flows from the way in which she combines ethnographic research with the insights of the Marxist version of historical-comparative theory. Marxist theories tend to emphasize how class inequality is reinforced through the history of economic and social relations. Some versions of Marxism, following in the tradition of his collaborator Friedrich Engels, attempt to explain the origins of the subordination of women in the history of the family. As such, Smith is part of this long tradition

of Marxist feminists. Her work combines a concern with how everyday gender relations are embedded in a broader history of what feminists call patriarchy: the legal, political, economic, and cultural dominance of men over women. Like Marx, Smith is concerned with changing society and not simply understanding it, and is one of the most influential sociological theorists today. She has attained her success partly because of the way she combines both the interpretive and historical-comparative traditions. In doing so, she argues against ethnographies and interpretive theories that do not link their observations to structures of inequality. Some sociologists feel that Smith's analysis is excessively subjective and does not make enough use of quantitative and traditional historical-comparative approaches. One could also argue that she does not give adequate weight to the changes in gender norms that the feminist movement created over the past 30 years. Despite these criticisms, Smith forged a sociology that would help to understand, and thus change, the experiences of women and disadvantaged people everywhere by understanding their place within powerful institutions.

Randall Collins's Micro Theory of Stratification

Not all combinations of interpretive and historical-comparative perspectives must be rooted in the Marxist tradition. Randall Collins's (1975, 2004) influential micro theory of **stratification** successfully combines Max Weber's theories of class, status, and power with the microsociology pioneered by Goffman. Traditional Marxist conflict theorists often stress how social classes (capitalists versus workers) are engaged in conflict over the control and use of economic resources and profit. From the Marxist perspective, those who control the means of production in society are accorded the most status, political power, and prestige, not to mention better meals and more fun at the cottage. Thus, for Marxists, economic well-being is the most important factor in determining status, power, and prestige. Following Weber, Collins stresses how status and power differences are played out in society over a broader range of conflicts than simply economic class alone. For Collins, society is pervasively dominated by battles over social prestige;

SOCIOLOGY IN ACTION
Karl Marx (1818–1883)

Born in England and educated in sociology at the London School of Economics and University of California at Berkeley in the 1950s and 1960s, Dorothy Smith has spent the most productive and innovative years of her career in Canada as our major feminist sociological theorist. Influenced by Marxism, the women's movement, and various micro-interpretive theories, Smith pioneered an approach to sociology that puts women's experience at the centre of the discipline. She taught one of the first Women's Studies classes in Canada at the University of British Columbia and taught for many years at the Ontario Institute for Studies in Education (OISE) at the University of Toronto. Though retired, Dorothy Smith continues to teach at the University of Victoria, and works with various former students on the development of what she calls 'institutional ethnography'.

racial, ethnic, religious, and gender differences; and local cultural distinctions. In addition, contemporary Weberian scholars such as Collins (1975) stress the importance of institutions—armies, the police, the state—that serve to control people through the use of force and violence.

Unlike Marxists, Collins believes that scholars should understand social inequality but not be primarily concerned with challenging it. Attempting to change society (the role of the activist) is a very different thing from trying to understand the world in an objective way (the role of the scholar). Thus, Collins combines the commitment to objective science with research into social inequality. Collins has studied topics as wide apart as the sociology of the family and sexual relations, the creation of 'credential inflation' in schools, and the fall of communism in the former Soviet Union. The common link across this work is a close attention to how conflicts of power, prestige, and economic resources play themselves out in society.

Collins's (2004) theory of inequality derives from Weber's emphasis on the importance of status and prestige as well as Goffman's micro-interpretive work. Most of the multivariate and historical-comparative theorists we have talked about tend to understand the world through a focus on large-scale structures of society. This tends to leave everyday interactions far less explored. Goffman's work in *The Presentation of Self in Everyday Life* (1959), you will remember, challenged this bias in traditional sociological theory. Collins follows this emphasis to extend the study of inequality to micro-sociological processes as well as macro-sociological structures. Traditional surveys, for example, tend to place people in one socio-economic category, which they are

supposed to carry around with them at all times. In reality, Collins argues, one's status is always connected to local interactions, something missed when one studies inequality with quantitative surveys. Thus, a professor may enjoy status and respect at the university but becomes a virtual unknown at a baseball game. This same professor would take on an even lower status while strolling through an inner-city ghetto, where he or she is forced to show deference to gangs on the street. To fully understand how social status plays out in real life, it is important to study work, leisure, and other ritual settings across a number of contexts that intersect in people's everyday lives.

Collins's (2004) focus on everyday interactions has provided interesting insights into the changing nature of status in society that the quantitative tradition is less likely to pick up. Have you ever noticed how informal servers in restaurants have become, often engaging in friendly and even personal interactions with diners? This is very different from the almost stiff formality one sees in old movies. In addition, movie stars and popular musicians today often appear in public unshaven and in torn jeans. This is something that would have been incomprehensible to someone from the generation of Marilyn Monroe or Frank Sinatra. Perhaps more dramatically, a politician today caught speeding in his or her private car would be far less likely now than in the past to escape a ticket. In the past, taking advantage of one's government authority to avoid paying the ticket might work, but today it would be seen as corrupt. Collins's theory of micro-stratification helps explain these examples of changing norms in everyday interaction as a function of larger transformations in societal

Social stratification has been a central concern of sociology since its founding. Even non-sociologists have long understood their lives are shaped by the class structure.
University of Washington Libraries, Special Collections, UW1535

attitudes towards elites, traditional authority, and the importance of formal hierarchies. The amount of status and power one has in a particular situation, Collins argues, is no longer so closely linked to the formal institutions and power relations of the larger society. Thus, from Collins's perspective, we need to do sociological work that looks closely at status and inequality in micro-interactions, as Goffman once argued. This means supplementing quantitative data on income or status with up-close observations of smaller contexts of interactions to see how social inequality plays itself out.

The Neglected Theory of W.E.B. Du Bois: The Problem of the Colour Line

Not all theorists are given as much recognition as they deserve. One of the most important sociological theorists is W.E.B. Du Bois. Du Bois was an African-Ameri-

[handwritten margin notes: "relate this / Du Bois theory / to current / day"; "historative"; "Systematic discrimination"]

ar who wrote at the same time as Durkheim r, but, for a variety of reasons, never gained the wn. For one thing, as a black scholar working ited States, Du Bois suffered from racial discrimination. In addition, Du Bois was a committed, political intellectual who spent much of his energy working on behalf of the movement for black rights in America. As a consequence, he did not formulate his theories as systematically as did scholars such as Durkheim or Weber. Moreover, as a researcher and theorist, Du Bois's contributions have had more influence in particular sub-areas of sociology (race relations, community studies, and historical sociology) than in sociological theory. Nonetheless, his legacy is impressive, and he exemplifies the need to combine the different logics of historical-comparative, multivariate, and interpretive theories.

Du Bois's *Black Reconstruction in America* (1935) is a historical analysis of the ways in which slaves were freed in the American South after the Civil War. He illustrates how blacks were first liberated from slavery, but then subordinated again through the creation of a system of legal segregation. Not satisfied with a purely historical approach, Du Bois's *The Philadelphia Negro* (1899) was one of the most important early urban studies to use up-close observations and interviews. It is also an excellent example of multivariate sociology; he gathered statistics regarding the black poor and presented a detailed ethnographic account of urban African-American Philadelphia. The study convincingly illustrates the lack of opportunities afforded to blacks at that time, and shows how their opportunities for employment were closely linked to their everyday deference to whites. Finally, *Souls of Black Folk* (1903) draws on the interpretive theories of the self learned from German scholars such as Weber and Simmel. Like many American sociologists in the early twentieth century, Du Bois visited Germany to become educated in social psychology. Du Bois uses Weber's insights to develop his own theory about the complicated psychology experienced by people who are discriminated against because of the colour of their skin. African Americans, Du Bois argues, were created by American history and became rooted in the United States after their ancestors were shipped to the New World from Africa as slaves. American blacks were part American then, since most of them, at the time Du Bois was writing, had been born and raised in the United States. The psychology of African Americans, however, has also been shaped by the experience of being looked down upon and discriminated against by the white majority. This is a condition that creates, Du Bois

argues, a complicated dual consciousness. In Canada, 'visible minorities' and Aboriginal Canadians experience a different psychology from the white majority because of similar dynamics of discrimination.

The irony here is that the major insight that Du Bois brings to contemporary sociological theory is the reason why he was ignored as a theorist for so long. Du Bois argued that the major theoretical, political, and moral problem of the twentieth century was 'the problem of the colour line'. Earlier theorists such as Weber, Marx, Simmel, Tocqueville, and Durkheim were white European theorists who tended to ignore the importance of race and racism. To be fair, both Marx and Tocqueville wrote critically about the domination of non-whites by the European great powers and in the United States. Nonetheless, only Du Bois made ra   tral to his sociological theorizing. In contempo   y, questions about racism directed at   mi   nts to Canada, the continuing tr   DS   ated deaths throughout Afri   ew ab t America that many m   world h d can be illuminate   n.

[handwritten note over text: "Theories are abstract ideas about the world"]

Putting   into Practic

For most sociologists, it is important that their research be closely connected with a **theory** or set of theories. Briefly, *theories* are abstract ideas about the world. Most sociological research is designed to evaluate a theory, either by testing it or by exploring the applicability of a theory to different situations. As can be seen throughout the many chapters in this text, sociologists investigate substantive problems and try to use their theories to help them understand these problems better. For instance, sociologists may be interested in understanding crime, the family, the environment, or education, and they will almost always use their theories to provide a deeper appreciation of these issues.

Sociologists use theories as models, or conceptual maps, of how the world works, and they use research methods to gather data relevant to these theories. Thus, theories and methods are always intertwined in the research process. There are hundreds of different theories in sociology, but most of them can be grouped into the four main theoretical perspectives that can be found throughout this text: structural functionalism, conflict theory, symbolic interactionism, and feminism. Theories cannot be tested directly because they are only abstract

ideas. _____ ervable ideas
before _____ translation is
called _____

Oper...

Operationalization is the process of translating theories and concepts into hypotheses and variables. **Concepts** are single ideas. **Theories** are abstract ideas composed of concepts. Usually, theories explain how two or more concepts are related to each other. For instance, Karl Marx used concepts such as 'alienation', 'exploitation', and 'class' to construct an abstract explanation (theory) of capitalism (see Chapter 6).

Once we have a theory, we need some way to test it. However, we are not able to test theories directly. We need an observable equivalent of a theory, or at least a set of observable statements that are consistent with our theory. These are called hypotheses. In the same way that theories express relationships between concepts, **hypotheses** express relationships between variables. Unlike the typical definition of a hypothesis as simply an 'educated guess', it is important to point out that hypotheses must be observable or testable. This means they must be composed of or express relationships between variables.

Variables are the empirical, or observable, equivalent of concepts. Variables must be observable and must have a range of different values they can take on. For instance, age, years of education, and annual income are variables. We can collect information on all of these items—that is, they are observable—and people can have different ages, incomes, and so on. 'Forty-five years old', '12 years of schooling', and '$50,000 per year' are not variables; although they are observable, they do not vary. They are *values* of variables, not variables in themselves, and it is important not to confuse the two.

In most cases, our hypotheses contain a minimum of two types of variables: independent variables and dependent variables. Independent variables are roughly equivalent to causes, and dependent variables are roughly equivalent to effects. Another way to keep these straight is to remember that the value of a dependent variable depends on the value of an independent variable. For instance, if you wanted to investigate differences between the average earnings of men and women, then sex or gender would be the independent variable and earnings would be the dependent variable. This is because peoples' earnings may depend on their gender. Indeed, it is easy to keep the independent and dependent variables straight in this example because it makes no sense to say that a person's gender can depend on his or her earnings.

● Research Techniques ● ● ●

Experiments

A popular idea is that the primary method scientists use to conduct research is the experi_____ vever, even in the natural sciences, ex_____ exception rather than the rule. A great _____ nomy, and other science is n_____ es, cannot be done—experi_____ ereotype persists, and has tr_____ gainst which science of all typ_____ measured.

The two mai_____ are that (1) experiments prov_____ in which it is possible to (_____ rs in an attempt to determi_____. Experiments can show the _____ variable on another variable quite convincingly because of these two features.

However, sociologists do not use experiments very often for two reasons. First, we cannot manipulate many of the variables we are interested in, for either practical or ethical reasons. Sociologists are often interested in the effects of variables like gender, ethnicity, and social class on other variables like educational outcomes, earnings, or health status. But it is neither ethical nor practical to alter peoples' ethnicity or gender just so we can observe what happens to their educational outcomes. Nor can we simply move a person from an upper-class home into a lower-class home (or vice versa) just so we can find out what effect this might have on his or her eventual choice of career.

Second, one of the enduring criticisms of experiments is that it is not always clear that what happens under the controlled conditions of an experiment will also happen when we try to apply our findings to the 'real world' (that is, external validity). For instance, many of the experiments in medical research are done first on rats and other animals. Will what happens to rats also happen to humans? Similarly, in social scientific research, it is never clear that what we observe in a controlled social experiment will also happen to people in their daily lives. Yet it is what happens in the real world that is often of most interest to sociologists. The findings from a social experiment may not be interesting for us until it can be shown that the results are relevant in the real world as well.

Despite the fact that sociologists do not use experiments very often, the logic of the experiment still dominates at least one of the major techniques of sociological research. Surveys almost always collect a great deal of extra information from respondents in an attempt to recreate the controlled environment of the experiment after the fact. Surveys are often referred to as *quasi-experimental* designs because they are only able to construct a controlled environment after the data have been collected. In other words, in true experiments, controlled conditions are set in place *before* the experiment is allowed to run, while in surveys, there is a set of 'naturally occurring' conditions, and some attempt is made to manage the effects of all the variables during the analysis.

Surveys

Surveys are the most widely used technique in social scientific research. Sociologists, economists, political scientists, psychologists, and others use them regularly (Gray and Guppy, 2003). They are an excellent way to gather data on large populations that cannot be studied effectively in a face-to-face manner. The goals of almost all social scientific surveys are to produce detailed data that will allow researchers to describe the characteristics of the group under study, to test theories about that group, and to generalize results beyond those people who responded to the survey.

Many 'surveys' are done for purposes other than social scientific research, and most of these will not produce data that are amenable to social science research. Designing and administering a good survey is much more difficult than it seems, but respondents rarely see all of the work that goes into producing a good survey. This may partly explain why surveys seem easy to create, and it may also contribute to the proliferation of pseudo-surveys in many different forms.

Constructing Survey Questions

Surveys consist mainly of questions, and there are many issues to consider in designing good survey questions (see Table 1.1).

At a first glance, it might seem that designing good questions for a survey would be easy. The reality, however, is that it is quite difficult. Sociologists can spend months trying to figure out what questions they will ask, how they will word them, and the order in which they will ask them. One of the reasons that it is so difficult is because each question must be unambiguous for both the respondent and the researcher. A question with several different

OPEN FOR DISCUSSION
Max Weber and *Verstehen*

In many of the chapters in this text, you will come across the ideas of Max Weber. One of his most enduring contributions to research methods in sociology is his elaboration of a concept he called '*verstehen*' (German for 'to understand'). His idea is that in order to properly study the cultures of other peoples, a researcher needs to develop more than knowledge, but an 'empathetic understanding' of their lives in order to see the world as that group sees it.

Verstehen became a cornerstone of qualitative sociology, as researchers tried to understand the lives of others 'from the inside'. In Weber's view, developing *verstehen* was a bit of an art, but in theory anyone who was good at it could understand the world view of any other group. In other words, the views of any group could be understood regardless of the personal characteristics of the researcher.

But this view has been criticized as too simplistic. That is, some researchers have argued that there are limits to *verstehen* because the personal characteristics of the researcher will affect how the group reacts to her or him. And this will limit the depth of

verstehen or understanding that a researcher can achieve. For instance, Margaret Mead's classic anthropological study in Somoa has been criticized because the Somoans later claimed that they were not completely honest with her. Similarly, men will be able to reach only a certain limited level of understanding with women. And because of this, it may not even be appropriate for men to study women, or vice versa. If we relate this to Killingsworth's (2000) study of mom and tot groups discussed in this chapter (page 24), it may be the case that as a male, he may not have had the same access to the ongoing discussions around motherhood and child care. On the other hand, are there factors that would also limit the level of *verstehen* that a researcher can achieve? And if so, what are those factors and how do we identify them? At its extreme, this would mean that a researcher would have to match up with her/his participants on everything from gender, to education level, to hair colour, to fashion sense. So neither extreme position is particularly convincing, but exactly where we draw this line remains 'open for discussion'.

interpretations is not useful because respondents may answer it from a different perspective than is intended by the researcher. Similarly, questions that are too complicated for respondents to answer, or that presume a level of knowledge that respondents do not have, will not produce useful data. There are many, many issues to consider in designing good questions and deciding on the order in which they will appear, but we will talk about just four of them.

First, sociologists must avoid the use of double-barrelled questions in surveys. *Double-barrelled questions* are those that have two or more referents or subjects, and that can therefore be answered honestly in more than one way. For instance, 'Do you think that the government should increase taxes so that it can spend more on environmental protection?' is a double-barrelled question. The problem is that a yes or no answer to this question is impossible to interpret. 'Yes' may mean that a person agrees with the whole statement, or only with the environmental protection component or only with the increasing taxes component. 'No' may mean that the person disagrees with increased taxes but may nonetheless want more environmental protection, or that he or she disagrees with the entire statement. A researcher will not know which of these interpretations is correct for any individual respondent. The way to avoid this confusion is to formulate two separate questions, one about tax increases and one for environmental spending.

A second problem occurs when researchers do not pay sufficient attention to respondents' abilities to answer questions accurately. It may seem straightforward to ask a person how much he or she earned last year, but very few people know to the actual dollar how much they earned over the previous 12 months. And even fewer people will be willing to look it up on their latest tax return. So, while you can ask people for their specific annual income, most of the answers you get will be wrong. Some people round-off their income to the nearest $1,000; others round it off to the nearest $5,000; still others simply guess at the actual dollar amount. You then have no way of correcting for these different reporting procedures. The solution is to offer people categories, because people often know to the nearest $5,000 or $10,000 how much they earn in a year.

Third, in some surveys, it is deemed necessary to ask people about uncomfortable topics and topics that they may perceive as threatening. Surveys of criminal activity, sexual practices, and criminal victimization imply socially threatening questions. However, it is impossible to predict how individuals will react to any question, and even the most innocuous question may be perceived

as threatening. Asking people about their incomes generally is perceived as somewhat threatening, and care must be exercised in how you ask about this.

Strategies for reducing the threat of questions include making the behaviour or attitude you are asking about less threatening by positioning the respondent at some distance—by asking about it in hypothetical terms or asking about it as one of a series of questions. For instance, instead of asking people directly if they have been victims of crime, you could ask people about how they feel about their own safety, how much media coverage of criminal activity they receive, and whether or not they have been victimized. It is important to note that no single strategy will work for every question, topic, or sample.

Finally, the order in which you ask questions can have a significant effect on respondents' answers, and even on whether or not they will complete the survey. As a general rule, it is better to ask threatening questions near the end rather than at the beginning of a survey. By asking easier questions up front, researchers have an opportunity to establish a rapport with the respondent, both in phone and interview surveys and through conversation and in paper surveys by leading the respondent to identify with the topics and issues on the survey. Second, if threatening questions discourage respondents so much that they refuse to participate further in the research, at least they will have completed part of the survey already. If they refuse at the beginning of the survey, no usable data are collected at all.

Random Sampling, Sample Size, and Response Rates

Random sampling is crucial to research because it is the only way that we can be confident that our sample is representative of, that is, that it looks like, the population we are interested in. If our sample is representative, then we can be fairly confident that the patterns we find among our sample also will be present in the larger population. If it is not representative, then we have no idea if what we found in our sample also is present in our population. Using a proper randomization procedure both ensures that we do not deliberately bias our sample and guards against any unintentional biases that may creep into our selection process. Although randomization does not guarantee that a sample will be representative, by minimizing both intentional and unintentional biases we maximize our chances that the sample will be representative. Remember, though, that randomization does not solve all problems in sociological research, and is not always appropriate or necessary in field research.

Table 1.1	Guidelines for Designing Good Survey Questions
Focus	Each question should have one specific topic. Questions with more than one topic are difficult to answer, and the answers are often ambiguous.
Brevity	Generally, shorter questions are preferable to longer questions. They are easier to understand for respondents. An important exception to this guideline is when asking about threatening topics, where longer questions are often preferable.
Clarity	Use clear, understandable words and avoid jargon. This is especially important for general audiences, but if you are surveying a distinctive group or population (such as lawyers), then specialized language is often preferable.
Bias	Avoid biased words, phrases, statements, and questions. If one answer to a question is more likely or is more socially acceptable than others, then the question is probably biased and should be reworded. For instance, if you are asking people about their religious preferences, do not use words like 'ungodly', 'heathen', or 'fanatic' in your questions, or else you will bias your answers.
Relevance	Ensure that the questions you ask of your respondents are relevant to them and to your research. Also, in most surveys, some questions will not be relevant to all respondents; filter questions allow people to skip questions that are not pertinent to them. For instance, if you want to know why some people did not complete high school, you should first filter out high school graduates and ask them not to answer the questions about not completing high school.

Source: Adapted from George Gray and Neil Guppy, *Successful Surveys: Research Methods and Practice*, 3rd edn (Toronto: Nelson Thomson, 2003).

There are many procedures for choosing a truly random sample, but all are based on the principle that each person (or element) in a population has an equal (and non-zero) chance of being selected into the sample. The simplest random-sampling procedure is known as *simple random sampling*: each person in a population is put on a list and then a proportion of people are chosen from the list completely at random. The usual way of ensuring that people are chosen at random is to use a table of random numbers either to select all of the people or to select the starting point in the list from which the sample will be chosen.

Actually, the adjective 'simple' in 'simple random sampling' does not refer to the degree of difficulty—simple random samples are quite difficult to construct. Generating truly random samples is not as easy as one might first imagine. The problem lies not in choosing the actual people or elements but in constructing a complete list of every person or element in the population. For this reason, other sampling techniques, such as stratified sampling and cluster sampling, are used to choose samples.

Sample size is an important consideration when designing a proper survey. One might first wonder 'How big a sample do you need in order to be able to generalize your results?' Actually, this is the wrong question to ask. It is not the size of the sample but rather how the sample is chosen that determines how confident you can be that your results are applicable to the population. That is, even a very large sample, if it is not chosen randomly, offers no guarantee about the generalizability of the results. On the other hand, a small, properly chosen sample can produce very good results. Never assume that a sample is representative just because it is large. Always find out how the sample was chosen before making any judgments about its generalizability.

Another crucial factor in determining the generalizability of survey results is how many people from the original sample actually complete the survey. This percentage is called the *response rate*, and is an important issue, although not the only issue, to consider in determining the generalizability of the results of a survey. It is important because unless a large proportion of the people in the original sample actually complete the survey,

Figure 1.1

"FILE THESE IN RANDOM ORDER LIKE YOU USUALLY DO."

Cartoon by Brenda Brown (http://webtoon.com).
Reprinted with permission.

it is quite possible that the people who do not respond are different from those who do respond.

Field Research

In surveys, the primary aim is to collect quantitative, numerical data that can be generalized to a larger population. In contrast, field researchers are concerned about collecting qualitative or non-numerical data that may or may not be generalized to a larger population. In field research, the aim is to collect rich, nuanced data by going into the 'field' to observe and talk to people directly. Researchers spend time getting to know their subjects in order to be able to capture their world view. Some of the classic sociological field studies, such as William Whyte's *Street Corner Society* (1943) and Elliot Liebow's *Tell Them Who I Am* (1993), are vivid portrayals of what life is like for certain groups of people—in the former case, the members of a lower-class urban community, and in the latter case, of homeless women.

Several separate techniques fall under the rubric of field research. These include participant observation or ethnography, in-depth interviewing, and document analysis. In many studies, more than one of these techniques is used.

Ethnographic or Participant Observation Research

In *ethnographic* or *participant observation* research, the researcher participates in the daily activities of his or her research subjects, usually for an extended period of time.

This may include accompanying them on their daily activities (such as following police officers on patrol), conducting interviews and discussions about their lives, and occasionally even living with them. During these activities, researchers take field notes (or make recordings) either during or after an episode in the field.

A good example of participant observation research is Killingsworth's (2007) study of how mothers interact with each other in a 'moms and tots' playgroup to construct ideas about what a good mother is, and how they can reconcile that perception with the consumption of alcohol. Killingsworth participated in a playgroup of mothers and toddlers in Australia over a period of several months. As is typical of participant observation research, he did not have a rigid research design that he followed strictly while he was in the field. Rather, his main interest was in the women's conversations about alcohol and their own personal consumption of it, and how they used these conversations to define, alter, and reconstruct ideas about 'good mothers'. He did not direct the women's conversations or ask them to focus their talk on particular issues. Instead, he simply participated in the playgroup and allowed the conversations to occur naturally. He found that the women were able to reconcile their understandings of good motherhood with the consumption of alcohol by recapturing the importance of alcohol to their previous identities as childless women and using that to build ideals of themselves as women first and good mothers second.

Killingworth's research is interesting for several reasons, but one reason is particularly relevant to his use of participant observation. By focring conversations, he was abl ideals about things like motherh embedded in and recreated by cussions among mothers. In o good mothers do not just appear pressure on people through 'no ideals about good mothers are reconstructed by actual people i

In-Depth Interviews

In-depth interviews are another popular field research technique and may be used in conjunction with participant observation. *In-depth interviews* are extensive interviews that are often tape-recorded and later transcribed into text. In some cases, these interviews are highly structured and neither the researchers nor the respondents are permitted to deviate from a specific set of questions. At the other extreme, unstructured interviews may seem like ordinary conversations in which researchers and _____ topics as they arise. In many _____ emi-structured in-depth interviews that ask _____ dents a basic set of questions but that also allow participants to explore other topics and issues. Striking the right balance between structured and unstructured questions can pose problems for sociologists, as can asking the right questions.

Elizabeth Murphy investigated the connections between health-care conversations (2000) and images of childhood (2007) and ideals about good mothers. Obviously, field research techniques can be used to investigate many more issues than motherhood, but Murphy's and Killingsworth's studies provide a nice illustration of how different field methods can be used to study similar topics. In her earlier article, Murphy used theories about how people understand and respond to risks as the basis of her research on breast-feeding and motherhood. In her later article, her focus was on how feeding, and breast-feeding in particular, allowed women to negotiate different conceptions of childhood. She interviewed 36 British mothers six times each, from one month before the birth of their babies to two years after birth. Each interview was semi-structured. In Murphy's sample, 31 women breast-fed their babies initially, but only six were still breast-feeding four months after birth. This is interesting in light of current medical advice about the importance of exclusively breast-feeding infants for at least four months, and many health practitioners recommend continuing up to two years of age. Did the women in this study who stopped breast-feeding before four months think of themselves as bad mothers? Or were they able to set aside this medical advice and still think of themselves as good mothers? Murphy found that almost all of the women who had stopped breast-feeding recognized formula feeding as inferior but that none of them perceived this as a threat to their status as good mothers. Rather, they were able to justify their decisions because other people were at least partly—and, in many cases, primarily—responsible for the switch to formula feeding. Also, breast-feeding and the demands of the children were critical in shaping how mothers viewed their children, in relation to 'Appolonian themes of natural goodness and innocence' (Murphy, 2007: 122). The interviews revealed that some women encountered health-care workers who were unsupportive of breast-feeding or who did not diagnose medical or mechanical problems that prevented breast-feeding. Other women had babies who were either uncooperative or could not do it because of 'incompetence' (Murphy, 2000: 317).

One of the strengths of Murphy's research is the flexibility of her semi-structured interview technique. By directing the women to discuss their breast-feeding decisions and then following their leads, Murphy was able to gain a much deeper understanding of these choices. Had she not imposed some structure on the interviews, it is possible that the women might not have talked about their breast-feeding choices at all. Instead, her research presents us with a better understanding of how women can reconcile individual decisions to stop breast-feeding with seemingly contradictory ideals about 'good motherhood'.

Document Analysis

In some field studies, researchers will have access not only to people, but also to documents. This is more common when studying formal organizations like police forces or law firms, but can also be true when studying churches, political groups, and even families. These documents (case records, files, posters, diaries, and even photos) can be analyzed to provide a more complete picture of the group under study.

The elaborate procedures needed to choose a sample for a survey are not necessary for selecting the research site and the sample in field research. Strictly following a randomization protocol is necessary only if statistical analysis and generalization are the goal of the research. Field research is done to gain greater understanding through the collection of detailed data, not through generalization. Nevertheless, it is important to choose both the research site and the subjects or informants carefully.

Conducting Field Research

The first criterion in choosing a site for field research is the topic of study. A field study of lawyers or police officers likely will take place at the offices and squad rooms of the respective groups. Choosing which offices and squad rooms to study depends on many factors, including which ones will be most useful for the purposes of the research. But a practical element impinges on much field research—the actual choice of research site can come down to which law offices or squad rooms will grant access. This is not a criticism of field research, but a recognition of the realities facing scholars doing this kind of research.

Once the site has been chosen, the issues of whom to talk to, what types of data to record, and how long to stay in the field become important. Some things can be planned in advance, but many things may be decided during the course of the field research. The selection of key informants—those people who will be most valuable in the course of the study—cannot always be made beforehand. Similarly, figuring out what to record in field notes and who to quote cannot always be determined until after the research has begun.

Deciding when to leave the field is almost always determined during the course of the research. Most researchers stay in the field until they get a sense that they are not gaining much new information. In many cases, researchers decide to leave the field when they find that the data coming from new informants merely repeat what they have learned from previous informants. This is often taken as a sign that the researcher has reached a deep enough level of understanding to be confident that he or she will not learn much from further time in the field.

This flexibility during the course of the study is one of the great advantages of field research over survey research. Mistakes in research design and the pursuit of new and unexpected opportunities are possible in field research but are not usually possible in quantitative survey research. Once a survey has been designed, pre-tested, and administered to a sample, it is impractical to recall the survey to make changes. This is one of the reasons why pre-testing is so important in surveys.

Existing Data

Both in surveys and in field research, sociologists are involved in collecting new, original data. However, a great deal of sociological research is done with data already collected. Of the several different types of existing data most are amenable to different modes of analysis. Some of the major types of existing data are official statistics and surveys done by other researchers; books, magazines, newspapers, and other media; case files and records; and historical documents.

Secondary Data Analysis

The analysis of official statistics and existing surveys—also known as *secondary data analysis*—has grown immensely with the development of computers and statistical software packages. It has become one of the most common forms of research reported in the major sociological journals, such as the *American Journal of Sociology* and the *American Sociological Review*. Statistical analyses of existing surveys also can be found in almost every issue of the *Canadian Journal of Sociology* and the *Canadian Review of Sociology and Anthropology* for at least the past 10 years.

Quantitative data can be presented in tables; however, tables can be designed in many different ways, and the type of information being presented will determine the types of comparisons that can be made. In Table 1.2, on marital status in Canada, comparisons can be made within or across the values of marital status (for example, how many people are married versus single), by sex, and across five different years.

As an example, we can see that the number of divorced males increased by over 93,000 between 1997 and 2001 (641,734 − 547,914 = 93,820) and the number of divorced females has risen by over 125,000 (868,037 − 742,671 = 125,366), while the numbers of married men and women have increased by 87,500 and 106,136 respectively. However, the table does not tell us anything about why these numbers may have changed, nor can we make any comparisons with the number of married and divorced people in other countries.

In Table 1.3, though, comparisons between countries are possible. Some of these results may seem surprising, depending on your impressions of high school graduation rates here in Canada versus other countries. Many media portrayals of the US school system suggest that it is inferior to the Canadian system, yet it has a higher graduation rate than Canada.

This table also reveals some of the problems tables may present, especially with data from different countries. First, the school systems vary widely between countries, and despite careful efforts by the Organisation for Economic Co-operation and Development (OECD) to standardize the data, all of these numbers should be viewed with caution. Many could change significantly depending on the way graduates are counted, and especially in reference to how each country reports its data to the OECD. Second, data may simply not be available, as in the case of Slovakia in Table 1.3.

Personal computers, statistical software packages, and the ready availability of many national and international data sets have made secondary data analysis possible for almost every social scientist. The advantages of secondary analyses are that the coverage of the data is broad and that the hard work involved in constructing and administering a survey has already been done, usually by an agency with far more expertise and resources than most individual researchers. The disadvantages are that the data collected are often not precise enough to test the specific ideas that interest researchers and that mastering the techniques to analyze the data properly can be challenging.

Historical Research and Content Analysis

The analysis of historical documents, print and other media, and records and case materials can be done by several methods. The two most common forms of analysis are historical research and content analysis. Historical sociology relies on *historical research* into all kinds of historical documents, from organizational records, old newspapers, and magazines to speeches and sermons, letters and diaries, and even interviews with people who

Table 1.2   Population by Marital Status and Sex, Canada, 1998–2007

	number of persons									
	1998	1999	2000	2001	2002	2003	2004	2005	2006	2007
Total										
Both sexes	30,248,412	30,499,323	30,770,834	31,110,565	31,413,990	31,676,077	31,995,199	32,312,077	32,649,482	32,976,026
Male	14,978,787	15,107,404	15,236,964	15,405,773	15,552,644	15,688,977	15,846,832	16,003,804	16,170,723	16,332,277
Female	15,269,625	15,401,919	15,543,870	15,704,792	15,861,346	15,987,100	16,148,367	16,308,273	16,478,759	16,643,749
Single										
Both sexes	12,797,263	12,911,946	13,031,272	13,175,106	13,304,129	13,231,209	13,368,674	13,507,149	13,653,059	13,800,997
Male	6,849,478	6,912,620	6,979,618	7,059,481	7,131,973	7,078,089	7,155,622	7,233,428	7,314,611	7,396,835
Female	5,947,785	5,999,326	6,051,654	6,115,625	6,172,156	6,153,120	6,213,052	6,273,721	6,338,448	6,404,162
Married[a]										
Both sexes	12,979,263	12,911,946	13,031,272	13,175,106	13,304,129	15,438,972	15,558,054	15,675,089	15,802,300	15,916,860
Male	7,299,132	7,337,226	7,381,266	7,431,522	7,476,537	7,701,393	7,752,882	7,803,419	7,860,087	7,910,554
Female	7,331,041	7,374,567	7,425,428	7,482,244	7,541,593	7,737,579	7,805,172	7,871,670	7,942,213	8,006,306
Widowed										
Both sexes	1,489,388	1,503,843	1,518,633	1,534,232	1,550,367	1,532,940	1,544,226	1,553,488	1,563,856	1,573,455
Male	263,490	269,220	274,910	280,748	286,940	288,816	295,446	301,404	307,050	312,357
Female	1,225,898	1,234,623	1,243,723	1,253,484	1,263,427	1,244,124	1,248,780	1,252,084	1,256,806	1,261,098
Divorced										
Both sexes	1,331,588	1,381,741	1,434,235	1,487,461	1,541,364	1,472,956	1,524,245	1,576,351	1,630,267	1,684,714
Male	566,687	588,338	611,170	634,022	657,194	620,679	642,882	665,553	688,975	712,531
Female	764,901	793,403	823,065	853,439	884,170	852,277	881,363	910,798	941,292	972,183

[a] Includes persons legally married, legally married and separated, and persons living in common-law unions.

Source: Statistics Canada, CANSIM, table (for fee) 051-0010.

Table 1.3	Percentage of 25- to 64-Year-Olds Graduating from Upper Secondary (High School) Programs, by Country, 1998
	Percentage Graduating from Upper Secondary
Canada	79.7
Mexico	21.2
United States	86.5
Japan	79.9
Korea	65.4
Australia	56.0
New Zealand	72.7
Belgium	56.7
Czech Republic	85.3
Denmark	78.4
Finland	68.3
France	60.7
Germany	83.8
Hungary	63.3
Italy	41.0
The Netherlands	64.3
Norway	83.0
Poland	54.3
Portugal	20.1
Spain	32.9
Slovakia	–
Sweden	76.1
Turkey	17.7
United Kingdom	60.2
OECD Mean	**61.2**

Source: Adapted from the Organisation for Economic Co-operation and Development (OECD). Data used by permission.

participated in the events of interest. In *content analysis*, documents such as newspapers, magazines, TV shows, and case records are subjected to careful sampling and analysis procedures to reveal patterns.

One of the major issues facing historical sociologists is that someone or some organization has created the records used in their analyses, but the potential biases and reasons for recording the information in the documents are not always clear. Further, some documents are lost or destroyed with the passing of time, so the historical sociologist must be aware that the extant documents may not give a complete picture of the events or time period under study. Why have certain documents survived while others have not? Is there any significance to the ordering or cataloguing of the documents? These and other issues must be dealt with continually in historical research.

Content analysis can be done in a number of ways, but it usually involves taking a sample of relevant documents and then subjecting these documents to a rigorous procedure of identifying and classifying particular features, words, or images in these documents. For instance, in studying political posters, content analysis could be used to determine whether the posters from particular parties put more emphasis on the positive aspects of their own party or the negative aspects of other parties. These results could then be used to better understand styles of political campaigning in a particular country or time period. In *manifest content analysis*, words, phrases, or images are counted to provide a sense of the importance of different ideas in the documents. In *latent content analysis*, researchers focus less on specific word or phrase counts and more on the themes implicit in the documents.

● Selecting ● ● ● ● ● ● ● a Research Method

All of the methods described in this chapter are used by sociologists to collect data on particular research problems; they use theories to help them understand or solve these problems. Any of these methods can be used to investigate problems from any of the theoretical perspectives encountered in this text, although some methods are almost never used in some perspectives. For instance, symbolic interactionists rarely, if ever, use quantitative surveys, while most conflict theorists prefer surveys to participant observation.

How do you know which method to use with which theory or theoretical perspective? The rule of thumb in sociology has been that you let the problem determine the method. For example, if you want to find out something about the national divorce rate and how divorced people differ from those who remain married, then you need a method that will give you data from people all over the country, such as a survey.

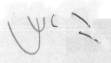

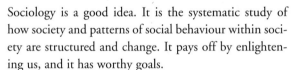

ime to Reflect

vere to read a piece of research, would you be more inclined to believe the results if they were based on
...ative analysis or on field research? Why?

But if you want to find out how nurses manage the many pressures of their jobs, then participant observation is a more appropriate method.

As with any generalization, there are exceptions. Sheldon Goldenberg (1992) and others have argued that letting the problem determine the method is not as straightforward as it seems. A sociologist can become overly comfortable using a particular technique. This leads to a tendency to frame research questions in ways that allow those familiar techniques to be used. In other words, the comfortable methods can come to determine the questions considered for investigation.

● Conclusion ● ● ● ● ● ●

Sociology is a good idea. It is the systematic study of how society and patterns of social behaviour within society are structured and change. It pays off by enlightening us, and it has worthy goals.

It is a broad field of study. This is obvious in the broad theoretical perspectives used to guide much sociological research. The breadth of the field of study is further evident in the idea that sociology highlights both micro- and macro-level analyses and the complex relationships between the two as highlighted in Mills's concept of the sociological imagination. Sociology also covers a broad

subject matter—consider the subject matter of the following chapters, ranging across deviance, family, education, religion, politics, the economy, health, and beyond.

Sociology allows people to move beyond a purely common-sense approach to better understanding social life. It allows them to use more powerful methods of investigation that reveal the multi-faceted and elaborate ways that aspects of social life are interconnected. In the process, much **common-sense knowledge** is shown to be faulty. Sociology will help you see that things are not always what they seem.

Sociology stresses the relationships among individuals, social structure, and culture. Social structure and culture are shown to constrain the behaviour of individuals, yet they are essential for the persistence of human life and society. In addition, social structure and culture are creations of humans through social interaction and, therefore, are subject to future change by individuals acting in group settings. Strong constraints are placed on certain forms of social and cultural change, however, by the actions of powerful interest groups.

Sociology has obvious personal relevance, since it addresses everyday life issues. And, finally, sociology has an important goal overall: to contribute positively to the future of humanity. Our sincere hope is that this text will set you on your way to developing your own sociological imagination.

Questions for Critical Thought

1. Durkheim emphasized the importance of ceremonies that encourage social solidarity in society, reducing the isolation of individuals. The presence of lonely and isolated individuals is often a serious problem on university campuses in North America. What can universities—administrations, faculties, and students—do to try and increase ceremonial activities in ways that might bolster social cohesion?

3. What are some of the strengths of each of the three major theoretical approaches we have discussed: multivariate, interpretive, and historical-comparative? What are some of the weaknesses of each approach?

4. When you read about a social scientific finding in the newspaper, what kinds of evidence convince you of its veracity? In other words, do you need quantitative, statistical results, are you convinced by detailed accounts of individuals, or are both equally convincing?

5. If you were going to investigate the effects of a person's ethnicity on his or her educational attainment throughout Canada, what method would be most appropriate? Why?

6. It was argued in this chapter that there is no single feminist method. Do you agree with this? Why or why not?

Recommended Readings

Robert Alford, *The Craft of Inquiry* (Oxford: Oxford University Press, 1998).

The argument that sociological theory can be divided into the three major approaches (multivariate, interpretive, and historical-comparative) is developed in this clearly written guide to the research process. Perhaps a difficult read on the first attempt, this book is extremely helpful when you are engaging in your own research. It outlines the process by which you can frame a research question using sociological theory and explains what methods to use to answer a question you are interested in.

Earl Babbie, *The Basics of Social Research*, 2nd edn (Toronto: Wadsworth Thomson Learning, 2002).

Babbie's books are used in more research methods courses across North America than those of any other author. This one is a comprehensive treatment of research methods.

Bruce Berg, *Qualitative Research Methods for the Social Sciences*, 4th edn (Boston: Allyn and Bacon, 2001).

Berg's book is the current standard for qualitative research methods courses.

George Gray and Neil Guppy, *Successful Surveys: Research Methods in Practice*, 3rd edn (Toronto: Nelson, 2003).

Gray and Guppy have written an accessible and comprehensive introduction to survey research methods. The book can be used as a step-by-step guide for conducting a basic survey.

Don G. McTavish and Herman Loether, *Social Research: An Evolving Process*, 2nd edn (Boston: Allyn and Bacon, 2002).

Another popular methods book, this one is more focused on quantitative methods than qualitative methods. Loether and McTavish have also written statistics texts that have been used in many social statistics courses across North America.

Fred Pampel, *The Sociological Lives and Ideas* (New York: Worth, 2006).

This is a well-written short introduction to the basic ideas of Marx, Weber, Durkheim, Simmel, Mead, and Du Bois. Following in the tradition of Coser, Pampel's text does a particularly nice job of linking the lives and historical context of each of these classical sociological theorists with their sociological concepts. If we were to recommend one short introduction to classical theorists, this would be it.

Shulamit Reinharz with Lynn Davidman, *Feminist Methods in Social Research* (New York: Oxford University Press, 1992).

Reinharz's book is the starting point for informed discussions of feminist methods. By reading this book first, you'll have a better appreciation of the more recent writings on feminist methods, many of which cite this book as a key source.

Irving Zeitlin, *Ideology and the Development of Sociological Theory*, 7th edn (Englewood Cliffs, NJ: Prentice-Hall, 2001).

Zeitlin, who taught at the University of Toronto for many years, is particularly valuable for highlighting the historical context for the emergence of sociological theory in the conservative reactions to the French Revolution. The ideas of Marx are given particular attention in this classic text.

● Recombined ● ● ● ● Websites

Émile Durkheim Archive
durkheim.itgo.com

Designed for undergraduate students, this site provides links to selections from Durkheim's major writings.

Inter-university Consortium for Political and Social Research www.icpsr.umich.edu

This is one of the first—and one of the best—social science data archives in the world. As a college or university student, you can use many of the datasets from the ICPSR for class and research purposes, at no charge.

Organisation for Economic Co-operation and Development (OECD) www.oecd.org

The OECD collects data on economic, political, social, environmental, and industrial conditions in member countries (including Canada) and non-member countries (particularly developing countries). Data, publications (online and paper), and special reports are available at this site.

PAR-L: A Canadian Electronic Feminist Network www.unb.ca/PAR-L/

PAR-L (Policy, Action, Research List) is a network of feminist groups and individuals engaged in research and policy discussions on women. This site is a great collection of links to feminist and advocacy organizations, as well as to publications and resources on feminist issues in Canada.

Research Methods Resources on the WWW www.slais.ubc.ca/resources/research_methods/content.htm

Although this site is no longer being maintained and has not been updated since June 2007, it presents a useful list of both qualitative and quantitative methods resources, originally developed at the University of British Columbia library. Resources include online books, data, journals, and more.

Sociosite: Sociological Theories and Perspectives www.sociosite.net/topics/theory.php

This resource is a valuable source on the most famous sociological theorists and their major ideas.

Statistics Canada www.statcan.gc.ca

This is one of the most useful sites on the Internet for Canadian sociologists. Many of the surveys listed at this site can be used for class projects and research papers through your university or college, at no charge to you. Ask at your computing centre or library for details on the Data Liberation Initiative. If you go to only one of the sites listed here, make it this one.

WWW Virtual Library: Sociology—Sociological Theory and Theorists www.mcmaster.ca/socscidocs/w3virtsoclib/theories.htm

A comprehensive website that provides links to the key texts of major sociological and social theorists.

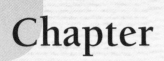

Chapter

Culture and Culture Change

Shyon Baumann

Learning Objectives

In this chapter, you will:

▶ see that culture has many meanings and dimensions;

▶ observe that culture is ubiquitous, thoroughly a part of our lives, and necessary
  for social life;

▶ learn that culture is powerful: it integrates members of society but can also cause
  great conflict;

▶ learn that culture quintessentially carries meaning and facilitates communication;

▶ see that change in culture is inevitable: it is within the nature of culture to evolve; and

▶ find that sometimes culture change is caused by socio-structural factors and other
  times culture change is spurred by other cultural factors.

● Why Study Culture? ●

Why do sociologists care about culture? Briefly, because **culture** is an amazingly powerful social force that influences events as diverse as whom we marry and whether we go to war. Marriage and war are interesting examples—while they seem unrelated, they are similar insofar as they both involve the bonds between people, in one case bringing people closer together and in the other pushing them further apart.

Let us consider how culture is implicated in each of these events. How we choose whom to marry is incredibly complicated, but what is clear is that, in general, people like to marry other people with whom they share interests and experiences. Such shared ideas and preferences create feelings of comfort and familiarity, which are things we enjoy about being with other people. If we like the same music and the same kind of movies, if we share a belief in the importance of family and the role of religion in our lives, if we share a notion of the different roles and responsibilities of men and women, and if we support the same political ideals, then we feel more connected to each other. In all these ways, culture is influencing how we relate to others. Culture includes all these preferences and ideas and notions, and these are the things that allow us, in our daily lives, to feel connections to other people. Cultural similarities influence our decisions not only about getting married, but about all kinds of connections—with whom we become and stay friends, even with whom we work.

Just as we often are brought closer to other people, so too do we often experience social divisions, some relatively minor and others quite significant. Like marriage, war is an enormously complicated phenomenon; it can result from a wide array of social, economic, and geopolitical factors. But it is also clear that culture can play a role in creating or worsening the divisions between groups or societies that can lead to war. While a conflict of material interests usually sets the stage for war, culture can play a large role in determining whether war is engaged. If we differ in fundamental **beliefs** about such things as democracy and human rights, if we speak different languages and cannot easily communicate, if we cannot understand others' religious concepts and practices or strongly oppose them, if we do not share preferences for what we consider to be the normal and good ways to live our lives, then we feel less connected to each other. In all these ways, culture plays a role in dividing us from others, and it is only in the presence of such divisions, when we feel essentially different and disconnected from others, that we are able to pursue as drastic a course of action as war. In addition, culture plays a role in many more minor social divisions that are not as significant as war, the various social cleavages between many **social groups** within the same society.

Culture, then, is important because it is the key to understanding how we relate to each other; specifically, it is behind both what unites us and what divides us. Our cultural differences and similarities are continually coming into play in our daily face-to-face interactions and on a global scale. To truly understand the dynamics of war and peace, love and hate, and more, we need to look at the ways culture facilitates or inhibits the bonds and the rifts between us.

The goals of this chapter are to review the many nuances to the meaning of culture and to explain how culture is implicated in many important social processes. First, we will further specify what culture is through a clear conceptualizing of culture's many dimensions. Second, we will summarize how culture is used in sociological theorizing about society and examine how culture fits into causal explanations of the way society works. In this chapter, we are also interested in a description of those realms of social life that are primarily cultural—the loci of culture. The nature of cultural change is a third focus of this chapter, and we will examine the reciprocal relationship between cultural change and social change. Finally, we will discuss the insights of this chapter as they pertain to Canadian culture.

● What Is Culture? ●

Think of the many different ways you might use the word 'culture' in conversation. You might use it to refer to the way that an entire society lives, visible most clearly when it is foreign to you, as perhaps in 'Thai culture'. You might use 'culture' to refer to the refined aesthetic productions that 'cultured' people enjoy, such as art shows, symphony concerts, or theatrical performances. Culture takes on a still different meaning in a phrase such as 'consumer culture', which focuses on a major pattern of people's behaviour and a set of economic institutions in contemporary society. Or, you might use 'culture' to refer to the practices and preferences of a subgroup of people, for example, 'jock' or 'geek' or 'skater' culture, who are nonetheless part of the larger society, in whose culture they also participate. Perhaps no term in the sociological vocabulary has as many meanings as 'culture'. Although some of these meanings are closely related to each other, others are remarkably divergent. For a concept that has traditionally been viewed as central to much sociological analysis, this is a strange state of affairs and one that complicates any attempt to provide a succinct and definitive summary of the sociology of culture. In lieu of a concise definition that would miss too many crucial nuances, this chapter will explain what culture is through a discussion of its most important dimensions.

Distinctively Cultural Elements of Social Life

Concepts like culture are most useful when it is clear what they do and do not refer to. At its most expansive, culture can be conceived of as the sum total of human creation; everything that is a product of a human mind, no matter how small or large, how concrete or abstract, how individual or widely shared, constitutes an element of culture. The first clear distinction, then, is between culture and the natural world as it exists apart from human interaction. For the purposes of sociological analysis, when we speak of culture we do not refer to the physical reality of our natural environment, the complex ecological system billions of years in the making. This first distinction, however, still leaves quite a lot under the rubric of culture, namely all of social reality, and this begs for further clarification.

Defining culture as the sum total of the human-influenced and human-created environment—anything and everything that is the product of a human mind—leaves us with a rather bloated notion of the term's meaning. This expansive definition rests on the notion that all of our thought processes are conditioned and shaped by the **social environment** into which we are socialized. Without this social environment, without this culture, we would have nothing to form our thoughts except for our natural instincts and desires. All human societies, however, develop distinctive ways of life that can significantly shape the minds of individuals and allow them to develop into socialized members of that society. Insofar as this **socialization process** influences all that we do—if not directly then at least indirectly—we can plausibly call all of social life cultural.

Although culture can mean all of this, the concept is really only useful for making sociological arguments and drawing sociological insights if we can limit it further. In practice, we are usually interested in determining the relative influence or functioning of cultural factors in society compared to other, non-cultural but still social, factors. We therefore often employ various, more restricted senses of the term and strive to set apart cer-

tain elements of social life as 'cultural' from those elements that are not. To add to the complicated nature of defining 'culture', among sociologists persists a certain amount of disagreement over which elements of social life are properly 'cultural'.

For the sake of giving initial form to the idea of culture as it is discussed here, we can create a list of specific things that are always or usually classified as 'culture' in sociology. Languages, symbols, discourses, texts, knowledge, values, attitudes, beliefs, norms, world views, folkways, art, music, ideas, and ideologies all are 'culture'. In sociological analysis, these social phenomena are differentiated on the basis of inherent cultural qualities. To better understand why these things are 'culture', we need to think about their characteristics.

Culture is different between places and at different times. We also need to examine the ways that sociologists distinguish between the cultural and the non-cultural. Two major distinctions employed in the sociological literature to specify the elements of culture are the difference between culture and structure, and the difference between the symbolic and the non-symbolic.

Pascal Deloche/Godong/Corbis

Culture in Place and Time

Culture quite often refers to the entire social reality of particular social groups in comparison to other social groups. Perhaps the largest cultural groupings frequently in use differentiate between large regions of the globe—Western culture, for example. While encompassing tremendous variation these groupings convey a notion that coheres in contradistinction to the history and present reality of, for example, Eastern and Near Eastern cultures. Such a broad distinction obscures the many similarities and historical continuities between these cultures and instead emphasizes how they differ. Nonetheless, it is a first step in limiting the concept of culture to a more useful definition, namely the entire social environment of people from within a circumscribed physical space.

It should be immediately clear that we often think of culture in more specific geographic terms than just Western or Eastern. We frequently think in national terms, with fairly strong ideas of what we mean by, for example, Japanese culture, Italian culture, or Mexican culture. These ideas exist in our minds as stereotypes or generalizations about the kind of lives inhabitants of these countries lead. Among many other things, we might think of Japanese rituals of politeness and a preference for sushi, the sights and sounds of Italian opera and the speed of Vespa scooters, and small Mexican towns where elaborate, solemn Catholic ceremonies can give way to lively and colourful festivals. Likewise, you might have noticed when talking to people from other countries that they sometimes impose expectations on you based on stereotypes of Canada and Canadians: 'Do you play hockey? Ski? Have a snowmobile?'

Whatever the accuracy or generalizability (frequently low) of such stereotypes as images of the typical culture of these countries, their pervasiveness points to the reality that culture can vary systematically between nations, even in ways we commonly are unaware of. Nation-states have often (although not always) coalesced around a common cultural foundation, or if one was not clearly defined from early on, they have tended to promote such a cultural foundation for the sake of national unity and cohesion.

Despite the definitional clarity that a notion of national culture offers, on closer inspection we can see that, like the larger generalizations of 'Western culture' or 'Eastern culture', national cultures also entail a great deal of regional and local variation. For example, in a large country such as the United States, the culture of the politically liberal, highly urbanized, economically successful Northeast can be contrasted with the culture of the politically conservative, less affluent states in the South. Such a contrast points to the differences between the whole way of life of northeasterners and southerners; however, we need to be mindful that both share a culture that is more generally 'American' and that they therefore share countless cultural features as well.

We can continue to spatially limit our concept of culture by pointing to the general social differences between various cities and even between parts of cities. The culture of downtown Toronto, for example, brings up notions of a lifestyle and a built environment that are business-oriented, cosmopolitan, and culturally rich. Toronto's **urbanism** is often cited for its impersonality and inward-looking character, and contrasts with the habits, manners, and interaction styles of, for example, St John's, Newfoundland. Remember that, as with the differences in regions, such local cultural variations exist in a broader cultural environment of greater similarities than differences.

However, just as with the differences between regions, we must be careful not to overstate the precision with which we can delineate a concept of culture based on physical space. Cultural similarities are bound to exist between various physical spaces—no matter how narrowly we draw our boundaries—on account of social spaces being shared. Just as we can identify culture as the human environment of specific geographic locations, so we can identify culture as the human environment of groups who are similar socially despite being geographically disparate. Therefore, we can think of the culture of, for example, adolescent males as distinct from adolescent females and from adult males, whether their geographic location is Vancouver or Halifax. (See also Table 2.1 on radio listening times across genders and age groups, broken down by musical genre.) Acknowledging culture's social—not just physical—boundedness provides us with a second dimension for understanding and limiting the meaning of culture.

Age and **gender**, the social groupings in the above example, are just two of many social boundaries that can differentiate between cultures. Other social lines along which cultural features may fall include **race** and **ethnicity**, sexual orientation, religion, and many other ways that people see fit to distinguish themselves. Another social space with important cultural implications is that of social **class**. Stereotypes of distinct working- and upper-class cultures are at least as pervasive as national stereotypes. We have firm ideas about the typical speech, mannerisms, dress, culinary preferences, occupations, and leisure activities of the working class and the upper class.

Table 2.1 — Radio Listening Time by Format and Age Group, Fall 2006

	All Ages	Teens 12–17	Men (18 and over)	Women (18 and over)
Adult contemporary	22.3	23.0	17.3	27.2
Album-oriented rock	6.0	9.3	8.0	3.8
CBC	11.6	2.7	10.7	13.1
Contemporary	8.8	24.8	8.5	7.8
Country	10.0	8.5	9.4	10.8
Dance	0.5	2.7	0.4	0.4
Easy listening	3.6	0.9	3.2	4.2
Golden oldies/rock	13.9	14.2	17.0	10.9
Middle-of-the-road	2.8	0.5	2.5	3.3
Sports	1.0	0.5	1.9	0.2
Talk	10.2	2.0	11.0	10.0
US stations	3.0	6.2	3.1	2.6
Other	6.3	4.6	7.0	5.8
Total listening time	100.0	100.0	100.0	100.0

Note: Figures may not add up due to rounding.

Source: Statistics Canada, at: <www40.statcan.ca/l01/cst01/arts17.htm?sdi=radio>.

At this point it is necessary to point out again that, just as the cultures of urban Ontario and rural Alberta share more similarities than differences, the culture of different social groups within a society likewise share more similarities than differences. By enumerating the ways in which, for example, social classes in Canada differ, we neglect myriad ways in which they are similar: difference in accent is trivial to the overall nature of a language; a similar reliance on automobiles overshadows any consideration of whether those automobiles are foreign or domestic; and a propensity to vote for different political parties cannot diminish the tremendous importance of a shared faith in parliamentary democracy.

In addition, it is necessary to point out that the dimensions of physical and social space are relatively, but not entirely, independent of each other. In some instances there is considerable overlap when a social grouping exclusively or almost exclusively inhabits a physical space.

For example, if we were to study the culture of retirement communities, we would see that these are physical spaces populated mostly by a specific social group defined by age. The social boundedness of culture by age (the culture of an older generation) overlays a physical boundedness of culture by residential location (the culture of a retirement community). Likewise, there is a great deal of overlap between, for example, the physical space of Anglican churches and the social space of Anglicans.

Notice that cases in which the physical and social spatial dimensions of culture intersect to the exclusion of other social groups are fairly narrowly circumscribed. For the most part, our social lives are messier, and different **subcultures** interact with each other all the time. Sometimes the young visit their grandparents in their retirement homes; quite frequently individuals of various social classes occupy the same classrooms, malls, arenas, and workspaces (although with different functions within those workspaces); segregation on the basis of race sometimes occurs residentially, though for the most part the common venues in which daily life is played out are racially integrated.

Adding to the fuzziness of cultural boundaries, borrowing across cultures happens all the time. Often such borrowing occurs without anyone noticing, but sometimes it can happen in ways that are thought to be illegitimate, leading to charges of cultural appropriation. In those cases, the borrowing of culture across social boundaries can offend a group's sense of identity and cultural heritage.

Finally, we can recognize that culture varies over time. The temporal dimension is an important qualifier because of the magnitude of differences that accumulate to produce cultures that are vastly different from what came before. In other words, culture evolves.

Leaving aside the precise mechanisms of cultural evolution for now, we can recognize that for the most part culture is never static. It is always developing new features and characteristics. Therefore, Western culture of today is remarkably different from 500 years ago and is in many ways quite different from even 10 years ago. The temporal dimension of culture is independent of its physical and social locations—culture changes over time in all countries and regions and for all social groupings. Norwegian culture today is different from what it was in 1900; French-Canadian culture, irrespective of actual geographic roots, has evolved over the century as well; and the culture of Canadians in their 60s has changed dramatically over time—the leisure and work options and the values and ideals of older Canadians bear little resemblance to what they were in earlier time periods. Many observers of culture argue that cultural changes are occurring more frequently in recent time periods—the rate of cultural change is increasing. When we turn to the specifics of cultural dynamics, we will learn more about the reasons behind this increase in the rate of change.

GLOBAL ISSUES
Fashion and Religion Don't Mix in Toronto

In their zeal to cash in on the trendiness of all things Bollywood, organizers of Toronto's biggest fashion event have stepped into a cultural minefield, outraging thousands of South Asians worldwide.

Hyped as a synergy of East and West—'Bollywood bling meets rhinestone cowboy'—the theme of this year's gala Fashion Cares has sparked an international protest among Hindus, who say the event appropriated their culture and was disrespectful to their religion.

About 5,000 people attended the annual fashion extravaganza organized by the AIDS Committee of Toronto (ACT) to raise money for AIDS prevention and treatment, held at the Metro Toronto Convention Centre on Saturday.

'The reaction is massive. It's not just locally people who are upset, it's internationally', said Tushar Unadkat, owner of a Toronto advertising agency. He said he has received thousands of e-mails from Canada, the United States, the United Kingdom and India since he posted a letter about the show on his website earlier this week.

The head of the Vishnu Hindu temple in Richmond Hill is organizing a protest to be staged in front of ACT offices. 'It's totally despicable to present a nude exhibition of a goddess. Hindus are docile and laid-back people, and they (ACT) obviously took advantage of that, but we won't stand for this', said Dr Budhendra Doobay, adding he wants a full public apology from ACT in the mainstream press.

ACT, which expects to raise more than $1 million from the event, has issued an apology on its website. 'ACT regrets any offence that was caused. Our intention was to have a great event to raise money for a worthwhile cause', said Karim Karsan, an ACT spokesperson and board member. . . .

Protestors say that despite the Bollywood theme, South Asians were largely absent from the show, aside from a performance by a hip hop bhangra group, a South Asian DJ spinning tunes and a song by a *Bombay Dreams* cast member. Clothes by South Asian fashion designers were not featured, and there were few South Asian models.

Some groups, like the National Anti-Racism Council of Canada, also found the pairing of cowboys and Indians, with its 'connotation of colonial conquest', problematic.

The cover of the Fashion Cares program, handed out at the show, depicts a model in a stylized pose of the multi-armed Lakshmi, goddess of wealth. She is sitting cross-legged in the lotus position and nude except for strategically placed sparkles.

'India has a very exotic image attached to it, especially now, and I'm totally for the mainstream embracing our culture, but they took it too far. These deities are sacred to us. How dare they do this', said Mitra Sen, a former director of the *Degrassi Junior High* television series, now a teacher in Toronto.

Unadkat said he was horrified to see drag queens dressed as the goddesses Durga, Saraswati and Lakshmi, smoking and drinking at the event, and white models dressed as Krishna and Radha, handing out postcards of Hindu gods and goddesses—images that had drinks spilled on them and were trampled underfoot when dropped. . . .

'I'm all for cultural fusion and all that fun stuff, but you can't mess with religion that way', said [Abhishek] Mathur, festival director of Masala! Mehendi! Masti!

About two dozen activist groups, including the Alliance for South Asian AIDS Prevention, brought the issues to ACT's attention a month before the show.

The storm began to brew after the Fashion Cares April 13 launch party, which featured white models dressed as goddesses, and go-go dancers with their skin painted in Krishna blue serving alcohol. Karsan now admits ACT should have consulted more broadly within the South Asian community before going ahead with the show. ACT made some changes to its marketing materials after it got negative responses, but it was too late to pull the program cover depicting a nude Lakshmi, he added.

The hullabaloo serves as a wake-up call to the sometimes complacent South Asian community, said Krishan Mehta, chair of the South Asian group. 'It's all about politics of inclusion. The mainstream still sees our culture as song-and-dance dinnertime entertainment, but if we want to be real players with a voice at the table, we need to push them to get beyond that.'

The incident shows how 'clued out' most so-called mainstream organizations, both corporate and non-profit, are when dealing with ethnic groups, said Andil Gosine, a professor of race and cultural studies at York University. 'They're not as engaged with the multicultural reality of Toronto as they ought to be, and they don't realize how much they're losing out because of that. The lesson here is to be really willing to deal with the people you claim to serve and not just have a distant relationship with them', Gosine said. 'My feeling is this kind of show results because there are not enough people of colour engaged in these institutions. They are so lost in how so much of Toronto's population thinks and reacts because of this.'

However, not everyone found the show offensive. Toronto filmmaker Deepa Mehta, who attended, said she doesn't know what all the fuss is about. 'This appropriation of culture makes me slightly uncomfortable, but surely we should be a bit more secure in our culture. Bollywood is good fun, glitzy, not to be taken seriously. It's just a fashion show, as opposed to an affront to our goddesses, and I'm a good Hindu', said Mehta.

In India, people are typically much more relaxed about such things, said Mehta, recounting a costume party she attended in New Delhi last year where everyone came dressed as a deity.

'We leave a culture behind in India and we become very protective about it, and we let that define who we are. I think it's very sad. When someone apologizes, we should accept it and move on.' . . .

Source: Abridged from Prithi Yelaja, 'For Hindus, it's fashion careless', *Toronto Star*, 9 June 2005, A1. Reprinted with permission—Torstar Syndication Services.

Culture and Structure

While a description of culture's dependence on time and location shows us the changing nature of culture, we also need a clear idea of what 'counts' as culture and what does not. To help us to draw this boundary, we can consider the distinction between *culture* and **structure**, two terms that have specific meanings within formal sociology. This distinction, as described by Philip Smith, sees culture primarily as the realm of the 'ideal, the spiritual, and the non-material' and opposed to the 'material, technological, and the social-structural' (2001: 3–4).

The meanings of these terms merit further elucidation. One might characterize the *ideal*, the *spiritual*, and the *non-material* as things that exist primarily in people's heads, limited to an essentially mental existence. That is to say, this version of culture privileges the distinction between thoughts, emotions, beliefs, and the more abstract elements of organized social life on the one hand and the 'concrete' elements of society that are embodied and enacted by actual things and people on the other hand. Drawing the boundaries of culture in this fashion allows us to classify, for example, attitudes about gender roles and about the kinds of work that are appropriate for men and for women as 'cultural'. Such attitudes are shared modes of thinking, and to the extent that they are only mental constructs, they properly are cultural.

At the same time, the fact that there exists a high degree of occupational segregation by gender, with some jobs primarily done by women (for example, elementary school teachers) and others primarily done by men (for example, elementary school principals), is not cultural. Rather, this segregation is 'structural'. It is an enduring pattern of social behaviour, existing primarily not at a mental level but at a level of lived experience. The idea that it is normal or proper for men to be principals and women to be elementary school teachers is a cultural value. The fact that this pattern exists in our society (although changing) is a structural property of our society.

We can find another example in the realm of **politics**. In Canada the widely held preference for representative democracy and a belief that it is a legitimate and necessary form of self-government represent a deep-rooted aspect of Canadian culture. This political orientation is related in a significant way to many other beliefs about authority, individual rationality, and justice, and so it is an element of culture that is enmeshed in a web of other important cultural elements. In contrast, representative democracy is not merely an idea, it is a practice that involves a tremendous amount of material resources and engenders long-standing patterns of social behaviour. Known in the sociological literature as **the state**, our democratic government is a structural dimension of social life. It is related in significant ways to many aspects of citizens' daily existence; it influences, among other things, our work lives, our consumption patterns, our health outcomes, and our educational outcomes, and so it is a material element of social life that is clearly enmeshed in a web of other important structural elements.

Culture as Symbolic

A second way in which culture frequently is defined in sociology is according to the role that it plays in creating meaning. In this view, culture is those elements of social life that act as symbols and are subject to interpretation. These elements are produced in order to be received and understood by individuals who derive meaning—a personal understanding—through the reception process. Any element of society that has meaning for its creator and its audience, even if there is a discrepancy between the intended and the perceived meanings, is part of the symbolic order. Culture, then, is both a product of **social interaction** and the social force that enables social interaction because it allows people to communicate meanings to each other.

In contrast to the symbolic, many things in life play an instrumental role for purposes other than communication or expression. For example, houses provide shelter from the elements, and planes exist to transport people and cargo. In these roles, houses and planes are not cultural. Admittedly, this is a fine distinction because meaning can often be found wherever we look hard enough, especially by those with a postmodern sensibility that encourages a view of all social objects as 'texts' that can be 'read' for the meanings that society has imbued them with. However, it is of practical importance to limit culture to those things that are intended to be interpreted and to hold meaning, even if people's interpretations of those meanings might vary.

Going back to the political example demonstrating the difference between culture and structure, we can see the state as an instrumental **social institution** designed to achieve governance. It does not qualify as culture because it is not in itself a symbol; it does not exist to be received and understood as having a meaning. However, there is no shortage of politically oriented culture or of political symbols existing in a wide array of forms. Political ideologies of the left, centre, and right, expressed in political discourses, conversations, newspaper articles, and books, both fiction and non-fiction, are squarely in the realm of culture. The national anthem and the Canadian flag are both explicit political symbols. The neo-Gothic Parliament buildings in Ottawa, while serving as the venue for federal politics, also serve as a political symbol, through the 'messages' associated with their stately, traditional, European style of architecture (they are not pagodas or pyramids) and because they are sufficiently well known to conjure an association with the federal government and so can represent the country as a whole. Their very image has gained interpretive currency and so can be effectively used as a tool for communication.

The symbolic view of culture bears much similarity to the view that opposes culture to structure. In both views, the roles of ideas and mental states are important elements of culture. The two views do differ, however. Where the opposition between culture and structure emphasizes the distinction between the material and the non-material, the symbolic view of culture, with its focus on the expressive function of culture, recognizes that meaning is conveyed through symbols that take material form.

By combining the insights of each perspective, we can recognize that culture is ideas, beliefs, emotions, and thoughts and their direct physical embodiments, such as paintings and newspapers. First, the two views together provide a more comprehensive description of what constitutes culture than either does alone, but without being unduly or impractically broad. Second, those manifestations that are clearly 'culture' from both perspectives are generally closer to the core of the concerns of the sociology of culture. For example, language—non-material words spoken or otherwise transmitted to convey meaning—is a phenomenon that is a cultural subject par excellence. Third, the two perspectives show us that there are multiple ways of viewing social phenomena. It is possible that certain things can be analyzed as culture while they are simultaneously understood as being outside the realm of culture.

To take a technological example, the automobile can be analyzed on different levels. On the one hand, automobiles are material objects that are instrumental in facilitating social needs. They are part of the structural side of social life, namely, our transportation system. On the other hand, automobiles are designed with an aesthetic dimension to them, and as such they are the embodiment of ideas about taste and style, which are cultural elements. They play a role in self-expression for many people. On a deeper level, attitudes towards automobile use and the kind of lifestyle that their use engenders are known as 'car culture', and in this sense automobiles are implicated in the realm of social culture in a second way.

● The Role of Culture ● ● ●
in Social Theory

Now that we have a clear idea of what culture is, we can gain an understanding of how it has figured in the works of some of the major sociological theorists. In this section, we will outline how these thinkers have employed culture in their writings about the fundamental driving forces of society.

Above all else, theories explain things. That is to say, the defining feature of a theory is that it tells why or how something is the way it is. Social theories, then, are explanations of social things—they tell us why certain aspects of society are the way they are. A great deal of social theory, it turns out, is strongly concerned with culture. This concern, however, appears in different forms: social theories are concerned with culture for a variety of reasons. Below, we consider the place of culture in five major social theoretical perspectives.

Orthodox Marxist and Neo-Marxist Theories

One of the most influential theoretical perspectives in sociology is **Marxism**. In developing his theory of society, Karl Marx was responding directly to previous philosophical arguments about the central role of ideas (squarely cultural) in determining the path of history and the nature of social reality. In such arguments, the general cultural environment worked at the level of ideas to shape people's thoughts and actions, and so was in principle the root cause behind events and social change. This 'spontaneous unfolding' of the spirit or culture of a given time could explain the course of history (Smith, 2001: 13).

By contrast, in Marxism, social reality is seen as determined primarily by the prevailing **mode of production**, evolving through history from agrarian societies to slave ownership to feudalism and then to industrial **capitalism**. This perspective posits that the best way to explain social facts—and all of history—is by recognizing that they are outcomes, direct or indirect, of the economic organization of society.

Societies shift from one mode of production to the next in a historical progression, the current state being industrial capitalism. The economic organization of society forms the base on which the rest of society, the superstructure, is founded. In a strict reading of Marxism, the superstructure responds to, but does not cause, changes in the base. Culture, in all its forms—ideas, beliefs, values, art, religion, and so on—is part of the superstructure and must be understood as essentially a product of the base.

In today's society, then, all aspects of our culture are shaped by the needs and dictates of industrial capitalism. One of the most important cultural productions of capitalism is the **dominant ideology**. This ideology is a system of thoughts, knowledge, and beliefs that serves to legitimate and to perpetuate capitalism. Our mental lives are shaped to minimize criticism of capitalism and to maximize participation in and support of capitalism.

Neo-Marxist perspectives do not adhere so strictly to the view that culture is entirely dependent on society's mode of production. While they borrow extensively from Marx's insights, they also modify these insights, and in so doing they provide a significantly different view of culture. These perspectives share with Marxism a focus on the role of culture in maintaining and supporting capitalism, but they differ from Marxism insofar as they seek to explain culture as more than simply the reflection of the underlying economic base.

Neo-Marxists recognize that culture can be shaped by specific groups and individuals who seek to achieve certain social outcomes. For example, Antonio Gramsci (1992) argued that in the 1920s and 1930s intellectuals within spheres such as politics, religion, the mass media, and education provided knowledge, values, advice, and direction to the general population that served to perpetuate the status quo and to suppress revolutionary tendencies. To take another example, members of the Frankfurt School, who began writing in the 1920s, identified pro-capitalist functions in much of popular culture, which promotes capitalist ideals and stifles critical independent thinking. The groups responsible for the creation and promotion of popular culture within the entertainment industry are themselves significant members of the **bourgeoisie**. In the view of the Frankfurt School, the entertainment industry is of great use to the capitalist order through the cultural products it creates.

It is important to note that neo-Marxists make a fundamental advance in their view of culture insofar as they see it as more than simply an artifact of the economic base. Culture, they argue, can also help to determine other facets of social reality—not merely reflective of other things in society, it also helps to shape society. A significant continuity between Marxist and neo-Marxist views of culture is that culture is implicated in the essentially conflictual nature of society. Culture, in a sense, supports dominant groups in their efforts to maintain their dominance.

Cultural Functionalism

A contrasting approach to understanding culture can be found in work that is based on the theoretical insights of Émile Durkheim. In contrast to the conflictual emphasis of the Marxists and neo-Marxists, the views on culture that are based on Durkheimian sociological insights focus on the integrative ability of culture. Rather than pointing to the ways in which culture can create social fissures, Durkheim (1995 [1912]) identified the ways in which culture can create social stability and solidarity, focusing on how culture unites us rather than on how culture divides us.

Culture, in terms of norms, values, attitudes, and beliefs, is not reflective of the economic mode of production. Instead, these cultural elements are generated according to the needs of society by its form as a more or less complex system. Culture rises out of a particular society's **social structure** to produce a general consensus about the goals and nature of society. As such, our values about, for example, the importance of education evolve in response to the changing needs of a modernizing society in which higher general levels of education allow for a more smoothly functioning society. In this sense, culture serves a necessary function: through common values and beliefs, society is able to remain coherent and all the different parts of society can effectively carry out their specific purpose.

Durkheim paid special attention to the role of religion as a motivating force in society, one that made possible the affirmation of collective sentiments and ideas, and one therefore that could play an important role in strengthening social bonds that then strengthened and reinforced the fabric of society.

Symbolic Interactionist and Dramaturgical Perspectives

A third important perspective treats culture as a product of individuals' interactions. In **symbolic interactionist** thought culture plays the role of a vehicle for meaning (hence 'symbolic') and is generated by individuals in face-to-face encounters (hence 'interactionist'). Culture is the enacted signals and attitudes that people use to communicate effectively in order to go about their daily lives. Body language and the signals we send through it, however subconsciously, are a clear element of culture in this perspective. The decisions we make and carry out to reveal or to suppress certain pieces of information about ourselves are also culture.

Social interaction can be analyzed to reveal layers of meaning behind routine actions. It becomes evident that there is a communicative element in a great deal of our interactions although we are not always conscious of its presence or of the nature of the messages we send. The result of our interactions is (usually) the successful management of our relationships with others.

In terms of its view on culture, the symbolic interactionist approach contrasts with Marxist and functionalist approaches insofar as it attributes more responsibility to individuals as the active creators and implementers of culture. Rather than originating from an economic order or indirectly from the general social structure, culture is a product of creative individual agents who use it to manage their everyday tasks and routines.

One of the most influential theorists to write about the interactions of individuals was Erving Goffman. Goffman developed an analytical framework that analogizes social interaction to what goes on in a theatre. For that reason, it is known as a dramaturgical perspective. In a theatre, there are actors with roles to play for an audience. Likewise, when we interact with people we assume a role for the situation we find ourselves in and perform that role according to a well-known script that defines the boundaries of what is expected and acceptable for the role. We learn these rules of social behaviour through the ordinary process of socialization. We use these rules to create meaningful and effective interaction with others. When we are interacting with others and are in our roles, we are managing impressions and performing in a front-stage area. When we let down our guard and behave informally and in ways that would embarrass us in front of others, we are in the back-stage area.

Culture plays a part in the dramaturgical perspective that is in one sense quite central: social order is constituted by the creation and use of meanings embodied in interaction. The sending and receiving of signals and messages is the key to understanding why society functions at all when there is so much potential for chaos. When you think about it, we are remarkably efficient at maintaining social order most of the time, and this achievement is made possible through the shared meanings in face-to-face interactions.

This view of culture, however, is one that is perhaps less rich than that offered by the cultural functionalist perspective. Rather than culture playing a fundamental role in shaping individuals' very consciousness, as the functionalist perspective would argue, the dramaturgical perspective sees culture as a tool for creative individuals to manipulate strategically. Rather than persons being fully subject to the influence of culture, culture is subject more to the influence of individuals.

The Cultural Studies Tradition

Cultural studies is a field with roots in British literary scholarship and in sociology. The 'Birmingham School' theorists at the Centre for Contemporary Cultural Studies at the University of Birmingham showed in the 1970s how subcultural groups on the margins of society, such as skinheads and punks, both appropriate elements of the dominant culture by imbuing them with alternative meanings and shape their own alternative subcultures in an attempt to create a separate space for themselves in the larger society. Much of the work accomplished in this tradition builds on the work of Marxism and neo-Marxists.

The specific insight that cultural studies borrows from neo-Marxists is that culture can be shaped and manipulated by dominant groups and employed to maintain hegemony. Cultural studies practitioners agree that culture can function to maintain social divisions, keeping some groups dominant over others. Where they break from Marxists and early neo-Marxists is in the recognition that class conflict is only one of many sites of ideological dominance. As Smith writes of cultural studies, 'a move has gradually taken place away from Marxism toward an understanding of society as textured with multiple sources of inequality and fragmented local struggles' (2001: 152). Dominant groups can be defined not only by class position, but also by race, gender, geography, and sexual orientation.

In addition to a focus on the multiple forms of domination, cultural studies has provided a more sophisticated understanding of the ways in which meaning functions in society. One of the main figures in this tradition from the Birmingham School is Stuart Hall, who has produced some of the seminal concepts of cultural studies. As Hall (1980) explains, communication of meaning requires both **encoding** and **decoding**. By this he means that such things as an advertisement or a television show are created in such a way as to convey a particular perspective. The predominant beliefs of the creators are encoded into these cultural productions (or texts) in subtle and sometimes subconscious ways. A fresh, critically informed reading of such texts is required to see how they encode assumptions and messages about such things as gender and social class relations. Another significant insight of Hall's is that meaning does not simply exist as part of cultural creations, but instead is constructed by individuals through the process of receiving and interpreting culture. Meaning is created by people while they make sense of the culture they consume or take in.

As evidence, note how the very same cultural products may carry very different meanings for different individuals or for different groups. For example, a study of the meaning of Hollywood Westerns showed that the movies were interpreted quite differently by 'Anglos' and by Native Americans: the films' messages about the frontier, Native–European relations, and the value of authority and independence were construed quite differently by the Anglo and the Native viewers (Shively, 1992). While those who create cultural products may intend them to convey a certain meaning, there is, nonetheless, opportunity for individuals to read or understand messages, texts, and symbols in oppositional or idiosyncratic ways, deriving meanings through a process that is influenced by the individuals' backgrounds and interpretive abilities.

The 'Production of Culture' Perspective

The 'production of culture' perspective takes as an object of study those aspects of culture that are created through explicit, intentional, and co-ordinated processes. This approach focuses on material culture, and studies taking this perspective focus on mass media, technology, art, and other material symbol-producing realms such as science and law. The guiding insight of this perspective is that culture is a product of social action in much the same way as non-cultural products are. The implication of this view is that culture is studied best according to the same methods and analysis that are standard in other fields of sociology.

A key figure in the development of the production of culture perspective, Richard A. Peterson (1994), notes that the perspective developed to account for perceived shortcomings in the prevailing 'mirror' or 'reflection' view that posited that culture was somehow a manifestation of underlying social-structural needs or realities. This view, held by orthodox Marxists and by functionalists, is quite vague about the specific mechanisms through which culture is created. The metaphor of a mirror is descriptive of the content of culture—it represents the true nature or character of society—but is mute about culture's production.

Such a view would find, for instance, that the contours of Canadian national identity are visible through studying the literary output of Canadian authors. As a body of work, Canadian literature takes on the characteristics of and reflects the essence of Canadian society. Likewise, Baroque art forms are seen as expressions of society in the Baroque period, and modernist art is explained as an expression of societal sentiments and values in the early decades of the twentieth century.

By contrast, the production of culture perspective is insistent on specifying all the factors involved not only in cultural production per se, but also in how culture is 'distributed, evaluated, taught, and preserved' (Peterson, 1994: 165). Through a thorough analysis of all these processes, we can better account for the specific content of culture. We need to examine the resources and constraints that specific actors were working with and that influenced the kind of art or other symbols that they created. In this way, the production of culture perspective provides us with the means of explaining the shape of culture.

Conflict, Integration, Origin, and Autonomy

It is useful to compare these various perspectives according to their views on several key features of culture. Marxists and neo-Marxists are clear in their argument that culture is a tool of conflict in society, a view that contrasts with functionalists, who emphasize the integrative function of culture. Functionalists are interested in explaining social order and they see culture as a key factor in creating social stability.

For symbolic interactionists, culture is primarily the means by which individuals create order out of potentially chaotic and unpredictable social situations, and so they support an integrative view of culture. The cultural studies tradition, building on the work of neo-Marxists, has an explicit focus on the many ways in which culture is implicated in various forms of domination and conflict in society.

The production of culture perspective has little to say about characterizing culture as integrative or as implicated in conflict. But while it has the least to say about that dimension of culture, it says the most about another dimension, the origin of culture, because it developed out of dissatisfaction with the views of Marxism and functionalism on the origin of culture. While these older perspectives relied on a 'reflection' metaphor to explain where culture comes from, the production perspective locates cultural origin in 'purposive productive activity' (Peterson, 1994: 164). Cultural studies does not provide quite so articulate an account of cultural origin, but neither does it merely rely on vague notions of reflection. Instead, it sees culture as originating in the work of hegemonic leaders who create the texts, symbols, and discourses that embody particular ideologies. Symbolic interactionists also provide an explanation for the origin of culture: it is produced in the meanings that people create through social interaction at the micro level.

Finally, the various perspectives place different emphases on what we can call the 'autonomy of culture'. *Autonomy of culture* refers to the place for culture within

■■ Time to Reflect ■■ ■■ ■■ ■■ ■■ ■■ ■■ ■■ ■■ ■■ ■■ ■

Which of the theoretical traditions do you find most useful for understanding culture's role in social inequality?

causal explanations. Is culture primarily a dependent **variable**, something that deserves to be explained but does not warrant recognition as a fundamental cause of social outcomes? Or is culture autonomous—does culture merit a place at the core of sociological explanation, wherein it is the key to understanding the contours of social reality?

Orthodox Marxism clearly denies the autonomy of culture by making it a reflection of the economic base of society. Functionalism views culture as far more autonomous: culture is, in and of itself, the predominant stabilizing force in society and can account for social order. Symbolic interactionists are less sympathetic to the auton-

omy of culture, preferring instead to privilege the role of spontaneous human creativity in understanding how social order is maintained. Culture is more appropriately viewed as the product of action than as the motivator of action. The cultural studies tradition gives us a view of culture as enjoying a significant degree of autonomy; the crucial role of ideology in various forms of dominance portrays culture as primarily shaping the conflictual nature of social life. The production of culture perspective, to conclude this summary, is largely concerned with the ways in which myriad social processes create cultural products, and so finds little room for the autonomy of culture.

OPEN FOR DISCUSSION
Uniting Iraq's Disparate Cultures a Challenge, Experts Say

24 April 2003

Constructing a representative government from the ashes of Saddam Hussein's totalitarian regime is a daunting challenge for Iraq. 'If you look at an ethnic map, you'd say that Iraq's political geography is at odds with its cultural geography', says geographer Harm De Blij, distinguished professor at Michigan State University.

'As with most of the nations in that region, the boundaries [of Iraq] are the result of political decisions, mostly arbitrary, by the colonial powers early last century', said James P. Reams, retired Army Artillery Field officer and former West Point geography instructor. 'That the boundaries have lasted into the 21st century is more a tribute to the series of local despots that have run these "countries" since the colonial powers left.'

Now that Iraq's regime has been toppled, the old cultural divisions are again surfacing. How and if different ethnic and religious groups can be united under one peaceful, stable system of government remains to be seen.

Modern Iraq was created after the defeat of the German-allied Ottoman Empire in World War I, when the victorious British and French carved up the territory of their defeated rival. One of their decisions was the establishment of the new nation of Iraq under the rule of King Faisal I. The monarch had led the Great War's Arab revolt—popularized by

Lawrence of Arabia—and had captured Damascus from the Ottomans in 1918.

Within the country's borders, three major groups—each with an identity and an agenda—occupy fairly distinct geographic regions: Sunni Muslims, Shiite Muslims, and Kurds. Each calls Iraq home, but each is unsure of what its role will be in the new Iraq. If the country's territorial integrity is to be respected, they must somehow work together.

In northern Iraq, the Kurds have recently begun to shake off decades of oppression. These traditionally pastoral people dwell in a region split by four different nations (Iraq, Iran, Turkey, and Syria). Though most Kurds are Muslim, they represent a unique group that has long held its own national aspirations. 'They are a distinct people with a distinct language (related to Persian or Farsi), much as Basques are different from Spaniards', explained David Miller, senior editor for National Geographic Maps.

The Kurdish minority was persecuted under the regime of Saddam Hussein. The Kurds took refuge in the mountainous north of Iraq where they enjoyed some degree of autonomy from Baghdad during the period between the Gulf War and the 2003 war that ousted the Hussein regime. . . .

'Numerically, they represent optimistically only a fifth of the population and that's not a lot', said Harm De Blij. 'Everyone talks about how much influence they'll have, but with their location and lack of presence elsewhere in the country I don't know how much they will be able to expect', De Blij said, while noting that the Kurds are themselves divided into two rival regional authorities. . . .

'They will demand no less autonomy than that which they had under Saddam', Reams said of the Kurds. 'However, I think they will realize that they cannot demand so much autonomy that they will incur Turkish wrath and even Turkish military incursions.' Turkey is ever wary of Kurdish aspirations because of the sizable and often restive Kurdish minority within Turkey. 'Since 1991, they've periodically staged raids into northern Iraq to get Turkish Kurd rebels who've fled to [Kurdish] Iraq to escape the armed forces', Miller added. 'Hussein's government had protested these incursions, but couldn't do much about them.' . . .

The rift between Iraq's Shiite and Sunni Muslims is primarily one of divergent religious viewpoints, which has its beginnings with the line of succession after the death of the Prophet Muhammad. Regional and cultural differences also exist, but Harm De Blij noted that the two lived rather harmoniously in Iraq until the rise of Baath Party power.

'What exacerbated this [difference] was a secular political movement—the Sunni Baath party. If there is one thing Shiites are not, they're not secular. As shown by the example of the Iranian revolution, religion is very central in their lives, and that's not the way Sunnis looked at it', De Blij said.

Saddam Hussein's sometimes brutal treatment of Shiites during his long reign has left a potentially deep rift between the groups—with many Shiites persecuted though they were numerically in the majority. 'It's one of the tragedies of Iraq', De Blij said, 'that because of that animosity a division was created that hadn't really been there before. . . .'

Salving these long-standing wounds won't be easy, as mistrust and animosity have grown over the years. Western officials at work in Iraq must recognize and account for such distinctions at all levels.

'Local ayatollahs toting sidearms with posses of loyal followers carrying AKs and knives will make these tribal and cultural differences an inescapable consideration in the attempts to transition to some form of democracy and representative government', said Reams.

A priority of any new Iraq government is balancing recognition and representation of the nation's distinct cultural entities with a central, national government that can rule for the good of all. How much regional autonomy is too much? How to get all groups fairly represented under the same tent? They are tough questions, but they should be at the forefront of rebuilding a nation that was from the beginning an amalgamation of disparate groups.

'The talking heads we see on TV have maps but they only seem to show tanks, planes, roads, and forts', said De Blij. 'I don't see many of them talking about the cultural, social geography of Iraq—and I hope somebody somewhere is looking at it that way.'

Source: Abridged from Brian Handwerk, for National Geographic News, at: <news.nationalgeographic.com/news/2003/04/0423_030423_iraqcultures.html>.

● Cultural Realms   ● ● ● ●

The stage is now set to discuss some of the attributes of those realms of social life most commonly located at the core of the sociology of culture. Although we could discuss the cultural dimension of almost any area of society, we will limit our discussion to language and discourse, the mass media, religion, and art. Within each realm, we will highlight the insights that the sociology of culture can bring to bear.

Language and Discourse

As mentioned above, language is a cultural subject par excellence. But before describing more fully the interest of sociology in language, it will be useful to distinguish it from the related concept of communication. *Language*, a system of words both written and spoken, is but one means of communication. **Communication** is the sharing of meaning, by which the thoughts of one person are made understandable to another. Communication can occur through a variety of signs and symbols, but we reserve a special place for the study of language because it is the primary means by which our communication takes place.

Languages are complicated systems of many symbols deployed according to a set of rules, and their use gives rise to a number of interesting social phenomena. It is argued, for instance, that the presence of language structures our very thoughts and consciousness, that without a vocabulary with which to label events (as is the case for infants) we cannot remember them. The character of social reality is tied to language insofar as we make sense of all our experiences in terms of the linguistic devices of and the logic made available through the language we speak.

As evidence of the consciousness-determining nature of language, we can point to examples of concepts and thoughts that exist in one language and are not entirely translatable to other languages, such as the German concepts of *Kultur* and *Geist*, or the French concepts of *ennui* and *joie de vivre*. Speakers of a language are said to share a certain mentalité that differentiates their mindset and world view. Likewise, it has been argued that the advancement of science in the West was in part related to the structure of European languages that encourages linear, causal thought patterns.

Discourse is a linguistic phenomenon that refers to a set of ideas, concepts, and vocabulary that recur in texts. A text can be broadly defined as any material or non-material communication act. Discourse is a habitual way of speaking about and understanding a topic or issue. Discourses abound in society. We encounter them constantly, but rarely do we explicitly recognize their features even when we are ourselves employing them. That is because it is natural for us to adopt a singular way of understanding an issue, and so a singular way of discussing or talking about an issue.

Take, for example, the issue of crime. In talking about crime, we might employ an *individualist discourse* that understands crime as the actions of a self-interested individual who is presented with options and makes certain choices. Crime in this discourse is conceived as something that one person does to one or more others, and it occurs in discrete instances. This discourse of crime encourages an understanding of the psychological factors involved in criminal behaviour and leads to solutions that work at the level of the individual. An individualist solution might suggest that if we alter the attractiveness of the option of committing crime by making penalties harsher for those who are caught, the individual will, we hope, no longer choose to commit crime.

In contrast, a *collectivist discourse* of crime also exists. This discourse views crime as a social problem. Crime is conceived as a feature of society that can be more or less prevalent. The focus is on crime rates and on the social conditions that influence the likelihood that crime will be committed in society. This discourse encourages a view more sociological than psychological of the factors contributing to crime, focusing on the social level rather than on the individual level. Just as the problem is conceived at the group level, so the ideas and terminology of a collectivist discourse promote a conception of solutions at the group level. For example, an effort to reduce crime might be based on information gained from a comparison of low- and high-crime societies to determine how certain social differences influence crime rates.

As the example of discourses about crime shows, discourses have the potential for great influence. The promotion of certain discourses throughout society, by those with the power to do so, can have the effect of setting the public agenda for certain issues. A discourse of abortion as an issue of privacy, for example, portrays the central concern as autonomy. It privileges the discussion of government impingement on the right of women to control their own bodies. But an opposing discourse surrounding abortion privileges a discussion of the social need to uphold all human life, no matter how inchoate that life appears to be. In this discourse, the primary concern is the idea that human life is so important to the society that it should not be compromised.

Such discourses play a role in the **social construction** of the categories and definitions we use to understand and to analyze social life. In our daily lives, we constantly refer to these categories and definitions in order to make judgments about good and bad, right and wrong, desirable and undesirable, how to distinguish between 'us' and the 'other', as well as to understand the very nature of things: Is abortion murder? Is killing in warfare murder? Are movies an art form, an educational medium, a propaganda tool, or entertainment? Is eating animals a question of morality? Is 'race' about biological differences? Is crime an individual failing? Is crime a collective failing of the society? For all these questions, our answers will be influenced by the way predominant discourses shape and frame our notions of the issues central to them.

Mass Media

The mass media are powerful social forces. They constitute a key realm of cultural production and distribution and can be seen to play a variety of social roles. The **mass media** are those technologically based methods and institutions that allow a single source to transmit messages to a mass audience. In Canada, the mass media include print (newspapers, magazines, books, and journals), film, radio, television (broadcast, cable, and satellite), and the Internet. The Internet is a special case because, although it can function as a mass medium, it is also much more—a network medium by virtue of its ability to allow multiple message sources. Potentially every person on the Internet can be a source of mass media content. (See Figure 2.1 on the ways in which Canadians are using the Internet.)

The mass media are a central cultural concern because of the nature of the content that they bring to the vast majority of people. That content can be categorized both as *information* and as *entertainment*.

Figure 2.1   Regular Internet Use in Canada, by Gender, Age, Education, and Household Income (%)

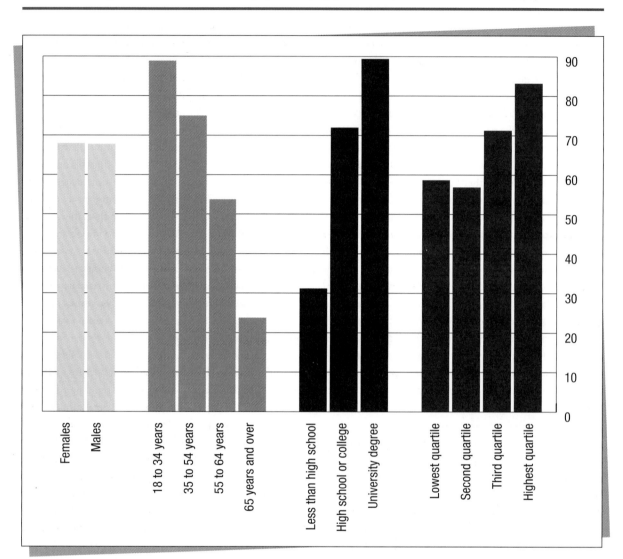

Let us first consider the mass media as the primary source of news information in society. They are the means by which we find out about important political, economic, and social happenings. We rely on them for the information we need to understand our local, regional, national, and global contexts. In addition to information that is delivered via news programs and in newspapers, the mass media provide us with a wealth of other information about the world that we might never have access to through first-hand experience. Through the mass media, we can read about the modernization of industries in China, we can see the skyline of Buenos Aires, we can hear about the best way to invest money in a sluggish economy, we can find information about our diagnosed disease and find a support group willing to share its experiences with the ailment. In short, the mass media bring a world of information to us, and their

capacity to do so has greatly increased with the advent of the Internet, which allows us to access only the information we desire, when we desire it, if we can locate it.

As the providers of so much information, the mass media have an enormous amount of influence on people's attitudes and behaviours, which are dependent on the state of our knowledge. For example, some people will alter their eating habits based on what they learn from magazine articles about the dangers and benefits of certain foods; some people will form an opinion about strengthening environmental protection regulations based on stories they watch on television news programs; and some people will relocate and change their lifestyles based on information about the effects of global warming. Because the mass media select a limited amount of information to present to audiences from a virtually infinite supply, they serve as informational gatekeepers (White, 1950). This gatekeeping function can account for much of their influence. However, just as important as what they present is the question of how they present media content. There is a connection here to the preceding discussion of discourses, because it is through the mass media that most discourses are disseminated to the general public.

The mass media are also the primary source for popular culture. While high culture (discussed below) is only rarely made available through the mass media, popular culture is everywhere. The popular culture productions brought to us by the mass media are argued to be linked to deep-seated social problems. This link is specified as the ability of the mass media to warp or corrupt our culture: television shows, movies, music, and so on are argued to have a profoundly negative impact on our entire way of life.

An important criticism of mass media content finds fault with the materialistic values the mass media explicitly and implicitly advocate. By constantly connecting depictions of happiness and success to material wealth, the mass media have been a principal cause of the development of a consumer culture that focuses our attention and energies on gaining and spending money and away from spiritual, moral, ethical, and social issues. The mass media also are blamed for a culture of violence: it is argued that they contribute to high levels of violence in society insofar as portrayals of violence incite violent acts and desensitize people to the presence of violence. At the same time, it is argued that the mass media contribute to an unhelpful, unrealistic, and shallow understanding of and response to this violence. The list of social problems linked to the ways in which the mass media may distort and negatively influence our culture is long, including such serious issues as body consciousness and eating disorders, racism, and sexism, exacerbated through stereotypical and misleading depictions.

Religion

Religion is a sociological subfield of its own but it merits inclusion in a discussion of culture because it has had such a large impact on the development of values and cultural traditions in most countries, Canada included. The case for the importance of religion as a cultural force was strongly made by Durkheim (1995 [1912]), who saw religion as providing the basis for social solidarity, as noted earlier in this chapter. More generally, we often characterize Western countries as belonging to a Judeo-Christian tradition, a tradition that denotes a specific history and related social institutions and dominant values. It is important to realize that it does not require a specif-

(Cultural functional-ism)

ically religious mindset to be influenced by Judeo-Christian values in general. These values permeate our culture and are seen in such things as predominant views on the role of authority; the moral code undergirding much of the legal system; beliefs in the value of punishment and the possibility of rehabilitation; social action on behalf of the underprivileged, sick, disabled, and terminally ill; and attitudes towards work and leisure.

Perhaps the best-known thesis in sociology regarding the influence of religion on culture is Max Weber's argument in *The Protestant Ethic and the Spirit of Capitalism* (1958 [1904]). Weber argues that several aspects of Protestant (specifically Calvinist) doctrine specifically encouraged the values and behaviour of economic rationalism, thereby promoting the rapid advancement of capitalism in Protestant societies. The accuracy of this argument and its strength as a single explanation of economic development has been questioned, but its importance for an understanding of the cultural role of religion remains.

Art and Aesthetics

In common usage, 'culture' often is synonymous with 'art', though for the reasons described in this chapter there is good reason for distinguishing between the two. Art is best seen as one element, albeit a unique element, of our larger culture, but most people use their artistic capacities in everyday life, just as they use their abilities to speak, write, and communicate in gestures and with facial expressions and other dramatic forms of movement. Children develop their artistic forms of expression in school; they go on to make choices about clothing, furniture, and personal and home accessories, and create environments in houses, gardens, and offices based on their personal aesthetics. They draw, paint, take photographs, make home movies, and make things of aesthetic appeal for themselves and others. Some use the skills they have developed therapeutically. Some turn these abilities towards commercial ventures in applications from letterhead and business cards to store window decoration, restaurant decoration, or other means of communicating with the buying public. However, one of the concerns of those who want to spend most of their time creating 'art' has always been, 'Will it sell?'

The realm of art is, above all, an expressive area of social life. Whereas much of our behaviour is oriented towards the practical achievement of a useful goal, art stands out as an activity that is done to communicate through **aesthetic** means and the goal may be no more (or less) practical than to induce feelings. The *New Shorter Oxford English Dictionary* (1993) defines *aesthetics* as 'a system of principles for the appreciation of the beautiful', which begs the definition by failing to define beauty! Today, many artists would eschew the word 'beauty' for 'important' (and some might narrow that idea to 'what is important to me'). Art, then, employs a set of rules or principles embodied in many different forms and pertaining to the artist's notions of what is beautiful or important. This makes art—whether visual, musical, or literary—a special form of communication: it is an expression of thoughts and emotions not communicated through the ordinary means of language. Instead, it relies on the much more implicit and intuitive rules that people in general use to assess beauty or truth or, for that matter, societal strengths, values, and shortcomings.

Art is an inherently imprecise form of communication, in which particular works carry implicit messages that may require an educated sense of appreciation for the aesthetic principles at play to be received. That is why we can read a novel and generate many different ideas about what the novel 'is really about' or what the author 'is really saying', just as we can for paintings, sculpture, plays, and other forms of art. Moreover, we tend to think of truly good art as the expression of artistic genius. 'Masterpieces', we tend to believe, are the works of geniuses, people of special technical and intellectual ability whose ideas and forms of self-expression represent ideals for human creativity and thought. The very best of art represents the very best of humanity, and so art occupies an honoured place in society.

As discussed above, we often distinguish between 'popular culture' and 'high culture'. This distinction points to the existence of a *cultural hierarchy*, in which certain forms of culture are granted greater legitimacy and prestige. Oil painting is higher on the hierarchy than filmmaking, which in turn is higher than television. Works by certain artists command higher prices than those of others. It is important to recognize that such status distinctions are themselves cultural productions. That is to say, our categories of 'high' and 'popular' or 'low' are socially constructed. These categorizations represent more than tangible differences in the characteristics of cultural productions. They also reflect differences in the social contexts in which the artifacts of culture are produced, distributed, and received.

Take, for example, Italian opera. North Americans have a clear notion of opera as high art. The dominant discourse of art portrays art as the product of artistic minds and as inherently special—there is something about art that allows us to recognize it when we see it. So long as we are informed about the value of art, we will never confuse Italian opera with popular culture. This discourse neglects the reality that our definitions involving status reflect an entire social process involved in bringing art to audiences. Our ideas about Italian opera as high art are based partially on an array of cues, such as its high cost, the status of its audiences, the costly training of its performers, the physically distinct and opulent venues in which it is performed, the extravagance of its production values, its non-profit status (we pretend to oppose art to commerce), and intellectual analyses of Italian opera to explain why it is great art. If one goes to Italy, however, one finds that opera is much more an art of the people. The audiences are much more broadly based in terms of class, and the vanishing of the language barrier removes an arcane quality to the production and demystifies both attendance and understanding of the production. People do not have to pay as much, relatively, to attend productions, and are much more likely to leave singing snatches of the arias without an appearance of flaunting class distinctions.

This approach to art highlights several of art's sociologically significant features. First, as explained by the production of culture perspective, art does not just spring out of a **collective consciousness**, or even out of an individual's consciousness. Instead, art is a collective activity that requires collaboration between many actors in an art world (Becker, 1982). It is this collective activity that helps to determine how artistic genres may be legitimated or become prestigious and how they may be viewed in the wider society.

Second, the socially constructed nature of distinctions between high and low in art also points to the significance of art in helping to determine the contours of social stratification. This link is rooted in the notion of **cultural capital**: the knowledge, preferences, and tastes that people have concerning art and aesthetics. Having abundant cultural capital usually means sharing the knowledge, preferences, and tastes that are common among those of high status in society. The link between cultural capital and stratification is based on the power of high cultural capital to provide access to informal interpersonal connections that can influence our occupational and economic prospects. Sharing similar artistic tastes and consumption patterns with those in economically privileged positions provides us with access to networks and opportunities not open to those who do not have the necessary aesthetic preferences and expertise. In sociological terms, our cultural capital can increase our economic capital. (This is an interesting inversion of the Marxist logic whereby the cultural realm is determining, or influencing, the economic realm.)

Third, and perhaps even more significant, is the role that artistic consumption plays in creating social groupings in society. The enjoyment of products of aesthetic quality is deeply related to our conceptions of our own identities, of who we really are, and of the kind of people with whom we wish to be associated. In this way, our tastes are profoundly implicated in how our lives are structured. We've already seen how artistic tastes can interact with our class position, but tastes can also be a way of expressing racial, gender, regional, and age-based identities.

Take the example of youth culture. Although this term refers to many aspects of how young people live their lives, one important way in which adolescents and young adults set themselves apart is through the music they listen to, the publications they read, the television shows and channels they watch, the films they see, and, increasingly, the websites they visit and create. Knowledge of and participation in this particular set of aesthetic preferences allow young people to experience group belonging. Through aesthetics, they can distinguish themselves from prior generations.

● Cultural Dynamics ● ● ●

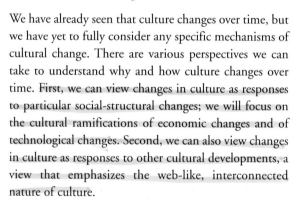

We have already seen that culture changes over time, but we have yet to fully consider any specific mechanisms of cultural change. There are various perspectives we can take to understand why and how culture changes over time. First, we can view changes in culture as responses to particular social-structural changes; we will focus on the cultural ramifications of economic changes and of technological changes. Second, we can also view changes in culture as responses to other cultural developments, a view that emphasizes the web-like, interconnected nature of culture.

Economic, Technological, and Cultural Change

At the most basic level, all of culture can be seen as human adaptation and ingenuity to better control and survive in the physical environment. Beyond that most basic level, but in keeping with the premise that culture allows us to deal with our surroundings, it also gives us the means to function effectively in our social environment, in our dealings with other people. Changes in that social environment, then, encourage and enable corresponding cultural changes.

The discussion of Marxism earlier in this chapter reviewed the case for the economic foundation of culture. In Marxism, culture is a reflection of the underlying economic basis of society. But it is not necessary to adopt Marxist assumptions of culture merely as a reflection of economics to see that important economic changes are capable of provoking specific changes in culture. An example of such a change is the liberalization of attitudes

towards women and work. In the mid- to late-nineteenth century and in the first half of the twentieth century, there was a strong belief in Western societies that it was most appropriate for women, especially married women, not to work outside the home but rather to find fulfillment in their roles as mothers and housewives. While the reasons for the change that has occurred in this attitude are many, it can be argued that an important cause of the change was economic. Maintenance of a middle-class standard of living increasingly required a second income. Changing attitudes about women and work, in this view, were an adaptive response to a changing economic reality.

Over the same period of time, rising levels of affluence made it possible for teenagers to possess a certain amount of disposable income. The development of youth culture, while deriving from various causes, was facilitated by the economic changes that created consumers out of young people and thereby encouraged cultural producers to target and cater to youth. The continued growth in spending power of teenagers has also allowed them to become the primary demographic target of Hollywood film studios. Because young people see films in theatres more often than do older groups, a great deal of film production is tailored to their tastes and expectations. This dynamic is representative of the more general dependence of the content of cultural industries on economic conditions.

Technological change can also be viewed as the source of a great deal of the change in our culture. Perhaps the clearest and most significant technological influence on culture has been the development of the mass media. The printing press, invented by Johannes Gutenberg in 1452, has been credited with transforming European culture in diverse ways. For example, the printing press—by making reproduction fast—reduced the value of a book and eventually brought the cost down to allow many people to personally own Bibles and read them and interpret them apart from what they were instructed by priests to believe and think: a precondition for the Protestant Reformation. The invention of the telegraph, which vastly hastened the speed with which information could travel over great distances, has been cited as changing our attitudes concerning the pace of life and punctuality, and even our very definitions of the proportions of space and time.

Television is arguably one of the most powerful technologies ever invented. It has wrought profound cultural changes. First, a specific form of cultural content has developed for the purposes of the medium, shaping our tastes for and expectations of dramatic entertainment, but also, and more fundamentally, influencing our perceptions of social reality and of the nature of the world

SOCIOLOGY IN ACTION
Patients with AIDS

AIDS presented a serious challenge to established identities—and patterns of trust and control—in the treatment domain. A knowledge and treatment vacuum emerged as a result of a very public display of scientific uncertainty and institutional impotence in the face of this new crisis. Suddenly, old understanding about who was knowledgeable, who could and could not be trusted, and who should and should not be granted control, were open to contestation. For example, early on in the epidemic, the expertise of the 'doctor' was in doubt. Not only did physicians *not* have the expertise to deal with this new challenge, some were patently unwilling to acquire it or even to act in the interests of their patients. Many early AIDS patients were abandoned, as discrimination, bigotry, and fear led to some doctors 'dumping' their patients.

PWAs ['persons with AIDS'] began to reject the identity of 'patient' and the victimhood it implied. 'Patients' (from the French '*patienter*', which means to wait, as in a physician's waiting room, and originally from the Latin, where it means 'to suffer')

would be 'patient' and suffer in silence no longer. '*Silence = Death*', an expression made popular by the activist group ACT-UP, became the call to action for HIV/AIDS patients seeking to redefine themselves and their role within the domain. Community members stressed that they were neither 'patients' nor 'victims', but 'people living with AIDS'. . . .

The identity of PWAs, collectively, is thus very different from that of traditional patient groups. The notion of patients as passive, ignorant, requiring the medical expertise of an elite was successfully deconstructed and replaced with a notion of a patient group as empowered, informed, and organized decision-makers.

Source: Steve Maguire, Nelson Phillips, and Cynthia Hardy, 'When "Silence = Death", Keep Talking: Trust, Control and the Discursive Construction of Identity in the Canadian HIV/AIDS Treatment Domain', *Organization Studies* 22, 2 (2001): 296. Reprinted by permission of Sage Publications Ltd.

outside our daily lives. Second, this technology has brought a major leisure activity into our homes, promoting the growth of television culture, in which we spend at least some of our free time in a one-way relationship with a screen rather than interacting with others or engaging in community-based activities.

It would be impossible to enumerate all the ways in which technology has created cultural change. To take an example of a broad cultural pattern, the very idea of 'nightlife' and all its attendant activities is predicated on the existence of electricity and the light bulb. Much more narrowly, the technological innovation of the electrification of musical instruments has influenced tastes in musical styles. Suffice it to say that technological change frequently has the potential to create cultural reverberations, sometimes of limited significance and other times life-transforming.

Recognition of the influence of technological, economic, and other (for example, demographic) changes on the shape of culture is in no way a denial of the trans-

formative power of culture. The relationship, to be sure, is reciprocal. Cultural changes can at times influence these very same structural features of society.

Change for the Sake of Change

Despite the strength of the relationship between culture and social structure, culture also has internal dynamics that can account for cultural change. In this view, cultural change is inevitable because culture, as representative of individual and collective self-expression, is inherently progressive, evolutionary, volatile, and unstable: it is the nature of culture to evolve.

The validity of this view is perhaps best exemplified by the phenomenon of fashion. *Fashion* is change for the sake of change in the realm of aesthetics. Ongoing change is built into the very idea of fashion. Moreover, fashion is not just the styles of clothes that are popular, although that is one of its most visible manifestations. Rather, elements of fashion can be found in a many areas of social life.

John Hills/www.Cartoonstock.com

Consider, for instance, how vocabulary choices acknowledge that some words are 'in' while others are 'out'. To express approval, one might have heard adjectives in the past such as 'swell', 'groovy', or 'mod', words that sound dated now despite the fact that the need to express approval has not gone away. New, more fashionable words do the job today. Consider also how changes in furniture and interior design occur gradually but consistently enough to evoke associations with particular decades. Few of these changes are linked to changes in function or technological innovations. Finally, consider how fashion operates to change the popularity of first names (Lieberson, 2000). The Ethels, Mildreds, and Eunices of yesterday are the Emilys, Hannahs, and Madisons of today (see Table 2.2). The function of naming remains constant, while the aesthetic element of naming reveals continuous modification. The kinds of aesthetic modifications that are made today are dependent on the nature of the aesthetic modifications of the past.

Although aesthetic changes do not serve any practical or functional purposes, they may still be related to a social purpose: they satisfy needs for self-expression. In this sense, the aesthetic dimension of life is symbolic—we communicate to others and articulate (however obliquely) for ourselves certain thoughts, values, identities, and senses of group affiliation. Change in aesthetics results from shifts in the meanings or understandings commonly attributed to certain aesthetic elements, such that they no longer connote what they used to.

To see how this is so, consider Georg Simmel's theory of fashion (1957). This argument has become known as the trickle-down model. In this model, fashion is triggered by the status concerns of high-status groups who seek to distinguish themselves by adopting a new fashion, which they have the means to afford.

Those elements of fashion that they adopt then come to connote high status by their association with a high-status group—that is the symbolism of the fashion. Lower-status groups then adopt this fashion for themselves to share in the high status, but in doing so they change the meaning of the fashion: it no longer expresses exclusiveness. High-status groups thus no longer find the fashion appealing or useful, and so they adopt a new fashion. Although this model cannot in fact explain much of the fashion world today, which often appropriates the symbols of lower-status groups, it is nonetheless a clear illustration of how culture can evolve according to an internal set of principles that do not reflect social-structural change.

● Canadian Culture ● ● ● ●

The concepts and arguments reviewed in this chapter can help us to understand the current state of Canadian culture, along with some of the more contentious issues facing Canadian society. Because of its unique history, Canadian culture is unlike any other national culture, with a unique set of challenges and a unique set of opportunities.

Distinct Societies

One of the defining features of Canadian culture is its basis in 'two founding peoples', French and English. The term *peoples* refers, of course, not only to the actual members of the French and English colonies, but also to their respective ways of life—their cultures. How different or similar are the cultures of French and English Canada? On a global scale, they are quite similar to one another in comparison with, for example, Pakistani or Indonesian culture. However, they differ in important ways. Most obvious is the linguistic basis for the distinction (see Table 2.3). As discussed earlier, language is a core component of culture, with significant implications for social life. The ability to communicate with verbal and written language is a key element to social bonding—without this form of communication, opportunities for social interaction are limited. Differences in other cultural traditions exist as well, ranging from cuisine and leisure activities to political values and views on marriage and family.

The challenge for Canada has been and continues to be the forging of a unified Canadian culture that respects the unique characteristics of both traditions. To this end, we employ a policy of **official bilingualism** and we foster cultural events and new traditions that embrace both French and English cultural elements.

Table 2.2   Top 20 Names for Baby Girls Born in Illinois by Race, 1989, 1940, and 1920

1989		1940		1920	
Shared by Blacks and Whites		**Shared by Blacks and Whites**		**Shared by Blacks and Whites**	
Ashley	Jessica	Barbara	Joyce	Alice	Helen
Brittany	Michelle	Beverly	Margaret	Anna	Margaret
Christina	Nicole	Carol	Mary	Catherine	Marie
		Dorothy	Patricia	Dorothy	Mary
		Joan	Sandra	Elizabeth	Mildred
			Shirley	Evelyn	Ruth
				Frances	Virginia
White Only	**Black Only**	**White Only**	**Black Only**	**White Only**	**Black Only**
Amanda	Alicia	Carolyn	Betty	Betty	Ethel
Caitlin	Amber	Donna	Brenda	Eleanor	Gladys
Catherine	Ariel	Janet	Dolores	Florence	Lillian
Elizabeth	Bianca	Judith	Gloria	Lorraine	Louise
Emily	Candace	Karen	Gwendolyn	Marion	Lucille
Jennifer	Crystal	Linda	Helen	Marjorie	Thelma
Kelly	Danielle	Marilyn	Jacqueline		
Lauren	Dominique	Nancy	Loretta		
Megan	Ebony	Sharon	Yvonne		
Rachel	Erica				
Rebecca	Jasmine				
Samantha	Kiara				
Sarah	Latoya				
Stephanie	Tiffany				

Source: Stanley Lieberson, *A Matter of Taste: How Names, Fashions, and Culture Change* (New Haven: Yale University Press, 2000), 204. Reprinted by permission of Yale University Press. Copyright © Yale University Press.

The great concern over the success of this endeavour has been with us for decades and remains. The movement for sovereignty within Quebec is, to a large extent, based on the belief that the health of French-Canadian culture, and especially the vigour of the French language in Quebec, can only be adequately maintained and nurtured separate from a wider Canadian culture. The challenge for our country is to capitalize on the potential for Canadian culture to unite us rather than to divide us.

Multiculturalism

The conception of two founding peoples can be seen as primarily a legal construct rather than as an accurate historical depiction. In reality, there have always been more than two cultural traditions in Canada. The Aboriginal cultures of **First Nations** and Inuit peoples were, of course, present before the idea of a Canadian society or culture was ever proposed.

More recently, increased immigration from a large number of countries and the formation of an equally large number of ethnic communities in Canada have added to the number of cultural traditions we have to work with (see Figure 2.2 on Canada's increasing linguistic diversity). As a society, we have adopted a stance of official **multiculturalism**, although the merits of this position engender a good deal of debate. We should distinguish between multiculturalism as a fact of contemporary Canadian society—there are ethnic subcultures that are thriving—and multiculturalism as a policy—the tolerance and encouragement of the maintenance of the national cultures that immigrants bring with them from their countries of origin.

Table 2.3 Population by Mother Tongue, Canada, 1996 to 2006

Years	English		French		Other	
	Number	%	Number	%	Number	%
1996	17,072,435	59.8	6,711,630	23.5	4,744,060	16.6
2001	17,521,880	59.1	6,782,320	22.9	5,334,845	18.0
2006	18,055,685	57.8	6,892,230	22.1	6,293,110	20.1

Source: Statistics Canada, Censuses of Population, 1996 to 2006, http://www12.statcan.ca/english/census06/analysis/language/tables/table1.htm

Proponents of multiculturalism point to its helpfulness in easing the transition of new immigrants into Canadian society. This happens through the fostering of ethnic communities that can provide social support. In addition, proponents argue that multiculturalism is a policy that is properly respectful to all Canadians and that enriches the wider Canadian culture. Detractors, on the other hand, argue that multiculturalism only makes it more difficult to create a unifying Canadian culture. Moreover, they question the wisdom of a policy that encourages, to however small a degree, self-segregation

rather than facilitating the full cultural integration of immigrants into Canadian life. Again, just as with the question of two founding peoples, the challenge here is to balance culture's potential for unifying us with our desire to maintain certain cultural partitions.

Globalization and American Cultural Imperialism ✳

Globalization typically refers to the fact that goods, services, information, and labour, now more than ever,

Figure 2.2 Changes in the Numbers of People Speaking the Ten Most Common Non-Official Languages, 1971–2006

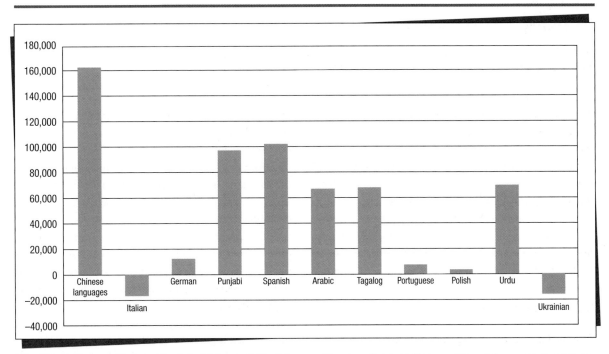

Note: 'Chinese languages' includes Mandarin, Cantonese, Hakka, Taiwanese, Chaochow (Teochow), Fukien and Shanghainese, as well as a residual category (Chinese languages not otherwise specified).
Sources: Statistics Canada, censuses of population, 1971, 2001 and 2006.

can easily flow between distant countries. Of particular concern for us is the cultural influence that globalization brings. There are various implications of globalization for Canadian culture. Technological advancements in mass media have made possible easy and abundant access to the sights and sounds of geographically distant locales. Through media representations we can be made aware of cultural elements from across the globe, and the potential exists to incorporate these elements into Canadian culture. In a sense, one effect of globalization is the internationalization of national cultures as they increasingly are exposed to one another. The mass media, then, are the key channels of the cultural diffusion occurring through the mutual influence of many national cultures.

Globalization, however, can bring with it many difficult cultural challenges. Chief among these challenges is the need to manage the global export of American popular culture. Popular culture, in the form of films, television shows, music, and websites, is one of the largest American exports, reaching every corner of the globe. The sheer volume of American cultural export has led to the term cultural imperialism, describing the scope of the global dominance of American culture.

The reaction to this state of affairs in Canada has been one of alarm and a concerted effort has been mounted to maintain the integrity of Canadian culture. The importing of American cultural products is seen as dangerous to Canadian culture because the many pre-existing similarities with American culture threaten to overwhelm the differences by which we recognize our culture as distinct and, for us, preferable. In order to promote Canadian cultural production, the federal government has, for several decades, enacted policies that require Canadian broadcasters to make a sizable proportion of their content of Canadian origin. In addition, a variety of programs exist to subsidize Canadian film, television, music, and book production (see Figure 2.3 on the relative costs of production).

This policy of Canadian cultural protectionism has clearly achieved some measured successes. Scores of Canadian artists have achieved a level of success that would have been unlikely if left to compete on the unequal playing field with American artists who are promoted by vast media conglomerates. Yet despite these successes, and despite the strict requirements of Canadian content regulations, Canadians consume tremendous amounts of American popular culture. There is no question that the continuing distinctiveness of Canadian culture and identity is threatened by the extensive consumption of American cultural products. There is an unfortunate contradiction between Canadians' preference for their own national norms, values, attitudes, and

Figure 2.3   Relative Costs and Revenues of Canadian Content and US Simulcasts in Television

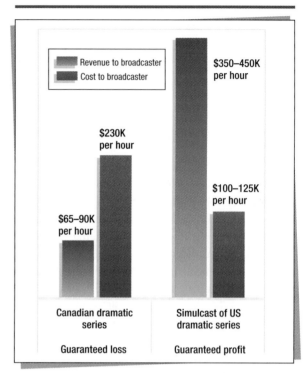

Source: CBC, *The Economics of Canadian Television* (CBC Fact Sheet) (2002); at <http://cbc.radio-canada.ca/htmen/pdf_rtf/CBCfacts-economics-finale.pdf>. Reprinted by permission of the publisher.

beliefs on the one hand and their preference for American popular culture on the other.

● Conclusion ● ● ● ● ● ●

Culture is undoubtedly one of the most difficult sociological terms to pin down—it has many meanings—but through careful analysis sociology can bring those multiple meanings into focus and can explain why we have them. Many different social phenomena can be called 'cultural'. We need to understand what those various phenomena have in common to cause them all to be considered 'culture'. Culture is always evolving and is intimately tied to other social changes and to other cultural changes. Finally, we need to be aware of the role of culture in social life because it is the key to understanding some of the most important events in our society and in the world today. Culture is implicated in the social dynamics both of conflict and of people coming together, and for that reason, as well as others, it is an essential subject for sociological analysis.

● Questions ● ● ● ● ● ●
for Critical Thought

1. What is Canadian culture, and what are its most important or distinctive facets?
2. What subcultures are you a member of? What are the characteristics of those subcultures? How did you enter them?
3. Where does culture come from? How could you begin to research such a question? What dimensions of culture are particularly amenable to such a research question?
4. How would you go about measuring cultural change? Moreover, how would you try to explain such change?
5. Is cultural change beneficial to society? Is it conceivable to have no changes in our culture?

● Recommended ● ● ● ● ●
Readings

Victoria D. Alexander, *Sociology of the Arts: Exploring Fine and Popular Forms* (Oxford: Blackwell, 2003).
This book is a clear, engaging, thorough, and sophisticated overview of this area of study.

Laura Desfor Edles, *Cultural Sociology in Practice* (Malden, MA: Blackwell, 2002).
Edles's book is a good survey of many issues and studies, both old and new, in cultural sociology.

Eric Klinenberg, *Cultural Production in a Digital Age: The Annals of the American Academy of Political and Social Science* (Thousand Oaks, CA: Sage, 2005).
Taking a broad view of what counts as culture, this edited volume investigates how the technological advances of the digital age have influenced the methods and outcomes of cultural production.

Nelson Phillips and Cynthia Hardy, *Discourse Analysis: Investigating Processes of Social Construction* (Thousand Oaks, CA: Sage, 2002).
This short book provides a concise and insightful review of the theory and research in sociology and related fields on the role of discourse in social life.

Lyn Spillman, ed., *Cultural Sociology* (Malden, MA: Blackwell, 2002).
Spillman provides an entertaining overview of many excellent empirical studies in the sociology of culture as well as many intriguing theoretical works.

● Recommended ● ● ● ●
Websites

Canadian Broadcasting Corporation (CBC) www.cbc.ca
In addition to finding the news, you will also find links to the corporate history of the CBC, the broadcasting entity charged with strengthening Canadian culture and identity.

Canadian Heritage www.canadianheritage.gc.ca
There are many agencies within this federal government department actively involved in promoting the health of Canadian culture.

Canadian Radio-television and Telecommunications Commission (CRTC) www.crtc.gc.ca
Here you'll find the public policy behind our broadcasting regimes. The CRTC is the quasi-independent agency responsible for regulating the entire broadcast industry.

Culture & Tradition www.ucs.mun.ca/~culture/
The bilingual journal *Culture & Tradition* focuses on both French and English Canadian folklore and folk culture.

National Film Board of Canada (NFB) www.nfb.ca
There are countless interesting links at the website of the NFB, which is especially renowned for its documentary and animated productions.

UNESCO www.unesco.org
The United Nations Educational, Scientific and Cultural Organization (UNESCO) deals with issues of cultural diversity and preservation.

• • • • • • • • • •

Socialization

Sue Wilson

Learning Objectives

In this chapter, you will:

▶ gain an understanding of the process of socialization;

▶ understand and develop the capacity to apply basic concepts in the study
of socialization;

▶ reflect on personal experiences growing up in terms of socialization;

▶ think about ways the hidden curriculum in educational institutions reproduces
inequalities of gender, class, and race;

▶ think critically about the ways in which the media both shape and reinforce
social values; and

▶ learn about the National Longitudinal Survey of Children and Youth as a resource
for studying Canadian children.

Photo: World of Stock

● Introduction ● ● ● ● ● ●

Peter Berger (Berger and Berger, 1975) defined **socialization** as the process by which people learn to become members of society. For every individual, this process starts at birth and continues throughout life.

The most intense period of socialization is infancy and early childhood. Almost from the moment of birth, children begin to learn the basics of **social interaction**; they learn to recognize and respond socially to parents and other important people in their lives. In the process of interacting with parents, siblings, and other caregivers, children typically acquire the necessary cognitive and emotional skills to get along in their society. Moreover, as they adjust to daily routines, they learn to conform to adult expectations about a wide range of behaviour: where and when to sleep and eat, what to wear and play with, what is funny and what is serious, and so on. At the same time, children develop an individual **identity**, a self-concept.

Language is an important aspect of socialization. As children learn to understand words and later to use them, they simultaneously learn to categorize their experience. Children also begin at an early age to evaluate their own behaviour and that of others. Indeed, one of the first words many children say is NO!

In time, children learn to identify social **roles**—first the roles of family members, and later, as their experience broadens, those of others with whom they interact. They begin to identify consistent patterns in relatives, teachers, doctors, religious leaders, and to know how they should act around these others. They also develop an understanding of status differences and the ways in which roles interact with **race**, **class**, and **gender** to create a complex social structure. When children respond appropriately, conforming to social expectations, they are said to have internalized behavioural **norms**.

Socialization patterns vary with class, ethnicity, family structure, gender, and birth order. The way people are socialized is therefore affected by whether they grow up in Vancouver or Moncton; whether they speak English or Cantonese at home; whether they worship at a church, a synagogue, a mosque, or not at all; whether they grow up in a single-parent or a two-parent household; and whether their parents are strict or lenient in their discipline, among many other factors. Despite such differences, the research cited throughout this chapter shows that there are certain interesting patterns in socialization practices and outcomes. According to Eleanor Maccoby, for example, as a result of socialization, most people acquire a package of attitudes, skills, and behaviours that enable them to '(a) avoid deviant behaviour; (b) contribute, through work, to the economic support of self and family; (c) form and sustain close relationships with others; and (d) be able to rear children in turn' (1992: 1006).

Parents (or parent substitutes) control much of the early learning environment of their children. But children are not simply passive receptors in the processes of socialization. Because of individual differences, some children thrive on routine; others resent it. Some grow up wanting to be like their parents; others react against parental models. Even within the same family, children will experience socialization differently.

Socialization, then, occurs in the process of social interaction. The two major accomplishments of socialization are the development of a self-concept and the internalization of social expectations. This chapter will examine some of the processes by which the complex learning that is socialization occurs and will discuss a number of theories of socialization. As you will see, families, schools, peer groups, and the media all play a part in socializing children. Moreover, adolescent socialization is a process that prepares young people for adult family and employment responsibilities. The chapter closes with a brief look at future directions in socialization.

● Forms of Socialization ● ●

Socialization is complex and multi-dimensional. In many ways, socialization is an umbrella concept: it takes in all social contacts and continues from birth to death. This section will consider the various forms of socialization experienced throughout life.

Primary Socialization

The most intense learning, **primary socialization**, occurs from birth through adolescence. The family is the most important agent of primary socialization. This socialization is both intentional and unintentional, imposed and reciprocal. Parents socialize their children intentionally in countless ways as they teach them how and what to eat, what to wear, what to play with, what is funny, what is sad, how to address and treat others, which behaviours are rewarded and which are punished, and so on. At the same time, unintentional socialization takes place as children learn about power and authority; gender, age, class, and ethnic differences; love, affection, and intimacy. Furthermore, the family's status in the community will affect the responses of others to the child, as well as where and with whom the child will play or go to school.

Although it is not entirely a 'top-down' process, primary socialization is largely imposed, because children have less power and are less competent than adults. Yet, although the relationship is far from equal, there will be some elements of reciprocity in parent–child interactions. On the other hand, the relative power of parents will not guarantee socialization outcomes: children do not simply absorb life lessons from their parents.

Secondary Socialization

Secondary socialization is an ongoing process of 'recalibrating' throughout the life cycle as people anticipate and adjust to new experiences and new situations. In changing jobs, marrying, having children, coping with life crises, and so on, people are continually being socialized.

In many ways, socialization is a reciprocal process: children learn from their parents, but parents also learn from their children. Thus, as children learn social interaction from their parents, parents learn how to parent. Reciprocal socialization is not confined to parents and children. Students learn from teachers, teachers from students. Family members, friends, and co-workers also socialize one another. In learning related to digital media, children are typically far more sophisticated than their parents and teachers. Much of this high-tech learning will involve children teaching adults.

Settersten (2003: 16) suggests that the life course provides a lens that shifts attention from a primary focus on childhood socialization to 'what adults learn in the central settings of their lives, why they learn it and how they learn it'. As Settersten points out, 'the socialization experience in childhood and adolescence is clearly not enough to meet the demands of the adult years' (2003: 16). In many cases, what is learned in childhood is outdated by adulthood.

In early adulthood we acquire new work and family statuses. Status losses (e.g., divorce or widowhood, the death of friends, or retirement) are more likely to occur later in life (Settersten, 2003: 21). Not all status losses carry regret. Some people will look forward to retirement or an empty nest. Some will move on with anticipation following divorce.

Adult socialization differs from childhood socialization because it is based on accumulated learning and previous experience. Frances Waksler likens the difference between primary and secondary socialization to the difference between being born into a religion and converting from one religion to another: 'In the latter process, one has both more choice (e.g., the very choice of converting or abandoning the endeavour) and more limits (e.g., the difficulty or even impossibility of coming to believe something that one had previously thought unbelievable)' (1991: 14).

Anticipatory Socialization

In most situations, previous experience provides the capacity to imagine new experiences, so people become adept at anticipatory socialization. People mentally prepare themselves for future roles and responsibilities by means of anticipatory socialization, which Robert K. Merton defined as 'the acquisition of values and orientations found in statuses and groups in which one is not yet engaged but which one is likely to enter' (1968: 438–9). Many college and university students, for instance, are engaged in anticipatory socialization as they acquire necessary academic skills and credentials for their future occupations.

The effectiveness of anticipatory socialization will depend on the degree of ambiguity of a new situation, as well as on its similarity to previous experience. According to Diane Bush and Roberta Simmons, 'if the individual is prepared ahead of time for a new role, in the sense of understanding the norms associated with the role, having the necessary skills to carry it out, and becoming aware of expectations and rewards attached to the role . . . he or she will move into the new role easily and effectively' (1981: 147). This sums up very well the assumption underlying the concept of anticipatory socialization.

Many vehicles exist to ease the process of anticipatory socialization. Familiar examples include high school and university orientations, new employee training programs, parenting courses, and pre-retirement courses.

▌▌ Time to Reflect ▐▌▐▌▐▌▐▌▐▌▐▌▐▌▐▌▐▌▐▌▐▌▐▌

Explain the difference between primary and secondary socialization. Think of an occasion when you have gone through an experience of resocialization. Perhaps it was moving away from home to attend university or college. What aspects of your early socialization had to be 'unlearned and relearned'?

Resocialization

Most people would not be able to anticipate successfully what it would be like to join the armed forces or a religious cult, to experience the sudden death of a loved one, or to be fired. When people encounter such situations, they must learn new rules. When new situations are so unique that people cannot rely on their previous experience to anticipate how to act, they may encounter a period of **resocialization**.

Some institutions, such as prisons and psychiatric hospitals, are specifically designed to resocialize 'deviants'. Timothy Seiber and Andrew Gordon (1981) introduced the idea of socializing organizations as a way of understanding socialization. Socializing organizations include institutions such as prisons, as well as schools, job-training programs, counselling centres, and voluntary associations. These organizations are formally mandated to bring about some change in their members, but often the explicitly stated aims are less important than the latent messages they impart. In the words of Seiber and Gordon, 'as recruits participate in the organization they learn its social and speech etiquettes, modes of self-presentation, rituals, routines, symbolic codes of deference, and other patterns of social relations' (1981: 7).

Therapy or self-help groups are significant sources of change for adults as they initiate self-resocialization to replace old beliefs with new ones. 'For many, adulthood is a period of recovery from negative childhood experiences; it is a period in which problematic early socialization must be unlearned and relearned' (Settersten, 2003: 33).

● Theories of ● ● ● ● ● ● Socialization

The questions sociologists ask, and often the methods they use, depend on which theoretical perspective they adopt. Some sociologists take **social structure** as their point of departure; others begin with individual interaction. Alan Dawe calls these two approaches, respectively, the *sociology of social system* and the *sociology of social action*: 'One views action as the derivative of system whilst the other views system as the derivative of action' (1970: 214).

These two contrasting views of socialization are the focus of this section. The sociology of social system— 'action as the derivative of system'—is best represented by the functionalism of Talcott Parsons (1955), who was interested in how individuals internalize social norms and become conforming members of society. **Symbolic interactionism**, by contrast with functionalism, explains how individual self-concepts develop in the process of social interaction.

The Functionalist Perspective

Sociologists who take the functionalist perspective, such as Talcott Parsons, describe socialization as a process of internalizing socially approved norms and behavioural expectations. People who grow up in a particular culture internalize a similar set of norms and values. The more widespread their acceptance, the more smoothly the group will function. Sociologists refer to a smooth outcome as *social integration*.

According to functionalist thinking, conformity is the consequence of internalizing behavioural expectations. This sounds very deterministic—as if norms necessarily make individuals conform. Indeed, the functionalist emphasis on individual conformity to group norms amounts to, as Dennis Wrong (1961) put it, 'an oversocialized view' of humankind. To say that people are socialized does not imply that they have been completely moulded by the norms and values of their culture.

The Feminist Critique

Sexist socialization practices were one of the first targets of **feminist** critiques of sociology in the 1970s. Feminists were highly critical of Parsonian analysis because of the implication that differences between men and women could be understood as differences in socialization. First, to describe inequities as the result of socialization avoided the issue of the structural barriers faced by women. Second, the socialization approach begged the question of change: how could parents socialized in traditional ways adopt non-sexist child-rearing practices? Therefore, feminists typically do not use socialization to explain gender differences, viewing them instead as consequences of systemic inequalities.

Gender socialization will be discussed in more detail later in the chapter. An extensive literature documents differential socialization practices, both implicit and explicit, and the ways these contribute to establishing gender differences in adolescents and adults.

The Symbolic Interactionist Perspective

The symbolic interactionist approach, in contrast to the functionalist perspective, assumes that individuals actively participate in their own socialization. George H. Mead and Charles H. Cooley, two American sociologists who were active in the early twentieth century, were leading figures in developing the symbolic interactionist perspective. Perhaps more than any other theorists, these two men influenced how most sociologists understand socialization.

Both Cooley and Mead were interested in the way individuals develop a sense of **self** and in the importance of family interaction in this process. Cooley believed that children were born with an instinctive capacity for self-development, which matured through interactions in *primary groups*, which he defined as 'characterized by intimate face-to-face association and cooperation' (1962 [1909]: 23).

Adults communicate their attitudes and values to their children primarily through language; children develop a self-concept on this basis. In other words, people begin to see themselves as they imagine others see them. This sense or awareness—'I feel about me the way I think you think of me'—Cooley called the **looking-glass self**. The looking-glass self has three elements, according to Cooley: 'the imagination of our appearance to the other person; the imagination of his judgment of that appearance; and some sort of self-feeling, such as pride or mortification' (1902: 184). The reaction of others, then, is important in determining how people feel about themselves.

Mead (1934) was also interested in the development of self-concept, which he considered to have two components: the *Me*, the socially defined self that has internalized society's norms and values, and the *I*, the spontaneous, creative self. The *I* is what makes every person different from others. The *Me* induces people to conform to behavioural expectations.

Mead emphasized the importance of children's imaginative play in early socialization, believing that through play children become sensitive to the responses of others. He believed that people learn symbolically, by taking roles, to present themselves in different social situations. This process consists of four stages. At first, children's behaviour is a combination of instinctive behaviour and imitation. This Mead called the *pre-play stage*. Later, when children pretend to be a parent, teacher, doctor, and the like, they are in effect role-playing. Mead called this the *play stage*, in which children learn to assume the roles of others and to objectify that experience by seeing themselves from the point of view of others. In the next stage, the game stage, children learn to handle several roles at once, to anticipate the behaviour of others and the expectations others have of them. Finally, children learn to internalize general social expectations by imagining how any number of others will act and react. At this

generalized other stage, a child has a sense of self and can react in a socially approved way.

Marlene Mackie (1987) regards the pre-play stage as lasting until the age of about two, the play stage as extending from two until the entry to school, and the game stage as continuing until puberty. Judy Dunn, however, argues that children have an early and sophisticated sense of the emotional states of family members, and respond appropriately. On the basis of her study of British families, Dunn asserts that by two years of age, children have developed 'powers to anticipate the feelings and intentions of other family members' and 'powers to recognize and transgress social rules and to understand that jokes about such transgressions can be shared with other people' (1986: 112). Nonetheless, because social meanings are based on assumptions concerning the understanding and intentions of others, they are always more or less ambiguous and subject to ongoing interpretation and reinterpretation.

Psychological Theories of Socialization

Sociologists owe a considerable debt to psychological theories of development, including the psychoanalytic theories of Sigmund Freud (1856–1939). According to Freud (1973 [1938]), the emotional development of children can be measured as a progression through five stages: oral, anal, phallic, latent, and genital.

The *oral stage* occurs in the first year when children are fed and experience positive sensations through suckling. At this stage, too, children begin to explore the world by putting objects in their mouths. The *anal stage* focuses on toilet training and is the child's first experience with self-control (Collier et al., 1991). Gender differences in development begin at the phallic stage, when children become aware of sex differences. This is followed by a latent period during which a child's sex drive is dormant before being awakened in adolescence.

Phase theories of development that focus on particular life tasks accomplished at specific stages in the life cycle inevitably build on Freud's work. Erik Erikson (1982), for instance, identified eight stages, or 'turning points', from infancy to old age. Each stage involves a conflict whose resolution creates a specific human capacity. For example, in the first phase, infants resolve the conflict between trust and mistrust, developing hope in the process. In the final stage, old age, the conflict is between integrity and despair, and people develop wisdom from the resolution of this conflict.

Another way Freud influenced the thinking of social psychologists was through his theory of personality development (Freud, 1974 [1923]). Indeed, awareness of the three components of personality (the id, the ego, and the superego) has seeped into popular culture and become part of everyday parlance. For Freud, the ego mediates between the id—our basic instincts—and the superego—internalized values. The insight for sociologists is that both the ego and the superego develop socially—in other words, in the process of socialization: 'One of Freud's central theses is that society forces people to suppress basic human impulses such as sex and aggression, so that they must find expression in indirect and often distorted ways' (Collier et al., 1991: 105).

Behavioural theories, by contrast, describe socialization as a process of learning through identification or reinforcement. Reinforcement, typically by parents, encourages some behaviours while discouraging others. Albert Bandura (1973), whose work on children's imitation of violence has been very influential, developed his social learning theory based on observations of children imitating parents and other models. While we have all seen children imitating parents, and may have family stories that centre on such imitative behaviour, it is hard to explain all learning in terms of this model.

There are, then, two views of socialization: action as derivative of system, and system as derivative of action. Those who focus on ways individuals *internalize* social norms and values fall into the first group. This perspective was the focus of early feminist critique of socialization theories. Mead and Cooley, in contrast, focus on ways individuals are active participants in socialization— that infants are born with the capacity for self-development. Students interested in understanding more about this topic are encouraged to read original versions of the work of Freud, Mead, Cooley, and Erikson.

● Agents of Socialization ● ●

Agents of socialization are those social institutions in children's environments that have the greatest effect on their socialization. The principal agents of socialization are family, friendship or peer groups, the education system, the media, religious institutions, and the neighbourhood or community. The socializing effect of these agents varies over time and is different for different children.

For most children, the family is the most important agent of socialization. Although it is reasonable to assume that children today spend fewer of their preschool years in the exclusive care of a family member, it is still the case that children learn basic life skills and develop their values and beliefs in the course of family interaction. The other important agents of socialization to be discussed here are schools (including daycare centres and preschool), friendship or peer groups, and the media. Parents and schools have legally defined responsibility for socializing children; peer groups do not.

The Family

Most children today have early and extensive experience of the world around them. Nevertheless, the family is still the most impressive agent of socialization. In families, children learn how to relate to other people, express intimacy, and resolve conflict. Parents play a major part in the lifelong social adjustment of their children. To cite Maccoby, 'successful socialization of children involves not only bringing about their outward conformity to parental directives, but also enabling them to become self-regulating, and motivating them so that they become willing to cooperate with parental socialization efforts' (1992: 171).

How do parents encourage their children to internalize social norms and values and to behave in socially appropriate ways? On the surface, it might seem that parental control of scarce resources would be sufficient inducement. However, asserting parental power is only effective in the short term. Longer-term effects are achieved when children have a say in setting the standards with which they are expected to comply (Maccoby, 1992). The parenting style that seems to be most effective in developing high self-esteem and encouraging self-regulating skills is a combination of warmth and discipline. Diana Baumrind (1971) called this style *authoritative parenting*. Authoritative parents are affectionate but clear in their expectations for pro-social, responsible behaviour. An authoritative parenting style is balanced between the two extremes of authoritarian and permissive parenting.

The family is the child's window to the world. A child's experience of the world will be framed by his or her family's social class, religion, ethnicity, and so on. 'Contemporary families are tall and narrow in form, with many generations alive at once, few members in each generation, and each generation significantly different from each other in age' (Settersten, 2003: 29–30). More of us are part of multi-generational households so that children are socialized by parents, grandparents, siblings, and so on—and they in turn socialize or resocialize their parents, grandparents, and even great-grandparents. Baker (1991) suggests that the influence of dead partners or relatives can be as great or greater than living family members. At best they can be influential role models; at worst they can prevent people from moving on.

Families today are also far more varied structurally than families in the past. More children are born to single women, live in single-parent households, or enter reconstituted families. What effect do these outcomes have on socialization? Do socialization practices differ by type of family? Many researchers have considered these questions. Sociologists Elizabeth Thomson, Sara McLanahan, and Roberta Curtin, for instance, argue that 'the most consistent findings from studies of family structure and socialization are that single parents exert weaker controls and make fewer demands on children than married parents' (Thomson et al., 1992: 368). The researchers wondered why this was so. Was it because one parent can exert only half as much control as two, or because single mothers have not been socialized to display traditional paternal control behaviours? They concluded that socialization differences are determined primarily by the structural conditions of being a single parent, not by gender. In other words, the primary reason for the greater leniency of single parents is their lack of time.

Does parenting style matter? According to the National Longitudinal Survey of Children and Youth, it does indeed. Sarah Landy and Kwok Kwan Tam (1996) looked at the effect of parenting style on children who were also at risk because of family characteristics. Four styles were identified: ineffective, aversive, consistent, and positive. *Ineffective parents* are often annoyed with their children and prone to telling the child he or she is bad, or not as good as others. *Aversive parents* raise their voices when children misbehave and use physical punishment. *Consistent parents* discipline the same way for the same behaviour. *Positive parents* praise their children and play and laugh together. Risk factors that might negatively affect physical or mental development include living in a single-parent household, having a teenage mother, family dysfunction, low social support, and low income (Landy and Tam, 1996: 103). Fewer than four per cent of the children in the survey were significantly at risk, and these children had four or more risk factors. The authors found that parenting practices had a greater impact on outcomes than risk factors. Indeed, positive parenting practices significantly contribute to child outcomes and protect children who are at risk: 'Children in at-risk situations who enjoyed positive parenting practices achieved [outcome] scores within the average range for children in Canada' (1996: 109). The parenting style that most strongly predicts delinquent behaviour in children aged 8–11 is the ineffective style, followed by the aversive and consistent styles (Stevenson, 1999; see also Table 3.1).

Do children learn to be violent from observing their parents? Moss (2004) used the National Longitudinal Survey of Children and Youth (see 'Sociology in Action' box) to investigate the effect of witnessing family violence

Table 3.1	Poor Parenting Practices		
	Children with Conduct Disorder		
Parenting Style Used	**Frequency**		**%**
Ineffective	Rarely		4
	Sometimes		24
	Very often		63
Aversive	Rarely		7
	Sometimes		22
	Very often		40
Consistent	Rarely		38
	Sometimes		24
	Very often		16
Positive	Rarely		27
	Sometimes		19
	Very Often		14

Source: Adapted from Kathryn Stevenson, 'Family Characteristics of Problem Kids', *Canadian Social Trends* (Winter 1999), Catalogue 11-008, 4.

on children's behaviour. The survey asked the person most knowledgeable—usually the child's mother—how often the child witnessed violence in the home. Although we might expect a certain degree of under-reporting, the results show that eight per cent of children aged four to seven years witnessed violence at home. Witnessing violence was related to poorer families and lone-parent families. Low education also made a difference. 'Higher rates of witnessing violence were reported for children whose parents gave little positive feedback, or were quite hostile or punitive in their interactions with the child' (Moss, 2004: 14).

Because data in the National Longitudinal Survey of Children and Youth is collected over time it was possible to see the effect of observing violence on subsequent violent behaviour. As we might predict, children who observed violence at home were more likely to show signs of bullying, fighting, and other aggressive behaviours. These children were also more likely to have higher levels of anxiety (Moss, 2004).

Children gradually move beyond their experience of the family. As they become involved in groups in the neighbourhood—other families, playgroups, school classes, church groups, and the like—they gain social experience, deal with conflicting demands, and become increasingly sophisticated social actors. Nevertheless, at the base of this experience of the world is their initial experience of family, which acts as a benchmark throughout life.

Media

The **mass media**, including newspapers, magazines, television, radio, films, and the Internet, are more than sources of entertainment or information. They are influential agents of socialization. The media are instrumental in transmitting and reinforcing certain values, social behaviours, and definitions of social reality. By focusing on some groups and not others or by stereotyping social characteristics, the media provide important lessons about power and influence. In this way, the media contribute to racial and sexual stereotypes. Stereotyped portrayals of men and women, racial or ethnic minorities, homosexual men or women, older people, or those with varying abilities shape viewer understandings and socializations. The impact is circular. Media representations are indicative of 'who counts' in our society and in turn provide lessons in who counts.

One of the first targets of feminist critique was the media, for contributing to the stereotyping of men and women. One would expect that there would be less stereotyping now than in the past because of this criticism and because women have made economic and political gains in the last four decades. It is therefore surprising to find that television commercials continue to reflect a gender imbalance. Robert Bartsch and colleagues (2000) replicated two earlier studies of stereotyping in television commercials and found that most

SOCIOLOGY IN ACTION
The National Longitudinal Survey of Children and Youth

The National Longitudinal Survey of Children and Youth (NLSCY) was initiated in 1994. Its purpose is to follow Canadian children by interviewing them every other year until 2018. The initial national sample comprised 22,500 individuals aged newborn to adult.

Information is gathered about the children and their families from the person most knowledgeable—usually the child's mother. Teachers and school principals also contribute information about school performance. Children aged 10 and 11 are asked about their experiences with friends, family, and school.

The study was designed to support the analysis of child and youth characteristics over time and to allow

for the investigation of the impact of social and physical environments on outcome measures such as sociability and success in school.

Longitudinal studies such as this one allow researchers to identify factors in a child's environment that affect later life abilities, capacities, health, and well-being. The NLSCY includes key development indicators such as family composition, employment, economic well-being, parenting styles, and community resources. Some of the research cited in this chapter is taken from this survey. To find out more about the survey, go to the study website: <www.hrdc-drhc.gc.ca/sp-ps/arb-dgra/nlscy-elnej/home.shtml>.

© iStockphoto.com/René Mansi

voice-overs continue to be male, and men are still more likely to appear in all commercials except those advertising domestic products. The authors did find some movement, however. The proportion of male voice-overs dropped from approximately 90 per cent to approximately 70 per cent, and the proportion of women advertising non-domestic products increased (2000: 739–40).

What about advertisements in non-Western media? In India, magazines, not electronic media, are the primary vehicle for advertising. Mallika Das (2000) studied changes in portrayals of men and women in Indian magazine advertisements in 1987, 1990, and 1994. Interestingly, the results showed that the 1990 ads portrayed women in less traditional situations than the earlier or later ads. At the same time, men were portrayed in more traditional ways in 1990 than before or after. In North American media, men and women are most typically shown in athletic roles in advertisements. This is far less evident in India. On the other hand, Indian women are less likely to be portrayed as sex objects than women in British media. Das writes, 'In India the trend seems to be to portray women less often as housewives or concerned with looks, but not more often in non-traditional, career-oriented, or authority figure roles' (2000: 713). Das suggests that this may reflect the patriarchal values of Indian society.

Concern about media violence has been long-standing. Today, concern focuses on violence and pornography in digital media; 20 years ago it was television, particularly music videos; but movies, comics, and magazines have all been considered potentially dangerous sources of influ-

ence, especially for young people. In the 1950s, Frederic Wertham published his book *Seduction of the Innocent* (1954) to protest violence in comic books, as there was a concern regarding the popularity of comic books and the rise of violence in the United States. Those concerned about media violence feel that the negative effects of the media are self-evident, that the sheer amount of violence speaks for itself. They are concerned that children will imitate what they see on television or on the Internet. A second, more subtle, more pervasive problem is the media's role in creating definitions of social reality. For example, we may tolerate high levels of violence because we have come to think that 'that's the way life is.'

Media effects have been studied by psychologists in laboratory experiments. Under laboratory conditions, subjects display more aggressive behaviour than control groups when exposed to television portrayals of violence (see Bandura, 1973). It is not clear, however, whether the kinds of imitative behaviour that occur in the laboratory also occur in normal social interaction. Experiments may confidently conclude that the response (aggressive behaviour) was triggered by the stimulus (violent media portrayals) but not that it will also occur outside the lab (Singer and Singer, 2000). In natural settings, the difficulty lies in controlling extraneous variables. In other words, how can we be sure that the behaviour we observed was, in fact, triggered by the media and not by something else?

Two social scientists at the Université de Montréal in Quebec studied the effect of listening to rap music on French-Canadian adolescents (Miranda and Claes, 2004). Adolescents listen to a great deal of rap music—some of which is explicitly anti-social in its messages. Does this encourage anti-social behaviour in young people, or are deviant adolescents drawn to particular kinds of music? The study found that rap music is related to deviant behaviours including violence, street gang involvement, and 'mild' drug use, such as tobacco, alcohol, and cannabis. Rap music that originates from France is more strongly associated with deviant behaviour while hip-hop/soul is significantly linked to less deviant behaviours. Miranda and Claes (2004: 120) suggest that adolescents who already present anti-social values select anti-social music because it reinforces their values. In this regard, it might be noted that rap had its origins in the 'toasts'—belligerent, boastful, misogynist, racist folk poetry—that developed out of the urban US black pimp/drug dealer subculture of a half-century and more ago (see, e.g., Abrahams, 2006 [1964]; Wepman et al., 1976).

Surveys indicate that television takes up the third largest amount of time in our lives, after work or school and sleep. Interestingly, the number of hours Canadians spend watching conventional television has decreased over the past two decades. Canadians watched television for an average of 21.4 hours a week in the fall of 2004—down slightly from 2000 (see Figure 3.1). The average ranged between 23 and 24 hours a week during the 1980s. Young men (aged 18–24) spent the least amount of time watching television—only 12.3 hours a week. Women watched an average of five more hours of television than men, although for both sexes viewing time increased with age (Statistics Canada, 2006a).

Television is the primary medium accessible to young children and is a potent agent of socialization. While we might worry about the amount of television children watch and about the way television contributes to a sedentary lifestyle, the amount of time children spend watching television has, like adult viewing, decreased. According to Statistics Canada figures, adolescents watch an average of 12.9 hours a week and children watch 14.1 hours. Both averages have dropped since 2000. One reason for the drop in viewing time was the cancellation of the 2004–5 NHL hockey season. Another obvious reason is the increased use of the Internet. Unfortunately, the survey did not ask about time spent playing video games, so we can only guess that this preoccupation accounts for another part of the decline.

In 1997, Statistics Canada began to collect data about Internet use. The 2007 Canadian Internet Use Survey, which included 30,000 respondents, provides an interesting picture of Internet use in Canada. In 2007, 73 per cent of Canadians used the internet. This is a five per cent increase in just two years. (The 2007 survey added 16- and 17-year-olds, which accounts for one per cent of the increase). Internet use is related to income, education, and age. Usage is highest for younger Canadians, and those with high income and high education. Almost all (96 per cent) of those aged 16–24 go online more than three times a week (Statistics Canada, 2008).

In his book *Growing Up Digital*, Don Tapscott (1998) refers to what demographers have called the *baby-boom echo generation* (born between 1977 and 1997) as the *Net generation*. The media sometimes call this group *screenagers*. While their parents, the baby-boom generation, were shaped by television, which influenced their values, their political beliefs, and how they spent their leisure time, the Net generation are immersed in digital media, with perhaps more far-reaching effects, for digital media are an educational tool in a way that television was never able to be. The Net generation also uses the Internet to communicate with friends and to establish and maintain community. Young people have, according to

Figure 3.1   Average Weekly Hours of Television Viewing, Canada, 1995–2004

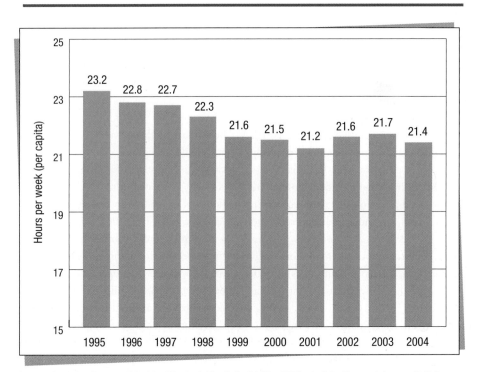

Source: Statistics Canada, 'Television Viewing', *The Daily*, 31 Mar. 2006, at <http://www.statcan.ca/Daily/English/060331/d060331b.htm>.

HUMAN DIVERSITY
Early Childhood Socialization and 'the Troubles' in Northern Ireland

Protestants and Catholics in Northern Ireland have been engaged in a long period of conflict. From the late 1960s until the mid-1990s the country was engaged in armed conflict, euphemistically called 'the Troubles'. Over 3,600 people died and thousands were injured during this 30-year period (Connolly et al., 2006: 265). A 1994 ceasefire signalled the beginning of a relatively peaceful period.

Little research has been done to find out the impact on young children of living in a divided society like Northern Ireland. One study (Connolly et al., 2002) found that it is not until age five or six that children develop a sense of 'us and them' in such a setting. While three-year-olds in Northern Ireland do not have a strong sense of the divisions, they implicitly have preferences for their respective communities (ibid.). When three-year-olds were shown the British Union flag and the Irish tricolour flag, most of the Protestant children (60 per cent) chose the British flag and the majority of Catholic children (64 per cent) chose the Irish one.

Recently there has been an effort to devise a way to encourage children in Northern Ireland to learn to respect diversity of race, ability, and religion. To this end, three one-minute cartoons were created for television accompanied by curricular materials developed for use in preschool. The program is

called the Media Initiative for Children—Northern Ireland. The decision to focus more broadly was taken to gain support for the program. It was anticipated that a program that focused only on religious difference would not gain acceptance among parents and would be stressful for children.

The short cartoons were developed using computer animation. The scripts were crafted by a storyteller respected by both Protestants and Catholics. The cartoons can be viewed on-line (www.pii-mifc.org). The four cartoon characters are Jenny, Jim, Kim, and Tom. Tom wears an eye patch. Kim is Chinese—the largest racial minority group in Northern Ireland. The other two characters wear soccer shirts that represent Protestant and Catholic teams.

A pilot project conducted in 2004 consisted of running the cartoons on television for six weeks and at the same time introducing the companion curricular materials in selected playgrounds. The evaluation of the pilot program showed that children who took part were better able to recognize instances of exclusion presented to them and better able to say how being excluded makes someone feel. They were also slightly more willing to include a person who was being excluded. Children in the pilot study showed that they were more likely to play with children who were 'different':

> The programme therefore appeared to have achieved some measurable success in terms of encouraging young children to be more inclusive of others in relation to disability and 'race', [but] it did not seem to have had any effect in relation to the third difference—Catholic and Protestant children's attitudes towards one another. (Connolly, 2006: 273)

Children in the pilot group were too young to have formed opinions about 'the other' in religious terms, although they already held such opinions about a child with a disability and a child of a different race. The initiative continues to be used throughout Northern Ireland, with an additional cartoon about bullying planned for the near future.

(The Canadian Press/AP/Peter Morrison)

Tapscott, become bored with the unidirectional medium of television, preferring the engagement required by digital technology. Indeed, they watch far less television than their parents did when they were young. The Net generation is also a sophisticated user of the new technology, far surpassing their parents or their teachers.

Two aspects of shifting media use are worth noting. The first is that media use is increasingly a solitary activity. Today there are more televisions and fewer people per household. In other words, more people are watching television alone. We also watch more videos and go to fewer movies. Again, going to the movies is usually a social activity; video viewing may not be. Typically, entertainment and communication on the Internet are solitary. The second point concerns what Tapscott (1998) calls the *digital divide*: the class and educational difference in digital media use. This has created a system of information haves and have-nots. The digital divide occurs within societies like Canada and the United States, and it occurs between societies where dramatic differences in access distinguish the developing and the developed world.

The Statistics Canada General Social Survey of 2000 asked Canadians about their Internet use. There were 3,300 young people (aged 15–24) among the respondents, 56 per cent of whom were connected to the Internet at home. Almost half of these young people used the Internet every day. Frequent users also access the Internet at school and at work. Nevertheless, those with home access indicated far more hours of use than those without home access. Men use the Internet for more hours per week than women. E-mail is the most popular Internet activity for young Canadians (Rotermann, 1999: 5–6). Internet use for 15- to 24-year-olds is lower in Quebec than in the rest of Canada. This is presumably because much of the content of the Internet is in English only, a factor that affects usage worldwide.

The Peer Group

Patricia Ramsay writes, 'For both children and adults, friends enhance our pleasure, mitigate our anxieties and broaden our realm of experience' (1991: 3). As you have seen, the family is the first reference group for most people, that is, the group with which children compare their behaviour, ideas, and values. But starting at an early age, the peer group also becomes very important. Because so many parents are now in the labour force, more children are spending more time with children of the same age, and at a younger age. Peer groups have therefore gained increasing recognition as important socializing agents for even very young children. The success of children's peer

relationships is linked to their later psychological development and to school success. It has also been suggested that children with poor peer relationships may experience job-related and marital problems in later life (Ramsay, 1991).

Playgroups provide important opportunities for children to learn to relate to others and increase their social skills. By interacting with their peers in playgroups, children develop a frame of reference not based on adult authority. Gerald Handel (1988: 17) asserts that 'it is in these peer groups that a child learns to function more independently, to acquire and test skills and beliefs that earn him a place among people of the same generation, to develop new outlooks that reflect youthful interests rather than adult ones.'

The peer group assumes great influence in adolescence. In developmental terms, the task of adolescents is to begin to establish emotional, social, and economic independence. By the age of 13 or 14, adolescents typically spend most of their leisure time with peers. In an international survey, Klaus Hurrelmann found, for example, that Western adolescents report spending more time talking to peers than on any other single activity—and are happiest doing just this (1989: 16).

Adolescence is commonly depicted as a period of testing limits. It is not a surprise that more adolescents are killed in accidents than die from health-related problems. If we were to rely on the mass media, we might be persuaded that youth violence is increasing in this 'age of Columbine'. Certainly there have been a few spectacular incidents of adolescent violence in Canada and in the United States. On the other hand, official statistics suggest that the incidence of violent crime is declining and that only a small proportion of young people are involved in physical violence. When Canadian sociologist Reginald Bibby surveyed Canadian young people, he found that many were fearful of encountering violence: 22 per cent of young people did not feel safe in school—a smaller proportion than found in comparable US studies (2001: 84, 88; see also Table 3.2).

Why is it that some adolescents resort to physical violence and others do not? The National Longitudinal Survey of Children and Youth (NLSCY) provides some interesting information about aggressive behaviour among Canadian pre-adolescents. Indeed, children become less, not more, violent as they become older. The age at which children are most likely to hit, bite, or kick was 27–29 months (Tremblay et al., 1996: 129), suggesting that most Canadian children 'benefit from the socializing impact of their families and other socialization agencies' (1996: 130). Children who are physically aggressive are also often hyperactive and suffer inattention problems. They also have lower self-esteem, tend to exhibit high levels of indirect aggression and high emotional disorder, and tend not to help other children (1996: 132).

Families have an important impact on the aggressive behaviour of pre-adolescents. Boys and girls who have siblings with behavioural problems are more likely to be aggressive themselves. They are also more likely to live in families with high levels of parent–child conflict and sibling conflict. Aggressive children have poor peer relationships and are more likely to be victimized by other aggressors (see Table 3.3). Will these young people outgrow their adolescent behaviour? Richard Tremblay and colleagues (1996) suggest that because the aggression stems from family interaction problems, this appears unlikely. Without support, these children are more likely

to continue aggressive behaviour into adulthood. It is, however, important to keep in mind that these children represent a small proportion of all Canadian children. Most children are not inappropriately aggressive. In addition, they are, as Bibby (2001) points out, highly resilient. In the face of family problems and economic and educational disadvantage, Canadian adolescents are optimistic about the future.

Judith Harris in *The Nurture Assumption* (1998) argues that children are socialized primarily by other children—not by their families. Others argue that Harris overstates the case. 'Socialization in families is a complex phenomenon encompassing multiple and interacting processes and mechanisms that are manifested in a number of domains with different effects' (Putney and Bengtson, 2003: 179). Although much is made of the idea of

Table 3.2	Teens' Concern About Violence by Region, Community Size, and Birthplace (Percentages)				
	School Violence a Very Serious Problem	Close Friend Attacked at School	Not Safe at School	Not Safe at Home	Close Friend Physically Abused at Home
Nationally	50	32	22	7	31
British Columbia	51	30	19	7	30
Prairies	49	32	17	5	30
Ontario	53	32	22	7	32
Quebec	43	33	27	7	33
Atlantic	54	30	21	8	27
North	53	34	19	2	31
Cities, towns					
<30,000	53	29	21	8	33
30,000–99,999	56	36	28	7	31
100,000–399,999	51	32	21	7	34
>400,000	44	35	21	5	32
Rural					
Non-farm	52	32	18	7	27
Farm	50	24	19	6	25
Born in Canada	50	31	21	7	32
Born outside Canada	47	35	26	6	28

Source: Reginald W. Bibby, *Canada's Teens* (Toronto: Stoddart, 2001), 84.

Table 3.3   Prevalence of Bullying and Victimization in Canada (Percentages)

| | Parent's Report | | Children's Self-Report[a] | |
	Boys	Girls	Boys	Girls
Ages 4–6				
Bullying	14.4	9.4	–	–
Victimization	4.9	4.4	–	–
Ages 7–9				
Bullying	14.8	7.9	–	–
Victimization	4.0	7.4	–	–
Ages 10–11				
Bullying	13.0	9.2	17.2	8.7
Victimization	8.6	9.1	13.6	8.1

[a] Self-report data were not collected in the 4–6 and 7–9 age groups.

Source: Wendy Craig, Ray Peters, and Roman Konarski, 'Bully and Victim: Child's Play or Unhealthy Schoolyard Behaviour?', from Human Resources and Social Development Canada, *Applied Research Bulletin* (Fall 1999): 17. Reproduced with the permission of Her Majesty the Queen in Right of Canada 2008.

adolescent rebellion, there will generally be considerable correspondence between parental and adolescent values. Because parents want their children to be well liked and want good relationships with them, they are generally supportive of their children's activities. Peer-group influence is tempered by parental influence because parents control scarce and valued resources, including their approval. Certainly some adolescents rebel, but for most young people learning to be independent adults, adolescence is not a particularly turbulent time.

School

Schools do more than instruct students in the three Rs; they also provide an important environment for the transmission of social values. Next to the family, the school is probably the most important locus of childhood and adolescent socialization because it is central to a young person's social life and acts as a filter for future occupational choice. Children's readiness to learn is an important factor in success at school. A recent study used the National Longitudinal Survey of Children and Youth to look at school readiness among five-year-olds. Not surprisingly there were significant gender differences. In factors that measure school readiness girls showed greater development regarding communication skills and greater attention to self-control and impulsive behaviour. Boys were

more developed in terms of curiosity. Children from affluent homes did better on many dimensions of readiness to learn. However, regardless of income—children who have been read to daily, who have positive interactions with their parents, or who are involved in sports or the arts show greater readiness to learn (Thomas, 2006: 49).

A key component here seems to be the effect of positive reactions by parents and teachers on a child's self-concept. Doris Entwisle and Leslie Hayduck (1988) report that parental and teacher reactions measured in Grade 3 had a significant effect on achievement almost a decade later. As they explain, children in the early grades are building their 'academic self-images'. During transitions, such as starting school, moving, or adjusting to family changes like a new sibling or a parental separation, children depend on significant others—family members, teachers—for support: 'getting off to a good start gives them a competitive advantage from then on' (Entwisle and Hayduck, 1988: 158).

Self-concepts are particularly fragile when adolescents are in middle school (senior public or junior high). David Kinney (1993) reports that older adolescents remember this as a difficult time. Students universally recall a rigid social structure dominated by a popular (and powerful) group. Unpopular adolescents remember being ridiculed, shunned, and ignored by their popular classmates. Fortunately, the impact of popularity is short-lived. In high school, student culture is more open and more diverse. There are far more reference groups with which to identify, and the social structure is less hierarchical (Kinney, 1993).

As children mature, they increase their experiences and contacts. However, these events and associations will not be random but, rather, are largely compatible with earlier experience. It is therefore unlikely that the school environment will promote different values from those already learned by a child. For example, middle-class children will attend school with other middle-class children, who for the most part will value school achievement.

Yet much of what is learned in school is implicit, sometimes referred to as the **hidden curriculum**. The hidden curriculum comprises unspoken rules and practices such as the acclaim given by students and teachers alike to academic versus athletic endeavours and the behaviours that are punished versus those that are excused; the age, sex, race, and ethnic structure of the administration, the teaching staff, and the student body; and the similarity or difference between the expectations for success held by a student's friends and those of his or her family. The greater the disjunction between the behaviours reinforced at school and those reinforced by the family or the peer group, the smaller the likelihood that the student will see success in school as relevant.

Parental involvement, including helping children with homework, encouraging them to study, having contact with the school and teachers, and attending events at the school, has a positive effect on children's academic performance. This relationship holds for younger as well as older students.

Many immigrant parents in particular have high expectations for their children regarding education. As shown in Table 3.4, the majority are actively involved in their children's education and want their children to go to university. Canadian-born children of Canadian-born parents are much less likely to want to choose their children's career or to expect their children to go to university. They are, however, among the most likely parents to help their children with school. L.P. Salazar and colleagues (2001) studied the family socialization processes used by Filipino-Canadian parents living in Winnipeg to motivate their children in school. The children, who were in Grades 7 through 12, completed a self-report questionnaire about parenting styles, parent involvement, the importance of family reputation, attribution of success, and student involvement. The results suggest that student involvement in school was promoted by parental involvement (as perceived by their adolescents) and authoritative (not authoritarian) parenting. Authoritative parents encourage psychological autonomy and exert firm behavioural guidelines. Authoritarian parents, in contrast, are strict, demand obedience, and are emotionally distant. Adolescents indicated that they felt obliged to do well in school to maintain their family reputation. Those students who were concerned about family reputation were inclined to believe that effort and interest, not academic ability, were the basis of student success. That these findings corresponded closely to findings of a study done of Filipino immigrants in San Francisco suggests that, indeed, the emphasis on family reputation as a mediating factor in school success may be characteristic of Filipino adolescent immigrants.

In schools throughout the world, adolescents are 'sorted' during secondary schooling. High school grades and course selection will determine whether a student attends a post-secondary institution, whether he or she graduates, and whether or not the student makes a successful transition to paid employment. One of the most important variables influencing which of these paths is taken is gender.

● Socialization Outcomes ● ●

This section will look at the effects of gender, race, and class on socialization practices. It will also examine how children learn to make gender, race, and class distinctions and how to understand their implications. For children, adolescents, and adults alike, gender identity and perceptions of socio-economic status are fundamental aspects of the development of self-concept. Gender and class infuse social interaction as children develop physically, cognitively, and emotionally and as they anticipate adult family and economic roles.

■■ **Time to Reflect** ■|■ ■■ ■|■ ■|■ ■|■ ■■ ■■ ■■ ■■ ■|■ ■■ ■■ ■|■ ■■ ■|■

When does the influence of parents on children's socialization shift to the peer group? Is this transition universal?

Table 3.4	Parental Expectations About Education and Career (% of Teens Agreeing)						
	Caribbean[a]	Chinese[a]	East European[a]	Latin American[a]	South Asian[a]	Canadian[b]	All
My parent(s) want to choose a career for me	15	26	17	19	26	8	19
My parent(s) expect me to go to university	69	89	70	68	77	45	70
My parent(s) think high marks in school are important	92	87	91	81	90	75	84
I feel a lot of pressure from my parent(s) to do well in school	50	55	49	52	60	45	52
If I have problems at school, my parent(s) are ready to help me	76	64	71	81	78	80	73

[a] Children not born in Canada or whose parents were not born in Canada.
[b] Children born in Canada to Canadian-born parents.
Source: Barbara Helm and Wendy Warren, 'Cultural Heritage and Family Life', *Transition Magazine* (Ottawa: The Vanier Institute of the Family, Sept. 1998): 7. Reprinted by permission of the publisher.

The Social Reproduction of Gender

Individuals develop an understanding of gender through a complex interweaving of individual and environmental factors, predispositions, and expectations. In the course of gender socialization, children are exposed to many models of behaviour and gain a sense of masculinity or femininity from a variety of sources. Furthermore, individuals receive inconsistent messages even from the same sources.

How much of what we are is determined by socialization, and how much is inborn? This question is often referred to as the *'nature versus nurture' debate*. The assumption that nature dominates is called **biological determinism**. The opposite of biological determinism is what is described as 'an oversocialized view' of human nature (Wrong, 1961) that implies that people are largely moulded by their socialization experiences.

In the past, people believed that behavioural differences were largely genetically determined, that children were born with certain aptitudes and dispositions—

including a predisposition to good or evil. This assumption of inherent characteristics was taken to apply to differences between races as well as between men and women. This line of reasoning is now regarded as fallacious. It is one thing to suppose that nature helps explain individual differences, quite another to say the same thing about group differences. Nevertheless, the question of nature versus nurture remains a focus of continuing research, with much attention given to differences between females and males. Are sex distinctions in adults better explained in terms of biological differences or in terms of differential socialization?

Gender differences have been the subject of thousands of studies. Much of the research has focused on the behaviour of infants and young children. Reviews of this body of work, including an early review by Eleanor Maccoby and Carole Jacklin (1974) of 1,400 studies, which found that few behaviours consistently differentiated males and females. In many cases, studies investigating similar behaviours have had contradictory results. For instance, consistent gender differences have been reported in aggression and in a preference for certain toys. In fact, most studies have found that the actual distinctions between boys and girls are minor. Most children are not aggressive, and they spend most of their time playing with toys that are not gender-related. Furthermore, since boys are handled more roughly from birth onward, it is predictable that there will be some sex-related differences in behaviours such as level of activity or aggressiveness; however, these differences may have more to do with socialization practices than with biology. Most adult behaviours do not have clear antecedents in early childhood. The important differences between adults—**status** distinctions, for example—are unrelated to the differences typically found in children.

Some researchers argue that gender differences develop because of parental reaction to innate differences (see Ruble and Martin, 1998). That is, girls become more verbally skilled because they are more receptive to verbal interactions, while boys become more physically aggressive because they respond more positively to aggressive play. Others argue that parents reinforce behaviour in a way that is consistent with their own expectations and stereotypes. Parents have different expectations of their infant boys and girls in language and in cognitive and social development (see Ruble and Martin, 1998). This may or may not also extend to motor development. E.R. Mondschein, K.E. Adolph, and C.S. Tamis-LeMonda (2000) measured mothers' expectations regarding crawling and compared this to crawling ability. Mothers of boys had higher expectations of their sons than did mothers of daughters regarding the crawling tasks. Although the infant boys and girls in the study did not differ in motor abilities, mothers expected them to differ. This difference in expectation has significant implications for later motor development and risk-taking.

Very young children show sex-stereotyped toy preferences and sex-stereotyped activities. Research evidence seems to favour a socialization explanation. Television ads, catalogue layouts, toy packaging, and the organization of toy departments all seem to collude to steer the toy purchaser in the direction of stereotyped choices. It is no surprise that toys and other aspects of the physical environment of very young children are differentiated according to gender. Andrée Pomerleau and colleagues (1990) found that boys under the age of two tended to be given sports equipment, tools, and large and small vehicles, while girls were presented with dolls, fictional characters, child's furniture, and other toys for manipulation. They also observed the traditional pink–blue differences in the room decoration of the children in their sample.

Socialization is, to a large extent, based on nuance and subtlety. By the age of two, children are perceptive readers of their **social environment**. They observe patterns of interaction in the home, including the gender-relatedness of household tasks. Even in homes where both parents are gainfully employed, women take greater responsibility for housework and child care than men. Socialization to such divisions of labour presumably affects the family and occupational choices of young people. Children grow up with gendered names, toys, clothes, games, and room decorations. By the time they get to school, **gender stereotypes** are well established. The structure and practices of education, then, reinforce rather than challenge these earlier perceptions.

As argued earlier in the chapter, the media are a significant source of gender stereotyping. Studies of media content continue to find that women are under-represented, stereotyped, and trivialized. Susan Losh-Hesselbart (1987) made the interesting discovery that heavy television viewers show more rigidity in gender stereotyping than occasional viewers. It is hardly surprising, then, that one of the women's movement's first targets among traditional socialization practices was the gender stereotyping in children's books and television programming. These criticisms have met with some success. A study of children's picture books by Carole Kortenhaus and Jack Demarest found that newer books show a greater representation of female characters: 'Prior to 1970, children's literature contained almost four times as many boys as girls in titles, more than twice as many boys in central roles, almost twice as many boys in pictures, and nearly four times as many male animals as female animals' (1993: 225). After 1970, there were more female characters in all categories—but still not an equal number. Kortenhaus and Demarest also noted that activities depicted in books were strongly stereotyped by sex, with males dominating in instrumental behaviours and females in passive, dependent roles. Again, however, they found some improvement over time.

Childhood experiences have lifelong implications. Patricia Coats and Steven Overman (1992) compared childhood play and other early socialization experiences of women in traditional and non-traditional professions. They found that women in non-traditional fields had received different forms of parental encouragement as children than women in traditional professions. Women in non-traditional (business) professions participated in more competitive activities as children and continued to seek competitive recreational activities as adults. The members of this group also had more male companions when they were children. Interestingly, the fathers of all the professional women encouraged their daughters' competitiveness. Mothers of women who entered non-traditional professions echoed that encouragement, whereas mothers of women who entered traditional professions encouraged more traditional values.

Data from a US intergenerational panel study of parents and children provide an opportunity to see the effect of childhood socialization practices regarding household division of labour on the next generation (Cunningham, 2001). Women in this sample were interviewed first in 1962 and again in 1977, and their 18-year-old daughters were interviewed in 1980. Indeed, the mothers' attitudes during their children's early years had a strong influence on the children's ideal division of household labour at 18. The family division of labour also had an important impact: adolescent women whose fathers had shared housework were more apt to support men's participation in stereotypically female household tasks.

A number of studies support the conclusion that black husbands and fathers do more housework than men of other races. This involvement seems to reflect early 'socialization for competencies' (Penha-Lopes, 2006). Penha-Lopes conducted in-depth interviews with 45 black fathers of young children to find out more about their engagement in housework and how they made sense of their choices. The majority (90 per cent) of the men in the study either shared (did at least 50 per cent of the housework) or helped (did at least one-third of housework) as adults. They had done housework from the time they were six and by age 10 or 11 were actively

involved in cooking and cleaning. Their parents did not have different expectations for sons or daughters, so the men in this study grew up with the expectation that they had a responsibility to help at home. Housework was not sex-typed in the homes they grew up in, 'regardless of their living arrangements, mothers' employment status, and the presence of sisters'. The men in this study 'formed ideas about housework as a matter of competence, self-sufficiency, and masculinity, rather than [as] the exclusive domain of femininity' (2006: 272).

Gender stereotypes continue to frame our understanding of the social behaviour of males and females from infancy to old age. Minor behavioural and attitudinal differences in childhood are reinforced through adolescence and become pronounced in adults. However subtly, people react differently to boys and girls, men and women, and in the process encourage different behavioural responses. The differential reactions may be quite unintentional. Parents tend to say they have similar expectations for their children with regard to dependency, aggression, school achievement, and so forth, although fathers are typically more concerned than mothers about gender-typed behaviour in their children.

The gender stereotyping of occupational choices has important implications for a young person's future. Occupational stereotypes frame educational, occupational, and interpersonal choices, especially for women, and are the basis of discriminatory practices in education and the workplace. Nonetheless, significant changes have occurred in the family and in the occupational

OPEN FOR DISCUSSION
Do the Media Contribute to Disordered Eating Among Young Adolescent and Pre-adolescent Girls?

Most women in fashion magazines, movies, and television are pencil-thin. Indeed, the media create an impression that thinness is highly valued in Western society. Viewers of all ages use these images as points of comparison when evaluating their own body image. No wonder body dissatisfaction is universal. Kevin Thompson and Leslie Heinberg (1999) connect exposure to unrealistically thin images in magazines and television with body dissatisfaction and disordered eating among girls and women. Their solution is to counter these extreme images: 'The media itself is one potential vehicle for

communicating productive, accurate, and deglamorized messages about eating and shape-related disorders' (ibid., 339).

What do you think about this issue? Are girls susceptible to images of ultra-thin models? Are girls more susceptible than young boys? In what other ways besides the mass media is thinness reinforced? How do we reconcile media images with reports of increased numbers of obese children and youth? Does the solution lie, as these authors suggest, in changing the images in the media, or is it a larger and more complex problem?

responsibilities of both women and men during the past three decades. These changes indicate that behaviour can be modified, even for those whose primary socialization was highly traditional.

The Social Reproduction of Race and Class

Racial socialization refers to all of the ways parents shape children's learning about race and race relations (Hughes and Johnson, 2001). Racial socialization is an important component of child-rearing among ethnic and racial-minority families. It appears that efforts to instill racial pride are successful. Generally, children whose parents have emphasized racial pride have higher self-esteem and greater knowledge of their ethnic or racial group (see Marshall, 1995).

Racial socialization, like gender and class socialization, is a repetitive process. Children are not simply sponges. Their reactions and needs interact with their parents' own experiences of being socialized and with their parents' experiences in the world to determine parental racial socialization strategies.

D. Hughes and D. Johnson (2001) used reports of 94 dyads of African-American parents and Grade 3, 4, and 5 children to determine if socialization practices were influenced by whether or not children had experienced racial **discrimination**. Most parents reported that they talked to their children about their own and other ethnic groups, and most talked to their children about the possibility that the child might experience discrimination. Only about one-fifth of parents reported that they had cautioned or warned their children about other racial or ethnic groups. Hughes and Johnson refer to this strategy of talking about the possibility of discrimination as 'promotion of mistrust'. Not surprisingly, promotion of mistrust was related to parents' reports that their children had received unfair treatment from adults as well as to children's reports of unfair treatment from peers. Interestingly, parental promotion of mistrust was not related to their own experiences of discrimination.

How does racial socialization work when parents and children are of different races? Tracy Robinson (2001) studied this issue by analyzing interviews of white mothers of mixed race (white–Maori) children in New Zealand. These mothers described the importance of exposing their children to both white (*Pakeha*) and Maori culture and their frustration in the face of the discrimination their children experienced. One woman discussed tearfully the difficulty her child encountered in finding an apartment. Her daughter had phenotypical characteristics (brown skin, dark hair, and brown eyes). One day the daughter said, 'Mum, you come along with me so that I can get the apartment' (Robinson, 2001: 180).

Another important context of socialization is socio-economic class. The kinds of work adults perform and the coping strategies they employ to make sense of their work have fundamental implications for the socialization of their children. As in gender socialization, children begin at a very young age to absorb the implications of class in society. They learn early 'who counts' and where they fit into the social hierarchy.

Alwin (1990) argues that there was a general shift in North American parental values over the five decades leading up to his study. Whereas parents used to want their children to be obedient and conforming, they were now more inclined to want to instill a sense of independence or autonomy. He looked at five studies measuring parental socialization values from the 1920s through the 1980s. Public opinion surveys done in Detroit in 1958, 1971, and 1983 revealed some interesting differences. Parents were asked the following question:

> If you had to choose, which thing would you pick as the most important for a child to learn to prepare him for life?
> (a) to obey
> (b) to be well-liked or popular
> (c) to think for himself
> (d) to work hard
> (e) to help others when they need help (Alwin, 1990: 365)

Respondents were asked to rank their top four choices. Alwin found that 'to think for himself' was the most preferred quality and that the number of parents citing it as most important increased over time. 'To be well-liked or popular' was the least preferred and became even less important over time. Obedience also decreased in importance, while hard work increased. The number of parents who valued the quality of helpfulness remained stable. In other Western countries, too, there seems to be a similar parental concern for developing independence in children (Alwin, 1990).

What accounts for this shift in focus? Alwin feels it results partly from increased education, partly from increased secularization. Predictably, increased education is associated with the valuation of autonomy and with a decrease in the value of conformity. Parental preference for obedience is linked to levels of church attendance, which have declined over recent decades. Finally, it is interesting that some evidence exists that the youngest cohorts are slightly more inclined towards conformity and obedience than older cohorts. Nevertheless, parental values are only one part of the equation. Myriad factors combine to influence children's behaviour. The fact that parents claim to value self-reliant behaviour does not necessarily imply that children will respond accordingly.

Social Reproduction of Adult Family and Work Roles

Childhood, adolescence, and adulthood are social constructs that broadly define periods of social, psychological, and biological development. They are generally, but not absolutely, determined by age. Because life-cycle stages do not follow a predictable or orderly track, there is no specific point at which an adolescent is declared to be an adult, for example. Some young people will have assumed adult roles of marriage, parenthood, or economic independence before their eighteenth birthday. Others remain in school and financially dependent on parents well into their twenties. Still others return to the parental home after divorce or job loss. Some of these adult children will have children themselves, thus creating a temporary three-generation household. During the past quarter-century, the transition from adolescence to adulthood has been altered by such trends as increased schooling and a rise in the age at first marriage. Now, young adults enjoy a period of independent living before marriage. Two or three decades ago, this period of independence was shorter, as both men and women typically married in their early twenties. Ceremonies such as graduation or marriage may therefore be more appropriate than age as signals of the transition to adulthood.

José Machado Pais (2000) has argued that the transition to adulthood takes longer now than in the past. One of the reasons for this is uncertainty about future education, work, and family roles. The transitional process from youth to adulthood is affected by past socialization experiences and by expectations about the future. To the extent that the future appears uncertain, the transition to adulthood is stalled. Leaving school, starting a job, or making a commitment to a relationship does not necessarily signal permanent departure or the assumption of adult responsibilities.

A second characteristic of the transition to adulthood today is that it is reversible. Education, employment, relationships, and living arrangements all are more transitory than they were in the past; young people may return to school, or again live with parents at the end of a romantic or employment relationship. Pais calls this reversibility the 'yo-yo-ization' of the transition to adulthood. Parents of youth in transition are also affected by this pattern because of the societal dominance of youth culture. Parents adopt aspects of youth culture in an effort to forestall aging.

One of the greatest challenges of adolescence is preparation for adult family and work responsibilities. Dating is one of the vehicles for this learning. Even though dating is much less formal than it was in the past, it still helps develop social and communication skills and contributes to the development of self-esteem. In our culture, dating provides opportunities for anticipatory socialization for future cohabitation or marriage.

Adolescents are also required to make decisions about educational options that will affect their future opportunities in the labour force. While not irreversible, decisions such as quitting school or selecting math and science rather than languages and history will open some doors and close others.

Not all of the socialization children receive for adult roles is positive. For instance, violent or abusive adults have internalized this inappropriate response to stress or frustration through socialization. In the area of family violence, researchers have just begun to clarify the links between experiences in childhood and adult behaviour. Judith Seltzer and Debra Kalmuss predicted that people who have experienced violence in their homes as children 'may incorporate abuse into the behavioural repertoires they bring to intimate relationships that they establish in adulthood' (1988: 475). Their findings support this prediction: 'Early childhood exposure to family violence has a substantially greater effect on spouse abuse than does . . . exposure to recent stressful experiences or chronic economic strain' (1988: 487). Furthermore, observing parents' marital aggression has more of an effect on children than being hit by a parent.

However, the relationship is not absolute. Some adults have violent marriages even though they did not grow up in violent homes. Moreover, not all children growing up in such homes become abusive adults. Extra-familial socialization agents, including peer groups, dating partners, and the media, explain the discrepancies (Seltzer and Kalmuss, 1988).

Socialization for Parenthood

Do adolescent boys and girls anticipate parenthood differently? A New Zealand study by Barbara Calvert and Warren Stanton found considerable evidence to support the conclusion that adolescent males and females were equally committed to becoming parents. Among the respondents, 89 per cent answered 'Yes' to the question, 'Would you like to have children of your own?' When asked whether they would want to adopt if they were unable to have children, 83 per cent of the girls and 72 per cent of the boys answered in the affirmative (Calvert and Stanton, 1992: 317). Both boys and girls wanted to have their first child when they were in their mid-twenties, and both genders listed 'fond of children' as an important quality in a spouse. All the young people in the study expected to combine family and employment responsibilities, although the majority thought that, ideally, one parent should stay home with young children. Interestingly, 82 per cent of the boys and 85 per cent of the girls said it did not matter whether the mother or the father was the caregiving parent (1992: 319). Other responses indicated that both girls and boys expected both parents to nurture and perform child-care tasks.

The major gender difference between these teenagers was not in attitudes, but in experience; the boys had considerably less exposure to young children and less experience in caregiving. As Calvert and Stanton suggest, this difference could result in a definition of the women as more expert and promote a gendered division of labour when the adolescents form families of their own. The study also found strong evidence to suggest that children will be strongly influenced by the child-rearing practices to which they were exposed when growing up: 'Most respondents expected to do pretty much as their parents had done' (1992: 325).

Studies of new parents find that many are ill-prepared for the time and energy demands of caring for a newborn. Not surprisingly, Renee Steffensmeier (1982) found that anticipatory socialization had a significant effect on the transition to parenthood. The more previous experience new parents had, or the better they were prepared by training for the experience of parenting, the more satisfying they found it. Jay Belsky (1985) found that women were more likely than men to experience a disjunction between their expectations and their experiences regarding childbirth and, consequently, to report less satisfaction. Since women hold the greatest responsibility for infant care, this is hardly surprising. While the household division of labour tends to become more traditional following birth, the mothers in Belsky's sample were more involved in infant care relative to the fathers than either the mothers or the fathers had anticipated, and this was a major source of dissatisfaction.

While most men marry, and while attitude surveys indicate that men give high priority to family life, early socialization does little to prepare them to be fathers. To some extent, low involvement by fathers is a self-fulfilling prophecy. Men have very little preparation for the care of infants or young children, and they are likely to feel awkward; they therefore experience failure in their attempts to help. Alice Rossi's investigations of interactions between fathers and infants suggest that men 'tend to avoid high

involvement in infant care because infants do not respond to their repertoire of skills and men have difficulty acquiring the skills needed to comfort the infant' (Rossi, 1984: 8). She sees a solution in teaching fathers about parenting and so encouraging their participation. Rossi assumes that men are not more active parents because they have not been socialized to anticipate this role.

In recent years, it has become more the rule than the exception for fathers to attend prenatal classes, to assist during labour, and to be present during the birth of their child. Other trends, such as high divorce rates, have brought about an increase in the number of 'weekend fathers'—divorced men who have periodic responsibility for their children. Such parenting experiences seem to pave the way for increased male involvement in child care.

However, no amount of compensatory socialization will alter the structural barriers to equal involvement in child care and other domestic tasks. Primary caregiving fathers in a study in Australia had made a decision to be involved in child-rearing and household tasks, although only half the sample defined housework and child care as their primary tasks (Grbich, 1992). In Australia, the role of caregiver is not considered appropriate for men. The fathers all recognized that parenting and housework have low status, and one-third of them were uncomfortable with their role for this reason. Some of the fathers mentioned that they received verbal put-downs from neighbours, shopkeepers, and others. They reported a number of subtle tactics used to marginalize them, including sexual labelling, avoidance, ostracism, active confrontation, lowered expectations of their performance or capabilities, and non-payment of child allowances (Grbich, 1992). Clearly, it will take much more than changes in individual behaviour to change the structures of sexual inequality.

Socialization for Employment

Professional schools are important socializing agents for adults. Medical schools in particular have been studied in this regard. What students learn during their years in medical school goes well beyond the acquisition of technical skills: they are learning to behave like doctors. Some researchers, however, feel that the similarities in attitudes and values among medical school graduates have more to do with selective recruitment of middle- and upper-class students than with any training they receive. In their panel study of Canadian medical students, Neena Chappell and Nina Colwill (1981) found that students recruited to medical schools shared certain attitudes at the outset. Interestingly, these viewpoints seemed unrelated to either social class or gender. Although the researchers do not discuss their findings in terms of anticipatory socialization, it seems that a medical student's orientation to the profession begins long before he or she enters medical school.

Frederic Jablin (1984) describes three stages of socialization to employment. The first is the period of *anticipatory socialization*. Prospective employees form expectations about the job on the basis of their education, training, and previous employment. The second stage is the *encounter phase*, during which the employees 'learn the ropes'—what the organization and its members consider to be normal patterns of behaviour. If anticipatory socialization experiences have created an accurate sense of the work environment, the encounter phase will be a relatively smooth transition. From the organization's point of view, effective socialization of new employees is a key to organizational stability. Most organizations therefore formalize the encounter phase through new employee orientation. The final *metamorphosis stage* continues throughout each employee's career in the particular organization.

Much adult socialization is self-initiated. Some is formal, such as the training provided in professional schools or work-related courses; some is informal. Increasingly, formal training is available in areas previously left to the family, the schools, or other agents of socialization, or in areas for which socialization was once taken for granted. Thus, prospective parents can take prenatal and, later, parenting courses, while people anticipating retirement can sign up for courses in retirement planning. When adults join such organizations as Weight Watchers or Parents Without Partners, they do so because they seek the social support these groups provide. It is during transition periods, as one moves from an established role to a new, possibly unexpected role, that this support is most needed.

● Future Directions ● ● ● ●

It is not new to suggest that family life has undergone major changes over the past few decades. Marriage rates have declined, while divorce rates have increased. More couples live together instead of marrying, and more children are born to single mothers. More children live independently, many of them on the street. At the same time, work demands and economic insecurities create stressful situations for many families. In the past decade, increased concern has been expressed for the plight of children worldwide, much of it arising from a concern about family instability and change. Thus, in the future, we might expect more research to focus on understanding the dynamics of early childhood development and

socialization in order to provide the kind of support to families that will optimize their positive development.

Sociology has been criticized for not paying sufficient heed to children, but this inattention is likely to change in the future. In an aging society such as that of Canada (and Western nations generally), with birth rates well below replacement levels, children will become an increasingly valued resource. An important goal for the future, then, is to create a central place in the discipline of sociology for children. This place should be based on a deeper understanding of the role of children, not just as recipients of adult socialization practices, but as active agents in the lifelong socialization of the people with whom they interact.

● Conclusion ● ● ● ● ● ●

Sociologists view socialization as a lifelong process influenced by all of an individual's social interactions. The two main accomplishments of socialization are the development of a self-concept and the internalization of social expectations.

Sociologists who take the functionalist perspective have tended to describe socialization as being imposed on individuals. By contrast, symbolic interactionists such as Cooley and Mead have helped to shed light on the active engagement of individuals in their own socialization.

All socialization takes place in a social context. For most people, the enduring and intimate nature of family relations makes socialization in the family the most pervasive and consequential experience of childhood. Parent–child interactions are differentiated by class, race, and ethnicity and are framed by the relationships between the family and the community. They are further affected by family size, birth order, family structure, and household composition. Patterns of influence are extremely complex, and become more so as children increase their contacts to include friends, neighbours, and schoolmates. The messages people receive from others are inconsistent and sometimes contradictory, and all draw their own conclusions from these competing influences.

Individual life chances are also strongly influenced by structural variables, the most important of which are gender and social class. Gender and social class have considerable influence on socialization and on the development of self-concept throughout life. The socialization of children and adolescents anticipates their adult work and family responsibilities. The competencies people develop in the course of primary socialization enable them to anticipate, prepare for, and deal with the ups and downs of adulthood.

● Questions ● ● ● ● ● ●
for Critical Thought

1. What are the implications of the research finding that few characteristics consistently differentiate very young females and males?
2. Why do gender stereotypes persist in the media despite the women's movement, the rise in female labour force participation, and other signs of structural change?
3. Talk to your parents and other family members about what they considered to be important values in your early development. What differences do you anticipate in raising your own children?
4. Ask students who have come to your university or college from another country to describe the resocialization they experienced in making the transition.
5. As you look back can you identify aspects of the hidden curriculum in your public school, your high school, or your university?

● Recommended ● ● ● ● ●
Readings

Reginald Bibby, *Canada's Teens: Today, Yesterday and Tomorrow* (Toronto: Stoddart, 2001).

Canadian sociologist Reginald Bibby has written a number of books based on his analysis of national surveys. This book documents attitudes and experiences of Canadian teenagers regarding violence, sex, and drugs and compares current patterns to past trends.

Gerald Handel, ed., *Childhood Socialization* (New Brunswick, NJ: Aldine Transaction, 2006).

This is a much-awaited second edition of what has been a classic reference in the study of socialization. The second edition adds 11 new readings to the anthology, retaining nine of the originals.

Don Tapscott, *Growing Up Digital: The Rise of the Net Generation* (New York: McGraw-Hill, 1998).

This book is an examination of the 88 million children of the baby boomers in the United States and Canada to have grown up with the Internet. This generation, Tapscott argues, is destined to be a force for social transformation.

Douglas Willms, ed., *Vulnerable Children: Findings from the National Longitudinal Survey of Children and Youth* (Edmonton: University of Alberta Press; Hull, QC: Human Resources Development Canada, Applied Research Branch, 2002).

This is a collection of papers based on the NLSCY, investigating the effect of community, family life, and school on the well-being of Canadian children.

● Recommended ● ● ● ●
Websites

Canadian Policy Research Networks
www.cprn.org/cprn.html

The family network at this site is dedicated to advancing public debate on policy issues that have an impact on Canadian families and on the circumstances in which they live. Its research ranges from public values about children and families to broader concerns of social cohesion within communities and society as a whole.

Childcare Resource and Research Unit (CRRU), University of Toronto
www.childcarecanada.org

Here you will find links to information about published and ongoing research, policy developments, and print materials related to child-care policy. The Resources section contains print and web resources, including bibliographies, complete texts of CRRU publications, and links to useful child-care, social policy, and research websites.

Health Canada
www.healthcanada.ca

Health Canada's website provides links to a wide range of information, including research reports about the health and well-being of Canadians of all ages.

The National Longitudinal Survey of Children and Youth (NLSCY)
www.statcan.gc.ca

The National Longitudinal Survey of Children and Youth (NLSCY) is a comprehensive longitudinal survey designed to measure and track the development and well-being of Canada's children and youth over time.

Vanier Institute of the Family
www.vifamily.ca

The vision of the Vanier Institute of the Family is to make families as important to the life of Canadian society as they are to the lives of individual Canadians. The Institute advocates on behalf of Canada's 8.4 million families because it believes that families are the key building block of society. This website is designed to help build public understanding of important issues and trends critical to the well-being and healthy functioning of Canadian families.

4 Chapter

• • • • • • • • •

Social Organization

Cheryl Albas, Dan Albas, and Lorne Tepperman

Learning Objectives

In this chapter, you will:

▶ learn what statuses, roles, and identities are and how they relate to each other;

▶ understand how it is possible to interpret statuses, roles, and identities from different theoretical perspectives;

▶ see how theoretical perspectives concerning statuses, roles, and identities can be used to understand face-to-face interaction in everyday life;

▶ see how statuses, roles, and identities constrain and shape us;

▶ learn about the different sociological 'sets' of people;

▶ distinguish between spontaneous and formal organizations;

▶ understand the characteristics of a bureaucracy;

▶ distinguish between the main points of organizational theories; and

▶ identify recent changes in the structure of organizations.

● Introduction ● ● ● ● ● ●

This chapter is about the most fundamental aspects of **social organization**—roles, identities, groups, and organizations.

This chapter argues that sociologists view roles and identities as the main ways in which social structure constrains and changes us. Roles and identities are just one part of the social structure that we enact and internalize. Just as they form the basic elements of social structure, they are also the basic elements of who we are and how we lead our lives. Roles and identities are, therefore, the meeting point of social structure, culture, and personality. You cannot understand social life unless you understand roles and identities, the building blocks of social structure.

● The Social Nature ● ● ● ● of Status, Role, and Identity

Identities are the names we give ourselves (female, male; child, adolescent, adult; friend, academic, worker, athlete; attractive, unsociable, ordinary, unusual) or who we announce ourselves to be in word, manner, and appearance that enable others to respond to or place us in particular ways (Stone, 1981).

Our first placement by others is when we are introduced to an expectant audience shortly after birth. As children learn the meaning of this placement by others, they usually identify with it and begin to present (or 'announce') themselves accordingly. By the time they are grown-ups they cannot interact comfortably with others without mutual identification in terms of their gender. Throughout a lifetime of establishing identities, we act parts in the game of life by playing out scripts organized in the form of normative expectations called roles, which are attached to social positions, or statuses. These roles include gender roles, age roles, occupation roles, and a multiplicity of others.

On the one hand, roles provide scripts that permit and oblige us to behave in certain ways. For example, at a party everyone can say, 'It's getting late; I've got to go to sleep'—except the host. On the other hand, roles can be thought of in a more dynamic fashion, as expectations that emerge in the give and take of social interaction. For example, a student reports that during an exam he was passed a note by his friend sitting in the next seat requesting 'help' for a particular question. Terrified that the instructor might notice the interaction, the student

attempted to resolve the dilemma by eating the note, mercifully 'very short and written on a small piece of paper' (Albas and Albas, 2005: 25).

Thus, *role enactment*, or *role-playing*, can be viewed either structurally, in terms of fixed expectations, or interactionally, as dynamic and developmental. In other words, we can view social behaviour as the learned performance of scripts that follow agreed-on rules or as negotiated arrangements that people work out with one another to solve unique problems of spontaneous interactions.

What is the use of studying the concepts of roles and identity? As agreed-to expectations for behaviour, roles generally facilitate interaction in society. We don't realize just how dependent we are on **role expectations** to coordinate our acts with others until those expectations are violated. Similarly, in order to play roles, we need to know the identities of others as well as our own. Roles may also polarize and distance people from one another. The expectations that persons may hold of others can work as barriers to both communication and socialization. We need to understand roles in order to avoid being unwitting slaves to them.

As we will see, roles and identities are complementary and intertwined. The roles we play give us a sense of what and where we are relative to others with whom we interact. This sense of identity allows us to act in ways that are coherent and purposeful. Every role we play has an identity awaiting us, and taking on that identity makes the role come to life. Consequently, when role expectations are breached, people are likely to feel as if trust has been betrayed and may feel bewildered and insecure. Unmet expectations lead us to question who we—and others in the situation—really are.

Consider an example of how roles and identities work. The American sociologist Harold Garfinkel (1997) believed that we could best understand the constraints of social structure by breaking the hidden rules. To do this, he instructed his university students to return to their homes and behave in ways that breached the normal expectations of their family lives: by acting as if they were boarders and their parents were the landlords. Students were to be extremely polite, addressing their parents formally as 'Mr' and 'Mrs' and speaking only when spoken to. Approximately 80 per cent of students who actually went through with the experiment reported that their parents were stupefied, shocked, and embarrassed. Many worried that their children had 'lost their minds'—that the pressures of school, work, and everyday life had 'gotten to them'. Others thought their children were being mean, inconsiderate, and impolite. In short, parents couldn't make sense of this rule-breaking behaviour.

How can we understand these common, disturbed reactions to **deviance** from the expectations people in society place on us? Sociology as a discipline offers a variety of perspectives. Also called *theoretical frames of reference* or **paradigms**, these perspectives vary from theorist to theorist and change from time to time. A number of different problems can be analyzed within the same paradigm, and any one problem can be analyzed from the standpoint of more than one paradigm. All discussions of problems involve concepts—their definitions, the ways they relate to each other, and the logical sense these relationships make for their solutions, in effect, construct theory.

Status, Role, and Identity

The Structural-Functional Paradigm

The structural-functional paradigm generally stresses the part played by factors that exist independent of individuals and that constrain them to act, think, or feel in particular ways. From this perspective, the roles of persons in 'real life' are described as 'expected behaviour corresponding to their positions in the "real world"', positions termed 'statuses'. The term *status* is also used to describe society's ranking of roles relative to each other, which, in turn, can determine a corresponding amount of prestige for the individual involved. Prestige adheres to the person who occupies high status and derives from it a degree of authority and the expectation of deference from others.

Émile Durkheim's initial orientation to the concepts of role and status was considerably elaborated, systematized, and reinforced by the anthropologist Ralph Linton (1936) as follows: status is a position to which are attached specific rights and duties, which, in turn, confer reciprocal rights and duties on others who occupy interacting statuses. From this perspective, then, in the case of students and teachers, teachers have the right to expect that students come to classes, are attentive during class, join class discussions, and study conscientiously: these are student duties.

An example of this mutual interplay of status and roles between teacher and students was observed in a large introductory-level university class. Two students started conversing with each other in tones loud enough to interrupt the order of the classroom and to distract the professor; that is, their behaviour constituted a breach of courtesy to the professor, a lack of considera-

tion for other students, and a violation of their duty as students to be attentive. The professor's response to the miscreants was a polite inquiry as to whether they had a question—intended also as a reminder that they were not fulfilling their duties. When the professor returned to lecturing, the students returned to their chatter. After class, the professor stopped them and reminded them of the requirement of considerate behaviour in class and of their duties to the other students in the class, to themselves as students, and to himself (the professor). The professor's suggestion that they no longer sit together in the class was met with the aggressive complaint that 'we weren't doing anything'—a clear breach of the students' duties of basic courtesy to the authority based on his status and a clear indication that they were failing in their own responsibilities to themselves as university students by engaging in disruptive behaviour. Their role enactment as students certainly was not 'ideal' role enactment, and as such, it would be termed 'dysfunctional'.

Students have reciprocal rights and expectations regarding their teachers. They can, for example, expect teachers to demonstrate expertise, mastery, and patience, to show up for class well-prepared, and to treat their students with respect and civility. These rights and obligations are well-known and accepted by everyone. When people do not fully know or embrace these agreed-on rights and duties, interaction breaks down and the situation becomes chaotic and confusing.

However, such breakdowns, at least according to the functional perspective, are remarkably rare. Sociologist Talcott Parsons (1949), perhaps the best-known structural-functionalist theorist, explains this by emphasizing that society is organized around many common values that are the source of stability and social order; this is Durkheim's concept of *exteriority* (1964 [1893]). It is only when socialization is imperfect or inadequate that people break the rules. Then others reinforce conformity by public sanctions, such as shame—Durkheim's concept of *constraint*.

One of Parsons's students, sociologist Robert K. Merton, makes more explicit this structural aspect of society in general, and of roles in particular. In fact, the problem facing us is that we all play so many different roles and, therefore, take on many different rights and responsibilities. Merton terms the specific collections of statuses we occupy as status sets, and the collections of roles in a specific single status (which Linton did not identify) as a *role set*: 'By role-set I mean that complement of role-relationships in which persons are involved by virtue of occupying a particular social status' (Merton, 1957: 110). The multiplicity of statuses and, consequently, of roles individuals occupy and play, respectively, in their lifetimes follow recognizable patterns that Merton terms *status sequences*.

These concepts of role sets, status sets, and status sequences underlie the recognition of order and structure in society as structural functionalists view it. More specifically, for example, a physician's status set may include the collection of statuses of a spouse, a parent, an administrator, and a soccer coach as well as a medical specialist. For each status in this status set, the physician has a number of roles to play, every one of which requires considerable expertise, tact, and discretion for its performance. This collection of roles is termed a role set.

A physician's role in a hospital or medical office involves interaction with a variety of other roles—nurses, paramedics, janitorial staff, clerks, medical colleagues, and patients—each interaction demanding different role behaviour. Consequently, physicians interact differently with each other than they do with other members of the medical team or with patients. Whereas physicians must routinely request that patients remove clothes so that their bodies can be examined, the same request to a ward clerk or nurse would be completely inappropriate to those role sets.

A good synonym for Merton's concept of status sequence is *career*. An individual progresses from high school student to university student to medical intern to medical resident to qualified physician. Each phase of the sequence carries with it specific rights, duties, associated prestige, and authority—generally, medical students do not have the right to carve up patients' bodies without supervision until they become fully fledged surgeons, at which time the carving process will be termed 'surgery' and the knife will be designated a 'scalpel'.

Role Strain

Despite the tendency towards order that was just described, a tendency towards disorder in every society and in every life may be observed. When roles compete, or even conflict, with each other, they produce *role strain* for the person. Strain above a critical level results in distress that we may describe simply as 'stress'. William Goode, Merton's student and a structuralist in the Mertonian tradition, states, 'Role strain—difficulty in meeting given role demands . . . is normal. In general, the individual's total role obligations are over-demanding' (1960: 485). Role strain may undermine the tendency towards order and interfere with people's ability to play their roles as expected.

Inadequate socialization, that is, people simply not knowing the rules of appropriate behaviour, is one of the major sources of strain constantly challenging the estab-

lished order. Consider this example: Almost three decades ago, a northern trapper came to the 'big city', and his son took him to a relatively posh restaurant for dinner. On the way home, the father admonished his son, saying, 'You're pretty careless with your money. You left some on the table, but I took care of it.' His isolated northern way of life at that time had taught him nothing about the convention of tipping; as a result, he violated the city restaurant rules. Both parties in this interaction experienced a degree of strain—the father because of his unfamiliarity with the restaurant setting, the son because he then felt responsible for **resocializing** his father.

Role conflict occurs when individuals are called on to play two or more roles that make incompatible demands such that conformity to one role necessarily means violation of the other. For example, an athlete who becomes the coach of the team and is required to select members for the next year will experience role conflict when choices must be made regarding whether to select outstanding new players or buddies and friends from the previous year. A student working for her father during the summer formed friendships with other employees. When those new friends disparaged her father, she found it particularly difficult to cope with roles both of loyal daughter and of friendly co-worker.

Role competition, which can also cause strain, exists for almost everyone because our many and varied roles compete continually for our energy and our time. For example, students might plan to spend a night with their books when friends call and ask them to go out. As long as there is enough time before the exam to study and catch up with work, they think they can do both. However, closer to the exam, they face role overload and must evaluate their roles as students and as friends and decide which roles to prioritize.

The same principle applies to workers—especially women, who are trying to balance multiple roles, such as paid worker, parent, spouse, elder caregiver, and household worker. They, too, are faced with choices between competing tasks and loyalties. They experience role overload in terms of their time or energy and must choose the demands of one role at the expense of others. Some women in a study by Hochschild and Machung (1989: 9) spoke longingly of sleep 'the way a hungry person talks about food'.

Merton (1957) identifies some social mechanisms that help people to articulate role sets and status sets more clearly, thus reducing strain. For example, people can appeal to hierarchies already established in society that distinguish between roles and order them in terms of institutional priority. In our society, the student role is valued and given high priority, so families and workplaces often give special concessions to students that allow them more study time.

Another way to reduce role strain is to abide by recognized **power** differences between roles. For example, school principals, who must mediate altercations between teachers and students, are almost always expected to support and defend teachers unless teachers' behaviour actually breaches the legal code for that role as, for example, by sexual misconduct. Few principals who fail to publicly support their teachers survive in their roles for very long. While this power relationship is being affirmed in the public schools, an aspect of the authority structure of society is publicly confirmed and reinforced.

Sometimes role strain is reduced when roles can be compartmentalized. Thus, families may separate and isolate the affectionate parent role from the affectionate spouse role and compartmentalize them into separate spaces in the home by installing locks on 'master', parental bedrooms.

Finally, role strain can be reduced by providing opportunities for relinquishing a role. When parental roles become overwhelming, some employers allow employees to take time off. Likewise, when life circumstances become generally overwhelming, employees may be granted some form of stress leave or offered compensation if they completely relinquish the role.

As adults performing multiple roles, we function better and make more fully informed choices when we understand what defines those roles, what they involve for ourselves and others, the strains inherent in the roles, the sources of those strains, and, sometimes, the societal mechanisms that can reduce some of those strains. Few of us in modern life have learned to play all our roles as smoothly and effortlessly as we should.

The Interactional Paradigm

The concept of role in sociology was borrowed from the world of the theatre to describe the behaviour of actors playing parts in the drama of life. As Shakespeare wrote in *As You Like It*:

All the world's a stage,
And all the men and women merely players.
They have their exits and their entrances;
And one man in his time plays many parts.

This analogy suggests two possible avenues of interpretation for the concept of role. In the theatre, an actor speaks or behaves in a particular way that produces a response from other actors on the stage. These speeches and responses are scripts, originally written on rolls

(which later came to be called 'roles'), which are spoken and acted out in such a way as to appear dynamic, changing, and spontaneous.

However, the difference between roles in the theatre and the roles people play in everyday life, from the interactional perspective, is that roles in society are not completely scripted. They have opportunities for mutual and reciprocal action and reaction to what other actors say and do. Thus, the social role is really a dynamic one in a constantly changing drama. George Herbert Mead (1934), the first social scientist explicitly to use the concept of role, refers to this ongoing drama as **role-taking**.

Mead and Turner

George Herbert Mead's outstanding contributions to role theory (1934) incorporate the concepts of significant **symbols** (language), role-taking, mind, self, and society. The concepts are linked theoretically as follows. First, intelligent human interaction rests on mutual understanding of the current symbols of meaning in society. Second, during interaction our response to others' behaviour towards us is based on our interpretation of it. Third, a further aspect of role-taking is the impression of **self** provided by the other's reaction to us. Fourth, when we have a distinct sense of self, we can name and recognize objects in the environment and make decisions about the appropriate reaction to them. We make these decisions in the process of an internal conversation with self—what Mead terms a **mind**.

Mead postulates that, as humans, we are universally vulnerable and our only hope for survival rests on our co-operation with others. In new situations, we use ingenuity to develop new ways of co-operating.

Meadian theory has been considerably refined and extended by Ralph Turner (1962), who regards the more structuralist approach put forth by Linton and Merton as being far too rigid and static. According to Turner, 'The actor is not the occupant of a [fixed] status for which there [are] a neat set of rules—a culture or set of norms—but a person who must act in the perspective supplied in part by his relationship to others whose reactions reflect roles that he must identify' (1962: 23). In effect, Turner shifts the focus from role-playing to the reciprocal joint processes of role-taking and **role-making**. He expands the concept of status from a static one to a dynamic one.

In role-making, we 'devise' performances on the basis of an imputed other role. Role-taking is the gestalt that we impute to be the role the other appears to be devising. As we might expect, there is the possibility of considerable inaccuracy and attempts to reinterpret the imputations involved. Turner refers to this process as

pattern, sum of parts, unified whole.

'shifting axis', which involves our continually testing the validity of our presumptions. Actors involved in role-making attempt to create a gestalt for each other so that they can more effectively role-take. To this end, they use the symbolism involved in things such as clothing, gestures, eye contact, and tone of voice to communicate clearly with each other.

A student illustrated the role-making/role-taking process involving a relationship between herself and a male friend, a relationship that, to this point (as she inferred from role-taking), had been on a casual level. They frequently attended movies together, visited in each other's homes, and engaged in games like pool. She assumed it was a non-romantic relationship and that he was a friend because this was the gestalt implied by his actions towards her to that point. Then, one evening as they walked towards a movie theatre, the axis shifted and the friend appeared to transform his role of friend into a role of lover. Instead of just walking side by side, he placed his hand on her upper hip. This unaccustomed and unexpected action on his part shocked her and presented her with a problem of how to validly interpret his role: he was clearly role-making, and she was attempting to role-take accurately, but was uncertain.

Was it an accidental slip of the hand, or was he attempting to demonstrate to approaching friends that they had become a couple? Had the relationship changed from friendship to romance? She looked for cues to help her define an accurate, valid interpretation of the situation: she glanced at him, he looked embarrassed and glanced away quickly, and when he finally did speak it was in a hoarse croak; she then noted with surprise that he was better dressed than usual; and when they reached the theatre, contrary to their custom of 'going dutch', he paid for her ticket to the movie. Further confirmation of the transformation of the relationship into a romantic one occurred when the movie began and he reached for her hand to hold.

Thus, Turner's approach to the concept of role is interactive and symbolic; it involves mutual testing of the images projected by symbols. Because of the tentativeness of meanings, interaction is always highly fluid. Although Turner's role theory deals mainly with interpersonal interaction at the individual level, it can also have a macro aspect in that the 'other' may be the '**generalized other**' constituted by society at large. Even self or 'ego' can be thought of as a group (for example, industrial workers) carrying on role-taking. Relationships between groups, like relationships between individuals, shift constantly and effect changes in the social order (shifting axes).

The Conflict Paradigm

W. Peter Archibald (1976, 1978) deals with the micro aspects of role from a conflict perspective and focuses on Marx's concept of **alienation** from others (Marx, 1964). According to Archibald, alienation from others is characterized by four features: (1) we feel indifference or separation; (2) when we approach others, it is for narrow, egoistic purposes; (3) when we interact with others, we are more controlled than in control; and (4) when we relate to others, it is with feelings of dissatisfaction and even hostility. Archibald develops these four features in generalizations that can also be considered aspects of the symbolic interactionist paradigm as it is elaborated by Erving Goffman in his chapter 'Nature of Deference and Demeanor' in *Interaction Ritual* (1967).

In the case of indifference or separation—really a detachment generalization—Archibald (1976) notes that people of different classes, statuses, and power groups tend to avoid each other. In factory settings, for example, management tends to have separate maintenance facilities, such as entrances, elevators, washrooms, and cafeterias. Similar principles apply in a **macrosociology** realm. For example, in her historical study of urban transformation, Lyn Lofland indicates that zoning ordinances emerged in the nineteenth century as a 'result of a desire on the part of the upper and middle classes to separate themselves from the "dangerous classes"' (1985: 74). Developers took these sentiments to heart and did their best, creating district after district of similarly valued homes and 'protecting' those values through covenants and 'gentlemen's agreements'.

Archibald (1976) argues that the two classes avoid each other because each feels threatened by the other. The position of the privileged depends on continued deference from the underprivileged. But such compliance is not always assured, and when it is not forthcoming it signals a loss of face and undermines one's superiority. In addition, revealing slips in the presence of subordinates give evidence that one may not be a superior person. At the same time, people in lower positions feel even more threatened by those in higher positions. Studies (see, e.g., Cohen and Davis, 1973) demonstrate that performing in front of high-status audiences is more anxiety-producing (as measured by the Palmar Sweat Index) than performing before an audience of peers. Interacting with, or at least within hearing distance of, bosses may result in giving out information that can be used against one. Consequently, avoidance is a useful strategy in dealing with enemies and rivals. As Goffman states, 'The surest way for a person to prevent threats to his face is to avoid con-

S
N
C
H

● ● OPEN FOR DISCUSSION
Philip Zimbardo's Stanford Prison Experiment

Commonly held stereotypes portray prisons as pathological places because of the personalities of the prisoners (low impulse control, problematic character structure, sociopathologies) and guards (surly, sadistic, megalomaniac). However, psychologist Philip Zimbardo and colleagues (1972) thought otherwise and suspected that social roles were the major factors in determining prisoner–guard interactions.

To test their hypothesis, they set up a mock prison and advertised in a local newspaper for subjects to participate in a two-week experiment on prison life in return for modest remuneration. All of the more than 75 male applicants were subjected to a rigorous screening process to ensure that they were mature, emotionally stable, and 'normal.' From this original group, 21 college students from middle-class homes were selected to participate in the experiment. Approximately half of the subjects (11) were randomly assigned to the status of prison guard, the remainder (10) to the status of prisoner. Guards were issued khaki uniforms, billy clubs, whistles, and handcuffs. Prisoners were dressed in smocks resembling hospital gowns and in nylon stocking caps.

Initially, subjects approached their role-playing in a light-hearted fashion, but it did not take long before they began to fall into stereotypical behaviour characteristic of their roles. The guards became increasingly callous and began to demonstrate inventiveness in the application of arbitrary power (Zimbardo, 1972). They refused prisoners permission to go to the toilet and forced them to do tedious and useless work (such as moving cartons back and forth, and picking thorns out of blankets that had been

dragged through thorn bushes). Guards issued commands to prisoners to do push-ups and occasionally stepped on their backs in the process. They also forced prisoners to do humiliating tasks such as scrubbing toilets with bare hands.

As early as the second day, the prisoners began to rebel, and the guards responded with increased force and threats of violence. In turn (given the reciprocal nature of roles), prisoners became increasingly passive and began to 'adopt and accept the guards' negative attitude towards them. . . . The typical prisoner syndrome was one of passivity, dependence, depression, helplessness, and self-depreciation' (Haney, Banks, and Zimbardo, 1973: 79).

The result was that prisoners began to develop serious pathologies. One prisoner developed a psychosomatic skin rash over his whole body, and others developed symptoms of severe depression and acute anxiety. The experiment had to be aborted after six days. As Zimbardo states,

At the end of only six days we had to close down our mock prison because what we saw was frightening. It was no longer apparent to most of the subjects (or to us) where reality ended and their roles began. The majority had indeed become prisoners or guards. . . . There were dramatic changes in virtually every aspect of their behavior, thinking, and feeling. . . . We saw some (guards) treat others as if they were despicable animals, taking pleasure in cruelty. While other boys (prisoners) became servile, dehumanized robots who thought only of escape, of their own individual survival, and of their mounting hatred for guards. (Zimbardo, 1972: 5)

tacts in which these threats are likely to occur' (1967: 15). Archibald concludes that 'avoidance as a self-protective strategy is . . . a very plausible explanation for the "detachment generalization"' (1976: 822).

Archibald's second principle is the means–ends generalization. That is, when the two classes do interact

there is a tendency (especially on the part of subordinates) for it to be on a role-specific basis rather than on a personal basis. As one former student said of his summer job, 'I am a very conscientious worker. When my boss asks me questions pertaining to work I'm happy to answer them . . . they make me look responsible . . . but

↳ seperation

I don't like him asking questions about my life outside of work. It's none of his business . . . it makes me look less responsible and reliable because I'm a teenager who loves to party and drink on weekends.'

Archibald's third principle is the control-purposiveness generalization. Archibald maintains that higher-class, higher-status, and higher-power individuals are more likely than lower-class, lower-status, and lower-power ones to initiate activity and influence others. Goffman notes that 'in American business organizations, the boss may thoughtfully ask the elevator man how his children are, but this entrance into another's life may be blocked to the elevator man, who can appreciate the concern but not return it' (1967: 64).

Archibald's fourth principle is the *feelings generalization*: an element of hostility underlies much and perhaps most interaction between non-equals; occasionally there is outright rebellion. An example would be low-power workers who rejoice at a manager's misfortune. In one instance, a lawyer had his parking privileges at work revoked because he used his wife's parking pass and attempted to gain the use of two spaces for the price of one. His misfortune gave so much satisfaction to his clerk in the law firm that she said she felt like a cat who just caught a mouse. Expressions of such feelings of hostility become particularly virulent during strikes.

The conflict paradigm provides a perspective to view status and role in their perhaps less acceptable, institutional aspects and to examine their underside of dissatisfaction, turbulence, and coercion—even their tendency to violence and revolution. So, while the structural-functional paradigm asserts that order in society is achieved by wide cultural consensus and achieves considerable stability and longevity, the conflict paradigm suggests that stability and any degree of permanence is achieved by the dominance of one group over the other and by the force used to maintain this dominance.

We turn now to the third element in our discussion of social structure and the way it constrains us. Identity is the way in which people define themselves and are defined by others. It is a result of the things people do (their roles) and the ways in which their acts are evaluated (accorded prestige) and reacted to. As John Hewitt says, 'A role in itself is lifeless—an unplayed part that has no substance until the individual claims it for his or her own and breathes life into it through identification with it' (2000: 97).

Hewitt (2000) classifies several aspects of identity. **Situated identity** focuses on identity as it emerges

(handwritten margin note: higher position more likely to initiate & influence)

SOCIOLOGY IN ACTION
Seymour Lieberman's Workplace Study

Seymour Lieberman (1956) studied the attitudes (that is, orientations towards a person, group, or social process) of 2,354 rank-and-file workers in an appliance factory towards unions and management. He demonstrated, as did Peter Archibald (1976) later, the Marxian hypothesis concerning the effect of status on attitudes and the resulting attitude of mutual hostility between upper and lower classes in society.

After the initial survey was completed, the usual workplace processes continued; 23 men were promoted to the rank of foreman and 35 people were elected by their work groups as shop stewards. After 15 months, promoted foremen and shop stewards whose attitudes had originally been recorded in the first survey were retested and the results compared with their answers on the first survey. The results of the second test showed an increase in pro-management attitudes on the part of the promoted foremen and an increase in the pro-union attitudes on the part of the shop stewards. How-

ever, the increase in the pro-management attitudes of foremen was greater than the increase in pro-union attitudes of the shop stewards. Lieberman says that these differences should have been predicted because the move from rank-and-file labourer to foreman is greater than that of worker to shop steward.

After two more years, business conditions for the company changed and fewer foremen were needed in the plant, so eight of them were demoted to their former positions. Lieberman then conducted a third survey to compare the attitudes of foremen who were demoted with those who retained their positions. The results indicated that individuals who were demoted now had much stronger pro-union than pro-management attitudes—a clear reversal compared to the situation when they were at the level of foreman. In effect, all of the test results in Lieberman's study support Archibald's (Marxian) theories of inter-class, particularly industrial world, attitudes.

through and affects face-to-face interaction with others. *Social identity* is based on identification with groups (e.g., family, ethnic, and occupational groups) and significant social categories (e.g., age and gender), which define us in terms of our similarities with some groups and our differences from other groups. *Personal identity* consists of factors that make us different from others (including physical characteristics such as height, weight, and skin colour) as well as aspects of our past we have incorporated into our sense of self based on how other people have reacted to us and typed us. Personal identity and social identity are parts of our *biographical identity* and, as such, provide continuity as we step into and out of various situated identities. Identities are established by our announcement of ourselves and by others' placement of us. Howard (1995) says that members of dominant groups are more likely to emphasize distinguishing achievement (i.e., personal identities) while members of oppressed groups are more likely to emphasize their similarities to others like themselves (i.e., social identities).

Classical Theorists on Identity: Cooley and Mead

Charles Horton Cooley (1902) is best known for formulating the concept of the **looking-glass self** to describe how identity is formed. Cooley states, 'Each to each a looking glass / Reflects the other that doth pass' (1902: 52). In effect, then, our identity is what we think others think of us. This reflected (hence 'looking-glass') self emerges as we imagine how we appear to others, then imagine how others judge that appearance, and finally come to some self-feeling such as pride or mortification.

Mead extended Cooley's ideas by emphasizing the cognitive skills acquired through role play and through learning the rules of games. Mead's best-known distinctions in the area of self-development are the definitions of the *play stage* and the *game stage* (1934). In the play stage, children 'play at' being, for example, a mother or father and speak to themselves as the mother or father might. Consequently, they assume for themselves the identity of the label applied by parents.

The development of identity, particularly biographical identity, is the result of a series of impulses to act and the resultant actual responses to those impulses. For the most part, the impulses are spontaneous and even unconscious, whereas reactions are more deliberate. Mead terms the spontaneous motivations of the individual the 'I' aspect of the self and the deliberately chosen behaviour the 'Me' aspect of the self. Over time, the chosen behaviour characteristics of an individual come to characterize that individual's self.

Contemporary Theorists on Identity: Blumer, Stone, Goffman

The structural view of interaction, as we have seen, emphasizes the relative stability and permanence of the social world. Symbolic interactionism, on the other hand, views social life as a series of processes involving continual interactions. Out of these interactions emerge new situations and new interactions within them, producing, in turn, different identities and coping strategies. Following the lead of Cooley and Mead, Herbert Blumer (1969) named this view of social interaction, that is, interaction as an exchange of meanings through symbols (i.e., words), *symbolic interactionism*, and he is considered the pre-eminent exponent of this school of social analysis. These situated coping strategies and identities rest on and are recognized additionally by material symbols, for example, the uniform identifying a police officer or the vestments identifying a priest.

In this ongoing social process, Gregory Stone (1981) recognizes two kinds of identity: *identification of*, when placement coincides with announcement, and *identification with*, when the person who does the announcing enjoys a comfortable compatibility with the one who does the placement. An identification of the other is necessary before role-taking can occur, which, in turn, makes possible an identification with the other.

One example of identification of and identification with is the process sometimes called 'gaydar' where gays and lesbians in public places signal their identities to one another (Nielsen, 2007). Nielsen notes that lesbians wear short hair, baggy jeans, masculine (i.e., comfortable) shoes, and adopt an 'open' body stance. This identity announcement is so effective, one lesbian said, she can 'spot queers a mile away' [identification of], which usually leads to feelings of **solidarity**. Another noted: 'I feel affirmed, energized, empowered and proud of myself and the lesbians I encounter. It makes me feel I'm not alone in the world and that I'm ok' [identification with].

Erving Goffman's research is perhaps the most lucid, imaginative exponent of identity analysis (though he does not label it as such); significantly for this discussion, his analysis also involves the concepts of role and status. Goffman places the concept of role squarely back on the stage, thus suggesting its structural aspect while also explicitly indicating an interactionist orientation. In the case of the structuralist aspect of self-presentation, Goffman (1959) uses theatrical analogies to distinguish the

'All the world is a stage', and people spend much time off stage or backstage, learning their lines, preparing their costumes, and readying themselves to play their 'big scene'. CuboImages srl/Alamy Images.

two zones of open and explicit role-making 'in the front stage' from the hidden role-making 'in the back stage'. Between the front stage and the back stage are 'barriers to perception' that buffer one area from the other.

Presentation of self in the front-stage area is analyzed in terms of three factors: (1) setting—the spatial aspects of things that function as sets and props; (2) appearance—the actor's age, sex, clothing, appearance; and (3) manner—behaviour indicating how one intends to perform the role, for example, haughty or friendly, formal or informal. These three factors combine to create *front*—a set of abstract, stereotyped expectations that prepare audiences for the ensuing performance and help them come to an appropriate definition of the situation (ibid.). Front adds 'dramatic realization' to performances because it helps performers convey everything they wish to convey on any given occasion.

Goffman's treatment of presentation of self and the establishment of identity involves the concepts of role, status, and prestige presented by an actor and recognized by an audience. Goffman states emphatically that

the recognition and granting of high status and the accompanying prestige it deserves are an actor's 'moral right': 'Society is organized on the principle that any individual who possesses certain characteristics has a moral right to expect that others will value and treat him in an appropriate way' (Goffman, 1959: 13). In the process of self-presentation to others, Goffman says that we overplay the two basic strategies of self-revelation and concealment. Self-revelation allows us to project ourselves in the best possible light when our worthy qualities might not be fully apparent to others, while concealment allows us to hide aspects of ourselves that could be discreditable.

Another aspect of identity projection is **altercasting** (Weinberg and Deutschberger, 1963). Altercasting is the strategy of projecting a characteristic of some kind—favourable or unfavourable, obligatory or privileged—onto another person with the object of achieving some advantage for oneself. It is the counterpart of Goffman's concept of **impression management**, whereby, in effect, actors engage in self-casting.

Identity Troubles: Embarrassment

Embarrassment occurs when an announced identity is not supported or is distorted, resulting in unsatisfactory placement (Gross and Stone, 2005). Typical instances of embarrassment resulting from dissonance between announcement and placement are a result of bodily accidents, which cause embarrassment because they project a less than fully mature persona, or possibly a careless one.

A second cause of embarrassment is insufficient support for identity announcement. Consider a self-confident student who consistently receives As emerging from the exam room proclaiming 'I aced it' only to find out when grades are posted that the performance was worthy of a mere B.

A third source of embarrassment is *mistaken identity placement*, in which a person may adequately document an identity but fail to have others place it because of distraction or inadequate attention.

Mismanagement of superfluous identities is a fourth cause of embarrassment. In most encounters there are more activities (roles) and identities than are necessary for ensuing transactions. For example, at parties people eat and drink (subordinate role) while they converse (dominant role). The subordinate roles and identities must be managed so that they remain in the background and don't interfere with what people have come together to do— their dominant roles. A misalignment of these subordinate and dominant roles and identities can result in embarrassment. This occurs when subordinate roles and identities impose themselves on dominant ones. A subordinate activity that properly belongs to a situation may suddenly become the dominant focus of the occasion.

Embarrassment also occurs when reserve identities inappropriately surface on the dominant identity (Gross and Stone, 1981). We also experience embarrassment when a relict identity—an element of our biographical identity we no longer wish to announce—resurfaces.

Identity Management: Defensive Practices

Goffman (1971) says that embarrassment causes us to 'lose **face**', and that when we do, we attempt to compensate for the loss by engaging in *remedial work*, that is, *face-work*, or face-saving. Remedial work manifests itself in a variety of forms, including avoidance, accounts (justifications or excuses), and disclaimers, all of which are designed to prevent or remedy damage to our identities (Goffman, 1971; Scott and Lyman, 1968; Stokes and Hewitt, 1976).

Avoidance

Goffman's term for face-saving work to prevent identity damage in the first place is *avoidance*. For example, university students who suspect they have failed an exam frequently do not attend classes on the day the tests are to be returned, and students who do attend class and find that they have received very low or failing grades generally attempt to avoid the students who received high grades. In other words, we attempt to avoid situations wherein we are likely to be embarrassed. Those students who bomb on tests and exams ('Test Bombers') not infrequently make remarks like 'You want to avoid them [Aces] because you emerge looking like the "dumb one"', or 'It makes you feel like you're lazy or unreliable.' Understandably, Bombers become particularly sensitive to the signs of success Aces display—things like 'sitting tall' at their desks, 'broad grins', 'sparkling eyes', and 'jaunty walks'. Bombers often use these signs as cues to identify whom to avoid (Albas and Albas, 2003).

Disclaimers and Accounts

Two related defence strategies to save face are disclaimers and accounts. *Disclaimers* are excuses that come before the act for which face-saving is expected to become necessary. *Accounts* are excuses and justifications that follow embarrassing acts. According to Stone (1981), both disclaimers and accounts can be verbal, in what he terms the *universe of discourse*, or they can be non-verbal mannerisms, in the *universe of appearance*. Until recently, almost all research in this area of identity has focused on verbal disclaimers and accounts in the universe of discourse. However, there has been increased interest in the non-verbal mannerisms we employ in public places where talk is difficult or impossible.

Verbal disclaimers—excuses that come before a potentially problematic act that may damage our identity—come in a multitude of forms. For example, when a professor asks a university class an 'open question', students who do take the risk and respond when they are not entirely certain they have the 'right' answer may attempt to set up the situation to defend their identity beforehand, hedging by using verbal disclaimers such as: 'I may be wrong on this, but . . .'. Another verbal disclaimer comes in the form of *sin license*, which occurs when we know we are going to break a rule, but we argue that we have a good reason to do so.

Verbal accounts are offered following a faux pas, and are 'statements made to explain unanticipated or untoward behavior' (Scott and Lyman, 1968: 46). Accounts, in turn, can be subdivided into excuses and justifications. *Excuses* are 'accounts in which one admits that the act in question is bad, wrong, or inappropriate but denies full responsibility' (1968: 47)—for example, 'I did not know' or 'I was coerced.' *Justifications* are statements wherein we accept responsibility for an act but deny the negative implications associated with it. For example, drivers may admit that they park in prohibited zones using a disabled notice, but argue that 'it's okay because I'm driving my mother's car and she really is disabled and might have been the person using the parking space.' People may mistreat others but argue that 'it's okay because they're not important enough to worry about anyway' or that 'they deserve what they get.' In all cases, accounts serve to 'repair the broken and restore the estranged' (Scott and Lyman, 1968: 46).

Disclaimer mannerisms (that is, excuses) prior to the problematic act can be seen regularly in traffic when a driver cuts in front of another vehicle and the offender then waves to the other driver, implying that the latter has generously allowed the privilege. It is possible that in this process ruffled feathers are smoothed and chances of road rage are decreased. Similarly, shoppers often take self-conscious precautions to avoid looking suspicious by making exaggerated shows of innocence, for example, by tying a knot at the top of every bag they are carrying to give a clear message that nothing else could have been added.

Identity Management: Protective Practices

Protective practices are, to some extent, altruistic and show consideration of the other. They function to protect the user as well as the communal assembly in which these practices are used because gaffes by a single person disrupt the interactional tone and thereby embarrass the entire group. Protective practices provide the user with some degree of self-protection because everyone is always vulnerable. Considerate people are more likely to have consideration directed to them than are people who are thoughtless and unsympathetic. As Goffman (1959) notes, actors form a moral pact to support each other's fostered impressions of themselves.

Protective practices include studious inattention to small lapses in appropriate behaviour of others. For example, we might pretend not to notice a quiet burp emitted by the person next to us. Goffman (1959) refers to this face-saving device as *studied non-observance*. Studied non-observance can also be active; women who need to breast-feed their infants in a public place usually appreciate a courteous lack of attention.

● Where Role and   ● ● ● ●
Identity Come Together

Three concepts that demonstrate strikingly how role and identity overlap are role distance, role embracement, and role exit. *Role distance* (Goffman, 1961b) designates the behaviour of actors who play roles in such a way as to announce identities that will have others place them at a distance from the identities they seemingly are announcing. *Role embracement* occurs when actors attempt to convey by their role-making actions the specific and correct self-images by which they wish others to identity them.

Goffman's examples of these concepts are based on his observations of boys on a merry-go-round. First, role embracement begins at about age four or five, when they have to expend every effort just to hang on to the reins, and often also to the horse's neck or ears, and so, literally as well as metaphorically, embrace the role of rider. As Goffman states, 'to embrace a role is to disappear completely into the virtual self available in the situation, to be seen fully in terms of the image, and to confirm expressively one's acceptance of it' (1961b: 106).

Role embracement represents the polar opposite of role distance; it can be observed when boys reach the age of 11 or 12 years. By this point, maleness 'has become a real responsibility. . . . It is necessary to stay away or exert creative acts of distance' from childhood (1961b: 108). Boys accomplish role distance by treating the wooden horse as if it were a racehorse, or by pretending they are stunt riders or comedians, jumping from horse to horse, all the while making faces at friends and passersby. The purpose of these acts, of course, is to display distance from the role of a merry-go-round rider.

A contemporary example of role distance is practised by teenagers who no longer wish to be viewed as children and instead want to establish an identity of independence and maturity, and do so in part by insisting that parents drop them off around the corner from their destination. David Snow and Leon Anderson found that role-distancing also is common among the homeless, especially the recently homeless; they quote one man as saying, 'I'm not like other guys who hang down at the Sally [Salvation Army]. If you want to know about the street people, I can tell you about them; but you can't really learn about studying street people from studying me, because I'm different' (1993: 349).

Role exit is the disengagement from a role that is central to one's self-identity (Ebaugh, 1988). This relinquishment usually brings with it a continuing identity 'hangover' from the past, which influences the playing of a new role. Helen Ebaugh, a former nun, used her own case as an example in her study and interviewed 69 other former nuns as well as another 116 'exes', including transsexuals, police officers, convicts, doctors, divorced people, and air traffic controllers. Drawing on Robert Prus (1987), she formulates a generic social process involved in becoming an 'ex'.

First, there are feelings of frustration, unhappiness, uncertainty, and burnout, which Ebaugh terms *first doubts*. This uncertainty on the part of people about to exit a role leads to what she terms *unconscious cueing*, whereby they begin to change the image they project to others. For example, nuns in this early phase of becoming an 'ex' begin to let their hair grow. Consequently, their announcement leads to a tacit placement, which accordingly encourages or discourages the contemplated move.

Second, depending on whether there has been encouragement or discouragement in the first phase, role alternatives are considered and weighed, and a new role identity is tentatively decided on. In this process, the person inevitably chooses and begins to identify with a new reference group, which will help to consolidate and confirm the new identity. For example, transsexuals, to identify with the opposite sex, cross-dress and take on new mannerisms and occasionally undergo sex-change surgery (Ebaugh, 1988). Role exit occurs after this anticipatory socialization in and by the contemplated new reference group, and finally the new reference group and the new membership group become one.

A fourth and final stage involves accommodating the new identity to the old one. This process is always problematic because the old identity constantly intrudes itself on the new one. Ebaugh cites examples of former police officers who find it difficult to interact affably with people they knew in their previous roles to be involved in shady activities.

Role exit is a predominant characteristic of modern society. In the past, people generally lived their entire lives in one community, gender, occupation, marriage, and religion. In today's society, these statuses and their accompanying roles and identities are taken on and shed with increasing frequency.

● Groups and Organizations

What ties these changeable roles and identities together into stable, predictable sets of behaviours? Groups and organizations. We are linked together in groups by interpersonal bonds of sentiment and exchange. Beyond that, we are linked together in organizations by rules and the allocation of resources. As we shall see, it is impossible to understand the functioning of groups and organizations without understanding the roles and identities that make them up. Equally, it is impossible to understand our face-to-face interactions—our enactment of roles and identities—without understanding the group and organizational contexts within which they take place. We begin this section by discussing different sets or ways of organizing people; they include networks, groups, and cliques. We start small and build up to bureaucracies, because the two sizes of organization—large and small—are more similar than you might think.

Sets of People

Imagine five sets of 20 people. Call them *categories, networks, communities, groups,* and *organizations*. Sociologists will study these five sets differently, because they are organized differently and have different effects on their members. This section will briefly discuss these sets and explain why they would interest sociologists in different ways.

Categories
Imagine, first, that these 20 people are a mere collection of people unconnected with one another—say, a random sample of Canadian 19-year-olds. Though unconnected, they fall into the same category: in this case, they are the same age.

This sample of teenagers is of interest to sociologists if they represent the attitudes and behaviours of 19-year-olds across the country. Knowing these attitudes and behaviours may help us predict the future behaviour or explain the current behaviour of 19-year-olds. It will be of particular interest to market researchers who want to

▮▮ Time to Reflect ▮▮▮▮▮▮▮▮▮▮▮▮▮▮▮▮▮▮▮▮▮▮▮▮

How would Blumer's, Stone's, and Goffman's theories of self each explain the process of role exit? Which perspective emphasizes which stage of role exiting?

sell products to 19-year-olds and to political pollsters who want to shape their voting preferences. However, for the most part, sociologists will not be interested in such samples of people. Since they are unconnected, people in categories have no social structure of interest, and it is **social structure**—the invisible feature of social life that controls and transforms our behaviour—that is mainly of interest to sociologists.

However, categories become sociologically interesting when societies dramatize (or socially construct) meanings for the boundaries between one category and another. No such meaningful boundaries exist for 19-year-olds, compared with 18- and 20-year-olds. However, important cultural boundaries exist between the categories named 'male' and 'female', 'young' and 'old', and, in some societies, 'white' and 'black'. As a result, these categories assume social importance. Yet, they assume importance only when the categorical differences are dramatized, the boundaries are enforced, and categorical differences result in social and cultural differentiation—for example, in the form of communities or of **social movements**.

Networks

Generally, sociologists are more interested in networks, or **social networks**. Imagine the same 20 people all connected, either directly or indirectly, to one another. By *direct connections*, we mean links of kinship, friendship, and acquaintance among all 20 people, each connected to the other. In this set of 20 people, there can be [20(19)]/2 = 190 such pairwise connections—obviously, many interesting relationships and combinations of relationships to study.

Indirect connections also are of interest to sociologists. In fact, some sociologists such as Mark Granovetter (1974) argue that *weakly tied networks*, based largely on indirect links, may be even more useful than *strongly tied or completely connected networks*. Information, social support, and other valuable resources flow through incompletely connected, or weakly tied, networks (see Figure 4.1). Also, rumours, diseases, innovations, and job information all spread geographically through (indirectly linked) networks of weak ties, because weakly tied networks have a vast outreach. They connect large numbers of weakly tied people (for example, acquaintances) at a few removes, unlike tightly connected networks, which tend to circulate the same information or resources repeatedly through the same set of people (for example, close friends).

The pairwise connections—called *dyadic relationships*—that make up social networks are based on regular patterns of social exchange. In stable dyadic relationships,

Figure 4.1   Social Networks for Social Support

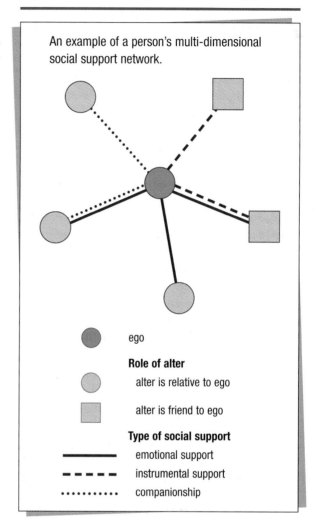

An example of a person's multi-dimensional social support network.

ego

Role of alter

alter is relative to ego

alter is friend to ego

Type of social support

——— emotional support

– – – instrumental support

·········· companionship

Source: Filip Agneessens, Hans Waege, and John Lievens, 'Diversity in Social Support by Role Relations: A Typology', *Social Networks* 28, 4 (Oct. 2006): 427–41. Copyright 2006, reprinted with permission of Elsevier.

people give each other things they want and need. So long as these relationships satisfy their needs, people stay in these relationships. People usually act in their own best interests—when they are aware of these interests. They are rational and sensible, and they preserve **social relationships** that are useful to them. So, people enter, leave, and stay in the social networks in which their valued dyadic relations are embedded. Over time, as people enter and leave relationships, networks change in their size and composition. This, in turn, affects the resources flowing to other members of the network.

In recent years, Internet-based social networking services such as LinkedIn, Friendster, and Facebook have rapidly increased in popularity. These services collect information from an individual's profile and their list of social contacts to create a display of their personal social

[handwritten margin notes: communities + groups — aware of memb. common identity]

network. This display publicizes how the contacts within the network are interconnected. These online services are often provided free to users, although individuals must disclose personal information to register and use the networking sites. These sites are built on the premise that individuals may merely be a few 'links' removed from a desirable business or social partner and not even know it. Such networking services claim that by allowing members to 'get to know one's friends of friends [they can] expand their own social circle' (Adamic and Adar, 2005: 188). Increasingly, people are setting up virtual networks of relationship in cyberspace, as well as real ones.

As you can see from this brief discussion, social networks are important and interesting. There is a growing sociological literature on social networks; however, much of social life is not well understood in terms of networks because networks lack several key characteristics. First, people in networks lack a sense of collective identity, such as a community would have. Second, people in networks lack an awareness of their membership and its characteristics, such as a group would have. Third, people in networks lack a collective goal, such as an organization would have.

Communities

Sets of people with a common sense of identity are typically called **communities**, and there is a long history of community studies in sociology. Imagine, for the sake of consistency, that we are thinking of a community of only 20 people—say, a community of like-minded people living together on the land (perhaps a commune in 1960s British Columbia or a utopian farming community in nineteenth-century upstate New York) or in the city (perhaps a community of anarchist or bohemian youth living in a broken-down squat in twenty-first-century Amsterdam).

These are likely to be people drawn together by common sentiments; or they may be people who have grown up together and share strong values uncommon to the rest of society. The nineteenth-century German sociologist Ferdinand Tönnies (1957 [1887]) took great pains to distinguish the foundations of community life, or what he called *Gemeinschaft*, from the foundations of non-community life, which he called *Gesellschaft*. Tönnies also associated community life with rural areas and non-community life with urban areas. At least since medieval times, the city has been represented as a place distinct from both rural communities and from the natural environment.

Gemeinschaft refers to the usual characteristics of rural and small-town life, which include a stable, homogeneous group of residents with a strong attachment to one particular place. Residents of the community interact around similar qualities and lead similar lives. Not only are their lives similar, they are also linked by intimate, enduring relationships of kinship, friendship, neighbouring, and (often) working together. Because rural people share so much, it is not surprising they also share similar moral values, and moral guardians such as the church, school, and local upper classes protect these values. In social structure, the *Gemeinschaft* is marked by dense or highly connected networks, centralized and controlling elites, and multiple social ties.

By contrast, the ties among people in a city take the form of a *Gesellschaft*. This includes a fluid, heterogeneous group of residents with a weak sense of place. According to Tönnies, the residents have different personal histories and impersonal, brief relationships. They interact around similar interests, not similar characteristics or histories. They share few moral values and few moral guardians to enforce a common moral code. In social structure, city networks are less connected, less centralized, less cliquish, and less redundant. In short, the *Gesellschaft* demonstrates less cohesion and has less social control.

The question that several generations of sociologists have debated since Tönnies is whether *Gesellschaft*—or city life—represents a loss of community or a new kind of community. Most sociologists in the first half of the twentieth century believed the former: they saw city life as disorganized and lacking in the cultural and social benefits of community. However, in the second half of that century, sociologists came around to another view. They showed that people are not as isolated and atomized in large cities as previously thought. Rather, the majority form small communities based on residential closeness and social likeness, or on friendship and support networks among geographically scattered people.

Communities, whether urban or rural, real or virtual, are important because people are aware of their membership in them. They want the community to survive and may make large personal sacrifices to see that it does.

Groups

Sometimes groups can be like small communities: engrossing and demanding of loyalty. In other cases, groups are much less so. What all groups have in common is an awareness of membership. Also, members are all connected with one another (directly or indirectly), and to varying degrees they communicate, interact, and conduct exchanges with one another. To continue our example, a 20-student classroom is one kind of group. It is more highly connected than a 20-person category, more self-aware than a 20-person network, but shows less solidarity (based on common values) than a 20-per-

[handwritten margin note, vertical right side: Ferdinand Tönnisl Gemeinschaft]

son community.

Since Cooley (1962 [1909]) wrote in the early twentieth century, sociologists have distinguished between primary groups and secondary groups. *Primary groups* are small and marked by regular face-to-face interaction; an example is a family household. Cliques, which we will discuss shortly, and work groups also fall into this category of primary groups. *Secondary groups* are larger; many members may not interact with one another on a regular basis. However, even in secondary groups there is a clear membership, at least some members interact, and there is an identifiable normative order and a shared sense of collective existence (as in a community).

Typically, groups are less engrossing than communities. However, they have organizational structures and do what social structures are expected to do: namely, control and transform their members. All groups, even small groups, have clearly defined familiar roles: for example, husband–wife, parent–child, or brother–sister in families, leader–follower in cliques, or teacher–student–teacher's pet in classrooms. These roles carry interactional expectations, and people are identified (and identify themselves) with the roles they play. Even in small groups, behaviours become scripted. Robert Bales (1950) found that in the discussion groups he studied, three roles—task leader, emotional leader, and joker—regularly emerged. Bales inferred that groups 'need' these roles to survive.

Secondary groups, though less strongly integrated than primary groups, are no less important. We spend most of our waking hours as members of secondary groups, interacting, communicating, and exchanging resources with other people. Secondary groups are also the staging area for much social learning. They bind people in fairly stable patterns of **social interaction**. Formal organizations, which will be discussed at length later, are subtypes of secondary groups, and bureaucracies are subtypes of formal organizations.

Organizations

As just noted, organizations are secondary groups that have a collective goal or purpose. An organization can be a giant **multinational corporation**, such as General Motors or a small corner variety store, a political party or a government, a church, a school, a sports club, or a search party. Given the endless variety of organizational forms and the millions of specific examples, what do all organizations have in common?

Every organization is a group of people working together and co-ordinated by communication and leadership to achieve a common goal or goals. Within this general definition, however, organizations vary considerably. The group of people in question—that is, the

social group—may come together spontaneously or deliberately. The division of labour within that organization may be crude or complex. The communication and leadership may be *informal* or *formal* (these terms will be defined shortly). The organization may have one specific goal or various loosely related goals.

One important distinction must be made between spontaneous and formal organizations. Both types fit the general definition of an organization, yet the two are different in important ways. A **spontaneous organization** is one that arises quickly to meet a single goal and then disbands when the goal is achieved, thought to be beyond reach, or when the organization is absorbed by a formal organization. A clique, though informal, is not a spontaneous organization. Perhaps the most commonly cited examples of spontaneous organizations are bucket brigades and search parties. Each has a single goal—keeping a barn from burning down or finding a lost child. Each arises spontaneously and its leaders emerge informally, without planning. Each has a crude division of labour—for example, filling buckets, passing them along, emptying them on the fire. Nevertheless, each is much more likely than an uncoordinated mob to achieve its goals. Compare the chance that a mob, running off in one direction, has of finding a lost child with that of a group conducting a coordinated search pattern. Spontaneous organizations disband as quickly as they form. The bucket brigade will scatter when it achieves its goal of putting out the fire or when the barn has burned down or when the fire department arrives on the scene.

Organizations that have loosely related goals and are fairly unstructured, with little differentiation between their members, are considered **informal organizations**. One familiar example of informal organization is the clique. Cliques seem very different from the formal organizations to be discussed in most of this chapter, yet, paradoxically, they share common features. Also, as we will discover later, cliques and other informal organizations can usually be found nested within formal organizations, doing much of the work.

Cliques (not a spontaneous organization)

Defining the Clique

Dictionaries variously define *clique* as 'a small exclusive set', a 'faction', a 'gang', or a 'noisy set'. This meaning comes from the French *cliquer*, meaning 'to click', or 'to make a noise'. People in cliques—especially the most popular ones—make a lot of noise pumping themselves up and ridiculing others.

To come closer to our current sociological meaning, we would define 'clique' as a group of tightly intercon-

You may have noticed, living in North America, that there seems to be an organization for every social ill, common interest, and shared goal. Is this a new phenomenon of the information age? Not at all. Alexis de Tocqueville, in his classic work, *Democracy in America* (1945 [1835, 1840]) noticed this trend while studying American society in the 1800s. He believed that individualism was a unique characteristic of democratic societies, such as the United States of America. He also believed that it could be very destructive, leading people to abandon societal concerns and turn inward to their own interests. Looking at the United States, he asked: 'how do the Americans combat the effects of individualism?' His answer was organizations, or, as he called them, 'free institutions'.

Tocqueville realized that urban life was much different from traditional rural living. People had fewer strong ties and often dealt with strangers in their daily work. This produced a new sense of individualism, where it became difficult for people to see that they were not independent of their fellow citizens. Organizations, Tocqueville said, helped people see that they were not as independent as they thought. These associations were often political, but he also saw how people organized in thousands of different ways—religious, moral, commercial, and otherwise.

Why were these groups so important in democratic societies? Coming from an aristocratic family himself, Tocqueville thought that voluntary associations performed the same function that the aristocrats did in traditional society: they served as an intermediary between the king and the people. In the case of the modern society, voluntary organizations were between the state and the people. Still, Tocqueville was a conservative at heart, and didn't think that these associations could replace what he saw as being lost in the move away from aristocratic society: community.

—Written by Matt Kopas

nected people—a friendship circle whose members are all connected to one another, and to the outside world, in similar ways. Usually, clique members feel strong positive sentiments or liking for one another and contempt for outsiders. They spend more time with one another than with non-clique members, share their knowledge with one another, and think and behave similarly. They try to ignore or exclude outsiders—people not like themselves, and not friends of their friends.

In short, cliques are groups characterized by friendship, likeness, interaction, exclusion, and the flow of valuable resources: information, support, and opinions (among others). In these respects, cliques are mini-communities, like mini-states. Like states, they amass **power** and resources. They receive, censor, and direct information flow. Like states, cliques remain distinct; resources (such as information) flow readily within the clique and less readily outside its borders. Cliques gather and redirect information. They also produce information, distort it, and send information out as gossip and rumour. Cliques, like other organizations, create and concentrate information flow. Because they produce and control the flow of information effectively, cliques are stable structures (on this, see Carley, 1989, 1991). They survive largely through what psychologist Irving Janis (1982) called 'groupthink'.

Though seemingly without goals, cliques have an unstated 'mission' or purpose: to raise the status of clique members at the expense of non-members. Though lacking an organizational chart or stated division of labour, school cliques have a clear hierarchy of influence and popularity, with the leader on top surrounded by his or her favourites. In this sense, then, a clique is a group of people working together and coordinated by communication and leadership to achieve a common goal or goals.

Cliques in School Settings

Cliques form in every area of life, even within bureaucracies and other formal organizations. However, cliques are most familiar to us from our childhood school experience. In school settings, cliques typically have a well-defined membership. Clique members are typically similar to one another in background and behaviour

(Ennett and Bauman, 1996). Cliques also have rituals that exclude outsiders and integrate insiders. Cliques usually have a leader who is the most popular member and who dominates the other members. Usually, the leader defines the group boundaries, invents group rituals, and chooses the membership.

Cliques are not only organizations: they are communities and miniature societies. In cliques, children first learn the rules and expectations of society outside their family home. Through games and play with clique members, children internalize the beliefs, values, and attitudes of their group. By these means, children also form judgments of themselves. For example, they learn what it means to be 'good-looking', 'sexy', and 'popular', to be chosen or passed over. Children's activities, their friendships, and their feelings about themselves are tied up with their involvement in the cliques that organize their social landscape (Crockett et al., 1984).

Cliques, though often supportive, can also offer excellent examples of structured cruelty, and they can be found everywhere, including cyberspace. Online bullying carried out by clique members is a new phenomenon and potentially just as damaging as the bullying that occurs face-to-face. With 'e-bullying', youth can constantly harass their victims over the Internet, through instant text messaging on cellphones and postings on bulletin boards and on their blogs. Thanks to technology, which makes more pervasive and unrelenting forms of bullying possible, victims are always within reach.

Cliques form when people meet others like themselves. The social structuring of activity itself—for example, grading of activities such as education, entertainment, or work by age—increases the likelihood that people will meet others like themselves (Feld, 1982). Also, since class or ethnicity often separates neighbourhoods, and since children usually attend neighbourhood schools, they are likely to meet other children of the same class and ethnic background. The more homogeneous the people they meet, the more children will form relationships with others who are similar. It is, first, this structuring of acquaintances that leads to creating cliques.

However, an element of choice is involved. Cliques carefully screen people for membership. Once formed, cliques preserve themselves by continuing to ensure that members remain similar. Cliques change as individuals enter and leave the group. Those at the clique's centre—the leaders—are most influential in the recruitment process. They use their power, based on their popularity, to decide which potential members are acceptable and which are not.

Cliques control their members by defining the behaviours that are proper and acceptable. Leaders are skilled in exercising control. They often do so by building up the clique members and then cutting them down (Adler and Adler, 1995). One technique is to draw new members into an elite inner circle, allow them to enjoy brief popularity, then humble them by turning the group against them. Leaders also take advantage of quarrels to divide and conquer the membership. They degrade and make fun of those who are lower in the hierarchy or outside the group. All of these tactics allow leaders to build up their own power and authority. Such rites of degradation also foster clique solidarity by clarifying the norms for acceptance and rejection.

The cohesion of a clique is based mainly on loyalty to the leader and loyalty to the group. This loyalty, in turn, is based as much on exclusion as it is on inclusion. First, group members hive themselves off from nonmembers. Lack of contact with outsiders allows members to believe that outsiders are different and less socially desirable than themselves. Furthermore, clique members use gossip to reinforce their ignorance of outsiders and keep social distance from them. They also use gossip to ridicule and spread nasty rumours about outsiders. Finally, they may pick on or harass outsiders. Doing so instills fear, forcing outsiders to accept their inferior status and discouraging them from rallying together to challenge the power hierarchy.

Cliques and the rituals of inclusion and exclusion on which they rely are more than mere children's games. They are small-scale models of how organizations state, teach, and enforce rules; as such, they provide a lesson in social control. Cliques remind us that every inclusive action is, at the same time, an exclusive action. Organizations like cliques can have shared goals that are unstated but real, norms that are unwritten but compelling, hierarchies that are undocumented but powerful, and divisions of labour that are effective but unplanned.

▋▋ Time to Reflect ▐█ ▐█ ▐█ ▐█ ▐█ ▐█ ▐█ ▐█ ▐█ ▐█ █

Do cliques provide useful socialization for children? What are the advantages and disadvantages of childhood exposure to cliques?

Bureaucracies

Formal Organizations

Organizations are *formal* if they are deliberately planned and organized. This planning may occur when people found a new university, for instance. Or it may occur gradually, as happens when the people who form a bucket brigade find that enough fires are starting that they would do better to organize themselves into a volunteer fire department.

Within formal organizations, communication and leadership are provided through consciously developed and formalized statuses and roles. Often formal organizations have multiple goals, and they usually have a long lifespan. The Roman Catholic Church is a formal organization that has lasted nearly 2,000 years. Besides this, formal organizations normally have access to far greater resources and more complex technologies than spontaneous organizations. We can define a **formal organization** as a deliberately planned social group in which people, resources, and technologies are consciously coordinated through formalized roles, statuses, and relationships to achieve a division of labour intended to gain a specific set of objectives. This is similar to the general definition of organizations. A formal organization will have an overarching set of goals framed by its leaders and more or less accepted by its members; however, we cannot assume that these are the only goals of the membership. Workers, professionals, and managers will have their own occupational goals as well.

There is a huge literature, containing many lively debates, that addresses the question of why some organizations are more successful and powerful than others. The most common explanations cite the degree to which an organization fills a social need (either real or successfully promoted by the organization itself), controls or has access to needed resources and technologies, tailors its goals to match the goals of its members, and adapts to or causes changes in its environment. The main form of the large, powerful, and long-lived formal organization in the twentieth century is the **bureaucracy**.

'Bureaucracy' has negative connotations for most people. In everyday use, the word carries little of its original meaning and is often used as a disparaging term. We hear about how bureaucracies impede business, how people battle against them, and, most of all, about how frustrating they are. The word calls to mind images of red tape, an overemphasis on rules and regulations, inefficiency, and unwieldy government organizations moving at a tortoise-like pace. To sociologists, however, a bureaucracy is merely a particular type of formal organization that

thrives in both the public and the private sectors, in capitalist and socialist societies alike. The fact that bureaucracy is the main organizational form taken by competitive corporations shows that it can be very efficient.

The Characteristics of Bureaucracy

Weber (1958 [1922]) first analyzed the particular features of the bureaucratic form of organization. In his study of the major organizations of his day, he identified seven essential characteristics of bureaucracy:

- a division of labour,
- a hierarchy of positions,
- a formal system of rules,
- a reliance on written documents,
- a separation of the person from the office,
- hiring and promotion based on technical merit, and
- the protection of careers.

Division of Labour

In earlier eras, to produce society's goods workers handcrafted specific articles from start to finish. Gradually, this production process gave way to specialization and the division of labour. Adam Smith noted the overwhelming productive superiority of specialization as long ago as 1776 (Smith, 1976 [1776]). A specialized division of labour became the foundation of modern industry and bureaucratization. An automotive assembly line is, perhaps, the typical modern example of such a division of labour.

As on an assembly line, every member of a bureaucracy performs named and distinguished duties. The bureaucracy itself provides the facilities and resources for carrying out these duties. Workers work with equipment they do not own; in other words, they are separated from the **means of production**. Also, administrators manage what they do not own. The goals of this combination—task specialization based on technical competence plus the centralized provision of resources—are increased efficiency and productivity.

Hierarchy of Positions

We can imagine the structure of an organization as a pyramid, with authority centralized at the top (see, for example, the organizational chart in Figure 4.2). Authority filters down towards the base through a well-defined hierarchy of command. Thus, the structure plainly identifies both the range and the limits of authority for people in each position. Within this hierarchy, each person is responsible *to* a specific person one level up the pyramid and *for* a specific group of people one level down.

The organizational chart of any large corporation is shaped roughly like a Christmas tree: the number of workers increases (and the division of labour specializes) as you move down towards the base of the hierarchy. With the other characteristics of bureaucracy, this feature serves to increase efficiency because all communications flow upward to 'control central' from large numbers of workers 'at ground level'. However, formal communication within a bureaucracy can be awkward. What if a sales representative in Halifax, Nova Scotia, wishes to discuss a special order with a craft worker in the Moncton, New Brunswick plant? Does the sales rep have to communicate through intermediaries, all the way up and down the structure, until he reaches the craft worker in Moncton? No. In real life, people work to avoid such unwieldy communication channels, often forming informal communication networks.

Rules

Bureaucracies work according to written rules. The rules allow a bureaucracy to formalize and classify the countless circumstances it routinely confronts. For each situation, decision-makers can find or develop a rule that provides for an objective, impersonal response. The

Figure 4.2   Ontario Municipal Board Organizational Hierarchy

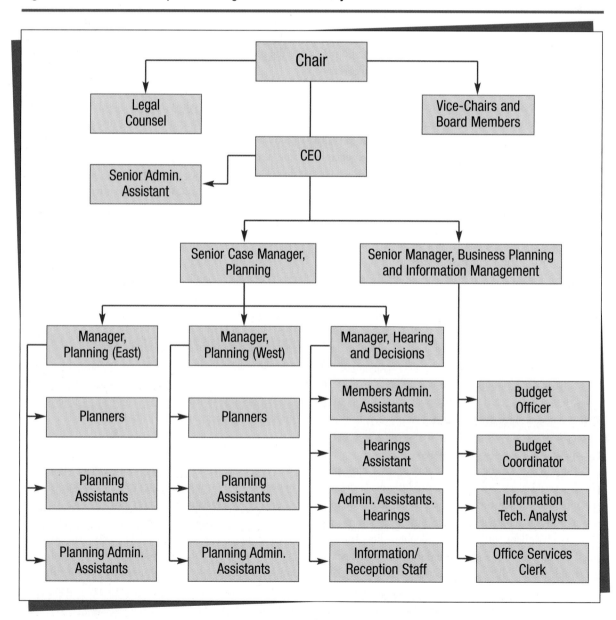

Source: Ontario Municipal Board, at: <www.omb.gov.on.ca/About/Annual%20Report/images/orgchart20012002.gif>. © Queen's Printer for Ontario. Reproduced with permission.

rules, therefore, guarantee impersonal, predictable responses to specific situations. Impersonality and objectivity help the organization to achieve its goals.

Separation of the Person from the Office

In a bureaucracy, each person is an office-holder in a hierarchy. The duties, roles, and authority of this office all are clearly defined. That is, the rights and responsibilities of a Level 3 supervisor are spelled out in relation to a Level 4 supervisor (her superior) or Level 2 supervisor (her subordinate). The relationships between positions in a bureaucracy are, thus, impersonal relationships between roles, not personal relationships between people. This separation of person and office means that people are replaceable functionaries in the organization: people come and go, but the organization remains intact. It also means that personal feelings towards other office-holders must be subordinated to the impersonal demands of the office. Equally, relationships are confined to the official duties of office-holders and—ideally—do not invade their private lives.

Hiring and Promotion Based on Technical Merit

A properly functioning bureaucracy hires on the basis of impersonal criteria such as technical competence, not by ascribed, inborn characteristics such as gender, race, or ethnicity. Promotion is based on technical competence, or sometimes on seniority. People are neither discriminated against nor favoured because of such personal criteria as their personalities or their kinship connection to a person at the top of the hierarchy.

Protection of Careers

The final characteristic of bureaucracies is that people's careers are protected within them. People can look forward to long careers in a bureaucracy because they are not subject to arbitrary dismissal for personal reasons. So long as they follow the rules attached to their office or position, they are secure in their jobs. Generally speaking, their income will continue to arrive at the end of each month.

Compare these characteristics with the cliques, communities, or spontaneous work teams considered earlier. In a bureaucracy, we find a much more detailed division of labour and a much longer hierarchy of positions than one finds in the typical clique, for example. The system of rules in a bureaucracy is formal, or written, unlike the informal rules in a clique. A bureaucracy separates the person from the office, whereas there are no offices in a clique, only distinct individuals. Hiring and promotion in a bureaucracy are based on technical merit; in a clique, they are based on popularity, friendship with the leader, toughness, or attractiveness. Finally, a bureaucracy pro-

vides people with secure, often lifelong careers; as we have seen, clique memberships may be brief and insecure.

How Bureaucracies Actually Work

Weber's concept of bureaucracy, as we have seen, is a very useful model for the study of this complex form of organization. It calls our attention to central features of bureaucracy. But it is a simplification, an idealization, like the notion of a perfect vacuum in physics or of a feather falling through space without meeting any wind resistance. Such images are good for starting to think theoretically, but they do not reflect the real world. In the real world, bureaucracies have flaws, and sociologists have spent a great deal of time discussing these flaws. This section presents the more obvious and troubling discrepancies between ideal bureaucracies and actual bureaucracies.

Ideally, every member of a bureaucratic organization is knowingly enmeshed in a network of reporting relationships. In graphic form, a bureaucracy is a Christmas-tree-shaped structure that repeatedly branches out as you go down the hierarchy. Thus, at the bottom of the hierarchy there are a great many people whose job it is to (1) carry out orders from above and (2) report work-related information up the tree to their superiors. At the top of the hierarchy, there are a few people whose job it is to (1) issue orders to their subordinates, (2) process information received from below, and (3) maintain linkages between the organization and its (political, economic, and social) environment. Also at the top, information is shared between the heads of planning, manufacturing, shipping, public relations, and other sectors of the organization.

In practice, organizations do not work this way, as sociologists since Weber have pointed out. They could not afford to work this way, and human beings aren't constructed to work this way. Thus, alongside the ideal or formal structure—which prescribes how a bureaucracy ought to work—there is an actual or informal structure, which is how it *really* works.

Actual Flows of Information

In theory, a failure to report information up the hierarchy would never occur. In practice, it occurs all the time. Workplaces are politically 'contested terrains' (Edwards, 1979), and controlling the flow of information from below is a means of changing the balance of power between superiors and subordinates. And, as the French sociologist Michel Crozier (1964) showed, bureaucracies work differently in different societies. This is because different cultures have different ideas about inequality, deference, openness, and secrecy. For example, people raised in France or Russia will be much more alert to the

inequality of bureaucratic relations and the power of information control to equalize relations than workers raised in the United States. French and Russian workers behave differently, and as a result bureaucracies work differently in these countries.

Bureaucracies also appear to work differently for men and women. When playing a managerial role, women adopt a collaborative, relational approach derived from qualities used in familial relations, whereas men emphasize purely economic considerations. Women's managerial styles emphasize the establishment of good employer–employee relations and the sharing of information and power (Occhionero, 1996).

In practice, workers everywhere make friends and acquaintances. As a result, they casually share work information. Much of the information that flows within an organization is shared orally, not in writing, to introduce civility and negotiation between work teams (Grosjean and Lacoste, 1998). In many cases, workers use information purposely to help one another. In a few cases, they may even leak information for personal gain or to subvert their boss or the organization as a whole.

Thus, within organizations based ideally on strangers relating to other strangers on the basis of written rules, we find workers forming what amount to secret organizations or sub-communities that obey their own rules. Political actors below the top level cannot employ routine channels or resources to negotiate in the idealized manner. 'Politics from below' includes all the actions that defy, oppose, or sidestep the rules or roles of the organization (Brower and Abolafia, 1997).

The basis of this informal organization is trust, which relies on friendship, acquaintanceship, and gossip about third parties that strengthens existing ties (Burt and Knez, 1996). In the end, the same materials that build cliques build the informal, often hidden, infrastructure of bureaucracies.

As in cliques, trust in bureaucracies is built gradually, maintained continuously, and easily destroyed (Lewicki and Bunker, 1996). When trust is violated, the result is often revenge or another disruptive response—confrontation, withdrawal, or feuding, for example (Bies and Tripp, 1996). Trust is easier to generate within organizations than across organizations, since it is within organizations that managers, serving as third parties, can monitor and enforce reciprocity. The result is that organizational boundaries work effectively to restrict intellectual diffusion (Zucker et al., 1996). Within organizations, the flow of information is harder to contain.

Often team structures are created by management to cut across the bureaucratic hierarchy, enabling workers to co-operate in the solution of a cross-branch problem.

This solution is undertaken with the recognition that requiring all information to flow to the top and then across is a slow and ponderous way of solving problems. Thus, increasingly, organizations have adopted horizontal, as well as vertical, reporting relationships. In many instances, this has improved organizational learning and given the organization a competitive advantage (West and Meyer, 1997).

Such temporary, cross-cutting groups rely on what is called *swift trust*. In these temporary systems, a premium is placed on making do with whatever information is available and in which swift judgments of trust are mandatory. Generally, trust develops most rapidly when (1) there is a smaller labour pool and more vulnerability among workers; (2) interaction is based on roles, not personalities; (3) behaviour is consistent and **role expectations** are clear; (4) available information allows a faster reduction in uncertainty; and (5) the level of interdependence is moderate, not high or low (Meyerson et al., 1996).

New information technology also makes it easier for horizontal groupings to form, since distant employees can easily exchange information through a large organizational computer network (Constant et al., 1996). New cultures emerge when computers, linked together to form intra-organizational networks, create a virtual organization parallel to, but independent of, the traditional bureaucratic hierarchical organization (Allcorn, 1997). As well, telecommuting now occupies an important place in the world of information work, posing new problems (Di Martino, 1996). It may reduce costs by externalizing or delocalizing work, but we are far from knowing how it will affect work organization and productivity (Carre and Craipeau, 1996). For example, the increased use of computer-mediated communication appears to increase user satisfaction in task-oriented organizational cultures and to decrease user satisfaction in person-oriented organizational cultures (Kanungo, 1998).

Nowhere is the role of new communication technology in organization more apparent than in the development of huge, seemingly shapeless 'virtual teams' of workers. Their size, ingenuity, and passion often produce unexpected discoveries.

Organizational Cultures and Flexibility

In temporary or other horizontal groupings, a worker reports to more than one superior. This may create conflicts or inconsistent demands. Sometimes, it becomes unclear where a worker's main duties lie and, therefore, how that person's work should be evaluated and rewarded. Greater flexibility and co-operation must be sought from the workers as well as built into the organizational structure itself.

Organizations require increasingly more flexibility from workers, which is possible only if those workers receive continuing education and training and participate in planning (de la Torre, 1997). Yet worker motivation, recruitment, and training all pose problems for bureaucracies. The motivational problem is greatest in organizations where professional expertise and judgment are most required, as in universities, law firms, and technology-development firms. There we find the greatest attention given to matters of organizational culture and career development. It is only by giving these workers considerable autonomy and rewards for strong identification with the firm that the most able workers can be induced to join, stay, and carry out their duties in conformity with organizational goals. Along with this structure comes a need for thorough organizational **socialization**, which begins at the stage of recruitment and interviewing and is never completed (Edwards, 1979).

Some organizational cultures are more effective than others in creating a high level of worker commitment and high rates of employee retention, and societies vary in their use of one or another kind of organizational culture. For example, in Japan, Korea, and China, people are more receptive to a collective (or group) culture than we find in North America.

Some organizations manipulate organizational culture to tackle the perceived shortcomings of bureaucracy and to empower the workers. They espouse open management, teamwork, continuous improvement, and partnership between customers and suppliers without replacing bureaucratic principles of standardization, differentiation, and control through a single chain of command. In the end, senior management has merely used these techniques to restructure management roles, justifying increased corporate control and intensifying work.

However, people usually form stronger attachments to other people than they do to 'the organization' as an abstract entity. Thus, patterns of clientelism develop even within bureaucracies. In the end, bureaucracies are organizations in which two principles—rule-based rationality and person-based clientelism—contend for dominance, with neither being able to win decisively at the expense of the other.

The Problem of Rationality

Bureaucracies are thought to be rational in the ways they make and execute plans. They are indeed more rational—in a limited sense—than patron–client relations. This is because, over the long term, by making impersonal decisions and rewarding excellence, they are more able to pursue long-term organizational goals with huge amounts of wealth and power.

However, the sheer size of large bureaucracies and their long-term outlook introduce certain types of irrationality that, in the end, may undermine the organization. A concern with the mere survival of the organization may undermine shorter-term concerns with the quality of decisions, products, and services the organization is providing to its customers. The much-hated 'red tape'—or administrative delay—by bureaucracies persists not because of inadequate technology or personnel, but because it serves positive (as well as negative) functions for the organization (Pandey and Bretschneider, 1997). The bureaucratic demand to eliminate subjectivity and individuality actually undermines the productivity of institutions. By creating boundaries between the institution and outside influences, the institution loses touch with the individuals who are both the subjects and the objects of their efforts (Imershein and Estes, 1996).

Managerial tools such as corporate statements, corporate culture, performance appraisal, and reward systems are means for the **social construction** of homogeneity. Obedience is valued because it is interpreted as the willingness to adopt and internalize dominant ideas, values, rationality, and, more generally, normative systems (Filion, 1998).

In bureaucratic organizations, the presumption of knowledge, heavy reliance on official records and procedures, and the predominance of routine all cushion 'paper-reality'—a world of **symbols**—from other forms of representation. This inhibits both forgetting and learning (Dery, 1998). Another result is the creation of a *bureaucratic personality*, which substitutes proceduralism at the expense of any moral impulse or ethical concern with outcomes (Ten Bos, 1997). Anonymity and distance from decision-making make moral indifference likely, if not inevitable. Rule-making and record-keeping proliferate, particularly in private organizations. There is evidence that managers who are more alienated and more pessimistic make more rules (Bozeman and Rainey, 1998).

The bureaucratic characteristic of relying on the rules as written can create another problem. As a bureaucracy grows and more rules are added, the system becomes increasingly complex. This can lead to a situation where no one person knows all of the rules and different offices act independent of each other, creating rules that conflict with one another.

Rule by offices undermines personal responsibility for decisions the organization may take. No member of the bureaucracy is asked, or obliged, to take responsibility for collective decisions. As a result, so-called collective decisions—typically taken by the top executives—are liable to be foolish, harmful, or even criminal. Corporate and government entities are unique in that their deviant behaviour may be caused by systemic patterns in their organizations rather than only by individual malfeasance. However, once deviant behaviour has occurred, they are well positioned to evade responsibility. Managers may often refuse responsibility by hiding behind organizational structures or by adopting the view that they were merely following orders. The deviant behaviour of big business and big government occurs because of limited information, the establishment of norms and rewards that encourage deviant outcomes, or the implementation of actions by organizational elites.

Such deviance, which is rarely prosecuted or punished, is usually initiated by managerial elites and subsequently institutionalized into organizational culture. It will normally continue unchecked until it is challenged from inside or outside the organizations. Organizations themselves are rarely penalized for deviant behaviour (Ermann and Lundman, 1996). A recent prominent example was the prosecution of top leaders of Enron for falsifying records and manipulating information for their own personal benefit, at the expense of thousands of investors and millions of American citizens. Enron's collapse in 2001 wiped out more than 5,000 jobs, more than $60 billion in market value, and more than $2 billion in pensions.

Twenty-four people besides the Enron president, Kenneth Lay, were convicted or pleaded guilty in Enron cases. Four of the 24 had convictions reversed on appeal, and more appeals are pending. Investors are suing to recover more than $30 billion in stock market losses. Lay, 64, died of heart disease while vacationing in Aspen, Colorado, in July of 2006. The government filed a civil forfeiture case in October 2006 against Lay's estate, seeking $12.5 million for victims of Enron's collapse. It sought a jury trial to re-establish Lay's responsibility for the fraud, though in May 2006 he had been convicted of 10 counts of fraud, conspiracy, and lying to banks in two separate cases. District Judge Simeon T. Lake III subsequently declared that Lay's death vacated his conviction on fraud and conspiracy charges because Lay couldn't challenge the conviction.

Even more recently, the US federal government has been equally assertive in its efforts to convict former Canadian businessman Conrad Black of white-collar crime. He faced 13 charges over claims he stole $60 million from investors in Black's newspaper firm, Hollinger International. Thanks to evidence from his former second-in-command, David Radler, the former media baron was found guilty of obstructing justice and of three counts of mail fraud. This followed a 15-week trial in Chicago and more than two weeks of jury delibera-

tion. In July of 2007, Black was found guilty of obstructing justice and three counts of mail fraud; he was acquitted on nine other charges. Radler pleaded guilty to fraud and received a 29-month sentence as part of an agreement to act as the key witness for the prosecution. Black was sentenced in December 2007 to 6½ years in prison and fined $125,000 US. Additionally, Black was ordered to repay $6.1 million US—the estimated amount of the fraud, according to a pre-sentence report.

As *The Financial Post* reported on 13 March 2008, 'Conrad Black, the disgraced former newspaper baron, noted historian and British peer who began serving his prison sentence Monday in Florida, could be feeding convicts or fixing their toilets.' However, this kind of story is rare. Despite a few headline-making 'successes' by the courts, historically, charges and convictions of white-collar criminals have been hard to secure. As a legal person, the corporation is able to employ many more resources than individuals who are seeking redress for their injuries by the corporation. The result may be fraudulent practices, dangerous commercial products, or even, as in Nazi Germany, death camps.

The administrative bureaucracies that carried out the extermination of the Jews progressed through several steps, ending in incarceration in concentration camps, starvation, and eventual annihilation. Once the machinery had been put into place, it was not confined to Jews but spread to treatment of other groups, including Gypsies, asocial individuals, and Polish prisoners of war. It is true that the managers responsible for this program experienced psychological repulsion. However, most managers rationalized their behaviour in terms of their duty in the bureaucratic system and the supposedly evil nature of the Jewish race (Hilberg, 1996).

Relations with the Outside World

Ideally, the bureaucratic organization relates to the outside world as though it is looking through one-way glass. The outside world, which is composed of competitors, customers, and other bystanders, cannot see into the organization. However, the organization can see out as well as it needs to. In principle, the main contact between the organization and the outside world is by means of its top executive. It is the top executive, in full possession of organizational intelligence, who can act publicly in the organization's interests.

The separation of decision-making authority from front-line experience is also likely to create an 'us versus them' point of view within the organization. As customers criticize the organization for unresponsiveness to

HUMAN DIVERSITY
Society and Bureaucracy in Ghana

Bureaucracy is a new and increasingly dominant form of human organization, but it is not the only one. Many communities and organizations function using a clientelist model, which emphasizes personal relationships, as opposed to the impersonal rules of bureaucracy. Traditional societies usually operated in such a manner, and there are even remnants of this model in our bureaucratic culture. It's easy to see how the rules that govern a bureaucracy can fail when met with the human element. Even as bureaucracy has become so prevalent in many societies, it causes problems when people ignore the rules in favour of other values. This raises the question: what would be the result of introducing bureaucracy into a society that is based on traditional familial obligations? Robert Price wrote about this issue in *Society and Bureaucracy in Modern Ghana* (1975), where he looks at the effects of implementing a bureaucratic civil service in Ghana.

In his study, Price discovered a conflict between the ideals and rules required to run a bureaucracy and the traditional values of Ghanaian society. There was also a conflict between the roles Ghanaian civil servants were expected to play—that of the bureaucrat and that of a family member. Price conducted the study in southern Ghana, where he said 'descent groups . . . are corporate in nature and are the foundation of social organization.' Thus, he found it hardly surprising that research pointed to family matters as the primary focus of traditional morality.

To study this conflict, he presented an imaginary situation where a civil servant experienced role conflict between bureaucratic and family roles. By presenting this situation together with various questions to civil servants, Price hoped to discover which role they thought should determine behaviour in a conflicting scenario. He also asked how respondents thought the typcial Ghanaian civil servant would act and how a family member would expect to be treated in the same situation. His findings showed that 75.3 per cent of the civil servants polled believed that universalistic behaviour was the legitimate one in the situation ('universalistic' meaning following the rules of bureaucracy that apply to all). Yet only 19.4 per cent thought that the typical Ghanaian civil servant would act in such a way.

The reason for this discrepancy is found in the last question asked. A full 92.6 per cent of respondents thought that the family member in the situation would expect the civil servant to act in a particularistic way (treating them as better than non-relatives). Thus, Price concluded that 'when presented with imaginary organizational situations involving conflict between bureaucratic and familial role obligations, there is a consensus among the civil servant respondents that the family role-set will consider its obligations binding, expect them to be fulfilled, and mobilize its considerable sanctional resources in instances of their violation.'

Source: Adapted from Price (1975: 56–82).

their concerns, the organization takes a stance of embattled resistance to change. Union-based protest and organized citizen or customer protest movements put pressure on the bureaucracy. The result may be 'groupthink', a resistance within the organization to taking criticism seriously, considering a wide variety of options, or conceding the need for change. Nowhere is this organizational strategy more starkly depicted than in what Erving Goffman has called *total institutions*.

Total Institutions

As Goffman (1961a) pointed out, mental hospitals, convents, prisons, and military installations have a lot in common as organizations. True, they have different institutional goals and provide different services to society; they also employ different kinds of experts and oversee different kinds of 'customers'. However, what they have in common organizationally far outweighs these differences.

First, they have total control over their 'customers'—whether mental patients, nuns, convicts, or soldiers-in-training. Twenty-four-hours-a-day, seven-days-a-week, they are able to watch and, if desired, control behaviour within the institution. Though they can see their customer pool perfectly, none of them—whether as psychiatrists or nurses, priests or mothers superior, guards or officers—can be watched unknowingly or unwillingly. Thus, their relationships in the flow of information are highly unequal.

Total institutions offer an extreme example of the bureaucratic organization and the bureaucratized society. They are founded on principles of efficiency and procedural rigidity that are potentially in conflict with the values to which public organizations are expected to assign priority: particularly, democratic participation by employees and by those affected by organization practice (Davis, 1996).

What Goffman (1961a) tells us about mental institutions and prisons reminds us of what we have heard about life in **totalitarian** societies like Nazi Germany and Soviet Russia. Under both Nazism and Communism, governance is further complicated by the competition between two bureaucratic hierarchies: the government (based on expertise) and the party (based on loyalty). (For details on East Germany, see Bafoil, 1996, 1998; on China, see Zang, 1998.) Moreover, in practice, both are dominated by a patrimonial ruler, making neither a true bureaucracy (Maslovski, 1996).

In fact, totalitarian societies are not only like total institutions, they also make liberal use of total institutions to punish, brainwash, and **resocialize** unco-operative citizens. Thus, as Weber warned, modern bureaucratic society is an 'iron cage' in which we are all trapped by aspirations to career, efficiency, and progress (1958 [1904]: 181). Bureaucracy has an enormous potential for enslavement, exploitation, and cruelty. It also has an enormous potential for promoting human progress through economic development and scientific discovery, high-quality mass education, and the delivery of humane social services to the needy. It is to gain the second that we have risked the first. The jury remains out as to whether, in the twentieth-first century, the gain justifies the cost.

● Conclusion ● ● ● ● ● ● ●

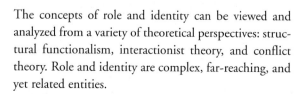

The concepts of role and identity can be viewed and analyzed from a variety of theoretical perspectives: structural functionalism, interactionist theory, and conflict theory. Role and identity are complex, far-reaching, and yet related entities.

Role is related to identity in that role involves a script of action, and that identity is a result of actions and how they are categorized, judged, and evaluated by others. Every role has an accompanying identity, and playing the role shapes both action and actor. We usually become that which we play at. Identity troubles, as manifested in episodes of embarrassment, make continued role performance difficult, if not impossible, raising the question of embarrassment management, which involves strategies such as avoidance.

The study of roles and identities stands at the intersection of society, culture, and personality. As such, it is inevitably connected with socialization—the process by which infants become socially competent—and with the formation and maintenance of communities. The process is social because it is through interaction with others and in response to social pressures that people acquire the culture—the language, perspective, and skills; the likes and dislikes; and the cluster of norms, values, and beliefs—that characterizes the group to which they belong.

As we have noted, wherever you turn these days, you see particularly visible groups—organizations. Large organizations are daunting: they have their own impersonal cultures, they bring together large numbers of strangers, and they devise special ways of maintaining social control. However, it is unclear whether small, tightly connected organizations, such as cliques, are any better than large, tightly connected organizations, such as bureaucracies.

We have reviewed a variety of different 'sets' of people. These included categories, networks, communities, groups, cliques, and organizations. Sets of people with a common sense of identity are typically called *communities*, and there is a long history of community studies in sociology. Communities, whether urban or rural, real or virtual, are important because people are conscious of their membership and make personal investments in remaining members. Formal organizations combine many of the features of networks, groups, cliques, and communities.

The main form of the large, powerful, and long-lived formal organization of the twentieth century is the *bureaucracy*. The goals of bureaucracy—task specialization based on technical competence plus the centralized provision of resources—are increased efficiency and productivity.

Finally, we considered *total institutions*. As Goffman pointed out, mental hospitals, convents, prisons, and military installations have a lot in common as organizations. These are all organizations that have total control over their 'customers'—whether mental patients, nuns, convicts, or soldiers-in-training. Myths and ideologies are propagated to justify the differences between the rulers and the ruled. Total institutions offer an extreme example of the bureaucratic organization and bureaucratized society.

Questions for Critical Thought

1. In the work world, what are the differences between workers and management? How are these differences expressed in roles?
2. What is the difference between the interactionist view of role and the structuralist view of role?
3. Where does one's sense of identity come from?
4. How is identity related to role?
5. What types of organizations would you expect to see in the absence of social order and control—for example, immediately after natural disasters? What is the 'natural' organization of human beings?
6. What is/are the main goal(s) of cliques? How do they control their members and interact with the outside world? What are the characteristics of leaders of cliques? How about members?

Recommended Readings

Bengt Ambrahamsson, *Why Organizations? How and Why People Organize* (London: Sage, 1993).

An in-depth look into organizational theory, this book offers cross-continental analysis of organizations and explores the universal functions of organizations and the social forces that regulate their operations.

Michel Crozier, *The Bureaucratic Phenomenon* (Chicago: University of Chicago Press, 1964).

The French sociologist Michel Crozier found that Weber's idealized bureaucracy in practice varies from one culture to another. Each bureaucracy is a political subculture nested within a larger culture; as a result, bureaucracies may operate differently in different societies, despite the same set of formal principles.

Erving Goffman, *Asylums: Essays on the Social Situation of Mental Patients and Other Inmates* (New York: Anchor Doubleday, 1961).

This classic work notes the remarkable yet often ignored similarities between institutions that, whatever their stated goal, act to warehouse and closely control large numbers of people. These institutions transform people's identities as inmates learn to lead new moral careers entirely defined by the organization itself.

Daniel A. Silverman, *Queen Victoria's Baggage: The Legacy of Building Dysfunctional Organizations* (Lanham, MD: University Press of America, 1999).

This book offers a cross-cultural analysis of what the author calls 'dysfunctional' organizations. Silverman examines the classroom and community as sites in which different cultural concepts of discipline exist.

Robert Westwood and Stephen Linstead, eds, *The Language of Organization* (London: Sage, 2001).

Taking a more micro approach, the articles in this collection focus on language as a form of social control. The volume looks specifically at the kinds of words we use to describe organizations generally, the day-to-day interactions within organizations, and the components of organizations.

Kath Woodward, *Understanding Identity* (London: Arnold, 2003).

This work explores personal and collective identities by drawing on experiences that highlight the importance of ethnicity and race, gender, and place in the production of meanings about who we are.

Recommended Websites

ALS Survival Guide
www.lougehrigsdisease.net/index.html

This website discusses how illness/disability is a master status that supersedes gender, race, and religion. It details the social, medical, emotional, and psychological aspects of Lou Gehrig's disease (amyotrophic lateral sclerosis).

Bureaucracy and Formal Organizations
www2.pfeiffer.edu/~lridener/DSS/formorg.htm

This website provides many links to relevant sites about bureaucracies and other formal organizations.

Encyclopedia of Organizational Theory
faculty.babson.edu/krollag/org_site/encyclop/encyclo.html

This site provides almost everything you need to know about organizations. Every concept and theory is summarized nicely.

Inside Canada's Prisons
www.cbc.ca/prison/index.html

The CBC offers an interactive tour of a Canadian prison, giving clues to how it would feel to be a prisoner. As well, this link offers articles and analysis concerning prisons and further links for those interested.

Managementlearning.com
managementlearning.com/index.html

This commercial site aims to educate users about behaviour within an organization. The main goal of the literature the site supplies is efficiency. Try following any of these sublinks: 'Research', 'Library', 'Articles', 'Topics'.

Chapter 5

Deviance

Vincent F. Sacco

Learning Objectives

In this chapter, you will:

▶ learn to define deviance and social control as sociological concepts,

▶ think critically about the images of deviance that we regularly encounter in the popular media,

▶ learn to describe the major problems confronting researchers who study deviance,

▶ identify the major questions that sociological theories of deviance and control are intended to answer,

▶ compare and contrast various sociological explanations of deviant behaviour,

▶ examine some of the social and demographic factors that are related to particular forms of deviant conduct,

▶ learn how behaviours and people come to be categorized as deviant, and

▶ study the ways in which people who are labelled 'deviant' cope with stigma.

● Introduction ● ● ● ● ● ●

In a suburban house on a quiet, tree-lined street, two teenagers sit in the kitchen and discuss how they will spend Friday night. They decide that one of them will try to get a fake ID in order to buy some beer for a party they are planning to attend. An older brother of one of the teenagers approaches the house. He picks the daily newspaper off the front step and glances at the front page, where the headline announces the mayor's resignation—it was discovered that the mayor had been giving untendered contracts to a construction firm owned by someone who made large, regular contributions to her recent political campaign. The teenagers stop discussing their plans when the older brother, who is a student at the local university, enters. He instructs them to stay off the computer because he is waiting for a 'very important' e-mail. What he doesn't tell them is that the e-mail is from a friend at another university who has promised to send a copy of an A+ essay, which the recipient plans to submit as his own work in a course he is failing.

Across town, in a gleaming corporate office, several managerial staff members of a clothing company meet to consider the bad press they have been getting since it was revealed that their clothing lines are made by children in sweatshops in developing countries. Rather than considering how they might improve employees' working conditions, they decide to launch a publicity blitz that denies the charges and calls into question the honesty and motivations of their accusers. One of the executives finds it difficult to concentrate on business because she is distracted by the situation at home. Her husband's occasional violent outbursts have become more frequent, and she worries that she and her children may be in some real danger. Before the meeting, she sneaked outside for a quick cigarette. She felt guilty doing it because she knows that the people with whom she works view smoking as a disgusting habit of weak-willed people. She hopes that the mint she has popped into her mouth will hide evidence of what she thinks of as 'my addiction'.

What do all of these situations have in common? On the surface, it might seem that the answer is 'very little'. However, some important common themes run through these examples and relate to the central concerns of this chapter: the sociological nature of deviance and control. All of these situations raise questions about the nature of disvalued social action, why some people engage in it, and why others react to it in particular ways.

This chapter will attempt to accomplish several objectives. First, it will explain what the terms **deviance** and **social control** mean when they are used in sociolog-ical discourse. Next, it will consider some of the major problems faced by researchers who are interested in the empirical investigation of deviance and social control. Finally, it will focus on the three major theoretical questions that occupy the time and attention of sociologists who study deviance.

● What Is Deviance? ● ● ●

Any discussion of the sociology of deviance and social control must begin with some consideration of what these terms mean. This is not a straightforward task. These terms have been defined in many different ways, both within and beyond the discipline of sociology. Formal sociological conceptualizations of deviance can be contrasted with more popular views that define *deviance* by illustration, statistically, and in terms of a notion of harm.

By Illustration

When students are asked to define *deviance*, a first response typically is to list types of people or types of behaviours they think deserve the label. Most of us would have no trouble coming up with a long list of deviants, which could include (but would not be restricted to) criminals, child molesters, drug addicts, alcoholics, the mentally ill, members of religious cults, chronic liars, and more. Of course, who goes on the list and who does not is very much a function of who is doing the listing and when and where the listing is being done.

The major problem with these stand-alone lists is that they are incomplete. On their own, they tell us nothing about why some types of people and behaviour are (and why other types are not) included. In short, we are left in the dark regarding the definitional criteria being employed.

In Statistical Terms

Statistical rarity suggests a more explicit way of thinking about the meaning of *deviance*. In this sense, deviant behaviour and deviant people are identifiable by their rarity. On the face of it, this makes a certain amount of sense. Many of the kinds of people we think of as deviant are, in a statistical sense, relatively unusual.

A major problem with statistical definitions of deviance is illustrated by Figure 5.1. The area between points X_1 and X_2 represents typical performance levels across some characteristic. The shaded area on the far left represents the minority of statistically rare cases that

Figure 5.1   The Normal Curve

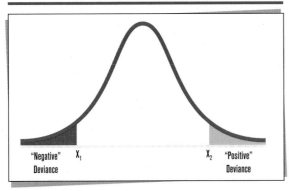

Statistical definitions of deviance make it difficult to distinguish 'negative' deviance from 'positive' deviance.

fall well below the average. On an examination of basic knowledge of their hometowns among Canadians, for instance, the people who fail very badly would be represented there. We might tend to think of such people as 'deviants' in the conventional sense of 'inferior'.

However, the shaded portion on the far right-hand side also suggests a statistically rare performance—but in the positive direction (Fielding et al., 2006; Spreitzer and Sonenshein, 2004). On an examination, these people would show superior knowledge about their town or city. Statistical definitions obscure distinctions between people who exceed and people who fall short of certain expectations.

As Harmful

Another familiar way of defining *deviance* is in terms of harm. In this sense, we equate deviant action with action that produces destructive outcomes. Once again, many of those who would appear on most shortlists of deviants would also seem to be encompassed by this definitional criterion. Murderers, thieves, liars, sexual abusers, and wife-assaulters all can be said to be authors of real and tangible harm.

But any attempt to equate deviance with harm also is fraught with difficulties. While many of the people treated as deviant in this society are the authors of harm, it also is true that many so treated are not. The developmentally delayed, the genius, the mentally ill, the exceptionally altruistic, gays and lesbians, the verbally unproficient, and many others outside of the mainstream are treated as deviant although it is difficult to ascribe harm to their differentness or to document the harm that they cause. In contrast, greedy corporate executives and unethical politicians may be able to manage how others see them so as to appear socially benign, even

though their actions may result in considerable damage to life and property. We tend to reserve the label of 'deviant' in our society for other categories of people (Pearce and Snider, 1995; Woodiwiss, 2005).

'Harm' may be as much a matter of judgment and opinion as is 'deviance'. Considerable disagreement persists in our society about what is and what is not harmful to the individual and to the society and whom we do and do not need to fear (Glassner, 1999; Siegel, 2005). Indeed, historical and anthropological evidence shows that judgments about harm may change over time and from one culture to another.

● Deviance as ● ● ● ● ● ● a Sociological Concept

As sociologists, we are interested in deviance as a product of **social interaction** and group structure. In other words, we understand the study of deviance to be the study of people, behaviours, and conditions that are subject to social control. Conversely, we can define social control as the various and myriad ways in which members of **social groups** express their disapproval of people and behaviour. These include name-calling, ridicule, ostracism, incarceration, and even killing. The study of deviance is about ways of acting and ways of being that, within particular social contexts and in particular historical periods, elicit moral condemnation.

When sociologists talk about deviance in this way, they sometimes create confusion for those who are used to thinking about the subject in a more conventional manner. When the sociologist says, for instance, that homosexuality is an appropriate subject for the scholarly study of deviance, the implication is not that the sociologist thinks of homosexuality as deviant; rather, that homosexuals are the targets of various forms of social control in our society. As sociologists, we are interested in why those with the power to exert social control regard gays and lesbians in this way and what the consequences of such actions are (Alden and Parker, 2005; Nylund, 2004).

In the study of deviance, it is important to distinguish between the *objective* and the *subjective* character of deviance (Loseke, 2003). The former refers to particular ways of thinking, acting, and being, the latter to the moral status accorded such thoughts, actions, and characteristics. It is important to keep this distinction in mind at all times. From the perspective of sociology, the 'deviant' character of certain behaviours or world views

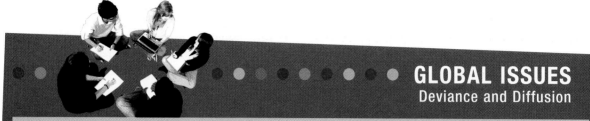

GLOBAL ISSUES
Deviance and Diffusion

Because we can think about deviance as resulting from a claims-making process, it is possible to conceptualize claims about the disreputability of behaviour as separate from the behaviour itself. This means that it is possible to ask questions about the 'performance' of these claims. Such questions have been posed by Joel Best (2001, 2008) and other writers who have attempted to determine how claims about deviance and social problems diffuse from one social setting to another. In other words, when a way of acting is seen as troublesome in one place, how do these definitions of the behaviour travel within and across national boundaries?

It is a reasonable question. After all, clothing styles, musical fashions, and other cultural trends certainly do travel in this way. There is every reason to expect that problem claims do also. The task of the sociologist interested in these issues is to understand the conditions under which such diffusion takes place and why some kinds of claims travel with greater ease or difficulty than others.

An interesting case study for the diffusion process concerns the relationship between Canada and the United States (Sacco and Ismaili, 2001). In this respect, it can be argued that many of the new forms of deviance that are constructed by the American cultural industries work their way northward in rather short order. For example, Canadians found themselves worrying about such problems as school violence, ritual abuse, stalkers, home invaders, rap music, and Internet predators quite soon after these issues had begun to attract widespread attention south of the border.

There are several reasons why this diffusion occurs as it does. Similarities in the linguistic and political cultures of the two countries facilitate similar styles of discussion and debate of such topics. In addition, the American mass media exert a remarkable influence on Canadian images of what is worrisome in the contemporary world.

However, differences in cultural settings can seriously impede the diffusion of claims about deviance. The moral panic about satanic crime that originated in the United States in the 1980s travelled easily to Canada, Great Britain, and Australia. Despite a remarkable lack of evidence, many residents of these countries, like the Americans who preceded them, came to believe that Satanists were kidnapping and molesting children, desecrating bodies, influencing the content of youth music and other forms of leisure, and conducting ritual human sacrifices. In France and elsewhere, however, these claims were met with ridicule and the satanic panic was never able to take root.

or physical features is not implicit in those behaviours, world views, or physical features, but is conferred on them by the society. To be deemed 'deviant' by a sociologist, a particular behaviour must not only hold the potential for being called deviant (e.g., be unusual or rare behaviour or be considered deviant in another society), but also must be labelled as 'deviant' by powerful others who are willing to use the labels.

Of course, as sociologists, we recognize the need to focus our attention on both sides of the deviance issue. We need to be alert to the fact that not everything that could be labelled 'deviant', say, statistically, is necessarily labelled 'deviant' by the society. In an East Asian neighbourhood, the blue-eyed and light-skinned person may be anomalous, but the neighbours probably do not consider that individual deviant. Or, the fact that women wore long skirts in the Victorian period and would have considered a woman with a knee-length skirt to be deviant does not mean that a contemporary woman in a short skirt will be considered deviant.

The ability of some in society to use available resources in order to resist the efforts of others to consider them deviant also is of sociological interest. For example, even though corporations engage in activities that undermine health or safety or that weaken the economic well-being of many in society, they are able to define themselves as moral and respectable corporate citizens. They do this, most commonly, through their support of sporting events, donations to universities and hospitals, and in public relations campaigns that promote a positive organizational image.

● Researching Deviance ●

Sociologists who undertake empirical studies of deviance attempt to make use of the same methodological tools employed in other areas of the discipline. These include, for instance, experiments, surveys, content analyses, and field research. However, attempting to study the degree to which people might be engaging in behaviours that excite widespread disapproval can create rather formidable problems. While the problems discussed in this section represent challenges to all forms of social research, they suggest special difficulties when the subject matter of the research is deviance.

Secrecy

Deviant behaviour often is behaviour that people wish to keep secret to protect themselves from social reactions. How do sociologists undertake valid research in a way that does not intrude excessively into the lives of those under study? There is no simple answer to this question.

Sometimes the researcher attempts to gain the confidence of the subjects by posing as one who shares their deviant status (Whyte, 1943). This involves some extremely hazardous ethical dilemmas. One much-discussed case in this respect is an early study by sociologist Laud Humphreys. His book *Tearoom Trade* (1970) is a study of impersonal sexual encounters between homosexual men in public washrooms ('tearooms'). In order to familiarize himself with the social character of these sexual encounters, Humphreys presented himself to 'tearoom' participants as someone who was willing to play the role of voyeur/lookout. This deception allowed him to observe the interaction between sexual partners in a way that did not arouse their suspicion. To compound the ethical problem, Humphreys recorded the licence-plate numbers of the men who frequented the 'tearoom' and was able to determine their addresses. After disguising his appearance, he went to their homes, under the pretense of conducting a public health survey, in order to learn more about them. Needless to say, when his

research techniques were discovered they provoked a firestorm of controversy. Generally, sociologists do not believe that such deception is ever excusable.

Discovery of Reportable Behaviour

If research subjects confide in the researcher and reveal information about illegal or harmful circumstances, does the researcher have an obligation to report that wrongdoing to authorities? The problem is brought about by the cross-pressures that the researcher experiences (Bostock, 2002). On the one hand, the researcher has a professional obligation to respect the confidentiality of information that research subjects divulge. On the other hand, one has a social and moral obligation to protect the safety of the public, including the research subject.

Some of the complexities relating to reportability are illustrated by the case of Russel Ogden, who in 1994 was an MA student in the School of Criminology at Simon Fraser University in British Columbia. Ogden's study involved an investigation of the process of assisted suicide among terminally ill HIV/AIDS patients. Shortly after he defended his thesis, he was summoned by a coroner's inquest, which asked him to reveal the sources of his information. Ogden refused, citing the pledge of confidentiality he had provided to his research subjects. He was subsequently charged with contempt of court. Despite his having little formal support from his university, he won the case. The court later ruled that social science researchers have a qualified privilege to maintain confidentiality because such research contributes substantially to Canadian society (Palys and Lowman, 2000).

Safety

Closely related to the problems of reportable behaviour are those related to the safety of respondents. In short, researchers should take no action that could result in harm to those who participate in the research. While we tend to think only of physical harm in this respect, the injunction is much broader and includes emotional, mental, and economic harm.

Research can put study subjects at risk in a more general sense as well. It is important to remember that, by definition, research into the disvalued nature of people and behaviour involves looking into the lives of the most vulnerable members of society. These could include the poor, the homeless, and others with whom society associates designations of deviance. The sociologist needs to remain aware that research findings can often be used *against* these vulnerable groups, especially when sufficient care is not taken to qualify conclusions or to suggest appropriate interpretations of research evidence.

● The Sociology ● ● ● ● ●
of Deviant Behaviour

We have defined *deviance* as ways of thinking, acting, and being that are subject to social control—in other words, as kinds of conditions and kinds of people who are viewed by most of the members of a society as wrong, immoral, disreputable, bizarre, or unusual. In so doing, we recognize that deviance has two distinct yet related dimensions: objective and subjective. *Objective* refers to the behaviour or condition itself, *subjective* refers to the placement of that condition by the members of society in their system of moral stratification.

To choose a simple example, sociologists do not confuse the physical act of someone smoking marijuana with the designation of marijuana-smoking as a deviant act. While each suggests a distinct realm of experience, each is an appropriate object of sociological attention. It is one thing to ask why people smoke marijuana, and it is quite another to ask why some (the social institution of the law, for example, and those who support it, for another) consider this deviant conduct. However, both types of questions are significant in sociology.

We can identify several problem areas that have been the focus of theoretical attention in the sociology of deviance. These include questions about (1) the causes and forms of deviant behaviour, (2) the content and character of moral definitions, and (3) the issues that arise over labels of deviance.

While sociologists are interested in a broad array of issues, questions about why deviants do what they do have attracted the lion's share of attention. However, the 'Why do they do it?' question contains a number of important (if unstated) assumptions: (1) It implies that most of us share a conformist view of the world in which the important thing to understand is why some deviant minority refuses to act the way 'we' act; (2) The moral status of deviant behaviour is never called into question. In a sense, the 'Why do they do it?' question proceeds from the assumption that—by and large—society is a pretty stable and orderly place, that there is generally widespread agreement about what is right and what is wrong, and that we therefore need to understand what pushes or pulls some off the path the rest of us travel.

Most (but not all) of the theoretical thought in this respect reflects the influence of functionalist perspectives. Three dominant ways of thinking about 'why they do it' can be identified—strain theory, cultural support theory, and control theory.

Strain Theory

Strain theory derives from the writings of the famous American sociologist Robert Merton, who in 1938 published a very influential paper entitled 'Social Structure and Anomie'. Merton sought to understand why, according to official statistics, so many types of nonconformity are much more pervasive among members of the lower social classes. Crime, delinquency, drug addiction, alcoholism, and other forms of deviance, Merton recognized, seem to emerge as more significant problems the further one moves down the socio-economic structure. As a sociologist, Merton was interested in trying to understand this issue in a way that made the structure of society—rather than the personalities of individuals—the central explanatory mechanism.

Merton argued that the answer could be found in the malintegration of the cultural and social structures of societies. In other words, it is the lack of fit between the *cultural goals* people are encouraged to seek and the *means* available to pursue these goals that creates a kind of social strain to which deviant behaviour is an adjustment. Merton's logic is elegant and compelling. In a society like the United States, there is little recognition of the role that **class** barriers play in social life. As a result, everyone is encouraged to pursue the goal of material success—and everyone is judged a success or a failure in life based on his or her ability to become materially successful.

Merton knew, though, that there are many people near the bottom of the class hierarchy who, because of their ethnic or regional or class origins, may not be able to achieve that overpowering social goal of material success. This, Merton said, is a type of socially induced strain to which people must adjust their behaviour, and often these adjustments take deviant forms. When people steal money or material goods, for instance, it can be said that they are attempting to use 'illegitimate means' to achieve the trappings of success. When they take drugs (or become 'societal dropouts'), they can be seen to have pulled out of the competition for stratification outcomes. For Merton, these problems are most acute in the lower social classes because it is there that people are most likely to experience the disjuncture between the things they aspire to and things that are actually available to them (see Table 5.1).

Table 5.1 Robert Merton's Paradigm of Deviant Behaviour

Robert Merton argued that there are essentially five ways of adjusting to a social structure that encourages large numbers of people to seek objectives that are not actually available to them. Four of these adaptations represent types of deviance. Each type can be understood in reference to the goals and means of the culture.

	Attitude to Goals	Attitude to Means	Explanation/Example
Conformity	accept	accept	Most people accept as legitimate the culturally approved ways of achieving those goals. In Merton's example, most strive for material success by working hard, trying to get a good education, etc.
Innovation	accept	reject	The bank robber, drug dealer, or white-collar thief seeks success, too, but rejects the conventional means for achieving that success.
Ritualism	reject	accept	Some people seem to simply be going through the motions of achieving desired social goals. In large organizations, we use the term 'bureaucrat' to describe people who are fixated on procedures at the expense of outcomes.
Retreatism	reject	reject	Some people adjust to strain by 'dropping out' of the system. Such dropping out could include losing oneself in a world of alcohol or illegal drugs or adopting some unconventional lifestyle.
Rebellion	reject/accept	reject/accept	Rebellion includes acts intended to replace the current cultural goals (and means) with new ones. In this category we might include the radical political activist or even the domestic terrorist.

stats re deviant behaviour may not always be accurate

Later critics have pointed out certain problems with Merton's arguments (Downes and Rock, 2003; Vold et al., 2002). Merton proceeds from the assumption that the distribution of crime and deviance we find in official statistics is accurate, which it may not be. Merton does not extend his argument to explain how it happens that acts of crime and deviance also occur within middle- and upper-class populations.

Despite these limitations, Merton's argument has had a great deal of influence on the way sociologists think about the causes of deviant behaviour (Laufer and Adler, 1994). For example, sociologists Richard Cloward and Lloyd Ohlin (1960) expanded on Merton's ideas in an effort to explain lower-class gang delinquency. They agree with Merton that juvenile crime is prompted by

the inability of lower-class youth to achieve the things that their culture encourages them to seek. However, they suggest that there is a need to explain why different kinds of delinquent behaviour patterns emerge in different types of neighbourhoods.

For these researchers, delinquency patterns are like rare plants that require specialized conditions to flourish. Cloward and Ohlin identify three kinds of delinquent adaptations. The first, which they refer to as the *criminal pattern*, is characterized by instrumental delinquency activities, particularly delinquency for gain, in which those involved seek to generate illegal profits. We might think of drug-dealing or the theft and fencing of stolen goods as examples of this kind of crime. The second, the *conflict pattern*, is characterized by the presence of 'fighting gangs' who battle over turf and neighbourhood boundaries. The third, the *retreatist pattern*, is organized around the acquisition and use of hard drugs.

A more recent version of strain theory has been proposed by Robert Agnew (1985, 2006; Agnew and Broidy, 1997). Agnew theorizes that the inability to achieve the things we want in life is only one type of socially induced strain and that there are at least two others. A second source of strain involves an inability to avoid or escape some negative condition. For example, the youth who cannot avoid an abusive parent or bullying at school might turn to drugs, run away from home, or become aggressive with others as ways of coping with the strain his living situation creates. A third kind of strain results from conditions in which individuals lose something that they value. For example, a child who is forced to move and thus leave important friendships, the person whose parent has died, and a boyfriend or girlfriend experiencing the breakup of the relationship all experience loss strain.

Despite differences, these arguments hold certain features in common. First, they take as their point of reference the need to explain why some individuals but not others behave in ways that invite social sanction. Second, they share an explanatory logic that focuses on how the organization of our social relations creates problems that require solutions. In this paradigm, the causes of deviant behaviour are located in patterns of social life that are external to but impact individuals.

Cultural Support Theory

A second explanation of deviant behaviour, **cultural support theory**, focuses on the way patterns of cultural beliefs create and sustain such conduct (Cohen, 1966). According to arguments of this sort, people behave in ways that reflect the cultural values to which they have been exposed and that they have internalized. In this way, it can be said that you are attending university or college because you value education and learning and come from a home or cultural setting that similarly values education and learning. If conventional values support conventional behaviour, it should also follow that deviant values support deviant behaviour. The important task of such theories is to understand how the cultural meanings people associate with deviant conduct make that conduct more likely.

One of the earliest explicit statements of this position was provided by a sociologist associated with the University of Chicago, Edwin Sutherland (Sutherland, 1947). Writing in the 1930s, Sutherland proposed that people become deviant because they have been exposed to learning experiences that make deviance more likely. In short, people end up deviant in the same way that they end up as Catholics, as stamp collectors, as saxophone players, or as French film fans—that is, as a result of exposure to influential learning experiences. People become deviant because they have learned in the context of interpersonal relationships how to become deviant.

But what does learning to be deviant actually involve? Most important, according to Sutherland, is the learning of what he called the 'specific direction of drives, motives, attitudes and rationalizations' (1947: 7). In other words, we must learn to think about deviant conduct as acceptable to ourselves. Why do we not kill people who make us angry? It cannot be because we don't know how (most of us do) or even, in many cases, because we fear getting caught. Most commonly, we refrain from murderous violence because we have come to define such action as morally repugnant, that is, as unacceptable to ourselves. For Sutherland, it was this learning to accept or to value criminal or deviant action that in a very real sense made such action possible.

Sutherland's cultural insights help us to understand how people come to value actions the rest of the society might despise. But other writers in this tradition have shown that the culture of deviant action is even more complicated. The complication concerns the fact that we live in a society that seems simultaneously to condemn and to support deviant behaviour. Is it possible to simultaneously believe in and to break important social rules? Most of us think, for example, that stealing is wrong, and we have learned to be wary of thieves. However, most of us also have stolen something of value (perhaps at work, perhaps from a corner store or a family member). This is possible because we have learned to define these deviant situations as ones to which the rules really do not apply. When we steal at work, for instance, we might not see this as theft. We tell ourselves (and others) that we are underpaid and deserve whatever fringe benefits we can get, or that our employers actually expect people to steal and build the cost of such losses into their budgets. From this perspective, the broader culture both condemns deviance and makes available for learning the techniques to neutralize the laws that prohibit deviant action (Sykes and Matza, 1957).

Like strain arguments, cultural arguments have been very influential in the sociological study of deviant behaviour (Akers and Jensen, 2006).

Some critics have charged, however, that arguments that use culture to explain deviance ultimately are tautological (Maxim and Whitehead, 1998), that is, employ a kind of circular reasoning. Cultural theories tell us that deviant beliefs and values are the source of deviant conduct. Yet, how do we ever really know what people's beliefs and values are? Usually, we observe how people behave and then, on the basis of their behaviour, infer that they hold certain values. Is it appropriate, then, to use the value we have inferred from observations of behaviour to explain that behaviour? If we observe people stealing and then infer that they have come to acquire values that are supportive of stealing and that these values explain the stealing, we have reasoned in a circle and have explained nothing at all.

On the other hand, arguments of this type have proven more useful than strain arguments in making sense of corporate crimes. Whereas strain theories typically proceed from assumptions of disadvantage as a cause of crime, cultural theories do not. One may argue that corporate crime, at least to some extent, is rooted in a 'culture of competition' that legitimates organizational wrongdoing (Calavita and Pontell, 1991).

Control Theory

The logic of the strain and cultural support theories contrasts quite sharply with the logic of a third point of view known as **control theory**. Advocates of control theory argue that most types of deviant behaviour do not require a sophisticated form of explanation. People lie, cheat, steal, take drugs, or engage in sexual excess when and if they are free to do so. Lying and cheating can be the most expeditious and efficient ways of getting what we want in life. Experimenting with drugs and sexual promiscuity can be more fun than working or studying. The important question we need to ask, according to control theorists, is not 'Why do some people break rules the rest of us abide by?' Instead we need to ask, 'Why don't more of us engage in "forbidden" behaviour?' For control theorists, deviant behaviour occurs whenever it is allowed to occur. Thus, we expect to find deviance when the social controls that are supposed to prevent or check it are weak or broken. Seen in this way, deviance is not a special kind of behaviour that requires a special kind of motivation. Rather, it is behaviour that results from the absence of pressures that would check or constrain it.

This idea is a very venerable one in sociology—it can be traced to the writing of Émile Durkheim (1966 [1897]). In his classic study of suicide, Durkheim sought to explain why some groups in society experience higher suicide rates than others and why suicide rates vary over time. Catholics, he found, have lower suicide rates than Protestants, and married people have lower

rates than single people. As well, suicide rates increase in times both of economic boom and of economic depression. What is varying in all of these cases? Durkheim suggested that the crucial variable might be social regulation (or what we call *social control*). Social regulation forces people to take others into account and discourages behaviours that are excessively individualistic. Catholicism—with its mandatory church attendance and practices such as confession—might suggest more social regulation than various strands of Protestantism. Married life implies more external regulation (in terms of obligations, duties, and so on) than single life. Periods of both boom and depression throw large numbers of people out of the customary social grooves in which they have been living their lives and disconnect them from social regulations. In short, suicide is more likely when people are left to their own resources.

In more recent times, sociologist Travis Hirschi (1969) has been the most influential social control theorist. Like many other sociologists interested in the study of deviant behaviour, Hirschi focused on the study of juvenile crime. In a very influential book published in 1969, Hirschi attempted to use social control logic to explain the conduct of youthful offenders. For Hirschi, the problem of juvenile crime could be understood in reference to the concept of the bond to conventional society. Each of us, to a greater or lesser degree, has a bond or connection to the world of conventional others. In the case of youth, the world of conventional others is the world represented by their parents, teachers, and members of the legitimate adult community. Hirschi reasoned that if youthful bonds to conventional others are strong, youths need to take these others into account when they act; if the bonds are weak, however, they are free to act in ways that reflect much narrower self-interest. Much of what we call crime and deviance, he reasoned, is evidence of this self-interested behaviour.

More recently, in collaboration with Michael Gottfredson (Gottfredson and Hirschi, 1990), Hirschi has proposed a general theory of crime and deviance that has been the object of a great deal of attention (Gottfredson, 2006).

Gottfredson and Hirschi argue that crimes of all types tend to be committed by people who are impulsive, short-sighted, non-verbal risk-takers. The underlying social-psychological characteristic of such people, they maintain, is low self-control. Further, individuals who have low self-control not only are more likely to commit crime, they are also more likely to engage in a wide range of deviant practices, including drinking, smoking, and activities that result in getting into accidents (Baron,

2003; Junger et al., 2001; Nakhaie et al., 2000). For Gottfredson and Hirschi, the problem of low self-control originates in inadequate child-rearing that fails to discourage delinquent outcomes.

Social control theories remain very influential, but they have been criticized for their assumption that motivation is essentially irrelevant to the study of crime and deviance (Bohm, 1997). As well, some writers argue that while these ideas make a certain amount of sense when we are talking about crime and deviance among the more marginalized segments of society, they do an inadequate job of explaining why those members of society whose bonds to the conventional world seem strongest also engage in prohibited acts (Deutschmann, 2007).

● The Transactional ● ● ● ● Character of Deviance

Despite their sociological character, strain, cultural support, and social control arguments tend to focus attention on the individual: people, according to these theories, commit deviant acts because they respond to strain, because they are exposed to learning environments that support deviance, or because they are free from social constraints. Other writers, however, encourage us to understand deviant behaviour as an interactional product. From this perspective, we understand deviant behaviour as a joint or collective, rather than individual, outcome.

Figure 5.2   Provincial Variations in Rates of Homicide (Number of Homicides per 100,000 Population), 2007

For reasons that are not entirely clear, the rate at which the situated transaction we refer to as homicide varies from province to province.

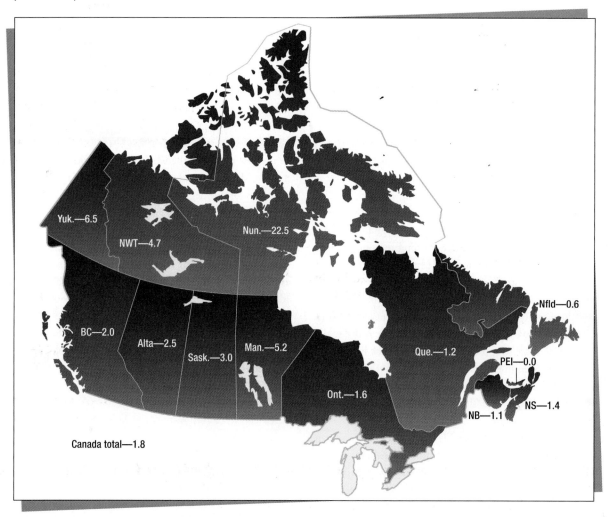

Source: M. Dauvergne (2008). *Crime Statistics in Canada, 2007*, 28 (7) Ottawa: Statistics Canada, page 12.

When most of us seek to explain murder, we tend to focus on the murderous acts of the individual (see Figure 5.2 for homicide rates in Canada). As sociologists, we might try to understand how people who commit acts of lethal violence do so in response to social strain (Pratt and Godsey, 2003) or as a result of an affiliation with a culture of violence (Chilton, 2004; Wolfgang and Ferracuti, 1967). Alternatively, we might try to understand how murder results from particular kinds of interactions.

David Luckenbill (1977), for example, has attempted to show how murder can in many cases be understood as a **situated transaction**. This means that some murder, at least, may be seen not as an individual act, but rather as an interaction sequence in which the participants (the eventual murderer, the eventual victim, and, perhaps, an audience) interact in a common physical territory. Based on a study of 70 homicides in the state of California, Luckenbill concludes that many murders move through six common stages:

- *Stage 1.* The transaction starts when the person who will end up the victim does something that the person who ends up the offender could define as an insult or as an offence to 'face'. This could be quite trivial. The victim might call the offender a liar, refuse to share a cigarette, or make a sexually suggestive comment about the partner of the eventual offender.
- *Stage 2.* The offender defines what the victim has said or done as threatening or offensive.
- *Stage 3.* The offender makes a countermove intended to respond and save face. This could involve a verbal response or a physical gesture.
- *Stage 4.* The victim responds in an aggressive manner. At this point, a working definition of the situation as one that will require a violent resolution seems to be emerging. The problems may be aggravated by the presence of onlookers who jeer the participants, offer to hold their jackets, or to block a convenient exit.
- *Stage 5.* At this stage, a brief violent exchange occurs. It may involve a fatal blow, a thrust with a knife, or the pulling of a trigger. Typically, it is over quickly.
- *Stage 6.* The battle, such as it was, is over and the offender either flees or remains at the scene.

Luckenbill's work shows us how murder can be understood as a social product. This does not imply an absence of guilt on the part of people who murder, and it is not offered as an excuse for killing. It does show that acts of deviance can be quite complex and can involve significant interactional dimensions. For this reason, some students of deviant and criminal behaviour argue that it is more useful to think of murder, or theft, or similar other forms of deviance as 'social events' rather than the acts of individuals in isolation (Sacco and Kennedy, 2008).

To say they are social events is to imply that they involve much more than an individual behaving badly. The outcome of a homicide event does not just depend on what the 'killer' does. It also depends on what bystanders do, whether the parties to the conflict are alone or with friends, how quickly the police or paramedics arrive, etc.

● Making Sense of the 'Facts' of Deviant Behaviour

Sociologists interested in the study of deviant behaviour have repeatedly demonstrated that deviant acts—especially the kinds of acts that seem to concern the average member of the society most—are not randomly distributed in the population. Instead, people with some kinds of social and demographic characteristics seem much more likely to be involved in such behaviour than others. The task for sociological explanations that focus on the deviant act is to explain these levels of differential involvement.

Gender

It is well-known that **gender** tends to correlate closely with a wide range of behaviours. This is no less true in the study of deviance than in the study of other areas in sociology. Males and females differ in terms of the amounts and the kinds of disapproved behaviours in which they engage.

Males are more likely to be involved in those behaviours of which most members of Canadian society would

▌▌▌ Time to Reflect ▌▌▌▌▌▌▌▌▌▌▌▌▌▌▌▌▌▌▌▌▌▌▌▌▌▌▌

Do you think that some explanations of deviant behaviour, such as strain theory, can be faulted for excusing such behaviour? Do theories that focus on situated transactions blame victims for their own victimization?

say they disapprove. Males are much more likely than females to be involved in criminal behaviour (crimes related to prostitution are an important exception in this regard). In 2003, males made up 81 per cent of persons charged by the police and this pattern is typical. The differential is greatest in cases of violence but is also very large for other kinds of crime (Gannon et al., 2005). While there has been some narrowing of the gender gap in recent years, crime remains very much a male-dominated activity (Sacco and Kennedy, 2007). Table 5.2 shows gender differences in crime for two of Canada's largest cities.

Males are more likely to consume both legal and illegal drugs, including tobacco, alcohol, marijuana, and cocaine (Canadian Centre on Substance Abuse, 2005). Males are more likely to commit suicide, and when they do so, they are more likely to use guns or explosives (Langlois and Morrison, 2002). Overall rates of mental illness do not differ markedly between men and women, although there are significant variations by type. Women are more likely to be diagnosed as suffering from depression and anxiety, while men are more likely to experience problems relating to various forms of addiction and psychosis (Health Canada, 2002).

Several feminist writers have argued that there has been a marked tendency in the sociological literature to systematically ignore the deviant behaviour of women (Miller and Mullins, 2006). To be sure, most of what is written about crime and deviance concerns the behaviour of men, both as deviants and as police and other agents of social control. Moreover, many sociologists have assumed that female deviant behaviour could be explained using the same theoretical ideas and models that have been used to make sense of male behaviour—a position with which many feminists do not agree.

The failure to be sufficiently attentive to the gendered nature of criminal and deviant behaviour has been an empirical problem, also. Most research has dealt with the actions of men, either explicitly or implicitly. Sociologists tended, historically, not to be terribly interested in acts of crime or deviance that did not have a significant male dimension (Boritch, 1997). Only through the work of feminist social critics did researchers come to focus on problems that affect women more directly. These include, for instance, various forms of deviance that tend to uniquely victimize women, such as intimate violence and sexual harassment (Chasteen, 2001; Comack et al., 2000).

Age

Age, like gender, is strongly associated with many kinds of deviant behaviour (Tanner, 2001). Crime rates are

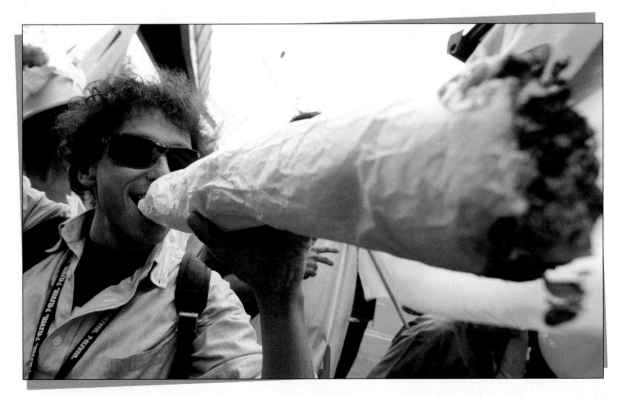

Illegal behaviours such as marijuana smoking are common among young people. Some believe marijuana use should be decriminalized since non-enforcement of the law brings all lawmaking into disrepute. Reuters/Daniel Aguilar

Table 5.2 — Gender Differences in Self-reported Delinquent Behaviours among a Sample of Toronto Youth in Grades 7-9 (Percents)

	Male	Female
Violent behaviours		
Snatching a bag, purse or something else from a person	3*	2*
Carrying a weapon, such as a stick, chain, or knife	15	5*
Threatening somebody to get money or something else from them	2*	2*
Participating in a group fight in a public place	22	10*
Intentionally beating up or hurting someone so badly they needed to see a doctor	3	1*
Total lifetime prevalence of violent behaviours	**30**	**15***
Property-related behaviours		
Damaging something intentionally	12	6*
Stealing something from a store	21	23*
Breaking into a building with the purpose of stealing something	1	—
Stealing a bicycle	4	1*
Stealing a motorcycle or car	—	—
Stealing something out of (or from) a car	2	1*
Intentionally setting fire to property (other than your own)	7	3*
Total lifetime prevalence of property-related behaviours	**30**	**26***
Drug-related behaviours		
Selling drugs, or acting as a middleman or go-between	3*	2*
Total lifetime prevalence of delinquent behaviours	**41**	**32***

* small numbers must be used with caution
— numbers are to too small to be reliably estimated
Source: J. Savoie, 2007. *Youth Self-Reported Delinquency*, 2006. Ottawa: Statistics Canada, page 12.

greatest during the late teens and early adulthood and decline very sharply after that (Sacco and Kennedy, 2007). This pattern characterizes even violence in the home: young husbands (those under 30) are much more likely than older husbands to treat their wives violently (Mihorean, 2005). However, this pattern does not hold for all kinds of crime. White-collar crimes (professional fraud, cheating on taxes, and so on) tend to occur somewhat later in the life cycle (Gottfredson and Hirschi, 1990).

Alcohol use and illicit drug use are more heavily concentrated among young people (Canadian Centre on Substance Abuse, 2005). But while suicide rates among young people are a cause of considerable concern, such rates actually tend to be lower among younger Canadians (Langlois and Morrison, 2002; see Figure 5.3). While older people are traditionally assumed to be those most likely to experience a variety of forms of mental illness, the onset of most mental illness occurs during adolescence and young adulthood (Health Canada, 2002).

Figure 5.3   Suicide Rates by Sex and Age (Rates per 100,000), 2004

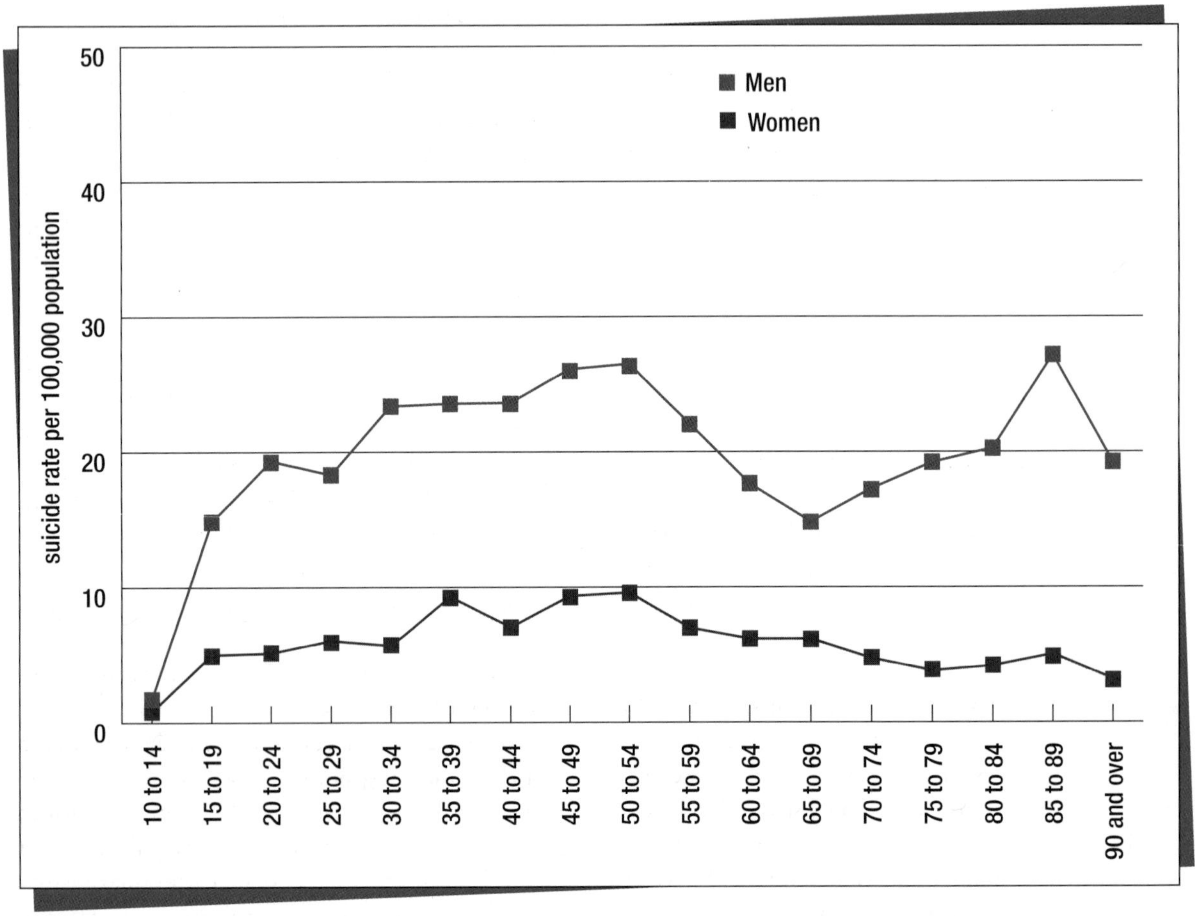

Source: Statistics Canada website (http://www40.statcan.ca/l01/cst01/perhlth66c.htm)

Class and Ethnicity

As with gender and age, relationships between indicators of socio-economic disadvantage and various forms of deviant behaviour are of considerable interest to sociologists. Many of the studies on this subject say that poorer people and people from minority groups are more likely to be involved in many forms of crime and delinquency, to use drugs and alcohol, and to develop various kinds of mental illness. Indeed, a great deal of sociological theorizing about the 'causes' of deviant behaviour has taken as its central issue the need to explain why social and economic precariousness is related to deviant outcomes. This is very clear, for instance, in most versions of strain theory.

However, a consensus in the research literature does not exist regarding how concepts such as poverty, economic inequality, ethnicity, or minority group status should be measured for research purposes (Braithewaite, 1979; Hagan and Peterson, 1995; Wortley, 1999), and there is less consistency in research findings. While some

studies seem to say that working-class youth are more likely to be delinquent, other studies tell us the opposite (Tittle et al., 1978). As well, while minority group status seems to be related to higher rates of crime in some cases, for example, with **First Nations** people, it seems to be related to lower rates of crime in others, for example, with Asian immigrants in British Columbia (Gordon and Nelson, 2000; Brzozowski et al., 2006).

Other interpretations of the significance of the relationship between social disadvantage and deviant behaviour point in the direction of a more general fault line that runs through the sociology of deviance. These other interpretations encourage us to ask different types of questions. Are poorer or minority people more likely to be deviant, or are they just more likely to get caught and labelled as 'deviant'? Even more profoundly, do our definitions of what constitute crime and deviance themselves reflect class biases? Poor people, for instance, are less likely to commit many kinds of crimes, such as fraud and embezzlement. They are even less likely to manufacture faulty products, to engage in false advertising, to profit from political corruption, or to engage in various kinds of stock market swindles.

These observations suggest that while questions about who commits deviant acts and who does not are interesting and important, there is a need to move beyond them and to ask questions about the subjective character of deviance. Why are some ways of thinking, acting, and being more likely than others to excite indignation and disapproval, and why are some people more likely than others to become the objects of social control? It is to these questions that we now turn our attention.

● The Sociology ● ● ● ● ● of Deviant Categories

As stated at the beginning of this chapter, the sociology of deviance is also the study of moral stratification. To call something or someone 'deviant' is to articulate a judgment that the thing or person is disreputable. An important set of issues in the sociology of deviance relates to the creation of categories—some deviant and some not—by which people and actions are sorted (Loseke, 2003).

In the course of living our lives day to day, we tend to treat these distinctions as common sense. The deviant qualities of people and acts, we convince ourselves, reside within the people and acts themselves. However, judged from another standpoint, known as **social constructionism** (Miller and Holstein, 1993; Spector and Kitsuse, 1977), this logic is flawed. Acts and people are not inherently deviant but are defined as such by those in society with the power to do so.

Proceeding from this assumption, we are led to another set of questions. For example, how do we make the moral distinctions that we make? This perspective maintains that there is nothing self-evident or commonsensical about the deviant quality of people and their behaviour. Instead, the deviant quality assigned to people and behaviour is itself problematic and requires investigation.

Further, we need to recognize that the character of social condemnation is fluid and dynamic over time (Curra, 2000). It is easy to think of behaviours that were once widely viewed as deviant but that have come to be considered much less deviant in recent years. 'Living together', having a child outside of marriage, or being gay might only a few years ago have been widely seen as grounds for social exclusion. While there is some resistance to these behaviours in the society at large (and a great deal of resistance in particular sectors of society), societal attitudes have moderated considerably.

At the same time, it is equally easy to think of many ways of acting or ways of being that were once widely tolerated but that now seem to draw considerable disapproval. One clear example is cigarette-smoking (Tilleczek and Hine, 2006; Troyer and Markle, 1983; Tuggle and Holmes, 1999). Only a few decades ago, cigarette-smoking was widely approved of, even imitated as glamorous. People smoked on elevators, in restaurants, and around children—even while attending sociology classes. That view of smoking contrasts sharply with the present-day view. Today, smokers are pariahs in many circles, and their habit is the object of scorn. Increasingly, they are the objects of a variety of forms of legal and extra-legal control (Wagner, 1997). Other examples of behaviour for which social tolerance has decreased in recent years include drinking and driving (Asbridge et al., 2004; Gusfield, 1981), wife assault (Johnson, 1996), and sexual harassment (Stewart, 2002).

Deviance as a Claims-Making Process

What are the sources of the distinctions that the members of a society make between what is and what is not deviant? Social constructionist writers understand this to be a **claims-making** process (Best, 2001; Spector and Kitsuse, 1977). This refers to the process by which groups assert grievances about the troublesome character of 'other' people or their behaviour. Claims-making thus involves the promotion of a particular moral vision of social life. In a practical sense, we recognize claims-making in many different sorts of activities that could include voting for 'reform' candidates in a local election, debating some exotic sexual practice on a daytime talk show, marching in protest to have the police do something about local crime, and providing expert testimony before a parliamentary committee. In short, claims-making is anything anybody does to propagate a view of who or what is deviant and what needs to be done about it (Loseke, 2003).

As a social process, claims-making is directed towards the achievement of three broad types of objectives:

1. *Publicizing the problematic character of the people with the behaviour in question.* Before they come to see people as troublesome, the members of a society generally need to be convinced that there is some tangible reason to regard those in question as troublesome. Claims-makers may endeavour to convince us that deviants are dangerous or irresponsible or that their behaviour is contagious (Best, 1999; Macek, 2006). In many cases, there is no objective basis to the claim, but the claim may

be understood by many as a valid statement about the world.

2. *Shaping a particular view of the problem*. Deviants can be defined in many different ways, and it matters greatly whether we see people as troubled or as troublesome (Gusfield, 1989). Generally, claims-makers want not only to convince us that certain people are a problem, but that they are problems of a particular type. 'Problem drinking', for instance, can be constructed in many different ways (Holmes and Antell, 2001). We might see it as a sin, which implies that it is a religious problem. We might see it as a crime, which implies that it is a legal problem. Or we might see it as a sickness, which implies that it is a medical problem. In all cases the behaviour in question remains the same, and in all cases it is seen as deviant. What changes is the kind of deviant the problem drinker is understood to be. These differing constructions have very different implications for what it is we think we need to do about the deviant person.

3. *Building consensus around the new moral category*. Claims-makers endeavour to build widespread agreement about the correctness of a particular moral vision (Heimer, 2002; Macek, 2006). This is accomplished by winning the support of the media, officialdom, and the general public (Hilgartner and Bosk, 1988). As consensus is built, dissenting views are relegated to the margins of legitimate discourse. It is precisely the establishment of consensus and the marginalization of dissenting views that give the deviant categories in our society their common-sense character.

Who Are Claims-Makers?

The movement to 'deviantize' people and behaviour originates in the perceptions (however narrowly shared at the outset) that something is troubling and needs correction. Howard Becker (1963) coined the term *moral entrepreneur* to describe those who 'discover' and attempt to publicize deviant conditions. Becker says that moral entrepreneurs are crusading reformers who are disturbed by some evil that they see in the world and who will not rest until something is done to correct it.

In the early stages, definitions of deviance often are promoted by those who have some direct connection to the problem. In the case of drinking and driving, for instance, claims-making to heavily criminalize this conduct originated with victim groups such as MADD (Mothers Against Drunk Driving), whose members had a powerful emotional stake in the issue (Reinarman, 1996). In contrast, many of those involved in the construction of deviance have no vested interest in or emotional connection to the problem or the outcome. Lawmakers, journalists, daytime talk show hosts, and the producers of television drama frequently play a very significant role in the promotion of particular designations of deviance (Hilgartner and Bosk, 1988; Sacco, 2005). However, their social distance from the issue is often greater than that of victims' groups, and for many of them, the construction of deviance is just another day at the office.

What Are Claims?

When social constructionists speak of *claims*, they are talking about the actual message content that conveys a moral vision of deviance and non-deviance. What do claims-makers say, for example, in interviews on television talk shows, in pamphlets, in newspaper editorials, and on picket signs to convey the message that something or someone deserves the appellation of 'deviant'? The study of claims is the study of rhetorical communication, since such communications—by design or in effect—persuade audiences.

Successful claims-making rhetoric can demonstrate the gravity of a problem in several ways, including these:

* *Using compelling statistics*. Statistics are used to impress on consumers of the media the size of a problem and that the problem is getting worse (Best, 2001; Gilbert, 1997). Statistical estimates of a problem's dimensions that suggest that a large problem is getting worse legitimate concern and provide compelling evidence of the urgency of a problem.
* *Linking an emergent concern to problems already on the public agenda*. In this way, familiar moral language can be used to provide ready reference points for the emergent problem. For instance, because addiction is widely recognized as a problem in North America, new problems may be described as 'addictions'. We use the term 'addiction' in a very liberal way and speak of, for instance, 'pornography addicts', 'gambling addicts', and 'Internet addiction' (Butters and Erickson, 2000).
* *Using emotionally compelling examples to typify the seriousness and character of the threat posed by the behaviour* (see Bromley and Shupe, 1981). For example, the killings at Columbine High School in Colorado are applied in a rhetoric to exemplify the problem of school violence, even though such incidents are extremely rare and most school crime in no way resembles this incident (Fox and Levin, 2001).

Deviance Ownership

Claims-making is not just a matter of seeing particular types of people or behaviour as problems; it is also seeing them as particular *kinds* of problems (Gusfield, 1989). What is at stake is the 'ownership' of the problem: how a problem is framed determines who will be responsible for responding to or dealing with the problem (Sasson, 1995). If problem drinking is understood as a legal problem, we might expect the courts and police to do something about it. If it is understood as a religious problem, then we look to the clergy and theologians for solutions. If it is understood as a medical problem, we turn to doctors and psychiatrists.

One dominant trend in the way we think about deviance solutions concerns *medicalization* (Adler and Adler, 2006; Conrad and Schneider, 1980). Increasingly, we have come to think that many behaviours are forms of medical disorder that require treatment rather than punishment (Dworkin, 2001). More and more, it seems we have come to use the language of sickness, health, and disease when talking about conditions as diverse as violence, gambling, obesity, drug use, underachievement, and rampant consumerism. It can be argued that this shift suggests a more benign approach to deviants, since it implies that individuals are not entirely to blame for their behaviour; the stigma associated with deviant conduct is therefore reduced (Appleton, 1995). At the same time, it can be argued that medicalization encourages us to ignore structural contexts when we think about various kinds of deviance. In other words, medical models imply that these problems occur because individuals 'get sick' and not because social structural conditions make some kinds of behaviour more likely, which would shift some of the responsibility for the condition of the individual onto society in general.

Deviance and Social Conflict

Moral differentiation suggests processes of social conflict. Disagreement exists in society regarding who or what should be seen as disreputable (Hier, 2002). These conflicts are evident in the battle over abortion, the movement to legalize marijuana, and efforts to control cigarette-smoking. In other cases, the conflict is less evident only because effective claims-making has resulted in consensus.

While sociology makes available to us a large number of versions of **conflict theory**, two broad types can be distinguished: conservative and radical (Williams and McShane, 2004). These theories suggest different ways of understanding the wider social dynamic of the claims-making process.

From the perspective of conservative conflict theory, social conflicts regarding the moral meaning of conduct emerge from diverse sources (Turk, 1976; Vold et al.,

2001). As members of various ethnic, religious, professional, lifestyle, or cultural groups seek to pursue their social interests, they may come into conflict with other groups over scarce resources. In the context of such models, **power** is seen as relatively diffuse and thus not concentrated in any one sector of the society (Gusfield, 1963). Instead, various **status groups** come into conflict, often over specific issues. From this perspective, the study of moral differentiation is the study of how some groups in society are able to influence systems of social control so as to allow them to compete more effectively in their struggle to achieve their goals.

The creation of new categories of deviance may facilitate the pursuit of social goals in many different ways. Social control bureaucracies may find that the resources made available to them become more plentiful when they can identify new forms of danger that require control (Becker, 1963; Jenkins, 1994). Alternatively, new or struggling medical specialties can find their social status enhanced if the members of a society become convinced that they are indispensable to the solution of some pressing social problem (Pfohl, 1977).

Often the struggle to define deviance reflects a much more evident cultural difference regarding what is or what is not moral. Contemporary debates over abortion, for instance, can be seen as debates about who will, in the end, get to call whom 'deviant'. Similarly, those whose cultural or religious beliefs lead them to oppose a movement for gay rights may think of gay people as deviants. At the same time, gays and lesbians (and others in society) may think of those who actively (or even violently) oppose the movement for gay rights as suffering from a psychological malady known as *homophobia*. Both examples suggest status struggles over whose moral vision shall prevail and, conversely, over who shall be thought of as deviant.

In contrast, radical conflict theory draws on the Marxian understanding of society (Spitzer, 1975). Thus, it views the economic organization of society as the key to understanding moral stratification. From this point of view, the **social construction** of deviance must be understood as reflecting the economic realities of capitalism and the class exploitation capitalism engenders.

From a Marxian position, the internal logic of capitalism gives deviance both its objective and its subjective character. Capitalism requires a large pool of labour that can be exploited by keeping wages low. But this means that there will always be more workers than jobs and some people inevitably will be marginalized. These marginalized populations will have little stake in the system and will be at greater risk of criminal involvement and of being labelled as criminal.

The Sociology of Deviant Stigma

A third key area of study in the sociology of deviance concerns the ways in which deviant stigmas are applied to people and how stigma is managed (see, for example, Table 5.3). This body of research and theory focuses attention on the social interaction between those who exercise social control and those who are thought of in society as disreputable. In this respect, questions about the application and consequences of deviant stigma tend to be more micro- than macrosociological.

The Process of Labelling

People come to be seen as deviant because of what others believe they have done or what others believe them to be. The labels of 'deviant' that are assigned to people are not benign. Rather, they are charged with a great deal of emotion. Such labels sort through the thousands of acts in which a person has engaged and indicate that the person's identity is best understood in terms of the act according to which the label is affixed (Erikson, 1966).

The assignment of stigma suggests what sociologists refer to as a **master status**. This means that the label of deviant overrides all other status considerations (Becker, 1963). To be known as a murderer, for example, is to possess a status characteristic that trumps any other status characteristics the person might have. Whatever else one might be (bright, interesting, poor, blond, left-handed), one is a murderer first.

Sociologists use the term **status degradation ceremony** to refer to the rituals during which the status of 'deviant' is conferred (Garfinkel, 1956). These ceremonies, like other public ceremonies such as marriage or graduation, publicly and officially acknowledge a shift in social **roles** and the emergence of a new identity. Status degradation ceremonies, including incompetency hearings, psychiatric examinations, and courtroom trials, mark the movement from one social position to another as the individual at the centre of the ritual is officially declared deviant. While we have designed ceremonies to move people into the status of 'deviant', we don't have comparable ceremonies to move them out of these statuses and back to 'normality'.

Resistance to Labelling

Of course, many people do not submit willingly to the imposition of labels of deviance. The ability of some in society to confer the status of 'deviant' on others reflects differentials in social power. When people have access to power resources, they are able to more effectively negotiate the status of 'deviant' (Pfuhl and Henry, 1993). A high-priced legal team can effectively counter-challenge efforts by the state to impose the status of 'deviant'. Plea-bargain negotiations, as the name implies, suggest straightforward attempts to negotiate moral status.

People might use a range of other strategies to avoid or negotiate a label of deviance. One obvious method involves efforts to undermine social control efforts through *evasion*. Such statuses are negotiated most effectively, perhaps, by avoiding their assignment in the first place. 'Successful' deviants learn to engage in prohibited conduct in ways that decrease the likelihood of getting caught (Becker, 1963).

Individuals also try to avoid or negotiate stigma through what Goffman calls *performance* (Goffman, 1959). Many of us are quite explicitly aware of the dramatic roles we might perform if we are stopped by the police officer who suspects we have been speeding; the performance is intended to neutralize the efforts of the police to impose a deviant designation (Piliavin and Briar, 1964). Under some conditions, people use what

Table 5.3	Types of Deviant Behaviour

Howard Becker (1963) suggested that once we recognize that deviant stigma is separable from the deviant act, it is possible to recognize at least four types of deviants. These types are created by the contrast between what people actually do (breaking rules or keeping them) and what they are perceived as (deviant or not deviant).

		Behaviour	
		Obedient	Rule-Breaking
Perception	Perceived as deviant	Falsely accused	Pure deviant
	Not perceived as deviant	Conforming	Secret deviant

HUMAN DIVERSITY
What's in a Name?

Does it matter how we label behaviour? Consider each of the pairs of labels below. In your view, do the labels in each pair refer to the same kinds of behaviour and people or to different kinds of behaviour and people? If they are different, then how are they different?

Terrorist	Freedom Fighter
Prostitute	Sex Worker
Sex Assault Victim	Sex Assault Survivor
Cult Leader	Religious Leader
Disabled	Differently-Abled
Pro-Life	Anti-Choice
Pro-Choice	Pro-Abortion
Addiction	Bad Habit

are called *disclaimer mannerisms*. These are actions intended to signal to agents of social control that they are not the appropriate targets of deviant attribution.

Deviant Careers and Deviant Identities

One potential consequence of the labelling process is what is known as *deviancy amplification*: the ironic situation in which the very attempt to control deviance makes deviance more likely (Lemert, 1951; Tannenbaum, 1938). Efforts to describe how labelling processes result in more rather than less deviance usually distinguish between primary and secondary deviance (Bernberg et al., 2006; Lemert, 1951). *Primary deviance* is the deviance in which we all engage from time to time and that has no real consequence for how we see ourselves or for how other people see us. For instance, all of us from time to time might lie, might cheat, might drink too much, or might engage in some other prohibited behaviour. *Secondary deviance*, in contrast, is marked by a life organized around deviance. Secondary deviance suggests emergence in a deviant role rather than ephemeral acts of deviance. It is one thing to steal on occasion; it is quite another to be a thief. While any of us might tell an occasional lie, most of us do not think of ourselves or are thought of by others as liars.

Some researchers have asked what sometimes turns primary deviance into secondary deviance. The answer is societal reaction. It is argued that the ways in which agents of social control respond to initial acts of deviance— through stereotyping, rejection, and the degradation of status—can actually make future deviance more rather than less likely (Markin, 2005; Tannenbaum, 1938).

One of the key intervening mechanisms in this process, it is argued, is the transformation of the **self**. Consistent with social psychological theories (such as the one advanced by Charles Horton Cooley, 1902) of how the self emerges and is maintained, labelling theorists have argued that individuals who are consistently stigmatized may come to accept others' definition of their deviant identity. To the extent that individuals increasingly come to see themselves as others see them, they may become much more likely to behave in ways that are consistent with the label of 'deviant'. In a sense, individuals become committed to a life of deviance largely because others have expected them to. Deviance becomes a self-fulfilling prophecy (Tannenbaum, 1938).

Managing Stigma

How do those who have been labelled 'deviant' manage these labels? People may employ various strategies that allow them to control information about their deviant identity or to alter the meaning of their stigma so as to reduce the significance of the deviance in their lives (Hathaway, 2004; Park, 2002).

In any discussion of stigma management, it is important to distinguish between the *discreditable* and the *discredited* (Mankoff, 1971). In the former case, we are talking about people who might become discredited if knowledge about their stigma were to become public. In the latter case, the stigma is either evident or it can be assumed to be known.

Because the discreditable and the discredited face different sorts of problems, they have differing options available to them for the management of stigma. For the discreditable, the pressing need is to control information others have about them. If people have a kind of stigma others may not know about, they face the constant worry that others they care about may reject them if information about this stigma becomes public (James and Craft, 2002). Victims of a sexual crime, those suffering from stigmatized diseases, and those who hold unpopular religious beliefs need, in many cases, to keep aspects of their lives secret because they fear the rejection of others.

In other cases, the discreditable may attempt to 'pass'—to fraudulently assume an identity other than the one for which they might be stigmatized. A gay man, for instance, might 'stay in the closet' to allow others to assume that he is 'straight'. An individual whose unpopular political opinions are kept secret may laugh publicly at the jokes directed at people who think the same way that she does.

The discredited face a different problem. Their stigma tends to be apparent, so there is no need to keep it secret. Rather, they need to restrict its relevance to the ways others treat them. One obvious way this might be accomplished is through some form of purification, in which the stigmatized individual attempts to convince others that he or she has left a deviant identity behind (Pfuhl and Henry, 1993). Some sort of redefinition of the self is intended to restrict the interactional relevance of the stigma by locating it in the past. This occurs when stigmatized individuals tell others that they have become religious or that they have 'finally grown up'. One of our contemporary definitions of a hero is someone who has left a deviant stigma behind. Helen Keller and Christopher Reeve, for instance, are thought of as heroic largely because they rose above the stigmatizing character of particular physical conditions.

The discredited may also invoke some collective form of stigma management. This means that individuals who are the bearers of stigma may join together to form some sort of association intent on changing public perceptions of their disvalued character. Organizations intended to 'undeviantize' behaviour have been formed in recent years, including the National Organization for the Reform of Marijuana Laws (NORML) and COYOTE (Call Off Your Old Tired Ethics), which promotes the rights of sex workers. Collective stigma management may involve attempts to influence media coverage of the group in question or the use of terms used to describe members of the group (Bullock and Culbert, 2002). For instance, groups organized around collective stigma management have advocated that the terms 'disabled', 'retarded', and 'AIDS victim' be replaced in popular and official discourse with 'differently abled', 'developmentally delayed', and 'AIDS survivor', respectively (Titchkosky, 2001).

● Conclusion

Our experience with deviance reflects the influence of the cultural context and the historical period in which we live. As times change, so do the categories of people and behaviour society finds troublesome. While gay and lesbian lifestyles were once viewed as highly deviant, today they are seen as less so. While drunk driving, wife assault, and cigarette-smoking were once regarded as normal, they are now viewed as highly deviant. Deviance is thus a dynamic process, and the future will present further permutations and innovations. By way of example, we need think only about the large number of newly constructed forms of deviance that we already associate with computer use, such as cyberporn, cyberstalking, and Internet addiction.

In the most general terms, the sociology of deviance is concerned with the study of the relationships between people who think, act, or appear in disvalued ways and those who seek to control them (Sacco, 1992). It seeks to understand the origins, the character, the consequences, and the broader social contexts of these relationships.

Deviance can be thought of as having two dimensions: the objective and the subjective. The objective aspect is the behaviour, condition, or cognitive style itself. The subjective aspect is the collective understanding of the behaviour, condition, or cognitive style as disreputable. A comprehensive sociology of deviance needs to consider both dimensions. Thus, we want to know why some people rather than others act in ways the society forbids, but we also want to know why some ways of acting rather than others are forbidden.

Correspondingly, it is possible to identify three major types of questions around which theory and research in the sociology of deviance are organized. First, how do we understand the social and cultural factors that make prohibited behaviour possible? Strain theory argues that people engage in deviant behaviour because it is a form of problem-solving; cultural support theories focus on the ways in which people acquire definitions of deviant conduct that are supportive of such behaviour; and control theories maintain that deviance results when the factors that would check or constrain it are absent.

Second, what is and what is not viewed as disreputable is not obvious and there is a need to explain the prevailing system of moral stratification. Definitions of deviance emerge from a process of claims-making. The establishment of consensus around such definitions gives categories of deviance a taken-for-granted quality.

Finally, we need to ask questions about the application and management of deviant stigma. Being labelled 'deviant' is a complex process that creates a large number of problems for the person who is the object of social control attention. It is important, therefore, to understand who gets labelled and how people cope with social control. In particular, we need to be alert to the manner in which the imposition of labels can worsen the very problems that the application of social control is meant to correct.

● Questions ● ● ● ● ● ● for Critical Thought

1. What images of crime and deviance dominate coverage in the local media of the community in which you live? What sorts of images do they create of troubled and troublesome people?

2. In your view, why are young males so much more likely than other groups in society to engage in a range of behaviours that many in society find troublesome?

3. What evidence do you see in your own social environment of the disvalued character of cigarette-smoking and smokers?

4. Aside from the examples given in the text, can you suggest behaviours or conditions that have undergone a shift in moral status in the last few years? How would you account for these changes?

5. How might Marxian and more conservative conflict theorists differ in their interpretations of the legal and moral battle in our society regarding the use of 'soft' illegal drugs, such as marijuana?

6. How might you explain to an interested layperson the difference between the ways in which sociologists think about deviance and the ways in which journalists do?

7. In your opinion, does it make sense to speak of something called 'positive deviance'? Why or why not?

● Recommended ● ● ● ● ● Readings

Francis T. Cullen, John Paul Wright, and Kristie R. Blevins, eds, *Taking Stock: The Status of Criminological Theory* **(Edison, NJ: Transaction, 2007).**

This collection of essays provides a detailed and comprehensive examination of the major varieties of sociological theories of nonconformity. Each of the theories is explained and assessed with respect to available empirical evidence.

John Curra, *The Relativity of Deviance* **(Thousand Oaks, CA: Sage, 2000).**

The aim of this book is to show that deviance cannot be considered an absolute and that what is subject to social control varies by time and place. The analysis of necessity calls into question many common assumptions about the nature of problematic people.

Frederick J. Desroches, *The Crime that Pays: Drug Trafficking and Organized Crime in Canada* **(Toronto: Canadian Scholars' Press, 2005).**

This book offers a systematic and highly readable treatment of the problem of organized drug-trafficking. The author's insightful analysis highlights the social organizational character of this kind of deviant activity.

Erving Goffman, *Stigma: Notes on the Management of Spoiled Identity* **(Englewood Cliffs, NJ: Prentice-Hall, 1963).**

This is the classic discussion of how people who are defined as 'deviants' by the society in which they live manage stigma. The book was formative in the development of the sociology of labels of deviance.

● Recommended ● ● ● ● Websites

Crimetheory.com crimetheory.com

This site provides a very comprehensive discussion of deviance and crime theory for educational and research purposes.

Society for the Study of Social Problems itc.utk.edu/sssp/

This is the main page for the Society for the Study of Social Problems (SSSP). The journal of this society, *Social Problems*, has been very influential in the development of the sociology of deviance.

The Surveillance Project www.queensu.ca/sociology/Surveillance/

This page contains a wealth of information relating to the Queen's University Surveillance Project. The project is concerned with the study of the increasingly large number of technologies and social practices employed for the purpose of social control.

Chapter 6

Class and Status Inequality

Julie Ann McMullin

Learning Objectives

In this chapter, you will:

▶ seek to understand Marxist conceptualizations of social class;

▶ examine Weberian conceptualizations of social class;

▶ differentiate between Marxist and Weberian conceptualizations of social class;

▶ learn about the feminist critique of traditional approaches to the study of social class;

▶ explore the relationship between social class and inequality in paid work, education, and health; and

▶ come to understand why 'class matters'.

● Introduction ● ● ● ● ● ●

Kimberly Rogers was born into a working-class family in Sudbury, Ontario, on 20 July 1961. She was raised by her mother and her stepfather; third in a line of four sisters. At the age of 18, Kimberly left Sudbury for Toronto, where she worked as a waitress, bartender, and receptionist. While working in Toronto, she also went to school and completed her high school diploma.

In 1996, she left Toronto and an abusive relationship, and returned to Sudbury. Upon returning to Sudbury, Kimberly could not find work and applied for social assistance. In the fall of 1996, Kimberly registered in the correctional services workers program at Cambrian College. She later changed programs and continued her studies in the social services program, from which she graduated near the top of her class, in the spring of 2000. By all accounts, she was a model student. As one of her teachers remarked, 'She was such an ambitious student . . . very thorough in her work and very supportive of others, which made her extremely popular with her classmates' (MacKinnon and Lacey, 2001: F1).

In order to pay for her education, Kimberly received student loans while receiving benefits under the general welfare program. This violated Ontario provincial law because the general welfare program does not permit recipients to receive student loans, nor does the Ontario Student Assistance Program (OSAP) permit recipients to receive welfare.

In November 1999, OSAP uncovered the fact that Kimberly had been receiving both OSAP loans and general welfare, and suspended her loan for the remainder of the academic year. Kimberly had to rely on two small grants obtained through the college to pay her tuition and books, and on charity for food. Because of her actions, Kimberly was also unable to benefit from the OSAP loan forgiveness program, and would have to repay the loan in its entirety (approximately $30,000) upon graduation. Ontario Works also began an investigation into Kimberly's actions and, in September 2000, she was charged with welfare fraud.

In April 2001, Kimberly pled guilty to the fraud charge. The judge sentenced her to six months house arrest and required her to pay restitution to welfare for the amount of benefits she received while she was in college, approximately $13,000. Because of her conviction for welfare fraud, Kimberly Rogers was automatically suspended from receiving social assistance for a period of three months. A new regulation, which came into force on 1 April 2000, required that persons convicted of welfare fraud committed prior to 1 April 2000 be suspended for a three- or six-month period, and that persons convicted of welfare fraud committed after 1 April 2000 be subject to a lifetime ban.

As a result of her conviction, Kimberly Rogers was required to stay in her apartment at all times, except for attending medical and religious appointments, and a three-hour period on Wednesday mornings, during which time she could run errands and buy groceries. But Kimberly Rogers had no money to buy the necessities of life. Even after her lawyers succeeded in having the court lift the ban on her benefits, her monthly benefits were reduced to collect a portion of the amount owing under the restitution order. After rent was taken into account, Kimberly Rogers was left with about $18 per month to buy food.

On 9 August 2001, while under house arrest, Kimberly Rogers died. She was eight months pregnant. Sudbury was suffering through a second week of temperatures over 30 degrees Celsius and Kimberly's apartment, which lacked air conditioning, was on the top floor of an old house. Responding to her death, Kimberly's lawyer stated that 'she would have been better off if she had committed a violent crime and been sent to prison. . . . If sentenced to jail, she would have had the necessities of life, she would have had access to medications. If something had happened to her, it wouldn't have been two days before her body was found' (MacKinnon and Lacey, 2001: F1).

On 20 December 2002, after a three-month coroner's inquest into her death, a coroner's jury determined that Kimberly Rogers had committed suicide. The jury heard testimony from an expert witness in suicidology, who explained that the suspension from benefits, the house arrest, the effects of a criminal conviction—which would effectively act as a bar from employment in the social work field—had acted as a crushing weight on Kimberly Rogers's spirit and played a decisive role in the decision to take her own life. At the conclusion of the inquest, the jury issued 14 recommendations, which they felt would prevent future deaths in similar circumstances. The recommendations included that the government remove the 3-month, 6-month, and lifetime bans for conviction of welfare fraud from the legislation, and that it increase welfare rates to reflect the actual costs of shelter and basic needs. Although the government initially refused to make these changes, in 2004 the Ontario government did remove the lifetime and temporary bans for fraud; three- and six-month suspensions are still in place for failure to comply with other rules.

I would like to acknowledge and thank Emily Jovic for her excellent research assistance and critical eye in assisting me with the revisions to this chapter.

Activist groups use Kimberly's death as political leverage in their fight against poverty and inequality. These groups blame the policies of an ultraconservative Ontario government for Kimberly's death. Indeed, the election of Mike Harris and his neo-conservative government in 1995 led to a 21.6 per cent cut to welfare benefits, a radical dismantling of welfare services, the institution of the Ontario Works Act and workfare program, massive cuts to social spending, and the deregulation of labour and other markets (Walkom, 1997). These social policy changes triggered massive protest movements. For instance, the Ontario Federation of Labour (OFL) sponsored Days of Action in most of Ontario's major cities, with participants from women's groups, unions, anti-poverty groups, and others (Munro, 1997). These were political strikes in which workers stayed 'away from their jobs not to make a point during negotiations in their own work-places or for their own contracts, but for the express purpose of making a point with an elected government' (Munro, 1997: 129). Clearly, this was not a government for the working-class people or those who were otherwise disadvantaged. As Kimberly Rogers's experiences demonstrate, this was a government whose policies helped make the rich get richer and the poor get poorer.

Social class, a structural pillar of inequality in Canadian society, influenced Kimberly Rogers's opportunities and experiences from the moment of her birth. It is not unusual, for instance, for people from working-class backgrounds to finish their education at the end of high school and to work at jobs such as bartending; their opportunities for anything else are often severely restricted. That Kimberly needed to rely on social assistance in the first place is also linked to her social class background.

This chapter considers the relationship between social class and inequality. From its inception, social class has been an important concept in sociology. Much has been written on the relationship between social class and politics and **social movements** (Curtis et al., 2004), voting behaviour (Andersen and Heath, 2002), educational attainment (Ali and Grabb, 1998), family (Fox, 2001a; Luxton, 1980), the nature of paid work (Rinehart, 2006), the process of professionalization (Adams, 2000), health (Davies and McAlpine, 1998; Turner and Avison, 2003), income (Allahar and Côté, 1998), **race** (Allahar, 1995), **gender** (Adams, 1998), and retirement (Myles, 1989; Street and Connidis, 2001). Yet, within this body of work, there is considerable debate about what **class** is and how best to conceptualize it. Hence, the first part of this chapter deals with various conceptualizations of social class. Then we consider the ways in which social class has been measured in the sociological literature and get to a working definition of *social class*.

Next we examine the relationship between social class and social inequality. Although many of the topics just listed touch on issues of inequality, it is well beyond the scope of this chapter to discuss all of them. Instead, the focus will be on paid work, education, and health. Finally, I will conclude this chapter by briefly considering an ongoing debate in sociology: Does class matter?

● What Is ● ● ● ● ● ● ● ● Social Class?

Many first-year sociology students are perplexed when they discover that they are not members of the middle class, as they had been led to believe, even though their family income was sufficient to provide them with the necessities of life and a university education. Unlike lay conceptions of social class that focus on income, sociologists define *social class* in relation to the paid work that people do. The general idea that people can be members of the working class without being aware that they are is sometimes referred to as **false consciousness**. Members of the working class who are living in a state of false consciousness have not developed a revolutionary, collective sense of their plight in a capitalist world (Hunter, 1981: 47–8).

As students try to make sense of their 'new' social class, a second thing they learn about is **social structure**. In learning about social structures, students begin to understand that individuals are not poor because they are lazy or stupid but because they are not afforded the same opportunities as others. Social life does not provide a level playing field for its players. Tommy Douglas (then Premier of Saskatchewan) nicely made this point at the beginning of one of his political speeches when he said, '"Everyone for himself", yelled the elephant, as he danced among the chickens' (cited in Hunter, 1981: 211). Kimberly Rogers was a chicken. She was a straight-A student who was an ambitious and hard worker. She died, in part, because she was poor.

Sociologists talk a lot about *social structures* in their work, but there is no single definition of them. Some argue that **social institutions**, such as the family and the educational system, are social structures. Others use the term *social structure* to refer to relatively long-lasting patterns that emerge among elements of society that may or may not be directly observable (Abercrombie et al., 2006). It is in the latter sense that the term **structure** is used in this chapter. Hence, *social structures* refer to how society is organized according to patterns of deeply held **beliefs**, of various **roles** and responsibilities of its mem-

OPEN FOR DISCUSSION
The Lessons of Kimberly Rogers's Death

It was sweltering hot this time last year when Kimberly Rogers, 40 years old and eight months pregnant, died in her Sudbury apartment. She was serving a six-month sentence of house arrest after pleading guilty to defrauding the Ontario Works program (she'd collected welfare while receiving student loans to cover her studies in the social services program at Cambrian College). . . .

What has society learned?

Ontario's welfare rates remain as low as they have been since they were cut by 21.6 per cent in 1995 (there hasn't even been a cost of living adjustment). A single person still receives a maximum of $520 per month.

Just months before Kimberly's death, Ontario introduced further amendments to its social assistance laws. Now, for anyone convicted of welfare fraud committed after April, 2000, there is a lifetime ban. Those convicted can never receive welfare again. Ever. Not even if they need it to survive. The fiscal savings that result from clamping down on welfare remain a greater political priority to government than the lives of citizens who are left without shelter and food.

And the Ontario government is still crowing about the success of 'workfare' in helping welfare recipients return to work. But the reality is different: Instead of integrating people into the new, knowledge-based economy, workfare is geared toward pushing people into low-paying, insecure jobs.

Still, some things have changed.

Opposition to the province's treatment of welfare recipients is growing. To date, 10 Ontario municipalities have passed resolutions to oppose the lifetime ban. Recently, the Court of Appeal determined that the province can't discriminate against welfare recipients simply because they are welfare recipients and dependent on government programs for support—in other words, a government does not have carte blanche to impose stricter conditions on welfare recipients than any other citizen. And later this year the Ontario Superior Court will consider the cases of three people who are appealing their lifetime welfare-benefit bans.

What the government did to Kimberly Rogers, it did in the name of Ontario's citizens. So her case forces all citizens to think about what kind of society we want. One that truly gives us all opportunities to participate in all aspects of society? Or one that condemns the most vulnerable to die alone? We cannot ignore these questions even if we wish to: An inquest into Kimberly Rogers's death is set to begin Oct. 7.

Source: Excerpted from JoAnne Frenschkowski, 'We've Learned Little from Kimberly Rogers's Death', *The Globe and Mail*, 9 Aug. 2002. Reprinted by permission of JoAnne Frenschkowski, staff lawyer, Income Advocacy Centre.

bers, and of sets of social behaviours. Social class may then be considered a social structure because our positioning within the social class system organizes and influences everything that we do. This idea will be developed throughout this chapter, but for now it is important to understand that the terms *social class* and *social structure* are highly interrelated.

Debates about how best to conceptualize social class stem from the sociological traditions of Karl Marx and Max Weber, both of whom arguably might be considered **conflict theorists**. The next sections consider these debates and outline the key themes that emerge from conflict and feminist accounts of social class.

Themes from Conflict Approaches to Social Class

Many of the debates about how to conceptualize social class stem from the work of Karl Marx and the subsequent critiques and elaborations of his views. Interestingly, although Marx discussed social class at length in his work, nowhere in his writings did he provide us with a succinct

Much inequality theory, from Marx to Weber, discusses the proletariat, or working class, but few people realize the devastating and long-lasting effects of such labour ghettoization. This working-class residence, close to Nova Scotia's defunct Sydney steel mill, captures the devastation. The Canadian Press/Andrew Vaughn

definition of what he meant by *social class*. Instead, scholars have had to piece together what they think he meant by the term from the various contexts in which Marx uses the concept. A now-famous quotation from the *Communist Manifesto* is often used in such assessments. Marx and Friedrich Engels (1983 [1848]: 203–4) wrote:

> The history of all hitherto existing society is the history of class struggles. Freeman and slave, patrician and plebeian, lord and serf, guild-master and journeyman, in a word, oppressor and oppressed. . . . Our epoch, the epoch of the bourgeoisie, possesses, however, this distinctive feature: It has simplified class antagonisms. Society as a whole is more and more splitting up into two great hostile camps, into two great classes directly facing each other—bourgeoisie and proletariat.

In these few lines, Marx emphasizes two issues that are central to his work on social class: first, he argues that society is characterized more by conflict than by harmony; second, he suggests that a distinctive feature of **capitalism** is the segregation of society into two central classes.

Few conflict theorists would disagree with Marx's view that society is characterized more by conflict than by harmony. Since the onset of industrial capitalism, workers and owners have fought over working conditions, pay, benefits, required hours of work, and so on (MacDowell and Radforth, 1992; Morton, 1998). Today, struggles continue over job security within the context of globalized economies and the rights of workers in **developing countries**.

The point on which scholars disagree is whether Marx's dichotomous conception of class is—or ever

▮▮▮ Time to Reflect ▮▮▮▮▮▮▮▮▮▮▮▮▮▮▮▮▮▮▮▮

Should Canadians blame individuals for their poverty or should society take some responsibility for ensuring a reasonable standard of living for all?

was—accurate. Some argue that these two basic class divisions still exist (Braverman, 1974), while others suggest that Marx's two-class conceptualization needs elaboration (Wright, 1997). Still others argue that Marx's two-category system was simply a theoretical abstraction and that he was well aware of the presence of middling classes and of the historical complexities of class formation (Giddens, 1971). Although such debates are interesting, they are complex and, as yet, unresolved. Hence, rather than delving into debates about how many classes there currently are in Canada, it is more fruitful to discuss the themes that are central to Marxist conceptualizations of social class.

First, Marx and Marxists argue that class is a social relation. Marx believed that society is divided into social classes that are defined by their relationship to the principal **means of production** in society (Giddens, 1971; Zeitlin, 1990). *Relations of production* refers to the idea that individuals who engage in production processes have various rights and powers over the resources that are used in production processes (see Wright, 1999). Under capitalism, those who own the means of the production (the **bourgeoisie**) exploit labourers (the **proletariat**), who have little choice but to sell their **labour power** to the bourgeoisie in order to survive. For Marx, class is not an economic relation but a social one. Hence, unequal access to the rights and powers associated with productive resources are class relations (Wright, 1999).

A second feature of Marxist accounts of class relations concerns who controls production processes (Poulantzas, 1975; Wright, 1997). *Control* refers to a specific form of authority. **Authority**, in turn, is connected to issues of **power**. More will be said on power as we move into a discussion of Weberian accounts of social class. For now, it is important to note that class relations reflect the amount of control that people have, over themselves and others, in doing the work that they do to achieve their means of subsistence. In other words, class relations reflect the relative amount of control that a person has over production processes.

Third, Marxists generally agree that **exploitation** is a central component of social class relations. According to Eric Olin Wright (Wright, 1997: 10), class-based exploitation occurs if the following criteria are met:

1. *The inverse interdependence principle*. The material welfare of one group of people causally depends upon the material deprivations of another.
2. *The exclusion principle*. The inverse interdependence in (1) depends upon the exclusion of the exploited from access to certain productive resources, usually backed by property rights.

3. *The appropriation principle*. Exclusion generates material advantage to exploiters because it enables them to appropriate the labor effort of the exploited.

If the first of these two conditions are met, 'non-exploitative economic oppression' (Wright, 1999: 11) occurs, but it is not technically a situation of class exploitation as such. Exploitation exists only when all three principles are operating simultaneously.

Note the relational component in each of these exploitation principles. Explicit in these statements is the idea that class exploitation involves **social interaction**. This interaction is structured by sets of productive social relations that serve to bind exploiters to the exploited (Wright, 1997). Class exploitation also highlights the presence of inherent conflict in class relations. Put simply, in a profit-driven capitalist system, owners want their workers to work longer and harder than the workers would freely choose to do. Hence, class conflict results, not simply over wage levels, but also over how much 'work effort' is expected (Wright, 1997: 18).

In summary, Marxist accounts of social class focus on the relationships between those who appropriate the labour of others to make a profit and those who need to sell their labour power. Furthermore, class relations may be assessed through the concepts of exploitation and control. As we have noted, control is related to power. Hence, one similarity between Marxist and Weberian scholarship, as we shall see, is that both schools agree that power is a central dimension of class relations. Weberians, however, have a somewhat different understanding of power than do Marxists, and Weberians focus more on distribution than on exploitation in their assessment of social class.

For Weber, classes are groups of people who share a common class situation. In *Economy and Society*, Weber (1978 [1908]: 57) defines *class situation* as:

> . . . [the] typical chances of material provision, external position, and personal destiny in life which depend on the degree and nature of the power, or lack of power, to dispose of goods or qualifications for employment and the ways in which, within a given economic order, such goods or qualifications for employment can be utilised as a source of income or revenue.

For Weber, class situations are market situations, and 'a class is simply an aggregate of people sharing common "situations" in the market' (Grabb, 2007: 48).

Weber further argues that there are three types of classes: property classes, income classes, and social classes. A *property class* is one in which differences in property ownership determine class situations. An *income class* is one in which 'the chances of utilising goods or services on the market determines the class situation' (Weber, 1978 [1908]: 57). A *social class* is a combination of the class situations created by property and income, whereby mobility between the social classes is a typical occurrence within either an individual lifetime or over successive generations.

Weber identified four main social classes: (1) the working class as a whole; (2) the petite bourgeoisie; (3) property-less intellectuals, technicians, commercial workers, and officials who may be socially different from one another depending on the cost of their training; and (4) classes privileged because of property or education. Although these social class distinctions are similar to those put forth by Marx (except with regard to the emphasis on education and the cost of training), Weber employs a different method in assigning groups of individuals to each class. For Weber, the emphasis is on the distribution of resources, whereas Marx is mainly concerned with the social relations of production.

Parties and **status groups** are other pillars of social power according to Weber. By *parties*, Weber means voluntary associations that organize for the collective pursuit of interests, such as political parties or lobbying groups. **Status** reflects an individual's position in society according to the relative prestige, esteem, or honour they are afforded (Clark, 1995; Turner, 1988). Samuel Clark argues that status varies along four dimensions: differentiation, criteria, ascription, and institutionalization. The meanings of these variables are summarized in Table 6.1.

Notably, Clark argues that status is a form of power—the 'power to elicit respect' (Clark, 1995: 15). A *status group* comprises a number of individuals who share a common status situation. Status groups 'are organized to maintain or expand their social privileges by a mechanism of social closure to protect existing monopolies of the privilege against outsiders, and by usurpation to expand the benefits by reference to proximate or superior status groups' (Turner, 1988: 8). Thus, aristocrats and the Hells Angels both are examples of status groups. Although members of a particular class may not be aware of their common situation, members of a status group usually are (Giddens, 1971; Grabb, 2007). And although classes, status groups, and parties sometimes overlap, this is not always the case. In Weberian scholarship, each is analytically distinct and central to class analysis (Weber, 1978 [1908]; see also Giddens, 1971; Grabb, 2007).

Weber's assessment of status groups and parties and the analytical importance that he attaches to these multiple bases of **power** point to the fundamental difference between his analysis of class and that of Marx. According to Weber, although status groups and parties are analytically distinct from classes, they are central to class analysis (Giddens, 1971; Grabb, 2007). For Weber, *status situations* are distinct but related to class situations; this term refers to the social status, prestige, and esteem that are associated with a social position. Unlike Marx, who believed that power is held by those who own the means of production, Weber felt that certain people in high-status groups derive power by virtue of their social position rather than through economic control.

The analytical importance that Weber attaches to the concept of power is evident in the preceding discussion. Unlike Marx, who believed that power relations are structural and cannot be separated from class relations, Weber defines *power* as 'every possibility within a social relationship of imposing one's own will, even against opposition, without regard to the basis of this possibility' (1978 [1908]: 38).

He goes on to clarify this broad definition of *power* by introducing the concept of *domination*. Domination exists in **social relationships** in which one actor (or

Table 6.1	Samuel Clark's Status Variables
Differentiation	The extent to which status is differentiated from other kinds of power, especially economic, cultural, political, and military power.
Criteria	What characteristics or possessions are accorded status (for example, wealth, erudition, military valour, athletic ability).
Ascription	Whether status is ascribed hereditarily.
Institutionalization	The extent to which stable norms and values regulate the distribution of status and the rights and duties associated with it.

Source: Samuel Clark, *State and Status: The Rise of the State and Aristocratic Power in Western Europe* (Montreal and Kingston: McGill-Queen's University Press, 1995), 17. Reprinted by permission.

group of actors) comes to expect that his or her orders will be followed by others or a group of others. *Domination* is a specific power relation in which 'regular patterns of inequality are established whereby the subordinate group (or individual) accepts that position in a sustained arrangement, obeying the commands of the dominant group (or individual)' (Grabb, 2007: 56). Weber states that although relations of domination are usually at work within associations or in cases in which an individual has an executive staff, other non-economic situations are also characteristic of relations of domination. One of the examples Weber mentions in this regard is that the head of the household exercises domination over the members of the household 'even though he does not have an executive staff' (1978 [1908]: 39).

Three themes emerge from Weber's conceptualization of class that separate his work from that of Marx. The first is Weber's insistence that classes, class situations, parties, and status groups must all be considered if we are to understand the class structures of societies and in this he differs significantly from Marx's view. The second is Weber's emphasis on and view of power. Marx felt that power was derived from an economic base and was largely structural. Weber, on the other hand, saw power as a multi-faceted concept that could be derived from many sources and has both structural and individual dimensions. Finally, unlike the social-relational approach to class in Marxist sociology, Weber focuses far more on distributional issues. For Weber, the ability of people to gain access to scarce resources such as income and education is central to class analysis.

Drawing on Weberian scholarship, Canadian sociologist Edward Grabb's work on social inequality and social class is worth considering. According to Grabb power is the 'differential capacity to command resources, which gives rise to structured asymmetric relations of domination and subordination among social actors' (2007: 211). In an elaborate scheme of power, domination, and social inequality, Grabb suggests that there are three means of power—control of material resources, control of people, and control of ideas—which correspond primarily with economic structures, political structures, and ideological structures respectively (see Figure 6.1). These structures of power are intersected by class and non-class bases of inequality that represent the 'human content' of power relations.

Grabb defines *class* on the basis of ownership, education, and occupation. For Grabb, these factors represent

Figure 6.1 Edward Grabb's Theoretical Framework on Social Inequality

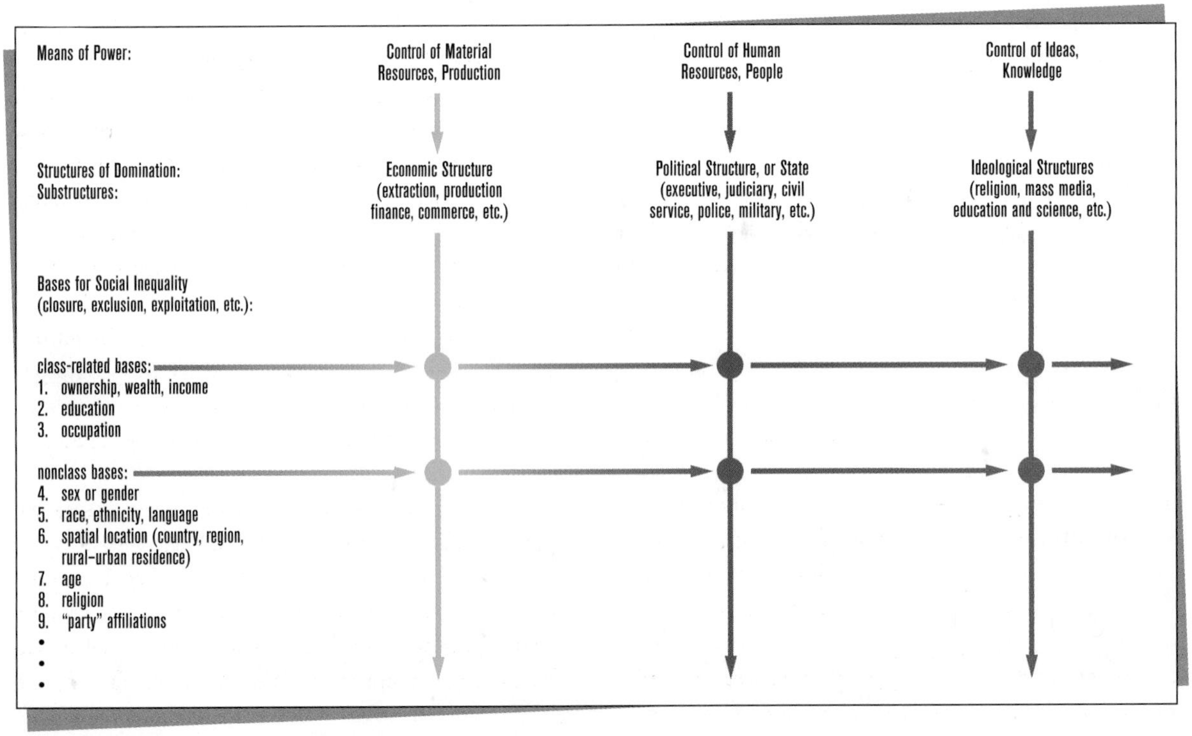

Source: 'The Major Means of Power, Structures of Domination, and Bases for Social Inequality' from *Theories of Social Inequality*, Fourth Edition, by Edward Grabb. © 2002. Reprinted with permission of Nelson, a division of Thomson Learning: www.thomsonrights.com. Fax 800-730-2215.

a synthesis of the key concepts in class analysis. *Owner-ship* includes ownership of property but also material possessions and income. *Education* comprises credentials and knowledge. *Occupation* includes distinctions such as manual versus non-manual labour, but also includes issues of skill. Grabb further suggests that, although classes should not be considered in static terms because they vary over time and space (that is, historically and in different regions and countries), there tend to be three main class categories in modern capitalist systems: an upper class, a heterogeneous central category, and a working class. He defines the *working class* as those who do not own capital, who have no special skills or creden-tials, and who sell their labour to make a living. The *upper class* is made up mostly of capital owners, although individuals with significant political or ideological power fall into this category as well. The *middle class* is a diverse group that may or may not have limited owner-ship but that is mostly distinguishable from the working class on the basis of credentials.

According to Grabb, the means of power (economic, political, and ideological) are differentially distributed along class lines. Of course, people in the upper classes control the means of material production or the eco-nomic structure by virtue of their ownership of the means of production. Middle classes may have some economic power depending on whether their incomes are sufficient to purchase desirable consumer goods and to the extent that their occupation confers upon them a certain amount of authority or autonomy. And working classes tend not to have economic power at all. In Grabb's scheme, class also crosses political and ideologi-cal structures of power. Hence, those in the upper class, by virtue of their capital, high levels of education, and good occupations, tend to control political and ideolog-ical institutions such as the judiciary and educational systems. Those in the working class tend not to have ide-ological or political power, and those in the middle vary in the extent to which they hold such power, again on the basis of class-related factors.

Grabb's work holds a great deal of appeal to those who assume that Marxist conceptions of social class do not go far enough in explaining social inequality and that social inequality is, instead, a multi-faceted phe-nomenon. Why? Because the central focus in his frame-work is on power, not class. The inherent problem with theories of inequality that begin with issues of class is that other bases of inequality, such as gender, race, **eth-nicity**, and age, carry less theoretical significance. Indeed, **feminist** scholarship has been critical of the lit-erature on social class for this reason.

Feminist Approaches to Social Class

Many theorists have worked to perfect the concept of social class. Researchers strive for a specific delineation of social class that corrects what they see as limitations in the classical work. But except among feminist sociologists and a few others (for example, Carroll, 1987; Cuneo, 1985), the exclusion of women and gender from class analysis has not traditionally been considered a theoretical limitation. Rather, if the social class of women is mentioned at all, it has been assessed using categories of analysis that were established to study men (Fox, 1989). Unwaged wives are assumed to take on their husband's social class, whereas women involved in the paid labour force are classed like men in what is assumed to be a gender-neutral class sys-tem (Acker, 1980, 1988, 1990; Fox, 1989).

Indeed, gender relations are intertwined with class relations in modern industrial capitalism. Particularly telling are the following research findings:

1. Housework and child care, which women are prima-rily responsible for, are productive activities that are important for capitalist production (Fox, ed., 1980). Hence, 'ignoring gender relations in general, and household labour in particular, produces distorted analyses of "the economy"' (Fox, 1989: 123).
2. Women are segregated into low-paying jobs both across and within broad occupational classifications (Bielby and Baron, 1984; Fox and Fox, 1986, 1987).
3. This segregation cannot be explained by status-attain-ment variables (England, 1982; England et al., 1988).
4. Often, the relations between men and women at work are antagonistic (Cockburn, 1983; Milkman, 1987).
5. The responsibilities that women have to their fami-lies are inextricably bound to their work lives: wives are more likely than husbands to work at home or to take time off from work to care for a sick child (Hochschild and Machung, 1989; Michelson, 1983), and their wages are influenced by the amount of time they spend engaged in household labour (Coverman, 1983; Shelton and Firestone, 1989).

Although this research demonstrates the prevalence of gender inequality within capitalism, feminists disagree over how these findings should be interpreted. Specifi-cally, there is a theoretical debate among feminists over whether **patriarchy** (male dominance) and capitalism are two systems of oppression that serve to subordinate women (this is called *dual-systems theory*) or whether women's oppression can be best understood by theorizing about a single system of inequality that simultaneously considers gender and social class relations. Patriarchy, an essential concept in dual-systems theories (see Hartmann, 1981), is at the heart of the feminist debates over the appropriateness of single and dual-systems approaches.

Patriarchy refers to 'the system of practices, arrangements and social relations that ensure biological reproduction, child rearing, and the reproduction of gendered subjectivity' (Fox, 1988: 175). The term *patriarchy* and the study of it has served a useful purpose in feminist theory because it gave women (although arguably only white, middle-class women) a political voice and also because it corrected some of the flaws of omission that were prevalent in social theory before the 1970s (that is, women were generally invisible; Acker, 1989). However, the concept of patriarchy is limiting in several respects.

Radical feminists conceptualize patriarchy as a 'universal, trans-historical and trans-cultural phenomenon; women were everywhere oppressed by men in more or less the same ways' (Acker, 1989: 235). The tendency in this view is to reduce male oppression of women to biological essentialism, and it is limiting because it does not consider historical or contemporary variations in women's situations (Acker, 1989). In light of these problems, dual-systems theorists attempted to conceptualize a system of patriarchy that was linked to household production. The tendency in this approach was to view patriarchy as a system of domination that operates alongside and interacts with the political-economic system. The roots of patriarchy are thought to be located within the reproductive sphere of the family, whereas the roots of the political-economic system are located in the **mode of production** (Acker, 1989; Fox, 1989). Thus, although surprising given its Marxist roots, this perspective considers gender in a more Weberian manner, as one of several sources of inequality.

Recognizing these problems, some feminists have argued against using the concept of patriarchy (Acker, 1989; Fox, 1988). These researchers argue for a single-system approach whereby the oppression of women cannot be separated from issues of social class. This requires a reconceptualization of social class that adequately considers gendered processes as they structure the class system (Acker, 1988, 1990; Fox, 1989).

Taking issue with dual-systems theory, Joan Acker sets out to develop a single-system theory of social relations that places equal emphasis on gender and social class. According to Acker, this requires a reformulation of Marx's conception of class that is best done by taking the social relations of distribution as well as the social relations of production into account. Relations of distribution 'are sequences of linked actions through which

people share the necessities of survival' (Acker, 1988: 478). According to Acker, the fact that there has always been a sexual division of labour suggests that in all known societies, the relations of distribution are influenced by gender and take on a gendered meaning. Gendered relations of distribution in capitalist society are historically rooted and they are transformed (like the relations of production) as the means of production change.

Acker suggests that the wage, which is rooted in the relations of production, is the essential component of distribution in capitalist society. The wage has developed historically as a gendered phenomenon because women have always been paid less than men and because gendered job segregation is typical. Thus, 'the wage and the work contexts within which it is earned are gendered in ways that re-create women's relative disadvantage' (Acker, 1988: 483).

Personal relations, marital relations, and state relations are the gendered processes through which distribution occurs. According to Acker, *personal relations of distribution* are held together by emotional bonds, usually between blood relatives, and are dependent on the wage. As a result of both the gender-based division of labour and the **ideology** of the family wage, gender serves to organize the personal relations of distribution. In its simplest form, this system requires that at least part of the male wage is distributed to women, who then redistribute it to the dependents in their families. The personal relations of distribution also often extend beyond the household. In instances where economic hardships are typical, women often maintain extensive kinship networks by means of which survival is ensured through the allocation of resources across households. Among the economically advantaged, gender-based personal relations of distribution also occur, helping to ensure the stability and reproduction of class.

Marital relations are the central component of distribution for married women who do not work for pay and are thus dependent on their husbands for their wage. According to Acker, unwaged housewives are connected to the production process through their husbands' wages. Although they share common standards of living with their husbands, they do not assume the same class because their situations, experiences, and activities are different. Unwaged wives have little control over their economic situation, although Acker suggests that this control likely varies by the men's and women's class.

State relations of distribution are the final type of distribution arrangement that Acker considers. The state relations of distribution are based in laws and governmental policies that have historically been developed in gendered ways. Policies and laws, established to alleviate the financial burden of the working class when the market fails, are based on gendered ideologies supporting the 'male breadwinner/dependent housewife' ideal. This renders some groups of women—those who remain unmarried, single mothers, poor working women—particularly disadvantaged. Women are further disadvantaged by the gendered nature of entitlement regulations because many social security programs are based on the labour force experiences of men.

For Acker, the culmination of these gendered relations structures social class. Conceptualizing class in this way allows unwaged persons to be included in the class structure. According to Acker, the aim of class analysis should not be to classify people into different categories; rather, class should be considered as 'processes that produce contradiction, conflict, and different life experiences' (1988: 496). Thus, to fully understand the 'links between gender and class, divisions must be changed. One way to do this is to see class as rooted in relations of distribution (as well as in relations of production) that necessarily embed gender, both as ideology and material inequality' (1988: 496).

Acker (2000) expands her analysis to include race and ethnic relations. Acker argues that to fully understand how class is gendered and racialized, a rethinking of class is necessary. This rethinking, according to Acker, should be informed first by a concept of class anchored within a larger notion of the economic than is now used' (2000: 54). This idea corresponds with Acker's promotion of a conceptualization of class whereby class relations encompass relations of distribution and production. Second, class, gender, race, and ethnicity must be understood from the standpoints of many different people within these categories (see Smith, 1987). In other words, the experiences of men and women of different classes and of different racial and ethnic groups need to inform class analysis. Third, class is not simply an abstraction into which people can be placed. Rather, it is an 'active accomplishment' (Acker, 2000: 53). Everything that people do and say is influenced by their class relations. Class is accomplished by people in interaction with one another. And fourth, class, race and ethnicity, and gender mutually constitute one another. That is, through structural processes and through processes of cultural representation and social interaction, race and ethnicity, class, and gender shape one another; they cannot be considered separately. **Identity** and meaning are not shaped simply by whether one is not a man or black or middle class, but by the interacting influence of all three of these things (see also Glenn, 2000).

To summarize, a central problem in much of the traditional class analysis and the key point of the feminist critique of social class is that the study of class has focused far too much on the relations of production (Acker, 1988, 2000). Feminist scholars argue that class relations are social relations that extend beyond the arena of production and that Marxist approaches that conceptualize social class simply as a relation of production are too restrictive. This is true, in part, because traditional class analysis excludes far too many people who are not directly linked to production processes, such as homemakers and retired individuals. Notably, scholars have tried to reconcile this problem by attributing the social class of homemakers to husbands and by assigning a class to retired persons based on their pre-retirement status. However, these approaches are unsatisfactory because they do not capture important distributive and status differences between a housewife and her husband or between a retired autoworker and her employed counterpart (see Acker, 1988; Estes, 1999).

With these caveats in mind, the remainder of this chapter will nonetheless focus on social class as it has been traditionally defined and conceptualized. The difficulties associated with rethinking social class in light of gender, race, ethnic, and age relations are far too complex for an introductory chapter on social class and inequality. Readers should refer to the chapters on gender, ethnicity, and race for more detail about how these factors structure social inequality.

● Defining and ● ● ● ● ● Measuring Social Class

Researchers study social class using both quantitative and qualitative methods. Qualitative approaches to social class often draw on the insights of **symbolic interactionism** and place emphasis on issues of meaning, experience, and identity. Such assessments do not attempt to succinctly categorize people into various classes but instead are concerned with the meaning, identity, and experiences of one class in relation to another. Qualitative historical work, for instance, has examined processes of class formation (Comninel, 1987) and how class relations structure professionalization projects (Adams, 1998, 2000). Using observation or in-depth interviewing techniques, other studies have explored the meaning and experiences of class relations in workplaces (Gannagé, 1986; Reiter, 1996; Rinehart et al., 1994) and in schools (Willis, 1977).

Quantitative work on social class tends to focus either on how class affects various outcomes of social inequality or on how the class structure has changed over time. Social class is defined differently depending on which of these particular focuses is at the heart of the research. In work on social inequality, for instance, proxies of social class (that is, such factors as income, education, and occupation that indirectly measure social class) tend to be used.

Social stratification approaches to social class have been very influential, particularly in American sociology. Stratification approaches conceptualize inequality as a hierarchical order (Davis and Moore, 1945) in which individuals are grouped into strata on the basis of their socio-economic status (SES) as measured through indicators such as income, education, or occupation. As a result, inequality tends to be conceptualized at the level of individual difference rather than in relational terms or on the basis of class structures (Grabb, 2007; Tilly, 1998).

Traditionally, stratification approaches have assumed that the rank ordering of people into socially defined strata is a universal and functionally necessary dimension of society (Davis and Moore, 1945). In other words, an ordering of people according to their worth, variously defined, is required for the smooth functioning of society. Certain positions in society are more valued than others because of the high level of skill that is attached to them. Only a few people can attain the skills required to fulfill these positions, and such attainment requires significant time commitment for the appropriate training. People who choose to invest the time in such training deserve higher-status positions in society and the resultant rewards attached to these positions. Furthermore, there is general agreement or consensus among the members of society that such stratification systems are acceptable (Davis and Moore, 1945).

There are two underlying assumptions in stratification research that set it apart from the Marxist or Weberian approaches to inequality. First is the tendency in stratification research to overemphasize the extent to which society operates on the basis of consensus rather than conflict. Second, and related to the first, is the under-emphasis in stratification research on issues of power and exploitation (see Grabb, 2007, for an extensive discussion of these issues).

The identification of problematic assumptions in stratification research has not, however, led to its demise. Stratification research has been influential in studies of inequality and informs much empirical research on the subject. Michael Grimes (1991) argues that many researchers apply stratification measures to the study of

class inequality either because they remain committed to certain aspects of functionalist thought or because stratification measures are often used in large surveys. It is important to clarify that stratification researchers do not suggest that they are studying class; class researchers, although they sometimes do stratification research, make the distinction between the two (Grabb, 2007). It is also important to clarify that regardless of one's theoretical perspective, quantitative measures associated with stratification research reveal much about social inequality.

The point that Grimes makes is nonetheless an important one and stems, perhaps, from a more general observation that researchers whose primary interest lies outside of class and stratification analysis tend to convolute the two approaches. This propensity is most likely a result of the significant overlap between the various social factors that are examined in these approaches. For instance, occupation, defined in various ways, tends to be at the core of research on social class regardless of theoretical or methodological perspective. Further, there is a general concern in all conceptual frameworks about the distribution of scarce resources such as income, education, and skill. Hence, the tendency to use stratification measures as indicators of social class likely stems from the continued use of traditional measurements in survey research and also from the fact that the indicators of social class are quite similar, *regardless of theoretical perspective.*

There is little doubt that stratification measures tell us something about class-based inequality. However, these indicators cannot fully capture the extent to which social class matters in contemporary Canadian society. Instead, a relational understanding of social class is necessary. Such an understanding of social class follows a long tradition in Marxist sociology that suggests that class is not merely an economic relation. Rather, social class manifests itself as people from various classes interact with one another in productive relations. Researchers who are concerned with the macro implications of the organization of the social relations of production **operationalize** social class using concepts such as power, exploitation, oppression, property ownership, and so on that are central in Marxist and Weberian scholarship.

Wright's work is an example of how social class can be assessed quantitatively in this way. For the past 20 years, Wright and his colleagues have been developing a typology of social class that relies on measures of occupation, authority, skill, and the number of employees who work at a particular locale (see Figure 6.2). This latter classification category reflects the number of people who are under the authority of each particular class location. For example, managers tend to have many employees over which they have authority and dominance, while non-managers have authority over no one. Owners are separated from employees in this scheme and are differentiated from one another only on the basis of how many employees they have. Hence, owners who have only a few employees are thought to be different from those who have many and from those who have none. Employees, on the other hand, are differentiated on the basis of number of other employees, skills, and authority. Expert managers have high levels of authority and of skill and tend to supervise many employees. They stand in most stark contrast to non-skilled workers, who have no authority or skill and who supervise no employees.

In this typology, the cells do not represent classes as such, but rather refer to class locations within the capitalist class structure. The distinction here is a subtle but important one that allows Wright to cover all of his bases. Unlike an earlier version of this framework, in which he refers to the various groupings in this model as classes (Wright, 1985), in his more recent work (Wright,

1997, 1999) he makes it clear that these cells represent class locations within an overriding framework of class relations. By doing this, Wright can stay true to a Marxist version of class relations in which exploitation is at the core, and at the same time identify contradictory places within class relations that individuals occupy.

Class has thus been used in many ways in sociological thought. For the purpose of this chapter, stratification measures will be used to assess the relationship between social class and each of income, education, and health. To assess class structure, a modified, more parsimonious version of Wright's conceptualization, as it is put forth by Wallace Clement and John Myles (1994) will be used. Clement and Myles develop a four-class model in which the *capitalist-executive class* controls both the labour power of others and the means of production (see Table 6.2). The *old middle class*—the 'petite bourgeoisie' in Marxist terminology—commands the means of production but not the labour power of others. The *new middle class* controls the labour power of others

Figure 6.2   Eric Olin Wright's Class Divisions

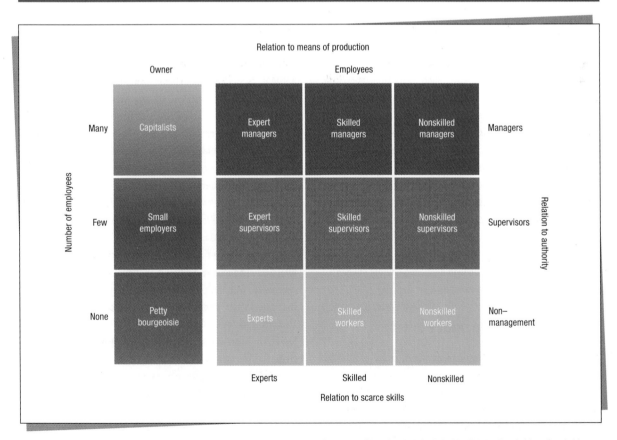

Table 6.2   Clement and Myles's Conceptualization of Social Class

	Command Labour Power of Others	
Command Means of Production	Yes	No
Yes	Capitalist-executive	Old middle class
No	New middle class	Working class

Source: Wallace Clement and John Myles, *Relations of Ruling: Class and Gender in Postindustrial Societies* (Montreal: McGill-Queen's University Press, 1994), 16. Reprinted by permission of the publisher.

but not the means of production. And, finally, the *working class* commands neither the labour power of others nor the means of production. The advantage of this approach to social class lies in its simplicity; it accurately reflects the 'relations of ruling' in Canada while at the same time eliminating the unnecessary and often tedious class location distinctions that are contained within Wright's approach.

● Social Class ● ● ● ● ●
and Inequality

Social inequality reflects relatively long-lasting differences between individuals or groups of people that have substantial implications for individual lives, especially 'for the rights or opportunities they exercise and the rewards or privileges they enjoy' (Grabb, 2007: 1; see also Pampel, 1998). So, for example, people who are a part of the working class earn less money, have less fulfilling jobs, do not have the same educational opportunities available to them, and have worse health than do people from the middle and upper classes. The next sections consider the relationship between social class and each of paid work, education, and health.

Paid Work, Income, and Poverty

Marx argued that as capitalism evolved, there would be an increasing polarization of workers into two central classes, the proletariat and the bourgeoisie. This polarization would involve at least three things: (1) a reduction in the proportion of small business owners and hence a shrinking of the old middle class; (2) increasing proportions of income going to the owners of large businesses and a reduction in the earnings of middle-class workers; and (3) continued deskilling of work and cor-

responding increases in the alienation of workers (Conley, 2004). We will consider each of these issues.

Class Structure in Canada

According to Clement and Myles's definition of social class, a slight majority of employed Canadians in the early 1980s formed the working class (57.6 per cent); almost 25 per cent formed the new middle class, 11.3 per cent the old middle class, and 6.2 per cent the capitalist-executive class (1994: 19).

Since the early twentieth century, the proportion of Canada's class structure comprising small business owners has declined considerably (Clement and Myles, 1994). Between the 1930s and the early 1970s, for instance, the proportion of the workforce comprising small business owners declined from approximately 25 per cent to between 10 and 12 per cent (Conley, 2004). Much of this decline occurred in the agricultural sector, where advances in farm technology made small-farm business unprofitable (Clement and Myles, 1994; Conley, 2004). Nonetheless, for much of the twentieth century it appeared that Marx's prediction regarding the shrinking middle class was right.

Since the mid-1970s, however, this trend has reversed. Indeed, the most significant change in the class structure over the past 20 years in particular has been the increase in the proportion of the class structure held by the old middle class. Clement and Myles report that the level of non-agricultural self-employment increased from 5.8 per cent in 1975 to 7.4 per cent in 1990 (1994: 42). When self-employed owners of incorporated businesses are included in this measure, the old middle class made up about 14 per cent of the total labour force in the early 1980s (Lin et al., 1999: 15). By 2008, 15 per cent of the total labour force was self-employed in both incorporated and unincorporated businesses (Statistics Canada, 2008). The majority of those who are self-employed either work on their own or hire fewer than three employees (Clement and Myles, 1994: 49; Hughes, 1999; Statistics Canada, 2006k).

Reactions to recent increases in the proportion of employed Canadians who primarily constitute the old middle class have been mixed. On the one hand, some hail these changes as positive. According to this school of thought, small business owners are free of the control of large capitalist enterprises and as a result have more autonomy in their work. Their conditions of work are less alienating, and this is a positive development of post-industrial capitalism. Others have argued that, far from being a positive occurrence, the rise of small business owners is the result of workplace restructuring whereby workers lose their jobs and are forced to earn a living without some of the rewards (such as pensions and benefits) that are associated with employment in large companies (see Clement and Myles, 1994, for an overview of these opinions). This suggests that the conditions under which one becomes a small business owner are important considerations when discussing the social implications associated with higher proportions of workers in the 'old' middle class.

Income and Poverty

There is a strong correlation between social class and income. Working-class jobs pay less than middle-class jobs, and owners of capital tend to have higher incomes than others (Krahn et al., 2007). For instance, in 2000, average annual earnings in Canada for dentists ($108,034), lawyers ($94,731), and managers ($61,412 in 2004) were much higher than were the average annual earnings for cashiers ($10,051), hotel clerks ($15,937), and hairstylists ($17,390) (Krahn et al., 2007: 109). These earnings stand in stark contrast to the incomes of the chief executive officers (CEOs) of large companies. In 2004, the average compensation package for the CEOs of 160 Canadian companies listed on the Toronto Stock Exchange was $5.5 million (Krahn et al., 2007: 111). Notably, a strong correlation between social class and income does not mean that it is a perfect correlation. There are certain jobs that, based on the definitions of social class defined above, would be considered working-class jobs even though they command a relatively high wage. For example, assembly-line workers in any of the 'Big Three' auto manufacturing plants are part of the working class, but because they are members of a relatively strong union they are paid a good wage and have good benefits.

Owners and executives of capital clearly have much higher incomes than do workers. The question that remains unanswered is whether there has been an increasing polarization of income over time. One way to address this issue is to divide Canadians into equal groups (typically either deciles or quintiles) on the basis of their income, calculate the proportion of the total income in Canada that each group accounts for, and then examine whether that proportion changed over time. In 1999, 45.3 per cent of all before-tax income was concentrated in the top quintile of the Canadian population, 24.3 per cent in the fourth quintile, 16.1 per cent in the third (middle) quintile, 10 per cent in the second quintile, and only 4.4 per cent in the lowest quintile. Between 1951 and 1999, there was a 3.0 per cent shift from the second and third quintiles to the two highest quintiles, while the proportion of income concentrated in the lowest quintile remained relatively stable. Moreover, between 1981 and 1999, the second, third, and fourth quintiles lost 3.6 per cent of their before-tax income, a total of $15 billion, to the upper quintile (Urmetzer and Guppy, 2004: 78). By 2003 families in the highest income quintile earned, on average, $12.90 of before tax earnings for every $1.00 earned by families the lowest income quintile. Between 1996 and 2002, the gap in after-tax income grew by 23 per cent between the richest and poorest families in Canada and then remained stable between 2002 and 2003 at $96,600 (Statistics Canada, 2005f). All told, these figures support the idea that there is increasing polarization of income in Canada.

The proportion of total before-tax income that is concentrated in the lowest quintile has remained relatively stable since 1951. What these figures do not tell us is that this stability has been maintained largely through government transfers such as tax credits, social assistance, and unemployment insurance. Indeed, for low-income families, the proportion of their total income from labour market earnings has declined since the 1970s (Picot and Myles, 1995). Hence, income polarization is not as serious as it could be because government policies are in place to ensure more equitable income distributions in Canada (Ross et al., 2000). But how equitable is a system in which the lowest quintile receives only 4.4 per cent of all before-tax income? And how equitable is a system in which the $15 billion gain made in the upper quintile during the 1980s and 1990s is equivalent to the amount of money it would take to eliminate poverty in Canada (Osberg, 1992)?

Poverty is a serious social problem in Canada. The National Council of Welfare reports that since a peak at 20.6 per cent in 1996, there were five consecutive years of declines in the poverty rate for all persons; a 12-year low of 15.5 per cent was set in 2001. In 2003, 15.9 per cent of Canadians lived in poverty; poverty rates for families are 12 per cent, and for unattached individuals they are 38 per cent (National Council of Welfare, 2006: 7).

Poverty rates vary on the basis of gender, family status, age, immigrant and minority status, health, education, and labour-force attachment. For instance, in 2003, the poverty rate for single-parent mothers was 48.9 per cent—more than four times the poverty rate for all families (National Council of Welfare, 2006: 12). Unattached women under the age of 65 are more likely to live in poverty than are their male counterparts (42.8 per cent versus 34.4 per cent), as are unattached women who are aged 65 and over (40.9 per cent versus 31.6 per cent) (National Council of Welfare, 2006: 13). Children (17.6 per cent) and the elderly (15.1 per cent) are somewhat more likely to be poor than are all Canadians (15.9 per cent) (National Council of Welfare, 2006: 8–10).

Gainful employment significantly reduces poverty rates among both unattached individuals and families. Yet more than 30 per cent of families who were living in poverty in 2003 were headed by people who were employed (National Council of Welfare, 2006: 5). The poverty rate for single-parent mothers who worked was 43.1 per cent (National Council of Welfare, 2006: 97). According to the 1996 census, some of the highest rates of poverty are found among Aboriginal peoples (43.4 per cent), members of visible minority groups (35.9 per cent) and persons with disabilities (30.8 per cent) (Ross et al., 2000).

Poverty rates also vary from province to province. In 2003, British Columbia had the highest poverty rate (20.1 per cent), followed by Newfoundland and Labrador (17.3 per cent) and Manitoba and Quebec (both 16.9 per cent). Prince Edward Island had the lowest poverty rate (11.8 per cent), followed by Ontario (14.3 per cent) and Alberta (14.6 per cent). (National Council of Welfare, 2006: 24). Provincial variations in poverty rates are a result of regional differences in economic structures, provincial inconsistencies in government policies regarding social welfare transfers, and access to other social and economic resources (National Council of Welfare, 2006).

Good Jobs/Bad Jobs

You will recall that Marx's third prediction with respect to the polarization of classes was that as capitalism developed, jobs would become increasingly deskilled and alienated. Indeed, skill and alienation are two characteristics of paid work that vary depending on social class. Generally, working-class jobs are characterized by low levels of skill required to do the job and by often corresponding high levels of alienation, whereas jobs held by those in the 'new middle class' and the 'old middle class' tend to require more skill and to be more intrinsically

rewarding. That said, for Marx's prediction to be supported, we must see evidence that middle-class jobs have become increasingly deskilled.

In 1974, Harry Braverman published his classic book *Labor and Monopoly Capitalism*. Taking issue with those who argued that rising white-collar employment was a positive effect of post-industrialism that resulted in an increasingly large middle class, Braverman convincingly argued that most white-collar jobs (such as clerical and retail jobs) should be considered working-class, not middle-class. White-collar jobs, Braverman argued, were increasingly being deskilled and organized according to **scientific management** techniques, thereby eliminating most of the control and autonomy that workers may have had over their work. Advances in new technologies contributed to this process by giving managers sophisticated tools through which they can monitor their employees' work. For example, before the advent of computerized cash registers, cashiers needed to know how to make change. Now cash registers inform cashiers how much change they need to give a customer. Further, cash registers can now monitor the speed of keystrokes and the number of customers that a cashier serves per hour. Managers, in turn, use this information in employee job-performance evaluations. Hence, new technology has been used to both deskill the work process and to monitor and control it.

One year before Braverman published his book, Daniel Bell published what was to become an influential text on post-industrial society. Unlike Braverman, who argued that occupations were becoming increasingly deskilled, Bell (1973) looked to the future and argued that knowledge, and hence skill, would become a highly valued commodity in post-industrial society. According to Bell, knowledge would be a basis of power much as the ownership of property had traditionally been, and knowledge workers would form a significant class (both in number and in power) in their own right. Bell argued that as the proportion of knowledge workers grew, the historical trend towards the polarization of society into two central classes, the bourgeoisie and the proletariat, would lose speed.

In the more than 30 years since Bell and Braverman published their books, debates have ensued over which thesis better explains the relationship between skill and class structure in post-industrial society. Although such debates are far from being resolved, Clement and Myles (1994: 72) note that the debate has unfolded as follows:

> We face either a postindustrial Nirvana of knowledge where everyone will be a brain surgeon, artist, or philosopher (Bell) or, alternatively, a post-industrial Hades where we shall be doomed to labour mindlessly

HUMAN DIVERSITY
Images of Child Poverty in Canada

Dirty, bare feet dangle over a licence plate in Prince Albert, Sask. A child plays with a lone tricycle on a cracked driveway in Winnipeg.

Those are images of some of the 1.3 million children in Canada who live in poverty, whose existence a group called PhotoSensitive is documenting in a cross-Canada exhibit.

The show was launched yesterday, in conjunction with a report on child poverty, released by Campaign 2000, that says nearly one in five children [was] living in poverty in 1999, compared with one in seven in 1989.

Campaign 2000 is a coalition of organizations formed to ensure that a 1989 House of Commons resolution to end child poverty by 2000 was implemented, a result still far from being realized, co-ordinator Laurel Rothman said.

'We are no closer [to ending child poverty]', she said. 'In 1989, we were at one in seven children living in poverty. Now we're at almost one in five.'

Samantha naps in the attic apartment she shares with her mother and three brothers in Edmonton. They will be moving soon. (© Chris Schwarz)

Ms Rothman said what is disturbing is that child poverty was prevalent even during the economic prosperity of the late 1990s.

'Governments have the option in the boom years of investing in children. Instead they took the strategy of cutting taxes, and in many cases, social services.'

The report says that despite a strong economy between 1998 and 1999, the child-poverty rate dropped only slightly to 18.5 per cent from 19 per cent. And with the latest economic downturn, 'those numbers are going to rocket up again', Ms Rothman said.

One positive number in the bulletin is the decrease in the depth of poverty, said Andrew Jackson, research director for the Canadian Council on Social Development, which compiled the data from several Statistics Canada studies.

In 1999, poor families saw an improvement of more than $500 in their depth of poverty over the previous year (to $9,073 below the poverty line in 1999 from $9,597 in 1998), but the gap between the rich and the poor in Canada is still far too wide, Ms Rothman said.

The report makes several recommendations to government, including the development of a national housing strategy.

And the photographs by the 24 members of PhotoSensitive remind people of the 'faces behind the numbers', Andrew Stawicki, photographer and founder of PhotoSensitive, said.

Source: Allison Dunfield, 'In 1989 We Were at One in Seven Children Living in Poverty. Now We're at Almost One in Five', *Globe and Mail*, 27 Nov. 2001, A11. Reprinted with permission from *The Globe and Mail*.

---

in the service of capital (Braverman). When drawn in these terms, the historical debate is now no debate at all. Bell is the clear winner. Although much less than a knowledge revolution, the net result of the shift to services has been to increase the requirements for people to think on the job.

In Canada, 42 per cent of jobs in the post-industrial service sector are skilled compared to only 26 per cent of those in the goods and distribution sector. And 55 per cent of 'new middle class' jobs are skilled, compared to only 23 per cent of working-class jobs (Clement and Myles, 1994: 76). Clement and Myles point out that the

■■ **Time to Reflect** ■█ ██ ██ ██ ██ ██ ██ ██ ██ ██ ██ █

Do you think that your university education will protect you from poverty?

growth in the service sector has brought both skilled and unskilled jobs, but they underscore the fact that in Canada and the United States, often unskilled service jobs are entry jobs for new workers rather than serving as a basis for working-class formation. This—combined with the fact that these service jobs are now often exit jobs for older workers who have been displaced, discouraged, restructured, or retired early—suggests that age may play a more significant role in labour market inequality in the years to come. Nonetheless, the point is that although the conditions of work in contemporary Canadian capitalism are far from ideal, the proletarianization of the labour force as predicted by Braverman has not occurred even though skilled jobs are concentrated in the new middle and executive classes (Clement and Myles, 1994).

In summary, considering debates about the deskilling of work in post-industrial capitalism, about whether the middle class is shrinking, and about the distribution of income and poverty, there is no consensus among sociologists about whether the class structure of Canadian society has become increasingly polarized. On the one hand, overall increases in the skill levels associated with many jobs and recent increases in self-employed small business owners suggests that the polarization thesis is incorrect. On the other hand, huge inequities in the distribution of income in Canada cannot be ignored. Furthermore, regardless of where one comes down on the debate about overall class polarization, the fact is that compared to 'middle-class' jobs, working-class jobs are characterized by low levels of income and other benefits, low levels of autonomy and control in the work process, poor working conditions, low levels of skill, and high levels of alienation. The combination of these things creates social disadvantage for members of the working class relative to members of the middle classes, which carries over to other social domains. Education and health are two areas of sociological study that stand out as sites of class-based inequality.

Education

Many Canadians believe that education is a vehicle through which occupational and income advantages may be attained (Wotherspoon, 2004). Over the last 30 years, more education has come to be required to perform jobs that were done well without as much educa-tion in years past (for example, needing a high school degree to work at an auto manufacturing plant). But regardless of this 'credential inflation' (Baer, 2004), there remain strong correlations between education, occupation, and income in Canada (Hunter and Leiper, 1993).

Typically, highly educated people are employed in well-paid jobs (Little, 1995) that have relatively high degrees of autonomy and authority associated with them (Butlin and Oderkirk, 1996). Of course, we have all either heard about or met a taxi driver who holds a PhD or a high school dropout who is the well-paid owner of a successful business. These examples illustrate the exceptions to the rules. Often, other extraneous factors account for these exceptions. For instance, in the case of the well-educated taxi driver, recent immigration status may affect his or her job prospects because of discriminatory hiring criteria (for example, a hiring requirement of Canadian education or work experience).

In light of the relationship between educational attainment and economic advantage, sociologists have long been concerned with the social determinants of educational attainment. Social class background, usually measured using SES indicators, is one such determinant. Two key measures of educational attainment are often considered in this regard: (1) whether young people complete high school and (2) whether young people continue with post-secondary education.

On average, Canadians are among the most educated people in the world (Looker and Lowe, 2001). High school completion rates continued to increase throughout the 1990s such that only 12 per cent of 20-year-olds did not complete high school in 1999, as compared to 18 per cent in 1991 (Bowlby and McMullen, 2002). The more educated parents are, the more likely their children are to complete high school (Bowlby and McMullen, 2002). Figure 6.3 shows data for 18- to 20-year-olds from the Canadian 2000 Youth in Transition Survey. Here we see that the highest proportion of both high school graduates (34.7 per cent) and high school dropouts (45.2 per cent) have at least one parent who graduated from high school. However, among those who have at least one parent who has completed either a college or a university program, the proportion of graduates is twice the proportion of dropouts (56.6 per cent versus 27.9 per cent). Among youth whose parents had not graduated from high school, the proportion of dropouts is three times the proportion of graduates (26.9 per cent versus 8.7 per cent). Furthermore, approximately 7 out of every 10 dropouts, compared to 4 out of 10 graduates, had parents who did not complete high school (Bowlby and McMullen, 2002: 31).

Similarly, mothers' and fathers' occupations are correlated with whether youth graduate from or drop out of high school. Mothers of high school dropouts were more likely to be working in sales and service jobs or in primary, processing, manufacturing, and utilities jobs. Mothers of graduates were more likely to be working in social science, government, art, culture, health, and applied science jobs. Fathers of dropouts were more likely to be working in trades, transport, and equipment-operating jobs, whereas fathers of graduates were more likely to be working in management jobs (Bowlby and McMullen, 2002).

Approximately 65 per cent of high school graduates enter post-secondary educational institutions in Canada (Looker and Lowe, 2001: 4). Among youth, the higher parents' measures of SES, the higher their children's expectations regarding post-secondary educational attainment (Looker and Lowe, 2001). Plans to attend college or university are correlated with whether youth actually attend such institutions. Hence, educational attainment, including participation in college and university programs after high school completion, is also influenced by class background, regardless of how it is measured (Ali and Grabb, 1998; Wotherspoon, 2004). Several studies have shown that financial situation is listed by youth as a key barrier to pursuing post-secondary studies (Bowlby and McMullen, 2002; see Looker and Lowe, 2001, for an overview). Furthermore, youth who are from families in the highest SES quartile are much more likely to attend university than are those in the lowest SES quartile (Chippendale, 2002; Statistics Canada and CMEC, 2000).

The preceding findings demonstrate that there is a clear relationship between parents' SES and children's educational attainment. A combination of economic, social, and cultural factors helps to explain the relationship between SES and educational attainment (Davies, 2004). In the first place, if parents are poorly educated and have low-paying jobs, families may not be able to afford to keep children in school. Poor families may need their children to drop out of high school and work to help with the family economy. In other situations, parents may not be able to help with the costs of post-secondary education, and the thought of excessive debt upon school completion may dissuade youth from continuing their studies. Notably, neither of these situations is likely to improve in the short term as rates of child poverty and the costs of post-secondary education continue to rise.

Besides economic factors, other social factors intersect with SES and social class to play a role in the educational attainment. To the extent that children and youth of similar SES and social class backgrounds are segregated into schools based on community residence, they will develop social ties with other children and youth of similar backgrounds. Lack of exposure to middle- and upper-class children and their parents limits access to **social capital**, the resources that are available through our connections to others. In other words, working-class children and youth may not have access to the information gained through social capital that is required for them to succeed in their educational careers. For instance, whereas middle-class children can turn to their parents and friends to learn about the intricacies of the educational system, working-class children do not have those social resources available to them and may not know how to find answers to questions that would help them succeed within school environments.

Finally, **cultural capital** also plays a role in educational attainment. Cultural capital is derived mostly from education and reflects middle- and upper-class **values**, attitudes, and beliefs regarding various aspects of social life. If education and related activities such as reading, discussing politics, and learning about the world and music are valued within a family and by the individuals within it, high levels of educational attain-

Figure 6.3   **Highest Education Attainment of Parents or Guardians of Dropouts and Graduates**

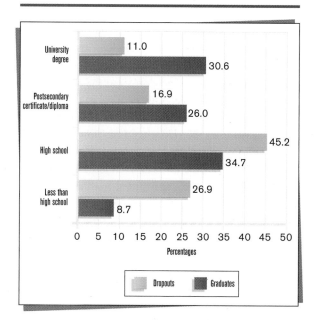

Source: Adapted from Jeffrey Bowlby and Kathryn McMullen, *At a Crossroads: First Results for the 18–20-Year-Old Cohort of the Youth in Transition Survey 2002* (Ottawa: Statistics Canada, 2002), 21.

ment are more likely. Working-class families tend not to expose their children to these activities to the extent that middle- and upper-class families do. Hence, the value of education is often not as strongly held in working-class families as it is in middle-class families, and working-class children may not be as inclined to continue with their education as a result.

Health

According to the World Health Organization, *health* is broadly defined as 'a state of complete physical, mental, and social well-being and not merely the absence of disease or infirmity' (2003), which suggests that multiple measures of health need to be examined in order to fully understand health and inequality. Income, status, and class advantages lead to better health outcomes within and across countries. Recent media and policy attention regarding the HIV/AIDS epidemics in developing countries suggests that developed countries need to pay more attention to the 'have-nots' who live beyond our national borders. Indeed, mortality and morbidity rates tend to be higher in developing than in developed countries, and biotechnology researchers are in search of methods to reduce the health gap between rich and poor countries.

Among the many indicators of health, mortality is one of the most studied. There is a well-known and consistent relationship between SES and mortality. Individuals who have lower incomes and less education tend to have lower life expectancies than individuals who have higher incomes and who are better educated (Mustard et al., 1997; Williams and Collins, 1995). Recent evidence suggests that the mortality gap between the rich and the poor is widening; this has been attributed to the more rapid gains for those with high SES relative to those with lower SES (Williams and Collins, 1995).

Recently, researchers have argued that beyond the simple relationship between SES and mortality, a socioeconomic 'gradient' also influences mortality. This *gradient effect* reflects the research finding that regions characterized by high levels of income inequality have higher death rates than do regions in which the income distribution is more equal. This suggests that the experience of disadvantage relative to others in a particular locale has an effect on mortality rates that cannot be explained by SES alone (Kawachi et al., 1999).

Morbidity generally refers to the presence of illness or disease, chronic symptoms, and general malaise. Regardless of how it is measured, there is also a strong and consistent relationship between SES and morbidity such that those who are more disadvantaged experience higher lev-

els of morbidity (Cairney, 1999; Humphries and van Doorslaer, 2000; Jette et al., 1996; MacMillan et al., 1996; Mao et al., 2000; Williams and Collins, 1995). Regional disparities regarding income and poverty have also been found to influence the experience of morbidity (Guernsey et al., 2000). Besides these differences in mortality and morbidity, individuals in lower-SES groups suffer poorer mental health (measured either as the presence of mental illness or as more generalized distress) than do those in higher-SES groups (Turner and Avison, 2003). Although there are debates about whether low SES causes poor mental health or whether poor mental health causes low SES, the correlation is strong.

What explains the strong and consistent relationship between SES and these various measures of health? People with lower levels of income and education and those employed in working-class occupations are more likely to experience malnutrition, disproportionately lack knowledge of health care practices, and are more often exposed to dangerous working and living environments. All of these things negatively affect health status. As well, research has shown that SES is associated with access to health care services even in countries such as Canada that have 'universal' health-care systems (Newbold, 1998).

● Conclusion: ● ● ● ● ● ●
Does Class Matter?

For decades, sociologists have quibbled over the relevance of social class as a marker of inequality (Clark and Lipset, 1991; Nisbet, 1959; Pakulski and Waters, 1996). Some argue that because false consciousness is so widespread within contemporary capitalism, political distinctions between the middle class and the working class have become negligible. Others suggest that because some working-class jobs are well-paid, distributive distinctions between the classes are becoming less significant. Still others purport that because most people report that they are members of the middle class, not the working class, and because working conditions are better now than they were a century ago, class is losing its significance as a basis of inequality in Canada and other Western industrialized nations (Pakulski and Waters, 1996). Indeed, Jan Pakulski and Malcolm Waters (1996) have gone as far as to proclaim the 'death' of class.

The claims in support of the 'death of class' are true to a certain extent. Indeed, the fact that many students first discover their working-class backgrounds in their first year of university may add some support to the argument that class does not matter. As well, the conditions of, and rewards for, work have mostly improved over the last century. Social security systems are better now than they were during the rise of industrial capitalism in Canada, which has reduced the risk associated with working-class membership.

That said, it is also true that after students are given social class as an explanatory tool, they better understand the circumstances of their lives. Furthermore, if given a choice, most employees would choose to work in non-working-class occupations that are better paid, more autonomous, and less alienating; working-class parents are not able to provide their children with the same educational opportunities that are afforded to middle-class children; and there are unique health risks associated with being a member of the working class. The culmination of this information suggests that although the nature of class-based inequality has changed over time, class remains alive and well.

● Questions ● ● ● ● ● ● ● for Critical Thought

2. Discuss the feminist critique of social class. How can social class be reconceptualized so that the experiences of women are fully integrated into a theoretical framework of social class?

3. Why are sociologists concerned about the polarization of social classes? What are the social implications of a shrinking middle class and a swelling working class?

5. Are there policies that could be put in place that could eliminate poverty? What might some of these policies be? Is the elimination of poverty a desirable social outcome?

6. Are there policies that could be put in place that could eliminate the relationship between social class and education? What might some of these policies be? Is educational equality a desirable social outcome?

● Recommended ● ● ● ● Readings

James E. Curtis, Edward G. Grabb, and Neil L. Guppy, eds, *Social Inequality in Canada: Patterns, Problems, and Policies* (Toronto: Pearson Prentice-Hall, 2004).

This is an excellent source of information on various aspects of social inequality in Canada.

Edward G. Grabb, *Theories of Social Inequality*, 5th edn (Toronto: Harcourt, 2007).

Grabb provides an excellent overview and analysis of classical and contemporary theories of social inequality.

Heidi Hartmann, 'The Unhappy Marriage of Marxism and Feminism: Towards a More Progressive Union', in Lydia Sargent, ed., *The Unhappy Marriage of Marxism and Feminism: A Debate on Class and Patriarchy* (London: Pluto, 1981), 2–41.

This classic socialist feminist article brings together, in a dual-systems theory, issues of patriarchy and capitalism.

Erik Olin Wright, *Class Counts: Comparative Studies in Class Analysis*, Student edn (Cambridge: Cambridge University Press, 1997).

This comprehensive book outlines Wright's ideas on social class.

● Recommended ● ● ● ● Websites

Canadian Labour Congress (CLC) www.clc-ctc.ca

Labour-related publications, media releases, and the history of the CLC are among the many resources available on this site.

Canadian Policy Research Networks www.cprn.ca

This is an excellent source of information regarding the relationship between social policy and social inequality.

Human Resources and Social Development Canada, Homelessness Partnering Strategy www.homelessness.gc.ca

Information is available on this site on the problem of homelessness among Canadians.

Make Poverty History www.makepovertyhistory.ca

This site includes information about poverty both in Canada and beyond, as well as ongoing campaigns and resources for anti-poverty activism.

Chapter 7

• • • • • • • • • • •

Gender
and Sexuality

Patrizia Albanese

Learning Objectives

In this chapter, you will:

▶ learn what is meant by sex, gender, and sexuality, and the diversity they encompass;

▶ learn that biology alone does not account for differences between males and females;

▶ appreciate some of the cross-cultural and historical diversity in attitudes and practices surrounding sex, gender, and sexuality;

▶ focus first on gender to see how child-rearing practices, the media, and the education system influence how children grow up to become gendered beings;

▶ examine gender segregation in the labour force, the home, and the political arena;

▶ consider why the life experiences of women are different from and more limited than those of men;

▶ compare various theoretical approaches to understanding sexuality; and

▶ identify some contemporary issues and trends in sexual attitudes and practices.

● Introduction ● ● ● ● ● ● ●

Human males and females are genetically almost identical. Yet, in most societies, men and women are treated as though they are *very* different. As a result, they lead considerably different lives. And though every society responds to the genetic differences between male and female somewhat differently, they all call attention to this difference. In most societies, this genetic difference becomes a social inequality. Sociologists want to know why sex differences almost always become gender and sexual inequalities, and why gender and sexual inequalities almost always favour males. In this chapter, we will explore some of the social and cultural answers to these questions. We will also see that differences result more from social relations and social structures than from biologically determined facts.

Typically, when we talk about sex, sociologists and other social scientists are referring to biological facts associated with being born male or female (including anatomical facts, hormonal facts, etc.). According to the World Health Organization (WHO) 'sex' refers to the biological characteristics that define humans as female or male, but WHO notes that while these are not mutually exclusive categories—there are individuals who possess elements of both—we nonetheless continue to differentiate humans as either male or female (WHO, 2008). In other words, considerable evidence indicates that despite the fact that we often think of male/female as a dichotomy, meaning that only two categories exist and that someone is born *either* male *or* female, some infants are born with 'ambiguous' genitalia—or genitalia that are variant or 'difficult to understand' (Morland, 2005: 335).

The socio-cultural designation of *masculine* and *feminine*, or the social and behavioural expectations, or conceptions of appropriate behaviour associated with being born male or female is referred to as **gender**. As a result of the dichotomizing of sex, we have also come to dichotomize gender. For example, many have come to believe and accept that men are rational and women emotional. Supposedly, men are strong and women are weak(er). Men are visual/tactile learners and women are verbal, and so on.

While some men and women appear to fit into these simplified categories, these are in fact **gender stereotypes**, or structured sets of beliefs about how women and men behave. Gender stereotypes are *descriptive* oversimplifications of socio-culturally accepted traits and attitudes, which become *prescriptive* as we come to *expect* men and women to behave in these socio-culturally predetermined ways. In fact, men vary in their strength just as they vary in their intelligence—along a normal or bell-curve—and so do women. So, even if it were true that men were, on average, stronger than women, many women would still be stronger than many men. Our simplification, by talk-

GLOBAL ISSUES
Changing Views of Men

While most of the research and writing on changing relations between the sexes has focused on women, in the last two decades there has been a flurry of publications that look at emerging patterns for men. Analysis of advertising offers just one example of this trend.

In her examination of the representation of males in advertising, Judith Posner (1987) found that the new male is smaller, has a less pronounced jaw, and is more likely to smile. He is also more likely to be found undressing or partially dressed, and he appears more vulnerable. Yet Posner concludes that this does not reflect a move toward equality, but rather demonstrates 'the increasing commercialization of sexuality' for both men and women (1987: 188).

In another analysis of advertising, Andrew Wernick argues that as women have moved into the labour force, men have become more involved in private consumption; this change has been reflected in 'a steady drive to incorporate male clothing into fashion, and mounting efforts to sell men all manner of personal-care products, from toothpaste and bath oil to hair dye and make-up' (1987: 279). Wernick suggests that men are being subjected to the same kind of 'intense consumerization as women and are no longer defined as breadwinners' (ibid.). More recently, however, Varda Burstyn (1999) has argued that both advertising in sports and the practice of sport promotes what she calls 'hypermasculinity.'

ing about ideals and averages, hides as much as it reveals.

Yet this simplification has consequences. We often feel obliged to conform to culturally defined norms and patterns of behaviours known as **gender roles**. People '*do gender*' by filling roles that are shaped by others around them. In other words, gender is an accomplished activity, not a fixed biological fact. Judith Butler (1990; 1999), for example, has argued that in doing gender we get caught up in a heterosexual matrix that has significant consequences for the construction and understanding of sexuality. She argues that gender ought not be constructed as a stable identity or locus of agency, but rather as an identity constituted in time and space through a stylized repetition of acts. These acts and gestures are 'performative' in the sense that the essential features of identity they *claim* to express are actually fabrications, manufactured and sustained through symbols and signs.

So, gender identity is not fixed or static. It varies from person to person, depending on the situation and culture, and is influenced by others around us. For example, have you ever heard someone say 'She is such a girly girl?' In saying such things, we are recognizing that people differ in the degree to which gender is a salient part of their identity. Studies show that in certain contexts we choose to present ourselves in more masculine or more feminine ways.

For example, one study found that when heterosexual women 'present themselves' to men who possess socially desirable characters, they alter their presentation. Men do the same when they interact with women they believe have desirable traits (Deaux and Major, 2004). Women eat fewer snacks at parties when they interact with desirable males, compared to less desirable ones, for example (DeAnna, Chaiken, and Pliner, 1987). Their goal is to appear delicate and 'feminine'. Though both men and women alter their gender behaviour to suit specific situations, gender identity is differentially important for men and women (Chodorow, 1990). When asked what identities are important to them, women are more likely than men to mention gender as a central identity (Deaux and Major, 2004).

● Heternormativity ● ● ● ●

Despite scientific evidence of the existence of diversity, we continue to dichotomize sex into male and female as measured by visible genital facts—the presence of a vagina or penis. And because our society has little tolerance for ambiguity, we typically reconstruct the genitalia, appearance, and personalities of intersexed infants—

those born with reproductive or sexual anatomy that does not seem to conform to typical definitions of female or male—to fit into one of the two boxes. Kessler (1998) estimates that genital surgery to 'fix' intersexed babies happened five times per day to infants in American hospitals in the 1990s.

Once we think of individuals as fitting into one of the two dichotomous sex categories, we also come to see men and women as naturally polar opposites of one another—note the term 'opposite sex'—who are inevitably assumed to be sexually 'drawn' to one another like magnets. As a result, in dichotomizing sex this way we have also dichotomized sexuality, sexual identity, and sexual orientation into heterosexual ('normal' sexual attraction to the 'opposite' sex) or homosexual (less 'normal' attraction to someone of the same sex), when in fact sexuality is considerably more complex than this. Furthermore, in doing this, almost all aspects of social life are constructed on the assumption that all ('normal') people are heterosexual. This has come to be called **heteronormativity**.

Sexuality has been defined by the World Health Organization as 'being a central aspect of being human, and encompasses sex, gender identities and roles, **sexual orientation**, eroticism, pleasure, intimacy, and reproduction' (WHO, 2008). The WHO explains that 'sexuality is experienced in thoughts, fantasies, desires, beliefs, attitudes, values, behaviours, roles, and relationships. . . . sexuality is influenced by the interaction of biological, psychological, social, economic, political, cultural, ethical, legal, historical, religious, and spiritual factors' (WHO, 2008).

Jeffrey Weeks (1993: 16) notes that the meanings we give to sexuality are 'socially organized, sustained by a variety of languages, which seek to tell us what sex is, what it ought to be—and what it could be'. He adds that these languages of sex 'embedded in moral treatises, laws, educational practices, psychological theories, medical definitions, social rituals, pornographic or romantic fictions, popular music and common sense assumptions (most of which disagree) set the horizon of the possible'. Sexuality therefore has to do with who we are and what place we (are allowed to) take within society.

Once people are snuggly packaged into boxes—male or female, masculine or feminine, heterosexual or homosexual—things like **sexism** (the subordination of one sex, usually female, and the perceived superiority of the other) and **homophobia** (an irrational fear and/or hatred of homosexuals and homosexuality) help reinforce rigid boundaries and keep people in their place. For example, a young person who challenges traditional gender ideology or practices is likely to be teased and taunted. In our society, boys, perhaps more than girls,

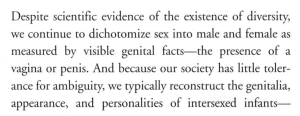

who cross the gender divide are often harassed back into stereotypically masculine behaviour. Children and youth learn quickly to avoid ridicule by conforming to pre-scribed gender and sexual norms. As a result, we come to see certain types of behaviour as normal, natural, and inevitable—the core or *essence* of femininity or mas-culinity, heterosexuality or homosexuality—when, in fact, we may have been encouraged or forced to suppress parts of our identities that cross the gender and sexual divide (see DeLamater and Hyde, 1998). We have learned to treat as natural, inevitable, or *essential* things that are cultural, learned, and open to change.

The Asymmetry of Gender-Typing

Not only have we constructed men and women as oppo-sites (the opposite sex) or two parts of the gender dichotomy, but we have created an asymmetrical dichotomy. According to Lesnick (2005), gender differ-ence always comes 'hooked to' gender inequality at home and in the workplace. In other words, men and women are seen and treated as not only different, but unequal.

This inequity stems not from biological or individ-ual differences, but from unequal power relations, opportunity structures, and everyday practices. Women have less socially sanctioned **power** than men, and as a result are less able to challenge existing norms and stereotypes (Lesnick, 2005). **Power** is often defined as the ability of an individual or group to influence others, despite resistance. In a **patriarchal** society, men as a group tend to have more power than women as a group. Men's greater control of resources, for example, influ-ences the amount of power they hold in relationships. As a result, when we carefully assess gender stereotypes, we find there is often more value, worth, and prestige asso-ciated with what are stereotypically masculine traits, compared to stereotypically feminine traits.

Gender in Childhood

Different societies respond to the genetic and biological differences between men and women somewhat differ-ently; however, they all call attention to differences. As previously mentioned, in most societies this biological difference becomes a social inequality. Unequal treat-ment of men and women is learned early in life. In childhood, we all learn to behave in patterned, culturally

prescribed ways through the process of **socialization**. What is deemed properly masculine and feminine is communicated to us through **gender socialization** via family, peers, media, and other institutions around us.

Gender socialization begins at birth and continues throughout our lives. If you ask parents today if they treat/raise their sons and daughters differently, many are likely to say 'no', and claim that they are gender-neutral or gender-blind. However, studies show that from a very young age girls and boys are handled and spoken to dif-ferently, are differently reinforced for their attention-seeking behaviour (Condry and Condry, 1976; Fagot, 1986; Mackie, 1991), and are granted different amounts of freedom and responsibility.

Compared to daughters, some parents handle their sons more roughly, speak to them to less often, allow them to respond in more aggressive ways, encourage them to risk more and cry less, and grant them more freedom than daughters. Parents are even likely to rate their male children as more intelligent than their female children (Furnham and Gasson, 1998). These attitudes and practices are products of the culture in which we live and shape us from a very young age (Martin and Ruble, 2004).

Gender and Education

In elementary school, children's formal and casual encounters are gendered and strongly separated by sex (Lesnick, 2005), to the point that it is 'meaningful to speak of separate girls' and boys' worlds' (Thorne, 1990: 61). According to Thorne (1990), at this time differences tend to be exaggerated and similarities ignored. Teachers, organizational structures, and students themselves create different types of opportunities and barriers for boys and girls. Teachers, for example, often use gender as a basis for sorting children into groups when organizing activities. Children, too, segregate themselves along gender lines in lunchrooms and playgrounds. In the elementary school classroom, boys tend to call out answers more often than girls, receive a disproportionate share of teacher atten-tion, and dominate class discussions, all encounters that foster independence in boys (Sadker and Sadker, 1991).

In high school, young men and women choose to study different subjects, begin making decisions about their futures, and interact with one another in gendered and sexualized ways. Researchers studying educational settings find gender inequality in classroom talk, assess-ment approaches, curriculum design, and educational policies (Lesnick, 2005; also see Kay and Knaack, 2008).

Increasingly, boys do more poorly than girls in formal education, with the result that more of them drop-out of school and get into trouble.

Over the past two decades, women have made tremendous strides when it comes to educational attainment. By 1996, the proportion of women with a university degree doubled from the previous decade (from 6 per cent to 12 per cent of all women, 15 years of age and older, according to Statistics Canada, 2000). By the late 1990s, women were the majority (55 per cent) of full-time students at Canadian universities. In 2001, just over 105,000 women received a degree, diploma, or certificate, accounting for 59 percent of the total number issued that year. In comparison, men received 72,900 (Statistics Canada, 2005b). Statistics Canada (2005b) data reveal that between 1996 and 2001, the number of women receiving a university degree increased by 2.0 per cent, while the number of men fell by 2.9 per cent (see Tables 7.1 and Figure 7.1). Some 77,600 women received a bachelor's degree, while 13,000 received a master's degree. By 2001 men outnumbered women only in the area of earned doctorates (Statistics Canada, 2005b).

However, even though men earned more doctorates, during this six-year period the number of men receiving a doctorate declined 17.7 per cent while the number of women receiving a doctorate increased 18.6 per cent (Statistics Canada, 2005b). Nonetheless, proportionally, more men received graduate level qualifications than women. Statistics Canada (2005b) noted that 16.3 per cent of men received a master's degree and 2.9 per cent received a doctorate; among women, 12.4 per cent received a master's, and 1.5 percent received a doctorate (Statistics Canada, 2005b).

Furthermore, for every woman who held a science or engineering doctorate in Canada in 2001, there were four men; earnings of female science and engineering PhDs were also significantly lower than those of their male counterparts (McKenzie, 2007). A study of earned doctorates in science and engineering found that for every dollar earned by a male doctorate holder, female doctorates earned 77 cents. In contrast, the average woman in the general labour force earned 71 cents for every dollar earned by a man (McKenzie, 2007).

While the number of women pursuing doctoral degrees in Canada is on the rise, traditional gender roles and gendered organizational hierarchies combine to make doctoral education an inherently different process for men and women (Wall, 2008). Wall (2008) studied the perspectives of female, Canadian PhD students in the arts and humanities and found that their program

choices, research interests, supervisors, perceptions of interpersonal and organizational social support, and career plans were unique, complex, and gendered. Wall noted that some female students received subtle and not-so-subtle messages from their departments about parenting during doctoral studies. One student recalls being told by her department chair: 'Don't have babies while you're doing your PhD' (Wall, 2008: 224). Following the shock and anger, one may begin to question one's decision to pursue doctoral studies.

Interestingly, a Canadian study found that the tendency of men and women with the same educational level to be married to one another has increased over the last three decades (Hou and Myles, 2007). In Canada, 54 per cent of couples under the age of 35 had the same level of education in 2001, up from 42 per cent in 1971. In 2001, 24 per cent of wives and 19 per cent of husbands finished university in Canada, compared with 4 per cent and 10 per cent, respectively, in 1971. As a result, wives now have a higher average educational level than their husbands, while the opposite was true three decades ago (Hou and Myles, 2007).

● The Adult World: ● ● ● ●
Gender and Paid Work

The past several decades have seen an increase in the proportion of women who are part of the labour force (see Table 7.2). Between 1976 and 1999, the proportion of women 15 and older in the paid labour force jumped from 42 per cent to 55 per cent, while the proportion of men working for pay decreased from 73 percent to 67 per cent (Statistics Canada, 2000). While fertility rates in Canada are declining, the proportion of women with young children in the labour force has been increasing steadily. Between 1995 and 2004, women's labour force participation rates increased, particularly for women aged 25–54 (Luffman, 2006). By 2005, this number had increased to 81 per cent (Marshall, 2006); 71.9 per cent of these women were mothers of young children (Roy, 2006). In 2006, women accounted for 47 per cent of the workforce, up from 37 per cent in 1976 (Statistics Canada, 2007d).

These changes reflect the changing roles of women in society, their increasing participation in post-secondary education, and their growing family economic need. In the past, women tended to leave paid work upon marriage to devote all their time to being wives and mothers. This is less true today. In fact, today a growing

Table 7.1   University Qualifications by Program Level and Gender

University qualifications awarded by program level and gender

| | | | | | % change[1] | |
| | | | | | 1996 to 2001 | 2000 to 2001 |
	1996	1999	2000[r]	2001		
Undergraduate level						
Total degree, certificate and diploma[2]	**149,700**	**143,500**	**145,300**	**146,300**	**-2.3**	**0.6**
Female	89,100	86,200	87,200	88,800	-0.3	1.9
Male	60,600	57,300	58,200	57,400	-5.3	-1.3
Graduate level						
Total degree, certificate and diploma[2]	**27,800**	**29,500**	**30,700**	**31,100**	**11.7**	**1.2**
Female	13,600	14,900	15,900	16,000	17.1	0.3
Male	14,200	14,600	14,800	15,100	6.6	2.1
Master's degree[2]	21,600	23,300	24,200	24,900	15.3	2.6
Female	11,000	12,100	12,800	13,000	18.3	1.2
Male	10,600	11,200	11,400	11,900	12.2	4.2
Earned doctorate	3,900	4,000	3,900	3,700	-5.4	-3.7
Female	1,300	1,600	1,600	1,600	18.6	-0.1
Male	2,600	2,400	2,300	2,100	-17.7	-6.2
Graduate certificate and diploma	2,300	2,200	2,700	2,500	7.2	-5.2
Female	1,300	1,200	1,500	1,400	5.2	-7.3
Male	1,000	1,000	1,200	1,100	9.9	-2.4

Notes:

1. Percentage are based on actual, non-rounded figures.

2. Total includes sex unknown.

3. Figures for totals may not add-up because of rounding.

r Revised data.

Figures are rounded to the nearest 100.

Source: Adapted from Statistics Canada. 2005. 'University degrees, diplomas and certificates awarded.' *The Daily*, 18 January 2005. Ottawa: Statistics Canada. http://www.statcan.ca/Daily/English/050118/d050118b.htm

proportion of women in the labour force are married women with very young children (Roy, 2006). The vast majority of mothers return to the labour force soon after childbirth. Among women who gave birth in 1993–94, for example, roughly one in five returned to paid work at the end of the first month after childbirth. Mothers who did not receive maternity benefits or who were self-employed were six and eight times, respectively, more likely than other mothers to return to paid work earlier (Statistics Canada, 2000). Even with recent improvements to maternity leave benefits (see Marshall, 2008), many return to work soon after childbirth, mostly due to economic necessity. Recent studies indicate that without women's income, the number of families living in

Figure 7.1 Proportion of University Graduates by Age Groups and Sex, Canada, 2006

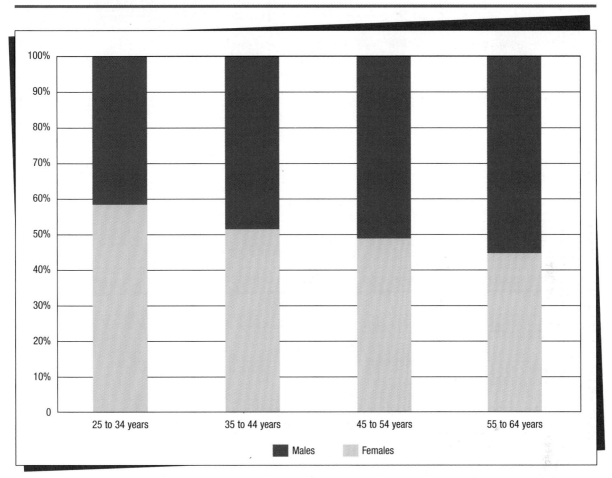

Source: Statistics Canada. 2008. Educational Portrait of Canada, 2006 Census: National picture. (Catalogue no. 97-560-X) Ottawa: Statistics Canada. http://www12.statcan.ca/english/census06/analysis/education/charts/chart2.htm

poverty would increase dramatically and many more would suffer significant setbacks in their standard of living (Chung, 2004; Statistics Canada, 2000).

Most employed women have one full-time, permanent, paid job, but a growing number of women work in *non-standard arrangements*—a category that includes part-time, temporary, self-employed, and multiple job holders. By 1999, 41 per cent of employed women had a non-standard work arrangement, up from 35 per cent in 1989 (Statistics Canada, 2000). Women remain more likely than men to have this kind of employment arrangement, and hold the majority of all part-time jobs (Bardasi and Gornick, 2008). Women are also more likely than men to have temporary employment. This is due to the changing nature of work and the relatively unchanging nature of family life and domestic responsibilities.

Today, more and more women enter the paid work force out of economic necessity and because of the decline in men's earning power. One salary is no longer sufficient to support an average family. As a result, the

wage gap between men and women has been closing. Much of this decline in men's earning power is linked to the disappearance of unionized secondary sector/industrial/manufacturing jobs, as many of these jobs have 'gone south' or offshore, to parts of the world where labour is cheaper.

Women are increasingly entering jobs traditionally dominated by men, particularly as their educational attainment surpasses men's (Alksnis, Desmarais and Curtis, 2008). But despite this trend, employed women still earn substantially less than their male counterparts (see Table 7.3). Interestingly, Statistics Canada research reveals that women's increased educational attainment has played a relatively small role in reducing the earnings gap since the 1980s. Frenette and Coulombe (2007) found that the earnings gap in the 1990s actually increased moderately for those with university-level education, but remained unchanged for those at the college level. This was, in part, explained by the fact that public spending cuts were felt by health and education graduates (female-dominated

Table 7.2   Total Employed (thousands) Women (Aged 15+) and Men (Aged 15+)

Year	Total employed (thousands) women	Percentage of all women employed	Total employed (thousands) men	Percentage of all men employed	Women as a percentage of total employment
1976	3,618.2	41.9	6,129.3	72.7	37.1
1977	3,729.3	42.3	6,187.9	71.9	37.6
1978	3,904.2	43.4	6,316.0	72.0	38.2
1979	4,139.9	45.1	6,528.7	73.1	38.8
1980	4,348.1	46.4	6,635.9	72.86	39.6
1981	4,556.6	47.7	6,748.4	72.8	40.3
1982	4,513.0	46.5	6,430.7	68.4	41.2
1983	4,605.7	46.8	6,416.3	67.4	41.8
1984	4,749.5	47.7	6,552.2	68.0	42.0
1985	4,942.7	49.0	6,684.5	68.5	42.5
1986	5,126.5	50.2	6,860.1	69.5	42.8
1987	5,307.7	51.3	7,025.3	70.3	43.0
1988	5,531.4	52.7	7,178.2	70.9	43.5
1989	5,704.2	53.6	7,292.0	71.1	43.9
1990	5,809.2	53.8	7,277.2	69.9	44.4
1991	5,790.5	52.8	7,066.9	66.9	45.0
1992	5,770.1	51.9	6,960.8	65.0	45.3
1993	5,798.7	51.5	6,994.0	64.6	45.3
1994	5,916.9	51.9	7,141.9	65.1	45.3
1995	6,034.6	52.2	7,260.8	65.4	45.4
1996	6,099.0	52.1	7,322.4	65.0	45.4
1997	6,235.4	52.6	7,470.7	65.5	45.4
1998	6,433.4	53.7	7,612.8	65.9	45.8
1999	6,609.6	54.6	7,797.2	66.7	45.9
2000	6,790.4	55.4	7,973.9	67.3	46.0
2001	6,910.3	55.6	8,035.8	66.8	46.2
2002	7,126.0	56.6	8,184.4	67.1	46.5
2003	7,324.2	57.4	8,348.1	67.6	46.7
2004	7,466.4	57.8	8,480.6	67.8	46.8
2005	7,575.0	57.8	8,594.7	67.7	46.8
2006	7,757.2	58.3	8,727.1	67.7	47.1

Source: Statistics Canada, 2007. Women in Canada: Work Chapter Updates, 2006. (Cat. no. 89F0133XIE) Ottawa: Statistics Canada.
http://www.statcan.ca/english/freepub/89F0133XIE/89F0133XIE2006000.pdf

fields), while the high tech boom helped engineering and other technology graduates (male-dominated fields) (Frenette and Coulombe, 2007).

In general, women come closest to earning parity with men during their younger years but lose significant ground later, when they leave the labour force because of childbirth and other family responsibilities (Meleis and Lindgren, 2002). Children have proven to be liabilities in women's careers because women often have to leave work to care for their children. In 1999, for example, paid female employees missed an average of seven days of work because of family obligations, up from four days in the mid-1980s. By contrast, employed men missed an average of only one day of work due to family commitments that same year (Statistics Canada, 2000). Since children and families continue to be seen as their responsibility, women continue to be seen as somewhat less committed to their paid jobs than men. As a result of this, women often end up in part-time employment or what some have called 'mommy-track jobs' or female job ghettos—low-paid, service-sector, dead-end jobs. These jobs tend to come with limited or no health benefits or leave time (Meleis and Lindgren, 2002; Brooks, Jarman, and Blackburn, 2003). In sum, men are still generally better-paid than women and more likely to hold full-time employment. They also experience continued upward mobility, while women, and especially those with children, are often said to hit the glass-ceiling.

Yet issues surrounding work are not limited to women: men also face considerable pressure when it comes to paid employment. Women are expected to marry, have, and raise children and (when possible) work for pay—the so-called double burden (Armstrong and Armstrong, 1994) or second shift (Hochschild, 1989)—but men are expected to work for pay from graduation until retirement, without interruption. They are expected to be self-supporting in their youth and primary breadwinners later in life, for as long as they are physically able to do so (Malenfant, Larue and Vézina, 2007). Unemployed or under-employed men are often stigmatized, viewed as undesirable marriage partners, and even as objects of scorn and ridicule (see also Waters and Moore, 2002).

Marshall (2006) found that over the last two decades, the average total workday for people aged 25–54 (including paid and unpaid work) increased steadily. In 2005, it amounted to 8.8 hours per day, on average, up from 8.2 hours in 1986 (Marshall, 2006). This amounts to over 200 extra hours in paid and unpaid work in 2005 compared to 1986—the equivalent of almost nine extra days. Most of this increase came from paid work, particularly among women, while most of the increase for men (while not as dramatic) came in the form of unpaid household work. The proportion of men and women (ages 25–54) who did some household work daily rose from 72 per cent in 1986 to 79 per cent in 2005 (Marshall, 2006). However, this increase was attributable to men, whose partici-

Table 7.3	Median Earnings, in 2005 Constant Dollars, of Full-time Full-year Employees[1] Aged 25 to 29 by Sex, Canada, 1980 to 2005		
	Median earnings in 2005 constant dollars		
Year	**Males**	**Females**	**Female–Male Earnings Ratio**
1980	43,767	32,813	0.75
1990	40,588	32,068	0.79
2000	38,110	32,579	0.85
2005	37,680	32,104	0.85

Note:

1. Full-time full-year employees worked 49 to 52 weeks during the year preceding the census, mainly full time (i.e., 30 hours or more per week). Individuals with self-employment income and those living in institutions are excluded.

Sources: Statistics Canada, Censuses of population, 1981, 1991, 2001 and 2006. Statistics Canada. 2008a. *Earnings and Incomes of Canadians Over the Past Quarter Century, 2006 Census.* Catalogue no. 97-563-X. Ottawa: Minister of Industry. Retrieved July 23, 2008. http://www12.statcan.ca/english/census06/analysis/income/pdf/97-563-XIE2006001.pdf

pation rate rose from 54 per cent to 69 per cent. The participation rate for women remained steady, at around 90 per cent (Marshall, 2006). Given these numbers, it was not surprising that the study found that women generally feel more time-stressed than men do, regardless of how long their paid workday was or if they had children (Marshall, 2006; also see MacDonald, Phipps and Lethbridge, 2005).

● Gender and Unpaid ● ● ● Household Work and Care Work

People today spend fewer hours on domestic work than they did in the mid-1960s (see, for example, Bianchi et al., 2000). The most dramatic reductions have occurred among women, who have cut housework hours in half since the 1960s because of their increased labour force participation, later marriage, and having fewer children. Changing gender attitudes have also been identified as a contributing factor (Artis and Pavalko, 2003).

Many think that given the changes in women's paid employment, the use of outside (paid) help, and technological changes, the gender balance in housework has been significantly transformed in recent years, with men doing more and women doing less. In reality, the gendered division of labour has not changed all that much; it resists technological innovation (Bittman, Rice, and Wajcman, 2004). While women are doing slightly less household work now than in the past (Statistics Canada, 2000), they still spend more time doing household work than men (Nordenmark, 2004). Women report spending an average of close to 15 hours a week on household tasks compared to men's 6.8 hours (Stevens, Kiger, and Riley, 2001). Not surprisingly, the more hours a woman works outside the home, the fewer number of hours of housework she performs (Stevens, Kiger, and Riley, 2001).

The true market value of this work is enormous. In 1992, economists valued the unpaid work done by women as 32–54 per cent of Canada's Gross Domestic Product (Statistics Canada, 2000; see also Chandler, 1994; Hamdad, 2003). There is general consensus that unpaid household work data of this type offers policy makers a powerful analytical tool, and a means of reframing basic policy questions regarding the (unequal) distribution of resources. As a result, a number of different approaches and techniques have emerged, both nationally and internationally, aimed at measuring the monetary value of unpaid household work.

The domestic division of labour also impacts marital relations. In short, too much housework, and too little fairness in the division of labour, makes both wives and husbands resentful. Said another way, the fewer hours of household work people do, and the more satisfied they are with household task arrangements, the more satisfied they are with their marriages. On a positive note, recent research shows that fathers are taking on more parenting responsibilities in their own new, different, and emerging way (Doucet, 2006).

Given the heavy burdens associated with domestic labour, many have viewed paid work as positively liberating. An American study confirms that paid work is associated with reduced depression among both husbands and wives, as long as the work hours are not excessive. By contrast, time spent on housework is found to be associated with increased depression (Glass and Fujimoto, 1994). Researchers find little evidence that an *equal* division of paid or unpaid labour inhibits depression, but *perceptions* of equity are significantly associated with lower levels of depression. In other words, a sense of fairness in the distribution of family workload contributes to well-being. In particular, husbands are strongly affected by perceived equity in the performance of *paid* work, while wives are strongly affected by perceived equity in the performance of *housework* (Glass and Fujimoto, 1994).

Both men and women look for ways to balance the demands of paid work and household work. According to MacDonald, Phipps and Lethbridge (2005), women more than men use strategies such as self-employment to improve work–family balance, but this has not proven to be as effective as anticipated.

● Why Gender ● ● ● ● ● Inequality?

In the past, much of science was sexist and supported biological explanations for the differential treatment of men and women. For example, early 'scientists' believed women's wombs controlled their minds and as a result, education was wasted on women. Whenever a woman stepped outside traditional roles or challenged social norms, she was deemed 'hysterical' and often 'cured' by the removal of her uterus. Even today, we still use the term 'hysterectomy' to refer to this womb-removal. And, early sociology proved to be no less sexist than other sciences. Many of the 'fathers' of sociology would have been considered sexist by today's standards. For example, Émile

Durkheim, the first self-identified sociologist, believed that women had smaller brains than men and were therefore intellectually inferior. Biological differences between men and women were almost always used to explain and justify why men and women lived different and unequal lives.

In the middle of the last century, **structural functionalists** (following Durkheim) were still treating the traditional two-parent nuclear family—with a breadwinner husband/father and nurturing, homemaker wife/mother—as a normal, inevitable, and functional institution within societies. When it came to gender relations, functionalists like Parsons and Bales (1955) argued that men and women perform separate and complimentary functions, or roles, within nuclear families which then benefit society as a whole. Women were expected to fulfill *expressive* (nurturing/domestic) roles and men, to fill *instrumental* (public/decision-making) roles, because this differentiation was natural and ideal.

Such differences were seen as biologically based and functionally necessary. Social stability was thought to be achievable only if men and women conformed to these traditional roles. To challenge or alter them was viewed as dysfunctional and became a problem for society as a whole. In other words, men and women had to live separate and different (unequal) lives for the greater good of society. A number of women and some men—past and present—have worked hard to challenge these types of assumptions. Some have identified the shortcomings in functionalist explanations of inequality, including their inability to recognize that men and women are neither equally valued nor hold the same amount and type of power in society (Kemp, 1994).

Conflict theorists, in particular, have called attention to a male monopoly on power; this power difference, not individual or biological differences, explains gender inequality in their view. These theorists note that men control more economic and political resources than women, giving them an ability to dominate women. Karl Marx and Friedrick Engels, for example, theorized that gender stratification and inequality result from men's private ownership of the means of production, which results in men's power over women. Engels in particular noted that before the advent of private property, under primitive communism, men and women were roughly equal. With the rise of private property, women were forced to accept monogamous marriage as the social norm, so that men could retain control over their property. This resulted in the institutionalization of male domination (Engels, 1972).

While most people today acknowledge there is social inequality on the basis of sex/gender and seek to eradicate it, not all agree on the cause of this inequality. Not even avowed feminists are in full agreement on these issues. They identify different sources or causes of inequality and therefore seek different ways to correct the problem. As a result, a number of different types of **feminism** co-exist.

Today, the word 'feminist' is used extensively, but at the same time, it has come to be treated as a four-letter word. While many people would support equality between men and women, few will actually call themselves a 'feminist'. As noted above, feminists come in many ideological stripes. All are likely to agree that feminism is a complex way of thinking about and acting upon the conditions of our lives (Rich, 1979). Feminists seek to understand the gendered nature of almost every aspect of social and institutional relations, and are committed to eradicating race, class, gender, and sexual domination wherever it exists. But different types of feminism have emerged throughout history, each focusing on somewhat different aspects of gender and sexual inequality. As a result, they have also sought different types of solutions (for a summary and simple overview of some differences, see Table 7.4 below). Some of the variants include liberal feminism, Marxist feminism, socialist feminism, radical feminism, anti-racist feminism, psychoanalytic feminism, and postmodern feminism. None of these approaches would seek to understand gender differences in life experiences to be the product of fixed, biological facts. All see inequalities as socially constructed and profoundly political—requiring social restructuring of power relations in all institutions and relations to destabilize the existing gender hierarchy. Let us take a look at two examples of how some feminist have understood and explained differences and inequalities.

Social and Biological Reproduction: Two Views on Gender Inequality

Social Reproduction

Social reproduction refers to the daily and generational production and maintenance of a population. Feminists have clearly demonstrated that this work is predominantly done by women (Bezanson, 2006). Having said that, our society continues to value and promote the advancement of paid work at the expense of the huge amount of women's work that goes into daily survival. With the neo-liberal restructuring of global economies (decreased state services and supports, and increasing economic insecurities), and with the distribution of paid and care work remaining inequitable, women have limited opportunities for social capital development (the development of networks often attributed to economic advancement) (Bezanson and Carter, 2006). These large and systemic inequities function to disproportionately disadvantage women.

Reproductive Capacity

On a slightly different note, some feminists have looked to the reproductive capacities of men and women as a way to explain inequalities. Mary O'Brien (1981) argued that the different roles women and men play in reproduction lead to different forms of consciousness and to men's efforts to control women. Not unlike Bezanson (2006), O'Brien noted that there are two kinds of labour: productive and reproductive labour. Only productive labour, seen primarily as men's domain, is explicitly recognized in society. Reproductive labour—predominantly done by women—has been and continues to be undervalued. In O'Brien's (1981) view, men experience reproduction mainly as alienation of their male seed, which in turn motivates them to seek control over both mother and child. While this has been very difficult to prove, a considerable amount of debate and theorizing, within feminism and beyond, has taken shape around our understanding of sexuality, sexual diversity, and sexual inequality. Many have wondered about whether men and women have different sexual needs, and if so, where these differences come from. Others have debated the 'naturalness' or 'inevitability' of heterosexuality. Let us consider some of these approaches.

● The Scientific ● ● ● ● ●
Study of Sex

Biomedical/Reproductive Approach

For most of human history, the scientific processes connected to procreation have remained a mystery. It was only in the late seventeenth century and early eighteenth century that the Dutch scientist Anton van Leeuwenhoek observed that sperm 'swam' in human semen. And it was not until 1875 that Oscar Hertwig became the first scientist to observe the fertilization of an egg by sperm—in sea urchins. Much of the early scientific research on sex focused on the biomedical aspects of sex and procreation. From there, some scientific work shifted focus towards 'sexual deviance', which included any and all acts that did not have reproduction as a possibility and goal. In other words, the development of sexology involved a shift in focus from reproductive processes to the study of sexual practices. For some time this branch of the field remained medical rather than social in orientation. Beginning in the latter half of the nineteenth century, as physicians sought to strengthen their hold on the medical profession and to extend their professional control over the human body and mind, 'sexual deviance' was seen as a mental illness, to be treated by medical interventions. Indeed, the American Psychological Association only removed homosexuality from its list of psychiatric disorders—found in the *Diagnostic and Statistical Manual of Mental Disorders*—in 1973.

This type of scientific approach to studying sex, which focused on sex for procreation in marriage as normal and all other sexual activity as deviant, was deeply ingrained in the social thinking until fairly recently. A 1967 academic textbook entitled *Human Sexuality: A Contemporary Marriage Manual* (McCary, 1967) included chapters on such topics as 'The Female Reproductive System', 'Fertilization, Prenatal Development and Parturition', 'Techniques in Sexual Arousal', 'Positions in Sexual Intercourse', and the last chapter, 'Sexual Aberrations', dealt with what was deemed to be deviant: sexual oralism, sexual analism (among a list of abnormal methods), homosexuality, zoophilia, necrophilia, masturbation (among a list of abnormal choices of sexual partners), and frigidity, promiscuity, and seduction (among a list of abnormal degrees of desire). The message of this scholarly text was clear, and not very different from the very earliest studies of sex: not only is human sexuality something that takes place between heterosexuals, but only within marriage, for procreation, and using prescribed and approved methods and positions.

▮▮ Time to Reflect ▮▮▐▮▐▮▐▮▐▮▐▮▐▮▐▮▐▮▐▮▐▮▐▮▐ ▮

Why does gender inequality persist? What are the most significant barriers to be overcome in achieving gender equity?

Table 7.4   A Comparison of Some Types of Feminism

	Liberal	Marxist	Radical	Socialist	Anti-racist/ Postmodern
General	Men and women essentially the same Concerned primarily with equal rights	Women as the first exploited class Subordination of women comes with the advent of private property	Men and women are different Patriarchy is not specific to capitalism, rather universal	Combines 'the best of' Marxist and radical feminisms	Critique of essentialism in other feminisms (not all women are the same, no single source of inequality Some men and women share oppression in complex ways
Why Gender Inequality?	Discriminatory legislation barring women from entering public life	Capitalism and private ownership	Patriarchy	Capitalism and patriarchy	Multiple inequalities: race, class, gender, sexuality, (dis)ability, etc. overlap in unique ways for different women
Key issues	Right to vote, access to education and paid employment, pay equity		Male control of female sexuality Women's reproductive capacity	Inequality as a result of the intersection of race, class, gender Inequality in paid and unpaid work, in the homeand outside	Post-colonial exploitation of women of colour
How fix?	Do not change the structure of society, just legislation barring women into public life The 'best women' like 'the best men' will rise to the top	Need to change the social structure: for example, abolish capitalism	Direct action, political opposition, radical social change	Attack both patriarchy and capitalism	No single solution for all women Need to address differences among women in a non-universalizing, non-essentialist way

Throughout the 1800s and into the 1900s, a number of prominent thinkers contributed to a growing body of sex research. Sigmund Freud (1856–1939), for example, the founder of psychoanalysis, produced a comprehensive theory of human development with sex at the centre. According to Freud, the development of a healthy adult personality depended on the successful navigation through various stages of psychosocial and psychosexual development, each involving the careful management of various aspects of the sexual instinct. In fact, many of the early theories of sexuality used the metaphor of repression, which comes from hydraulics, and included the idea or image of a gushing energy that must be held back and controlled. Sexuality, historically, has been perceived as an innate 'force' that needs to be regulated and successfully manipulated or (re)directed towards acceptable channels.

Social Survey Approach

The American biologist Alfred Kinsey (1894–1956) broke new ground in the scientific study of sex by challenging some of the accepted norms of his time. For example, he argued that 'biologists and psychologists who have accepted the doctrine that the only natural function of sex is reproduction have simply ignored the existence of sexual activity which is not reproductive' (Kinsey et al., 1953: 448). He was critical of biologists and psychologists who assumed that heterosexual responses are part of an animal's innate or instinctive equipment, and was especially critical of their treatment of non-reproductive sexual activity as perversions of normal instincts (Kinsey et al., 1953).

In 1947, Kinsey founded the Institute for Research in Sex, Gender and Reproduction at Indiana University, now called the Kinsey Institute. Kinsey is famous for surveying approximately 18,000 Americans in the 1940s on their sexual practices. Through the survey he found, among other things, that there were significantly different class patterns among men in the incidence of masturbation, homosexuality, oral sex, sex with prostitutes, and premarital and extramarital sex. For women, their age and gender ideologies were significantly more important than social class in explaining variations in sexual preferences and practices. He was also famous for his 'Heterosexual–Homosexual Rating Scale', a seven-point continuum representing a considerably more complex approach to understanding sexuality and sexual orientation than was typical at the time.

He proposed that males do not represent two discrete populations—heterosexual and homosexual—and that the living world is a continuum in all its aspects (Kinsey et al., 1948). As such, he emphasized a continuity of the gradations (a scale) between exclusively heterosexual and exclusively homosexual life histories. Note that he did not say 'exclusively heterosexual individuals' but rather 'histories'. This was intentional because Kinsey argued that an individual may be assigned a different position on the scale for different periods in his life. On the scale, zero refers to exclusively heterosexual with no homosexual experiences; 1 is predominantly heterosexual, and only incidentally homosexual; 2 is predominantly heterosexual but more than incidentally homosexual; 3 is equally heterosexual and homosexual; 4 is predominantly homosexual but more than incidentally heterosexual; 5 is predominantly homosexual and only incidentally heterosexual; and 6 is exclusively homosexual (Kinsey et al., 1948: 638).

Laboratory Approach

Other noted sex researchers include William Masters (1915–2001) and Virginia Johnson (1925–). In 1957, William Masters hired Virginia Johnson as his research assistant in studies of human sexuality. After years of working together, Masters and Johnson left their respective partners and married; Masters and Johnson subsequently divorced in 1993. Together, they founded the Reproductive Biology Research Foundation in St Louis, Missouri, later renamed the Masters and Johnson Institute. In their early laboratory research they recorded data, based on direct observation, on the anatomy and physiology of human sexual response (including the nature of female arousal and orgasm). They began by observing and documenting the stages of sexual arousal and orgasmic responses of 382 women and 312 men. Among other things, they observed and reported on the sexual responsiveness of older men and women, including elderly individuals—noting that many older men and women are perfectly capable of excitement and orgasm (typically following more direct genital stimulation) well into their seventies. They observed and measured masturbation and sexual intercourse in laboratory settings. In doing this, they treated and wrote about sex as a healthy and natural activity, enjoyed for pleasure and intimacy. They also developed a clinical approach (sex therapy) to the treatment of 'sexual dysfunction' or 'sexual problems', including premature ejaculation, impotence, and female frigidity. Given the voyeuristic nature of this research, it is not surprising that their work was more trendy and 'popular' than of long-lasting importance.

Ethnographic/Anthropological Approach

Although anthropologists such as Margaret Mead (1901–78) would not be considered 'sexologists', they have, nonetheless, done extensive research documenting the sexual lives of people across diverse cultures. In doing so, they have contributed a body of research that challenges the view that sex and sexuality are biological (fixed, innate) facts. Mead, for example, wrote hundreds of articles and dozens of books documenting the lives, including the sexual lives and practice, of diverse cultures of the South Pacific. In *Coming of Age in Samoa* (1928), she shocked some of her American readers (from the 1930s into the 1950s) when she wrote about her observations of young Samoan women who deferred marriage while enjoying casual premarital sex before eventually marrying. She documented the impact of variations in culture (rather than biology) in the construction of sex roles, including sexuality, in *Sex and Temperament in Three Primitive Societies* (1935). Similarly, Clellan Ford and Frank Beach (1951), in an extensive survey of over 200 societies, produced anthropological evidence of striking diversity and variation in sexual practices and norms. The amount of variation across and within cultures is one way in which we know that sexual responses are learned and not innate.

Photo #KI-HI:1061 by William Dellenback. Reprinted by permission of The Kinsey Institute for Research in Sex, Gender, and Reproduction, Inc.

Sociology of Sex: Theoretical and Methodological Approaches

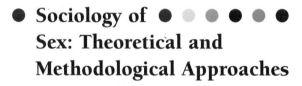

Like Mead, most sociologists today would argue that sexuality involves much more than an understanding of biological aspects of physical attraction. Sociologists, like anthropologists, frequently stress the social and cultural relativity of norms surrounding sexual behaviour and the socio-historical construction of sexual identities and roles. Within sociology, sexuality is typically studied and understood as being intricately connected to cultural, economic, political, legal, moral, and ethical phenomena. Janice Irvine (2003: 431), for example, notes that from a sociological perspective, 'sexuality is a broad social domain involving multiple fields of power, diverse systems of knowledge, and sets of institutional and political discourses.' While sociology may have been comparatively slow to enter this field of study, it has gone a long way to address, explain, and understand some of these diverse issues and dimensions. But it does so from a number of different theoretical and methodological perspectives.

In tracing the history of sociological theorizing and research on sexuality, Irvine identified five broad themes in the sociological literature: (1) the denaturalization of sexuality (a shift away from biological explanations); (2) the historicization of sexuality; (3) the analytic shift from the study of 'sexual deviants' (the individuals) to the study of 'sexual deviance' (the rule-making strategies or social systems that define people as deviant or stigmatize them), thus challenging the pathologizing categories of sexuality and blurring the status of insider/outsider; (4) the destabilization of sexual categories and identities, with new emphasis on the fluid and diverse meanings of sex and sexuality; and (5) the theorizing of sexuality (and gender) as performance.

Denaturalization

Structural Functionalist

Early sociologists, especially some structural functionalists, made liberal use of biological models and metaphors but did not wholeheartedly embrace simple biological explanations of social reality. When the American structural functionalist Kingsley Davis wrote about

Figure 7.2   Kinsey's Heterosexual–Homosexual Rating Scale . . . Applied

Heterosexual–Homosexual Rating Scale

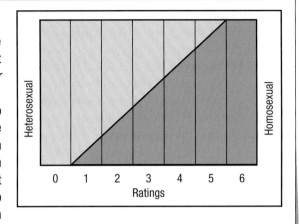

One theoretical construct designed by Alfred Kinsey is the 'Heterosexual–Homosexual Rating Scale', a seven-point continuum originally published in Kinsey's *Sexual Behavior in the Human Male* (1948).

Fernando Luiz Cardoso (2002) applied this scale to his six-month field study of 41 men living in a remote fishing village in southern Brazil. Cardoso found that in this society many 'straight' men customarily had sex with local 'gay' men, called '*paneleiros*'. He found at least three different categories of male sexuality: men who have sex only with men, men who have sex only with women, and men who have sex with men and women. Cardoso noted that 'they believe, a "real" man is somebody "who has never been @#$%&* but can @#!* whoever is available"' (ibid., 57). For them, masculinity is determined by sexual function and position, and not by the sex of the partner. The same was true in ancient Greece, where social class and authority determined who would penetrate and who would be penetrated.

Source: Diagram from <www.kinseyinstitute.org/about/photo-tour.html>. Reprinted by permission of the Kinsey Institute for Research in Sex, Gender, and Reproduction, Inc.

human sexuality, he looked at sexual intercourse as more than a biological exchange or a simple response to natural urges. He instead saw it as a social exchange, often involving 'the employment of sex for non-sexual ends within a competitive-authoritarian system' (Davis, 1937: 746). In his classic article, 'The Sociology of Prostitution', Davis asked the question: why is it that a practice so thoroughly disapproved, so widely outlawed in Western civilization, can yet flourish so universally?

Davis noted that where the family is strong, there tends to be a well-defined system of prostitution. He explained that the family is an institution of status that limits the variety, amount, and nature of a person's satisfaction. Through prostitution, a man is paying for the privilege to demand what he wants. Davis suggested that 'the sole limitation on [a man's] satisfaction is not morality or convention, but his ability to pay the price' (Davis, 1937: 753). To a certain extent, then, prostitution served to keep nuclear families together and 'strong'. When men could not have their sexual needs met within marriage, prostitution functioned to fill that role. He also added that prostitution served a number of other functions in economical ways: 'enabling a small number of women to take care of the needs of a large number of men, it is the most convenient sexual outlet for an army, and for the legions of strangers, perverts and physically repulsive in our midst. It performs a function appar-

ently, which no other institution fully performs' (Davis, 1937: 755). He warned, however, that a decline of the family and a decline of prostitution are both associated with a rise of sexual freedom, and explained that 'unrestricted indulgence in sex for the fun of it by both sexes is the greatest enemy, not only of the family, but also of prostitution' (Davis, 1937).

More recently, using a structural-functionalist perspective, Davidson and Hoffman (1986) conducted a survey of 212 married female graduate and undergraduate students at a Midwestern commuter university in the United States to see what meaning and function sexual fantasies played in marital satisfaction. They found that, contrary to popular belief and some previous studies, engaging in sexual fantasies did not negatively affect married women's mental health, including level of guilt, sexual adjustment, and overall satisfaction with their current sex life. They found no significant differences between frequency of sexual fantasizing and marital satisfaction. Respondents who reported being satisfied with their current sex life fantasized about their current sex partner, and those who were dissatisfied were much more likely to fantasize about a more affectionate partner. Davidson and Hoffman concluded that their data strongly suggest that sexual fantasies function to help achieve sexual arousal irrespective of satisfaction or dissatisfaction with married women's current sex lives.

HUMAN DIVERSITY
Incest and Taboo

In the following excerpt, Clifford Bishop (1996: 120–1) describes the variation in the practices and beliefs of different peoples surrounding the issue of incest.

Some form of prohibition against incest is the nearest thing to a universal human taboo. People such as the !Kung of Southern Africa think of incest as 'dangerous, like going up to a lion,' and the Comanche of North America used to consider it neither a crime nor a sin, but simply impossible. However, there are numerous examples of incest being allowed, or even encouraged, in a culture. The most famous instances are the incestuous marriages of the royal houses of ancient Egypt and Inca Peru, in which brother and sister were required to continue the dynastic line. Half-sibling marriages were quite common in the ancient Near East and Europe, among the Persians, Greeks and Hebrews. In Bali, although half- and full-sibling marriages are forbidden, it is assumed that opposite sex twins have already been intimate in the womb, so they are allowed to marry as adults; by contrast, the Marshallese of the Pacific believe that such *in-utero* incest is cause to kill the male twin. Other peoples, such as the Lamet of Asia, define kinship socially rather than by blood, and allow sibling marriage if the boy and girl have been raised in different households.

Sex between a father and his daughter is more rarely sanctioned in any society, but is, in practice, the most frequent form of incest. A survey in the United States in the mid-1980s concluded that 10 to 14 per cent of under-18-year-olds had experienced some form of incestuous attention, and that most were girls and young women abused by their fathers and stepfathers.

The rarest matings of all are between mother and son. Travelers' tales relate examples of this union worldwide, but there are probably only two plausible institutionalized examples. The Kubeo of South America require a boy to sleep with his mother to mark the beginning of his official sex life (although marriage between them is forbidden), and an east African Tutsi cure for impotence on the marriage night involves the man sleeping with his mother.

But even those societies that selectively sanction breaches of the incest taboo enforce it in all other cases . . . .

Source: Clifford Bishop, *Sex and Spirit* (Alexandria, VA: Time-Life Books, 1996), 120–1.

Conflict Approaches

We often think of Friedrich Engels in relation to his work with Karl Marx, writing about social class inequality. However, his famous work, *The Origin of Family, Private Property and the State* (1990 [1884]), has a great deal to say about sexuality, private property, power, and subordination. Engels notes that in tribal societies with no concept of private property, promiscuous intercourse prevailed so that 'every woman belonged equally to every man and every man to every woman' (Engels, 1990 [1884]: 142). He adds that among the Iroquois, for example, a man considered his own and his brother's children his children, and they would all call him father. Paternity was no mere honorary title linked to procreation, but rather carried serious mutual obligations, essential for the social constitution of these people (Engels, 1990 [1884]: 141). Engels explains that with the advent of private property, this changed. As the desire for the accumulation of wealth increased, men gained greater status in the family than women. This also created a stimulus for men to overthrow traditional communal forms of inheritance in favour of their children. To do this, men would have to ensure paternity as a biological rather than social category, and did so through the introduction of monogamy, the repression of women's sexual freedom, and the rise of the patriarchal family as a dominant family form (Engels, 1990 [1884]: 164–5).

Engels states that the final outcome of 3,000 years of monogamy is the bourgeois family, where men have exclusive domination over women, including over women's sexual autonomy. He predicted that monogamy and women's sexual oppression would disappear when the economic cause—private property ownership—disappears. The revolutionary overthrow of capitalism and the abolition of private property would mean that the individual family would cease to be the economic unit of society. Engels explains that then 'society takes care of all children equally' and 'the anxiety about the 'consequences,'' which is today the most important social factor—both moral and economic—that hinders a girl from giving herself freely to the man she loves, disappears.' He then proclaims: 'Will this not be cause enough for a gradual rise of more unrestrained sexual intercourse, and along with it, a laxer public opinion regarding virginal honour and female shame?' (Engels, 1990 [1884]: 183). Engels's views on 'individual love sex' or free love were adopted by a number of others, including left-wing feminists Alexandra Kollontai and Emma Goldman.

More recent conflict theorists have focused less on sexual freedom and more on understanding the link between sexuality and social class differences. An American study of sexual behaviour and attitudes found that people from higher social classes and white men had greater access to sexual capital than black men and black women, white women, and men and women in lower classes (Gonzales and Rolison, 2005). Gonzales and Rolison (2005) found, among other things, that study respondents with higher socio-economic status (SES) reported thinking about sex more frequently than other respondents. They also found that the higher a respondent's SES, the more frequently he or she reported masturbating and the more likely the individual was to report finding a significantly greater variety of sexual acts more appealing than others. Gonzales and Rolison (2005) concluded that sexual behaviour and attitudes in the US reflect patterns of dominance and inequality, and these 'structures of sexual inequality are enshrined in taken-for-granted American moral dispositions' (Gonzales and Rolison, 2005: 716). In other words, these differences reflect their position in a stratified society, and 'private' choice is conditioned by race, class, and gender dominance.

Interactionist Sociology and Sexual Scripts

John Gagnon and William Simon, both of whom trained at the University of Chicago and later worked at the Kinsey Institute (1965–8), have been identified as 'fathers' of the sociological study of sex in North America. Going much further than Park, they openly challenge the biological determinism of most sexologists, arguing that if sex does play an important part in shaping human affairs it is because societies have created its importance, not because of rigid biological grounding (Simon and Gagnon, 2003). For them, sex is neither a dangerous instinct that needs curbing nor a passionate impulse that needs liberating. They further argue that neither sexual activities nor body parts are inherently sexual; rather they become sexual when social meanings are attributed to them. While sexual activity most often takes place in private settings, they argue that 'the sexual encounter remains a profoundly social act in its enactment and even more so in its antecedents and consequences' (Simon and Gagnon, 2003: 492). In other words, the language and actions that make up sexual encounters, and their rules, restrictions, and **taboos**, are socially constructed and part of socially defined **sexual scripts** or road maps for sexual activity (Gagnon and Simon, 1986). The script concept implies a complex construction of culturally defined socio-sexual roles. For example, while this may be changing (also evidence of the fact that these are constructed roles), men are/have been expected to conduct themselves assertively and to make the first move, and women are/have been expected to be passive, compliant, and more responsive as the interaction progresses. Scripts also include internal dialogues about desire and resistance (Weis, 1998).

Destabilizing Sexual Categories: Feminists, Queer Theory, and Beyond

Many feminists have questioned and challenged, among other things, the social construction of sex and sexuality, the control of women's bodies and reproduction, the objectification of women, sexual double standards, the link between sex and power, and sexual abuse and oppression (Millett, 1969; Greer, 1984; Weitz, 2002). Holly Benkert notes that 'the basis for oppression of women is deeply rooted to our sexuality, the very source of our primary "difference"' (Benkert, 2002: 1197). Some, however, have pointed out that, since the 1960s, feminists in North America have understood sexuality as both 'an arena for women's liberation' and 'a crucial vector of women's oppression' (Marcus, 2005: 193). Some feminists have attempted to deconstruct and then reclaim women's rights to sexual pleasure, autonomy, and knowledge (Bell, 1994; Eaves, 2002), while others have challenged the forces that stood against women's autonomy, including pornography, rape, and sexual harassment (Brownmiller, 1975; Dworkin, 1981; MacKinnon, 1989).

The debates around pornography have been especially divisive. Some, like Dworkin and MacKinnon, consider pornography to be demeaning and degrading to women and representative of male power over women. For others, the freedom to explore diverse representations of sexuality, including pornography or erotica, is seen as liberating to women, and challenges restrictions placed on women's sexuality (Bell, 1994;

Zimmer Gunsel Frasca Architects LLP · ARC/Architectural Resources Cambridge · BraytonHughes Design Studios · CBT/Childs Bertman Tseckares · Wolcott Architecture Interior · RTKL Associates Inc. · STAFFELBACK · Ted Moudis Associates · Tobin + Parnes Design Enterprises · VOA Associates Incorporated · Wolcott Architecture in · Margulies Perruzzi Architects · McCarthy Nordburg · NELSON · OWP/P · Partridge Architects Inc. · Perkins+Will · Rotter Studio – Architecture and T · Valcarcel, Architects, PC · H. Hendy Associates · HLW International LLP · HOK · Huntsman Architectural Group · Ken R. Harry Associates, Inc. · LS3P ASSOCIATES · Resources Cambridge · BraytonHughes Design Studios · CBT/Childs Bertman Tseckares · Francis Cauffm · FXFOWLE Architects LLP · Gensler · Gerner Kro · Associates · Tobin + Parnes Design Enterprises · VOA Associates Incorporated · Wolcott Architecture Incorporated · Zimmer Gunsel Frasca Architects LLP · ARC/Architecture in

Sprinkle, 1991). The African-American social theorist and feminist critic bell hooks explains that many feminists, in fact, stopped talking about sex publicly because it exposed 'our differences' (hooks, 1994: 79); however, challenging patriarchal definitions and restrictions on women's sexual autonomy has been a unifying theme within feminism.

Writers such as Judith Butler (1990) have argued that categories like 'heterosexual' and 'homosexual' are used to control and constrain individuals and therefore should be challenged on a number of fronts. Some, like Carr, promote the notion of a 'fluid conception of sexual identification' that is subject to 'the flux and flow of life' (Carr, 2004: 17), allowing for the possibility of individuals to change from one identification to another. Queer theory calls for this type of challenge and change.

The use of the term 'queer' within the gay community began as a ploy to reclaim a slur and highlight the multiple ways that sexual practices, sexual fantasy, and sexual identity 'fail to line up consistently' and 'expresses an important insight about the complexity of sexuality' (Marcus, 2005: 196). Queer theory derives part of its philosophy from the ideas of Michel Foucault (1990), who saw homosexuality as a strategically situated marginal position from where it may be possible to see new

and diverse ways of relating to oneself and others. Queer politics rejects forms of gender and sexual oppression, but it intentionally does so from the margins in order to maintain a critical outsider perspective (Baird, 2001).

Sexual Citizenship and Sexuality in Canada

Former Prime Minister Pierre Trudeau, when he was Justice Minister in 1967, played a key role in helping to legally redefine sexuality for Canadians. For the first 100 years after Confederation, homosexuality was illegal in Canada and considered to be a mental illness. In December of 1967, Trudeau introduced a controversial new omnibus bill in the House of Commons (Bill C-150) that challenged this and some other restrictions placed on sexuality. Trudeau's legislation brought issues like abortion, homosexuality, and the divorce law to the forefront, changing the sexual landscape of Canada. At the time, Trudeau famously stated that 'there's no place for the state in the bedrooms of the nation.' Despite considerable opposition, by 1969 homosexual acts had been decriminalized and women had more control over sexual reproduction and their bodies. It was not until the 2000, however, with the passing of Bill C-23, that same-sex

SOCIOLOGY IN ACTION
Sexual Scripts and Sexual Double Standards in Popular Magazines

A number of content analyses of women's and men's magazines have found that stories, advice columns, and advertising reinforce dominant gender and sexual norms (Carpenter, 1998; Reichert and Lambiase, 2003; Jackson, 2005; McCleneghan, 2003). For example, Jackson (2005), analyzing young women's letters to the advice pages of a magazine (and the published responses from 'agony aunts'), found that while young women's letters suggest attempts to 'do' (and understand their) sexual desire, agony aunts often contributed to an 'undoing' of desire. Discourses of romance, sexual safety, and adolescence functioned to undermine the young women's expressions of desire. For example, compulsory heterosexuality was reinforced when one young woman asked about her attraction to girls over boys. Similarly, masturbation was endorsed, particularly as a substitute for sexual

contact with others, and expressions of sexual desire were sidestepped, often by advocating the need for a loving relationship (Jackson, 2005).

In contrast to this, the relatively new and rapidly growing popular genre of men's magazines (often referred to as lad magazines, which include *Maxim*, *Stuff*, and *FHM*), while seeming to focus on what women want sexually, actually often privilege a fairly narrow male heterosexuality, oriented towards sexual variety (Taylor, 2005), and reinforce the objectification of women (Krassas et al., 2003). In brief, while the magazines targeting young women promoted heterosexual exclusivity and traditional sexual scripts, the men's magazines promoted more permissive (hetero)sexual attitudes and the desire to seek sexual sensation more frequently and with a greater number of sexual partners.

couples were granted the same rights and obligations as common-law couples. In 2005 the Liberal government passed 'equal marriage' legislation and on 20 July 2005, Bill C-315, The Civil Marriage Act, recognized the right of same-sex couples to have access to civil marriage.

Over the past 40 years there have also been changes to the laws governing the legal age of consent to have sex in Canada, with major changes in 1988. That year, the introduction of Bill C-15 created the offence of 'sexual interference' and prohibited adults from engaging in virtually any kind of sexual contact with either boys or girls under the age of 14, regardless of consent. The notion of 'sexual exploitation' was also included, making it an offence for an adult to have any sexual contact with boys or girls ages 14–18, where a relationship of trust or authority exists (teachers, coaches, etc.). The law added that consensual sex with those 12–14 'may not be an offence' if the accused is under 16 and less than two years older than the complainant. This clearly attempted to reflect some of the trends in early sexual engagement among teenagers today.

Sexual Activity among Youth

Findings from the National Longitudinal Survey of Children and Youth in Canada revealed that an estimated 12 per cent of boys and 13 per cent of girls have had sexual intercourse by the age of 15 (Garriguet, 2005; Statistics Canada, 2005c). The study also found that characteristics associated with early sexual activity differed for boys and girls. That is, the odds of early intercourse among girls were high for those who at 12 or 13 had reached puberty, or were not overweight, but also for girls whose self-esteem was weak at ages 12 and 13. In regards to self-esteem, the opposite was true for boys. The association between smoking and early intercourse was also strong. Furthermore, for girls, having tried drinking alcohol by the age of 12 or 13 was also associated with having intercourse by age 15, while drinking alcohol was not associated with boys' sexual activity (Statistics Canada, 2005c). Girls in the eastern provinces and Quebec were more likely to report being sexually active than those in Ontario and the western provinces (Garriguet, 2005). Boys with poor relationships with their parents were more likely to report early sexual activity.

A study of teenagers' perception of parental disapproval of their initiation of sexual intercourse found that well over half of the 2,353 Grade 10 and 12 students interviewed anticipated parental disapproval of their behaviour, but about 44 per cent of the total had had sexual intercourse nonetheless (Hampton et al., 2005). Coincidentally, a report by the Vanier Institute of the Family found that Canadian adults under the age of 35 were considerably less likely than older Canadians to express disapproval and non-acceptance of their children having premarital sex at any age, engaging in homosexual acts, learning that their children are gay or lesbian, the arrival of grandchildren when their sons and daughters are not married, and having their children live together in common-law situations (Bibby, 2004; see Table 7.5). In fact, it has been found that attitudes towards sexuality have shifted considerably when we look across various generations of Canadians (see Tables 7.6 and 7.7). Some historical examples demonstrate that the shift or change has more to do with perceiving rather than with 'doing' sex differently.

Statistics Canada notes that 28 per cent of 15–17-year-olds reported having had sexual intercourse at least once, and by the ages of 20–24, 80 per cent had had sexual intercourse. One-third of 15–24-year-olds reported having had more than one sexual partner in the previous year, and 30 per cent of those who had sex with multiple partners in the past year had not used a condom the last time they had intercourse (Statistics Canada, 2005c). Having sex without a condom was more common among older youth: 44 per cent of sexually active 20–24-year-olds reported having sex without a condom compared to 33 per cent of those aged 18 and 19, and 22 per cent of those 15 to 17 (Statistics Canada, 2005c). Researchers speculate that those in older age groups are more likely to be in longer-term relationships and so perceive condom use as less necessary. Indeed, Netting and Burnett (2004) found that condom use tended to be low among monogamous sexually active students.

While there are clearly shifts in attitudes and practices when it comes to sex and sexuality, do these amount to another sexual revolution? Connell and Hunt (2006) note the sexual revolution of the 1960s weakened the link between sex and marriage. In their analysis of sex advice literature, they identify a clear shift from 'marriage manuals' to 'sex manuals', with the new sex manuals investing heavily in the ideology of interpersonal responsibility and mutuality, and often emphasizing the giving or sharing of pleasure. Connell and Hunt (2006) suggest that these new manuals consciously refused to confine sexual pleasure to marriage, yet the traditional script persisted of the male as initiator and the female as responding to his initiative. They explain that the idea that men need to court women with romantic tactics continued to 'pervade the discursive construction of heterosexuality', and this dominant paradigm was only occasionally challenged (Connell and Hunt, 2006: 37). Despite the fact that newer and even recent manuals more openly discuss

Time to Reflect

Why do you think the word 'queer' was adopted in the gay community and among homosexual writers? Does this help us to rethink sexuality? How? Why?

the female orgasm and women's sexual desires, the dominant gendered paradigm of the heterosexual encounter has shown remarkable persistence. Connell and Hunt (2006) conclude their analysis of sex advice literature by stating that 'the cult of sexual pleasure retained much of its gendered configuration and thus undermined the apparent commitment to sexual egalitarianism' (Connell and Hunt, 2006: 41).

Sex and the Workplace

A number of scholars of sex and gender have argued that many different workplace and organizational cultures play key roles in creating, maintaining, and undermining sexual identity and inequality at work (Hearn and Parkin, 1987; Woods and Lucas, 1993; Welsh, 1999; Dellinger, 2002). Dellinger (2002) suggests that instead of simply looking at sexuality as something individuals bring to work, we can, and some have, examine how customs and practices in a workplace constitute a type of **organizational sexuality** or social practice that determines explicit and culturally elaborated rules of behaviour to regulate sexual identities and personal relationships. In other words, different occupational cultures hold different and specific social rules about what constitutes 'appropriate' or acceptable sexuality. Workplace norms about sexuality regulate who we say we are, who we 'date', how we dress, and how we understand and experience sexual harassment in the workplace.

Woods and Lucas (1993) write about the 'corporate closet', which strongly encourages gay men in some professions to keep their sexual identities and relationships hidden. In such work contexts, gays and lesbians intentionally pass as heterosexuals because of the pervasiveness of heteronormative discourses and **heterosexism** in the workplace (Johnson, 2002).

Ironically, heterosexist norms in the workplace, which assume that everyone is heterosexual, may at times make sexual interaction between co-workers of the same sexual orientation somewhat less problematic than sexual interaction between heterosexual co-workers. Some workplaces actively discourage the sexual involvement of heterosexual colleagues even when there is sex-

ual consent between the individuals involved. The issue is, of course, very complex. Some 'pro-sex' feminists argue that women should be free to express their sexuality, and that women are oppressed by restrictions on sexual expression, including in the workplace, since such restrictions are often supported by social and political conservatives seeking to promote the image of women as pure and virtuous (Williams et al., 1999). In contrast, Catherine MacKinnon and Andrea Dworkin, among others, argue that heterosexuality is oppressive to women and that sexual consent is only possible between equals and, therefore, impossible in workplaces dominated and controlled by men. Williams and colleagues (1999: 76) explain that 'workers themselves often conceive of sexual behaviors at work along a continuum, ranging from pleasurable, to tolerable, to harassing.'

Sandy Welsh (1999), writing on sexual harassment, explains that some organizations actually mandate the sexualization of their workers, and as a result, in some sexually charged work cultures, degrading and/or sexual behaviours become an institutionalized component of work. Thus, for example, a waitress at *Hooters* is required to wear short shorts and a top that shows cleavage, but this is not considered sexual harassment. Of course, for some women who work at *Hooters* bar-restaurants such a requirement may be demeaning and objectifying; for others, however, this might not be the case. Researchers such as Dellinger (2002) have noted that most workplaces, either formally or informally, convey rules of dress, and that dress is a well-recognized site of gender construction and sexual identity. Dellinger finds that dress norms and local workplace norms 'influence people's definition of pleasurable, acceptable, and unacceptable sexuality at work' (2002: 23). As a result, workplace norms and organizational culture affect how sexuality is negotiated at work and, in part, determine what counts as sexual harassment.

Welsh (1999) reminds us that heterosexual norms in the workplace often exclude or sexualize women, silence or closet gay man and lesbians, and work to constrain the behaviour of heterosexual men who are at times labelled 'unmasculine' when they choose not to participate in 'hypermasculine' stereotypical behaviour.

Table 7.5   Disapproval and Non-Acceptance of Children's Sexual Behaviour by Age, Gender, and Religious Service Attendance

	Total	18–34	35–54	55+	18–34			
					Female	Male	Weekly+	<Weekly
Engaging in premarital sex proir to age 18	29%	19	28	40	18	20	57	11
Engaging in premarital sex when 18 or older	11	9	9	18	8	10	37	3
Engaging in homosexual acts	45	27	45	63	24	31	71	18
Informing you that they are gay or lesbian	22	12	23	32	12	13	29	9
Having children without being married	17	8	16	30	8	7	28	3
Living with partner without being married	12	9	10	17	8	10	37	3
Having sexual relations other than with spouse	74	69	74	79	74	63	90	65

Notes: Percentages are for those who disapprove and do not accept. Gender breakdown and religious service attendance shown only for 18–34 age group.
Source: Bibby (2004), at: <www.vifamily.ca/library/future/section_2.pdf>. Reprinted by permission of the Vanier Institute of the Family.

Table 7.6   Discussing Sexuality by Age and Region

'Do you—or did you, or do you plan to—talk about sexuality with your children?'				
	A Fair Amount	A Bit	Little/None	Totals
Nationally	**54%**	**34**	**12**	**100**
18–34	66	31	3	100
35–54	35	39	26	100
55+	35	39	26	100
Atlantic	60	28	12	100
BC	57	32	11	100
Prairies	57	32	11	100
Ontario	54	33	13	100
Quebec	47	41	12	100
18–34	*62*	*34*	*4*	*100*
35–54	*47*	*42*	*11*	*100*
55+	*33*	*48*	*19*	*100*

Source: Bibby (2004), at: <www.vifamily.ca/library/future/section_2.pdf>. Reprinted by permission of the Vanier Institute of the Family.

Table 7.7 — Acceptance of Sexual Relations and Approval of Legal Abortion by Age Cohorts, 1975 and 2000*

	1975	2000
PREMARITAL RELATIONS		
Nationally	68%	84
18–34	90	93
35–54	65	89
55+	42	74
HOMOSEXUAL RELATIONS		
Nationally	28	73
18–34	42	75
35–54	25	64
55+	12	42
LEGAL ABORTION A POSSIBILITY . . .		
"If her own health is seriously endangered"		
Nationally	94	94
18–34	97	98
35–54	92	95
55+	93	90
"If she is married and doesn't want more children"		
Nationally	45	52
18–34	47	51
35–54	43	44
55+	45	48

*Sexual relations: % indicating '*not wrong at all*' or '*sometimes wrong*' versus 'always wrong' or 'almost always wrong'; legal abortion: % indicating '*yes*', it should be possible.

Source: Bibby (2004), at: <www.vifamily.ca/library/future/section_2.pdf>. Reprinted by permission of the Vanier Institute of the Family.

Sexual Offences

For some radical feminists, such as Andrea Dworkin and Catherine MacKinnon, pornography—online or offline—'reveals that male pleasure is inextricably tied to victimization, hurting, exploiting' (Dworkin, 1981: 69). Others have not gone so far, but have pointed out that pornography often contains sexual violence (Barron and Kimmel, 2000; Palys, 1986) and that this may have a negative effect on men's attitudes towards women. But whether pornography actually causes its consumers to engage in sexual violence is still debated (McKee, 2007). Having said this, sexual assault and abuse continue to be a problem in Canada, especially for younger victims.

In 1983, Bill C-127 introduced a three-tiered structure of sexual assault offences designed to improve legal processing of rape cases (see DuMont, 2003). Today, under Canadian criminal law, a broad array of activities qualify as sexual assault, ranging from unwanted touch-

ing to sexual violence resulting in serious injury, with penetration not being an essential component (Johnson, 2005). A Statistics Canada report pointed out that the rate of sexual offences, including sexual assaults, reported to police declined by 36 per cent between 1993 and 2002 (Kong et al., 2003). In contrast, sexual offences against children and youth were alarmingly high. Police reports and victimization surveys reveal that young women and girls are at the highest risk of sexual assault victimization, and rates of sexual offending were highest among male teenagers (Kong et al., 2003). As a result, a majority of sexual assaults today are committed against children and youth (AuCoin, 2005). In Canada, six of every 10 victims of sexual offences reported to police in 2002 were children and youth under 18 (Statistics Canada, 2005d). Girls made up the majority of victims (85 per cent), with the highest rates among those aged 11–19 (with the peak at 13 years of age). For male victims, rates were highest for boys aged 3–14 (Kong et al., 2003). Boys aged 13–14

Figure 7.3   Percentage of Canadian Grade 9 and 11 Students Who Have Had Intercourse, 1988, 2002

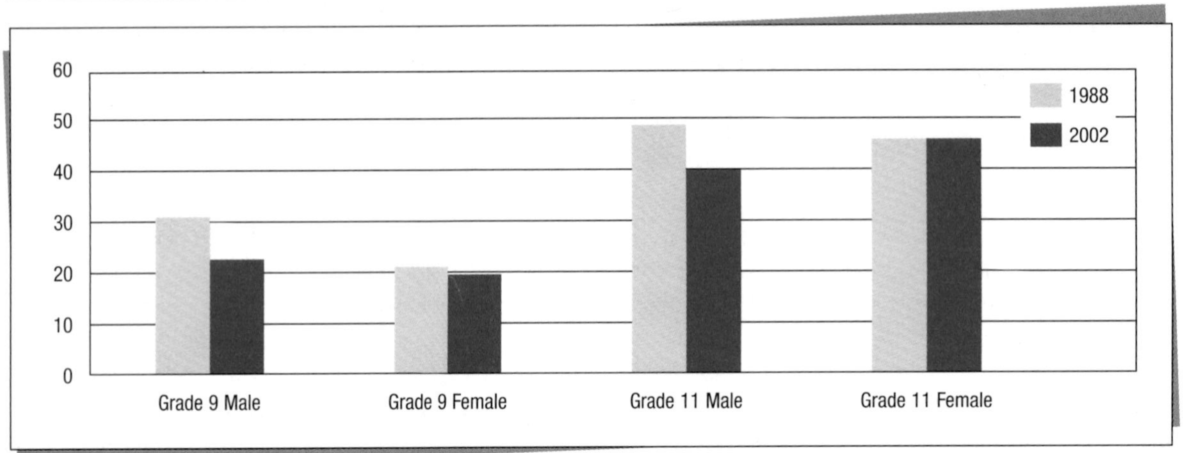

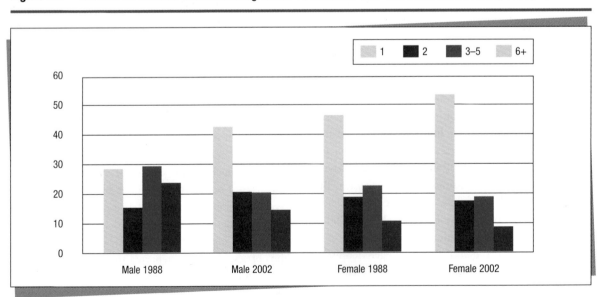

Source: Boyce et al. (cited in McKay, 2004: 74, at: <www.sieccan.org/pdf/mckay.pdf>). Reprinted by permission of the publisher.

were at highest risk of committing level 1 sexual offences (level 1: minor or no physical injuries to victim; level 2: sexual assault with weapon; level 3: wounding or endangering the life of victim).

Younger victims were more likely to be sexually assaulted by a family member. In fact, only 4 per cent of female victims under the age of six and about 10 per cent of victims 6–13 years old were sexually assaulted by a stranger (Statistics Canada, 2005d). Those of ages 12–17 were most often sexually victimized by peers and acquaintances (Kong et al., 2003). In sum, 86 per cent of cases of sexual assaults were perpetrated by an individual known to the victim (AuCoin, 2005). At the same time, it should be noted that increased attention is being placed on the sexual victimization of children and youth by strangers via the Internet. Future research is likely to focus on this relatively new and growing form of sexual exploitation.

Figure 7.4   Number of Sexual Partners among Grade 11 Students Who Have Had Intercourse, 1988, 2002

Source: McKay (2004: 74), at: <www.sieccan.org/pdf/mckay.pdf>. Reprinted by permission of the publisher.

● Mission Accomplished?● ●

In 1970, we saw the publication of the *Report of the Royal Commission on The Status of Women in Canada.* The Royal Commission on the Status of Women in Canada was set up in February 1967. Its goals included documenting the status of women at the time, and making recommendations on a number of legislative changes and practices, with the goal of improving the position of women in Canada. Following a series of public hearings, hundreds of witnesses, hundreds of briefs, and thousands of letters of opinion from across the country, the Commission noted that the lives of women are rapidly changing and that Canadian society—its laws, policies and practices—should also change to accommodate and reflect this. It reported on and suggested improvements on women's access to education, employment, rights within their families, taxation, child care, poverty, public life, immigration and citizenship, and criminal law.

Since then, Canadian women have fought for and achieved notable improvements in access to education, workplace discrimination, sexual harassment, wife abuse, and reproductive rights. Many have come together to achieve improvements in access to equal pay, maternity leaves, same-sex marriage, etc. On the other hand, women continue to be underrepresented in politics and public life; affordable child care remains outside the reach of many families; we continue to see high rates of poverty among women and children, particularly among female-headed, single-parent families; and the division of household work remains inequitable. Individually and collectively—as communities and as a society—there is a considerable amount of work yet to be done.

● Conclusion ● ● ● ● ●

The lives of men and women in Canada have been changing dramatically over the past few decades. In some ways, including education, paid employment, health, stress, and longevity, their lives have become more similar. In other ways, their lives remain very different—almost worlds apart and, surprisingly, relatively unchanged. In this chapter we have looked at the different, but related concepts of gender, sex, and sexuality. We have seen how all three concepts are variable, across time and space, and therefore *not* fixed, biological facts, as we are at times lead to believe.

Sociology has been a relative latecomer to the study of sex and sexuality, but over the course of the chapter we have seen that the discipline has come a long way in (re)defining, theorizing, and researching sex and sexuality. Most sociologists today, unlike many early sexologists, would argue that sexuality involves much more than an understanding of biological aspects of (heterosexual) physical attraction (in marriage and for procreation), and would, like many anthropologists, stress the social and cultural relativity of norms surrounding sexual behaviour, identities, and roles. This is doubly true when it comes to gender roles and relations.

Throughout the chapter, we have seen some of the work, at the individual and structural level, that goes into making us masculine, feminine, and sexual beings. Knowing this, it is important to note that as attitudes and practices surrounding gender and sexuality get 'made', there is still considerable room for them to get 'unmade' and 'remade'. And this is a comforting thought for some.

● Questions ● ● ● ● ● ● ●
for Critical Thought

1. The World Health Organization and many sociologists have noted that sexuality is influenced by the interaction of biological, psychological, social, economic, political, cultural, ethical, legal, historical, religious, and spiritual factors. What does all of this mean? Give an example of the influence on sexuality for each of these definitional terms.
2. There are clearly very different scientific approaches to the study of sex and sexuality. How do biological and psychoanalytic explanations compare to social survey and ethnographic approaches? What are the key factors that set them apart? Do you see any similarities? Which approach do you think best explains sexuality?
3. Do you think it is possible to separate nature from nurture, biology from culture, when it comes to gender and sexuality? Explain your reasoning.

● Recommended ● ● ● ● ●
Readings

Kate Bezanson, *Gender, the State, and Social Reproduction: Household Insecurity in Neo-Liberal Times* (Toronto: University of Toronto Press, 2006).

Bezanson's work convincingly demonstrates that the economic and political discourse of neo-liberalism has re-shaped the Canadian state, labour market and family/household relations.

Vanessa Baird, *The No-Nonsense Guide to Sexual Diversity* (Toronto: Between the Lines, 2001).

This book, one in a series of 'No-Nonsense Guides', provides a history of sexuality, with international examples of the 'war' against sexual non-conformity.

Donna Bulman, Diana Coben, and Nguyen Van Anh, 'Educating Women about HIV/AIDS: Some International Comparisons', *Compare* 34, 2 (2004): 141–59.

The authors note that the determinants of HIV infection include gender and status, poverty and inequity, education, access to health care, including reproductive care, human rights, and social disruption. They compare strategies in Canada, the UK, and Vietnam, arguing that the creation and implementation of gender-specific and gender-sensitive strategies are essential in preventing the spread of HIV.

Judith Butler, *Gender Troubles: Feminism and the Subversion of Identity* (New York: Routledge Classics, 2006 [1990]).

Butler's groundbreaking work challenges some traditional feminists' assumptions about the 'naturalness' and essentialism of sex and gender. She argues that the masculine and feminine are not biologically fixed categories, but rather are culturally determined.

Andrea Doucet, *Do Men Mother? Fathering, Care, and Domestic Responsibility* (Toronto: University of Toronto Press, 2006).

In this award winning, and very readable book, Canadian sociologist Andrea Doucet decodes male and female parenting styles. Using interviews with primary-caregiver fathers, she documents the ways male and female parenting roles have changed, differ and overlap.

Michel Foucault, *The History of Sexuality: An Introduction* (New York: Vintage Books, 1990).

This is the first volume of Foucault's three-volume study of sexual history, presenting a detailed, critical, and provocative account of the changing attitudes and discourses surrounding sexuality and sexual repression. His purpose is 'to show how deployments of power are directly connected to the body' (p. 151).

Edward Shorter, *Written in the Flesh: A History of Desire* (Toronto: University of Toronto Press, 2005).

In contrast to other books listed here, *Written in the Flesh*, a finalist for a Governor General's literary award in non-fiction, argues that sexual behaviour is a product of biologically driven desire rather than of fashion or social conditioning. In other words, Shorter supports the nature side of the nature–nurture debate, underscoring that desire is a brain-driven longing for sensuality.

Statistics Canada, *Women in Canada: A Gender-Based Statistical Report* (Ottawa: Statistics Canada, 2006).

This compilation of data on the status, health, education, income, and family status of women is accompanied by useful, descriptive text. There are also important chapters on Aboriginal and immigrant women, visible minority women, and senior women.

Shannon Winnubst, *Queering Freedom* (Bloomington: Indiana University Press, 2006).

Winnubst looks at contemporary categories of difference such as sexuality, race, gender, class, and nationality and how they operate within the politics of domination.

● Recommended ● ● ● ● Websites

Centres of Excellence for Women's Health
www.cewh-cesf.ca

This website offers access to a wide range of materials on women's health issues. Women's health is broadly defined to include factors that influence health as well as male/female differences in health.

Egale Canada www.egale.ca

Egale Canada is a national organization that advances equality and justice for lesbian, gay, bisexual, and trans-identified people and their families across Canada. The site includes summaries of key court cases, press releases, and information on local, national, and international campaigns and events.

Joint United Nations Program on HIV/AIDS (UNAIDS)
www.unaids.org/en/

UNAIDS brings together the efforts and resources of 10 UN organizations to the global AIDS response. The website includes international data on HIV and an extensive range of publications/materials (research reports, best practices, etc.) on a variety of topics related to HIV/AIDS.

Kinsey Institute for Research in Sex, Gender, and Reproduction www.indiana.edu/~kinsey/

The Kinsey Institute at Indiana University promotes interdisciplinary research and scholarship in the fields of human sexuality, gender, and reproduction. The website includes an abundance of resources and information on research and publication, interdisciplinary conferences and seminars, opportunities for graduate students, etc.

Status of Women Canada (SWC) www.swc-cfc.gc.ca

SWC is the federal government department that promotes gender equality and the full participation of women in the economic, social, cultural, and political life of the country. SWC focuses its work in three areas: improving women's economic autonomy and well-being, eliminating systemic violence against women and children, and advancing women's human rights.

Women Watch www.un.org/womenwatch/

The United Nations Convention on the Elimination of Discrimination Against Women can be found on this site, along with routes to a variety of documents the United Nations produces on the current situation of women in the world.

World Health Organization (WHO)—Sexual Health
www.who.int/topics/sexual_health/en/

The World Health Organization, a UN agency, provides information on a wide range of health topics, including sexual health and sexual violence. Included here are fact sheets, reports, and publications on a wide range of topics such as adolescent sexual and reproductive health, sexually transmitted diseases, female genital mutilation, etc.

Ethnic and Race Relations

Nikolaos I. Liodakis

Learning Objectives

In this chapter, you will:

▶ learn that the meaning of the terms 'ethnicity' and 'race' are historically specific, and are important bases for the formation of social groups;

▶ discover that ethnic and racial hierarchies exist in society;

▶ understand how Canada has been shaped by the colonization of Aboriginal peoples, the requirements of 'nation-building', capitalist economic development, and discriminatory immigration policies;

▶ find out that multiculturalism is an ideological framework within which government policies and programs attempt to manage ethnic and race relations and provide social cohesion;

▶ come to appreciate how, despite improvements in immigration policy and government integration efforts, discrimination and racism continue to permeate many aspects of Canadian social, political, and economic life; and

▶ learn about different theoretical approaches that attempt to explain the economic inequalities among and within ethnic and racial groups.

Photo: World of Stock

● Introduction ● ● ● ● ● ●

Canada is, demographically, one of the most multicultural countries in the world. Our population is now approximately 32 million people. With the exception of Aboriginal peoples, everyone else is either an immigrant to this country or the descendant of one. Today, almost one in four people in Canada has been born outside the country. Over the past 100 years, more than 13 million immigrants have arrived here from all corners of the earth to start a new and hopefully better life for themselves and their children (Statistics Canada, 2007b). Recent data show there are over 200 different ethnic groups in Canada, speaking more than 100 languages (Statistics Canada, 2007c). Since Confederation, the majority of immigrants have come mainly from Europe, especially during the first half of the twentieth century. More recently, non-Europeans have been accepted in larger numbers either as skilled workers, business immigrants, refugees, or family members of previous immigrants (Statistics Canada, 2007b).

The examination of ethnic and race relations is crucial to our understanding of Canadian society. As sociologists, we are interested in analyzing social relations, that is, relations of power (domination and subordination) among individuals and social groups. We cannot understand current economic, political, and social relations or conflicts in Canada without a comprehensive understanding of ethnic and race relations. For example, we cannot understand the current struggles of Aboriginal peoples with various levels of Canadian government over their land and self-determination without examining the legacy of colonization and the long-lasting effects it has had on their cultural, economic, and social lives. We cannot begin to talk about the formation of the Canadian state without reference to historical British–French conflicts. Modern Canada is constituted as a political entity, in large part, as a result of the struggles and the uneasy union between the charter groups—the French and English—at the expense of Aboriginal peoples. Moreover, our existing demographic makeup is a product of our history; it is a reflection of Canada's immigration policies and practices even before Confederation, many of which have been outright discriminatory and racist, at least until the mid-1960s.

Similarly, current problems in the economic, social, and political integration of visible minority groups may be attributed in part to racism. The economic and social hardships facing migrant agricultural labourers in Canada today may be the result—to a great extent—of current neo-racist immigration policies of the federal government (Simmons, 1998). It is not surprising, then, that the field of ethnic and race relations has been central and continues to enjoy growth and importance within Canadian sociology. Let us begin by briefly examining how sociologists define the concepts of ethnicity and race, and how we can approach the study of ethnic and race relations theoretically.

● A Brief History ● ● ● ● ●
of Ethnicity and Race

Sociologists argue that the terms 'ethnicity' and 'race' have historically specific significations, i.e., their meanings differ in time and space. They mean different things to different people at different times and in different places. Ethnicity and race are not constant or monolithic concepts, but represent dynamic social relations in flux. Thus, as people's understandings of these two terms vary considerably, they are not readily or succinctly defined. Popular uses of the terms tend to differ from social scientific definitions (Miles and Torres, 1996). **Ethnicity** refers to social distinctions and relations among individuals and groups based on their cultural characteristics (language, religion, customs, history, etc.), whereas **race** refers to people's assumed, but socially significant, physical or genetic characteristics (Satzewich and Liodakis, 2007: 10). The term 'ethnicity' comes from the Greek word *ethnos* and means a large group of people. The ancient Greek historian Herodotus, in the fifth century BC, was the first to study **ethnic groups**. In his *Histories*, we find many passages where several ethnic groups are mentioned, some of which reside in the large urban Canadian centres today (e.g., Greeks, Persians, Arabs, Egyptians, Chaldeans, Assyrians, Indians, Ethiopians, Libyans, etc.). He described their languages, gods, some of their customs, their 'idiosyncrasies', their geography and contacts with other groups, their history, politics, other social arrangements, and their economies (Herodotus, 1996: Books 1–9). He also provided an explanation of what comprises an ethnic group. For example, recognizing that ancient Greeks were geographically and politically fragmented, still, he argued, they constituted an ethnic group because they were of common biological descent, had a common language, common gods, sacred places, and sacrificial festivals, and customs or ways of life and 'the common character they bear'—their sameness (Herodotus, 1996: Book 8). In short, they shared a sense of 'belonging together'.

Émile Durkheim, one of the founders of sociology, used the concept of collective consciousness as a primary source of identity formation. In his classic work *The Division of Labour in Society* (1964 [1893]), he tried to explain what made pre-modern societies so cohesive and he emphasized the importance of community or group sentiments over individual ones. Social solidarity is based on sameness and the conformity of individual consciousness to the collective. Furthermore, similarities among members or sameness within the social group lead members to differentiate between themselves and others (non-members) and to prefer their 'own kind' over others. Durkheim believed that the collective consciousness of people leads them to 'love their country . . . to like one another, seeking one another out in preference of foreigners' (1964 [1893]: 60). This is an 'us' versus 'them' feeling, important in social group formation, reproduction, and maintenance.

Max Weber, another famous sociologist, argued that social group formation is associated with social practices of inclusion/exclusion, important in turn for the production and distribution of scarce valuable resources (goods, services, wages, social status and status symbols, economic and political power, equality, voting rights and citizenship, access to social programs, human rights, self-determination, autonomy, etc.). This practice of inclusion/exclusion constitutes the basis upon which decisions about rewards and sanctions are made. According to Weber (1978 [1908]), common descent, tribe, culture (which includes language and other symbolic codes), religion, and nationality are important *ethnic markers* and determinants of ethnicity. He wrote:

> We shall call 'ethnic groups' those human groups that entertain *a subjective belief in their common descent* because of similarities of physical type or of customs or both, or because of memories of colonization and migration; this belief must be important for the propagation of group formation; conversely, *it does not matter whether or not an objective blood relationship exists.* Ethnic membership differs from the kinship group precisely by being a *presumed identity*. (1978 [1908]: 389; emphasis added)

Ethnicity should be seen as a subjective, presumed identity based on what Weber called a 'folk-feeling', not (necessarily) on any blood ties. Ethnic identity is often linked to people's 'primordial attachment'. Whereas *hard primordialism* holds that people are attached to one another and their communities of origin because of their

blood ties, *soft primordialism*, as Weber argues, proposes that people's feelings of affinity, attachment, acceptance, trust, and intimacy towards their 'own kind' are not mediated by blood ties (Allahar, 1994). Here is a historical example of presumed identity: in early Christian times, like today, people's religion was important in designating social groups, social positions, and hierarchies. Those who were not Christians were called *ethnics* (a stigmatizing, derogatory term at that time), although, of course, none of these large groups shared common, identifiable blood ties.

Weber used the term 'race' to denote common identity of groups based on biological heredity and endogamous conjugal groups. Not only customs but also visible similarities and differences, however minor, serve as potential sources of affection and appreciation or repulsion and contempt (Driedger, 1996: 5). Weber wrote: 'Almost any kind of *similarity or contrast of physical type* and of habits can induce the belief that affinity or disaffinity exists between groups that attract or repel each other' (Weber, 1978 [1908]: 386; emphasis added). Cultural and physical differences, produced and reproduced over time, constitute the foundations upon which a 'consciousness of kind' can be built. Such traits, in turn, 'can serve as a starting point for the familiar tendency to monopolistic closure' (Weber, 1978 [1908]: 386). Monopolistic closure refers to economic, political, and social processes and practices, often institutionalized, whereby members of the in-group ('we'/'Self') have access to the scarce valuable resources mentioned above, while members of the out-group ('they'/'the Other') are excluded. The former monopolize, the latter are left out. Social boundaries, then, have been set and reproduced over time.

Today, sociologists use the term **racialization** to refer to sets of social processes and practices through which social relations among people are structured 'by the signification of human biological characteristics in such a way as to define and construct differentiated social collectivities' (Miles and Brown, 2003: 99). Invariably, these 'collectivities' are the majority, who are advantaged by racialization of others, and visible minorities, who are disadvantaged by their observable difference from the majority. We can also speak of ethnic or minority labelling in general, because cultural and other social characteristics also are used to identify social collectivities. An important part in long, historical processes of this labelling of social groups is the creation of hierarchical social dichotomies by the attribution of negative intellectual, moral, and behavioural characteristics to subordinate populations and the attribution of positive or not-negative characteristics to the dominant group(s) (those who label or stereotype). Social *positions* of superiority and inferiority are thus created and a social order is built (Li, 1999).

Ethnicity and race, therefore, are central factors in relations of power; they are socially constructed categories used to classify human populations and create social hierarchies. Like most social relations of power, they are not only setting boundaries, but they are also designating hierarchical positions of superiority and inferiority among and within social collectivities. As such, the meanings of the categories and the populations they describe or 'contain' are not fixed in time and space. In ancient Greece and Rome, unlike today, physical characteristics such as skin colour did not appear to be socially important in setting group boundaries or in creating social positions of superiority and inferiority (Snowdon, 1983). Herodotus, for example, differentiated between Greeks and 'barbarians', but his was not a racial hierarchy; it was based on the notion of freedom (Goldberg, 1993). The Greeks were free; the barbarians were not. The former had desired characteristics, often deemed superior (a better language, cleverness, bravery, adventurousness, piety, cleanliness, the favour of [their] gods, etc.) to those of the barbarians (lacking in intellectual capacity, dressing strangely, dirtiness, cowardice, trickiness, irreverence, bloodthirstiness, raw-meat eaters, etc.).

When I ask my students how many races there are, they usually answer only one: the human race. But when we begin to discuss the legacy of colonialism, or issues of inequality among social groups, terms such as 'white', 'black', 'visible minorities', 'Asians', and 'Aboriginals' cannot be avoided. These terms connote race as real. The physical characteristics of humans that have been used to classify social groups have included skin colour, eye colour, hair type, nose shape, lip shape, body hair, and cheekbone structure (Driedger, 1996: 234–5). Using the term 'race' as a means of categorizing human populations is definitely linked to the European 'voyages of discovery' or, to be historically accurate, to the colonization, exploitation, domination, and often the extermination of indigenous peoples by the colonizers.

The meanings of the term 'race' have shifted and continue to shift even today. Here are a few historical examples. For a long time, race simply meant descent or lineage and was attributed to groups with a common history. It was not seen as a real, objective biological category (Banton, 1987). But by the end of eighteenth century in Europe, there was an obvious shift in the meaning of 'race'. European pseudo-science was preoccupied with the explanation and classification of the physical and cultural diversity of the newly 'discovered' peoples, just as researchers in the natural sciences, led by Linnaeus, sought to classify and give Latin names to the flora and fauna of the natural world. Categorizing and naming the previously unknown and exotic helped to make it known and understandable—and within the namer's control. The concept of race was increasingly used to explain human physical, social, moral, and intellectual variation among peoples.

After the era of colonization and during the advent of capitalism as a new mode of production, a new social dichotomy slowly emerged, one based on definitions of 'Self' and 'Other'. The 'Self' referred to dominant European populations and cultures and was considered superior; the 'Other' referred to non-Europeans, who were seen as inferior and subordinate. Prior to the emergence of capitalism, race was used in a legal sense to describe people with common lineage and as a self-identification label for the aristocracy (a category that defined the Self), but with the emergence of the bourgeoisie in France the term was used to define 'Others', 'others' being 'Negroes', 'Jews', 'Arabs', 'Asiatics', etc. It became an externally imposed label. The classification of certain groups as races was coupled with negative evaluations of their members' biological and social characteristics, just as Herodotus had characterized the barbarians more than 2,000 years earlier.

If we look closely into Canadian history, we find that notions of ethnicity and race have also changed over time. For example, in the aftermath of the Upper and Lower Canada rebellions of 1837, Lord Durham attempted to explain the British–French conflict in terms of racial, not ethnic, differences. It was believed, then, that despite their physical similarities, the British and the French constituted different races, not different ethnic groups, as we call them today (Satzewich and Liodakis, 2007: 28, 32–3). In the first half of the twentieth

▮▮ Time to Reflect ▮▮▮▮▮▮▮▮▮▮▮▮▮▮▮▮▮▮▮▮▮▮▮

Do you believe that races exist? If so, how many races are there? Could all human populations be categorized in terms of inherited physical characteristics? Should they be?

century in Quebec, this notion of the British and French as different and *unequal* races (i.e., the inferiorizing of the latter) found social expression in the reality of 'capital speaking English' and 'workers speaking French' (Whitaker, 1993: 22).

In Canada, social class position, coupled with prevailing notions of femininity and masculinity, has also been used to 'describe' and define races as social groups. In British Columbia, at the beginning of the twentieth century, the Chinese immigrants were labelled a 'feminine' race by European-origin Canadians because of the large numbers of Chinese males found in occupations traditionally associated with 'female labour': doing laundry, cooking, cleaning, or waiting tables in restaurants (Vorst et al., 1991). Canadian immigration policies—for a very long period of time—were saturated with notions of race as a real biological category, with the idea that certain ethnic and racial groups are superior to others, and with practices of inclusion/exclusion. As a consequence, until policy changes in 1967, members of 'preferred' groups were allowed to immigrate to Canada freely; 'non-preferred' groups could not make Canada their home so easily, as we will see below.

● Building One Nation or Two: Canada's Development through Immigration

Canada is not, of course, the only country in the world that has admitted and continues to admit large numbers of immigrants, but we are a major immigrant-receiving country, and for good reason. Why do we admit immigrants in the first place? Today's reasons are not that much different from those of the nation-building era. State formation requires more than a stable political territory, an army, political institutions, and government buildings. It also needs people. It needs the creation and management of human populations, national identities, and citizens. In the late nineteenth and early twentieth centuries the federal government endeavoured to increase its population base, build the country's infrastructure, and develop the economy by promoting capitalist development, domestic and international trade, manufacturing, commercial farming, mining and other resource extraction industries, and generally, to engage

Sikh passengers aboard the *Komagata Maru*. Vancouver Public Library, Special Collections, VPL6231

in the activities that build nations. Today, in the context of global economic competition, Canada still needs a growing population to keep labour costs down, increase the tax base, finance social programs, increase international competitiveness, and maintain its comparative advantage in the oil and gas industries and in other resource extraction. In short, it needs immigrants. But what explains the present demographic constitution of Canada? In other words, what could account for the cultural, ethnic, and racial makeup of the country today? Why are certain groups in Canada more populous than others? Why have there been dramatic changes in the patterns of immigration to Canada? Some answers to these questions are provided below, where we examine briefly the particular role that immigration policies have played in Canadian nation-building.

Until the 1960s, the image of Canada as a nation was based on the idea that the British and French peoples founded this country. These two **charter groups**, by this thinking, built the country; everyone else 'joined in' later. The 'two founding nations' thesis endures even today, but, in part, it is historically inaccurate. To be sure, the French and the British colonized Canada and sent settlers to this land. But this was done at the expense of the Native peoples who were already here. Not only did they lose their lands through colonization, warfare, and deceitful treaties, but 'efforts to assimilate *them*' into the dominant aspects of the British and French cultures (Christianity, private property, competitive individualism, etc.) left Aboriginals with long-lasting cultural trauma and without the communal economies that had sustained them for centuries. In addition, immigration from other countries began in earnest around the time of Confederation. Nation-building required the creation of a national transportation infrastructure (roads, railways, canals), the development of commercial agriculture in western Canada, and capitalist industry in major urban centres. In the minds of government policy-makers, these requirements, in turn, necessitated the large influx of mostly Northern and Central European and American immigrants (except blacks), since, what was left of the once-thriving Aboriginal population, it was believed, either did not have the necessary skills or could not adapt to the British/French 'ways of doing things'. More often than not, Canada's first peoples were seen and treated as 'uncivilized savages'—very much 'others'.

Cultural compatibility was a requirement for immigration to Canada. The offer of free land to European and American settlers (land that was taken away from Aboriginals) resulted in the first wave of immigration to

Canada, from 1896 to the beginning of World War I. The federal government passed Immigration Acts (1906, 1910) that set the terms under which immigrants other than the charter groups, called *entrance groups*, were accepted in Canada. In 1913, 400,000 immigrants arrived in Canada. During the years of World War I, the Great Depression, and World War II, immigration almost ceased (see Figure 8.1).

Immigration picked up again in the 1950s, when Canada admitted almost half a million immigrants from Europe. As mentioned earlier, however, not everyone has always been welcomed in Canada. The Immigration Act of 1910 prohibited the immigration of people who were considered 'mentally defective', 'idiots, imbeciles, feeble-minded, epileptics, insane, diseased, the physically defective, the dumb, blind, or otherwise handicapped' (McLaren, 1990: 56). A 1919 amendment to the Immigration Act decreed that people with 'dubious' political loyalties were also excluded outright, or, if already in Canada, were subject to deportation. Individuals who sought to overthrow Her Majesty's governments or possessions by force or violence, or who promoted the destruction of private property, by words or acts, or attempted to create riots or public disorder, were 'deemed to belong to the prohibited or undesired classes' (Roberts, 1988: 19). Early immigration policies, therefore, created categories of desired and undesired immigrants. Race and ethnicity were also critical in determining who was allowed into Canada and who was not. Until the liberalization of immigration in the 1960s, successive Canadian governments, Liberal or Conservative, exercised exclusionary policies. At the end of the nineteenth century and the beginning of the twentieth century, the admission of immigrants was based on a social hierarchy of ethnic and racial groups. Some groups were preferred (mostly Northern and Central Europeans, as well as Americans). Others were labelled as 'non-preferred' and were thus systematically excluded (Chinese, black Americans, Eastern and Southern Europeans, people from India, etc.). Members of the former groups were seen as good workers, law-abiding people, and desirable future citizens, whereas the latter were regarded as culturally, ethnically, or racially 'unsuitable' and only would be admitted to Canada as a last resort.

Immigrants from China and India were of particular 'concern' to xenophobic immigration authorities because the former were seen as unable to assimilate and thus unsuitable for permanent residence. In the 1880s, Chinese immigrants were allowed into the country because of the growing demand for cheap and disposable labour in the building of the transcontinental rail-

Figure 8.1 Levels of Immigration to Canada, 1997–2007

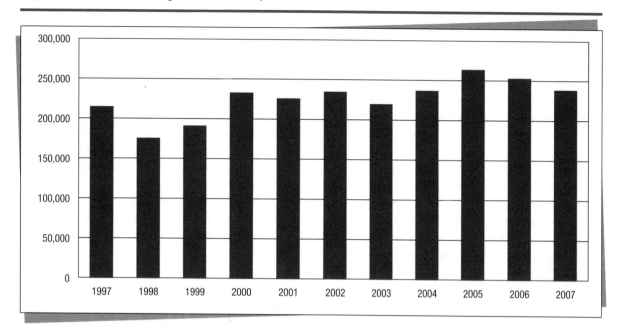

way. From 1880 to 1884, approximately 16,000 Chinese immigrants arrived in Canada, mainly in British Columbia, to work in railroad construction. Employers and railroad contractors saw an opportunity to exploit Chinese labourers and called for increases in Chinese immigration. Labour unions, on the other hand, opposed the influx of Chinese workers; increases in the supply of immigrant labour led to stiffer labour market competition and kept wages low. The government, exploiting xenophobia, popular anti-Chinese sentiments, and unfounded fears ('worries' about the 'dilution of our British character', the presumed cultural, ethnic, and racial homogeneity of Canada), restricted immigration from China by imposing the now-infamous Chinese head tax. Introduced first in 1885 at $50, it increased to $100 in 1890 and to $500 per person in 1903. By 1923, Chinese immigration was prohibited until after World War II. In other words, only the Chinese who could afford the head tax could immigrate to Canada. Their social class background and gender were especially important since Chinese businessmen who either invested in or established businesses in Canada were exempt from the head tax and were allowed to immigrate to Canada even after 1923. The immigration of Chinese women was also restricted because of fears they would reproduce the 'yellow peril' and lead to the propagation of 'alien' cultures and races, thus undermining the image of Canada as a 'white' settler society. It is believed that the federal government collected a total of $23 million for the period the head tax was in effect

(Satzewich and Liodakis, 2007). In today's dollars, this would amount to approximately $1.2 billion.

The case of immigrants from India also demonstrates the **racism** prevalent in immigration policies. By the 1910s, around 5,000 immigrants from India had arrived in British Columbia to work in the lumber and mining industries. The government could not introduce outright anti-Indian immigration legislation because India was part of the British Empire, so, for the sake of appearances, it opted for the covertly discriminatory policy of the so-called 'continuous journey stipulation'. An Order-in-Council passed on 9 May 1910 stipulated that only people who had made a non-stop journey from their country of origin to Canada would be allowed in as immigrants (Basran and Bolaria, 2003: 99). Not surprisingly, there were no direct sailings between India and Canada. Canadian steamship companies were 'persuaded' by the government to end all direct travel from India. Indians who wanted to come to Canada as immigrants had to travel via Hong Kong or Hawaii, but that did not constitute a continuous journey. Immigrants from India, thus, were not admitted. Indeed, when this policy was tested by an enterprising Sikh, Gurdit Singh, who organized the immigration to Canada of 340 fellow Sikhs, the Japanese-registered freighter, the *Komagata Maru*, which sailed from Hong Kong in April 1914, with stops in Shanghai and Japan, was refused landing at the Port of Vancouver. After a tense standoff lasting two months, extensive world press coverage, and rapidly deteriorating conditions aboard the vessel anchored in Vancouver harbour, the *Komagata Maru* returned to Asia with its passengers (Buchignani et al., 1985: 54–61).

The end of World War II saw some minor improvements in Canadian immigration policy. It did not end **discrimination**—that started slowly in the 1960s—but Canada began by repealing the Chinese Immigration Act (1947) and the continuous journey stipulation. A quota of 150 Indian immigrants per annum was set in 1952, which was later raised to 300 (Basran and Bolaria, 2003: 104). Gradually, some non-whites were allowed to immigrate. Small numbers of black women were admitted as domestic workers, typists, and nurses. But even as late as 1952, the government could still (and did) prohibit immigration based on people's nationality, citizenship, ethnic group, occupation, class, geographical area of origin, 'peculiar' customs, habits, modes of life and methods of holding property, low probability of becoming readily assimilated or to assume the duties of citizenship, and unsuitability to the climatic, economic, social, industrial, health, and educational conditions prevailing in Canada (Satzewich, 1991: 124–5). In short, the government could choose from a large pool of legally sanctioned 'reasons' to reject certain 'types' of (undesired) immigrants. It was not until 1962 that the government initiated the elimination of racist criteria in the immigrant selection process, and not until 1967 that the familiar points systems was introduced, which relied on more objective criteria and assigned more weight to the applicant's age, educational credentials, job skills, work experience, and English- and/or French-language abilities, rather than to a person's country of origin. These changes eventually led to a large increase in the numbers of Southern Europeans (Italians, Greeks, Portuguese, and, to a smaller extent, Spanish) in the late 1960s and early 1970s, and the moderate rise of non-white immigration to Canada.

● The New Mosaic: ● ● ● ●
Recent Canadian
Immigration Trends

The 'colour' of Canadian immigration has changed since the 1980s. Immigration from the traditional European (white) source countries has diminished substantially, since their standard of living has improved markedly, even in Southern Europe and especially after the emergence of the European Union. As shown in Table 8.1, there has been a remarkable shift in the geographical regions from which Canada admits immi-

grants. During the 1950–5 period, for example, the United Kingdom and the rest of Europe accounted for 88 per cent of all immigration to Canada, but for the 2000–4 period the percentage of European immigration had dropped to 19.7 per cent. US immigration has dropped from 6.3 per cent to 2.6 per cent. Similarly, when comparing these two periods, we find that immigrants from Africa and the Middle East accounted for only 0.4 per cent of all immigration in the first period, but 50 years later these source regions accounted for 19.1 per cent of all immigration. Most remarkable is the change for Asia and the Pacific. The percentage of all immigration for the aforementioned periods has increased from 3.6 to 50.3 per cent. For South and Central America the percentages are 1.5 and 8.3, respectively. As Table 8.1 shows, immigration to Canada from Europe and the United Kingdom dropped even further in 2006 to only 15.1 per cent of total immigration in 2006. In contrast, US immigration increased to 4.4 per cent. Immigration from Africa and the Middle East increased

Table 8.1	Permanent Residents Admitted in 1950–5, 2000–4, and 2006, by Country of Origin		
Area	**1950–5 (%)**	**2000–4 (%)**	**2006 (%)**
Africa and the Middle East	0.4	19.1	20.6
Asia and the Pacific	3.6	50.3	50.2
South and Central America	1.5	8.3	9.7
United States	6.3	2.6	4.4
Europe and the United Kingdom	88.0	19.7	15.1
Other/not stated	0.2	0.0	–

Source: Figures for 1950–5 compiled from Canada, Department of Manpower and Immigration, *Immigration Statistics*; figures for 2000–4 compiled from Citizenship and Immigration Canada, *Facts and Figures 2004*: Immigration Overview, at: <www.cic.gc.ca/english/pub/facts2004/permanent/12.html>; figure for 2006 from Citizenship and Immigration Canada, *Facts & Figures 2006*

GLOBAL ISSUES
The Points System for Skilled Workers: Would You Make It?

Do you think you would qualify as an immigrant to your own country? Test yourself to find out if you would qualify as a skilled worker for admission to Canada. The table below outlines the various categories of qualification for which points are rewarded. For example, if at present your education consists of a secondary school diploma, but no further diplomas, certificates, or degrees, you will get 5 points in this category; under language, if you can read, write, speak, and understand English with complete proficiency, you will get 16 points, and total proficiency in French will give you an additional 8 points. You will need at least 67 points (out of a possible 100) to be admitted to Canada as a skilled worker. For a complete breakdown of the points system, go to the following website: <www.canada-immigration. biz/permanent_skilled.asp>.

Selection Criteria		Points Awarded
Education	5	up to 25
Knowledge of official language(s)	16	up to 24
Work experience	0	up to 21
Age (applicants 21–49 years of age receive maximum points; 2 points are deducted for each year under 21 or over 49, so that someone 16 or younger or 54 or older will receive no points)	4	up to 10
Arranged employment in Canada	0	up to 10
Adaptability		up to 10
Spouse's or common-law partner's education	0	3 to 5
Minimum one-year full-time authorized work in Canada	0	5
Minimum two years post-secondary study in Canada	0	5
Maximum points awarded		100
Minimum required to pass for skilled worker immigrants		67

to 20.6 per cent and from South and Central America to 9.7 per cent. Immigration for Asia and the Pacific remained stable, at 50.2 per cent.

Canada today admits approximately 260,000 immigrants per year. Table 8.2 lists the top 10 source countries of immigrants to Canada for 2007. Together, these 10 countries accounted for more than half of all immigrants. The top source country is China (11.4 per cent of all admitted immigrants that year), and the second highest percentage belongs to India (11.0 per cent). We have certainly come a long way since the era of the Chinese head tax and the continuous journey policy. The UK, France, and the US are still found in the top 10 source countries, but their percentage contributions are small (3.4, 2.3, and 4.4 per cent, respectively).

Immigrants are divided into four major categories (often called immigration classes): skilled workers, business immigrants, the family class, and refugees. Figure

Table 8.2   Permanent Residents Admitted in 2007, by Top 10 Source Countries

Country	Number	Percentage	Rank
China, People's Republic of	27,014	11.4	1
India	26,054	11.0	2
Philippines	19,064	8.1	3
United States	10,450	4.4	4
Pakistan	9,547	4.0	5
United Kingdom	8,128	3.4	6
Iran	6,663	2.8	7
Korea, Republic of	5,864	2.5	8
France	5,526	2.3	9
Colombia	4,833	2.0	10
Total–Top Ten Countries	123,143	52.0	
All Other Source Countries	113,615	48.0	
Total	236,758	100	

Source: Citizenship and Immigration Canada, *Facts & Figures 2007*, p. 30. Reproduced and adapted with the permission of the Minister of Public Works and Government Services Canada, 2009.

8.2 shows the numbers and percentages for each category of immigrants admitted to Canada in 2007. Contrary to public misconceptions about the people admitted, the largest immigration class was that of skilled workers (121,069 people), who constituted 51.1 per cent of total immigration. Skilled workers are independent applicants who are admitted by the use of the point system.

The family class (66,230 people) was second, with 28.0 per cent of total immigration. These immigrants are admitted if they have close relatives (spouses, children or parents) in Canada who are willing to sponsor them to come and to support them financially for a period of 3–10 years after they arrive. Refugees (27,956 persons) accounted for 11.8 per cent of total immigration. Canada is a signatory to international treaties and is obliged by international law to provide asylum to those who have demonstrably genuine refugee claims. Usually, these are people who come from countries with known records of human rights violations. They are called convention refugees since they fall under the provisions of the 1951 United Nations Convention relating to the Status of Refugees and the 1967 Protocol to the

Convention that extended its scope and time frame beyond refugees in Europe following World War II. Finally, business immigrants (10,179 people), comprised 4.3 per cent of the total 2007 immigrants to Canada, and are divided into three subcategories: (1) investors who have business experience, are worth at least $800,000, and must invest at least half of that in the country; (2) entrepreneurs who are worth at least $300,000 and must create and manage a company that will create at least one full-time job in the country (other than their own); and (3) the self-employed category, who must demonstrate to immigration officials that they have the skills and experience to start up a business that will create employment for themselves.

Once in Canada, most immigrants in 2007—over 80 per cent—settled in Ontario, British Columbia, and Quebec (Figure 8.3). The distribution of immigrants across Canada, therefore, is decidedly uneven. From Ontario's high of 47.0 per cent of all immigrants, after Quebec (19.1 per cent) and BC (16.5 per cent), only Alberta (8.8 per cent) and Manitoba (4.6 per cent) attracted more than 2 per cent of the total immigration.

Figure 8.2   Categories of Immigrants Admitted to Canada, 2007

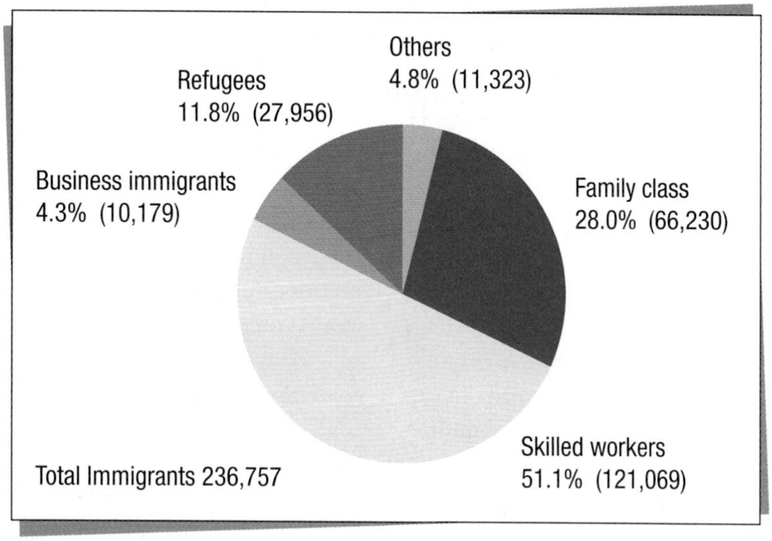

Others
4.8% (11,323)

Refugees
11.8% (27,956)

Business immigrants
4.3% (10,179)

Family class
28.0% (66,230)

Total Immigrants 236,757

Skilled workers
51.1% (121,069)

Source: Source: Citizenship and Immigration Canada, *Facts & Figures 2007*, p. 8. Reproduced and adapted with the permission of the Minister of Public Works and Government Services Canada, 2009. http://www.cic.gc.ca/english/resources/statistics/facts2006/

This uneven distribution, of course, influences variably the ethnic and racial makeup of certain parts of Canada. There is also a clear urban/rural divide. Immigrants are attracted to major urban centres because they will usually find more economic opportunities and other immigrants from their own part of the world. Today, for example, the majority of Torontonians have been born outside Canada, whereas almost all of the residents of Hérouxville, a small farming community in Quebec, are Canadian-born.

Figure 8.3   Canada, Permanent Residents [Immigrants] by Province or Territory, 2007 (Showing Percentage Distribution)

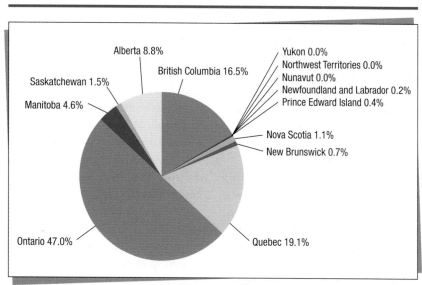

Alberta 8.8%

British Columbia 16.5%

Saskatchewan 1.5%

Manitoba 4.6%

Yukon 0.0%
Northwest Territories 0.0%
Nunavut 0.0%
Newfoundland and Labrador 0.2%
Prince Edward Island 0.4%

Nova Scotia 1.1%

New Brunswick 0.7%

Ontario 47.0%

Quebec 19.1%

Source: Source: Citizenship and Immigration Canada, *Facts & Figures 2006*, p. 35. Reproduced and adapted with the permission of the Minister of Public Works and Government Services Canada, 2009.

● Multiculturalism ● ● ● ●
and Its Discontents

The meanings and social content of ethnicity and race are not monolithic or static but dynamic and fluid. There is no simple, one-to-one correspondence between individual people, their culture and ethnicity, and the 'nation' to which they belong. Culture is not static, uniform, or homogeneous. Rather, it is a set of dynamic social processes and practices; it is a collective response of socially constituted individuals to their ever-changing external conditions, largely determined by pre-existing social structures. Cultural values in Canada have changed over time. Prior to the advent of official **multiculturalism** in 1971, to which we are so accustomed today, there had been the long, hard years of Anglo- and/or Franco-cultural conformity. It is historically inaccurate to believe that the values and attendant practices of ethnic pluralism, tolerance for others, and multiculturalism have always been present or dominant in Canada. Canadian society has been characterized by ethnocentrism from the era of colonization to the early 1970s. An individual is ethnocentric when he or she evaluates (usually negatively) the culture of others based on criteria derived from his/her own. The charter groups have set the terms for the entrance of all others into the country. There has always been sustained pressure on Aboriginals and minority group newcomers to adopt the dominant British and French cultural values, customs, and symbols. In short, 'others' had to conform; they had to assimilate to the norms of the 'Self'.

'Assimilation', a term always encountered in race and ethnic relations discourses, is usually defined as the processes and social practices by which members of minority groups are incorporated into the dominant culture of a society (Isajiw, 1999: 170). Sociologists distinguish between behavioural assimilation ('acquiring' the values of dominant groups) and structural assimilation (the integration of 'others' into the economic, social, and political life of a country).

But assimilation has not always been a simple matter of choice for minorities; often it was forceful and violent, as was the case with Aboriginals, for example, through the residential schools and the banning of Native customs and ceremonies such as the thirst dance and the potlatch. Early Canadian government efforts to assimilate Aboriginals and other immigrants somewhat resemble American **melting-pot policies**. Robert Park, the noted Chicago School sociologist, argued that when members of different ethnic groups come into contact (because of colonization or migration), competition and conflict usually occurs among their members. Writing in the US of the early twentieth century, and having worked with blacks in the South and Polish immigrants in Chicago, Park (1914) represented the interaction of whites and blacks in terms of a race relations cycle. The same cycle has also been applied to ethnic relations. It included several stages, two different routes, but one outcome: that of fusion or assimilation, where the subordinate minority groups assimilate to the dominant majority group. Initially, contact between the two groups creates competition for access to and acquisition of scarce valuable resources. This competition can lead either to accommodation and eventually fusion/assimilation, or to conflicts over the social and material resources (remember Weber's monopolistic closure) that in turn lead to accommodation and then fusion/assimilation. Underlying this cycle is the position that the 'new' culture that emerges from their fusion is good for both and certainly good for the 'nation'. Fusion also implies social harmony, even equality. This is the melting-pot metaphor of American society. The present generation in Canada has been brought up within the multicultural framework and even the idea of a melting pot is alien. But multiculturalism is a fairly recent policy development.

'Multiculturalism' is one of those elusive terms that we use everyday, but it means different things to different people. In sociology, we understand the term as having four interrelated meanings:

> It is a demographic reality.
> It is part of pluralist ideology.
> It is a form of struggle among minority groups for access to economic and political resources.
> It is a set of government policies and accompanying programs. (Fleras and Elliott, 1996: 325)

It can be defined as an ideology, based on Canadian social reality, that gives rise to sets of economic, political, and social practices, which in turn define boundaries and set limits to ethnic and racial group relations in order to either maintain social order or manage social change (Liodakis and Satzewich, 2003: 147).

First, when we say that multiculturalism is a fact of Canadian society, we mean that the Canadian population comprises people who come from over 200 ethnic groups. Canadian society has never been ethnically homogeneous, as some would like to believe. Demographically, Canada was a multicultural country long before the implementation of multiculturalism as policy. Second, as an ideology, multiculturalism includes normative descriptions about how Canadian society *ought to be*. The basis of multiculturalist ideology is cultural pluralism, which advocates tolerance of cultural diversity and, most importantly, promotes the idea that such diversity is compatible with national goals, especially those of national unity and socio-economic progress (Fleras and Elliot, 1996). The basic principles of multiculturalism rest on the notion of cultural relativism, as opposed to ethnocentrism. Cultural relativism promotes tolerance and diversity in order to achieve the peaceful coexistence of groups in ethnically and racially heterogeneous societies. As opposed to ethnocentrism, cultural relativism argues that we should not judge other cultures by our own norms and criteria. If we recognize the right of all people to self-identify and promote their own culture, then, it is hoped, the same courtesy would be extended to individuals who share different cultural norms and values. Third, multiculturalism is also a process and a terrain of competition among and between minority groups for valuable economic and political resources. As such, it is used by governments as a mechanism for conflict management and resolution. Multiculturalism was not exactly given as a gift to minority groups; historically, it emerged for several reasons:

> During the 1960s, immense political pressure was exerted on the federal government by the 'other' ethnic groups (e.g., the Ukrainians and Germans in the West, who were dissatisfied with the Royal Commission on Bilingualism and Biculturalism of 1963–9) for the recognition of their contributions to Canadian society.
>
> It became a political necessity to counterbalance western alienation and Quebec nationalism, and multiculturalism appeared to be a logical avenue for this counterbalancing.
>
> The Liberal Party of Canada sought to acquire greater electoral support from immigrants in urban centres, and this was a logical step in that direction. (Fleras and Elliot, 1996: 335)

Finally, multiculturalism refers to all government initiatives and programs that seek to realize multiculturalism as ideology and to transform it into a concrete form of social intervention.

As policy, it is a relatively recent aspect of Canadian state activity. It was introduced in 1971 by a very charismatic Canadian Prime Minister, Pierre Elliott Trudeau. Ironically, and contrary to what we may think today, it was not the historical legacy of racism, discrimination, and **prejudice** in Canada that multicultural policy initially aimed to redress. In fact, these issues did not figure

at all into the framework for the initial development of multicultural policy. Three stages of multicultural policy development have been identified by Fleras and Elliott (1996). From 1971 to 1980, policy was essentially folkloric (ethnic food, costume, and dance) and focused on 'celebrating our differences'. At this time, cultural diversity was seen as the core of 'Canadian identity', of being Canadian. The years of Anglo- and Franco-conformity had passed. We no longer had an official culture. All cultures were seen as equal. Four basic principles guided federal multiculturalism at this time:

> The federal government would support all of Canada's cultures and seek to assist the development of those cultural groups that had demonstrated a desire and effort to continue to develop a capacity to grow and contribute to Canada as well as a clear need for assistance.
>
> The government would assist all cultural groups to overcome the cultural barriers to full participation in Canadian society.
>
> The government would promote creative encounters and interchange among all Canadian cultural groups in the interest of national unity.
>
> The government would continue to assist immigrants to acquire at least one of Canada's two official languages in order to become full participants in Canadian society. (Hawkins, 1989: 220)

Culture had become an issue of personal choice, and there was no shortage in the Canadian ethnic supermarket. In this light, individuals were protected against any discrimination stemming from their cultural choices, and they were strongly encouraged to cultivate and promote their cultures, and to participate fully in all aspects of Canadian life.

In the 1980s, the second phase of multicultural policy—the process of institutionalization—was developed. This phase entailed a number of new developments. First, there emerged an explicit concern over race relations. Second, in 1988 the Progressive Conservative government passed the Multiculturalism Act, which essentially turned a *de facto* policy into a *de jure* legal framework (see page 215), thus elevating multiculturalism to equality with the principle of bilingualism. Third, renewed calls of Quebec nationalism were countered by the repatriation of the Constitution (1982) and the inclusion of the Charter of Rights and Freedoms in the Constitution Act, 1982. Section 27 of the Charter stated that its interpretation, i.e., in Canadian courts and legislatures, 'shall be . . . in a manner consistent with the preservation and enhancement of the multicultural heritage of Canadians.' In other words, multiculturalism had become a fundamental and legally contestable characteristic of Canadian society.

Finally, multiculturalism was increasingly cast in economic terms. Consistent with neo-conservative economic doctrines was the attempt to justify the 1988 Multiculturalism Act not only in terms of pluralist ideology, but also in terms of potential economic benefits to the country. This involved a shift in emphasis away from a 'culture for culture's sake' perspective towards a more instrumentalist view of the benefits of multicultural policy. Canada is full of people who speak innumerable languages and keep in touch with their homelands. Simply put, the Mulroney government of the day strongly believed that multiculturalism could and did mean business—increased business, more economic opportunities, and greater prosperity for all. Cultural pluralism and the image of Canada as an equal, tolerant, and fair society were defined by the government as a unique Canadian asset within the emerging global economy (Moodley, 1983). What the Conservatives failed to recognize was that most of Canada's global competitors are now multicultural in fact, if not in official policy terms, and so this might not have been as much of an advantage as initially thought.

Since the 1990s, a third stage of multiculturalism has developed. This 'civic multiculturalism' can be defined as a stage during which folkloric and institutional multiculturalism are coupled with notions of social equality and citizenship. The focus of civic multiculturalism is society-building; today, fostering a common sense of identity and belonging is considered essential for the participation and inclusion of all Canadians in national institutions (Fleras and Elliott, 1996: 334–5). During this stage, governments have moved away from the initial folkloric focus, which has meant a withdrawal from all programs associated with it (e.g., funding for cultural festivals).

The policy of multiculturalism has been critiqued since its introduction. There has never been agreement about the effectiveness, desirability, or necessity of the policy and its accompanying programs. Simply put, some argue that multiculturalism makes Canada a unique and great country, while others say that multiculturalism is useless, unnecessary, and ineffective. In the post-9/11 context, debates about multiculturalism have acquired renewed political importance.

Aboriginal Peoples, Québécois, and Multiculturalism

Another criticism is that multiculturalism detracts from the special claims that francophones and Aboriginal peoples have in Canadian society. In Quebec, multiculturalism was seen as an attempt by the federal government to undermine the legitimate Quebec aspirations for 'nationhood'. Indeed, its direct growth out of the fourth volume of the Bilingualism and Biculturalism Commission report, on the 'other' ethnic groups, which seemed to be an extension beyond the mandate the Commission name implied, made this a reasonable charge. By severing

Figure 8.4   Permanent Residents by Top 10 Mother Tongues, Canada, 2007

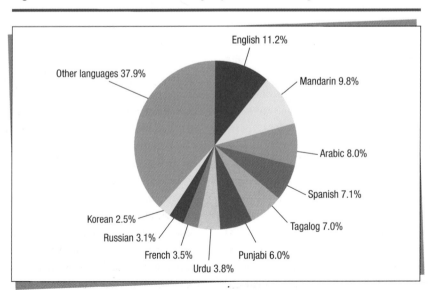

Source: Source: Citizenship and Immigration Canada, *Facts & Figures 2007*, p. 52. Reproduced and adapted with the permission of the Minister of Public Works and Government Services Canada, 2009.
http://www.cic.gc.ca/english/resources/statistics/facts2006/permanent/28.asp

culture from language, multiculturalism rejected the 'two founding nations' metaphor of Canada's historical development and reduced the status of French Canadians from that of 'founding people' to just another ethnic group (Abu-Laban and Stasiulis, 1992: 367). Multiculturalism also became a mechanism to buy allophone votes. Multiculturalism, it is claimed, has had an adverse effect on the Quebec collectivity by reducing the Québécois to one of many minorities within Canada. Assimilationist Quebec language policies directed towards allophones can be understood in this context.

Successive Quebec governments have pursued a policy of *interculturalism* (prominent in Europe), instead of multiculturalism. According to Kymlicka (1998), interculturalism operates within three important principles: (1) it recognizes French as the language of public life; (2) it respects the liberal-democratic values of political rights and equality of opportunity for all; and (3) it respects pluralism, openness to, and tolerance of the differences of others. These principles constitute a 'moral contract' between the province of Quebec and immigrant groups. Interculturalism may sound a lot like the federal policy of multiculturalism, but there are some nuanced differences. For example, it promotes *linguistic assimilation*. The 'centre of convergence' for different cultural groups in Quebec is the 'collective good' of the French language, which is seen as an indispensable condition for the creation of the *culture publique commune* (common public culture) and the cohesion of Quebec society. The French language needs to be protected and promoted. It constitutes the basis for the self-definition of Quebec as a political community and as a nation. Particular emphasis is placed on the educational system. As Stéphane Lévesque (1999: 4) has argued, 'common blood or ethnicity hardly creates social cohesion or nationhood, but an education system with a common language does make a "homeland". . . . It is language, more than land and history, that provides the essential form of belonging.' Federal multiculturalism promotes individualist approaches to culture, whereas interculturalism focuses on the collectivity.

Interculturalism does not reduce calls for Quebec separation or more political autonomy to an ethnic phenomenon; it discourages ethnic enclaves (Abu-Laban and Stasiulis, 1992: 368). Like multiculturalism, it promotes cultural exchanges in the hope that, as people of different cultures are exposed to various elements of other cultures, the ensuing dialogue may lead to an understanding and acceptance of the 'Other', not merely to tolerance. The result should lead to a fusion of all commonalities of cultures (in a francophone frame-

work). As a policy, interculturalism also aims to overcome prejudices and fight racism.

Finally, some researchers have argued that interculturalism is the most advanced form of pluralism today (Karmis, 2004: 79). It is claimed that it combines multiculturalism and multinationalism and is more inclusive than either. It does not apply only to ethnic groups or nations but also to 'lifestyle' cultures and world views associated with new social movements, including cultural gay, punk, environmental, feminist, and other non-ethnic-based identities. In principle, no cultural community is excluded from Québécois identity. Whereas multiculturalism is believed to undermine the national claims of peoples within Canada by juxtaposing communities composing the Canadian mosaic, interculturalism seeks to intertwine them, recognizing that most individuals have multiple identities and that no one identity is so dominant as to subordinate others (Karmis, 2004: 79–80).

Canadian Aboriginal peoples and their organizations are similarly critical and have similar reservations about multiculturalism. Aboriginal leaders argue that multiculturalism reduces them to 'just another minority group' and undermines their aspirations for self-government (Abu-Laban and Stasiulis, 1992: 376). They claim that they possess a distinct and unique set of rights—now enshrined in the Constitution—that stem from their being the first occupants of Canada. Since Aboriginal peoples do not consider themselves to be part of the so-called mainstream Canadian pluralist society, but as being distinct peoples, multiculturalism is seen as an actual threat to their survival. They prefer to negotiate their futures in a binational framework with federal (and provincial) governments that recognizes their collective rights to special status and distinctiveness (Fleras and Elliott, 1996: 343).

Multiculturalism in a Changing World

Many countries now officially celebrate their multicultural makeup, and some have policies designed to promote the peaceful coexistence of diverse groups. However, a number of events over the past few years have provided a context for renewed questions about, and attacks on, policies of multiculturalism both in Canada and abroad. Certainly, the attacks on the World Trade Center in New York and the Pentagon on 11 September 2001 put many Western governments on alert about the threats that cultural and religious 'Others' may pose to the 'peace and security' of their countries. In the post-9/11 era of Islamophobia and 'big brother' surveillance, two criticisms of multiculturalism are also prevalent:

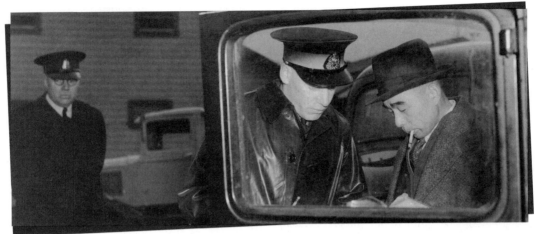

Racism has always been a part of Canadian society. In this historical photograph, dated 1942, Vancouver police harass a Japanese man and confiscate his vehicle. After Pearl Harbour, Canada expelled or interned 22,000 Japanese immigrants and Japanese Canadians. Vancouver Public Library, Special Collections, VPL1326

(1) that multiculturalism encourages and tolerates the promotion of cultures and religions that are decidedly intolerant; and (2) that multiculturalism is a recipe for homegrown terrorism. Such critiques are often concealed forms of racism. No country has arrived at an ideal management of ethnic and racial diversity. Canada's multicultural approach to diversity issues may not be perfect, indeed, it is rather limited, but many other far more problematic approaches to diversity exist (the US and France spring readily to mind) that we can take pride in having avoided so far. Let us now turn, then, to the unresolved issues of racism.

● Prejudice ● ● ● ● ● ● ● and Racism

Racism is based on 'othering' (Simmons, 1998). According to Stuart Hall, it is 'not a set of false pleas which swim around in the head . . . not a set of mistaken perceptions . . . . [Racist ideas] have their basis in real material conditions of existence. They arise because of the concrete problems of different classes and groups in society. Racism represents the attempt ideologically to construct those conditions, contradictions, and problems in such a way that they can be dealt with and deflected at the same moment' (in Li, 1999: 325). Many sociologists have suggested (e.g., Bolaria and Li, 1988; Li, 1999) that race problems often begin as labour problems. Competition for employment among workers from different ethnic/racialized (and gender) groups keeps wages low and profits for employers high. Workers usually participate in a *split labour market*, in which more members of the dominant groups may have more secure, full-time, and high-paying jobs, whereas minorities are found in largely part-time, low-paying, insecure, menial occupations. Expressions of working-class racism may be attributable to labour market conditions of inequality (see Dunk, in Satzewich, 1998).

This labour market split develops over long periods of time and is reproduced by prejudice and discrimination. Processes of racialization are coupled with preconceived notions of what people are, not who they are, and are associated with everyday racist social practices. Often, we have preconceived notions about ethnic/racialized groups. Members of some groups are seen through the prism of stereotypes (Driedger, 1996). Some are deemed as 'hard-working', 'law-abiding', 'smart', 'moral', etc. Others are seen as 'lazy', 'smelly', 'dirty', 'stingy', 'criminals', 'promiscuous', 'uncivilized', and the like. Ethnic jokes, which might amuse us uncritically, are based on these stereotypes. Negative stereotypes are often reserved, by the majority group, for minority groups; positive stereotypes are related to dominant groups, although minority groups use positive self-stereotypes to resist racism. Discrimination refers to behaviours and policies that reproduce ethnic and racial social stereotypes as well as economic and political inequalities. We also use the term 'prejudice' to refer to the negative views of and attitudes about members of various minority groups. 'Prejudice' comes from the Latin word for 'prejudgment'. Also associated with this term is the *ecological fallacy*, which is the assumption that an individual member of a social group (in our case, an ethnic/racialized group) has the social characteristics associated with that group. As such, stereotypes, discrimination, and prejudice maintain and reproduce racism.

We can speak of two types of discrimination against minorities: *de jure* (i.e., by law) and *de facto* (in fact). Historically, in Canada and elsewhere, government policies have explicitly discriminated against specific groups, such as against blacks during the apartheid era in South Africa; in Nazi Germany, where the Nuremberg Laws of 1935 restricted the movement, occupations, education opportunities, and other rights and freedoms of Jewish people; and in the US, where in the South, especially, until the 1960s blacks were segregated from other Americans and often were denied the right to vote. In Canada, many Aboriginals experience varying degrees of racism in their daily lives, but as a group, First Nations people have been singled out for unequal treatment by Canadian governments. Their lands have been taken away (presumably legally, through 'treaties'), they have been forcefully segregated in reserves, and, for many, their children were sent to residential schools for most of a century, depriving generations of their own cultural heritage. During the two world wars of the twentieth century, members of other ethnic groups (Germans, Italians, and Japanese) were singled out for internment by Canadian authorities, and members of other ethnic groups (e.g., Russians, Ukrainians, Jews) were seen as harbouring Communist political beliefs and often were not allowed to immigrate to Canada, or, when they were involved in labour strife, they were quickly deported. Canada would accept only a relative handful of European Jewish refugees in the 1930s, and, as we saw earlier, government policy in the first half of twentieth century excluded Chinese and South Asians.

Today, a more subtle type of discrimination permeates Canadian life. De facto discrimination is more difficult to resist and fight against because it is covert. Canadian law prohibits overt discriminatory acts in employment, social services, and education, but the reality is that some members of minority groups face issues of *systemic discrimination*—impersonal, covert practices that penalize members of certain groups. Also called *institutional racism*, this is the outcome of the inner workings of institutions (the economy, education systems, the government) that disadvantages particular individuals and groups. For example, in the labour market, a minimum educational requirement of a high school diploma may exclude from unskilled jobs some members of minority groups with low educational attainment (e.g., Aboriginals and blacks). Recent immigrants may be excluded from getting good jobs when government and employers require long years of 'Canadian experience'. Members of some minority groups may be excluded from Canadian police or firefighting

forces on the basis of a minimum height requirement (similar regulations have kept large numbers of women out of these forces for a long time). Not recognizing the educational credentials of immigrants attained abroad (especially from developing countries) keeps large segments of visible minority immigrants from secure, well-paying jobs. In aggregate terms, we can often detect systemic discrimination in the under-representation of minorities in some better-paid, more prestigious segments of the workforce.

A lot of people believe that, since the term 'race' has been discredited today, and its analytical utility is limited, modern Canadian society is not as racist as it used to be (Levitt, 1994) and that racism may be a thing of the past. This view is wrong. Many modern versions of individual and institutional racism exist. For example, in terms of immigration policy, despite changes to immigration regulations that were considered anti-racist, Simmons (1998) has noted that the Canadian government still is not granting migrant agricultural workers from the Caribbean landed immigrant status. This is a neo-racist policy. In addition, although we do not have lists of preferred and non-preferred countries from which we choose immigrants today, Canadian governments do not invest in adequate personnel and the required resources for immigration offices in developing nations, thereby setting systemic limits to the numbers of (racialized) immigrants we accept into the country.

In addition, as Henry and Tator (2005) argue, there is a peculiar form of racism in Canada today: *democratic racism*. Democratic racism is not necessarily based on old racist notions of the biological and social superiority of whites over racialized minorities, but, rather, on contradictions about and conflicts over social values. For example, Canada supposedly is committed to justice, equality, and fairness, but these values coexist with differential treatment and discrimination against minorities. Democratic racism is an ideology and a mechanism for reducing the conflict inherent in maintaining a commitment to both liberal and non-egalitarian values. As an ideology, it permits and sustains the rationalization, justification, and maintenance of two apparently conflicting sets of values (liberal-democratic versus negative judgments about people of colour).

Attitudes, values, and assumptions about minorities may lead to their differential treatment and discrimination. Racism is reflected in the systems of cultural production and representation and in the codes of behaviour of the dominant culture. Henry and Tator argue that they are 'embedded in the values and meanings, policies and practices of powerful institutions' (2005: 90). Racialized discourse and racist practices in Canada are marked by a history of oppression, domination, and resistance. Society gives voice to racism through words, images, stories, explanations (or silences), categorizations, justifications, and rationalizations, which in turn produce a shared understanding of the world and of the (inferior) status of people of colour in that world (2005: 91). This discourse is used to extend or defend the traditional interests of the dominant culture.

Some examples of democratic racism include the following: (1) Many people, usually members of dominant groups, claim that they do not 'see' colour. This claim of colour-blindness may be true, but it obfuscates the reality of the pervasiveness of the historical 'baggage' of colour in our everyday lives—the policies, programs, and practices that continue to be racist. (2) The discourse of equal opportunity expresses a value dear to Canadians, but it is often assumed that we do not have to dismantle dominant (white) institutions of power in order to achieve it. Egalitarianism somehow will manifest itself without any social or political struggle. (3) Just because we exalt tolerance of others through the language and policy of multiculturalism, this does not mean that multiculturalism necessarily leads to social harmony. The new buzzword—'reasonable accommodation'—is a hoax (see 'Open for Discussion' box). We continue to use the dominant values, beliefs, and ideas as measuring sticks for evaluating others. In addition, multiculturalism conceals the structural, economic, and political inequalities in Canada. Multiculturalism does not combat racism. (4) The discourse of national identity tends to be racist since it erases or silences the contributions to the Canadian national identity of ethnic/racialized minorities. When we continue to reproduce the two founding nations concept of Canada, this myth ignores the 'First Nations'—Aboriginal groups (Satzewich and Liodakis, 2007: 155–6).

Finally, it should be kept in mind that racism is not found exclusively among members of dominant groups. There also exist intra- and inter-group racisms. For example, some members of the same group may exhibit racism towards other members because of regional, linguistic, religious, or political differences. We often encounter inter-minority group racism. Members of groups who had been marginalized in the past (Irish, Greeks, Italians, etc.) identify today more with their skin colour than with their ethnic background and thus reproduce the racial dichotomy of 'us' versus 'them'. They have changed from being 'micks', 'wops', and 'macaronis' to being racists. There is a broader theoretical issue here: the tendency to view racism as a binary opposition between racists and those who are racialized.

Culturalism and Political Economy: Explanations of Socio-economic Inequalities

Broadly speaking, two major theoretical frameworks attempt to explain ethnicity and race as social phenomena. One emphasizes the role of culture; the other that of social structures, which is often linked with a political

OPEN FOR DISCUSSION
Reasonable Accommodation, Xenophobia, and Islamophobia

'Reasonable accommodation' is the new mantra used by proponents of Quebec interculturalism. The term implies that government policies and programs will endeavour not just to tolerate, but also to accommodate the cultural differences, the 'otherness', of new immigrants, in the spirit of pluralism. The debate on the usefulness of this policy is ongoing. The Quebec government has actually institutionalized this debate by holding public hearings. Not all Quebecers agree with reasonable accommodation. In fact, a clear urban/rural cultural split reflects current socio-demographic realities: urban centres, like Montreal, have sizable immigrant populations and are more accepting of difference; rural areas are largely homogeneous and culturally conservative, and they would like to keep it that way. For example, in January 2007, Hérouxville, a small (population 1,338) Quebec farming community of almost exclusively white, francophone, nominally Catholic residents located 180 kilometres north of Montreal, gained notoriety when its town council passed a resolution prescribing a code of conduct for potential immigrants. It set conditions under which new immigrants could be admitted to their town. Specifically, the resolution stated that immigrants who 'cover their face', 'carry weapons to school', 'stone or burn alive women', or 'perform female genital mutilation' were not welcome in their community. As André Drouin, a town councillor, put it, reasonable accommodation had reached a state of emergency in Quebec. The implication was clear: apparently, interculturalism and reasonable accommodation have gone too far, since, it is presumed, they 'allow everything'. Quebec Premier Jean Charest suggested that Hérouxville's 'measures' may be drastic and exaggerated, and not representative of Quebec society.

The reaction of minority communities was swift. A delegation of women from the Canadian Islamic Congress visited Hérouxville and met with the town council and some local residents to discuss the issue, in the spirit of cultural understanding. The resolution was clearly directed against Muslims and other peoples from Northern Africa, the Middle East, and Asia. Its intentions were discriminatory. It was a concrete example of xenophobia and Islamophobia. After the exchange of niceties and gifts, the town resolution was watered down, but the controversy remained and sparked debates in other parts of the country among politicians, the media, students, professors, and many others.

The Hérouxville incident is not the only example of attempts to discriminate against Muslims. In the post 9/11 world, xenophobia and Islamophobia are on the rise worldwide. In particular, the 'veil' issue has sparked debates in the UK and France. Politicians such as former UK Prime Minister Tony Blair and his ex-Minister of Foreign Affairs, Jack Straw, have asked Muslim women to remove their veils in their presence 'in order to improve communication'. A Muslim teacher in the UK was required by law to remove her veil in the classroom, since, it was argued, 'it hindered student learning.' In France, Nicolas Sarkozi, the new President, has made similar calls and is now considering proposals for DNA tests to 'scientifically ascertain the blood relationship of parents and kids' from Muslim North Africa (ex-French colonies with mostly Muslim populations) before they are admitted to France as family members of legal immigrants.

In Canada, no one has called for such DNA testing (yet). But the veil issue attracted media attention recently. In September 2007, three federal by-elections took place in Quebec. Marc Mayrand, Canada's Chief Electoral Officer, was under pressure from politicians, the media, and 'concerned citizens' to take a stance against allowing veiled Muslim women to vote unless they first showed their faces. Should women with their faces covered be allowed to vote? How could their identity be verified? He decided, in the spirit of being reasonable, that veiled Muslim women have the same rights as everyone else. After this decision, Mayrand held a press conference in Ottawa to address some of the criticisms he had received. Allegedly, the Chief Electoral Officer had 'flouted the will of Parliament' by his loose interpretation of the Elections Act (*National Post*, 10 Sept. 2007). According to Mayrand, there is nothing in the current electoral law to prevent veiled people from voting. Moreover, the law allows citizens—for religious reasons—to vote with their face covered provided they show two pieces of valid ID and swear an oath. After all, said Mayrand, in the previous federal election, 80,000 people cast votes by mail (*Toronto Star*, 10 Sept. 2007). Prime Minister Stephen Harper and Official Opposition leader Stéphane Dion disagreed with this interpretation of the law, and argued that people must show their faces when voting to maintain integrity in the election process. Mayrand countered that if parliamentarians did not like his interpretation, they should have changed the law when they had the chance. On the other hand, John Ivison, a writer for the *National Post*, pointed out that neither has Parliament ruled 'on voting by comic book characters but if Batman and Robin turned up in the polling booth, one hopes that Elections Canada staff would force them to reveal their secret identities' (*National Post*, 10 Sept. 2007).

Do you think that veiled women want to hide their identities? Or is veiling based on religious beliefs and/or cultural traditions? Canada is considered a tolerant society, has an official policy of multiculturalism, and freedom of religion is protected by the Charter of Rights and Freedoms. So, should we allow veiled citizens to cast ballots? Before you grapple with this last question, you should know that both the Canadian Islamic Congress and the Canadian Council of Muslim Women agreed that veiled women should show their faces before voting. What do you think are the implications of this issue for the study of race and ethnicity in Canada? Who decides what is 'reasonable' in reasonable accommodation? What are the criteria? What should they be?

economy perspective. Culturalism has been an important discourse in the social sciences. It attempts to explain the behavioural, moral, intellectual, and socio-economic characteristics of ethnic and racial group members in terms of their culture. Its central argument can be summarized as follows: ethnic and racial groups share common values, religion, beliefs, sentiments, ideas, languages, historical memories and symbols, leaderships, a common past, and often the same geographical territory. They have specific and distinct ways of responding to their external conditions that vary and are shaped by their own environment. In short, they have a common culture. If we want to explain their differential socio-economic achievements, we must look into their culture, the key to understanding their differences. Culture is considered the *explanans* (that which explains), not the *explanandum* (that which must be explained). Cultural values (often linked to biological traits) affect the psychological composition of their members and produce, it is claimed, 'differences in cognitive perception, mental aptitude, and logical reasoning' (Li, 1999: 10). In turn, such differences are thought to affect subsequent educational and economic achievements. Thus, some groups, on average, are doing better than others in school and the labour market. Some cultures foster values conducive to economic achievement (in capitalist conditions); others do not.

Two examples from the 1950s are instructive in this regard. Rosen (1956, 1959) studied the relative upward social mobility of six groups—Greeks, Jews, white Protestants, French Canadians, Italians, and blacks—and found that the former three groups had higher mobility rates than the latter three because of what he asserted were differences in achievement motivation, achievement values, and educational aspirations. He did not examine or show differentials *within* these groups. Presumably, then, if all members of an ethnic group share the same culture and have the same achievement motivation, values, and educational aspirations, there should not have been any differences *within* these groups. Did all Greeks score high on his scales? Did all French Canadians score low? Weren't there any highly motivated Italians in the sample? How could we explain, based on culture alone, those French Canadians with high educational credentials? How could we explain, based on culture alone, variations in the educational and economic achievement within the same ethnic or racial group?

Wagley and Harris (1959) used the term 'adaptive capacity' as an explanatory device. Some groups, according to this line of thinking, are able to adapt to their new external conditions better and more readily, and perform better in education and the labour market than others, because their own cultural values prepare them to do so. They argued, for example, that the French-Canadian and Jewish cultures had higher adaptive capacity than those of Aboriginals and blacks. Hence, the former groups enjoyed higher socio-economic status than the latter. Again, however, there seem to be important differences *within* these groups that cannot be accounted for by culture alone. Not all Jewish Canadians or French Canadians are well-educated and/or have high incomes. Some Aboriginal and black people in Canada are well-educated and/or earn high incomes. By itself, culture cannot account for the internal socio-economic differences of ethnic/racial groups. It has been argued that the links between culture and ethnicity are tenuous at best (Li, 1988). Moreover, culture is not static, monolithic, uniform, or homogeneous. It is a set of ever-changing social processes and practices; it is a dynamic response of socially constituted individuals to their ever-changing external conditions, largely determined by social structures.

Political economy approaches, on the other hand, tend to focus more on the historical development of the terms 'ethnicity' and 'race', as well as on the social inequalities among and within such social groups. The political economy perspective encompasses a wide and varied corpus of literature with the following characteristics: (1) it tends to be rooted in the conflict theories of Marx and Weber and their contemporary variations and proponents; (2) as such, it focuses on the study of differential allocation of economic, political, and ideological power among individuals and groups in society; (3) in turn, social relations based on the ownership and control of private property, their historical development, and their manifold ideological and social manifestations and/or embodiments are examined. The political economy perspective begins with the tenet that socially constituted individuals belong to inherited social structures that enable but also constrain their social actions. Examples of these structures include those built on social relations of class, gender, race/ethnicity, age, sexual preference, physical ability, mental health/illness, etc. Societies are characterized by the unequal distribution of property, power, and other resources (both natural and socio-political). Who owns and controls what, when, why, and how are central concerns of political economy (Satzewich, 1999: 314). The analysis of intergenerational endowments of these resources is also imperative in understanding relations of social inequality. To paraphrase Marx, individuals are born into a web of unequal social relations, inherited from the past, and beyond their immediate control, at least until they understand them and try to change them. Although these social relations are malleable, it takes concerted social action—it takes social *praxis*—to bring about social change.

With regard to ethnic and race relations, then, we must begin by trying to understand historically what processes have brought about the differentiation and classification of human populations, their social impact, and their conditions. Hence, political economy approaches the subject by asking, for example: Who has historically defined certain human populations as superior? Which ones have been defined as inferior, and on what basis? Peter Li has argued that skin colour, for instance, becomes a physical characteristic of classifying human populations only if it is deemed *socially important* (1988). What makes it socially important? Why isn't shoe size a socially or culturally 'necessary' criterion? That would definitely signify a discernibly *different* classification of human populations. We must look into the legacy of colonialism and slavery to understand the historical roots of the social construction of the term 'race', as well as the racialization/ethnicization or the reduction to minority status of social groups by dominant groups and their hegemonic ideologies. Historically, under capitalism in the West, the white (see how we cannot escape racist language?), male, capitalist class has been in control of the means of production and reproduction, as well as the political and ideological tools of domination. This domination, by and large, has been a catalyst in creating and sustaining the coupling of people's cultural and physical characteristics with presumed behavioural, moral, and intellectual traits, justified by racism. As Brown (1995) has argued, the assignment of significance to biological or physical attributes (and arguably cultural ones) is itself a cultural, ethnocentric choice.

The political economy approach perceives race and ethnicity as *relational* concepts. Goldberg (1993) has argued that race (and ethnicity also) can be seen as social status in the Weberian sense and as class in the Marxist sense. Goldberg writes that social status, race, and ethnicity can be seen as an 'index of social standing or rank reflected in terms of criteria like wealth, education, style of life, linguistic capacity, residential location, consumptive capacity, or having or lacking respect. Status has to do with one's ranking in a social system *relative to the position of others*, where the ranking involves . . . [positive] self-conception and (de)valuations of others' (1993: 69; emphasis added). Most immigrant groups have been primarily associated with the lower classes because of the menial (yet highly important) jobs they have done upon arrival in the host country—the Irish 'navvies' laboured in the building of canals in central Canada in the first half of the nineteenth century; Chinese workmen were instrumental in the completion of Canada's first transcontinental rail line; Ukrainians and other Central and Eastern Europeans settled and farmed the prairies; Italians were among the principal labourers when the Toronto subway system was first constructed in the 1950s.

In contrast, members of the charter groups have been associated with the upper classes and with less labour-intensive and more prestigious occupations. There appeared to be an overlap between lower-class membership and membership in a minority ethnic/racial group. John Porter, in *The Vertical Mosaic* (1965), although he emphasized structural conditions in explaining income inequalities (e.g., patterns of immigration, labour market participation, occupational attainment, monopolistic closure), could not resist the temptation of relying—to some extent—on cultural explanations as well. He argued that people's ethnic affiliation was a determinant of their social class membership and prevented the upward mobility of certain groups, partly because they had not *assimilated culturally* to the new conditions of capitalist development in Canada. This is the 'blocked mobility thesis'. We shall examine the economic dimensions of ethnic/racial inequalities below.

The Vertical Mosaic Then and the Colour-coded Mosaic Today

Over the years, most research on social inequality in Canada has focused on the economic performance of ethnic groups to determine whether Canadian society is hierarchically structured (Agocs and Boyd, 1993: 337). Prior to Porter's famous work, *The Vertical Mosaic*, the attention of most politicians and researchers focused on the role of ethnicity in Canadian society, underestimating the importance of social class in determining the location of ethnic group members in the social hierarchy. Porter argued that immigration and ethnic affiliation were important factors in the process of social class formation in Canada, especially at the bottom and elite layers of the stratification system (Porter, 1965: 73). His argument was based on an analysis of census data from 1931, 1951, and 1961. As the title suggests, Porter argued that Canadian society, understood as an ethnic mosaic, is hierarchically structured in terms of the differential distributions of wealth and power among its constituent ethnic groups. Examining the Canadian labour market from a Weberian perspective, Porter found that ethnic groups were unequally represented in the occupational structure.

Four of his findings are noteworthy. First, the charter groups (British and French) had appropriated positions of power and advantage in the social, economic, and political realms and had designated the 'entrance status' groups to lower, less preferred positions. Over time, reinforced by stereotypes and social images, these divisions in status were hardened and perpetuated. Second, 'less preferred' groups that arrived in Canada later than the charter groups were relegated to a lower, 'entrance status'. That is, they were employed in lower-status occupations and were subject to the assimilation processes laid down by the charter groups (Porter, 1965: 63–4). Third, ethnic affiliation implied blocked social mobility. Upward mobility of ethnic groups depended on the culture of the ethnic group in question and the degree to which it conformed to the rules of assimilation set by the charter groups. The improvement in the position of entrance status groups over time could be determined by their 'assimilability' or their behavioural and structural assimilation (Porter, 1965: 67–73). In terms of the relative hierarchical position of ethnic groups in the occupational structure, which he regarded as a crude substitute for class, Porter found a persistent pattern of ethnic inequality. Canadians of Jewish and British origin were at the top. They were persistently over-represented in the professional and financial occupations (higher status and income) and under-represented in agricultural and unskilled jobs (lower social and income). The Germans, Scandinavians, and Dutch were closest to the British. Italians, Polish, and Ukrainians were next, with other Southern Europeans (Greeks and Portuguese) near the lower end of the spectrum (Porter, 1965 90). The French, somewhere between the Northern and Southern Europeans, were under-represented in professional and financial occupations and over-represented in agricultural and unskilled jobs, a result of historical and sociopolitical factors. Aboriginal people were at the bottom of the hierarchy. Fourth, in regard to the charter groups, the British were more powerful than the French (Porter, 1965: 73–103). In fact, despite the considerable influence exerted on the political system by French Canadians, not only in Quebec but also at the federal level (Porter, 1965: 417–56), and their access to high-status political positions and the media, the British dominated Canada's economic life and were over-represented in elite positions (Porter, 1965: 201–308, 337–416, 520–59).

Since Porter's influential publication, sociologists have paid attention to the relationship between ethnic origin and class in Canadian society, and a number of significant questions have been raised regarding his findings and treatment of the data. Subsequent analyses have shown that his claims might have been exaggerated (Brym and Fox, 1989: 93–9, 103–19). A detailed account of criticisms of Porter is not our aim here (see, e.g., Ogmundson 1991, 1993; Ogmundson and McLaughlin, 1992). Some researchers have suggested that, since the 1960s, an equalization of earnings has occurred among ethnic groups. Others argue that ethnic earnings inequalities persist. Ornstein (1981) has shown that ethnicity alone does not explain much of the variation in earnings. He argues that much of what appear to be ethnic differences in earnings may be attributed to place of birth, place of education, and language. Subsequent research (Ornstein, 1983) has demonstrated that class and gender, along with labour market variables, are more important determinants of earnings than ethnicity.

Weinfeld (1988), examining 1971 and 1981 census data, has argued that in that 10-year period income inequalities among ethnic groups diminished. When sex, nativity, occupation, age, education, and number of weeks worked are statistically controlled, ethnic groups not considered visible minorities had almost the same income, whereas the earnings gap experienced by visible minorities had narrowed. What mattered, according to Weinfeld, was the percentage of the foreign-born within visible minorities and their amount and type of educational attainment (1988: 603–5).

Even though questions have been raised about the persistence of the **vertical mosaic** for European-origin ethnic groups, some suggest that the vertical mosaic persists in a racialized form and that Canada is characterized today by a *colour-coded vertical mosaic* (Galabuzi, 2006: 7). In 1984, the Royal Commission on Equality in Employment, using 1981 census data, found that among men, visible minorities such as the Indo-Chinese, Central and South Americans, and blacks had incomes below the national average and were at the bottom of the income hierarchy. Among women, Aboriginal people, Central and South Americans, the Indo-Chinese, and Koreans had the lowest incomes (Royal Commission on Equality in Employment, 1984: 84–5). These income disparities were attributed to **systemic discrimination** in the workplace. Visible minorities were sometimes denied access to employment because of unfair recruitment procedures and were more likely to be unemployed. Often, education credentials acquired outside Canada were not recognized in the labour market or by governments. Sometimes, Canadian experience was required unnecessarily (1984: 46–51). For Aboriginal peoples, the situation was even worse.

Aboriginal men earned 60 per cent of the earnings of non-Aboriginal men; Aboriginal women made 72 per cent of what non-Aboriginal women earned (1984: 33). And this spoke only of those who had jobs—a high percentage of Aboriginal people then and now, isolated in peripheral locations far from job markets, are unemployed and not seeking employment, and therefore are not counted in unemployment statistics. Educational opportunities and training for Aboriginals were seen as inadequate responses to the problem of inequality (1984: 34–5). Aboriginal people were more likely to be found in part-time or seasonal employment and less likely to move up the promotional ladder (1984: 37). Lian and Matthews (1998) examined 1991 census data and analyzed ethnic inequalities in earnings, studying the relationship between ethnicity and education and between education and income. They argue that race is now *the* fundamental basis of income inequality in Canada. The French now earn more than the British, and there is a general trend of convergence of earnings among the European groups. Visible minorities, however, in all educational levels receive lower rewards, substantially below the national average (Lian and Matthews, 1998: 471, 475). Controlling for a number of variables, such as gender, age, marital status, province and place of residence, and year of immigration, Lian and Matthews suggest that in most of the 10 categories of educational level they examined, visible minorities make less than non-visible minorities (1998: 473, Table 5). These findings led them to conclude that the old ethnic vertical mosaic may be disappearing, but it is being replaced by a strong 'coloured mosaic'.

Li (2003) has shown that in 1996 immigrant men and women in medium-sized and large metropolitan areas earned less than their Canadian-born counterparts. Also, the earnings of Canadian-born and immigrant men exceed the earnings of comparable groups of Canadian-born and immigrant women. In addition, Li found that white Canadian-born men tend to do better than white immigrant men, and that visible minority Canadian-born men do better than visible minority immigrant men. On the other hand, although white Canadian-born men do better than visible minority Canadian-born men, visible minority Canadian-born women tend to do better than white Canadian-born women. This is an interesting finding that tends to undermine the colour-coded vertical mosaic thesis. Finally, Li showed that white and visible minority immigrant women have roughly the lowest levels of earnings of all groups. These patterns are complex, but one of the things that Li has demonstrated is that when other individual and job market variables are taken

into account, immigrants do less well in every Canadian CMA than the Canadian-born. Yet, if Canadian society rewarded everyone equally on the basis of the training and skills that they bring to the labour market, the net differences between groups should be minimal.

More recently, Galabuzi (2006) has found substantial evidence to support the colour-coded vertical mosaic claim. Comparing after-tax income of racialized and non-racialized persons in Canada in 2000, he demonstrated that the average after-tax income for racialized persons was $20,627, 12.3 per cent less than the average after-tax income of $23,522 for non-racialized persons. Differences in after-tax income can even be found when higher education is taken into account. Among university degree-holders in 2000, racialized individuals had an after-tax income of $35,617, while non-racialized individuals had an after-tax income of $38,919, an 8.5 per cent difference.

● Earnings Differentials within Ethnic Groups

Apart from a few notable exceptions (Li, 1988, 1992; Nakhaie, 1999, 2000), the class dimension of ethnic earnings inequality in Canada has not been adequately examined. Porter (1965: 73) argued that ethnic groups have internal hierarchies and are themselves stratified. They are not homogeneous. Among other characteristics, they are differentiated by religion, dialects, regions of origin, whether they are recent or earlier arrivals to Canada (Porter, 1965: 72), by social class (Li, 1988, 1992), gender (Boyd, 1992), age, and place of birth (Liodakis, 1998, 2002). Even if we accept that there was a period in the history of Canada when ethnic group membership overlapped with class position, there was never a one-to-one correspondence of the concepts and their social content. In other words, despite the fact that there was never empirical evidence to support the notion that one ethnic group was associated with one class only, ethnicity became a proxy of class. Ethnic groups became 'statistical classes' that exhibited differential socio-economic performance and held differential amounts of political and economic power.

For the 2006 census, the variable visible minority contained the categories Chinese, South Asian, black, and other visible minority. This taxonomy creates categories so broadly defined that the considerable internal socio-economic heterogeneity within groups is concealed (Boyd, 1992: 281; Liodakis, 2002). The term 'visible minority' emerged in the 1970s in response to the use of pejorative terms such as 'coloured' or non-white and was used by activists and scholars who were fighting racism and other forms of social inequality. The term is now embedded not only in census questions but also in state policies of employment equity and multi-culturalism (Synnott and Howes, 1996: 137), and, by extension, in the language of social scientists and non-academics. A person is officially a member of a 'visible minority' group if s/he is 'non-white' in 'colour' or 'non-Caucasian' in 'race', other than Aboriginal.

The problem with this social construction of the concept of 'visible minority', according to Synnott and Howes, is that when attempts are made to refer the concept of 'visible minority' back to the social reality it is supposed to describe, 'it falls apart' (1996: 138). It does not have a social referent. It tends to homogenize and racialize diverse groups of people. Census-taking is not an innocent exercise of simply counting people. As Melissa Nobles (2000) has argued, censuses help to shape and reproduce a racial discourse that in turn affects public policies that either restrict or protect the rights, privileges, and experiences we commonly associate with citizenship. Statistics Canada is not necessarily a politically neutral institution that simply 'counts' Canadians in an objective sort of way. It creates the conditions under which people will identify themselves so that Statistics Canada can count them afterwards. The terms 'ethnicity', 'visible minority', 'whites', and 'non-whites' are, irreducibly, political categories that construct racial and ethnic groups, often with government approval (Nobles, 2000). In general, the term 'visible minorities' also homogenizes the 'non-visible' category. Synnott and Howes argue that visible minority groups are diverse in terms of their place of birth and place of residence as well as their length of residence in Canada, not to mention their age, class, and gender composition. This is also true, of course, of non-visible groups. Such divisions, however, have important implications for their employment and level and type of education, as well as earnings. For example, there are different unemployment rates within the category of visible minority. In 1991, the unemployment rate of people who reported Japanese ancestry was only 6 per cent, below the national average, whereas that of Latin Americans was 20 per cent, almost double the national average (Synnott and Howes, 1996: 139, Table I).

The colour-coded vertical mosaic thesis does not fully explain the patterns of earnings inequality in Canada. In fact, the racialized vertical mosaic thesis

seems to overlook anomalies that undermine the thesis. In much of the literature on social inequality, Southern European groups—the Greeks, Portuguese, and to a lesser extent the Italians—are not as well educated as the rest of the European groups and do not earn as much; many studies have shown that they are not as well educated and are earning less than some visible minority groups (Li, 1988: 76, 78, 82, 84, 88, Tables 5.1–5.5). In Boyd's (1992) research, non-visible minority women of Greek, Italian, Portuguese, other European, and Dutch origin made less than the average earnings of all women. Finally, as noted above, Li's data from the 1996 census show that visible minority native-born women make more than their non-visible counterparts.

Central to the analysis of social inequality is the understanding that the production and reproduction of the conditions of people's existence is social. Individuals are interacting social subjects, situated in class, gender, and ethnic social locations (Satzewich and Wotherspoon, 1993: 13). Social inequality is a social reality. In most advanced, liberal-democratic societies like ours, all social relations have class, gender, and race/ethnic elements. It is not claimed that class is the only, or the most important, dimension of social inequality. We do claim, however, that, along with gender, it accounts more for the earnings differentials among and within ethnic and racial groups than do any of the other dimensions. Ethnicity or visibility alone is not a good 'predictor' of earnings inequality in Canada (Li, 1988, 1992).

In actual societies, class locations (bourgeoisie, petite bourgeoisie, proletariat) contain sets of real people: men and women who come from different ethnic backgrounds and whose actual lives do not fit neatly into one exclusive category. Whereas earlier traditions have tended to emphasize the 'mosaic' dimension of inequality and to examine the earnings inequalities *among* ethnic groups, the 'vertical' dimension also is worthy of examination to discover the earnings inequalities both among and *within* ethnic groups. These ethnic inequalities do not occur in a social vacuum but take place within a class society. The approach proposed here suggests that within each structural locational basis of inequality (ethnicity, gender, or class), the other two coexist. All classes have gender and ethnic segments. Gender groups have class and ethnic segments. All ethnic groups are permeated by class and gender differences.

To simplify our argument, we do not examine the class structure of every ethnic group in Canada. Instead, we selectively examine the social class composition of the following groups: Aboriginal (not considered a 'visible minority' by Statistics Canada), British, Caribbean, Chinese, Filipino, French, Greek, Italian, Jewish, Portuguese, and South Asian. These choices are based on the fact that the British and the French are the so-called charter groups, were part of the original vertical mosaic thesis, and feature prominently in all subsequent analyses of ethnicity. They have conventionally constituted the frame of reference for all comparisons. Jews, on the other hand, albeit accorded an 'entrance status', have tended to outperform both charter and all other groups in terms of educational attainment and earnings. They represent an 'anomalous' case for proponents of the vertical mosaic thesis and/or its assimilationist versions. The three Southern European groups—Greek, Italian, and Portuguese—are undoubtedly the least studied European groups. Some evidence indicates that Greeks may represent an anomalous case as well, which poses problems for the proponents of the racialized vertical mosaic argument (Liodakis, 2002). Often, because of their poor socio-economic performance, they do not very well fit the visible/non-visible dichotomy used by some researchers (Li, 1988; Hou and Balakrishnan, 1999; Lian and Matthews, 1998). The four visible minority groups—Caribbean, Chinese, South Asian, and Filipino—represent the most populous of all other single-origin 'visible' groups in Canada.

● Conclusion: The Future of Race and Ethnicity

In this chapter we have argued that ethnicity and race are social relations. As such, they are about power among individuals and social groups. Notions of ethnicity and race are about domination and subordination; they are rooted in the history of colonialism and associated with the development of capitalism. Historical processes that have made some people 'minorities' have led to and continue to inform and reproduce the formation of the social, political, and economic dichotomies of the 'Self' and the 'Other'. Canada's current socio-demographic makeup is linked to the historical (and ongoing) 'othering' of Aboriginal peoples, the usurpation of their lands, the destruction of their cultures, and government policies of forced assimilation. It is also intertwined with racist immigration policies that, for a long time, excluded visible minorities and other 'non-preferred' groups from immigrating to Canada.

Race and ethnicity are bases of social inequality. They inform and are part of its class and gender dimensions. In Canada, some groups are doing better than others. If we consider ethnic and racial groups as homogeneous entities, there appears to be a binary social hierarchy based on visibility. When we examine the internal class and gender differences among groups, it is apparent that the Canadian-born, males, managers and supervisors, professionals, and small employers do better than the foreign-born, females, workers, and the petite bourgeoisie. Canada now has an official policy of multiculturalism that attempts to integrate minorities to the social fabric. But the policy does little to address the economic inequalities of Canadian society, and has not been very successful in combating racism or promoting the institutional integration of minorities.

Recent efforts of 'reasonable accommodation' have sparked more debates. This is by no means an exclusively Canadian phenomenon. The wider global context is interesting: in the postmodern, globalized world, the hegemonic economic, political, and cultural powers (e.g., the US, the European Union, Japan) have increasingly pushed for world economic integration through free trade, the free movement of capital across nation-states, the control and surveillance of international labour migration, the weakening of the role of the nation-state, as well as the rise of supranational organizations like the World Bank, the International Monetary Fund, and the World Trade Organization. A trend towards global cultural homogenization is partly attributable to the export of consumer popular culture to developing nations.

In the past two decades the world has witnessed the destruction of the Soviet Union, the triumph of capitalism, and the dominance of Western culture. And yet, the world does not seem to be any more peaceful or more egalitarian. Nor have ethnic/racial and cultural identities or racism disappeared. On the contrary, in the past two decades we have witnessed the rise of nationalisms; ethnic cleansing; the rise of racism, xenophobia, and Islamophobia (especially after 9/11); the war in Afghanistan; the war in Iraq; and a general thrust against the protection of individual and group rights and freedoms in all Western, liberal-capitalist democracies—all in the name of fighting 'terrorism' and 'exporting' what is claimed to be democracy. At the heart of all these matters are race and ethnicity, a major field of study within the social sciences, especially within sociology.

Table 8.3   Median[1] Earnings of Recent Immigrants and Canadian-born Earners, Both Sexes, Aged 25 to 54, With or Without University Degrees, 2005

Geographic name	Canadian-born		Immigrant population		Recent immigrants[2]	
	With university degree	Without university degree	With university degree	Without university degree	With university degree	Without university degree
Canada	$ 51,656	$ 32,499	$ 36,451	$ 27,698	$ 24,636	$ 18,572
Newfoundland and Labrador	$ 50,117	$ 21,188	$ 58,155	$ 23,582	$ 50,087	–
Prince Edward Island	$ 44,012	$ 23,719	$ 40,580	$ 17,447	–	–
Nova Scotia	$ 45,367	$ 26,561	$ 38,317	$ 24,322	$ 23,874	$ 18,263
New Brunswick	$ 48,984	$ 25,037	$ 42,316	$ 25,101	$ 28,790	$ 17,379
Quebec	$ 48,987	$ 30,041	$ 29,695	$ 20,952	$ 20,081	$ 16,053
Ontario	$ 55,992	$ 36,532	$ 38,976	$ 30,027	$ 26,330	$ 19,335
Manitoba	$ 48,045	$ 29,968	$ 34,470	$ 26,223	$ 23,442	$ 20,124
Saskatchewan	$ 49,017	$ 29,493	$ 39,140	$ 24,828	$ 25,572	$ 16,142
Alberta	$ 54,953	$ 36,832	$ 38,982	$ 29,532	$ 27,432	$ 21,415
British Columbia	$ 47,279	$ 33,840	$ 33,512	$ 25,703	$ 22,920	$ 17,786
Yukon Territory	$ 55,622	$ 35,710	$ 40,110	$ 30,673	–	–
Northwest Territories	$ 73,176	$ 44,941	$ 64,019	$ 35,057	–	–
Nunavut	$ 80,316	$ 29,998	–	–	–	–

Sources: Statistics Canada, censuses of population, 1996 to 2006.

Notes:

1. Medians are not available for counts less than 250. Earnings are in 2005 constant dollars.

2. Recent immigrants for 2005 is defined as immigrants who immigrated between 2000 and 2004; recent immigrants in 2000 are those that immigrated between 1995 and 1999 and recent immigrants in 1995 are those that immigrated between 1990 and 1994.

● Questions ● ● ● ● ● ● ● ●
for Critical Thought

1. What criteria would you use to differentiate human populations and why?
2. What makes you a member (or not) of an ethnic and/or racial group? Should Ontarians be considered an ethnic group? If yes, why? If not, why not? Try to apply the criteria listed in the first part of this chapter to answer these questions.
3. The Canadian policy of multiculturalism is better than the American view of their society as a melting pot. Do you agree or disagree with this statement? Why?
4. What is the notion of reasonable accommodation? Who decides what is reasonable? With this in mind, try to explain the rise of xenophobia and Islamophobia in the post-9/11 world of control and surveillance in the US, Canada, and other parts of the world. Choose a particular issue (e.g., the veil or the *hijab*) and survey the opinions of your friends and family. What do you conclude?

● Recommended ● ● ● ● ●
Readings

Grace-Edward Galabuzi, *Canada's Economic Apartheid: The Social Exclusion of Racialized Groups in the New Century* (Toronto: Canadian Scholars' Press, 2006).
In this controversial argument that supports the view of Canada as characterized by a new colour-coded vertical mosaic, Galabuzi presents evidence of persistent income inequalities between racialized and non-racialized Canadians.

Frances Henry and Carol Tator, *The Colour of Democracy: Racism in Canadian Society*, 3rd edn (Toronto: Thomson Nelson, 2005).
This thorough and caustic critique of racism in Canadian policies and institutions points to the contradictions of multiculturalism and democratic racism in Canadian society.

Peter Li, *Destination Canada: Immigration Debates and Issues* (Toronto: Oxford University Press, 2003).
This is an excellent and up-to-date review of the major debates about the social and economic consequences of immigration to Canada.

● Recommended ● ● ● ●
Websites

Assembly of First Nations www.afn.ca/
This excellent website of the national organization for status Indians, established in 1982 out of the earlier National Indian Brotherhood, includes press releases, publications, news, policy areas, information on past and future annual assemblies, and links to provincial and territorial organizations. You also might want to check out the fine websites for the other two national Aboriginal organizations in Canada: Inuit Tapiriit Kanatami, at <www.itk.ca>, and Métis National Council, at <www.metisnation.ca/>.

Canadian Heritage: Multiculturalism www.canadianheritage.gc.ca/progs/multi/index_e.cfm
This federal department site includes information on multicultural programs, definitions of multiculturalism and diversity, news releases, publications, and links to numerous Canadian and international organizations.

Canadian Race Relations Foundation www.crr.ca/
The CRRF, established by an Act of Parliament in 1991, is the lead government agency that aims to eliminate racism in Canada. Its site outlines programs, includes publications, and has useful links to other sites.

***Global Networks* www.globalnetworksjournal.com/**
Global Networks journal, founded at Oxford University in 2001, provides links to sites on transnational movements of goods and people and on globalization, as well as journal contents.

International Organization for Migration www.iom.ch/
This intergovernmental organization, with 120 member countries, provides news of interest and information on policy and research, as well as 'Quick Links' to such topics as international migration law and United Nations resolutions and reports related to migration. The organization is premised on the liberal-capitalist belief that 'humane and orderly migration benefits migrants and society.'

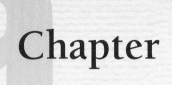

Chapter 9

Families and Intimate Relationships

Maureen Baker

Learning Objectives

In this chapter, you will:

▶ learn to differentiate popular myths about family life from actual research results,

▶ gain a clearer understanding of variations in family life,

▶ understand how sociologists have conceptualized and explained family patterns,

▶ gain some insight into several contentious issues in Canadian families, and

▶ identify current demographic trends in Canadian families.

● Introduction ● ● ● ● ● ●

This chapter defines families and outlines some of the variation in family structure and practices. The different ways that sociologists have discussed and explained family patterns are introduced before we turn our attention to five issues in family life: sharing domestic work, low fertility and assisted conception, child-care concerns, the impact of divorce and re-partnering on children, and wife abuse. Some general comments are made about family policies before turning to a prediction of what families will be like in the future.

● Family Variations ● ● ● ●

What Are Families?

Many different definitions of family have been used in academic and government research, as well as in the delivery of government programs. Most definitions focus on legal obligations and family structures rather than on feelings of attraction, love, and obligation or the services intimates provide for each other. These definitions always include heterosexual couples and single parents sharing a home with their children, but until recently, few definitions encompassed same-sex couples. Most definitions include dependent children, while some also take into account childless couples or those whose children have left home. Still others extend the definition of family to grandparents, aunts, uncles, and cousins who are sharing a dwelling.

Sociologists and anthropologists used to talk about 'the family' as a monolithic **social institution** with one acceptable structure and common behavioural patterns (Eichler, 2005). Academic researchers used to assume that family members were related by blood, marriage, or adoption and that they shared a dwelling, earnings, and other resources; that couples maintained sexually exclusive relationships, reproduced, and raised children together; and that family members cherished and protected each other. Nevertheless, academics have always differentiated between **nuclear families**, which consist of parents and their children sharing a dwelling, and **extended families**, which consist of several generations or adult siblings with their spouses and children who share a dwelling and resources. Both kinds of families continue to be a part of Canadian life although the nuclear family is more prevalent.

The most common definition used in policy research is Statistics Canada's **census family**, which includes married couples and cohabiting couples who have lived together for longer than one year, with or without never-married children, as well as single parents living with never-married children. As of 2006, couples can be same-sex or heterosexual but this definition says nothing about the larger kin group of aunts, uncles, and grandparents, or about love, emotion, caring, or providing household services. Yet a common definition must be agreed upon when taking a **census** or initiating policy research.

The Canadian government also uses the concept of **household** in gathering statistics relating to family and personal life. Household refers to people sharing a dwelling, whether or not they are related by blood, adoption, or marriage. For example, a boarder might be part of the household but not necessarily part of the family. Table 9.1 shows the percentage of Canadians living in various family types in 2006 compared to 1981.

In a culturally diverse society such as Canada, it is inaccurate to talk about 'the family' as though a single type of family exists or ever did exist. In fact, cultural groups tend to organize their families differently, depending on their traditions, religious beliefs, socio-economic situation, immigrant or indigenous status, and historical experiences, though most Canadians live in nuclear families comprising parents and their children (VIF, 2004).

Nevertheless, the extended family, in which several generations (or siblings and their spouses and children) share a residence and co-operate economically, remains important as a living arrangement as well as a support group, especially among recent immigrants from parts of the Middle East or South Asia. Even when family members do not share a residence, relatives may live next door or in the same neighbourhood, visit regularly, telephone daily, assist with child care, provide economic and emotional support, and help find employment and accommodation for one another (Paletta, 1992). When relatives do not share a household but live close by and rely heavily on one another, they are said to be a **modified extended family**.

In the 1950s, American sociologists lamented the isolation of the modern nuclear family, suggesting that extended families used to be more prevalent prior to industrialization (Parsons and Bales, 1955). Since then, historians have found that nuclear families were always the most prevalent living arrangement in Europe and North America (Goldthorpe, 1987; Nett, 1981), but extended families were and still are widespread among certain cultural groups, such as some **First Nations** peoples, Southern Europeans, and some Asians. They are also more prevalent among those with lower incomes and at certain stages of the family life cycle, for example, in

Table 9.1 — Percentage of Families in Canada by Type, 1981 and 2006

Type of Family	1981	2006
Legally married couples with children	55	39
Legally married couples without children	28	30
Lone-parent families	11	16
Common-law families with children	2	7
Common-law families without children	4	9
Same-sex couples as % of all couples	—	0.6
% of male same-sex couples with children in household	—	3.3*
% of female same-sex couples with children in household	—	15.2*
Stepfamilies as % of all families	—	12*

* 2001 data

Source: Vanier Institute of the Family 2004: 40, 42, 58; www.vifamily.ca/library/facts/facts/html (accessed 16 July 2008). Reprinted by permission of the publisher.

order to provide low-cost accommodation and practical support for young cash-strapped couples, lone mothers after separation, or frail elderly parents after widowhood.

Many immigrants come to Canada from countries where people live in extended families, yet the percentage of 'multi-family households' (a term used by Statistics Canada that approximates an extended family) declined from 6.7 per cent in 1951 to 1.1 per cent in 1986, when immigration rates were high (Ram, 1990: 44). The explanation for this decline is that more Canadians began to live alone during that period and that immigrants tend to change their family practices to fit in with the host country. In a study of immigrants who came to Canada in 1985, 43 per cent initially lived with established relatives in 1986, but this declined to 26 per cent by 1996 (Thomas, 2001: 18). In contrast, only 11 per cent of Canadian-born people lived with relatives in 1986 compared to 13 per cent in 1996. Living with relatives was more prevalent among female immigrants and among those with lower educational qualifications and lower incomes (Thomas, 2001: 21).

In this chapter, the term 'families' will be used in the plural to indicate the continued existence of different family structures. Qualifying phrases, such as 'male-breadwinner families', 'lesbian families', and 'stepfamilies', will be used for clarification. Although sociological definitions formerly focused on who constitutes a family, more researchers and theorists now emphasize what makes a family. This approach downplays the sexual preference of the couple and the legality of the relationship, focusing instead on patterns of caring and intimacy (Eichler, 2005).

Monogamy and Polygamy

In Canada it is against the law to marry more than one spouse at a time but **polygyny**, or having several wives at a time, is practised in some countries in Africa and Western Asia, especially those using Islamic law. In sub-Saharan Africa, about half of married women aged 15–49 were in polygynous unions throughout the 1990s in Benin, Burkina Faso, and Guinea, and over 40 per cent in Mali, Senegal, and Togo (UN, 2000a: 28). Wealthy men are more likely than those with fewer resources to take on more than one legal wife (Barker, 2003).

Polygynous unions, which lead to a proliferation of stepchildren and step-relatives, tend to be associated with patriarchal authority and wider age gaps between husbands and wives. They are more common among rural and less-educated women, as well as among those who do not formally work for pay outside the household (Barker, 2003). Multiple wives, who are sometimes sisters, may resent their husband taking a new partner but they may also welcome her assistance with household work, child care, and horticulture, and may value her companionship in a society where marriage partners are seldom close friends. Furthermore, the husband's second marriage elevates the rank of the first wife, who then becomes the supervisor of the younger wife's household work.

Polygamy refers to the practice of having more than one spouse at a time but polygyny is much more prevalent than **polyandry** or marriage between one woman and several husbands. When polyandry does occur, the husbands are often brothers and the practice may relate to the need to keep land in one parcel (Ihinger-Tallman and Levinson, 2003). However, most societies prefer polygyny because more children can be born into marriages with multiple wives and this could be important if children are the main source of labour for the family or community. Also, the identification of the father is particularly important in **patrilineal** societies because children take their father's surname, belong to his kin group, and inherit from him, and married men are responsible for supporting their children. Knowing who the father is would be difficult with multiple husbands, so this is not usually an acceptable form of marriage in patrilineal systems. As most societies have been patriarchal, men have ensured that marriage systems suit their own interests.

Arranged versus Free-Choice Marriage

Marriages continue to be arranged in many parts of the world in order to enhance family resources, reputation, and alliances, and because parents feel more qualified to choose their children's partners. The family of either the bride or the groom may make initial arrangements, but marriage brokers or intermediaries with extensive contacts are occasionally used to help families find suitable mates for their offspring.

Middle Eastern and South Asian immigrants living in Canada sometimes have their marriages arranged, which may involve returning to the home country to marry a partner selected by family members still living there, or being introduced to a suitable partner from the same cultural group living in Canada. Young people expect to have veto power if they strongly object to their family's choice, but in the home country considerable pressure exists to abide by the judgment of elders (Nanda and Warms, 2004).

Family solidarity, financial security, and potential heirs are more important in arranged marriages than sexual attraction or love between the young people. New partners are urged to respect each other, and it is hoped that love will develop after marriage. Often, arranged marriages are more stable than free-choice unions because both families have a stake in marriage stability. Furthermore, divorce may be legally restricted, especially for women, and may involve mothers relinquishing custody of their children and struggling to support themselves outside marriage.

In cultures with arranged marriage systems, dowries have sometimes been used to attract a partner for daughters, to cement alliances between families, and to help establish new households. Dowries involve payments of money or gifts of property that accompany brides into marriage and become part of marriage agreements. Although the types of payment vary considerably, they might include household furnishings, jewels, money, servants, or land. If a woman has a large **dowry**, she can find a 'better' husband, which usually means one who is wealthier, healthier, better educated, and from a more respected family. In some cultures, the dowry money becomes the property of the groom's family and in others

HUMAN DIVERSITY
A Maori Lone-Mother Family on Social Assistance, New Zealand

'. . . from Friday to Sunday it's pretty much mayhem here. I can have anything up to 13 kids. Nieces, nephews, the *mokos* (grandchildren), the neighbours. Last weekend I had their baby, a 15-month-old baby from next door. Because they were having a big party and they were out of babysitters and I said, well just chuck him over the fence and we'll be right and she can sleep here the night so you can . . . pick her up in the morning. So they did that. My niece had to go to a funeral and she's got a three-week-old baby and she popped her over to me with a little bottle of breast milk as well. So I had those two babies and . . . my son had his friend over for the night because his mother was next door partying and so while everybody does their thing, I have the kids and I had another little girl 'cause her mother was there too and I don't really know them.'

Source: Excerpt from an interview with a Maori lone mother on social assistance in New Zealand, Maureen Baker, 2002.

it is used to establish the bride and groom's new household. Dowries have also been used to provide brides with some measure of financial security or insurance in case of partner abuse, divorce, or widowhood, but this depends on how much control women have over the money or property (Barker, 2003).

In other societies that practise arranged marriage (such as eastern Indonesia), the groom's family is expected to pay the bride's parents a **bride price** for permission to marry their daughter. If the bride is beautiful or comes from a wealthy or well-respected family, the price rises. If the groom and his family are short of assets, the bride price could sometimes be paid through the groom's labour.

Although dowries and bride prices are associated with arranged marriages, free-choice marriages have retained symbolic remnants of these practices. For example, trousseaus, wedding receptions, and the honeymoon are remnants of dowries, while the engagement ring and wedding band given to the bride by the groom are remnants of a bride price.

Patterns of Authority and Descent

Most family systems designate a 'head', who makes major decisions and represents the group to the outside world. In both Western and Eastern societies, the oldest male is typically the family head, in a system referred to as **patriarchy**. An authority system in which women are granted more power than men is a **matriarchy**, but matriarchal systems are rare. Some black families in the Caribbean and the United States have been referred to as matriarchal, or at least **matrifocal** (Smith, 1996), as have been the Tchambuli people of New Guinea (Mead, 1935). In both examples, wives and mothers make a considerable contribution to family income and resources as well as to decision-making. Although Canadian families used to be patriarchal, men and women now have equal legal rights and men are no longer automatically viewed as family heads; however, in some cultural communities, men are still regarded as family heads.

When Canadian youth marry, they usually consider their primary relationship to be with each other rather than with either set of parents or siblings. In most cases, however, the newly married pair is expected to maintain contact with both sides of the family and to participate in family gatherings, and could inherit from either side of the family. This situation is termed a **bilateral descent pattern**. In some other societies, the bride and groom are considered to be members of only one kin group, in a system called patrilineal descent if they

belong to the groom's family, matrilineal descent if they belong to the bride's. Patterns of descent may determine where the couple lives, how they address members of each other's family, what surname their children will receive, and from whom they inherit.

In Canadian families, bilateral descent is common for kinship and inheritance, but **patrilineal descent** has been retained for surnames. The surname taken by a wife and by the couple's children has traditionally been the husband's name—a symbol of his former status as head of the new household. This tradition has been changed in Quebec, where brides are required to retain their family name. In Ontario, brides have a choice between keeping their family name or taking their husband's name. Where there is some legal choice, couples may also abide by their cultural traditions.

● Explaining Family ● ● ● ● Patterns and Practices

All social studies are based on underlying philosophical assumptions about what factors are responsible for the structure of human society, what influences social change, and what should be the focus of social research. These assumptions, often called theoretical frameworks, cannot be proven or disproven but guide our research and help to explain our observations (Klein and White, 1996). In this section, several theoretical frameworks used to study families will be examined, including their basic premises, strengths, and weaknesses.

The Political Economy Approach

The basic thesis of the political economy approach is that people's relation to wealth, production, and power influences the way they view the world and live their lives. Family formation, interpersonal relations, lifestyle, and well-being are all affected by events in the broader society, such as economic cycles, working conditions, laws, and government programs. This perspective originates in the nineteenth-century work of German political philosophers Karl Marx (1818–83) and Friedrich Engels (1820–95). In *The Origin of the Family, Private Property and the State* (originally published in 1882 but reprinted in 1942), Engels discussed how family life in Europe was transformed as economies changed from hunting-and-gathering societies, to horticultural, to pre-industrial, and finally to industrial societies.

The political economy approach has been debated and modified over the years. Political economists argue that social life always involves conflict, especially between the people who have wealth and power and make social policies and those who do not. Conflicting interests remain the major force behind societal change. In the nineteenth century, men's workplaces were removed from the home, which gradually eroded patriarchal authority and encouraged families to adapt to the employer's needs. Furthermore, many of the goods and services that people formerly had produced at home for their own consumption were eventually manufactured more cheaply in factories. This meant that families eventually became units of shared income and consumption rather than units of production. Once the production of most goods and services took place outside the home, people began to see the family as private and separate from the public world of business and politics. Nevertheless, the two are actually related, as unpaid labour within the family helps keep profits high and wages low in the labour market (Bradbury, 2005; Luxton and Corman, 2001).

The impact of industrialization and workplace activities on family life become the focal point of the political economy approach, as well as the belief that economic changes transform ways of viewing the world. Political economists would argue, for example, that the surge of married women into the labour force after the 1960s occurred mainly for economic rather than ideological or feminist reasons. The service sector of the economy expanded with changes in domestic and foreign markets, requiring new workers. While married women had always worked as a reserve labour force, the creation of new job opportunities, as well as inflation and the rising cost of living, encouraged more wives and mothers to accept paid work. These labour market changes led to new **ideologies** about family and parenting. Political economists focus on the impact of the economy on family life, on relations between **the state** and the family, and on the social conflict arising from these political and economic changes. In doing so, they downplay voluntary behaviour and interpersonal relations.

Structural Functionalism

The basic assumption of structural functionalism is that behaviour is governed more by social expectations and unspoken rules than by economic changes or personal choice. Individuals cannot behave any way they want but must abide by societal or cultural guidelines learned early in life. Deviant behaviour that violates rules is always carefully controlled.

Within this approach, 'the family' is viewed as a major social institution that provides individuals with emotional support, love and companionship, sexual expression, and children. Parents help to maintain social order through socializing and disciplining their children. Families co-operate economically and help each other through hard times by sharing resources. They often protect their members from outsiders. Finally, people acquire money and property through inheritance from family members, which suggests that social **status** is largely established and perpetuated through families.

Talcott Parsons and Robert F. Bales (1955) theorized that with the development of industrialization and the shift to production outside the home, the small and relatively isolated nuclear family began to specialize in the **socialization** of children and in meeting the personal needs of family members. These authors assumed that the family has two basic structures: a hierarchy of generations, and a differentiation of adults into instrumental and expressive **roles**. Parsons and Bales argued that the wife necessarily takes the expressive role, maintaining social relations and caring for others. The husband, on the other hand, assumes the instrumental role, earning the money for the family and dealing with the outside world (Thorne, 1982).

Structural functionalists have been criticized for their conservative position, as they often write about the family as though there is one acceptable family form rather than many variations. They believe that behaviour is largely determined by social expectations and family upbringing, and, therefore, is difficult to alter. Structural functionalists have also implied that a gendered division of labour was maintained throughout history because it was functional for society, when it may actually have benefited heterosexual men more than others (Thorne, 1982). In addition, change is seen as disruptive rather than as normal or progressive, and individual opposition to social pressure has been viewed as deviance. Consequently, structural functionalists have not dealt with conflict and change as well as have those who take a political economy approach. Nor have they focused on the dynamic nature of interpersonal relations. For these reasons, many researchers who want to examine inequality, conflict, and change find this theoretical perspective less useful than others to explain the social world.

Systems theory accepts many of the basic assumptions of structural functionalism but focuses on the interdependence of family behaviour and the way that families often close ranks against outsiders, especially when they are in trouble. This approach has been particularly useful in family therapy.

Social Constructionist Approach

The **social constructionist** approach refutes the idea that people behave according to unwritten rules or social expectations. Instead, it assumes that we construct our own social reality (Berger and Luckmann, 1966). Life does not just happen to us—we make things happen by exerting our will. This approach, also called **symbolic interactionism**, originated with the work of Americans Charles H. Cooley (1864–1929) and George Herbert Mead (1863–1931), who studied how families assist children to develop a sense of **self**. Within this perspective, the way people define and interpret reality shapes behaviour, and this process of interpretation is aided by non-verbal as well as verbal cues. Social constructionists also theorized that part of socialization is developing the ability to look at the world through the eyes of others and anticipating a particular role before taking it (called **anticipatory socialization**).

Studies using this approach often occur in small groups in a lab setting, using simulations of family interaction and decision-making. Researchers observe the interaction in this kind of setting between parents and children, among children in a playgroup, and between husbands and wives. Sometimes behaviour will be videotaped and the subjects will be asked to comment on their own behaviour, which is then compared to the researchers' observations. Research is often centred on communication processes during everyday experiences, but it is not enough to observe what people do. In addition, it is essential to understand how they feel and why they feel this way. People's perceptions and their definitions of the situation, rather than events or constraints in the external world, are thought to influence their actions or behaviour. This perspective could be seen as the precursor of postmodernist theory, to be discussed later in this chapter.

Feminist Theories

Feminist theorists have focused on women's experiences, on written and visual representations of women, and on socio-economic differences between men and women. These perspectives developed and proliferated as more researchers concluded that women's experiences and contributions to society have been overlooked, downplayed, or misrepresented in previous social research.

Some feminist researchers have used a **structural approach** to analyze the ways in which inequality is perpetuated through social policies, laws, and labour market practices (Baker, 1995; O'Connor et al., 1999). Others have concentrated on interpersonal relations between men and women, examining non-verbal communication, heterosexual practices, and public discourse (Baines et al., 1998; Krane, 2003). Still other feminist theorists are attempting to create a more interpretive feminist analysis that takes women's experiences and ways of thinking and knowing into consideration (Butler, 1992; D. Smith, 1999).

Feminists typically argue that **gender** differences are social and cultural, are developed through socialization, and are maintained through institutional structures and practices. Most argue that differences in interests, priorities, and achievements between girls and boys grow out of their unique psychological and sexual experiences, which are shaped by different treatment by parents, teachers, relatives, community leaders, and employers (Brook, 1999). Nancy Chodorow (1989) combines psychoanalysis and feminist theory, showing how unconscious awareness of self and gender, established in earliest infancy, shapes the experiences of males and females as well as the patterns of inequality that permeate our culture. Carol Gilligan argues in *In a Different Voice* (1982) that women's moral development is quite different from men's: while men tend to focus on human rights, justice, and freedom, women's sense of morality is typically based on the principles of human responsibility, caring, and commitment. Feminist scholars have also argued that whatever is considered 'feminine' in our culture is granted lower status than 'masculine' achievements or characteristics.

Feminists note that housework and child care are unpaid when performed by a wife or mother but paid when done by a non-family member but that, in both cases, the work retains low occupational status and prestige. Although most adult women now work for pay, they continue to accept responsibility for domestic work in their own homes (Bittman and Pixley, 1997; Fox, 2001a; Hochschild, 2001). The unequal division of labour within families, as well as women's 'double shift' of paid and unpaid work, is considered to interfere with women's attempts to gain employment equity.

Post-feminists question the very nature of feminist analysis by arguing that vast differences remain between individual women depending on their unique experiences, social position, and cultural background (Fraser and Nicholson, 1990). Others criticize the feminist perspective because it glosses over men's experiences or does not always compare men with women, but feminists argue that men's experiences and views are already well represented by traditional social science. Much of social science is now permeated by feminist ideas and the work of female scholars. The incorporation of this perspective into mainstream academic theory has been promoted by greater acceptance of the postmodernist idea that there is no absolute truth and that perception and knowledge depend on one's social position.

Postmodernist Approaches

The postmodernist analysis of families argues that truth is relative and depends on one's social position, gender, race, and culture. Furthermore, vast differences exist in family life, and the traditional nuclear family is more a myth than a historical reality. In contemporary countries of the Organisation for Economic Co-operation and Development (OECD), sexuality is increasingly separated from marriage, and marriage is being reconstructed as a contract that can be ended. Child-bearing and child-rearing are no longer necessarily linked with legal marriage, and the division of labour based on gender is continually renegotiated (Beck-Gernsheim, 2002). These demographic and social trends have led to a theoretical reworking of what defines family in the twenty-first century.

Another focus is on how families are constructed in everyday language and policy discourse (Muncie and Wetherell, 1995). By deconstructing—or analyzing the origins and intended meanings of beliefs about the family, researchers are able to see how images of this institution have been socially constructed and are historically situated. Nancy Fraser (1997) argues that historical conceptions of the nuclear family, upon which many Western countries built their welfare systems, were premised on the ideal of the male-breadwinner/female-caregiver family. Labour market changes (including the casualization and feminization of the workforce) and new lifestyle possibilities have encouraged both men and women to question this gender order. Fraser suggests that we need to rethink the social construction of gender and the organization of work in order to facilitate a new order based on equity and recognition of the interdependence of work and family.

The legal assumption of the heterosexuality of couples has also been criticized, and Martha Fineman (1995) proposes a reconceptualization of family away from the current focus on sexual or horizontal intimacy (between spouses or partners). She argues for abolishing marriage as a legal category and placing greater emphasis on a vertical or intergenerational organization of intimacy (between parents and children). This would redirect attention away from sexual affiliation and encourage policy discussions about support for caring. Elizabeth Silva and Carol Smart (1999) suggest that 'normative heterosexuality' is being challenged by lesbians and gays who dispute the old saying, 'You can choose your friends, but you can't choose your relatives.' These families embrace friends, lovers, co-parents, adopted children, children from previous heterosexual relationships, and offspring conceived through alternative insemination (Weeks et al., 1998). Critics of the postmodernist approach often argue that too much emphasis is placed on personal choices and minority family situations rather than focusing on the ways that most people live or the practical constraints on their life choices (Nicholson and Seidman, 1995; Baker, 2007).

● Recent Issues ● ● ● ● ●
in Canadian Families

In the past few decades, many aspects of family life have come to be seen as conflicted, or even as social problems. In this section, we consider a number of these, with specific reference to Canadian families. First, we examine issues relating to the gendered division of labour.

Sharing Domestic Work

Over the past 20 years, patterns of paid work between husbands and wives have changed dramatically. While 50 per cent of families depended only on the husband's income in 1975, by 2002 only 15 per cent had a single male earner because so many wives have entered the job market (Statistics Canada, 1998a: 22; VIF, 2004: 83). The second earner in a dual-earner family with children increased the household income by 35 per cent (VIF, 2004: 87). Fathers are still more likely than mothers to be working for pay, regardless of the age of their children. In

▮▮ Time to Reflect ▮▮▮▮▮▮▮▮▮▮▮▮▮▮▮▮▮▮▮▮▮▮▮

Which theoretical approach to the study of families do you find of most relevance to your own experience as a family member? Why?

addition, fathers are more likely than mothers to work full-time and overtime and to earn higher wages. Table 9.2 shows that mothers with younger children are less likely to be employed but more have entered paid work in recent years.

Canadian adolescent women expect to have paid jobs in the future. They tend to perceive household tasks as 'women's work', but not as a viable option for themselves, except among working-class girls (Looker and Thiessen, 1999). Furthermore, both adolescent males and adolescent females see jobs normally done by women as less desirable than those usually performed by men.

Research typically concludes that most heterosexual couples divide their household labour in such a way that husbands work full-time and perform occasional chores around the house, usually in the yard or related to the family car. Most wives are employed for fewer hours per week than their husbands, but they usually take responsibility for routine indoor chores and child care, even when employed full-time. Wives are also expected to be 'kin keepers' (Rosenthal, 1985), which includes maintaining contact with relatives, organizing family gatherings, and buying gifts. In addition, wives and mothers usually retain responsibility for emotional work, such as soothing frayed nerves, assisting children to build their confidence, and listening to family members' troubles (Ranson, 2005).

Despite this prevalent division of labour, wives who are employed full-time tend to perform less housework than those who work part-time or who are not in the labour force, and employed women did less housework in 2005 than in 1986 (Statistics Canada, 2006c). Wives employed full-time may lower their housework standards, encourage other family members to share the work, or hire someone to clean their houses or care for their children. Yet most women continue to retain all or most of the responsibility for indoor housework and child-rearing tasks, including the hiring and supervision of cleaners and care providers (Bittman and Pixley, 1997; Luxton, 2001; Ranson, 2005). Many employed mothers report feeling exhausted and drained by their attempts to earn money while also accepting most of the responsibility for child care and homemaking.

Younger, well-educated couples with few or no children tend to share domestic work more equitably. However, some wives in dual-earner families are employed full-time but still retain sole responsibility for housework, especially older women and those who did not complete high school. Wives' bargaining power may increase slightly when they earn an income comparable to their husbands', as these wives are better able to persuade their husbands to do more housework (Statistics Canada, 2006c) and they tend to be less willing to relocate with their husbands' jobs. An unsatisfactory division of housework with their partner was given as a valid reason for divorce by 17 per cent of respondents in a 1995 Canadian study, but men were more likely to hold this attitude than women (Frederick and Hamel, 1998).

Why do wives accept the responsibility for housework even when they work for pay and prefer more sharing? Lorraine Davies and Patricia Jane Carrier (1999) examined the division of labour in dual-earner Canadian and US households using 1982 data, which allows them to say little about the current division of labour. Nevertheless, they concluded that the hours of work and the income earned by marital partners are less important than marital power relations in determining the allocation of household tasks. These power relations are influenced by gender expectations, opportunities, and experiences in the

Table 9.2   Percentage of Women Employed by Age of Youngest Child, Canada, 1976 and 2004

Age of youngest child	1976	2004
Under 3 years	28	65
Under 6 years	31	67
Under 16	39	73
No children under 16 at home*	61	79

* Includes only women under 55 years of age

Source: Derived from Statistics Canada. 2006. Women in Canada, 5th edition. Catalogue 89-503-XIE, pages 105–7.

larger society, and gender intersects with race, ethnicity, and social class to influence these relations.

Only one per cent of Canadian families have adopted a role reversal, with the husband performing domestic work and child care at home while the wife works full-time (Marshall, 1998). In these families, most of the men are unemployed and have not necessarily chosen this lifestyle. Other North American research suggests that unemployed husbands feel that they would lose power in their marriages if their wife earned most of the household income, and that this view is shared by the wider community (Potuchek, 1997).

Low Fertility and Assisted Conception

Common-law marriage, same-sex partnerships, divorce, and remarriage have complicated marriage and family relationships in the twenty-first century, but reproductive and genetic technologies may be in the process of fundamentally reshaping families (Eichler, 1997). This reshaping includes separating biological and social parenthood, changing generational lines, and creating the possibility of sex selection. A wide range of procedures have now become routine, such as egg retrieval, in vitro fertilization, and reimplantation into a woman's womb. Frozen sperm and embryos make conception possible after their donors' death, post-menopausal women can bear children, and potential parents can contract surrogates to bear children for them (Baker, 2005).

Eichler (1996) argues that reproductive technologies tend to commercialize human reproduction: we can now buy eggs, sperm, embryos, and reproductive services—all of which are produced and sold for profit. These technologies tend to raise the potential for eugenic thinking and enable us to evaluate embryos on their genetic makeup. Prenatal diagnoses allow us to determine whether or not a fetus is worthy of being born (Eichler, 1996). However, we have very little research on the impact of these technologies on family life, such as how parents involved in artificial insemination reveal their children's background to them and how children deal with this knowledge.

Most men and women intend to reproduce. Fertility is important for social acceptance and gender identity, and conception problems contribute to feelings of guilt, anger, frustration, and depression and to marital disputes (Doyal, 1995). Low fertility may be caused by many factors, including exposure to sexually transmitted diseases, long-term use of certain contraceptives, workplace hazards, environmental pollutants, hormonal imbalances, and lifestyle factors such as tobacco smoking, excessive exercise, a large consumption of caffeine or other drugs, and prolonged stress (Bryant, 1990). The probability of conception also declines with women's age. Some couples spend years trying to become pregnant, while others place their names on adoption waiting lists. The number of infants available for adoption, however, has dramatically decreased in the past two decades with more effective birth control, greater access to abortion, and social benefits enabling single mothers to raise their own children. Consequently, more couples with fertility problems are turning to medically assisted conception.

Infertility is usually defined as the inability to conceive a viable pregnancy after one year of unprotected sexual intercourse, although many fertile people take longer than that to conceive. This short-term definition encourages some fertile couples to seek medical attention prematurely. Access to reproductive technologies is often limited to those considered most acceptable as parents: young heterosexual couples in a stable relationship with no previous children. Private clinics charging fees, however, may be less selective, and many women around 40 years of age approach fertility clinics for assistance. Most treatments last for several months and involve the use of drugs that can produce side effects such as depression, mood swings, weight gain, and multiple births. Some treatments continue for years (Baker, 2005).

Fertility treatments are also expensive, although those who end up with a healthy baby may find these costs acceptable. Many individuals pay privately for medically assisted conception but any complications will probably be treated within the public health system. The chances of complications following in vitro fertilization (IVF) are higher than with natural conception; about 25 per cent of IVF pregnancies end in miscarriage (Baird, 1997). Furthermore, the success rate is not always as high as couples anticipate. British research indicates that in vitro fertilization ends in success for less than one-third of those who embark on it (Doyal, 1995: 149) and for only about 15 per cent per treatment cycle. In Australia, the viable pregnancy rates were 14.9 per cent after one cycle of IVF, 15.9 per cent for insemination with sperm, and 18.1 per cent for egg transfer. If these products are frozen or thawed, the pregnancy rates fall (Ford et al., 2003: 100). Australian research also shows that adverse infant outcomes, such as pre-term delivery, low birth weight, stillbirth, and neonatal death, are higher among assisted conception births compared to all births (Ford et al., 2003). Medically assisted births and their complications tend to use greater public health resources and also place financial and time constraints on new parents.

Those unable to reproduce even with the assistance of medical technology have sometimes turned to surrogacy arrangements. Surrogate mothers are usually low-income women who view pregnancy and childbirth as a relatively easy way to earn money, while the childless couple is often financially comfortable (McDaniel, 1988). Patricia Baird (1997) suggests that commercial surrogacy arrangements are unethical because they are premised on the idea that a child is a product that can be bought on the market and because they allow women to be exploited. In the United States, the substantial cost of surrogacy arrangements means that the commissioning couple is likely to be of a much higher economic and educational status than the woman gestating, and the brokers work on behalf of the paying couple (Baker, 2001).

Eichler (1997) argues that reproductive and genetic technologies represent a quantum leap in complexity by blurring the role designations of mother, father, and child. For the child in a surrogacy relationship, who is the mother—the woman who gave birth or the woman who was part of the commissioning couple? What does it now mean to be a father? Does a man become a father if he impregnates a woman but has no social contact with the child? Does he become a father when he contracts another woman to use his sperm to make a baby, which he then adopts with his legal wife? Although sociologists have always been interested in the impact of absent fathers on family life, they are now talking about the 'new absent fathers': sperm donors (Jamieson, 1998: 50). Social researchers are also interested in the increasing number of lesbian couples who are using self-insemination to create families without men (Albury, 1999; Nelson, 1999).

Sociologists and feminists have been ambivalent about medically assisted conception. On the one hand, it offers hope and opportunities for parenthood for those who might otherwise be excluded. However, some of the technologies are experimental and intrusive. These technologies also medicalize the natural act of child-bearing, reinforce the pressure for all women to reproduce, and provide costly services unavailable to the

OPEN FOR DISCUSSION
Medically Assisted Conception

'We tried IVF [in vitro fertilization] and we got pregnant the first time. So it was very successful and obviously we are very pleased. I would say the IVF process was very cruel, even though we succeeded. I take my hat off to people who have it two or three times because it was extremely tough. It is very impersonal. You can't fault the treatment or the staff, but all the injection, different phases—it's like a roller coaster. You think you're ahead. Then you have a setback, bad news. One of the most stressful times for me was when I was in the room and they were harvesting the eggs from [my wife's] ovaries the first time—one egg. It felt terrible because we were hoping to get 12. We got five off the second so that was great but you still feel pretty disappointed. Then they fertilize and you only get two embryos and we were pretty depressed. Then a day later, we were up to four, so we were elated. Their goal was to try for five or six to choose. We had four but one was a bit dodgy so we had three good embryos—you get that news a day later and you're down a little bit. Then during the IVF we had always envisaged that they would insert two embryos, which is extremely common—most people have two put in. We only had one because [my wife's] uterus is a bit dodgy and they didn't want twins with a uterus shaped like that. They didn't want a prem baby [premature] so all of a sudden you think that your chances are halved, which wasn't quite true. Then we had three great embryos and they chose the best one and it took, which is very pleasing. The other two are cryogenically frozen just like Austin Powers, waiting for their day in the sun.'

Interviewer: 'Amazing isn't it when you think of the technology?'

'Yes it is and we wouldn't have got pregnant otherwise. . . . One of the senior doctors said that this was just the start and there were plenty more ups and downs. We are in the process now where there is lots of worry. [My wife] is worried about what she should and shouldn't eat. She worries that the baby will be born with some fault because she didn't take enough care. I'm very much in the reassuring mode—I'm sure it will be fine. I'm sure that once it is born then more worries start. It is an intriguing game, becoming a parent, I'd say.'

Source: Interviews with couples experiencing fertility treatments in Auckland, New Zealand, Maureen Baker, 2002.

poor. Feminist scholars have also been concerned that patriarchal societies will use sex selection to reinforce the cultural preference for sons rather than daughters and that working-class women will be exploited, both financially and emotionally, through surrogacy arrangements. These scholars seem to be most supportive of new reproductive technologies when they discuss self-insemination within lesbian relationships (Nelson, 1999), perhaps because of the assumption that unequal power relationships and coercion are minimized.

Affordable and Regulated Child Care

The dramatic increase in the proportion of employed mothers within the past 40 years has led to a higher demand for non-family child care and to public concerns about the need to regulate the quality of care. Yet the demand still outstrips the supply, the assurance of quality continues to be a problem, and child-care costs are unaffordable for many parents. Since the 1960s, Canadian governments have subsidized child-care spaces for low-income and one-parent families, generally in not-for-profit centres or licensed homes. However, there are insufficient spaces for eligible families and two-parent families with higher incomes must pay the full cost (Clevedon and Krashinsky, 2001).

Canadian governments offer two forms of support for child care: a federal income tax deduction of up to $7,000 per child for employed parents using non-family care (with no family maximum), which is most useful for middle-income families paying higher taxes. In addition, the provincial governments (assisted by federal transfers) subsidize child-care spaces for low-income families and for sole parents (Baker, 2006). Unlike other Canadian provinces, Quebec offers heavily subsidized child care for all parents who need it, regardless of their household income or work status, at a cost to parents of only $7 per day (Albanese, 2006). Not surprisingly, the employment rates of mothers with children under six are much higher in Quebec than in the rest of Canada (Statistics Canada, 2006d).

Across Canada, many not-for-profit child-care centres have long waiting lists. Furthermore, they do not usually accept children under the age of two unless they are toilet-trained. Even if space is available, parents want to ensure that the centre employs an adequate number of staff to keep the infants clean, fed, and stimulated. In addition, some parents are concerned about the spread of infectious diseases in centre care. Finding a qualified babysitter to come to the child's home or who will welcome an extra child in her home is also difficult,

although licensed family homes are available in most jurisdictions (Doherty et al., 1998).

Sitter care is unregulated by any level of government, yet it remains the most prevalent type of child care for employed parents. Grandparents (usually grandmothers) are sometimes able and willing to provide child care while the parents are at work, and care by grandmothers can save money, provide culturally sensitive care, and create a more solid bond between generations. Yet it could also lead to disagreements about child-rearing techniques between the parents and the grandparent, who is likely to have retained more traditional cultural values. Child-care concerns have encouraged some mothers to remain at home to care for their own children, although most can no longer afford this option.

Most centre-based care operates during regular office hours, but some parents need child care in the evening and weekends. In two-parent families, employed parents may be able to share child-rearing if they work on different shifts, but it is difficult to maintain their own relationship or to engage in family activities. Parents whose children have special needs also experience problems. Before institutions and hospitals were built in the 1960s, mothers were the main caregivers of these children. This source of unpaid labour is once again being examined as a way to reduce health and chronic-care costs with policies of deinstitutionalization since the 1980s. Yet many mothers are now in the labour force, and without some remuneration and community assistance, they will be unable to supervise their disabled children (or frail relatives) because of their own work responsibilities.

Many parents and activists are concerned about the quality of care both in licensed centres and by babysitters in private homes. In some jurisdictions (such as Alberta), neither the employees of child-care centres nor babysitters are required to have special training. These jobs pay the minimum wage or less and have difficulty attracting and retaining trained workers. A number of advocacy groups have formed around child-care concerns. These groups have asked governments to tighten regulations; to improve training, fringe benefits, and pay for child-care workers; and to allocate more public money to child care for employed parents. However, the extent of government involvement in the funding and regulation of child care remains contentious in many jurisdictions.

In the early 1980s, two Canadian commissions studied child-care issues, and after considerable lobbying by child-care advocacy groups the Conservative government under Prime Minister Brian Mulroney introduced a National Strategy on Child Care in 1987. However, only the tax reforms were implemented from this Strategy and the proposed national child-care program was delayed. As child care falls under provincial jurisdiction, the federal government was unable to persuade the provinces to create a program with national standards. This meant that federal child-care subsidies to the provinces continued to be channelled through the Canada Assistance Plan, which was a program for funding welfare.

Since this program ended in 1996, the federal government has been giving block grants to the provinces to use for a variety of health, social, and educational services. Friendly (2001) argues that after many years of lobbying, Canadian child-care programs have not developed beyond a rudimentary level and even deteriorated in the 1990s. She attributed some of the problems to disputes over federal–provincial jurisdiction. In recent years, child-care shortages have become election issues yet the shortage of childcare spaces continues with rising demand.

Some conservative politicians still argue that child care is a family matter that should be of no concern to governments or employers. Yet conservative women's lobby groups, such as REAL Women of Canada, have argued for more income-tax relief for single-earner families and for higher social benefits to allow women to make a choice about working for pay or caring for their children at home (Baker and Tippin, 1999). For governments to provide mothers with a real choice, however, the social benefits would need to approximate women's potential earnings. This suggests that taxes would have to rise considerably.

Divorce and Repartnering: The Impact on Children

When divorce rates increased in the 1970s and 1980s, researchers began to devote their attention to the social consequences, especially for children. In 2001, researchers estimated that about 38 per cent of marriages would be expected to end in divorce before their thirtieth anniversary, but only half of all Canadian divorces involve children (VIF, 2004: 33). Many studies have concluded that children from one-parent families experience more negative outcomes than do children from two-parent families, including lower educational attainment, behavioural problems, delinquency, leaving home earlier, premarital pregnancy for girls, and higher divorce rates when they marry. The main research question typically focuses on whether negative outcomes result from the parental conflict during marriage, the trauma of separation, the absence of a father, or some other factor. As Figure 9.1 shows, mothers typically retain custody of the children.

Despite negative media attention given to single-parent families, most children from these families do not experience problems, although they have a higher risk of problems than do children from two-parent families. Furthermore, when studies control for changes in household income after marital separation, the incidence of problems declines, although it does not disappear (Elliott and Richards, 1991; Kiernan, 1997). The Canadian National Longitudinal Survey on Children and

Figure 9.1 Dependent Children by Party to Whom Custody Was Granted, 1995 and 2002

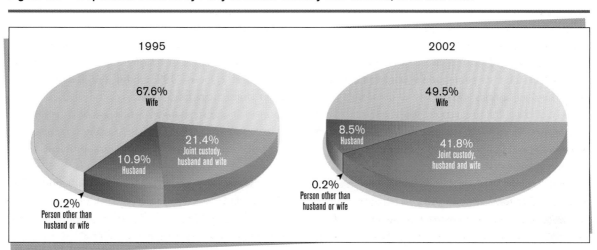

Source: Adapted from Vanier Institute of the Family, *Profiling Canada's Families III* (Ottawa: Vanier Institute of the Family, 2004), 38. Reprinted by permission of the publisher.

Youth (NLSCY) found that about 19 per cent of children from low-income families headed by a lone mother experience a conduct disorder, compared to 9 per cent of children from two-parent families. For those from higher-income families, this percentage drops to 13 per cent for lone-mother families and 8 per cent for two-parent families (Lipman et al., 1996: 88). Socio-economic conditions, however, are not always held constant in research projects.

Many lone-parent families experience economic disadvantage before divorce as well as after, as people from lower socio-economic groups tend to have higher rates of bereavement, separation, and divorce (Pryor and Rodgers, 2001). When children are raised in low-income families, they are more likely to suffer disadvantages that continue into adulthood. Using British National Child Development Study data, Kathleen Kiernan (1997) found that children from separated families were more likely than those from intact families to experience low earnings, low family income, unemployment, and social housing as adults. As Table 9.3 indicates, most children in one-parent families live in poverty in Canada and the English-speaking countries, especially if their mother is not working for pay.

Distinguishing between the impact on children of low socio-economic status and of parental separation is difficult for researchers. Lower status after separation seems to be a mediating factor for some outcomes but not for others. It accounts for a decline in educational attainment but not for rates of delinquency, psychosomatic illnesses, cigarette smoking, or heavy drinking in adulthood (Hope et al., 1998). Even in intact families, being raised in lower socio-economic households is associated with negative behavioural outcomes. These include delayed school readiness, lower educational attainment, a greater number of serious childhood illnesses, higher childhood accident rates, premature death, high rates of depression, high rates of smoking and alcohol abuse as young adults, and more trouble with school authorities and the law, to name only a few (NLSCY, 1996). For this reason, social researchers and theorists must consider socio-economic status as an important variable in all discussions of the outcomes of children after divorce.

Many studies indicate that children who live with their mothers after divorce are likely to experience diminished contact with their fathers and to suffer distress from this loss (Cockett and Tripp, 1994; Smyth, 2004). As children grow older, the time they spend with the non-resident parent decreases, and about a third lose contact completely (Amato, 2004). However, father/child contact is not the deciding factor in children's adjustment after their parents separate. Frequent contact with their father may negatively impact on children's well-being if there is a high amount of conflict between father and child or between parents over the children. If conflict is absent or contained, children want and benefit from frequent contact with both parents (Amato, 2004). In general, a close relationship with both parents is associated with a positive adjustment in children after divorce (Pryor and Rodgers, 2001). Furthermore, whether or not the father continues to pay child support may influence both the children's adjustment and the socio-economic status of the lone-parent family.

Adult children of divorced parents are more likely than those from intact marriages to end their own marriages with divorce (Beaujot, 2000). This may result from poor role models in childhood, from the simple observation that there is life after marriage, or from the fact that divorce becomes more personally acceptable as a solution to an unhappy marriage if it has already happened in one's own family.

There is no simple or direct relationship between parental separation and children's adjustment, although many studies do find differences between children from intact and separated families. Parental separation clearly adds stress to children's lives through changes in relationships, living situations, and parental resources. Although most studies find that psychological and behavioural stress are prevalent for children from separated parents, few studies conclude that psychological disturbance is severe or prolonged (Emery, 1994). Instead, most research finds that the first two years after separation require adjustments by both parents and children.

Never-married mothers who become pregnant before their education is completed are particularly vulnerable to low income as well as to disciplinary problems with their children. These mothers often re-partner within a few years of the child's birth, but the socio-economic disadvantages of bearing a child at a young age may linger (Dooley, 1995; Edin and Kefalas, 2005). Their children are most likely to spend their childhood in one or more stepfamilies, which are often conflictual (Marcil-Gratton, 1998). These factors may partially account for higher rates of behavioural problems in the children of never-married mothers.

Research suggests that stepfamilies are difficult to establish and that considerable negotiation is required to maintain them. Children living in stepfamilies are at the same risk of behavioural problems and distress as children growing up in lone-parent families. Neither a higher household income nor having two adults in the home ensures good outcomes for these children (Pryor and Rodgers, 2001). One explanation is that parental conflict

Table 9.3	Poverty Rates of Households with Children in Various Countries, by Working Status of Parents					
Country	1 parent, no worker	1 parent, 1 worker	2 parents, no worker	2 parents, 1 worker	2 parents, 2 workers	Poverty rate for all children
United States	93.8	40.3	77.9	30.5	8.3	21.7
Canada	89.7	27.7	75.3	22.9	3.5	13.6
United Kingdom	62.5	20.6	37.4	17.6	3.6	16.2
Australia	58.7	11.7	43.3	5.4	3.3	11.6
Netherlands	42.8	17.7	50.7	7.8	1.7	9.0
Finland	25.0	7.2	25.8	5.4	1.3	3.4
Sweden	34.2	5.6	13.7	8.2	1.1	3.6

Source: Based on EQ3.2, 'Poverty rates are much higher for families with jobless parents' (p. 57), from *Society at a Glance: OECD Social Indicators 2005*, © OECD 2005.

and separation have a lasting effect on children. Another is that step-parents do not relate to their stepchildren with the same warmth and concern as they do with their biological children because they do not see them as their own children and have not spent their formative years together.

Although researchers usually study separation and divorce as negative life events, parents often experience relief and contentment after the initial adjustment of leaving an unhappy marriage. This is reflected in their general outlook and in their interactions with their children. Consequently, most researchers agree that children living in stable lone-parent families are better off than children living in conflict-ridden two-parent families (Booth and Edwards, 1990). Furthermore, children of employed lone mothers tend to accept more egalitarian gender roles, as they see their mothers supporting the family and managing tasks that were previously defined as men's jobs (Baker, 2001). This suggests that separation and divorce could have positive as well as negative outcomes for both parents and children.

Wife Abuse

Beginning in the 1980s, when domestic violence appeared to be on the increase, sociologists became more interested in studying this phenomenon. Feminist sociologists argued that the very term 'family violence' implies that this behaviour is randomly distributed within families, when men actually are the perpetrators

in the vast majority of cases that come to the attention of police and social workers (Dobash et al., 1992).

The Canadian Urban Victimization Study found that in cases of 'spousal violence', physical abuse is not an isolated event. Some abused women are assaulted on numerous occasions by their male partners and have sought help many times from friends, neighbours, social workers, and the police. Furthermore, separated women are more likely to be assaulted than divorced or married women (DeKeseredy, 2005). Women are also more vulnerable if they see their partner as the head of the household, if they are financially dependent on him, or if they live in a housing development with other single mothers. Violence may also become normalized when it is continually viewed as a form of entertainment in films and sports events.

Murray Strauss and Richard Gelles (1990) found that marital violence actually decreased in the United States throughout the 1980s even though the reporting of this behaviour increased. They argued that reporting was influenced by the women's movement, by police campaigns to prosecute perpetrators, and by the availability of more options for women wishing to leave violent marriages. Yet they also made the controversial claim that women are as likely as men to abuse their partners, although they acknowledged that this behaviour is less likely to be reported to the authorities, is less consequential in terms of physical harm, and often is a form of self-defence. Walter DeKeseredy (2005) criticized the conflict tactics scale used by Strauss and Gelles, which counts incidences of violence but fails to examine their social context. He agreed that women's 'violence' against men often is in self-defence.

Wife abuse may represent men's rising concern that they are losing authority in their families, especially those men who are experiencing unemployment or other personal problems. This kind of violence is also aggravated by alcohol and substance abuse but represents much more than an interpersonal problem. The fact that most victims of reported violence are women and that separated women are often the targets indicates important social patterns in this behaviour relating to gender and power.

In the past, the police failed to respond in a serious way to calls about violent wife abuse because they thought women did not want charges laid or would later withdraw them (Strauss and Gelles, 1990). Policies have now been implemented in most jurisdictions for police to charge men who batter. Yet many wives remain with abusive partners because of shortages of low-income and temporary housing, an inability to support themselves and their children, and a lack of knowledge about where to turn for assistance. Abuse is also permitted to continue because some women feel that they deserve it, especially those abused as children and those who suffer from low self-esteem. In addition, many women fear reprisal from spouses or former spouses who have threatened to kill them if they go to the police or tell anyone about an incident. The enormous publicity recently given to women killed by their partners indicates that, in many cases, fear of reprisal is entirely justified.

Women's groups, social service agencies, police, and researchers have developed new ways of dealing with violence against women in intimate relationships. Many of the programs are crisis-oriented and focus on women, helping them develop a protection plan that could involve laying charges against a spouse or ex-spouse, finding transitional housing, engaging a lawyer, and, if necessary, acquiring social assistance to cover living costs. Through either individual counselling or group therapy, battered wives are also helped to restructure their thinking about violence and to view it as unacceptable regardless of their own behaviour.

The male abuser is now more often charged with an offence. He is also given opportunities for counselling, including accepting responsibility for his acts of violence rather than blaming his partner, learning to control his emotions, developing better communication skills, and learning non-violent behaviour from positive male role models. Action against family violence has also included sensitization workshops for professionals, such as teach-ers and judges, to increase their knowledge of program options and of the implications of this form of violence for women, their families, men who batter, and the wider society (Strauss and Gelles, 1990). In addition, more support services have been provided for families in high-risk circumstances.

Although governments at all levels have voiced their concern about violence against women and children, money is a major impediment to establishing new programs and transitional housing. Transition houses are usually funded by private donations, staffed by volunteers, and operated with uncertain resources. Follow-up therapy and counselling may also be necessary for the entire family, but these services also cost money to establish and maintain. Despite the serious nature of marital violence, new program funding for the rising number of reported victims and their abusers is difficult to find (Se'ver, 2002).

A correlation has been noted between 'courtship' violence and marital violence. K. O'Leary and colleagues (1989) found that the probability of spouse abuse in the United States was over three times greater if violence had also occurred during courtship. They also found that adults who abuse their spouses or children have often come from families where their parents engaged in similar behaviour.

Three broad explanations of marital violence arise from these studies. The intergenerational theory suggests that solving conflicts through physical or verbal violence is learned from early family experiences. The solution within this perspective focuses on improving conflict resolution and parenting skills in order to reduce marital violence. A second theory sees marital violence as a misguided way of resolving conflicts that is used by husbands who feel that their authority within the family is being threatened. The solution to the problem within this system's framework is to offer therapy sessions to men or couples to improve their communication skills, learn to control emotions, and become more assertive about their feelings and needs without resorting to violence.

In contrast, feminist theories argue that marital violence is actually violence by men against their female partners. This behaviour is symptomatic of women's lack of interpersonal power in families, the way in which the patriarchal state has permitted husbands to control their wives, and the social acceptability of violence towards those considered most vulnerable (Se'ver, 2002). Changing public attitudes towards physical and sexual abuse means that more people now report such activity and that social services are needed to assist them. Consequently, this kind of behaviour, which always existed, now appears more prevalent.

These theories are not entirely incompatible: not everyone becomes abusive who has witnessed abuse or who feels threatened by lack of power in their workplace or at home. Furthermore, everyone lives in a society that condones certain kinds of violence and a lower status for women. None of the theories can explain by itself the perpetuation of violence in intimate relationships. Yet it is clear that violence against women and children cuts across national, cultural, and class boundaries and that it is not confined to marriage or cohabitation. In fact, separated women are more vulnerable than married women.

Reforming Canadian Family Policies

When Canada was established as a nation in 1867, jurisdiction over policy was divided between the federal and provincial governments. Over the years, new social policies and programs were established to meet the needs of the changing society. In the nineteenth century, the federal government developed ways to count the citizens and to require them to register marriages, births, adoptions, divorces, and deaths. The provincial governments also enabled married women to control their property, equalized the guardianship rights of mothers and fathers over their children, and established basic social services in the 1920s. As Table 9.4 indicates, income security programs for families were developed by both levels of government, mainly from the 1940s to the 1970s, but these have been modified considerably since then. Provincial governments have also tightened abuse and neglect laws as well as the enforcement of child support and eligibility for 'welfare' during the 1980s and 1990s (Baker, 2006; Ursel, 1992).

In recent years, the extent of government intervention in family life has been questioned but there will always be a need to regulate certain aspects of family life, especially to protect vulnerable family members, and to assist those in serious financial difficulty. Families also require health and social services to ensure healthy and safe pregnancy, childbirth, and childhood, and these services need government regulation and financial support. Regulation of life events by the state is designed to prevent incestuous and bigamous marriages, adoptions by inappropriate parents, and hasty divorces, and to ensure that spouses and parents understand and fulfill their basic support obligations. Governments also need to gather basic statistics about populations in order to plan future social services and facilities. They must be able to predict the size and structure of the future labour force and the numbers of future voters, taxpayers, and consumers. Some of these statistics also prove useful for the business sector in their marketing and growth plans.

Since the 1980s, labour markets have been restructured, full-time jobs have become harder to find, and more households now need two or more earners to pay the bills, but high rates of marriage instability mean that more households contain only one parent. These socio-economic trends have raised the cost of social programs for governments, encouraging more taxpayers and politicians to express concern about the high levels of taxes needed to maintain the welfare state at existing levels and to question the effectiveness of anti-poverty strategies. In addition, many politicians and researchers continue to worry about the state's ability to sustain social programs with an aging population, growing structural unemployment, and high rates of marriage dissolution. While several provincial governments have cut back on 'welfare' benefits since the 1990s, the federal government has tightened eligibility for unemployment benefits but enhanced child benefits. However, Canadian parents are increasingly expected to rely on their own resources for family well-being rather than depending on state assistance.

Throughout Canadian history, the desirability of government involvement in family life has been debated, although these debates have usually focused on the cost of state income support. Recently, federal and provincial governments have trimmed the costs of social services and focused more on personal and family responsibility rather than on state support. At the same time, they have tightened laws on spousal and child abuse, but these laws have been difficult to enforce because this behaviour often occurs within the privacy of people's homes and without witnesses. The careful monitoring of at-risk families suggests that the state regulates family life as a form of social control as well as merely for assistance, information-gathering, and future planning.

Conclusion

Intimate relationships remain central to most people, yet family life has changed substantially over the past few decades. Cohabitation and divorce are now more prevalent than a generation ago, while legal marriage and fertility rates are declining. Cultural variations are becoming more noticeable with new immigration sources. In addition, more people are creating or modifying their own intimate arrangements in response to changes in the larger society, but governments continue

Table 9.4   The Establishment of Social Benefits in Canada

Family Allowance	This universal allowance was created in 1945 and paid to mothers for each child.
Old Age Pension	Originally established in 1926 as a pension for those with low incomes, in 1951 it was converted to a universal pension.
Mothers'/Widows' Pensions	These pensions were developed around 1920 but the date varies by province.
Unemployment Insurance	UI was established as a federal social insurance program in 1941; in 1971 maternity benefits were added.
Hospital/Medical Insurance	Hospital insurance was established in 1958; universal medical insurance (medicare) was established in 1966.
Canada Pension Plan	This broad social security program, effectively a retirement program, began in 1966, financed by contributions from employees and employers and from government; CPP also pays survivor benefits and disability benefits to contributors.
Spouses Allowance	Set up in 1975, this is an income-tested pension for spouses (mainly women) aged 60–4 of old-age pensioners.
Child Tax Benefit	The former Family Allowance and tax deductions/credits for children were rolled into this targeted tax benefit for lower- and middle-income families in 1993.
Parliamentary Resolution to end 'Child Poverty'	An all-party agreement was passed in 1989 to end child poverty by the year 2000.
Canada Child Tax Benefit	The Child Tax Benefit and Working Income Supplement were rolled together to form this benefit in 1998.

Sources: Ursel (1992); McGilly (1998); Baker and Tippin (1999).

to clarify the rights and responsibilities of family members within these new arrangements.

Social scientists have used different theoretical frameworks to study changes in family patterns and practices, each emphasizing different aspects and issues. The five theoretical frameworks presented in this chapter suggest that family theorists differ in their focus. This chapter also discussed five of the many conflictual issues in family life. The first is the sharing of domestic work; despite dramatic increases in women's paid work, wives still do the major portion of housework and child care. The second issue relates to the apparent rise in infertility and to feminist and sociological concerns about medically assisted conception. The third issue relates to the high cost and quality of care of the children of employed parents, making it difficult, especially for mothers, to combine paid work and child-rearing.

The fourth discusses the contradictory evidence of the impact of separation, divorce, and repartnering on children, suggesting that separation is not always a negative solution, but neither is remarriage always the best solution for children. And the fifth issue relates to wife abuse and why it continues despite public efforts to reduce it.

This chapter has shown that more people now cohabit, separate, re-partner, and live with more than one partner over their lifetime. Nevertheless, not all of our family circumstances represent personal choices. Most Canadians still hope to develop loving and stable intimate relationships and to watch their children grow into adults. However, few people anticipate the ways that work requirements, money problems, social policy changes, new ideas, and the actions of other people shape their family experiences.

Questions for Critical Thought

1. In your opinion, does the way in which family is defined make a difference? Why or why not?
2. Would you expect societies that practise arranged marriages to have more stable and happier marriages than societies that allow free-choice marriage? Why or why not?
3. How would you explain the rise in maternal employment, with reference to (a) feminist perspectives, (b) structural functionalism, and (c) political economy theory?
4. Why are more young people living together? Does this behaviour indicate a rejection of marriage?

Recommended Readings

Lynn Jamieson, *Intimacy: Personal Relationships in Modern Societies* (Cambridge: Polity Press, 1998).

> The author discusses whether a new type of intimacy is being sought in Western societies or if relationships are still fundamentally shaped by power and economic considerations.

Susan A. McDaniel and Lorne Tepperman, *Close Relations: An Introduction to the Sociology of Families*, 2nd edn. (Scarborough, Ont.: Prentice-Hall Allyn and Bacon, 2004).

> This Canadian text provides an overview of research on and theories of family life.

Jan Pryor and Bryan Rodgers, *Children in Changing Families: Life after Parental Separation* (Oxford: Blackwell, 2001).

> This book, which covers international research on the impact on children of parental separation and stepfamily formation, offers insights into why some survive family change better than others.

Vanier Institute of the Family, *Profiling Canada's Families III* (Ottawa: Vanier Institute of the Family, 2004).

> This book contains numerous tables and charts about family trends and patterns, accompanied by a discussion of their relevance.

Recommended Websites

Campaign 2000 www.campaign2000.ca

> Campaign 2000, created in 1989 to monitor 'child poverty' in Canada, publishes an annual report card.

Centre for Families, Work and Well-Being www.worklifecanada.ca

> The website of the Centre for Families, Work and Well-Being at the University of Guelph contains information about research projects.

Child and Family Canada www.cfc-efc.ca

> This website offers public education from numerous non-profit organizations.

Childcare Resource and Research Unit www.childcarecanada.org

> The website of the Childcare Resource and Research Unit at the University of Toronto includes Canadian and cross-national research and other material on child-care issues.

Chapter 10

● ● ● ● ● ● ● ● ●

Health Issues

Juanne Clarke

Learning Objectives

In this chapter, you will:

▶ see how health, illness, and disease are distinct in the sociology of health, illness, and medicine;

▶ learn that health, illness, disease, and death are integrally related to social inequality throughout world through a number of intermeshing levels;

▶ examine medicare as a system that embodies five principles: portability, universality, comprehensive coverage, public administration, and accessibility;

▶ see how privatization is increasing in the Canadian medical system;

▶ learn that medicalization is a powerful cultural force; and

▶ discover that there are significant problems in the medical profession.

WELCOME TO

insite

OPEN DAILY
10:00AM - 4:00AM
Front door closes at 3:15 am daily
Ph: 604.OUR.SITE

● Introduction ● ● ● ● ● ●

Health is linked inextricably to the social order. Its very definition, its multitudinous causes, and its consequences all are social. What is considered healthy in one culture or society may not necessarily be considered to be healthy in another. What was thought of as good health at one time is not the same as what is considered to be good health at another. Rates, as well as understandings, of sickness and death vary across time and place. Social classes differ in their definitions of good health. What a woman considers health may be different from a man's definition of health. Moreover, **class** and **gender** differences lead to varying levels of health and sickness and different rates of death.

Stories of the experiences of new immigrants from various parts of the world to all of the provinces in Canada would provide interesting insights into some of the culturally distinct threads of the Canadian 'mosaic' of health's meanings. The interpretation of health varies not only historically and culturally, but also between men and women, people of different educational and social class backgrounds and religious traditions, and so on. Think about how your male and female friends, your brothers and sisters, and your parents differ with respect to how they think, talk about, and act with regard to what they consider sickness. Think, too, about how illness and medicine are portrayed on popular television programs such as *Grey's Anatomy*. The first part of this chapter will examine several health issues: the changing health of Canadians over the nineteenth and twentieth centuries, environmental health problems in different parts of Canada, social inequality, **social capital** and health, and the sense of coherence.

The sociology of health issues is not only about **health**, illness, and **disease**, but also about medical or health systems of diagnosis, prognostication, and treatment. Conventional medicine—sometimes called **allopathic medicine** because it treats by means of opposites, such as cutting out or killing germs, bacteria, or other disease processes through medications, surgery, or radiation—is taken for granted in much of the Western world. In fact, much of the history of the sociology of health and medicine is based on assuming the primacy of the work of the allopathic system and its practitioners. However, naturopathic (treatment through 'natural' remedies and procedures, such as herbs or massage), chiropractic (treatment through spinal adjustment), and homeopathic medicine (treatment with similars) all are examples of CAM, or *complementary and alternative medicines* and are of increasing importance in the Western world.

The second part of this chapter will investigate some of the most important trends and social policy issues in the area of medical sociology, including **medicalization**, the future of the health-care system, and **privatization**.

● Theoretical Perspectives ● ●

Four theoretical **paradigms** of sociological thought are considered to be the most significant approaches to understanding health and medicine sociologically: structural functionalism, conflict theory, symbolic interactionism, and feminism.

Structural Functionalism

From the **structural functionalist** perspective, health is necessary for the smooth running of the social system. In a stable society, all institutional forces work together to create and maintain good health for the population. Your university or college assumes your good health—you probably have to get a letter from a doctor for exemption from writing a test or an exam. The smooth functioning of societies depends on the good health of their members. Societies are organized to support a population up to an average **life expectancy** and at a given level of health and ability. This normative standard of health and normative age at death are reinforced by political, economic, cultural, and educational policy.

It has been suggested, for example, that the reason governments continue to allow cigarette smoking is because to do so reaps economic benefits for **the state** through the high levels of taxation. Not only does the availability of cigarettes with their high taxation rate contribute to the income of the state, but the relatively fast death from lung cancer as compared to other cancers, for instance, saves the government in health-care costs. Although some may find this too cynical an analysis, it does make clear that there are interesting and thought-provoking social structural ways of thinking about the potential relationships between the health and life expectancy of a population and institutional and political forces.

Assertions about the interrelationships among institutions all fit within the structural functionalist theoretical perspective. A classic statement of this perspective is found in the work of Talcott Parsons (1951), in particular in his concept of the sick role. The sick role is to be thought of as a special position in society. It exists to prevent **sickness** from disrupting the 'ongoingness' of social life. The sick role also provides a way of institutionalizing what might otherwise become a form of deviant behaviour. It does this by articulating certain rights for those who claim sickness in a society, as long as they fulfill certain duties.

Specifically, in Parsons's thinking, there are two rights and two duties for those who want to claim sickness and engage in the sick role. The rights include the right to be exempted from normal social **roles** and the right to be free of blame or responsibility for the sickness. The duties are to want to get well and to seek and co-operate with technically competent help. However, that these theoretically derived ideas do not always have empirical support is evident in a number of ways. For example, it is well known that the right to be exempt from the performance of social roles depends in part on the nature of the sickness. A hangover, for instance, may not be considered a good enough reason to claim the sick role as an excuse for an exam exemption. There is also a great deal of evidence that people with AIDS were seen as culpable, especially in the early days of the disease in North America—in fact, it was called the 'gay plague' by some (Altman, 1986). And, with respect to duties, not everyone is expected to want to get well. Indeed, those with a chronic disease such as multiple sclerosis are expected to accept their condition and to learn to live with it. Parsons assumed the dominance of allopathic medicine in his statement that a sick person was to get technically competent help. Today, however, many people believe that the best help may not always come from allopathic medicine even though it is the state-supported type of medical care. Indeed, a substantial minority—approximately 40 per cent—of North Americans now rely on complementary and alternative medicines, or CAMs (Statistics Canada, 2001a: 17; Eisenberg et al., 1998) and between one-fifth and one-quarter of Canadians use alternative health-care providers (Statistics Canada, 2006g: 161).

Conflict Theory

From the perspective of **conflict theory**, health and ill health result from inequitable and oppressive economic conditions. The primary focus of analysis is the distribution of health and illness across the **social structure**.

Questions driving this perspective include: Are the poor more likely to get sick? Is the **mortality rate** (the frequency of death per a specified number of people over a particular period of time) among the poor higher than among the rich? Are women more likely than men to get sick? Do men die at younger ages? Does racism affect the **morbidity rate** (the frequency of sickness per a specified number of people over a particular period of time)? In this perspective, health is seen as a good that is inequitably located in society.

A classic statement of this position is found in the work of Friedrich Engels, who often wrote with Karl Marx. In his book *The Condition of the Working Class in England* (1994 [1845]), Engels demonstrates the negative health consequences of early **capitalism**. He describes how the development of capitalism advanced mechanism in agriculture and forced farm workers off the land and into the cities to survive. Capitalists in the cities sought profit regardless of the costs to the well-being of the workers. Owners maintained low costs for labour through poor wages and long hours of back-breaking work in filthy and noisy working conditions. Even children worked in these unhealthy circumstances.

As a consequence, poor labourers and their families lived exceedingly rough lives in shelters that offered little or no privacy, cleanliness, or quiet. They had very little money for food, and the quality of the foodstuffs available in the cities was poor. The slum-like living conditions were perfect breeding grounds for all sorts of diseases, and because of the high density of living quarters, the lack of facilities for toileting and washing, and the frequent lack of clean drinking water, the morbidity and mortality rates in the slums were very high. Infectious diseases such as tuberculosis (TB), typhoid, scrofula, and influenza spread quickly and with dire results through these close quarters and malnourished populations.

Epidemics were almost common in nineteenth-century industrial cities where overcrowding, overflowing cesspits, garbage piled all around, and unsafe water were the norm. It was only when there were new discoveries in bacteriology and it became clear that many of the worst diseases were spread by bacteria and viruses in the water, air, and food that governments enacted public health measures. These new prevention policies

▄▄▄ Time to Reflect ▄▄ ▄▄ ▄▄ ▄▄ ▄▄ ▄▄ ▄▄ ▄▄ ▄▄ ▄▄ ▄▄ ▄▄

Why do you think a growing number of people choose to go to alternative health-care providers? Use sociological reasoning.

included sewage disposal, garbage removal, clean filtered drinking water, and the hygienic handling of food. The death rates began to abate (Crompton, 2000). Even in the 1920s in Canada, infectious diseases such as influenza, bronchitis, and pneumonia, TB, various stomach and digestive ailments such as gastritis, and communicable diseases were significant causes of death.

Conflict theory has also been given a feminist emphasis, as in the work of Hilary Graham. In *Women, Health and the Family* (1984), Graham documents how inequality affects the various types of home health-care work done by women in order to protect the good health of their families. In particular, she articulates four different components of women's home health-care work: (1) maintaining a clean, comfortable home with an adequate, safe, and balanced diet as well as supportive social and emotional intra-familial relations; (2) nursing family members when they feel ill or are debilitated; (3) teaching family members about health and hygiene, including such things as sleeping, bathing, cleaning, and toileting; and (4) liaising with outsiders regarding the health-care needs of family members, such as taking children or a partner to the doctor, clinic, hospital, or dentist.

As Graham notes, the ability of women to fulfill these four roles varies significantly depending on the socio-economic, health, spiritual, and emotional resources that women have or to which they are able to gain access. Moreover, these resources are inequitably distributed over the socio-economic hierarchy.

Symbolic Interactionism

Interpretation and meaning are the hallmarks of sociology within the **symbolic interactionist** perspective. What is the meaning, for example, of anorexia and bulimia? Are they medical conditions? Are they the result of a moral choice? Or could they be considered 'socio-somatic' conditions, that is, caused by society (Currie, 1988)? Various authors have attributed them to women's 'hunger strike' against their contradictory positions, against culturally prescribed images, and against lack of opportunities in contemporary society. They have been conceptualized as a means 'through which women, both unconsciously and consciously, protest the social conditions of womanhood' (Currie, 1988: 208). Dias (2003) has documented the way many people with various eating disorders support their 'lifestyle choice' through involvement in pro-ana (anorexia) websites.

Stigma often is attached to the person with HIV/AIDS, cancer, depression, inflammatory bowel disease, diabetes, or asthma. By some, these diseases are thought to have connotations of morality or immorality.

Good health is even associated with being a good person. The following research addresses some of the paradoxes of stigma in respect to Asperger's syndrome, often considered to be a mild form of autism. This study, in the symbolic interaction tradition, is an analysis of the blogs of people who self-identify as having Asperger's (AS) and parents or caregivers of those thought to have the disorder (Clarke and Van Amerom, 2008). It used a qualitative content analytic technique to describe and compare the similarities and differences between people self-identifying as having AS and their parents or caregivers. The findings indicate that these two groups held not only different but even oppositional views regarding AS. People who self-identified as having Asperger's rejected the stigma of AS. They called themselves Aspies and called others NTs or neurotypicals. They said they were proud of who they were and of the way they thought. They also said that they felt the major problems they faced were not due to the 'disorder' or the 'limitatations' they suffered because of AS but resulted from the stigma of AS and the way that others perceived and acted towards them. Parents and caregivers, on the other hand, expressed worry about their children's problems in schooling and in their social lives. They accepted the dominant, pathologizing view of AS, while the bloggers who self-identified as having AS expressed pride and mutual solidarity. This research demonstrates the value of an 'up close and personal' investigation of the world views of people, particularly those who are vulnerable to stigmatization or marginalization.

Feminism

Feminist health sociology recognizes the centrality of gender to social life as well as to inequity in the worlds of and in relations between men and women. Feminist health sociology investigates whether, how, and why men and women have different health and illness profiles, as well as different causes and average ages of death. Feminist health sociology also includes consideration of such things as **ethnicity**, sexual preference, and ability/disability as fundamental characteristics of social actors and social life. These axes of inequality, therefore, are central issues to be included in designing research, uncovering social injustice, and planning and making social change.

Women's health has been a central issue and in many ways a major impetus for the recent women's movement. The health-related book *Our Bodies, Our Selves* became a major rallying document for women when it was published in 1971. Translated into many languages, and more recently revised and updated, this book from the Boston Women's Health Collective offers a radical critique of medical practice and medicalization and provides women's views of their own health, sickness, and bodies.

Another example of work within the feminist paradigm is Anne Kasper and Susan Ferguson's *Breast Cancer: Society Shapes an Epidemic* (2000), which suggests that among the reasons for the growing incidence (number of new cases in a year) and prevalence (number of cases within a given population) of breast cancer is that it is largely a women's disease and is therefore not given the serious, systematic research attention that it would receive if it were primarily a male disease. Contributions to this book by scholars and practitioners from a wide variety of fields, including sociology, zoology, social and health policy, anthropology, law, and biology, examine the social and political contexts of breast cancer as a social problem, arguing that gender, politics, social class, race, and ethnicity have affected the type of research that is done, the types of treatments that have become dom-

inant, the rates of growth in the morbidity and mortality of breast cancer, and even the ways in which the disease is experienced by women. Indeed, they suggest that one of the reasons for the continuance of the epidemic is that it is not only primarily a women's disease but that it is located in their breasts.

Kasper and Ferguson's collection provides a thought-provoking look at one of the major causes of worry, sickness, and death among women in Canada and the United States. Despite the fact that both heart disease and lung cancer are more frequent causes of death for Canadian women, women in Canada fear breast cancer more and even think of their breasts as essentially flawed and vulnerable to disease (Robertson, 2001). This is undoubtedly related to the enormous mass media attention the disease has received in the last 15 years or so. During this time, first in the United States and then in Canada, powerful lobby groups of women activists

GLOBAL ISSUES
Warfare and Human Health

Human health depends on the complex interaction of manifold social determinants that operate across a number of levels as portrayed in Figure 10.1. An important part of this picture is international and intra-national conflict. The twentieth century was the most violent century in history. Almost three times the number of people who had died in conflict in the previous four centuries died in the twentieth century. This is partly due to the huge numbers massacred in World Wars I and II and partly due to the overall frequency of conflict. The Rwandan genocide in 1994, for instance, resulted in the deaths of approximately 1 million people. The civil war in the Democratic Republic of the Congo decimated 7 per cent of the population of that country and the several-decades-old conflict in Sudan has resulted in 2 million deaths and the displacement of 6 million people. Over time, conflict has increasingly occurred in the poorest countries of the world. By the 1990–2003 time period low-income countries accounted for more than half of the world's conflicts. In fact, approximately 40 per cent of the world's conflicts are in Africa.

The consequences of conflict for health are many. Wars inevitably result in death, disability, and rape. They also result in the destruction of the infrastructure necessary for everyday living for the masses of people affected. This decimation occurs in food production, storage, and distribution systems. It occurs in limiting or obviating access to potable water, sewage systems, and electricity, not only for homes but for hospitals. Fundamentals such as roads, homes, schools, and health-care facilities are also affected and frequently destroyed or damaged. Other negative consequences include chronic and acute psychological trauma and distress. The majority of the countries that have experienced war have child death rates that have either stagnated or worsened after the conflicts.

The World Bank has suggested that a civil war reduces the growth of a nation's economy by about 2.2 per cent per year and costs an average of $54 billion for a low-income country. The longer a conflict lasts the greater the toll on all fronts, from the human to the economic. Violence also sets in motion uncertainty about the future that inevitably has long-term health consequences for people within the countries engaged in the conflict as well as interacting countries around the world.

founded highly successful breast cancer advocacy coalitions, lobbied governments and corporations, and received substantial increases in the funding levels for research into the disease and its treatment. There is, of course, a painful irony in the fact that the increased attention and financial investment have been coupled with a proliferation of stories in the mass media that have served to increase anxiety and fear of risk of disease among Canadian women. King, in *Pink Ribbons, Inc.*, also demonstrates how the focus on consumer activism in the breast cancer movement, 'shaped as it is by an ideology of individualism and an imperative for uncomplicated, snappy marketing slogans, has allowed for the emergence of a preoccupation with early detection to the virtual exclusion of other approaches to fighting the epidemic (e.g., prevention) and a failure to address the barriers, financial or otherwise, to treatment' (King, 2006: 117–18). She argues that the corporations involved in breast cancer awareness and fundraising have benefited from their involvement. It is possible that this corporate advantage has been to the detriment of accessibility to treatment for all American women equally.

● The Sociology of Health, Illness, Disease, and Sickness

At the broadest level, sociologists compare within and between societies around the world and over time with respect to the rates of, causes of, and treatments for health and sickness and to rates and causes of death. Here, factors such as wars, famine, drought, epidemics, natural disasters, air and water quality, quantity and quality of foodstuffs, transportation safety, level and type of economic development, technology, available birth control, immunization, antibiotics, medicalization, culture, and political economy all are considered relevant.

At the next level, sociologists examine morbidity and mortality within societies and cultures and compare people of different social class, educational levels, genders, religiosity, rural/urban locations, occupations, ethnicities, family statuses, and so on. A further level of investigation concerns the way socio-psychological factors, such as level of stress and sense of coherence, are implicated in illness, disease, and sickness.

The next level is an examination of the relationships between various 'lifestyle' behaviours, such as smoking, seat-belt use, alcohol consumption, diet, risk-taking behaviours, sexual activity and protection, drug use, and

health. Finally, the existential considerations, including the meaning and the experience of morbidity and mortality to individuals, are studied. Figure 10.1 shows these links, beginning from the person.

Comparative Analyses

The Changing Health of Canadians

People generally are living longer, healthier lives today than they did in the past. The increase in health and the decrease in mortality rates over the past 150 years have been substantial. In the nineteenth century, infectious and communicable diseases such as cholera, typhoid, diphtheria, and scarlet fever were responsible for enormous suffering and death for early Canadians. Wound infections and septicemia were frequent results of dangerous and unhygienic working, living, and medical

Figure 10.1   Components of Health

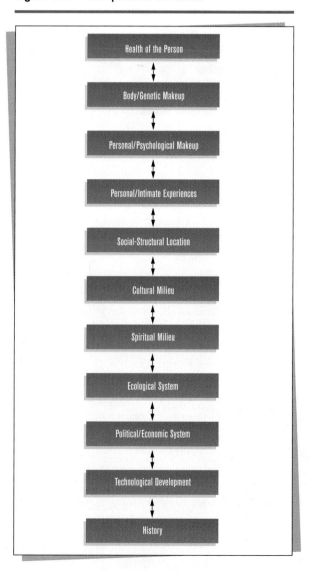

conditions. Puerperal fever killed many women during and after childbirth. The health experiences of early Canadians have been described well in some general non-fiction (see, e.g., Bliss, 1991, 1992) and in personal memoirs, such as Susannah Moodie's *Roughing It in the Bush* (1995 [1852]), on settler life in the 1800s. Even fiction can help us understand how people have experienced health. Margaret Atwood's *The Edible Woman* (1994 [1968]), for example, foreshadows the contemporary issue of eating-disordered attitudes and behaviours.

In 1831, the average life expectancy for Canadian men and women was 39.0 years—38.3 for women, and 39.8 for men (Clarke, 2000: 50). Today, life expectancies are about double this for Canadian men and women. Today's women can expect to live to 82, men to 77 (Statistics Canada, 2006g: 161). What has happened to cause this dramatic shift? You might think first of medical interventions and vaccinations. However, the most important causes of the increase in life expectancy are related to public health measures that were able to forestall the spread of disease. These included improved nutrition, better hygiene through sanitation and water purification practices, and advances in birth control. Interventions such as these brought the average life expectancy to 59 in the 1920s and, largely because of dramatic declines in infant mortality, to 78 in 1990–2 (Crompton, 2000: 12).

In the 1920s, the most common causes of death became heart and kidney disease, followed by influenza, bronchitis, and pneumonia, and the diseases of early infancy. Widespread use of newly discovered vaccines and antibiotics (vaccines against diphtheria, tetanus, typhoid, and cholera were developed in the late nineteenth and early twentieth centuries, and antibiotics were introduced in the 1940s and 1950s) made a significant difference in the twentieth century (Crompton, 2000). While heart disease remains the most common cause of death, it has declined dramatically over time, probably as a result of lifestyle changes such as declines in smoking and dietary fat, improvements in exercise, and better medical treatments. Lower infant death rates today have resulted primarily from better nutrition and improved hygiene in pregnancy, secondarily from medical and technological advances. For example, prematurity, a frequent cause of infant death in the past, is now more often prevented through educational programs and prenatal care, and effective management in hospitals.

The incidence of diseases such as measles, scarlet fever, and whooping cough was cut virtually to zero until some people abandoned the vaccines in the 1990s. For a short time, the incidence of these diseases increased, but by the late 1990s they had declined again when public health authorities were alerted to the issue and became more diligent about universal vaccinations in Canada.

One other important feature of the declines in mortality or gains in life expectancy is the gap between men and women and how this gap has changed over time. From 1920 to 1922, women lived an average of two years longer than men; from 1990 to 1992, they lived an average of six years longer than men. Part of the explanation for women's greater benefit from the changes of the twentieth century relates to the decline in maternal mortality over this period. Another part of the explanation is the greater tendency for men to engage in risk-taking behaviours such as cigarette smoking and drunk driving.

Today, among the most important causes of death are, for men, cardiovascular disease, followed by diseases

Table 10.1   Health Indicators: Canada, 2003

	Males	Females
Life expectancy at birth (years)	77.4	82.4
Health-adjusted life expectancy at birth[1] (years)	68.3	70.8
Infant mortality rate (deaths per 1,000 live births)	5.7	4.8
Babies with low birth weight (%)	5.4	6.3
Total fertility rate (number of live births per woman)	—	1.5
Daily smokers (%)	19.4	16.2

[1]Data for 2001.
Source: Statistics Canada, *Canada Year Book*, 2006, Cat. 11-402, p. 160, released 28 June 2006.

of the heart and then cancer, and for women, cardiovascular disease, followed by cancer and then diseases of the heart. The rates per 100,000 for men are 316.9, 238.7, and 234.7, and for women, 193.8, 150.3, and 134.8, respectively (Statistics Canada, 2001a).

But these rates do not take age into account. Potential years of life lost, or **PYLL**, is a statistical representation of death that does take age into account: the younger the average age of death for a given disease, the greater the number of years of life lost. PYLL allows us to see the years of life lost by disease type, taking 70 years as the cut-off point for age. Here, the importance of suicide and accidents, occurring as they often do among younger people, increases (see www.statcan.ca/english/freepub/82-221-XIE/2004002/hlthstatus/deaths4.htm).

These two sorts of information have different implications for such things as government health promotion planning. For example, the PYLL figures tell us that younger people are more likely to die of accidents and suicide and that the numbers of deaths in these categories are large. One can then consider what might be done to prevent different sorts of accidents and suicides as compared to the chief causes of death—those sometimes called 'diseases of civilization'—cancer and cardiovascular and heart diseases.

Intra-societal Analyses

Social Inequality and Health

The degree of economic inequality has been increasing in Canada, especially in the last decade of the twentieth century and into the twenty-first century. Consider the following statistics. In 1996, the top 20 per cent of the Canadian population earned 43.2 per cent of the total income, while the bottom 20 per cent earned 2.3 per cent (Ross and Roberts, 1999: 26). Many people are aware of the widening gap between the rich and the

Table 10.2   Leading Causes of Death, Canada, Twentieth Century

	Cause of Death[a]	Rate per 100,000
1921–5	All causes	1,030.0
	Cardiovascular and renal disease	221.9
	Influenza, bronchitis, and pneumonia	141.1
	Diseases of early infancy	111.0
	Tuberculosis	85.1
	Cancer	75.9
	Gastritis, duodenitis, enteritis, and colitis	72.2
	Accidents	51.5
	Communicable diseases	47.1
1996–7[b]	All causes	654.4
	Cardiovascular diseases (heart disease and stroke)	240.2
	Cancer	184.8
	Chronic obstructive pulmonary diseases	28.4
	Unintentional injuries	27.7
	Pneumonia and influenza	22.1
	Diabetes mellitus	16.7
	Hereditary and degenerative diseases of the central nervous system	14.7
	Diseases of the arteries, arterioles, and capillaries	14.3

[a]Disease categories are not identical over time.
[b]Rates are age-standardized.
Source: Adapted from the Statistics Canada publication, *Canadian Social Trends*, Catalogue 11-008, Winter 2000, p.13.

▪▪ Time to Reflect ▪▪ ▪▪ ▪▪ ▪▪ ▪▪ ▪▪ ▪▪ ▪▪ ▪▪ ▪▪ ▪▪ ▪▪

What might be some of the other sociological explanations for the growing gap in life expectancy in men as compared to women?

poor, the 'haves' and the 'have-not's in Canada. What you might be less familiar with is that there is a direct link between income inequality and health. A classic illustration of this relationship can be found in the Whitehall studies, which followed the health of more than 10,000 British civil servants for nearly 20 years, and found that both the experience of well-being and a decline in mortality rates were associated with increases in the ranks in the occupational hierarchy of the British civil service (Marmot et al., 1978, 1991). Positive health benefits were found *in each increase in rank*. Remember,

too, that this is a study of the civil service. Thus, all of the jobs under scrutiny were white-collar, office jobs with 'adequate' incomes. It is interesting that this finding held true even among people who engaged in health-threatening behaviours such as smoking. Thus, for instance, 'researchers found that top people who smoked were much less likely to die of smoking-related causes' than those nearer the bottom who did not smoke (National Council of Welfare, 2001–2: 5).

Poverty exacerbates health problems from birth onward. In 2006, approximately 10.5 per cent of Canadians

A heroin addict in Vancouver's Downtown Eastside, a neighbourhood notorious for its drug addicts and dealers. The area is also home to North America's first safe injection site, set up to counter the spread of HIV and AIDS among the neighbourhood's drug users. Christopher Morris/Corbis

had 'low-income' and 11.3 per cent were Canadian children (Statistics Canada, 2008b). The rate of poverty for children from one-parent families is 60 per cent as compared to 13 per cent for those from two-parent families. According to the Canadian Institute of Child Health (CICH) 43 per cent of children of visible-minority parents and 52 per cent of Aboriginal children live in poverty. Poor women are more likely to bear low-birth-weight babies, and low birth weight is associated with myriad negative health, disability, learning, and behavioural effects. Children born in the poorest neighbourhoods in Canada (the lowest 20 per cent) live shorter lives, by 2 to 5.5 years. They also tend to spend more of these shorter lives with some degree of disability. Children at the lower end of the social hierarchy have a greater variety of health and developmental deficits than those higher up on the socio-economic status ladder. It is also important to notice that these results, like the Whitehall study results, are situated in the context of a nationally funded medical care system. Moreover, the number of children living in poverty grew by 700,000 between 1981 and 1996. It is also interesting to note that in a global context the rate of childhood poverty is high. It is also important to point out that the rate of childhood poverty in Canada is *higher* than in other developed nations such as Sweden, where the incidence of childhood poverty is 3 per cent; the Netherlands, where it is 6 per cent; France and Germany, 7 per cent; and the United Kingdom, 10 per cent (CICH, n.d.).

Even though there are substantial links between income inequality and both ill health and death, Canadian health policy continues to involve substantial investments in the health-care system rather than in community-level interventions such as a guaranteed annual wage, job creation, a national daycare program, or proactive prenatal care for low-income mothers. This is despite the fact that repeated studies have documented that interventions at these levels would have more widespread effects on the health of the population than do medical initiatives directed towards individuals.

Social Capital

It is clear from all types of research done today and in the past, and in this and other societies, that social status and health are related. Much of this analysis compares individuals who differ in health and **social status**. When the level of analysis moves from the individual to the society as a whole, however, the link between status and health remains. Societies with greater degrees of inequality have poorer overall health outcomes regardless of their overall wealth. Thus, for rates of health and illness, the overall wealth of a society appears to be less important than the degree of inequity among societal members with respect to rates of health and illness.

This interesting paradox needs clarification. Explanations for the individual-level correlation have suggested that people with higher incomes, higher occupational prestige scores, and higher educational levels are more able to prevent ill health through eating and drinking wisely, avoiding serious threats to health such as cigarette smoking and excessive alcohol consumption, and engaging in prescribed early detection such as mammograms and PSA (a test for prostate cancer). When those in these higher levels are sick, they are able to get immediately to the doctor and take advantage of the most sophisticated and effective new treatments. They are also, as the Whitehall studies intimated, able to maintain a sense of well-being through various socio-psychological processes.

Why would the degree of inequality in a society be more important than the average living standard and income of persons in a society in predicting health and illness outcomes? A recently developed theoretical explanation is that it is the degree of social cohesion, social capital, or trust that is the link between inequity and health (Mustard, 1999). A society characterized by inequity is one in which 'there is a pronounced status order' (Veenstra, 2001: 74). As people compare themselves to one another, it is possible—indeed, likely—that those lower in the status hierarchy 'will feel this shortcoming quite strongly, given the width of the gap, and consequently will suffer poorer health' (Veenstra, 2001: 75). This may result from 'damaging emotions such as anxiety and arousal, feelings of inferiority and low self-esteem, shame and embarrassment, and recognition of the need to compete to acquire resources that cannot be gained by any other means' (Veenstra, 2001).

A number of researchers have suggested that societies with high degrees of inequality are also low in *social cohesion* (or *social capital*), and it is social cohesion that mediates between social status and illness. Social cohesion is thought to be evident in societies to the extent that people are involved in public life and volunteer to work together for the good of the whole. A society with little social cohesion might, for instance, be dominated by market values and characterized by transactions in the interest of profit. Current social policies in Canada that favour market dominance over state intervention exacerbate the degree of inequity in society.

Many researchers are now looking at the processes whereby societies with high degrees of citizen involvement, communication, and community feeling (social cohesion or social capital) maintain relatively high levels of good health.

The Existential Level

How do you experience illness? What sorts of illnesses have you had? Have you always gone to the doctor when you have felt ill? Have you gone to a naturopath, chiropractor, or acupuncturist? Have you always been able to get a diagnosis when you have sought to find out what is wrong with you? People around the globe and even within the variety of cultures and classes within Canada experience illness in different ways. There are competing and overlapping popular conceptions of illness, too. One compilation of popular notions of illness includes illness as choice, illness as despair, illness as secondary gain, illness as a message of the body, illness as communication, illness as metaphor, illness as statistical infrequency, and illness as sexual politics (Clarke, 2000).

Illness as choice refers to the notion that we choose when to become sick, what type of illness we will have, and so on. In other words, illness episodes are viewed as a reflection of the deep tie between the mind and the body. That illness is a sort of despair is a related notion. Primarily, however, the idea is that illness results from emotional misery. It reflects unresolved grief and unhappiness.

The notion of secondary gain emphasizes the idea that people sometimes benefit from illness—for instance, an ill student might not be able to write an exam for which he or she also happens to be unprepared. Closely related to this notion is the philosophy of illness that suggests physical symptoms are a means through which the body communicates a message to the consciousness. And related to this, in turn, is the idea that the symptoms are meant to reflect a particular message, a particular set of unmet needs. For example, a cold, with its running nose and eyes, may be said to represent a frustrated desire to cry.

Susan Sontag (1978) has described some of the metaphors attached to diseases such as tuberculosis, AIDS, and cancer. One illustration of disease metaphor is the idea of a disease as an enemy and the subsequent necessity for a war against the disease. Illness as statistical infrequency, in contrast, is simply a numerical definition that names as 'illness' a bodily functioning or symptom that is infrequent in the population.

Finally, the idea that illness reflects gender politics is related to the **patriarchy** of the medical profession and its consequent tendency to see women's bodies as basi-

cally flawed and women's behaviours as more likely to be pathological (for example, meriting psychiatric diagnosis) than those of men. These medical views reflect gender and gender roles in society (see Clarke, 2000).

All of these different popular conceptions of illness have been taken up at one time or another by Canadians.

Sociology of Medicine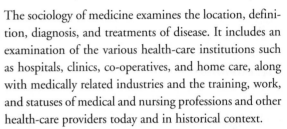

The sociology of medicine examines the location, definition, diagnosis, and treatments of disease. It includes an examination of the various health-care institutions such as hospitals, clinics, co-operatives, and home care, along with medically related industries and the training, work, and statuses of medical and nursing professions and other health-care providers today and in historical context.

Because the history of the twentieth century has been characterized by the increasing dominance of allopathic medicine and its spreading relevance to more and more of life (Zola, 1972), the term **medicalization** (the tendency for more and more of life to be defined as relevant to medicine) has provided an important conceptual framework for critical analysis. In this part of the chapter we will discuss the medical care system in Canada today.

The Canadian Medical Care System

Our present medical care system was first implemented in 1972 after a Royal Commission on Health Care (Hall, 1964–5), under Justice Emmett Hall, recommended that the federal government work with the provincial governments to establish a program of universal health care. While hospitalization and some medical testing had been covered before that, the new program was designed to cover physicians' fees and other services not already covered under the Hospital Insurance and Diagnostic Services Act (1958).

Four basic principles guided the program. The first was universality. This meant that the plan was to be available to all residents of Canada on equal terms, regardless of prior health record, age, income, non-membership in a group (such as a union or workplace), or other considerations. The second was portability. This meant that individual benefits would travel with the individual across the country, from province to province. The third was comprehensive coverage: the plan was to cover all necessary medical services, including dentistry, which required hospitalization. The fourth was administration. This referred to the fact that the plan was to run on a non-profit basis.

The Canada Health Act of 1984 added a fifth principle: accessibility. The costs of the plan were to be shared by the federal and provincial governments in such a way that the richer provinces paid relatively more than the poorer provinces; thus, the plan would also serve to redistribute wealth across Canada. Doctors, with few exceptions (found mostly in community health clinics), were not salaried by the government. Instead, they were and continue to be private practitioners paid by the government on a fee-for-service basis.

Privatization

Despite the presence of the universally available and federally supported national medical care system, there is considerable evidence of privatization within the system. Moreover, the degree of privatization varies across the provinces. By the late 1990s approximately 75 per cent of the Canadian system was public, 25 per cent private (Fuller, 1998). These figures, however, exclude physicians, who are in a somewhat anomalous position

because, though most receive money from the state, they do so as private entrepreneurs compensated on the basis of the number of patients they see and the type of diagnosis and treatment they offer.

The private aspects of the Canadian system are dominated by multinational corporations involved in providing a variety of health-related goods and services, including additional medical insurance, information technology services, food and laundry for hospitals, long-term and other institutional care, drugs, medical devices, and home care (Fuller, 1998). The most important impetus for growth in the medical system is in the private sector, particularly in drugs and new (and very expensive) technologies such as MRI, CAT scan, and mammography machines and other increasingly popular diagnostic technologies, such as the PSA test for prostate cancer (Fuller, 1998).

Table 10.3 describes the relative increase in personal expenditures for health care products and services in the years from 1999 to 2007. It may also reflect the growing privatization of medical care as more and more of the costs may be covered by individuals and not by the tax-supported medicare system. Both the overall growth from 4.8 per cent to 5.5 per cent in personal expenditures, as

Table 10.3   Personal Expenditure on Medical Care and Health Services, 1999 to 2007

	1999	2001	2003	2005	2007
	$ millions				
Total personal expenditure on consumer goods and services	560,884	620,614	686,552	759,239	852,770
Total personal expenditure on medical care and health services	26,913	31,042	35,440	40,760	47,282
Medical care	12,656	14,485	15,906	18,354	21,083
Hospital care and the like	1,265	1,493	1,653	1,911	2,234
Other medical care expenses	3,817	4,139	4,856	5,403	5,926
Drugs and pharmaceutical products	9,175	10,925	13,025	15,092	18,039
	%				
Percentage of all personal expenditure on medical care and health services	4.8	5.0	5.2	5.4	5.5

Source: Statistics Canada, CANSIM, table 380-0024.

well as the overall cost increase from $560,884 million to $852,770 million, indicate substantial increases over a relatively short period of time. Note, too, that the growth in drugs and pharmaceutical products represents the highest levels of growth in the categories listed.

There is considerable debate today about whether or not Canada can continue to afford a publicly funded, universally available medical care system. The mass media are full of stories of overcrowded emergency rooms and impossibly long waiting lists. These sorts of concerns often seem to lead to the argument that the problem is the publicly funded system. Consistent with the move to the political right both in Canada and throughout the Western world is an emphasis on the value of the free market, arguing that a private health-care system would be both more efficient and more cost-effective. However, evidence from a wide variety of sources does not support this point of view (Canadian Health Services Research Foundation, 2002). For example, Calgary recently moved to some degree of privatiza-tion: cataract surgery services are now bought from private companies. This has resulted not only in more costly cataract surgery, but also in longer waiting times than in the nearby cities of Lethbridge and Edmonton.

US studies on the effect of governments' buying of medical services from private companies also demon-strate problems with privatization. For instance, dialysis and kidney transplants are funded through the federally run Medicare program, which buys services from both for-profit and not-for-profit dialysis centres. Johns Hop-kins University researchers compared over 3,000 patient records and found that the for-profit centres had higher death rates, were less likely to refer patients for trans-plants, and were less likely to treat children with the dialysis method most likely to be of benefit to them (Canadian Health Services Research Foundation, 2002).

Most US-based research suggests that for-profit (pri-vate) care costs more, pays lower salaries to staff, and incurs higher administrative costs but does not provide higher-quality care or greater access. Between 1990 and 1994, for-profit hospitals billed approximately $8,115 (US) for every discharged patient, whereas not-for-profit hospitals charged $7,490 per person even though qual-ity of care, according to some indices, was better in not-for-profit institutions. For instance, not-for-profits tend to provide higher rates of immunization, mammogra-phy, and other preventive services (Canadian Health Services Research Foundation, 2002). On average, peo-ple lose two years of life when they are treated in for-profit hospitals (Devereaux et al., 2002: 1402).

Some claim that private systems offer more choice. The inference is that public systems are restrictive because of bureaucratic government interference. How-ever, the interference by insurance companies in medical decision-making in private, for-profit systems appears to be more problematic than state interference. The other aspect of the argument for choice is that a combined sys-tem would allow individuals the possibility of choosing between private and public services for different services. This argument, by and large, flies in the face of the repeatedly confirmed value orientations of Canadians, who continue to identify medicare as one of Canada's most important social programs.

Medicalization

Medicalization is the tendency of more and more of life to be defined as relevant to medicine. Irving Zola (1972) is a social theorist who has been critical of this process. He defined medicalization as including the following four components:

1. an expansion of what in life, and in a person, is rele-vant to medicine;
2. the maintenance of absolute control over certain tech-nical procedures by the allopathic medical profession;
3. the maintenance of almost absolute access to certain areas by the medical profession;
4. the spread of medicine's relevance to an increasingly large portion of living.

The first area of medicalization is the expansion of medicine from a narrow focus on the biomechanics of the human body to a broader concern by medicine with the 'whole' person. The second area refers to the fact that there are things that only doctors are allowed to do to the human body, such as surgery. The third refers to the fact that doctors, through medicine, have been able to transform into medical problems areas of life such as pregnancy and aging that were formerly viewed as normal, neither as pathological nor as med-ically relevant processes. The fourth pertains to the way in which medicine increasingly has jurisdiction in areas formerly considered to be of relevance to the criminal justice or religious systems, such as criminality and alcohol addiction.

Medicalization has been shown to be evident in the tendency for more and more of life to be defined by the medical profession. Ivan Illich (1976) attributes the growth of medicalization to bureaucratization. Vincente

OPEN FOR DISCUSSION
The Power of Medicalization

The power of medicalization can be illustrated by the case of Tyrell Dueck. He was 13 when, in early October 1999, he was diagnosed with osteogenic sarcoma or bone cancer. Treatment upon diagnosis usually begins immediately with chemotherapy to shrink the tumour and stop the spread of the disease. Surgery is used next to remove the tumour or sometimes the whole limb if the disease is found to have spread. Chemotherapy may then continue. With immediate treatment and localized disease the prognosis can be excellent for full recovery.

At the point of diagnosis Tyrell's father, Tim Dueck, said that the family did not want Tyrell to undergo chemotherapy and surgery but wanted him to try alternative treatments. By 11 December the hospital went to court in Saskatchewan and received a court order giving the Saskatchewan Minister of Social Services guardianship over Tyrell. This gave the minister the right to consent to treatment on Tyrell's behalf. After two rounds of chemotherapy doctors decided Tyrell's leg would have to be amputated and that this surgery would give him a 65 per cent chance for survival. The doctors were also clear that they believed that he would die without the amputation of his leg.

Nevertheless Tyrell decided that he did not want to have his leg removed. Nor did he want more chemotherapy. This created a new dilemma. The court order of guardianship had taken the power of consent for treatment from Tyrell's parents. It had not taken it from Tyrell himself. Another hearing began on 13 March. A psychologist and a psychiatrist gave contradictory evidence regarding whether Tyrell was legally mature and thus capable of making the decision against treatment on his own. The media were highly involved by this time and debate raged about the issue. It became clear that the Duecks believed that a combination of prayer and complementary health care in Mexico would heal Tyrell.

By 18 March the court decided that Tyrell was a 'mature minor' and therefore was to be required to have the prescribed medical treatment. But by this time further medical investigations revealed that the time lapse had decreased Tyrell's chances for survival to 10 to 15 per cent. At this point the Minister of Social Services withdrew the order of treatment and the Duecks were free to pursue alternative treatment in Mexico. They did so. Tyrell received the treatment. Nonetheless, Tyrell died a few months later (Rogan, 1999: 43–52).

Who do you think should have the power to decide in a situation like this, the state, the doctors, the parents, or the young person?

Navarro (1975) claims that medicalization, or medical dominance, is more related to class and class conflict, in particular the upper-class background and position of physicians. He also relates medicalization to the work of physicians who operate as entrepreneurs in the definition of health and illness categories and their relevant treatments.

Disease Mongering

Furthering this argument about the role of capitalism in the growth of medical dominance is the instrumental role that the pharmaceutical corporations play in 'disease mongering'. Through a series of suggestive anecdotes, Ray Moynihan, Iona Heath, and David Henry (2002) argue for critically examining the ways in which the pharmaceutical industry plays a significant role in defining as diseases conditions for which they have developed an effective drug. The researchers illustrate this practice through descriptive case histories of a process whereby a drug is manufactured and then a disease is newly highlighted as problematic. Three cases are highlighted: a baldness tonic for men, a drug for 'social phobia', and osteoporosis medication for aging women.

Counterthink: 'Disease Mongers, Inc.' By Mike Adams.
Reprinted by permission of Natural News Network

Ostensibly involved in public education about new diseases and treatments, and often working alongside doctors and consumer groups, the pharmaceutical industry has promoted as problematic conditions that may well be better seen as part of life. For example, the medicalization of baldness by Merck occurred after the development of their anti-baldness drug, Propecia, in Australia. Around the time of the patenting of the drug, a major Australian newspaper reported on a new study that indicated that about one-third of men experienced hair loss (Hickman, 1998). Further, the article emphasized, hair loss sometimes led to panic and other emotional difficulties and had a negative impact on job prospects and well-being. At the same time, the paper featured news of the establishment of an International Hair Study Institute. What the newspaper failed to report was that both the study and the institute were funded by Merck and that the 'expert' quotations were from the public relations firm hired by Merck.

These two steps are just illustrations of some strategies used by pharmaceutical industries that have been advised in Britain's *Pharmaceutical Marketing* magazine to 'establish a need and create a desire' (Cook, 2001). The report cited is based on several anecdotes. More and systematic research on the extent of these practices is needed, but even these few examples raise questions about what may be invisible and unregulated attempts to 'change public perceptions about health and illness to widen markets for new drugs' (Cook, 2001: 891).

The Socio-economic Background of Medical Students in Canada

There are substantial differences between the backgrounds of medical students and those of the rest of the Canadian population. Doctors are not drawn, in a representative way, from across the socio-economic and socio-demographic variation of the whole population of citizens.

Specifically, medical students have been more likely to have had fathers who were doctors. This continues to be true today. In 1965, 11.8 per cent of medical students had fathers who were doctors; today, 15.6 per cent have (Dhalla et al., 2002: 1032). Rural students, in contrast, were underrepresented in the mid-1960s and continue to be underrepresented today. Whereas 30.4 per cent of Canadian high school students lived in rural areas in 1965–6, only 8.4 per cent of the medical students did. Rural students are slightly better represented today (Dhalla et al., 2002). In 1965–6, the fathers of 7.5 per cent of the population had attended university, while 38.0 per cent of the fathers of medical students had done so. Today, 39.0 per cent of the fathers of medical students earned graduate or doctoral degrees, compared with only 6.6 per cent of the whole population of the same age (Dhalla et al., 2002). With respect to gender, however, significant changes have occurred. In 1965–6, 11.4 per cent of the medical students were female. Now about half are (Dhalla et al., 2002). Medical students continue, however, to be less likely than the general population to be Aboriginal or African Canadian.

These findings are important in practical terms as well. For example, medical students who are from rural areas are more likely to practise in (underserviced) rural areas. And poorer people have poorer health outcomes, yet students from the poorest neighbourhoods are seven times less likely to attend medical school than those from the richest neighbourhoods (Dhalla et al., 2002).

The trend towards privatization in Canadian universities can only exacerbate these discrepancies in adequate representation of medical students. Rising tuition fees in Ontario since 1997 have already affected the equitable representation of doctors such that there has been an increase in the self-reported family incomes of students in medical schools while they are graduating with more

You have probably heard the concern voiced that the health-care system will be stressed as the population ages in the next several decades in Canada as a result of the increase in age among the baby-boom generation. In fact, people over 65 are no more likely to be ill than adults at other ages. They are, however, more likely to use the health-care system when they are ill. Recent research from the Canadian Health Services Research Foundation demonstrates that the increasing utilization by seniors is not the result of their increasing numbers in the population but rather their relatively higher utilization rates. There is evidence that it is not the sick seniors who are responsible for the increase in costs but rather healthy seniors. The rate of doctor visits among the well, for example, in Manitoba between the 1970s and 1983 increased 57.5 per cent among specialists and 32 per cent for general practitioners. Unhealthy seniors' rates increased only 10 per cent or less. It appears that the elderly routinely receive more care than they formerly did. The cost of health-care increases, due to the simple aging of the population, is estimated to be only 1 per cent of the total health-care costs. The significant impact of population aging, then, appears to be the result of some degree of over-treatment of the elderly. Although such

interventions as flu shots, hip replacement, and cataract surgery may be necessary, others may not (www.chsrf.ca/mythbusters).

Examine the following figure. What is the obvious explanation for what is portrayed? Having read the above paragraph, what do you think are the more complex and interesting explanations?

Figure 10.2   Increase in Medical Use by Seniors in Good and Bad Health, Manitoba, 1971–83

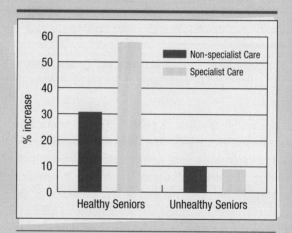

Source: Reproduced by permission of the Canadian Health Services Research Foundation, copyright 2002.

debt, are more likely to consider finances when choosing a place to practise, and are more likely to report financial stress while in school (Kwong et al., 2002).

● Conclusion ● ● ● ● ● ●

In many ways, health issues are fundamentally social issues. The rates, definitions, and meanings of illness, sickness, disease, and death have varied and continue to vary around the world and over time. Within Canadian society, these differences, particularly in rates, reflect culture and social structure and mirror inequality and marginalization. They are affected by large external physical forces such as characteristics of the physical

environment and by smaller lifestyle, existential, and psychosocial factors.

Medical care is dominated by allopathic medicine today. However, a sizable minority of Canadians are now choosing complementary and alternative care. Still, there is continuing evidence of the dominance of medical definitions of reality (medicalization) in many parts of life. As well, evidence increases of the manipulation of medicalization by the pharmaceutical industry and its entrepreneurial disease-defining work. While there is substantially more privatization in the Canadian medical care system today, it has tended not to reduce costs or to provide better medical service but the reverse. Finally, it appears that doctors in the system are experiencing low levels of job satisfaction and morale today.

Questions for Critical Thought ● ● ○ ● ● ● ● ●

1. What are the implications of developing health policy on the basis of the mortality rate from the chief causes of death in Canada as compared to PYLL?
2. Discuss the evidence for an increasingly medicalized society.
3. What are the costs and benefits of medicalization?
4. Compare the sense of coherence and social cohesion. To what extent are these concepts related to one another?

Recommended Readings ● ● ○ ● ○ ●

Pat Armstrong, Hugh Armstrong, and David Coburn, eds, *Unhealthy Times: Political Economy Perspectives on Health and Care in Canada* (Toronto: Oxford University Press, 2001).

This is a fascinating book on the ways that economics and politics influence health in Canada and globally. Topics covered include globalization and its impact on health and the health-care system, the pharmaceutical industry, health-related ideologies such as neo-liberalism, the impact of capitalism on the curriculum of pharmaceutical sciences, women's health issues related to health-care reform, the relationship between work and health globally, environmental contamination and political ecology, and poverty, social disintegration, and health among Canadians.

Colleen Fuller, *Caring for Profit: How Corporations Are Taking Over Canada's Health Care System* (Vancouver: New Star, 1998).

Fuller is a health-care activist and researcher who wrote this book while she was a research associate at the Canadian Centre for Policy Alternatives. After discussing the beginnings of the medicare system in Canada, Fuller charts medicare's history up to the current period of privatization. She documents examples of privatization across the country to demonstrate that medicare is no longer a universal system.

Samantha King, *Pink Ribbons, Inc.: Breast Cancer and the Politics of Philanthropy* (Minneapolis: University of Minnesota Press, 2006).

This book examines the corporate face of fundraising for breast cancer with a series of interrelated papers on various aspects of funding medical research.

Recommended Websites ● ● ○ ● ○ ●

Health Canada www.hc-sc.gc.ca

Health Canada, a government department, provides health-related information on topics such as healthy living, health care, diseases and conditions, health protection, and media stories. You can also find here the latest statistics regarding health, illness, death, PYLL, medical care system characteristics, and current issues.

***Globe and Mail*
www.theglobeandmail.com/health/**

This is the website of Canada's national daily newspaper. It provides journalistic accounts of the latest in important health-related news stories in Canada.

National Institutes of Health www.nih.gov

The National Institutes of Health in the US provides access to research, health news, and various health-related resources.

**National Network on Environments and Women's Health
www.yorku.ca/nnewh/english/nnewhind.html**

This is one of the five federally funded Centres of Excellence for Women's Health. It focuses on women's health and workplaces, including paid and unpaid work, unemployment and labour force restructuring and adjustments, health systems (both conventional and unconventional forms of health care), formal and informal practices, women's understandings of health and health risks, and policy.

**Public Health Agency of Canada
www.phac.asac.gc.ca/**

The Public Health Agency of Canada offers access to research and working papers on the social determinants of health, health promotion, and population health perspectives.

Chapter 11

••••••••••

Education

Terry Wotherspoon

Learning Objectives

In this chapter, you will:

▶ understand how and why formal education has become a central social institution in Canada and other nations;

▶ identify the main dimensions and challenges associated with the growth of formal education systems;

▶ gain a critical understanding of various forms of lifelong learning beyond formal education;

▶ understand the major theoretical perspectives and theories that sociologists employ to explain educational institutions, practices, and outcomes;

▶ understand the relationships between education and social inequality;

▶ explore how education and educational outcomes are shaped by relationships between educational institutions and participants and how the social contexts within those institutions operate; and

▶ critically evaluate contemporary debates and controversies over major educational issues.

● Introduction ● ● ● ● ● ●

The chief economist for the World Bank recently highlighted the importance of education as 'critical to participation and productivity in economic life'. 'A healthy, literate labor force', he said, 'will both increase the amount of growth realized from establishing a sound investment climate and strongly reinforce the poverty reduction benefit from that growth' (Stern, 2002: 21). Probably few people would take issue with these comments. What do they mean, though, to people in different situations?

Sociologists are interested in several issues associated with educational processes and outcomes and in the environments within which education operates. This chapter examines several key questions that sociology addresses in its concern to understand education:

* Why is formal education so important in contemporary societies, and how did it get to be that way?
* What are the main dimensions of education and education systems in Canada and other nations?
* How do sociologists explain the growth of education systems and the outcomes associated with education for different groups?
* What are the main educational experiences and outcomes for different social groups?
* What are the main challenges facing education systems in Canada and other nations?

● The Changing ● ● ● ● ● Face of Education

Education is generally understood as the formal learning that takes place in institutions such as schools, colleges, universities, and other sites that provide specific courses, learning activities, or credentials in an organized way. Informal learning also occurs as people undertake specific activities to learn about distinct phenomena or processes. Both formal and informal education are part of the broader process that sociologists typically call **socialization**, which refers to all direct and indirect learning related to humans' ability to understand and negotiate the rules and expectations of the social world.

Nearly all Canadians engage in formal education for extended periods of time, a situation that was not always the case. In the late nineteenth century, educational participation tended to be secondary to other pressing concerns. Ian Davey observes that factors such as 'cyclical depressions and crop failures affected school attendance because in good times more parents sent more of their children to

school and sent them more regularly. Yet, lower attendance during bad times resulted largely from a magnification of those factors which caused irregular attendance throughout the nineteenth century—transience and poverty' (1978: 230). At the beginning of the twentieth century, only three out of five pupils enrolled in public school attended on a regular basis, and many of those were not in school for extended periods during the school year. Many communities lacked schools or qualified teachers. Children often did not begin their **schooling** until they were seven or eight years old; typically, they left school by their early teen years (Guppy and Davies, 1998).

A comparison of today's educational settings and classrooms with those of a century ago yields both striking similarities and profound differences. Massive, architecturally designed complexes have replaced self-contained one- or two-room wooden buildings; sophisticated equipment often takes the place of chalk and slate boards; and most students are exposed to a diverse range of teachers, subject choices, and work projects unthinkable in 1900. Today's students and teachers are likely to exhibit a far greater array of personal, stylistic, and cultural variation than was apparent a century ago, and they have access to many more learning and community resources.

Despite these changes, the casual visitor to classrooms in either time period is not likely to mistake schools for other settings. Groupings of children and youth, under the instruction and regular scrutiny of adult teachers, are guided both through regimented activities—at least for part of the time in rows or other arrangements of desks—and through periods allocated for recreation or personal expression. Education is a unique social institution at the same time as it reveals characteristics that are integral to the society in which it operates.

Dimensions of Educational Growth

Educational expansion accelerated rapidly after World War II. In 1951, over half (51.9 per cent) of all Canadians aged 15 and over had less than a Grade 9 education, while just under 2 per cent had a university degree and only about one in 20 aged 18 to 24 was enrolled in university (Clark, 2000: 4–6; Guppy and Davies, 1998: 19). At the beginning of the twenty-first century, by contrast, Canadians have unprecedented levels of education, distinguishing Canada with one of the most highly educated populations in the world.

Table 11.1 provides an overview of the increasing educational attainment of Canadians in the last half of the twentieth century. The proportion of the population who had less than a Grade 9 education diminished rapidly, especially in the 1960s and 1970s. By contrast, very

A century ago, schools were often segregated by class and age. Here, young ladies are learning to sketch a live model—a skill that will give them cultural capital when they pass into adult social life.
Courtesy of the Bishop Strachan School Museum & Archives.

few had taken or completed post-secondary studies at the start of the period, whereas nearly half of the population now holds post-secondary credentials. The average number of years of formal education held by Canadians has risen from just under 12.5 at the beginning of the 1990s to over 13 a decade later, ranking Canada sixth among highly developed nations in 2004, just below Norway at 13.9, Denmark and Germany at 13.4, and the United States and Luxembourg at 13.3, but above the average for the developed countries of the Organisation for Economic Co-operation and Development of 11.9 (OECD, 2006: 41). Growing emphasis on the importance of formal education and credentials has been matched by three interrelated factors: the overall expansion of educational opportunities and requirements, increasing levels of educational attainment among people born in Canada, and recent emphasis on the selection of highly educated immigrants.

The fact that many people did not have substantial amounts of formal education in the late nineteenth and early twentieth centuries was not as significant as it may seem in retrospect because only a few occupations required educational credentials. Most people relied on schools to provide some basic skills and knowledge, discipline, and social training, and as a service to provide something for children to do when their parents were too busy to attend to them. Formal learning was often subordinate to other concerns. School superintendents and other educational authorities devoted their efforts to enforcing school attendance and improving the quality of instruction in schools. Annual reports and other documents maintained by provincial education departments

■■┃ Time to Reflect ┃■┃■┃■┃■┃■┃■┃■┃■┃■┃■┃■┃■┃■┃■┃■

What is the difference between education and socialization? How has the introduction of formal schooling influenced the relationship between these two phenomena?

Table 11.1   Educational Attainment in Canada, by Percentage of Population Aged 15 and Over, Selected Years, 1951–2005

	Less than Grade 9	Grades 9–13	Some Post-secondary	Post-secondary Certificate or Diploma	University Degree	Median Years of Schooling
1951	51.9	46.1	–	–	1.9	–
1961	44.1	53.0	–	–	2.9	–
1971	32.3	45.9	11.2	5.8	4.8	10.6
1981	20.1	44.3	16.1	11.5	8.0	11.8
1986	17.7	42.5	19.3	12.3	9.6	12.2
1991	14.4	43.8	8.8	21.9	11.4	12.5
1996	12.3	39.4	8.9	25.9	13.3	12.7
2001	9.7	36.9	9.2	28.3	16.0	13.0
2005	8.4	35.0	8.6	29.8	18.2	–

Note: Figures are rounded.

Source: Compiled from Statistics Canada, census data (1951–86) and labour force survey, annual averages (1991–2005).

are filled with references to concerns such as the need to maintain proper order and discipline in the classroom; attention to habits and duties; routine procedures and daily records of pupil attendance, school visitors, and recitations drawn from various subjects; and the desire for teachers who were not so much good instructors as proper role models with good manners and high moral standing (for examples, see Lawr and Gidney, 1973).

Early advocates of public schooling undertook a mission to convince the public, and especially members of influential groups, of the merits of the educational system. They promoted schooling as an efficient enterprise that would serve the public or general interest. Other institutions or sites, such as families, churches, and businesses, were by contrast more narrow and selective in scope.

Education systems adopted a degree of flexibility that made it possible to integrate new tasks and curricula. School authorities had to make concessions when funds to build and run schools or hire the preferred quality of teachers were scarce. Some people resented having to pay or be taxed for schooling. Schools could also be victims of their own success, as demands for education or population growth in communities outpaced the ability to provide school facilities, textbooks, teaching materials, and qualified teachers. In many parts of

Canada, especially in smaller communities and rural areas, school operations remained highly uncertain or irregular until well into the twentieth century because of sporadic pupil attendance, resignation of teachers or the community's inability to attract teachers, lack of funds, or disputes between school board and community members. A single teacher provided the schooling that was offered for all grades in rural one-room schools, whereas cities and larger districts tended to have better-equipped schools with a full range of programs and a complement of trained, more specialized teachers.

Centralized schools and districts gradually replaced smaller units across Canada. School district consolidation began in 1900, though amalgamation into larger schools and school districts did not fully take hold until the period between the mid-1940s and the late 1960s. Amalgamation has continued since then, accelerating in the 1990s as the number of school boards declined in each province, in many cases by as much as half to two-thirds; New Brunswick abolished all school boards between 1996 and 2001 (Pierce, 2003). Consolidation was hastened by financial and administrative difficulties in many districts and by the development of transportation networks and support linkages that made it easier to concentrate schools in selected centres. By 1970/1, there were just over 16,000 public schools in Canada (a figure that has since declined by a further 500), nearly 10,000 below the number that had operated a decade earlier (Statistics Canada, 1973: 104; Statistics Canada, 2005a).

Pressure to build and maintain larger schools intensified as more people began to stay in school longer, extending into and beyond the high school years. The **baby boom** that occurred after World War II resulted in unprecedented sizes of cohorts of children who were entering and moving through the school system. The figures in Table 11.2 demonstrate that, while total enrolment in Canadian public elementary and secondary

Table 11.2	Full-Time Enrolment in Canada, by Level of Study, Selected Years, 1870–2003 (000s)				
	Pre-elementary	Elementary and Secondary	Non-university Post-secondary	University Undergraduate	University Graduate
1870	–	768	–	2	–
1880	–	852	–	3	–
1890	–	943	–	5	<1
1900	–	1,055	–	7	<1
1910	–	1,318	–	13	<1
1920	–	1,834	–	23	<1
1930	–	2,099	–	32	1
1940	–	2,075	–	35	2
1950	–	2,391	–	64	5
1955	103	3,118	33	69	3
1960	146	3,997	49	107	7
1965	268	4,918	69	187	17
1970	402	5,661	166	276	33
1975	399	5,376	221	331	40
1980	398	4,709	261	338	45
1985	422	4,506	322	412	55
1990	468	4,669	325	468	64
1995	542	4,895	392	498	75
2000	522	4,867	408	522	81
2003*		5,289	461	616	101

*Pre-elementary figure for 2003 is included in elementary and secondary total.

Sources: Compiled from various editions of Dominion Bureau of Statistics/Statistics Canada, census data, 'Education at a Glance', *Education Quarterly Review*; Patric Blouin, Marie-Josée Courchesne, and Isabelle Thony, *Summary Public School Indicators for the Provinces and Territories, 1997–1998 to 2003–2004* (Ottawa: Minister of Industry); and Canadian Association of University Teachers, *CAUT Almanac of Post-Secondary Education in Canada 2006* (Ottawa: CAUT, 2006).

schools in 1950 was just over double what it had been in 1900, enrolment doubled again over the next decade and a half. The average number of pupils per school increased from 66 in 1925–6 to 156 in 1960–1; it then nearly doubled over the next decade to reach 350 in 1970–1, a level that has remained relatively stable since then (Manzer, 1994: 131).

The data in Table 11.2 demonstrate how formal education has expanded throughout the life course. Children have begun their schooling at progressively younger ages over the past five decades. Kindergarten is now compulsory in most Canadian jurisdictions, and many children also attend various preschool and early childhood education programs.

Meanwhile, people have been extending their formal education well past high school into post-secondary studies. The larger cohorts of students moving through schools and completing high school, combined with an increasing emphasis on higher education in particular fields and more general reliance on educational credentials as a means for firms to select employees, contributed to massive growth in post-secondary studies. The data in Table 11.2 demonstrate that, whereas in 1950–1, only about 69,000 people were enrolled in full-time university studies, university enrolment exploded to over 200,000 by the mid-1960s, and has now surpassed 700,000 (with over 100,000 in graduate studies alone).

A similar pattern followed in other post-secondary institutions, which until the 1960s had encompassed mostly specific occupational and vocational certification programs in areas such as nursing and teacher education as well as pre-university studies in Quebec and other provinces. However, the introduction and expansion of the community college system in the 1960s and 1970s provided numerous options for post-secondary study both for students seeking certification in specialized trades or vocations and for students taking courses that could then be applied towards university credit. Sociologists have been concerned with issues related to the bureaucratic organization of education and educational inequality as school size and complexity increased.

Education in the Learning Society

The organization and nature of schooling across Canada remain varied. Initiatives to implement greater conformity and consistency across jurisdictions run parallel with increased numbers of alternative schools and educational services. Educational diversity is a product, in part, of the fact that elementary and secondary education is a formal jurisdiction of the provinces under constitutional legisla-

tion, while other forms of education, including adult and post-secondary education and vocational training, are controlled, operated, or funded by a variety of governments (federal, provincial, and First Nations) and by private sources. Increased emphasis on education and training has been accompanied by considerable expansion of educational opportunities and programs offered at all levels. Many people are turning to additional sources, such as distance education and Internet-based course offerings that originate both within and outside Canada.

Formal schooling is compulsory for Canadians aged 6 to 16 in most provinces (with an overall range between 5 and 18 years). However, most people engage in education well beyond these limits. The growing popularity of terms such as *information society*, *learning society*, and **lifelong learning** signifies the central place that education holds within the context of what is commonly designated as the **new economy** or *knowledge-based economy*. The new economy has gained prominence through increasing reliance on rapidly changing information technologies and scientific advancements that have affected not only business and the workplace, but virtually every major sphere of social life. Learning is central to all dimensions of the new economy, including the need to train qualified personnel; to conduct research for continuing innovation; to develop, test, and market new products and services within firms; to process the vast amounts of new information being created; and to ensure that people have the capacities to employ new technologies at work and at home (Wolfe and Gertler, 2001). In this climate, what counts is not so much the knowledge that we acquire, as the capacity to learn and apply that knowledge to emergent situations. People are expected not simply to learn more, but to develop different ways of learning and transferring knowledge.

These expectations have contributed to extensive levels of and variations in educational qualifications and experiences. With respect to formal learning, nearly 6.5 million Canadians (about one-fifth of the entire population) identified in Table 11.2 are engaged in full-time schooling; well over 300,000 more are involved in part-time studies. About half of the Canadian population aged 16 to 65 (ranging between less than one-quarter of those with the lowest literacy levels and over two-thirds of those with the highest levels of literacy) indicate, as well, that they are involved in some adult education, whether in the form of in-person, correspondence, or private courses, workshops, apprenticeships, or arts, crafts, or recreation programs (Desjardins et al., 2005: 98).

The phenomenon of informal learning has also attracted growing attention. *Informal learning* involves distinct efforts arranged and undertaken by individuals or groups to acquire new knowledge that can be applied to work, personal, or community circumstances. Such activities include initiatives to learn a new language on one's own or with other people, to learn computer skills or software programs, or to gain competencies that can be used for volunteer work or family situations. Surveys in Canada and the United States estimate that over three-quarters of the adult population undertake well over 300 hours of informal learning projects per person every year. Nearly all people, regardless of education, are heavily involved in informal learning activities although, as with adult education, there is a general pattern of correspondence between levels of active participation in informal learning and formal educational attainment (Livingstone, 2004: 36–7; Desjardins et al., 2005: 89).

Canada ranks high on international comparisons of education, although Canadians are not unique in their growing pursuit of education and training. Among the OECD nations represented in Figure 11.1, Canada has the highest proportion of the population with formal educational credentials beyond high school, but it ranks behind the United States, Denmark, the Netherlands, and Iceland with respect to the percentage of the population with a university degree, and it is also lagging behind many nations in the advancement of literacy levels across the population.

Emphasis on formal training and lifelong learning is a phenomenon associated with **globalization** and competitiveness across national settings. Throughout the twentieth century, the degree to which a population was educated came to be recognized as a significant indicator of modernization and development status. The more education one has, the higher the chances of having a job, better income, good health status, and many other factors positively associated with a high standard of liv-

Figure 11.1 Level of Education in Selected OECD Countries, 2004

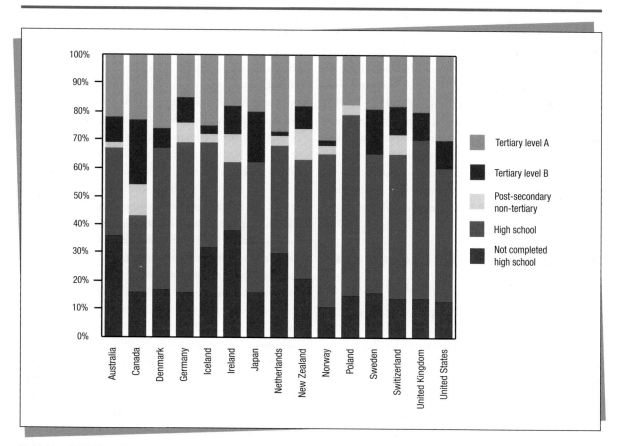

Percentage distribution of the population 25 to 64 years of age, by the highest completed level of education.

Tertiary level A: equivalent to university, including advanced research programs.

Tertiary level B: equivalent to community college in Canada.

Post-secondary non-tertiary: similar to CECEP in Canada.

Source: Based on data in OECD (2006).

ing. Conversely, rates of poverty, unemployment, crime, serious illness and injury, and other less desirable indicators rise when formal education is limited.

Many nations are accelerating the pace of educational advancement as they undertake economic and human resource development strategies aimed at the production of new knowledge and a more highly trained workforce. The importance of education for the new economy is highlighted in the titles of numerous recent research reports and discussion papers produced by governments; Canadian examples include *High School May Not Be Enough* (Human Resources Development Canada and Statistics Canada, 1998), *Learning a Living: First Results of the Adult Literacy and Life Skills Survey* (Desjardins et al., 2005), and *Knowledge Matters: Skills and Learning for Canadians* (Human Resources Development Canada, 2002). Consequently, governments, businesses, and agencies concerned with economic development stress the need to expand education well beyond compulsory levels in order to foster both economic growth and non-economic benefits such as improved health, the ability to use skills for non-monetary purposes, and the intrinsic desire to learn (OECD, 2001). The prevailing sentiment is that, with a few variations, 'overall, individuals will need more and more knowledge and skills, and our society will need a class of highly educated and trained people to prosper' (LeBlanc, 1994: 15).

Regardless of the widespread acceptance of and participation in education as an essential feature of contemporary life, not everyone encounters and benefits from education in the same way. Educational experiences, outcomes, and achievements differ considerably among individuals and groups and are interpreted in different ways.

● Alternative ● ● ● ● ● ● Accounts of Educational Growth and Development

Several major theoretical perspectives that have been applied to an understanding of the education system are outlined here: the structural-functionalist approach, symbolic interactionist and interpretive theories, conflict theory, feminist theories, and more recent integrative orientations to the analysis of education.

Structural Functionalism

Structural functionalism is concerned primarily with understanding how different parts of the entire social system are interconnected in order to keep the system going. It addresses questions of how societies perpetuate themselves, how individuals come to be integrated within social frameworks, and how social change can occur without upsetting the social order. Structural functionalism examines education, like any other aspect of society, in terms of its contributions to social order and stability. Education gains importance in modern societies as an institution that provides participants with the core understandings, capabilities, and selection criteria necessary to enable them to fit into prescribed social and economic roles. As society becomes more complex and specialized, schools and other educational institutions take on many of the functions previously managed by families, communities, and religious organizations to ensure that children and youth—and eventually adult learners—are equipped for work and adult life.

The structural-functionalist perspective presents an image of the properly functioning society as one in which the **transition** from early childhood and family life into schooling and eventually the labour force is relatively seamless, relying on the co-ordination and integration of all of the significant contributors. Disruptions and changes are posed as problems of adjustment, either within the social system or within individuals who do not 'fit'. Social pathologies must be monitored, like periodic automobile maintenance or health check-ups, and repaired through proper diagnosis and treatment in order to maintain the system in a state of healthy balance.

In the early twentieth century, Émile Durkheim (1956 [1922]: 123), who wrote extensively about education in his efforts to establish sociology as a distinct scientific discipline, described education as 'the means by which society perpetually re-creates the conditions of its very existence'. Education cultivates within each person knowledge as well as moral obligation and commitment to other members within a social framework governed by definite rules, regulations, and expectations.

Talcott Parsons (1959) later extended this analysis to a North American context, highlighting the two central functions that schooling fulfills within contemporary societies. First, schooling allocates individuals into selected occupational pathways and social positions in order to match social requirements with the available pool of skills, talents, and interests. Second, it socializes people by providing them with the general aptitudes and knowledge that they need to operate successfully in their society and by preparing them more specifically for the adult roles that they will occupy. Schooling is organized in such a way that people move in the primary grades from home environments where highly

Nations on a global scale have identified the establishment of access to basic education and improvements in educational standards as core priorities. In 2000, an agenda entitled 'Education for All' was adopted by 192 nations co-ordinated through the United Nations Education, Science and Cultural Organization (UNESCO), highlighting six main priorities targeted for achievement by 2015: (1) expanding and improving comprehensive early childhood care and education; (2) ensuring access to and completion of free and compulsory primary education of good quality for all children; (3) ensuring equitable access to appropriate learning and life-skills programs for all young people; (4) achieving a 50 per cent improvement in levels of adult literacy, especially for women, and equitable access to basic and continuing education for all adults; (5) eliminating gender disparities in primary and secondary education (by 2005), and achieving gender equality in education by 2015, with a focus on ensuring girls' full and equal access to and achievement in basic education of good quality; (6) improving all aspects of the quality of education and ensuring excellence of all so that recognized and measurable learning outcomes are achieved by all, especially in literacy, numeracy, and essential life skills.

As indicated in this summary from the monitoring report (UNESCO, 2006: 63), based on 2004 data, there are strong disparities across nations and regions with respect to educational access, attainment, and quality:

- Pre-primary enrolments are up, but not very significantly. In some regions, pre-primary education has become the norm (e.g., North America and Western Europe, Latin America, and the Caribbean); in others it is still very rare (e.g., sub-Saharan Africa).
- Access to primary school is improving, a fact reflected in data on new entrants and on primary enrolments, especially in the three regions that were, and remain, farthest from the goal: sub-Saharan Africa, South and West Asia, and the Arab States. Primary school progression and completion remain major concerns, however, especially in these same regions but also to some extent in Latin America and the Caribbean. The lack of data for a number of countries, mainly in sub-Saharan Africa, that are

or have recently been affected by conflict also means the global picture is not as positive as that painted by examining only countries for which data exist.

- The number of children not in school has declined but remains much too high. Moreover, there is some evidence that countries which are getting within closing distance of UPE are finding it very difficult to succeed in the final stages of attracting the most marginalized children and retaining them through the full primary cycle.
- Considerable progress is being made towards gender parity, in particular in countries where gender differences in education are still high, but disparities remain predominant, particularly in secondary education. About two-thirds of countries with data available for 2004 have achieved gender parity in primary education; in the remainder, the disparities mainly favour boys. However, in only one-third of the countries with data available for secondary education has gender parity been reached at that level, and disparities in secondary are much more pronounced than in primary education; they can favour either girls or boys.
- No major new information is available on learning outcomes, but new analyses of past assessments, together with a new evaluation report from the World Bank, confirm that quality remains a major issue, particularly for children from poorer backgrounds. Key teacher indicators suggest the same: while pupil/teacher ratios have generally improved slightly, they remain much too high, as do the proportion of teachers who are not qualified and trained, and the rate of teacher absenteeism. The issue of quality is not confined to the three regions with the greatest enrolment challenges. It is also a concern in East Asia and the Pacific, and in Latin America and the Caribbean.
- The scope of the global literacy challenge remains much as depicted in the 2006 Report, which had literacy as its special theme: about one in five adults is still not literate (one in four adult women) and those who are not literate live mainly in South and West Asia, sub-Saharan Africa, and the Caribbean.
- Monitoring instruments remain to be developed for the learning needs of youth and adults, and for the literate environment.

personal, emotional ties prevail, through the senior grades marked by progressively greater degrees of competition, merit, and instrumentality intended to prepare the individual for integration into work and other institutional settings crucial to adult life.

Robert Dreeben (1968) shows further the importance of school practices, in and out of the classroom, in cultivating characteristics essential for contemporary work and public life. Four essential **norms** are independence (students' acting according to expectations without supervision), achievement (students' actions to meet accepted standards of excellence), universalism (students' impartial treatment of others based on general categories), and specificity (students' developing selected individual characteristics as opposed to the person as a whole). Teachers are expected not only to convey knowledge and the opportunity to practise these norms for their students, but to model these behaviours for them as well.

Structural functionalism offers a possible explanation of educational expansion both by connecting schooling with the growth of complexity in the occupational structure and by highlighting its increasing importance to citizenship in industrialized societies. A related form of analysis, sometimes referred to as *technical functionalism*, links educational growth with the increasing technical sophistication of jobs and knowledge production (Bell, 1973). Functionalist analysis typically assumes a broad social consensus about what should be taught in schools and how educational institutions should be organized. Moreover, it tends not to question either the legitimacy of educational credentials to determine entry into specified labour market positions or the fairness of the way the education system operates.

Functionalist analysis tends to portray deviation from these ideals as abnormalities or temporary problems that warrant minor reforms rather than as challenges to the education system as a whole. It tends to descriptions of what schools should be like, within liberal democratic ideologies, than to explanations of how schooling came about. Functionalism presents education as a meritocratic ideal, a means of enabling people to gain opportunities for social or economic success regardless of their social backgrounds. Societies require a careful fit among capability, talent, effort, training, and jobs as social tasks become more complex and specialized. These claims have led to subsequent research into the definition and measurement of educational inequality, calling into question the degree to which educational realities match the needs of industrial democratic societies.

Human capital theory, an approach with some affinity to structural functionalism, emphasizes education's role as a critical tool for developing human capacities to create and apply new knowledge. The human being is regarded as an input, along with material and economic resources, that contributes to economic productivity and development. **Human capital** can be enhanced when adequate investment is made in the form of proper training, education, and social support; this approach has been used to justify massive investment by governments that contributed to the significant enrolment growth in post-secondary education discussed earlier and observed in Table 11.2. Modified versions of human capital theory have gained renewed currency as attention turns to the importance of advanced training and educational credentials in 'knowledge-based' societies.

Despite evidence that levels of employment, income, and other benefits improve with educational attainment, structural functionalism and related theories, such as human capital theory, are unable to account for the presence of persistent inequalities in educational opportunities, outcomes, and benefits. The theoretical emphasis on consensus limits consideration of differences in educational values, content, and practices; of how some things get incorporated into schooling while others do not; and of how these differences affect people from different social backgrounds. Alternative theoretical approaches to education attempt to address some of these issues.

Symbolic Interactionism and Microsociology

In contrast to structural functionalism's focus on education systems and institutional arrangements, *microsociology* or *interpretive theories* are concerned more with interpersonal dynamics and how people make sense of their **social interactions**. **Symbolic interactionism**, the term applied to one of the most influential branches of microsociology, focuses on how meanings and **symbols** are integral to social activity. Symbolic interactionism moves the analysis directly into the lives and understandings of social participants.

Interpretive analysis examines diverse questions central to the sociological study of education, such as how schooling contributes to the development of personality and **identity**, how some forms of knowledge and not others enter into the curriculum, and how students and teachers shape the learning process in and out of the classroom. This work stresses the importance of examining the meanings and possibilities that social actors bring to social settings. Willard Waller depicts schools as 'the meeting-point of a large number of intertangled social relationships. These social relationships are the paths pursued by social interaction, the channels in which social influences run. The crisscrossing and inter-actions of these groups make the school what it is' (1965 [1932]: 12). Peter Woods (1979) explores schooling as a series of **negotiations** among teachers, students, and parents, expressed in such phenomena as how pupils select the subjects they take, the role of humour and laughter in the classroom and staff room, and teacher reports on student progress. Howard Becker (1952) shows how teachers' backgrounds influence their con-struction of images of the ideal pupil, which in turn affect how they treat and assess students.

These examples illustrate symbolic interactionists' depictions of societies and institutions as fluid rather than as fixed entities. Institutional patterns are the result of recurrent daily activity and of people's capacities to shape, interpret, reproduce, and modify social arrange-ments through their social relations. *Ethnomethodology*, a variant of interpretive sociology, examines in detail the methods or approaches that people draw on to construct a sense of reality and continuity in everyday life. Under-stood this way, the likelihood that classrooms in one place resemble those in another is less a product of a given model of schooling than an outcome of actions based on images about what is expected of us and how we are supposed to act.

Symbolic interactionism and ethnomethodology offer interesting insights, but they tend to fail to account for broader concerns and limiting factors by focusing too much on the details of ongoing social activity. Class-room dynamics or how one interprets the curriculum cannot be understood fully without reference to educa-tional policy, power structures, social change, and per-sistent social inequalities that strongly influence educational processes and outcomes.

Some researchers have combined interpretive sociol-ogy, with its insights into practical social activity, with other approaches that pay greater attention to the social contexts in which social action takes place. Several British sociologists, under the banner of the 'new sociol-ogy of education', extend this analysis by attempting to break down barriers between **micro-** and **macrosociol-ogy**, and by shifting attention away from educational problems defined by educational administrators and policy-makers. Their concern is how society constructs educational knowledge and practices and makes them part of the taken-for-granted assumptions that guide the actions and understandings of teachers and other educa-tional participants. This work has focused 'on the cur-riculum, on the "educational knowledge" imparted by

the school, and on the school's conception of "what it is to be educated"' (Blackledge and Hunt, 1985: 290). Furthering this analysis, Basil Bernstein (1977) high-lights the various ways that **power** and control enter into the authority structure of schools and classrooms as well as through the expectations and assumptions around which the curriculum and educational policies are framed. Bernstein's contributions to a systematic under-standing of micro and macro levels of analysis have influenced writers working within diverse theoretical traditions (Sadovnik, 1995).

Conflict Theory

Conflict theory, arising in Marxism, encompasses approaches to social analysis that emphasize competition between and power relations among social actors, groups, or forces. Much greater concern prevails in con-flict theory than in other approaches regarding how institutional structures and social inequalities are main-tained or changed through conflict and struggle.

Samuel Bowles and Herbert Gintis, like structural functionalists, emphasize schools' role as mechanisms that select and prepare people for different positions in labour markets and institutional life. Their Marxist ori-entation reveals schools' inability to fulfill the demo-cratic ideology they purport to enact, namely, that all students have fair chances to succeed. Their view is that the labour market is conditioned more by capitalist interests than by general consensus about social values and needs. Bowles and Gintis (1976: 49) posit educa-tion, historically, as 'a device for allocating individuals to economic positions, where inequality among the posi-tions themselves is inherent in the hierarchical division of labor, differences in the degree of monopoly power of various sectors of the economy, and the power of differ-ent occupational groups to limit the supply or increase the monetary returns to their services'.

Conflict theorists emphasize that education-related inequalities are not simple imbalances that can be erad-icated with minor modifications or reforms. Deeply rooted relations of domination and subordination create persistent barriers to opportunity and advancement. This critical sociological orientation denies the function-alist and human capital theory accounts of educational expansion as being a result of rising technical require-ments of jobs. Different **social groups** are understood to employ education and educational ideologies as tools to pursue their own interests. Employers rely on formal educational credentials—regardless of the skills demanded by the job—to screen applicants and assess a person's general attributes. Professions control access to education and certification as a way to preserve the status and benefits attached to their occupations. New knowledge and technological advancements in areas such as medicine, nursing, teaching, engineering, and information-processing may appear to produce a demand for increasingly more advanced, specialized training. But more often, credential inflation occurs as occupations preserve special privileges by simultaneously claiming the need for superior qualifications and restricting entry into these kinds of jobs (Collins, 1979).

Technological developments are not necessarily accompanied by increasing skill requirements for many jobs. Machines and information technology often substitute their routine technical operations for human input or influence the content of 'new jobs' in which people are required to do little but read gauges, respond to signals, or key in information. Under these conditions, schools may function more as warehouses to delay people's entrance into the labour force and to dissipate their dissatisfaction with the economy's failure to provide sufficient numbers of satisfying jobs than as places where effective learning and occupational training take place. Harry Braverman suggests that 'there is no longer any place for the young in this society other than school. Serving to fill a vacuum, schools have themselves become that vacuum, increasingly emptied of content and reduced to little more than their own form' (1974: 440). **Capitalism**, in this view, has contributed less to skills upgrading through technological advancement than to an ongoing process that erodes working skills, degrades workers, and marginalizes youth.

Other conflict theorists highlight the biases and inequalities that are produced directly or indirectly through the curriculum and classroom practices. Students and parents have different understandings, resources, and time that affect the extent to which they can participate in and benefit from educational opportunities. Government cutbacks and changes to school-funding formulas exacerbate many of these inequalities. In Ontario, for instance, many schools report difficulty raising funds even for basic school materials and supplies: 'funding levels are so low, parents are having to make up for programs that aren't paid for—so then it depends on where you live and who you are. . . . There is a growing concern about equity. There is a growing gap between the "have" and "have-not" schools' (L. Brown, 2002: A1, A26).

In post-secondary education, decreased government funding has led to rising tuition fees, which, accompanied by higher costs for textbooks and technology support, living expenses, and other factors, make it increasingly diffi-

cult for students without sufficient resources or unable or unwilling to take on mounting student loans to attend colleges and universities. Conflict analysis also points to concern about the growing reliance by educational institutions on corporate donations and sponsorships to make up for shortfalls in government funding.

Conflict theories of education, in short, stress that expectations for schooling to fulfill its promise to offer equal opportunity and social benefits to all are unrealistic or unattainable within current forms of social organization. Barriers that exist at several levels—access to schooling, what is taught and how it is taught, ability to influence educational policy and decision-making, and differential capacity to convert education into labour market and social advantage—deny many individuals or groups the chances to benefit from meaningful forms and levels of education. Conflict theories offer varying assessments of what must be done to ensure that education can be more democratic and equitable. Some analysts stress that educational institutions and organizations themselves must be transformed, while others suggest that any kinds of school reform will be limited without more fundamental social and economic changes to ensure that people will be able to use, and be recognized for using, their education and training more effectively.

Feminist Theories

Feminist analyses of schooling share similar observations with other conflict theories, though with an explicit emphasis on the existence of and strategies to address social inequalities based on **gender**. Feminist theory stresses that social equity and justice are not possible as long as males and females have unequal power and status through **patriarchy** or gendered systems of domination. In the eighteenth century, Mary Wollstonecraft (1986 [1792]) saw access to education as a fundamental right for women; by being denied such a right historically, women were degraded as 'frivolous', or a 'backward sex'. Later waves of feminism have continued to look to education as a central institution through which to promote women's rights, opportunities, and interests.

There are multiple feminisms in the analysis of education, rather than a single feminist orientation; each poses different questions for educational research and proposes different explanations and strategies for change (Gaskell, 1993; Weiner, 1994). In general, though, feminist analysis shows that influential mainstream studies of schooling have most often concentrated on the lives of boys and men, with little recognition that girls and women have different experiences and little chance to voice their concerns. Much research in the 1970s and 1980s focused on how such things as classroom activities, language use, images and examples in textbooks and curriculum material (including the absence of women and girls in many instances), treatment of students by teachers, and patterns of subject choice reflected gender-based stereotypes and perpetuated traditional divisions among males and females (Kenway and Modra, 1992).

Feminist analysis seeks to do more than simply demonstrate how these social processes contribute to inequalities in order to change the conditions that bring these practices about. This focus has shifted as some aspects of the agenda on women's rights and issues have advanced successfully while specific barriers continue to restrict progress on other fronts. For instance, school boards have policies, enforced through human rights legislation, to restrict sexist curricula and to prohibit gender-based **discrimination** in educational programs and institutions. Educational participation rates of and attainment by females have come to exceed those for males. Yet, gender parity has not been achieved in several important respects, as reflected in concerns that relatively few females take courses or programs in areas such as computer programming, engineering, and some natural sciences, that some gender-based barriers exist in other areas of schooling, and that educational achievements do

SOCIOLOGY IN ACTION
Dimensions of Educational Participation

In Canada and most other nations, educational participation rates and attainment levels are increasing, regardless of social background. Sociologists have debated the extent to which these trends do or do not reflect the ability of education to fulfill its promise to provide social and economic opportunity, especially in relation to demands associated with labour markets that require more skilled and highly qualified workers.

Exploration of these issues offers a useful opportunity to apply a *sociological imagination*, described by C. Wright Mills (1959) as the ability to link one's personal biography or background and circumstances with historical sensitivity to wider social structures and processes.

Begin by examining your own educational and career pathways. What level of formal education have you attained so far? What level would you like to attain? What other kinds of education (such as informal learning through self-directed or group study, special interest courses, adult education, or on-the-job training) have you engaged in? Have there been any gaps or interruptions in your studies? What experiences (positive or negative) have affected your interest and ability to gain the level of education you desire or have completed? What jobs (if any) have you been engaged in? What is the relationship between your educational background, including any specific skills, knowledge, or credentials you have, and the job itself? (Examine both the starting qualifications for the job and the actual tasks involved in the job.) What future employment do you desire, and how is this related to your educational plans and qualifications?

Second, consider your own educational experiences in relation to your social background and context. How typical or different are your own educational and work experiences in comparison with your family and members of other social groups you have associated with (such as your grandparents, parents, childhood peers, and community members) or those you consider yourself part of now? Relate your educational experiences and aspirations with other important characteristics or aspects of your social background (including your gender, race, ethnicity, family income, regional and national origin, place of residence such as urban or rural, age, and other factors you consider important).

Third, engage in broader comparisons between your own education and working experiences and those of others. Examine data from various studies cited in this chapter and from extensive records maintained on the Statistics Canada website. What is the relationship between your experiences, those of other persons from your family and home community, and wider trends evident from these data?

Finally, explain the major patterns and conclusions derived through your inquiries. What do these findings reveal about the nature of education and its social and economic importance?

not always contribute equitably to successful social and economic outcomes.

Feminist analysis of education also explores the gender structure of the teaching force. The feminization of teaching, as female teachers came to outnumber male teachers by the end of the nineteenth century, carried significant implications for the occupation and its members. Teachers often lack the professional recognition that might otherwise accompany the demands and training their work involves. Teachers—women teachers in particular—have been heavily regulated by governments and by school boards. During the early part of the twentieth century, guidelines often specified such things as what teachers could wear, with whom they could associate, and how they should act in public (Wotherspoon, 1995). Until the 1950s, legislation in many provinces required women to resign their teaching positions upon marriage. Although today's teachers have much greater personal and professional autonomy than those of the past, teachers' lives and work remain subject to various forms of scrutiny, guidelines, and informal practices that carry gender-based assumptions or significance. Female teachers predominate in the primary grades, while men tend to be overrepresented in the upper grades and in post-secondary teaching positions, especially in the most senior teaching and educational administrative positions.

Feminist analysis also addresses interrelationships among gender and other social factors and personal characteristics. Gender-based identities, experiences, and opportunities are affected by race, region, social class, and competing expectations and demands that people face at home, in the workplace, and in other social spheres (Acker, 1999). Students and teachers from different backgrounds encounter diverse experiences, concerns, and options, even within similar educational settings, which in turn impact subsequent educational and personal options.

Emerging Analysis and Research in the Sociology of Education

Educational researchers make distinct choices about which theoretical positions are most useful or relevant to their analysis. Since theory is a tool to help understand and explain phenomena and guide social action, sociologists commonly employ insights from several models or orientations.

Critical pedagogy is an approach that draws from different theoretical positions, including conflict theory, feminist theory, and postmodernist challenges, both to explore how domination and power enter into schooling and personal life and to seek to change those aspects that undermine our freedom and humanity (Giroux, 1997; McLaren, 1998; Darder et al., 2003). Anti-racism education shares similar orientations, further stressing the ways in which domination builds on notions of racial difference to create fundamental inequalities among groups that are defined on the basis of biological differences or cultural variations (Dei, 1996).

Pierre Bourdieu (1997a; Bourdieu and Passeron, 1979) has explored how **social structures** (the primary focus of structural functionalism and conflict theory) become interrelated with the meanings and actions relevant to social actors (the main concern of symbolic interactionism or interpretative sociology). As a critical theorist, Bourdieu emphasizes that education contributes to the transmission of power and privilege from one generation to another because it employs assumptions and procedures that advantage some groups and disadvantage others. Educational access, processes, and outcomes are shaped through struggles by different groups to retain or gain advantages relative to one another. However, the mere fact that people hold varying degrees of economic, social, and cultural resources does not guarantee that these will be converted automatically into educational advantage. Competition for educational access and credentials increases as different groups look to education to provide a gateway into important occupational and decision-making positions.

Canadian research, influenced by Bourdieu's analysis and other integrative approaches such as life course theory, demonstrates the complex interactions among personal and social structural characteristics that affect the pathways taken by children and youth through education and from schooling into work and other life transitions (Andres Bellamy, 1993; Anisef et al., 2000). In order to understand schooling fully, it is necessary to take into account several interrelated dimensions:

- how educational systems are organized and what happens inside schools;
- how school experiences are made sense of and acted on by various educational participants;
- the relationships between internal educational processes and external factors, including governments and agencies that set and administer educational policy, employers that demand particular kinds of education and training and that recognize particular types of credentials, political frameworks composed of competing values and ideologies about what education should be and about how resources should be allocated for education

in relation to other priorities, and broader structures of social and economic opportunity and inequality;

* the relations among transformations occurring on a global scale with more specific economic, political, and cultural structures that alternatively provide opportunities for, and systematically exclude, democratic participation by specific social groups (Apple, 1997; Torres, 1998).

● Educational ● ● ● ● ● Participants

Educational institutions reveal considerable complexity in their organization and composition. Comprehensive schools may have 2,000 to 3,000 students and dozens of teachers and support staff, while colleges and universities can exceed the size of small cities. Consequently, sociologists are interested in questions related to the changing nature of who attends and works in these institutions (with respect to gender, racial, ethnic, religious, socio-economic, and other factors), what positions they occupy, and what barriers and opportunities they encounter.

Increasing diversity in education is a consequence of several factors. The educational participation of girls and women has increased significantly since World War II, especially at the post-secondary level. Immigration has also contributed to changing educational profiles, particularly in the largest cities. The immigrant population, in turn, contains increasing numbers and proportions of students classified as visible minorities and of those who speak languages other than English or French when they arrive in Canada. Combined processes of rural-to-urban migration, policy changes, and population growth have increased the concentrations of Aboriginal students in elementary and secondary schools, especially in western and northern Canada. Economic changes have exacerbated many inequalities, including the perpetuation or magnification of gaps between high- and low-income families. Poverty and economic marginalization affect up to one-quarter of Canada's children. Classrooms today integrate students who historically have been excluded, such as teen parents or those with physical or learning disabilities. Numerous additional factors such as religious orientations, the health of regional economies, and distance to essential educational and support services affect educational participation and outcomes.

Significant questions arise concerning how educational institutions attend to the diverse circumstances and needs of their student bodies. Sociologists are interested in much more than simply how the curriculum and formally structured activities affect students' learning and chances for success. Educational organization, rules, expectations, and practices also contain a **hidden curriculum**, the unwritten purposes or goals of school life. School life has a daily rhythm, through repeated variations between structured learning situations and informal interactions, channelling students into selected directions and contributing to taken-for-granted understandings about order, discipline, power relations, and other aspects of social life (Lynch, 1989). These educational processes are likely to reflect selected interests or issues while they ignore others. Benjamin Levin and J. Anthony Riffel observe that 'low socio-economic status is more strongly associated with poor educational outcomes than any other variable. Yet educators are quite ambivalent about the meaning of poverty for their work and the conduct of schooling' (1997: 117). Schooling often has limited connection with—and produces negative consequences for—the students and communities it is intended to serve (Dei et al., 2000; Royal Commission on Aboriginal Peoples, 1996).

Two mechanisms—referred to as *silencing* and the *banking model*—illustrate how common educational practices can have indirect and unequal consequences for students, their identities, and their educational experiences and outcomes. *Silencing* refers to practices that prevent educational participants from raising concerns that are important to them (such as when teachers do not give students the opportunity to talk about current events or matters of student interest), as well as to indirect processes that make students question their own cultural background or that discourage parents from talking to teachers because of their discomfort with the authority represented by the school. The *banking model* of **pedagogy** (Freire, 1970) refers to educational practice in which material is pre-packaged and transmitted in a one-way direction, from the educator to the student. This practice limits the forms of knowledge that are presented as valid, leaving students from alternative backgrounds with a sense that their experiences, questions, and capacities are invalid or irrelevant.

Many educators have modified their approaches as they have gained sensitivity to the impact of their actions on students and have responded to new skill priorities in areas such as critical thinking. However, educators are under considerable pressure to balance public demands for improvement in the quality of education with attention to the multi-faceted problems and interests they must deal with in their work. As resources and energies are directed to special needs students or to programs to accommodate students from diverse cultural backgrounds, there tends to be less time and funding for core areas that must also be covered.

The high profile given to concerns such as bullying and violence in the classroom and schoolyard is, in part, symptomatic of tensions encountered both by staff and by students. Teachers are becoming increasingly frustrated with many aspects of their jobs as they find they are given little time and recognition for all that they are called on to do (Council of Ministers of Education Canada, 1996). While teachers are considered to be professionals, with the expectation that they are responsible for planning and carrying out educational functions, their professional status is constrained by extensive regulations and scrutiny.

● Educational Policy, ● ○ ●
Politics, and Ideologies

Educational policy is established and administered in quite different ways in other countries. Many nations, such as Sweden and Japan, have highly centralized systems of education. Canada and the United States, by contrast, do not have uniform or centralized education systems because education is constitutionally defined as an area of provincial and state authority. Canada exhibits what Paul Axelrod describes as an 'educational patchwork, particularly in comparison with the more uniform approaches of other countries' (1997: 126). In nearly all nations, however, competing demands for more co-ordinated educational planning, national standards, and consistency across jurisdictions coexist with competing reforms seeking greater responsiveness and **accountability** to local concerns (Manzer, 1994).

Provincial and territorial governments in Canada have the authority to create legislation and guidelines that outline virtually all aspects of the education system, including how it is organized, the length of the school year, curriculum and graduation requirements, teacher qualifications and certification, and educational funding. The specific details related to setting and carrying out educational policies and operating schools are normally delegated to elected local school boards or similar regional bodies.

In recent years, almost all provinces and territories have begun to propose and initiate significant changes in the ways education is organized and administered, particularly at the school board or district level. Along with a shift to larger school units, noted earlier, new bodies, including parents' advisory councils and community school programs have been established to seek greater local representation (Council of Ministers of Education Canada, 2001).

Public education at elementary, secondary, and post-secondary levels has experienced significant financial changes since the early 1990s. Total education spending, estimated to be over $80 billion in 2006, has risen by nearly $30 billion since 1991. However, the rate of increase has slowed considerably (with education expenditures falling for a brief period in the mid-1990s), with education spending as a proportion of the nation's gross domestic product (GDP, or total expenditures) declining from 8 to 6 per cent since 1992 (Statistics Canada, 2004a: 54). Education spending now represents about 6 per cent of GDP although total educational spending has recovered and increased in the new century, often through more selective or targeted forms of funding. Selected educational priority areas, such as materials, innovation, and training related to new technologies, have expanded, whereas other areas have languished. Figure 11.2 shows that the predominant source of education funding in Canada is provincial/territorial governments, but a reliance on private and individual sources is growing.

These fiscal trends have placed higher burdens on students and others who have come to be defined as 'educational consumers'. Educational inequalities increase when students from less privileged backgrounds cannot afford to enroll and remain in advanced educational programs. Post-secondary tuition fees doubled during the 1990s and have continued to grow dramatically. Increases in the numbers of students incurring student debt and in the extent of student debt loads have accompanied rising costs of education and living expenses (Allen and Vaillancourt, 2004).

Elementary and secondary schools are facing difficult choices as they weigh the costs and benefits of seeking higher taxes to finance schools, increasing school fees, fundraising, relying on corporate sponsors to cover educational expenses, or cutting school programs and

■■ Time to Reflect ■■■■■■■■■■■■■■■■■■■■■■■■

What does an understanding of the hidden curriculum tell us about the nature and purposes of schooling?

Figure 11.2 Total Educational Spending in Canada, by Direct Source of Funds

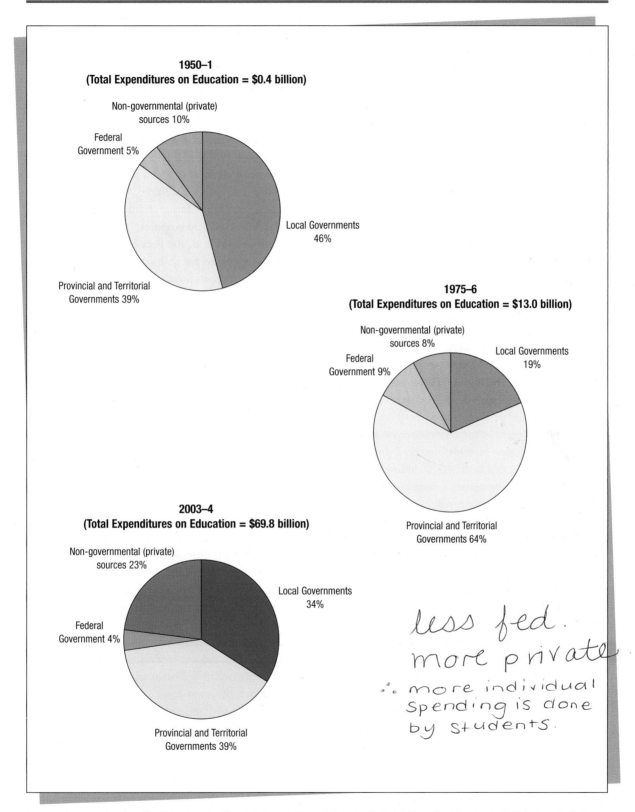

Sources: Based on data from Statistics Canada, *Historical Compendium of Education Statistics: From Confederation to 1975* (Ottawa: Statistics Canada, 1978); Statistics Canada, *Advance Statistics of Education* (Ottawa: Statistics Canada, annual); and estimates calculated from OECD (2006) and Statistics Canada CANSIM data tables 385–0002 and 385–0003.

services. Following changes to its provincial school funding formula, Ontario has concerns about what some observers have identified as an increasing inequity between 'have' and 'have-not' schools (L. Brown, 2002: A26). Similarly, results from a national survey by the Canadian Teachers' Federation (2006: 12–13) demonstrate fundraising initiatives, once employed primarily for school trips or extracurricular activities, are being relied on increasingly to cover core areas:

- 49 per cent of all schools reported fundraising for library books (including 60 per cent of elementary schools);
- 24 per cent of all schools reported fundraising for school programs, and 18 per cent for school supplies;
- 92 per cent of full-time educators contribute some of their own money (an average of $344 each in the 2004–5 school year) for classroom materials and class-related activities for their students.

Educational funding decisions are accompanied by growing concern over the extent to which education systems are able to prepare learners for contemporary economic and social conditions. There are competing viewpoints (often expressed through concerns about educational quality and excellence) about what role governments should play within this changing environment.

Neo-liberal critics promote the need for governments and the services they deliver, including education, to operate more like businesses guided by market principles. High-quality education is defined in terms of the excellence of educational 'products', measured by such things as standardized test scores, parental choice, and public accountability. Parents and learners are commonly viewed, in this way, as 'consumers' who should have the opportunity to approach education like decision-making about other purchases, with the added importance that it is their children and not some material object that is of concern, with the tools to make personal choices about the kinds of schooling they desire.

These criticisms have had some impact on education systems, particularly as governments look for ways to restrict expenditures and reorganize public services. Some observers view the recent directions in educational reform as a dangerous shift in public priorities to serve the needs of vocal interest groups who are more concerned with their own economic interests or catering to narrowly defined family and group demands rather than a commitment to community participation and high-quality education (Osborne, 1999). Matters of educational quality, accountability, and choice often are framed by a limited number of factors that can be measured in quantifiable terms, such as standardized test results. These kinds of indicators, and the manner in which they are interpreted, can be misleading when they do not account for the full range of activities and competencies encompassed by schooling. Ironically, many reformers who claim to increase educational 'choice', public accountability, and decentralization of educational decision-making in fact concentrate control over such matters as finance, curriculum, and provincial testing at the provincial or territorial level or in central bodies outside of formal education systems (Gidney, 1999; Kachur and Harrison, 1999; Sears, 2003).

Education is the focus of intense debate in part because of its social and economic importance. It is both a central institution in the lives of children and youth and a strategic focus for policy related to emerging economic realities. Given these concerns, it is important not to forget that there has been fairly consistent consensus over time about the general nature and purposes of education: schooling is to be responsive, as much as possible, to the needs and interests of the communities it serves while it must also prepare people for effective participation in broader social, cultural, and economic contexts.

Education, Work, and Families

Changes in the nature and composition of learners' families and the varied demands from workplaces for particular kinds of qualified labour-force participants have made it even more crucial to understand how education systems interact with other institutions.

The nature of childhood and adolescence is changing profoundly as students and their families experience various life challenges. Few people experience 'traditional' linear pathways from home to school to work. Periods of work and study often overlap. Children and their parents undergo substantial stress as they experience family breakdown, economic crises induced by job layoffs or persistent poverty, or difficulties in securing adequate child-care arrangements. Family, work, and community responsibilities create multiple demands on both children's and parents' time, often making it difficult to provide strong support for learning and extracurricular activities that rely on extensive student–parent interaction. Tensions often spill over from one site of social life to another, expressed in public concern over phenomena such as bullying, violence, gang warfare, and 'risk' among children and youth. Unfortunately, these issues may be regarded in a highly sensationalist way that distorts the true nature of childhood and youth activity and that ignores the strong motivations and positive contributions to leadership and mutual support prevalent among much of the student population.

Students, teachers, and educational environments face additional stresses through the growing general emphasis on education as an entry point to subsequent occupational and economic success. Taking their cue from the market model of education, many parents view their children's education as an investment, making significant demands both on their children (in order to guarantee high performance) and on teachers and educational administrators (in order to deliver a high-quality product that will yield the best results in the marketplace). Parental education, along with emphasis on early reading and literacy skills, factors heavily as an influence on children's subsequent educational attainment and success (Statistics Canada, 2006e). Parents and community members from diverse backgrounds frequently have divergent expectations about the way education should be organized and delivered. Some immigrants, for instance, may feel the Canadian education system is too unstructured and undemanding in comparison with the systems they were familiar with prior to arriving in Canada, while others take the opposite view (Campey, 2002). Aboriginal people look to schools to reconcile the need to prepare youth for a meaningful place in global society with the need to make strong connections with Indigenous people, their cultural heritage, and their contemporary circumstances (Royal Commission on Aboriginal People, 1996).

● Education and ● ● ● ● ● New Technologies

Education, like other institutions, has been significantly affected by the introduction of computers and other new technologies. Information technology, in a few cases, has revolutionized education. Some institutions have replaced traditional instructional settings with fully wired teaching/learning centres in which participants can not only communicate with each other, but also draw upon material and interact with individuals on a global basis (Gergen, 2001). Schools in remote regions have gained access to varied learning resources and connections

through the Internet and through initiatives such as SchoolNet, which aims to provide web-based learning resources to all Canadian schools. Adults can subscribe to an unprecedented range of continuing and post-secondary study options. Schools and universities are just beginning to explore the opportunities that new technologies are making available to them (even though the origins of the World Wide Web lie, in part, in the development of a tool that could be used to produce and share new knowledge among university-based researchers).

New technologies and their use in and impact on education give rise to several important questions. Levin and Riffel, reviewing different perspectives on the role that new technologies play in school settings, conclude that 'it may be that technology is not living up to its promise because it has been seen as an answer to rather than a reason to ask questions about the purposes of schools and the nature of teaching and learning' (1997: 114). Two issues are especially critical in this respect.

First, a significant 'digital divide' separates those who have access to computers and electronic connections—and the skills and know-how to use and take advantage of new technologies—and those who do not. This divide is most commonly posed in global terms, distinguishing richer, more technologically developed nations, such as those in North America, Europe, parts of Southeast Asia, and Australia and New Zealand, from developing nations in Asia, Africa, and Latin and South America. Canada, in this regard, is in a highly favourable situation in comparison to all or nearly all other nations, with one of the highest proportions of its population who use and own computers and employ Internet connections at home and at work. However, even within regions and nations, regular access to computers and the ability to employ them regularly at higher levels depend on such factors as a steady job, income and education levels, gender, social class, and racial characteristics (see Table 11.3).

A second issue related to the impact of new technologies on education arises from an examination of how and why new technologies are being adopted as tools and expectations in education. Clearly, information technology offers many advantages to users, contributes to important educational innovation, and may provide greater employment and economic opportunities outside of school. The rapid expansion of new technologies and applications, from text messaging, blogging, and communities involved in the dissemination of public information resources such as Wikipedia, to gaming and electronic surveillance devices, is transforming everyday life for students and their families. However, students

Table 11.3   Summary of Digital Divide: Inequalities in Internet Access in Eight Countries

Country	Socio-economic Status	Gender	Life Stage	Region
US	Declining yet persistent	No appreciable divide	Declining yet persistent	Declining yet persistent
UK	Increasing	Declining yet persistent	Declining yet persistent	Declining yet persistent
Germany	Increasing	Increasing	Declining yet persistent	Declining
Italy	Large divide based on education	Increasing	Younger use the Internet more	Northern Italy leads the south
Japan	Declining yet persistent	Declining yet persistent (reversed digital divide in mobile Internet	Younger use the Internet more	Major cities have higher Internet diffusion than smaller cities
Korea (Rep.)	Increasing	Persistent	Increasing	Declining: Seoul still the most wired city in country
China	Huge yet slightly declining	Declining yet persistent	Slightly declining	Huge, yet slightly declining
Mexico	Huge	42 per cent of Internet users are women	Younger make up the majority of Internet users	Very uneven: users still concentrated in centre, Guadalajara, and Monterrey

Source: Chen and Wellman (2004: 43). Reprinted by permission of the publisher and the authors.

and teachers are not always equipped and supported to use such technologies to their advantage, or to understand fully their implications and limitations.

Issues related to the adoption of computer technologies in education reflect more enduring concerns about the relationship of what happens in the classroom with structures and processes outside of schooling. Educational practices are strongly influenced by social, technological, and economic developments and innovations, though they also reveal their own peculiarities and rhythms. Demands for education to prepare people for the changing workplace sit side by side with parallel demands for producing better citizens and persons with multiple competencies to function in a global society.

● Educational ● ● ● ● ●
Opportunities
and Inequalities

Questions about the relationship of education to social inequality and opportunity structures have long been central to the sociological study of education. This is due, in large part, to public expectations about education's contributions to social and economic advancement in post-industrial or knowledge-based societies. Despite compelling evidence that much of this promise has been fulfilled, significant inequalities persist in educational experiences and outcomes.

Differences between groups are apparent within the significant increases in levels and rates of educational participation and attainment across the population as a whole. One of the most striking trends within the general pattern of educational growth has been the strong advancement of educational opportunities for women, particularly in post-secondary education. With respect to the increase in overall education levels during the period between 1951 and 1991, Neil Guppy and Scott Davies point to two key trends related to gender: 'First, at the low end of the educational distribution, men remained less likely than women to complete at least Grade 9 and this difference did not narrow over the 40-year interval. Second, at higher education levels, women have surpassed the lead that men clearly held in 1951' (1998: 87). Among persons most likely to have completed their education recently, the proportion of the population in the 20–29-year-old age cohort with a post-secondary degree or diploma increased from 37 per cent for both men and women in 1981 to 54 per cent for women and only 45 per cent for men in 2001 (Statistics Canada, 1998b: 1; Statistics Canada, 2006e). In 2003, 60 per cent of all persons who received university degrees were women, although the reverse was true at the highest end, where 58 per cent of PhDs were awarded to men (Statistics Canada, 2005f; see also Table 11.4).

The shift in the gender balance of educational attainment has drawn attention to other aspects of education. Findings from numerous surveys that girls have begun to outperform boys on a number of indicators have generated controversy over suggestions that gender inequality has reversed to the point that the education system is now 'failing' boys. For example, the comprehensive Programme for International Student Assessment (PISA), conducted in 2000 and 2003 to compare student performance in core areas, has posed a concern for policymakers that girls in Canada and at least 30 other participating nations consistently demonstrate stronger test outcomes in reading (Bussière et al., 2001; Bussière et al., 2004: 38). However, the findings from PISA and similar studies also demonstrate the complex nature of gender inequalities in education. For instance, in most provinces, and in many dimensions of mathematics and science performance, relatively few pronounced gender differences appear while in some instances boys outperform girls. Moreover, the survey highlights how similarities and differences based on gender cannot be understood without reference to a broad array of other family, school, and individual characteristics, notably family socio-economic background (Bussière et al., 2001).

Many gender-related differences are obscured through simple comparisons between boys' and girls' test results (Epstein et al., 1997). Women outnumber men in post-secondary enrolment and graduation, but there are strong gender differences in fields of study and types of training programs (see Table 11.3). Programs in areas such as business, management, and commerce, some arts and social sciences, protection and correction services, and languages are relatively popular among both men and women. Women are much more heavily concentrated in a few fields such as education, nursing, and social work or social services. Men tend to be more widely dispersed over more fields but outnumber women considerably in areas such as engineering and electrical technologies, computer science, and primary industries.

Differences in fields of study reflect a combination of personal choices and circumstances, institutional characteristics (such as cues or levels of comfort and discomfort that direct students into some areas and away from others or the compatibility between particular programs and responsibilities to care for dependent children), and broader socio-economic factors (Statistics Canada, 1998b; Wotherspoon, 2000). Employment options and life pathways are generally associated with the kinds of education and credentials that people attain. Nonetheless, rising levels of education do not always translate fully into gains in labour market positions, incomes, and other equitable outcomes for women (Kenway et al., 1998).

Parallel with gender comparisons, educational differences between racial and ethnic groups appear to have disappeared or diminished significantly in recent decades (Guppy and Davies, 1998). Immigration policies have simultaneously emphasized the recruitment of immigrants with high educational credentials and made Canada less dependent on immigrants from Western Europe and the United States. These policies have contributed to a growing proportion of highly educated or professionally qualified visible-minority immigrants who place a high value on their children's educational advancement. Racial diversity has been accompanied by increasing sensitivity to the impact of racial discrimination and other mechanisms that historically have excluded or discouraged racial minority students from advancing through the Canadian education system.

Nonetheless, as in the case of gender inequalities, much of the analysis of racial and ethnic inequality in education points to a complex series of factors and interactions that do not lead to any straightforward conclusions. The short answer to the question of whether some groups are advantaged or disadvantaged in relation to racial and ethnic criteria is, 'It depends.' Guppy and Davies (1998), in common with many other commentators who have reviewed census data and education indicators over time, observe that Canadians in most categories (based

Table 11.4   University Degrees Awarded by Field of Study and Gender, Canada, 2004

Field of Study	Number of Graduates	Rank Order for Female Graduates	Female Graduates in Field as % of All Female Graduates	Females as % of All Graduates in Field	Rank Order for Male Graduates	Male Graduates in Field as % of All Male Graduates	Males as % of All Graduates in Field
Business, management and public administration	43,200	2	19.0	54.9	1	23.2	45.1
Social and behavioural sciences, and law	41,800	1	22.4	66.7	2	16.4	33.0
Education	25,400	3	15.5	76.0	7	7.2	24.0
Humanities	22,400	5	11.6	64.7	4	9.3	34.8
Health, parks, recreation and fitness	20,100	4	12.2	75.6	8	5.8	24.4
Architecture, engineering, and related technologies	17,500	8	3.5	25.1	3	15.6	74.9
Physical and life sciences, and technologies	15,200	6	7.0	57.2	6	7.6	42.1
Mathematics, computer and information sciences	11,100	9	2.6	29.7	5	9.1	69.4
Visual and performing arts, and communications technologies	7,300	7	3.9	67.1	9	3.0	34.2
Agriculture, natural resources and conservation	3,600	10	1.5	52.7	10	2.0	47.2
Other	1,700	11	0.8	58.8	11	0.7	35.3
All Fields	209,100		100.0	59.7		99.9	40.3

Source: Compiled with data from Statistics Canada, 'University Enrolment', *The Daily*, Cat. 11-001, 7 Nov. 2006, at <http://www.statcan.ca/Daily/English/061107/d061107a.htm>.

HUMAN DIVERSITY
Education for Canada's Aboriginal People

The educational experiences of Aboriginal people in Canada are instructive for an understanding of how education can both advance and restrict social and economic opportunities. Historical practices and inequities have contributed to a legacy of widespread failure, marginalization, and mistrust, but considerable optimism also accompanies many new initiatives.

Many Aboriginal people in the late nineteenth century looked to schooling as a way to ensure integration into contemporary societies. Tragically, while some education-related treaty promises were fulfilled, the residential school system and continuing problems with other forms of educational delivery had devastating consequences that many Aboriginal communities and their members are still struggling to cope with. The report of the Royal Commission on Aboriginal Peoples (1996) endorsed the long-standing principle of First Nations control over education along with other measures to ensure that all educational institutions would provide more receptive schooling for Aboriginal people.

Mixed results have been accomplished so far, as one of the co-chairs of the Royal Commission has observed:

Considering the primary importance of children in aboriginal cultures, it is not surprising that education was one of the first sectors where aboriginal nations and communities are now administered locally, and where possible they incorporate aboriginal languages and cultural content in the curriculum. . . . More young people are staying in school to complete a high-school diploma, though a gap still exists between graduation rates of aboriginal and non-aboriginal people. . . . Aboriginal youth are especially vulnerable. They are less likely than mature adults to have attained academic and vocational credentials and they are hardest hit by unemployment. (Erasmus, 2002: F6–7)

The accomplishment of educational improvement is a difficult one in the context of considerable diversity among Aboriginal populations and their educational options, aspirations, and circumstances. Some successful schools or programs, for instance, have developed strong foundations in Aboriginal cultures and indigenous knowledge systems, while others have been more concerned to provide services oriented to students' immediate needs and future plans. Marlene Brant Castellano, Lynne Davis, and Louise Lahache, reviewing recent trends, conclude that:

the promise of education is that it will enable Aboriginal people to sustain well-being while meeting their responsibilities in the circle of life. Those responsibilities are seen to reach further today than in any previous generation. Fulfilling the promise will require preparing successive generations to participate fully in their own communities and to assume their place as Aboriginal citizens and peoples in global society. (2000: 255)

However, the legacy of failed promises continues, according to a 'report card' issued by the Assembly of First Nations (2006: 16–17) on the tenth anniversary of the Royal Commission report, which assigned failing grades to all but three of 11 specific recommendations in the section on education.

on gender, race, region, age, class, and other factors) have benefited from the expansion of education systems. However, specific groups, including Aboriginal people, those from working-class backgrounds, francophones within Quebec, Portuguese Canadians, and the disabled, continue to face strong disadvantages relative to most other groups. Social class has a strong impact on post-secondary attendance and educational attainment. These general trends are compounded by considerable variation in educational success and attainment within groups.

Research on education for Aboriginal people is instructive in this regard. Many significant initiatives have been undertaken as researchers, policy-makers, and educators have come to acknowledge the combined impact of significant barriers to educational advancement faced by Aboriginal people. Education has long been regarded by Aboriginal people, as for any other group, as an important vehicle for gaining meaningful employment and social participation. Many First Nations, for instance, expressed their desire in the treaty-making process in the nineteenth century to have access to formal education in order to keep pace with contemporary social and economic demands.

However, subsequent developments, including the often damaging legacy of residential schooling, lack of acceptance or discriminatory treatment in provincial schools, and other social, cultural, and economic factors, have left Aboriginal people's overall education levels (especially for registered Indians who live on reserve) well below national levels (Schissel and Wotherspoon, 2003). Data from the 2001 census reveal that, despite continuing increases in the levels of educational attainment by Aboriginal people, Aboriginal people aged 25–40 years remained two-thirds as likely as non-Aboriginal people to have a post-secondary degree or diploma, one-quarter as likely to have graduated from university and over twice as likely not to have completed high school (based on data in Hull, 2005: 6).

Sociologists and other researchers have identified numerous factors, such as cultural differences, lack of individual motivation and family or community support, and social and educational discrimination, to explain these educational inequalities. These typically occur through a complex chain of interrelated cause-and-effect mechanisms. Increasing attention has been paid to the importance of early childhood development and to the family and social environments in which children are raised for the development of literacy and language skills, thinking processes, and other capacities that are central to educational success. These conditions, in turn, depend on the socio-economic circumstances of parents, the availability of support networks in the home and community, labour market opportunities for parents and students coming out of the education system, the extent to which people in particular communities or regions have access to high-quality educational programs and services, and numerous other factors. There are strong associations between social class or socio-economic background and educational attainment. Parents' education levels and household income are strong predictors, both independently and in combination with one another, of the likelihood that a person will continue into post-secondary education (Knighton and Mirza, 2002).

Educational institutions are implicated in these broader processes in several ways. Schooling makes a difference in many ways, such as how well institutions are equipped to deal with students from diverse cultural and social backgrounds; the kinds of relationships that prevail between and among teachers, parents, and students; curricular objectives and materials; standards for assessing and evaluating students; and the general social climate within educational institutions. Social class and cultural differences are evident, for instance, in the grouping and **streaming** of students into specific educational programs that contribute, in turn, to diverse educational pathways.

There is general agreement, in the context of global economic developments that place a premium on knowledge and learning, that education is important for all people. The same consensus does not exist, however, with regard to how education should be arranged to fulfill its promise on an equitable basis.

● Conclusion   ● ● ● ● ● ●

This chapter has examined several dimensions of education and its relevance for sociological inquiry. It has highlighted the phenomenal growth of formal systems of education since the nineteenth century and the accompanying increases in general levels of education throughout the population. It has linked that growth to a strong degree of public faith in the ability of education to contribute simultaneously to individual development and to address social needs for knowledge, innovation, and credentials. Educational growth, processes, and outcomes have been understood from four major theoretical perspectives: structural functionalism, which analyzes education in terms of its contributions to dominant social and economic requirements; symbolic interactionism and microsociology, which highlight the roles and interactions of various participants within educational processes; conflict theories, which emphasize education's contributions to social inequality and power relations; and feminist theories, which stress gender-based educational differences. The chapter has also addressed the changing significance of formal schooling to the experiences and social and economic opportunities of different social groups, particularly with respect to gender, race and ethnicity, and social class. All groups have benefited from educational expansion, though in varying degrees. Adequate sociological analysis of education requires an ability to integrate an understanding of what happens in and as a result of formal education with the social context in which education is situated.

Questions for Critical Thought

1. Why is education in most nations organized formally through schools and related institutional structures rather than through some other arrangement, such as families or community-based agencies? To what extent should education be a private as opposed to a public responsibility?

3. Compare and contrast schooling (formal education) with other major social institutions, including businesses, families, prisons, and religious organizations. Describe and explain the major similarities and differences.

6. Discuss the extent to which education is, and should be, organized in the interests of the communities in which educational institutions are located as opposed to interests shaped by national and global concerns. Illustrate this with reference to your own educational experiences.

7. To what extent has education in Canada fulfilled its promise to provide greater opportunities for social and economic advancement to all social groups? Explain your response with reference to at least three different theoretical frameworks.

Recommended Readings

Paul Anisef, Paul Axelrod, Etta Baichman-Anisef, Carl James, and Anton Turrittin, *Opportunity and Uncertainty: Life Course Experiences of the Class of '73* (Toronto: University of Toronto Press, 2000).

A comprehensive account of the life transitions that people undergo after high school, this book traces for a period of over two decades the educational, work, and family dynamics experienced by Ontario students who were in Grade 12 in 1973.

George J. Sefa Dei, Irma Marcia James, Leeno Luke Karumanchery, Sonia James-Wilson, and Jasmin Zine, *Removing the Margins: The Challenges and Possibilities of Inclusive Schooling* (Toronto: Canadian Scholars' Press, 2000).

Diverse research and experiential backgrounds highlight the authors' call for a more inclusive form of education. The work outlines a series of strategies that can enable schools to benefit all students by drawing from the varied resources and capacities available in diverse community settings.

Neil Guppy and Scott Davies, *The Schooled Society: An Introduction to the Sociology of Education* (Toronto: Oxford University Press, 2006).

The authors integrate their discussion of core concepts and theories in the sociological analysis of education with material drawn from research and case studies, both historical and contemporary.

D.W. Livingstone, *The Education–Jobs Gap: Underemployment or Economic Democracy* (Toronto: Garamond, 2004).

Livingstone systematically analyzes both education and the extent to which it is related to actual employment situations. His analysis integrates statistical data with people's accounts of their own education and work experiences.

Terry Wotherspoon, *The Sociology of Education in Canada: Critical Perspectives*, 2nd edn (Toronto: Oxford University Press, 2004).

Various dimensions of Canadian education are explored from a critical orientation that emphasizes inequalities based on class, race, gender, region, and other factors. The book addresses contemporary aspects of Canadian education in the context of various theoretical perspectives and historical factors.

Recommended Websites

Canadian Teachers' Federation www.ctf-fce.ca/

This website provides an educators' perspective on important educational matters, ranging from factual information on education systems and significant educational developments to position papers and analyses of pressing educational issues.

Council of Ministers of Education, Canada www.cmec.ca

The Council of Ministers of Education provides access to major reports and studies conducted through that organization, as well as links to each of the provincial and territorial ministries of education and other important Canadian and international education bodies.

Educational Resources Information Center (ERIC) www.eric.ed.gov/ERICWebPortal/Home.portal

The ERIC database is a comprehensive collection of information (mostly abstracts of journal articles and reports) on various aspects of and fields related to education, including the sociology of education.

12

Chapter

• • • • • • • • • • •

Work and the Economy

Pamela Sugiman

Learning Objectives

In this chapter, you will:

▶ come to understand the different types of paid and unpaid work that people carry out in this society;

▶ examine the different ways in which work has been socially organized by employers;

▶ be introduced to some of the main concepts that are used in the sociological analysis of work;

▶ learn some of the recent trends in employment;

▶ highlight the ways in which workers experience work and sometimes resist; and

▶ recognize the impact of the new flexibility strategies on workers who are located differently in a society stratified by race, gender, and class.

● Introduction ● ● ● ● ● ● ●

Most of us will spend the better part of our lives working, because work is central to our economic well-being. Work is a social product and, as such, it is subject to **negotiation** and change by human actors. People seek meaning in the work that they perform and, as a result, there is a close relationship between work, life, and **identity**.

In recent years, some social commentators have predicted the demise of work. In this view, people will invest more time in leisure activities and will be shaped primarily by their relationship to the consumer economy. But try to imagine a life without work. What would it be like if you never held a job? Unless you were incredibly wealthy, unable to work as a result of disability or poor health, or willing (or forced) to live on social assistance or handouts on the street, it is unlikely that you could live without work. If you are like most people, you have no choice but to work in order to secure for yourself the basic necessities (food, clothing, a hospitable living environment). Most of us will spend most of our days working; the majority will work for someone else, on another's terms. This holds true whether you bus tables, drive a truck, trade on Bay Street, or teach in a school. The very wealthy rely heavily on investment income for their economic well-being, and the extremely poor depend on social welfare (transfer payments). But the majority of people in the middle- and highest-income groups in Canada (from $50,000 to over $100,000 household income per year) count on wages and salaries for their existence (Jackson and Robinson, 2000: 11). A recognition of the strong link between work and life calls for a critical examination of the world of work. It is imperative that students today confront the topic because it has strong implications for how you will live your lives.

Most Canadians view the work they do as a given. Work is something that we either have or do not have (Gorz, 1999), that we must prepare ourselves for, that we may escape at the end of a day or the end of a career. Discussions of work, therefore, tend to revolve around a specific, narrowly circumscribed set of concerns, namely, job growth, unemployment, and job-related training (Lowe, 2000). But just as we need to accept that work is what we will do for the good part of our lives, it is also important to understand that there is nothing inevitable about how work presently is organized. Work is a social product. The way work is structured, the nature of jobs, the rewards of work—these are the products of **social relationships** between different groups of people. Hence, over time and across cultures, work has taken varied forms. Students

need to examine critically its current forms and organization with the knowledge that these can be questioned and perhaps even transformed.

Although most of us work in order to survive and to live comfortably, we also work for more than mere economic survival or comfort of living. Sociologist Graham Lowe (2000) highlights the importance, therefore, of moving discussions about the quantity of work (unemployment statistics, job counts, and work hours) to its quality. After all, the quality of work matters to workers, young and old. According to Workplace 2000, this country's first national work-ethic study, when Canadian workers were asked what they would do if they won a million dollars, only 17 per cent said that they would quit their jobs and never work again; 41 per cent of respondents claimed that they would remain in their current job, 17 per cent would embark on a different career, and 24 per cent would start their own business (Lowe, 2000: 52). Canadians have a strong attachment to their work.

In order to understand work fully, it is necessary to think about the wider economy in which it is situated. We may define the *economy* as a social institution in which people carry out the production, distribution, and consumption of goods and services. Discussions of the economy sometimes are presented in inaccessible language that easily mystifies those untrained in the discipline. Talk of gross domestic product, gross national product, inflation, and recession can be confusing. Yet it is critical that we understand how economic systems function because they have a direct bearing on how we live. The economy and our location in it shape what we may or may not enjoy of, for instance, the quality of health care, housing, diet and nutrition, consumer spending, and the accoutrements of lifestyle. The economic system is, furthermore, linked to a nation's political system, to people's conceptions of democracy and citizenship, and to general measures of success and failure.

● World ● ● ● ● ● ● ●
Economic Systems

Economic systems are not abstract entities. They are structured and contested, shaped and reshaped, by the people who inhabit them. They further reflect relations of **power** and inequality. In Canada, we presently live in a society that is based on a system of **capitalism**. As such, it is a society in which there are both blatant and subtle manifestations of inequality. We observe extremes of wealth and poverty every day. On the highway, a shiny new Porsche whirs by a 1989 Chevy Impala. A businessman rushing to pick up a $3,000 suit from Holt Renfrew walks quickly past a homeless person squatting on the corner. A Filipina nanny on a temporary work permit spends her days taking someone's children to Montessori school, piano lessons, and dance class. On her way home, she buys their groceries. At night, she returns, tired, to her small room beside the furnace in the basement of the family's well-appointed home. We live in a society in which economic inequalities are complexly wound up with inequalities based on **gender**, **race**, and **ethnicity**.

Pre-industrial, Pre-capitalist Societies: Hunting and Gathering

Early human societies rested on a system of production and exchange called *hunting and gathering*. Hunting-and-gathering (also called *foraging*) societies were characterized by a simple *subsistence economy*—relatively small groups of people lived off the land (gathering nuts, berries, and other forms of wild vegetation), hunting game, and, in some cases, fishing. Such societies were characterized by considerable physical mobility as groups would move from one geographic location to another in accordance with the food and water supply. Production among hunter-gatherers was largely for *consumption*, or immediate use. In other words, food gathered would be divided among people and eaten with little excess, or surplus. Without the accumulation of surplus, a system of exchange was minimal, and there was no private accumulation of wealth. Hunting and gathering societies are thus considered to be among the most egalitarian in human history.

Furthermore, the division of labour among hunter-gatherers was simple, based on sex and age. Women tended to perform gathering activities, often with children in tow, while men hunted. Some anthropologists have argued that this sex-based division of labour did not translate, however, into inequalities between the sexes. While men and women performed different functions, the divisions were not as rigid as they are currently. The work that women performed was not devalued. Indeed, insofar as hunting-and-gathering societies looked largely to vegetation (and not scarce meat) for their dietary needs, women made a greater productive contribution to the maintenance of the group than did men.

Agricultural Societies

The development of *agriculture* (the breeding of animals, the cultivation of plants, and human settlement) brought about many changes in the social and economic organization of societies. These changes were connected to an increase in productive power, a more dependable and stable food supply, and the accumulation of surplus leading to the establishment of market exchange.

Prior to the nineteenth century, Canada was largely an agricultural society based on a family economy: most economic activities were located in or nearby family households. The **household** thus served both as a place of work and of residence. This type of economy, furthermore, featured a more elaborate division of labour (than in the past) based on age and sex (Nelson and Robinson, 2002). Family survival during this period, though, depended on the interdependent and collective labours of household members. Work was organized according to the market, but also according to nature, seasonal cycles, and personal need.

Capitalism

Unlike earlier economic systems, capitalism is based on private ownership of the **means of production**, an exchange relationship between owners and workers, an economy driven by the pursuit of profit, and competitive market relations.

In order to understand capitalism, let us turn to the ideas of the social theorist Karl Marx. Marx (1967 [1867]) wrote about the profound changes he observed in nineteenth-century England. He witnessed a gradual but dramatic transition from a feudal agricultural society to an industrialized, capitalist economy. Under capitalism, the capitalist class (or **bourgeoisie**) owns the means of production while the majority of people, the working class (or **proletariat**), does not. Means of production is a concept that refers to wealth-generating property, such as land, factories, machines, and the capital needed to produce and distribute goods and services for exchange in a market. While many of us own a car, a computer, or perhaps a house, these items do not constitute the means of production insofar as they are for our personal use only (a place to live, a tool for writing your research papers) and not for the production of wealth.

In a capitalist society, furthermore, capitalists and workers are engaged in a relationship of unequal exchange. As workers do not own the means of production, they have no choice but to sell their labour to a capitalist employer in exchange for a wage. Working people are forced into this relationship because in this type of economy, it is almost impossible to survive without money. One can try to feed a family with the produce from a home vegetable garden, wear home-made clothes, and live without electricity, but at some point it is necessary to purchase market goods and services. For example, you will need to buy fabric, sewing needles, seeds, and a plot of land.

The capitalist class organizes production (work) with the specific goal of maximizing profits for personal wealth. For this reason, it structures work in the most efficient way imaginable, pays workers the lowest possible wages, and extracts the greatest amount of labour from the worker within a working day. And, lastly, capitalism is based on a freely competitive market system and therefore a laissez-faire ('hands-off') government. Under capitalism, the market forces of supply and demand are supposed to determine the production and distribution of goods and services, with no government interference.

Capitalism and Industrialization

People sometimes use the terms capitalism and industrial society interchangeably. Conceptually, however, they are distinct. While capitalism is a broad economic system, industrialization refers to a more specific process that has consequences for the nature and organization of work as well as for the division of labour.

In Canada, as in England, industrialization resulted in a transformation of capitalist production. The rise of industrial capitalism in the late nineteenth and early twentieth centuries constituted one of the most fundamental changes in our society. Industrialization involved the introduction of new forms of energy (steam, electricity) and of transportation (railroads), **urbanization**, and the implementation of new machine technology, all of which contributed to the rise of the factory system of production and the manufacture and mass production of goods. These changes greatly facilitated and heightened capitalist production. As well, and in profound ways, they have shaped the ways in which people worked and organized their lives.

The proliferation of factories led to the movement of work from homes and small artisanal workshops to larger, more impersonal sites, to the concentration of larger groups of workers under one roof, and to the introduction of *time discipline* (by the clock), in addition to a more specialized division of labour.

This movement of work, furthermore, resulted in the departure of men from the home and family. While single women were employed in some textile factories, married women were prohibited from most factory jobs. Many women thus continued to work in the home or were employed as domestics in private households,

took in boarders, or did other people's laundry in exchange for a small cash sum (Bradbury, 1993). These changes in the economy had far-reaching consequences for the construction of femininity and masculinity, marriage, and family life.

During the period of industrial capitalism economic inequalities became increasingly visible and conflict between classes grew. While successful capitalists made huge amounts of money, working-class men toiled in factories or mines for a pittance, women combined long hours of domestic drudgery with sporadic income-generating activities, and children were sent off to factories or domestic work. Many people lived in poverty and misery.

Family Capitalism

In the mid- to late nineteenth centuries, industrial capitalism was in its early stages. Throughout this period, a small number of individuals and families owned and controlled most of the country's wealth—major companies and financial institutions. Because wealth accrued from business enterprises was passed on within families, from generation to generation (for example, the Fords and Rockefellers in the United States and the Eatons and Seagrams in Canada), this era is aptly termed that of *family capitalism*.

Corporate Capitalism

The subsequent phase of economic development, occurring in the late nineteenth to mid-twentieth centuries, is called *corporate* (or *monopoly*) capitalism. This phase witnessed the movement of ownership from individuals and families to modern corporations (and their shareholders). A *corporation* is defined as a legal entity distinct from the people who own and control it. As an entity, the corporation itself may enter into contracts and own property. This separation of enterprise from individuals has served to protect owners and chief executives from personal liability and from any debts incurred by the corporation.

Insofar as the Canadian economy has traditionally been resource-intensive, many of the corporations that have dominated our industrial development have been American-owned. Consequently, Canadians have witnessed the establishment of numerous branch plants of companies whose head offices are located in the United States (for example, IBM Canada and GM Canada). This fact has raised important concerns about our political sovereignty, our culture, and our distinctiveness as a people and a nation.

Under corporate capitalism, furthermore, there has been a growing concentration of economic power (that is, power in the hands of a few large corporations). One way in which capitalists have increased their economic power is through mergers. By merging, large corporations have been able to create situations of monopoly and oligopoly. We have a monopoly when one corporation has exclusive control over the market. Obviously, this situation is undesirable for consumers, as it restricts their market 'choices'. The Canadian government has, as a result, implemented various controls to curb the monopolization of an industry.

An *oligopoly* exists when several companies control an industry. The insurance, newspaper, and entertainment industries are characterized by oligopolistic control. An increased revenue by way of mergers and acquisitions obviously is desirable to corporate owners but may occur at the expense of industrial development and employment. In 2005, profits of the top 500 firms internationally reached a halting $610 billion. In fact, these economically powerful firms, known as the Fortune 500, have doubled their economic power over the last half-century. In 2005, Fortune 500 revenues were up by 10.2 per cent. Yet, during this same period, employees or what economists term 'head count', increased by a mere 2 per cent. Although the 10 largest employers provided jobs for 5 million workers, these employers included such companies as Wal-Mart, McDonald's, Sears, Home Depot, and Target, all of which are retailers known for offering low wages and few opportunities for training and advancement. Workers have not benefited from this growing wealth (Labour Research Association, 2006; see also Table 12.1).

Welfare Capitalism

In the real world, of course, examples of pure capitalism and pure socialism cannot be found. In Canada, as well as in parts of Western Europe, the economy is market-based; at the same time, the government intervenes with regulations and controls. Economists call this type of system *welfare capitalism*. Under this system, state-sponsored programs such as universal health care and public education address the needs of different groups of people within the country. Many government controls, such as tax credits for corporations, act in the interests of business.

As well, in our society, the means of production are owned by both private citizens and governments. In spite of moves towards their **privatization**, we still have a number of *Crown corporations* (businesses owned by the federal or provincial governments) such as Canada Post, the Canadian Broadcasting Corporation (CBC), and the Canada Mortgage and Housing Corporation (CMHC).

Socialism

Marx (Marx and Engels, 1986 [1848]) believed that in a capitalist society, workers would eventually revolt against their **exploitation**, develop a consciousness of themselves as a class, and overthrow the system of capitalist production, replacing it with a socialist economy. It was not clear how this revolution was to proceed (except that it would be led by a communist party). In the first stages after victory, workers would establish a 'dictatorship of the proletariat' and the economy would be socialized. This would involve the elimination of private property and public ownership of the means of production (in other words, workers' control). Once this had been accomplished, the state would gradually wither away and socialism would give way to *communism*. Under communism, work would be organized on the basis of a radically different division of labour. In particular, the production and distribution of goods and services would be in accordance with ability and need within the population, rather than shaped by market forces and the pursuit of profit for individual gain.

Like capitalism, socialism and communism have never existed in a pure form. Many revolutions, successful and not, have been attempted in its name (for example, the Bolshevik revolution in Russia in 1917, China's in 1949, and Cuba's in 1959), but these societies have never reached the vision laid out by Marx. During the 1980s, the Soviet Union experienced a series of economic and political crises that ultimately led to the disintegration of its economic base and political structures. This economic crisis was based on the inability of this form of 'command economy' to adapt rapidly to the changing global economy. The last two decades have witnessed the breakup of the Soviet empire and attempts by Russia and the various 'new' countries, such as Hungary, Czechoslovakia, Poland, Ukraine, Latvia, Estonia, and Lithuania, to make the transition from command to capitalist economies, or some variation between the two (Storey, 2002).

● The Global Economy ●

Today, economic activity knows no national borders. Most large companies operate in a global context, setting up businesses in Canada, the United States, and various parts of Asia, Africa, and India. These companies may be called *transnational* or *multinational*. The head offices of transnational corporations are located in one country (often the United States), while production facilities are based in others. We see the products of the

Table 12.1   The 25 Largest Employers in Canada, 2007

Rank	Company (Year End)	Number of Employees	Location of Head Office	Revenue per Employee ($)	Profit per Employee ($)
1	Onex Corp. (De06)	167,000	Toronto, Ont.	$120,341	$6,000
2	George Weston (De06)	155,400	Toronto, Ont.	$207,857	$779
3	Magna International (De06)[a]	83,000	Aurora, Ont.	$292,253	$6,361
4	Royal Bank of Canada (Oc06)	70,000	Toronto, Ont.	$514,929	$67,543
5	Metro Inc. (Se06)	65,000	Montreal, Que.	$168,398	$3,892
6	Alcan Inc. (De06)[a]	64,700	Montreal, Que.	$365,394	$27,604
7	Canadian Tire (De06)	56,559	Toronto, Ont.	$146,203	$6,270
8	Bombardier Inc. (Ja07)[a]	56,000	Montreal, Que.	$267,375	$4,786
9	BCE Inc. (De06)	54,434	Montreal, Que.	$326,469	$36,870
10	Bank of Nova Scotia (Oc06)	53,251	Toronto, Ont.	$422,189	$67,210
11	Toronto-Dominion Bank (Oc06)	51,147	Toronto, Ont.	$436,037	$89,996
12	Garda World Security (Ja07)	50,000	Montreal, Que.	$13,660	$421
13	Jean Coutu Group (My06)[a]	47,115	Longueuil, Que.	$236,714	$2,203
14	Shoppers Drug Mart (De06)	44,040	Toronto, Ont.	$176,804	$9,593
15	Sears Canada (De06)	41,107	Toronto, Ont.	$144,752	$3,712
16	CIBC (Oc06)	40,559	Toronto, Ont.	$497,202	$65,238
17	Alimentation Couche-Tard (Ap06)[a]	39,500	Laval, Que.	$257,438	$4,967
18	Empire Company (My06)	37,000	Stellarton, N.S.	$356,565	$8,022
19	Quebecor Inc. (De06)	36,588	Montreal, Que.	$268,911	$–2,566
20	Bank of Montreal (Oc06)	34,942	Toronto, Ont.	$519,518	$76,212
21	Nortel Networks (De06)[a]	33,760	Brampton, Ont.	$343,661	$829
22	Extendicare REIT (De06)	33,700	Markham, Ont.	$51,794	$–1,060
23	Thomson Corp. (De06)[a]	32,375	Toronto, Ont.	$205,869	$34,595
24	ACE Aviation Holdings (De06)[b]	32,256	Saint-Laurent, Que.	$331,318	$12,649
25	Telus Corp. (De06)	30,000	Vancouver, B.C.	$289,777	$37,417

[a]Company reports in US dollars.

[b]Figures have been annualized in previous 3 through 5 years.

Figures for fiscal periods other than 12 months are annualized for rankings and calculating returns. Foreign currencies are converted into Canadian dollars at the end of the relevant period for balance sheet items and at the average exchange rate for the relevant period for earnings items.

Source: Excerpted and adapted from 'The Top 1000', *Globe and Mail Report on Business Magazine* (2007); available at <http://www.reportonbusiness.com/v5/content/tp1000-2007/index.php?view=top_50_employers>. Reprinted with permission from The Globe and Mail.

global economy everywhere we turn. Look at the clothes you wear, the car you drive, the food you eat. Where are they from? Products of the new global economy typically move through many nations.

Clearly, the goal of transnational corporations is profit. Capitalists are rapidly moving beyond national boundaries in an effort to secure the cheapest available labour, lowest-cost infrastructure (power, water supply, roads, telephone lines), and production unencumbered by health and safety regulations, minimum-wage, and hours-of-work laws, maternity provisions, and the like. Unprotected by legislation and typically without union representation, labour in **developing countries** is both cheaper and easier to control than workforces in Canada.

GLOBAL ISSUES
Global Sweatshops: Nike in China

Nike's presence in China is estimated at 50 contracted factories, manufacturing sneakers and clothing and employing approximately 110,000 workers. Forty per cent of Nike's footwear is produced in China. The Sewon factory is a South Korean investment that has produced exclusively for Nike since 1989. Average wages for a worker in a shoe factory in South Korea are US $2.49/hour, or more than twelve times the cost at Sewon. Is it any wonder that Nike produces such a considerable amount of shoes and garments in China?

The New York-based National Labor Committee (NLC) researchers uncovered that working time is excessively long and three factories show evidence of gender and age discrimination. These factories prefer to hire young, single women, specifically stating in job recruitment advertisement that proof of marital status is necessary for the application. One company fires employees at the age of 25 when they become 'used up' (exhausted).

Nike's Code of Conduct guarantees that '. . . partners share the best practices and continuous improvement in . . . management practices that recognize the dignity of the individual' and that 'there shall be no discrimination based on race, creed, gender, marital or maternity status, religious or political beliefs, age, or sexual orientation.' Obviously, on these points, Nike has failed in China.

Source: Canadian Labour Congress, 'Nike in China', *Sweatshop Alert* (Nov. 2000): 9; at: <www.clc-ctc.ca>.

Nike in China: Five Factories

Factory	Location	No. of Workers	Wages ($US)	Working Hours	Time Off	Remarks
Sewon	Jiaozhou City, Shandong Prov., Liuhizai Ind. Area	1,500, mostly women aged 18–25	Base wage: 20¢/hr	11- to12-hr shifts, 6 days/wk	1 day/wk	Sewon would not hire 27 yrs of age
Hung Wah & Hung Yip Keng Tau	Huijou City, Guangdong Prov.	2,000–2,500, mostly women aged 16–32	Average: 22¢/hr	Peak season: 15-hr shifts, 7 days/wk	1 day/mo.	Workers never heard of Nike's Code of Conduct; 12/room
Keng Tau	Keng Tau Industrial Zone	1,000–1,200	11–36¢/hr	Peak season: 14 hrs/day, 7 days/wk	1 day/mo.	No overtime premium; 16/room
Tong Ji	Chongzhan Prov.	500 migrant workers	Average: 27¢/hr	57.5 hrs/wk	1 day/wk	Nov. 1999: 72.5 hrs/wk
Wei Li	Guangdong Prov.	6,100, mostly women aged 16–25	Average: 56¢/hr	Normal: 8 hrs/day, 5 days/wk; Peak: 12-hr shift	Normal: 2 days/wk; Peak: 1 day/ 2 wks	Employs only single women; requires certificate of marital status

Source: China Labour Bulletin and National Labour Committee.

Critics have pointed to the negative cultural, social, and economic consequences of **globalization**. Some argue, for example, that globalization has resulted in a homogenization of **culture**. Media giants Time Warner and Disney, for instance, distribute many of the same cultural products (television shows, films, videos, books) to audiences across the globe. Among many other holdings, Time Warner owns well over 1,000 movie screens outside of the United States and the second-largest book publishing business in the world. The company furthermore boasts that CNN, its popular news network, aggregates approximately two billion audience impressions worldwide every day (www.timewarner.com/corp/businesses/detail/turn_broadcasting/index.html). Admittedly, corporate capitalists of the early twentieth century wielded great power, but the power of transnational firms in the current era is immense. According to Anthony Giddens, 'half of the hundred largest economic units in the world today are nations; the other half are transnational corporations' (2000: 315).

Furthermore, global capitalism has had an uneven impact on different groups of people both within Canada and around the world. Media exposés of children sewing Nike soccer balls in Pakistani sweatshops for the equivalent of six cents an hour have brought worldwide attention to sweatshop abuses in the garment and sportswear industries. More hidden, says the Maquiladora Solidarity Network, are the teenage girls, often single mothers, who sew clothes in the maquiladora factories of Central America and Mexico for major North American retailers such as Wal-Mart, The Gap, and Northern Reflections (Maquiladora Solidarity Network, 2000). Some of these are 12- and 13-year-olds working illegally, while others, 15- and 16-year-olds, are legal employees. Both groups of young people, however, work 12–18-hour days, often without overtime, under unsafe conditions and in the face of physical, verbal, and sometimes sexual abuse.

It is no coincidence that many sweatshop employees are women, and of colour—people who have no choice but to endure these conditions in order to survive. Garment manufacturers in Central America's free-trade zones, Mexico's maquiladora factories, and Asia's export-processing zones say that they prefer to hire young girls and women because 'they have nimble fingers. Workers suspect that children and young people are hired because they are less likely to complain about illegal and unjust conditions. And more importantly, they are less likely to organize unions' (Maquiladora Solidarity Network, 2000). We are seeing the intensification of divisions of labour, globally, along the lines of class, sex, and race.

These developments, furthermore, have direct consequences for the organization of work, and for the collective power of working people in Canada. Many Canadians now work under the constant threat of company relocation to lower-cost areas. And this has resulted in a weakening of the political power of workers and their unions. In light of this threat, many people in Canada have agreed to concessions (that is, giving up past gains) such as pay cuts, loss of vacation pay, and unpaid overtime. In a study of clerical workers employed at a major telecommunications firm, Bonnie Fox and Pamela Sugiman (1999) found that top management relied on television monitors in the employee cafeteria to broadcast warnings that jobs would be lost if the workers did not make special efforts (including concessions) in the interest of the firm's survival. One employee explained, 'the axe is falling. People are afraid. . . . They'll do what they need to do to keep their jobs' (Fox and Sugiman, 1999: 79). In the long term, the lingering threat of job loss affects the standard of living in the country as a whole.

● **The Capitalist Economy: Where People Work**

Most of us contribute to the economy in one way or another. Just as the economy undergoes change throughout history, so does our relationship to work. With the expansion of some economic sectors and the contraction of others, our opportunities for certain kinds of jobs also change. Social scientists identify four major economic sectors in which people in this country find employment: primary and resource industries, manufacturing, the service sector, and social reproduction (see Table 12.2).

Primary Resource Industry

Years ago, most Canadians worked in primary (or resource) industry. It is likely that your grandparents or great-grandparents performed primary-sector work. Though not always for pay, **First Nations** people have had an important history in the resource industry (Knight, 1996). Work in the primary sector involves the extraction of natural resources from our environment. Primary-industry jobs may be found, for instance, in agricultural production (farming, skilled and unskilled agricultural labour), ranching, mining, forestry, hunting, and fishing.

Table 12.2   Employment by Industry and Sex, 2007

	Number Employed (000s)		
	Both Sexes	Men	Women
All industries	**16,866.4**	**8,888.9**	**7,977.5**
Goods-producing sector	*3,993.0*	*3,070.8*	*922.1*
Agriculture	337.2	233.0	104.2
Forestry, fishing, mining, oil and gas	339.3	277.1	62.2
Utilities	138.0	99.0	39.1
Construction	1,133.5	996.9	136.6
Manufacturing	2,044.9	1,464.8	580.1
Services-producing sector	*12,873.5*	*5,818.1*	*7,055.4*
Trade	2,682.4	1,357.6	1,324.8
Transportation and warehousing	822.8	625.6	197.2
Finance, insurance, real estate, and leasing	1,060.4	442.1	618.3
Professional, scientific, and technical services	1,136.9	657.0	479.9
Business, building, and other support services[1]	702.1	379.0	323.1
Educational services	1,183.2	414.0	769.1
Health care and social assistance	1,846.1	322.2	1,523.9
Information, culture, and recreation	782.0	412.5	369.5
Accommodation and food services	1,069.4	433.9	635.5
Other services	723.5	343.1	380.4
Public administration	864.6	431.0	433.5

1. Formerly Management of companies, administrative and other support services.
Source: Statistics Canada, CANSIM, table (for fee) 282-0008. http://www40.statcan.gc.ca/l01/cst01/labor10a-eng.htm.

Throughout the eighteenth and nineteenth centuries, the primary sector represented the largest growth area in Canada. However, in the twentieth century, it began to experience a dramatic decline. Many forces have contributed to its contraction, notably the demise of small family farms and small independent fishing businesses, along with a corresponding rise in corporate farming (or 'agribusiness') and large fishing enterprises. These developments have resulted in dwindling opportunities for many people. Moreover, because of the geographic concentration of primary-sector jobs, this decline has devastated some towns (for example, Elliot Lake, Ontario) and entire regions (for example, Atlantic Canada).

Manufacturing

Into the twentieth century, growing numbers of Canadians began to work in the *manufacturing* (or *secondary*)

sector. Manufacturing work involves the processing of raw materials into usable goods and services. If you make your living assembling vans, knitting socks, packing tuna, or piecing together the parts of Barbie dolls, you are employed in manufacturing. Though the popular image of a manufacturing employee is a blue-collar male, the industry's workforce now reveals much more diversity along the lines of sex, as well as race and ethnicity.

On the whole, the manufacturing sector in Canada has experienced a slower decline than primary industry. The decline in manufacturing began in the early 1950s. In 1951, manufacturing represented 26.5 per cent of employment in Canada, but by 1995, the employment share of manufacturing had been cut nearly in half, to 15.2 per cent (Jackson and Robinson, 2000: 11). The industry nonetheless continues to be an important employer of Canadians. Job losses in manufacturing are largely attributable to technological change and the relocation of work to various low-wage sectors in Mexico, parts of Asia, and the southern United States.

The Service Sector

In *The End of Work* (1995), Jeremy Rifkin wrote about the relationship between job loss and technological change. Rifkin predicted that technological innovation would result in the loss of a great many jobs (except for an elite group of knowledge workers such as computer technicians and scientists) and would thus constitute an end to work. For various reasons, Rifkin's predictions have not come true. First, many employers prefer to hire dirt-cheap human labour rather than purchase expensive machines. Second, unions have exerted some power in resisting the wholesale implementation of technological change. And third, a massive number of new jobs have been created in the rapidly expanding service (or tertiary) sector. Study after study demonstrates that employees who lost jobs in manufacturing have been absorbed by the service industry. Indeed, many of you are no doubt currently employed in part-time or temporary service jobs. If so, you are not unlike many Canadians.

In recent years, the service sector has expanded dramatically. Among the world's largest industrialized economies—Canada, France, the United States, and the United Kingdom—the percentage of employment in the service sectors now surpasses 70 per cent. In addition, in Germany and Japan, service-sector work constitutes between 67 and 69 per cent of total employment (http://www.business.nsw.gov.au/aboutnsw/labour/c20_employment_by_ind_sector.htm). The rise of the service industry has been linked to the development of a post-industrial, information-based economy and to the rise of a strong consumer culture. All of this has resulted in a growing need for people to work in information-processing and management, marketing, advertising, and servicing. In the course of a day, you will encounter dozens of service-sector employees. Airline reservation agents, taxi drivers, teachers and professors, daycare staff, bank employees, computer technicians, crossing guards, librarians, garbage collectors, and Starbucks baristas—all these are service workers.

The experience of service work is also qualitatively different from that of manufacturing. Much service employment involves not only the physical performance of a job, but also an emotional component. In the face of an intensely competitive market, how does a company vie for customers? Service. And service rests on a big smile and (artificially) personalized interactions. In *The Managed Heart* (1983), Arlie Hochschild explored the emotional work of flight attendants. According to Hochschild, emotional labour, typically performed by women, is potentially damaging to workers because it involves regulating one's emotional state, sometimes suppressing feelings and often inventing them.

Also problematic is the frequently tense relationship between workers and their bosses. Low-end service work is characterized by low-trust relationships. With the expectation that their workforces will have only weak loyalties to the company and its goals, managers attempt to control employees largely through close direction and surveillance (Tannock, 2001). It is now common practice for employers to use electronic equipment to monitor telephone conversations between employees and clients and to install video security cameras to keep an eye on retail clerks. Another form of surveillance, more common in the United States than Canada, is drug testing (through urinalysis) of prospective employees. Such testing is standard, for example, at Wal-Mart stores (Ehrenreich, 2002; Featherstone, 2004). But at the same time that such work is subject to routinization and close surveillance, it necessitates high levels of self-motivation and investment on the part of the workers. In consequence, the most common complaint among workers in low-end service jobs is a high level of stress (Tannock, 2001).

Social Reproduction

All the work we have discussed so far is conducted in what social scientists call the *sphere of production*. Production typically occurs in the public world of factory, office, school, and store. Moreover, it involves monetary exchange. The study of work in this country has largely been biased towards production. When we think of work and workers, who comes to mind? Steelworkers, garment workers, plumbers, secretaries, farmers, and lawyers. What is common to all of these occupations? They are all done in exchange for money—a wage, salary, or income.

However, in Canada as well as in other parts of the world, many people spend hours and hours each day doing work that is not officially recorded as part of the economy. This type of labour may be called **social reproduction**. Social reproduction involves a range of activities for which there is no direct economic exchange. Often, though not always, this work is performed within family households. Typically, it is done by women. We do not view as economic activity the hours women (and, less often, men) spend buying groceries; planning and cooking meals; washing dishes; washing and folding laundry; chauffeuring children; buying clothes; vacuuming, washing floors and sinks, and cleaning the toilet bowl; managing the household budget; caring for aging relatives; and supervising homework. The instrumental value of such activities has long been hidden. Rather than being viewed as work, they are deemed a labour of love (Luxton, 1980).

But what would happen if women and other family members no longer performed this labour? How would it get done? Equally important, who would pay for it? If capitalist employers or the state had to ensure that workforces got fed, clothed, nurtured, and counselled, what would be the cost? These kinds of questions perplex economists and social statisticians. Says economist Marilyn Waring, breast-feeding, for example, is 'a major reproductive activity carried out only by women, and this thoroughly confuses statisticians' and economists' production models. The reproduction of human life also seems conceptually beyond their rules of imputation. But bodies most certainly have market prices' (1996: 86). In the United States, the cost of reproducing another life through artificial insemination ranges from $1,800 for artificial insemination to $10,000 to over $30,000 for a surrogate mother to carry the child (en.wilkipedia.org/wilki/Surrogatemother). According to a Canadian estimate, if unpaid work were replaced for pay, it would be worth $275 billion to the Canadian economy (GPI Atlantic, n.d.).

The system of capitalism benefits tremendously from the performance of unpaid labour. Yet the unpaid services of housewives and other family members are not only excluded from traditional economic measures, for many years sociologists did not even consider them to be 'work'. This is perplexing insofar as such work is essential to basic human survival and to the quality of our lives.

The Informal Economy

Also hidden from official growth figures—as well as from the public conscience—is a wide range of economic activities that are not officially reported to the government. These activities make up the **informal** (or

underground) **economy**. Some are legal; others are not. They include, for example, babysitting, cleaning homes, sewing clothes, peddling watches, playing music on the streets, gambling, and dealing drugs. As you make your way through the downtown areas of most major cities in Canada and the United States and almost anywhere in the developing world, you will see people of all ages trying to eke out a living in the informal sector.

Of course, we do not know the precise size of the underground economy. We have only estimates of its share of officially recognized economies and see much variation across the globe. According to the International Labour Organization, (ILO), in developing countries as a whole, the informal economy has been estimated to involve one-half to three-quarters of the non-agricultural labour force. In North Africa, it represents 48 per cent of employment; 51 per cent in Latin America, 65 per cent in Asia, and 72 per cent in sub-Saharan Africa. Furthermore, in the developing world, informal employment is generally a larger source of employment for women than for men. For example, in sub-Saharan Africa, 84 per cent of female non-agricultural workers are active in the informal economy compared to 63 per cent of male agricultural workers; in Latin America, these informal workers' statistics are 58 per cent for women and 48 per cent for men; and in Asia, the proportion of women and men in the non-agricultural informal economy is roughly equivalent (International Labour Association, 2002).

Informal economies have flourished for a long time in most nations, but this sector has been growing in importance, largely because of economic hardship related to restructuring, globalization, and their effects of dislocation and forced migration. Increasingly, people are turning to 'hidden work' in order to survive in the midst of contracting opportunities in the formal economy. It has become a safety net of sorts for the poorest groups in society. Without doubt, workers in this sector have had to be enterprising. Some are highly motivated and possess valuable skills; others lack formally recognized credentials. Unfortunately, most people who rely on the informal economy for a living face precarious, unstable 'careers' in unregulated environments.

▪▪ Time to Reflect ▪▪▪▪▪▪▪▪▪▪▪▪▪▪▪▪▪▪▪▪▪

What is the difference between social reproduction and the informal economy? Do these concepts overlap? Are there more similarities than differences?

● Managerial ● ● ● ● ● ● Strategies of Control

Scientific Management

To assess the new world of work, it is important first to understand the old one. So, let us go back in time. Since the days when Marx observed the rise of the factory system, capitalist goals of efficiency and profit-making have shaped the organization of work. Writing in the nineteenth century, Marx declared that work should be a central source of meaning and satisfaction in a person's life. In his words, 'the exercise of **labour power**, labour, is the worker's own life-activity, the manifestation of his own life' (cited in Rinehart, 2001: 13). But he noted that for most labouring people, work had lost meaning and creativity. Under capitalism, the worker 'works in order to live. . . . Life begins for him where this activity ceases' (cited in Rinehart, 2001: 3).

By the early twentieth century, with the spread of mass production, much work (most notably in manufacturing) was being further divided into ever more unconnected and meaningless parts. The twentieth century witnessed the large-scale implementation of so-called **scientific management**, one of the most influential and long-lasting managerial strategies. Scientific management was a method of organizing work and controlling workers introduced by American engineer Frederick Winslow Taylor; scientific management is also referred to as *Taylorism*.

Taylor applied the principles of 'science', or efficiency, to the human performance of labour. On the basis of his close observations of workers performing their jobs, he broke work processes down into simple tasks, each of which could be timed and organized into formal rules and standardized procedures. Taylor believed that once the work was subdivided, workers did not need to understand the entire process of production. Scientific management, in this sense, resulted in the separation of mental and manual labour, the conception of work from its execution. In short, it contributed to the deskilling of the worker.

Also in the twentieth century, Henry Ford, founder of the Ford Motor Car Company, applied the principles of scientific management (in tandem with the bureaucratic organization of work) to mass production of the automobile. Even if you have never stepped foot in an auto-manufacturing plant or other mass production facility, you are probably familiar with the assembly line. Richard Edwards (1979) called the moving assembly line an example of *technical control*. Technical control refers to the control of a workforce not directly by supervision (for example, by a foreperson), but indirectly by a machine.

While early researchers highlighted the application of Taylorism to manufacturing, this principle is now applied to many different types of work. In one form or other, scientific management has been implemented in offices (Lowe, 1987), schools, hospitals, and restaurants. Esther Reiter (1991) describes how the fast-food industry has carefully broken down the process of serving a burger from laying down the buns to evenly spreading the ketchup to distributing precisely half an ounce of onions. The total preparation time for a Burger King Whopper is 23 seconds—no more, no less.

Though efficient and 'rational', critics have argued that work broken down into simple parts results in degradation and dehumanization (Braverman, 1974). The minutest opportunities for individual decision-making and judgment are subverted. Marx introduced the concept of 'alienation' to describe the consequences for working people. **Alienation** is a structural condition of powerlessness that is rooted in a worker's relationship to the means of production. Insofar as workers have little or no control over their labour, work is no longer a source of fulfillment. According to Marx, under these conditions, workers become estranged from the products of their labour, from the work process itself, from each other, and from themselves (Rinehart, 2001).

Faced with the problem of alienated workforces, some employers have attempted to motivate workers with financial incentives. In the 1930s, Henry Ford introduced the 'Five Dollar Day'. In that era, five dollars constituted a relatively high rate of pay that would supposedly cover the living costs of not only the male autoworker but also his (dependent) wife and children. Decades later, J.H. Goldthorpe and colleagues' study of workers' orientations to work (1969) further supported the view that some people have an instrumental relationship to work. In this view, people can be compensated for meaningless work. Work can be a means to an end rather than an end in itself.

Two central problems contend against the assumption that money makes up for the meaninglessness of work. First, only a minority of employers do in fact compensate their employees for performing degraded and dehumanized work. In the popular media, we hear stories about $30 hourly wage rates for auto and steelworkers. But we must keep in mind that Ford, GM, and Stelco workers represent the privileged of the working class. The fact is that most employers are not willing to pay high wages—though they can be forced to do so, under the pressure of strong unions such as the Canadian Auto

HUMAN DIVERSITY
Offshore Migrant Farm Workers: A New Form of Slavery?

What does slavery have to do with a free and democratic country like Canada? Slavery did exist in the eighteenth and early nineteenth centuries in Canada, and some people think that there are groups of people who continue to work in this country under conditions that bear a strong resemblance to slavery. Slavery involves the ownership of one person by another, and is a form of unfree labour. Unfree labour refers to working arrangements where individuals are not allowed to freely circulate in the labour market and where they face political and/or legal constraints regarding where, and how, they work.

Most people in Canada work as 'free labourers'. This does not mean that they work for free, but rather that they are free to choose whom they work for. They can also decide where they want to live, what they eat and drink, and what they do in their leisure time. As a result, if they do not get along with their employer, or feel that they are underpaid and would be better off financially in another job, there is nothing stopping them from quitting and finding a new job. In other words, most Canadians are free workers because they are able to circulate in the labour market and do not face political or legal constraints in shaping their decisions about where to work.

Who, if anyone, are the new slaves in Canada? While they are not really slaves in the classical sense of the term, the 16,000 workers who come to Canada every year from the Caribbean and Mexico to work in Canadian agriculture are a form of unfree labour. Slavery may be too strong a term to describe who they are, but their condition of unfreedom does bear a strong resemblance to slavery.

What makes these workers different from other Canadians, and from immigrants who come here to build better lives for themselves? Migrant workers from the Caribbean and Mexico come to Canada under labour contracts. These contracts specify how long they can remain in the country and the conditions under which they must work. Workers are allowed to stay in Canada for between three and eight months every year. When their contracts expire, or if they breach one of the terms of their contracts, they are expected to leave the country. Workers pay for a portion of their transportation, and must pay their employers back to help them cover the costs of accommodation. In some cases, workers bunk five or six to a room and live in hot, overcrowded conditions. However, the main reason why they are considered to be unfree labourers stems from their inability to quit or change jobs in Canada without the permission of their employer and a representative of the federal government. If they do quit their jobs with a Canadian employer without permission, they are subject to deportation from the country.

Why does this condition of unfreedom matter? After all, some people think that compared to where they come from, migrant workers have it good here. They invariably make more money here than they would have back home so they should be grateful for the opportunity to come here to work, even if it is only temporarily. Even though no one is forcing them to sign a labour contract and come to Canada to work, it does matter that they are a form of unfree labour. Their lack of choice when it comes to whom they work for and their inability to vote with their feet and find better-paying jobs in other sectors of the Canadian economy mean that farm employers have a tremendous amount of power over migrant workers. In many cases, workers are fearful of saying 'no' when they are asked to do jobs that are dangerous and might harm their health. And employers who have a captive labour force do not have market incentives to improve wages or working conditions.

Some church groups in places where migrant workers live, support groups, and labour unions like the United Food and Commercial Workers Union are organizing to try to help improve the wages and working conditions of these unfree migrant workers.

Source: Vic Satzewich, McMaster University. Reprinted by permission of the author.

Workers and the United Steelworkers of America. Consequently, the majority of people do not receive high monetary compensation. Most Canadians perform boring jobs and are not paid handsomely for doing so.

Second, this view overlooks the importance of workers' needs for *intrinsic satisfaction*—the need of human beings to find meaning in the work that they perform. As stated, whether they are Supreme Court judges, car assemblers, letter carriers, caretakers, or retail clerks, people need to find meaning in the work that they perform day in and day out. We have a basic human need for respect and dignity at work (Hodson, 2001). This holds true whether you are a man or woman, Canadian-born or a recent immigrant or a migrant labourer, in middle age or youth, in a part-time job or a career.

The Early Human Relations School

In the 1930s, social psychologists and managerial consultants began to recognize this basic human need. In a series of experiments at the Western Electric Company's Hawthorne plant in Chicago, an industrial psychologist named Elton Mayo discovered that attention to workers resulted in a significant improvement in their productivity. The Hawthorne studies played an important role in spawning a new school of management thought known as the **human relations** approach. The basic idea on which the human relations approach rests is that if managers want productive, motivated workers, they should recognize workers' social needs.

In contemporary workplaces, many early human relations principles are embedded in an array of organizational initiatives such as 'human resource management', 'total quality management', and 'quality of work life' programs. Employee-of-the-week schemes, employee suggestion boxes, quality circles, and job enrichment all reflect such managerial methods. All of these schemes highlight employee motivation by promoting a discourse of co-operation (rather than of conflict) between managers and workers, with the belief that happy workers are better workers.

A fundamental problem with the human relations approach to managing, however, is that such programs do not constitute real workplace democracy. Under such schemes, employers often create the illusion that workers are important and respected, their ideas valued and rewarded, but there is no real redistribution of power and control. Over time, employees begin to recognize the limits of their involvement. Moreover, some research has demonstrated that workers' suggestions for organizing work may backfire against them, resulting in layoffs

for some and in the further rationalization of the work process for those who remain (Robertson et al., 1993).

● The Social ● ● ● ● ● ● Organization of Work Today

Revolutionary New Technology

Today, popular writers and scholars alike are talking about the emergence of a new world of work, one that is rooted in a 'knowledge society'—a world that offers opportunity, an increase in leisure time, an experience of work that is far more positive than in the past. Are these assertions founded? Do people now have better jobs than their parents and grandparents? Have we rid the economy of many of the low-paying, dead-end, and routine jobs that characterized the past? In short, has work been transformed?

According to Daniel Bell (1973), the answer to these questions is 'Yes'. In *Post-Industrial Society*, Bell argues that we are now living in a post-industrial era, a new information economy, one based on the use of sophisticated microelectronic technology. With the decline of Taylorized manufacturing jobs and the rise of knowledge work, argues Bell, people are becoming highly skilled and jobs are becoming intrinsically rewarding.

Admittedly, most people agree that the new technology may eliminate routine, repetitive tasks, thereby freeing people to perform more challenging work. Think, for example, about preparing a research paper without a computer, printer, and access to the Internet. Moreover, the technology has had a positive impact on job creation. In fact, in Canada, information technology has created more jobs than it has eliminated. In a comparison of firms that relied extensively on sophisticated information technology with other, low-tech firms, the Conference Board of Canada found that the former produced more jobs than the latter (Lowe, 2000).

Notwithstanding these findings, some sociologists argue that, at the same time, the technology has created new forms of inequality and exacerbated old ones. While it has resulted in new, more challenging jobs for some people, many others have lost their jobs (or skills) as a result of technological change in the workplace. In the **service economy**, for instance, employers have relied extensively on computers and the new microelectronics to streamline work processes. In banking, many of the decisions (such as approving a bank loan) that used to be made at the discretion of people are now computer governed. And the introduction of automated bank machines has made redundant the work of thousands of tellers. As well, in various industries, computers have taken over the supervisory function of employee surveillance. With state-of-the-art computer equipment, and without the direct intervention of a supervisor, firms can now effectively enforce productivity quotas and monitor workers, especially those who perform highly routine tasks (Fox and Sugiman, 1999).

Another problem is that the technology is rapidly changing. Competence with the technology thus necessitates continually learning new skills and making ongoing investments in training. Often workers themselves assume the costs of such training. In the past, says Graham Lowe, employment was based on an implicit understanding of loyalty in exchange for job security; today, this idea has been replaced with a system based on 'individual initiative and merit'. Workers who go above and beyond, who contribute what managers sometimes call 'value added', who hone their skills—these are the workers who will be recognized and rewarded (Lowe, 2000: 61).

Moreover, opportunities for extra job-related training are unequal. Not surprisingly, they are closely linked to an employee's income and level of education. Lowe notes that only 3 in 10 Canadian workers annually receive training related to their present or future employment (Lowe, 2000: 65). University graduates are twice as likely as high school graduates to be involved in such training. One in five workers who earns less than $15,000 participates in training, compared to half of those earning in excess of $75,000.

Flexible Work

Alongside information technology, some writers are extolling the benefits of related innovations in management methods. In business circles today, one hears buzzwords such as 'workplace restructuring', 'downsizing', and 'lean production'. All of these concepts are part of a relatively new managerial approach called flexibility. Flexibility (most often in tandem with technological innovation) has, as they say, 'held out the hand of promise'. It has been promoted as an improvement over the old human relations approach and an alternative to the Taylorist and Fordist methods that have long stripped workers of control and dignity (Sennett, 1998). Critics, on the other hand, say differently. Smart, young managers trained in the postmodern language of flexibility may introduce seemingly new forms of managing and organizing work and adapt them to an increasingly com-

petitive and precarious global context, but on close inspection, they claim, such strategies are firmly grounded in earlier approaches.

Most contemporary flexibility strategies are based on one or a combination of two approaches: *numerical flexibility* and *flexible specialization* (also called *functional flexibility*). Numerical flexibility involves shrinking or eliminating the core workforce (in continuous jobs, and full-time positions) and replacing them with workers in *non-standard* (or *contingent*) *employment*. Non-standard work is a term used to describe various employment arrangements such as part-time work, temporary (seasonal and other part-year) work, contracting out or outsourcing (work that was previously done in-house), and self-employment. Non-standard work is, in short, based on an employment relationship that is far more tenuous than those of the past (Jackson and Robinson, 2000; Vosko, 2000, 2003).

When you hear about non-standard work, what comes to mind? If you are like most Canadians, you think of jobs in the fast-food or retail industries—'McJobs'. But in the current economy, non-standard work arrangements now characterize most spheres of employment. We need look no further than the university or college, for example, to see the employment of people in non-standard jobs. In these institutions of higher learning, you may discover that many of your courses are taught by part-time or sessional instructors, some of whom hold PhDs, others of whom are graduate students. These individuals are paid by the university to teach on a course-by-course or session-by-session basis. Sessional or part-time instructors typically do not work on a full-time basis, and they seldom receive assurances of stable employment.

According to the Economic Council of Canada, non-standard labour represents the fastest growing type of employment in this country (Duffy et al., 1997: 53). While six per cent of all employed persons worked part-time (fewer than 30 hours per week) in 1975, that proportion had risen to over 18 per cent by 1997 (Nelson and Robinson, 2002: 239). Today, non-standard work represents over one-third of all jobs. Though this form of employment may be found in all industries, non-standard workers are most likely to be found in the primary and utilities industries, accommodation and food services, and construction or trades (Statistics Canada, 2004c).

Many writers have cogently argued that the growth of non-standard work is closely linked to the corporate goals of flexibility and global restructuring (Harvey, 1989). Not unlike the 'reserve army of labour' described by Karl Marx, non-standard employees provide owners and managers with a ready supply of labour to 'hire and fire' as the market demands. Employers invest minimally in these workers and offer them only a limited commitment. In order to remain competitive in the global market, it is argued, corporations must reduce labour costs through downsizing, that is, laying off permanent, full-time workers and replacing them with part-time, temporary, and contract labour (Vosko, 2000).

Yet, unyielding market forces notwithstanding, there is also evidence that 'precarious jobs have become the norm much faster in some countries than in others' (Jackson and Robinson, 2000: 50). For example, in the United States, non-standard work grew quickly in the 1980s, but in comparison to Canada, in the 1990s, its growth has been limited by low unemployment. Moreover, in much of Europe, unions and employment laws have (until recently) limited the growth of contract work and substandard part-time work. In the Netherlands, a country known for having one of the most flexible labour markets in continental Europe, part-timers receive equal wages and benefits with full-time employees, and contract workers must be given a permanent job within a specified time period (Jackson and Robinson, 2000).

Another offshoot of the increasingly precarious relationship between employers and workers is the growth in self-employment. In the 1990s, one driving force behind self-employment was the move of large firms and governments to contract out work that formerly had been performed in-house by a core workforce (Jackson and Robinson, 2000). In fact, throughout the 1990s, growth in self-employment was a leading labour market trend. In 1998, self-employed individuals accounted for 18 per cent of all employment in Canada, and between 1989 and 1997, self-employment constituted about 80 per cent of all job growth (Lowe, 2000; see also http://www40.statcan.gc.ca/101/cst01/labor64-eng.htm).

Contrary to romantic images of the self-employed as benefiting from flexible work schedules, autonomy, and economic success, research indicates that they are not always better off than their waged or salaried counterparts. Most self-employed people work alone, often in small enterprises. Only a minority run companies that employ others (Lowe, 2000). Furthermore, they tend to work excessively long hours and, on average, accrue about the same earnings as regular employees. In addition, gender-based pay differentials are more pronounced among the self-employed, and work is highly polarized. In other words, recent growth in self-employment has been especially strong at the top of the job hierarchy (for example, among engineers and accountants) and at the bottom (for instance, among domestic cleaners and salespeople).

Part-time and temporary workers tend to be women and young people, though not exclusively (see Table 12.3). Because of these demographics, people assume that the casual employment relationship is not problematic; indeed, some believe it to be desirable. Admittedly, there are individuals who choose non-standard work in the hope that it will offer heightened flexibility to facilitate the competing demands of job and family or job and school. Yet, many other people accept these employment terms on an involuntary basis, largely because they have no alternatives. Moreover, studies suggest that many non-standard work arrangements do not in fact provide employees with greater flexibility (Vosko, 2000) or that they offer flexibility only to favoured employees (Sennett, 1998).

Furthermore, non-standard workers as a whole receive relatively low wages and few benefits. Consequently, many people who rely on this type of work must resort to holding multiple jobs in an effort to make ends meet. People carve out a living by stringing together a host of low-paying, part-time, and temporary jobs. Often this involves moonlighting or doing shift work, situations that no doubt put added strain on families.

Interestingly, along with the expansion of the non-standard workforce, there has been an increase in overtime work for full-time employees. And while there has been a significant rise in overtime hours for both sexes, men are especially likely to work beyond the standard 40-hour week. As well, the lengthening of the work day has been more pronounced among managers than among employees. And on the whole, more of this overtime is unpaid. Paid overtime tends to be concentrated in unionized workplaces and in blue-collar manufacturing and construction jobs (Jackson and Robinson, 2000). Unpaid overtime, in comparison, is more marked in the female-dominated public sector such as in teaching and social work (suggesting that women are more likely to put in overtime without pay), as well as among managers and professionals.

There are many reasons for the recent increase in overtime work. First, as a result of downsizing and restructuring, people simply must put in longer hours to get the job done. Say Andrew Jackson and David Robinson, 'the survivors have to pick up the work of those who have left as a result of layoffs or early retirement' (2000: 86). Fear of future job loss is also a potent factor behind putting in extra hours. In a 'survival-of-the-fittest' corporate culture, long hours are viewed as evidence of effort and commitment. Undoubtedly, many workers also internalize the ethic of doing more with less, particularly those who are serving the public and helping to make up

Table 12.3 Full-time and Part-time Employment by Sex and Age Group, 2002–2007 (000s)

	2002	2003	2004	2005	2006	2007
Both sexes						
Total	15,310.4	15,672.3	15,947.0	16,169.7	16,484.3	16,866.4
15–24 years	2,399.1	2,449.4	2,461.0	2,472.5	2,535.8	2,589.4
25–44 years	7,575.6	7,571.5	7,594.0	7,597.5	7,610.7	7,658.9
45 years and over	5,335.7	5,651.4	5,892.0	6,099.7	6,337.8	6,618.2
Full-time	12,439.3	12,705.3	12,998.1	13,206.2	13,509.7	13,803.1
15–24 years	1,323.1	1,344.3	1,361.4	1,370.2	1,419.8	1,435.1
25–44 years	6,627.0	6,624.7	6,671.2	6,684.7	6,730.9	6,774.4
45 years and over	4,489.1	4,736.3	4,965.5	5,151.3	5,359.0	5,593.6
Part-time	2,871.1	2,967.0	2,948.9	2,963.5	2,974.7	3,063.3
15–24 years	1,076.0	1,105.1	1,099.6	1,102.3	1,116.0	1,154.3
25–44 years	948.5	946.8	922.8	912.8	879.9	884.5
45 years and over	846.6	915.0	926.5	948.4	978.8	1,024.5
Men						
Full-time	7,287.9	7,423.0	7,559.3	7,664.0	7,781.0	7,909.9
15–24 years	763.9	774.9	781.2	782.5	809.2	828.5
25–44 years	3,831.1	3,832.2	3,834.1	3,832.6	3,845.6	3,840.2
45 years and over	2,692.9	2,815.9	2,944.1	3,048.9	3,126.2	3,241.3
Part-time	896.5	925.0	921.3	930.7	946.1	979.0
15–24 years	460.4	468.3	467.1	456.5	467.7	484.8
25–44 years	197.4	196.9	189.8	199.5	189.7	192.5
45 years and over	238.8	259.8	264.4	274.7	288.7	301.7
Women						
Full-time	5,151.4	5,282.3	5,438.8	5,542.3	5,728.7	5,893.2
15–24 years	559.2	569.4	580.2	587.8	610.5	606.6
25–44 years	2,796.0	2,792.5	2,837.2	2,852.1	2,885.3	2,934.2
45 years and over	1,796.2	1,920.4	2,021.4	2,102.4	2,232.8	2,352.4
Part-time	1,974.6	2,041.9	2,027.6	2,032.8	2,028.5	2,084.3
15–24 years	615.6	636.8	632.4	645.8	648.4	669.5
25–44 years	751.2	749.9	733.0	713.3	690.1	692.0
45 years and over	607.8	655.2	662.1	673.7	690.0	722.8

Source: Statistics Canada, at: <www40.statcan.ca/l01/cst01/labor12.htm>.

for cuts through unpaid work. In short, in the face of general labour market uncertainty, many core employees feel pressured to work overtime, whether or not they so desire. As a result, we now have, 'side by side, underemployment and overemployment, with high levels of insecurity and stress on all sides' (Duffy et al., 1997: 57).

In light of these trends, for most Canadians, the concept of a career is a remnant of the past. The gold watch for 50 years of continuous service to the same company is not attainable in the new workplace sce-

nario. Says Richard Sennett, 'flexibility today brings back this arcane sense of the job, as people do lumps of labor, pieces of work, over the course of a lifetime' (1998: 9). Living in this era of economic uncertainty, with the attendant worry about layoffs and job loss, is, not surprisingly, a major source of stress for people in Canada (Jackson and Robinson, 2000).

Another component of the new flexibility is **flexible specialization** (or *functional flexibility*, often called *flex spec*). Flexible specialization involves multi-skilling, job rotation, the organization of workers into teams, and the concentration of power—without the centralization of power. Flexible specialization has been called the antithesis of the system of production embodied in Fordism (Sennett, 1998). Under the new system, the old auto assembly line has been replaced by 'islands of specialized production'. These new work units, or *islands*, allow businesses to respond quickly to fluctuations in market demand, especially in industries such as fashion and textiles where there is a short product life.

Typically, flex spec is also accompanied by a goal of co-operation and flexible arrangements between labour and management rather than adversarial relations based on strict contractual agreements. Where Taylorist management strategies have rationalized production by eliminating the need for workers to make decisions, a flex-spec organization attempts to eliminate 'waste' by employing workers' knowledge of their jobs in the rationalization process. Working in teams, employees are given responsibility for scheduling, planning the work, rotating workers among jobs, and meeting quotas (Fox and Sugiman, 1999). By increasing workers' responsibility, team organi-

zation diminishes the need for supervision—although it provides employees with no added authority.

Finally, information technology has been an integral component of flexibility strategies. Flexible specialization is suited to high technology: 'Thanks to the computer, industrial machines are easy to reprogram and configure. The speed of modern communications also has favoured flexible specialization, by making global market data instantly available to a company' (Sennett, 1998: 52). Unlike the earlier mechanization, the new telecommunications technology enables employers to relocate work easily from one site to another, thereby scattering workforces to various parts of the country, continent, or world. As a result of teleworking, you can make a hotel reservation or check your credit level from Picton, Ontario, and be speaking to a reservation agent or debt collector in Tennessee. Likewise, with the availability of portable computers, fax machines, cell phones, Blackberries, and other Internet connections, some people may simply do their work from home rather than in an office or factory. Work can now follow people home.

When you next order a pizza, complain about the non-arrival of a package, or report a lost credit card, you may find yourself talking to someone in India—thanks to the globalization of work and the export of Canadian jobs. Amit Bhargava/Corbis

Flexibility for Whom?

We may now point to a polarization of jobs. At one end of the spectrum are the good jobs, at the other the bad. There is no bulging middle. There has, in other words, been a widening of inequalities. Good jobs offer decent pay and intrinsic rewards (fulfillment, autonomy, the opportunity to exercise knowledge and acquire skill). But while the new information society has created some good jobs, these are not held by all, or even most, people in this country. And whether they work in the primary, manufacturing, or service economy, as manual labourers or as professionals, people are facing increasing uncertainty in the labour market.

Downsizing, the resulting increase in non-standard employment, and the **globalization of work** have all contributed to this uncertainty. Says Sennett, 'What's peculiar about uncertainty today is that it exists without any looming historical disaster; instead it is woven into the everyday practices of a vigorous capitalism. Instability is meant to be normal' (1998: 31).

● The Changing ● ● ● ● ● Face of Labour: Diversity among Workers

Just as places of work have changed dramatically over time, so too has the workforce. Workplaces today, whether they are offices, factories, hospitals, or classrooms, are becoming increasingly diverse. Only a minority of families rely on a single paycheque. First Nations people make up a growing proportion of the paid labour force in certain geographic areas. People of colour, some of whom are immigrants to this country, many Canadian-born, currently have a stronger-than-ever presence, particularly in big cities such as Vancouver, Toronto, and Montreal. As well, the workforce has become more highly educated and younger. As a result of these changes, students of work must turn their attention to some pressing new problems.

Gendered Work

The participation of women in the paid labour force has increased steadily over the past four decades. In Canada today, women constitute approximately 47 per cent of the labour force (see http://www.statscan.ca/Daily/English/060615/d060615c.htm). Most striking has been a rise in the employment rates of married women and mothers of children under the age of six. Recent census data indicate that the two-breadwinner (also called *dual-earner*) family is now the norm.

Decades—indeed, over a century—of struggle and activism by feminists have resulted in important gains. Paid work is one arena in which these gains have been most prominent. In Canada, we now have employment equity legislation (albeit limited) in the federal government and laws enforcing equal pay for work of equal value. It is important to remember, though, that many of these breakthroughs are relatively recent. Into the 1950s, companies and governments still restricted the employment of married women, overtly defined work as 'female' and 'male', and upheld gender-based seniority systems (Sugiman, 1994).

Today, many young women and men entering the labour force are unaware of the blatant sexual inequalities of the past. Whether or not they self-identify as feminists, women today are building their careers on a feminist foundation. If not for the challenges posed by women's rights activists, university lecture halls would be filled exclusively by men, women would not be permitted entry into the professions or management, and paid employment would simply not be an option after marriage.

But just as women's historical breakthroughs are instructive, so, too, are the persisting inequalities. In spite of a dramatic increase in female labour-force participation, women and men are by no means equal in the labour market. The **social institution** of work is still very much a gendered one. It is important that women have made inroads in non-traditional fields of manual labour, the professions, and management and administration, but the majority of women remain concentrated in female-dominated occupations such as retail salesperson, secretary, cashier, registered nurse, elementary school teacher, babysitter, and receptionist, while men are more commonly truck drivers, janitors, farmers, motor vehicle mechanics, and construction trade helpers, for example. Particularly troubling is the finding that Canadian women who have completed university or community college are three times more likely than their male counterparts (24 per cent and 8 per cent, respectively) to move into a clerical or service job (Nelson and Robinson, 2002: 226). To the extent that occupational segregation by sex has lessened somewhat over time, it is more because of the entry of men into female-dominated occupations than the reverse.

As well, women (as well as youth of both sexes) are more likely than men to be employed on a part-time and temporary basis. For years now, women have made up approximately 70 per cent of the part-time workforce in Canada. And while the majority of the self-employed are men, the 1990s witnessed a rapid growth in women's self-employment. In comparing the sexes, we also see that self-employed men are more likely than self-employed women to hire others—male employers outnumbered females three to one—and that businesses operated by men are more likely to be in the goods sector whereas female-run businesses are likely to be in the less lucrative service sector (Nelson and Robinson, 2002: 242).

These trends—labour market segregation by sex and the overrepresentation of women in precarious employment—have contributed to gender-based differences in earnings. While the pay gap between women and men employed full-time and full-year has narrowed over time, on average, women still earn less than men even when we take into account, occupation, age, and education. Furthermore, the narrowing of this wage gap was largely the result of an increase in time worked for women and of falling or stagnant wages for men, with only a modest increase in women's earnings. In addition to this, gender-based earnings differentials may, to a large degree, be attributed to women's concentration in part-time and temporary work. When we compare women employed on a full-time basis with their male counterparts, the gap narrows—though, as noted above, it does not disappear. Currently, a woman employed full-time earns 72.5 cents for every dollar earned by a man (http//www.statcan.ca/english/freepub/75-001-XIE/01201/ar_ar_200112_01_a.htm.).

All women are not, of course, in the same position. Immigrant women, women of colour, and Aboriginal women bear the brunt of income and occupational polarization by sex. In consequence, their average annual earnings are disproportionately low. In her research on various categories of women, Monica Boyd (1999) concludes that earnings differentials increase between Canadian-born women and foreign-born women, especially when members of the latter group are of colour and when they are not fluent in English or French. In addition, foreign-born women who are currently residents of Canada are more likely than Canadian-born women to be employed in particular segments of the service sector—namely, those that are typically labour-intensive, poorly paid, and dominated by small firms (Vosko, 2000). While men of colour are concentrated in either professional occupations or service jobs, women of colour are more likely than Canadian women as a whole to perform manual labour. Aboriginal women likewise are concentrated in service or clerical work (Aboriginal men are more likely to perform manual labour than other kinds of work).

Faced with multiple forms of **discrimination**, working-class women of colour and some female immigrants have come to occupy job ghettos. Indeed, many of the jobs that typically are performed by working-class people of colour have a 'hidden' quality: the work they do is not noticed; the workers are rendered invisible. All too often, we regard private domestic workers and nannies, hotel and office cleaners, taxi drivers, health-care aides, and dishwashers—all of whom perform indispensable labour—as simply part of the backdrop (Arat-Koç, 1990; Das Gupta, 1996). Not only are they physically out of sight (in basements, in kitchens, working at night when everyone else has gone), they are out of mind.

In documenting sex-based inequalities in employment, social scientists have produced reams of statistics. But there are many other ways in which we may speak of the gendering of work, some not easily quantifiable. Joan Acker (1990) writes about the process by which jobs and organizations come to be gendered, regardless of the sex of job-holders. The bureaucratic rules and procedures, hierarchies, and informal organizational culture may rest on a set of gender-biased assumptions, for example. In *Secretaries Talk* (1988), Rosemary Pringle highlights the ways in which gendered family relationships are reproduced in workplace relations between bosses (fathers) and secretaries (wives, mistresses, daughters). Pringle describes how male bosses determine the boundaries between home and work, public and private, whereas 'secretaries do not have this luxury. Male bosses go into their secretaries' offices unannounced, assume the right to pronounce on their clothes and appearance, have them doing housework and personal chores, expect overtime at short notice, and assume the right to ring them at home' (Pringle, 1988: 51).

There are many formal and informal mechanisms that prevent women from entering male-dominated occupations. Cynthia Cockburn (1983) explores the ways in which a culture of manhood became very much a part of the printing trade. For years, the link between masculine identities, masculine culture, and the printing trade was so strong that it made the occupation completely impenetrable to women. Sugiman (1994) describes how women attempted to carve out for themselves 'pockets of femininity' in the male-dominated auto plants of southern Ontario during World War II. By the war's end, however, women's presence was no longer welcome. Most were hastily dismissed from the industry.

Today, many young women plan to both have a professional career and raise a family, but they are not quite sure how they will combine the two. Feminist researchers have demonstrated how the very concept of 'career' is gendered, built on a masculine model. Career success depends on the assumption of a wife at home—a helper who will pick up the children from school, arrange dinner parties, and generally free the 'breadwinner' to work late at nights or on weekends and for out-of-town business travel.

Furthermore, feminist analysis has called attention to the complex link between paid and unpaid labour, employment and family. With two breadwinners, both of whom are spending increasing hours in their paid jobs, families are under enormous pressure (see Figure 12.1). While the demands of paid work have risen over time, so too have pressures on family life. Government restructuring and cutbacks in resources have affected public daycare, after-school programs, special needs programs, and care of the elderly and the disabled. Who picks up the slack? The family. One consequence has been an intensification of (unpaid) family work and growing tensions within families as people try to cope.

In a study of working-class families in Flin Flon, Manitoba, Meg Luxton (1980) introduced the concept of a *double day* of labour—the combination of paid and unpaid labour that must be performed in the course of a day. Usually, notes Luxton, this double burden is carried by women. Every day, millions of people put in a 'second shift' of unpaid labour after they get home from their paying jobs. According to Hochschild and Machung, (1989), this second shift amounts to one extra month of 24-hour days of work per year. Hochschild (1997) also speaks to the experiences of millions of North American families in her study of the 'time bind'. The time bind has resulted in overworked,

stressed people and in the downsizing and outsourcing of family responsibilities. Children are cranky, parents are rushed, and the concept of 'leisure' is laughable. Hochschild suggests that rather than leave families with the 'leftovers' of paid work, people should start challenging employers to more seriously consider the conflicting needs of family and employment.

Race and Racialized Work

The trends we have so far discussed (precarious work, heightened job insecurities, and underemployment) have had a disproportionate impact on groups who have long faced discrimination in the labour market and in society as a whole: women, people of colour, and indigenous people. But though we now have an abundance of research on the gendering of work, sociologists in Canada have paid far less attention to the relationship between race, citizenship, and employment.

Barriers faced by people of colour, by Aboriginal Canadians, and by some immigrant groups are most often demonstrated in unemployment and earnings disparities. Aboriginal peoples comprise only a tiny percentage of the working-age population, yet this group is growing rapidly and already constitutes a sizable share of the labour force in some cities (Jackson and Robinson, 2000: 70). **Unemployment rates** for Aboriginals are disturbingly high, more than double that for the Cana-

Figure 12.1 Measures of Time Scarcity

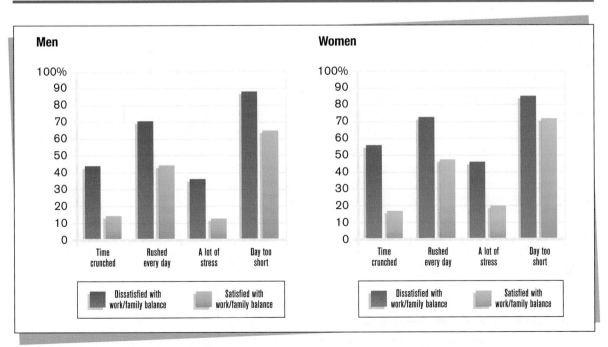

Source: Adapted from Statistics Canada, *General Social Survey*, 1998.

dian population as a whole (24 per cent for Aboriginal men and 22 per cent for Aboriginal women. In addition, over half of Aboriginals are in part-time employment—jobs that offer little security—and they are concentrated in marginalized sectors of the economy where they face low pay, seasonal jobs, and high levels of discrimination in hiring (see http://www12.statcan/english/census01/Products/Analytic/companion/abor/canada.cfm). Furthermore, the economic prospects for those who live on reserves are even more bleak. Close to half of the off-reserve Aboriginal population lives in poverty (Jackson and Robinson, 2000: 71).

The category 'people of colour' is quite diverse, containing significant differences according to class, education, and citizenship status. In Canada, about 1 in 10 workers is defined as being of colour (the official census term is 'visible minority' and excludes Aboriginal Canadians), and over 80 per cent of this group are relatively recent immigrants (Jackson and Robinson, 2000: 69). Today, immigrants of colour (compared to earlier generations of immigrants) are finding it extremely difficult to close the employment gap with native-born Canadians, as it is, more generally, for visible minorities in Canada (see Figure 12.2). In 2000, the average annual earnings of Canadian-

born workers of colour was $21,983, compared to $25,205 for immigrant workers of colour and $30,141 for other persons born in Canada (labourfutures.ca/Section%206.pdf). And these gaps persist even when we control for age and education. Typically, recent immigrants are younger than the labour force as a whole, but they also have more schooling. One problem is that foreign credentials are not always respected in Canada, thus contributing to a high concentration of immigrants of colour in low-wage jobs (Jackson and Robinson, 2000: 69–70).

Likewise, recent immigrants are far more likely to experience unemployment in their first five years in Canada as compared to migrants who have been in this country for longer. For example, in 2001, the unemployment rate among men aged 25–44 who arrived between 1996 and 2001 was 11 per cent. Among women it was even higher at 15.8 per cent. These statistics merit concern about whether certain immigrant groups are being constrained from converting relatively high human capital (such as a university education) and a desire to work, into strong economic performance and socio-economic mobility. Equally alarming is the finding that immigrants who arrived in this country in the latter part of the 1980s and through the 1990s, have faced an even greater earn-

Figure 12.2   Distribution of Annual Earnings, Visible Minorities and Non-Visible Minorities, 2001

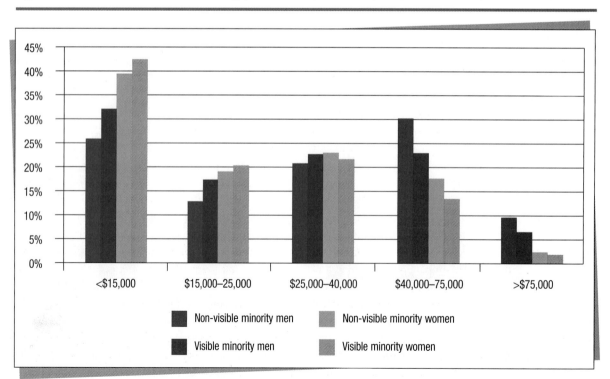

Source: Adapted from Statistics Canada, *Statistical Area Classification: Highlight Tables, 2001 Counts, For Canada, Provinces and Territories*, 2001 Census, Catalogue no. 97f0024, 27 Feb. 2004.

ings gap relative to native-born Canadians. Moreover, this gap has not rapidly closed as immigrants spend more time in this country (Ray, 2005).

It is not surprising, then, that many immigrants who reside in large cities such as Toronto, Montreal, and Vancouver experience high levels of poverty. While low-income rates among the Canadian-born generally dropped across the country, throughout the last decade low-income rates for people living in our major cities actually rose, as did the low-income rate for immigrants who have resided in Canada for fewer than 20 years (Ray, 2005).

Strong economic need also is experienced disproportionately by some groups of native-born Canadians. Roughly 45 per cent of black households in Canada, for example, live in poverty. Furthermore, there is evidence of race-based inequities in earnings. On the whole, people of colour earn about 15 per cent less than the total Canadian workforce (Jackson and Robinson, 2000: 70). And among this group, the pay gap is much greater for men than women (though we must consider that women generally have much lower earnings than men). These lower earnings are in part a result of this group's concentration in low-paying, relatively low-skilled jobs, their underrepresentation in skilled jobs, and their higher rates of unemployment.

Though telling, these statistics reveal only one dimension of the research on disadvantaged groups. It is equally important to recognize that because of racial and cultural differences, people experience the work world in distinct ways. In their study *Who Gets the Work*, Frances Henry and Effie Ginzberg (1985) found a striking incidence of discrimination directed at job seekers. For example, when whites and blacks with similar qualifications applied for entry-level positions that had been advertised in a newspaper, jobs were offered three times more often to whites than to black applicants. Similarly, of the job seekers who made inquiries by telephone, those who had accents (especially South Asian and Caribbean) were often quickly screened out by employers.

Furthermore, the role of the Canadian state historically in promoting or facilitating racialized work has been documented extensively (Schecter, 1998). Agnes Calliste (1993) notes that between 1950 and 1962, Canadian immigration authorities admitted limited numbers of Caribbean nurses, but under rules different from those for white immigrant nurses. Black nurses were expected to have nursing qualifications superior to those demanded of whites. Several scholars (Arat-Koç, 1990; Bakan and Stasiulis, 1994, 1995; Daenzer, 1993) have also discussed the role of the Canadian state in addressing the need for cheap child-care workers by importing women from the developing world (the Caribbean and the Philippines, in particular) to perform domestic labour, without granting them full citizenship rights.

Often, jobs and occupations come to be racialized (that is, to adopt a racial label) as a result of formal and informal barriers that prevent their holders from exiting (Calliste, 1993; Das Gupta, 1996). In a study of black workers in automotive foundries, Sugiman found that after years of intense discrimination, workers themselves may come to circumscribe their 'choices'. Over the course of many decades, most black men remained where they had started—in the foundry. In the words of one foundry worker, 'Their idea was, "well, the white man don't want you up there no how, so why . . . put yourself in a position where you know you're not wanted"' (Sugiman, 2001: 102).

Youth

In Canada today, youth (persons 15–24 years old) constitute a much smaller share of the population than in past years (Lowe, 2000: 110). Nevertheless, the youth labour market is expanding at a significant rate. Curiously, young people still receive relatively little attention in studies of work. But young people today are facing harsh economic conditions, with the youth unemployment rate roughly 50 per cent higher than that of the population as a whole. Throughout the 1990s, in Canada, the overall high unemployment rate, government deficit-cutting, public- and private-sector downsizing, and various other wage-reduction strategies resulted in a contracting job market. In consequence, large numbers of youth withdrew from the labour market, returning to school or staying in school for longer periods (Lowe, 2000: 109).

The research presents us with a woeful picture. Study after study suggests that young people are in important ways no different from the majority of Canadian workers. They want high-quality work—work that is interesting and challenging and that provides a sense of accomplishment (Lowe, 2000). And youth have been increasing their human capital to acquire such jobs. Notably, young people are acquiring more education. (While a university degree does not guarantee a job, young people are still better off if they have the formal credentials.) But while Canadian youth are better-schooled on the whole, they are also working less, and in jobs for which they feel that they are overqualified. Young people are most likely to be employed in low-paying service-sector jobs such as fast food restaurants, clothing stores, and grocery stores. For most students, contingent work is all that is available.

Some writers argue that the youth labour market makes a perfect accompaniment to the new goals of managerial flexibility. Employers invest in the belief that young people will have a limited commitment to the goals of the firm and that they expect to stay in jobs temporarily, as a stop-gap measure discontinuous with their adult careers and identities (Tannock, 2001). Stuart Tannock explains that youth themselves partially accept the popular **ideology** that positions them 'as a separate class of workers who deserve less than adult workers do. Good jobs are predominantly the privilege of adulthood. Young workers must be content at first to spend their time in a tier of lower-quality service and retail employment. Dreams of meaningful work must be deferred' (Tannock, 2001: 109). Many young people compare themselves not to other workers across the spectrum, but exclusively to other youth workers (Sennett, 1998). Consequently, youth are more pliable and passive. Also, because their jobs are viewed as transient, youth are not as likely to become unionized. All of these features render them an extremely exploitable source of labour.

But as Tannock points out, youth are not stop-gap workers simply because they are young: they are also stop-gap workers because of the poor conditions under which they have to labour—conditions that have been created by employers in the service sector. But despite the popular view that young people are not especially concerned about their conditions of work, there is now much evidence that points to the contrary: 'Teenagers and young adults working in these industries, who expect to have long lives ahead of them, worry that their jobs, which are supposed to be meaningless, stop-gap places of employment, will have lasting and detrimental effects on their bodies and future life activities' (2001: 54).

● Workers' Coping ● ● ● ● and Resistance: The Struggle for Dignity and Rights

Finding Meaning in Work

Regardless of the many differences among Canadian workers today, one point remains clear: most Canadians want work that is personally fulfilling (Lowe, 2000). People have a powerful desire to maintain dignity at work (Hodson, 2001). Some of us are fortunate to hold jobs that offer challenges, jobs in which we can exercise autonomy, and jobs from which we can reap fruitful economic rewards. But even the 'good jobs' are not

always meaningful. And there are many jobs that are rarely rewarding. How do people cope with their work?

Sociologists have found that no matter how meaningless the job, people seek meaning in their work. Sometimes this is done through the culture of the workplace. People who have boring, routine jobs, for example, may make a game out of their work, varying repetitions, altering pace and intensity, imagining the lives of customers. As well, the social component of work (peer relations) is frequently a source of pleasure. In some workplaces, employees regularly exchange gossip, flirt, engage in sexualized play, share personal problems, debate politics, and ridicule management. Relationships with co-workers often make the job itself more bearable, if not meaningful. In cases where the organization of work permits such exchanges, the lines between employment and leisure can become blurred.

Job satisfaction studies suggest that work is not all that bad. Most people report that they are generally satisfied with their jobs (Lowe, 2000). On close examination, though, discontent broods near the surface. At the same time that they report satisfaction, a majority of workers say that their jobs are somewhat or highly stressful, that they are not sufficiently involved, recognized, and rewarded, and that their talents are underutilized (Lowe, 2000). In addition, there are high rates of absenteeism, oppositional attitudes, slacking off, pilfering, and even destruction of company property. Some workers simply quit their jobs. But in the face of a competitive job market, family responsibilities, consumer debt, and, for some, few marketable skills, this is not a viable option. Furthermore, it is telling that even though they themselves claim to like their jobs, many people add that they do not want their own children to end up doing the same kind of work (Sennett, 1988).

Faced with unfair, unsafe, and sometimes unchallenging work, workers will be discontent. They will find ways to make changes, to resist. The question is, how? Individual acts of coping and resistance may give workers the feeling of agency and control, but insofar as they are individual acts, they rarely result in a fundamental or widespread change in conditions of work. In order to effect large-scale change, people must resort to collective measures.

Professions and Negotiating Professional Control

Securing professional control is an option for middle-class people who possess formally recognized credentials and can claim expertise in an area. When we think of a *professional*, who comes to mind? Physicians, educators, psychiatrists, dentists, lawyers, engineers, accountants. Some sociologists (proponents of trait theory) have attempted to define professionals with reference to a checklist of characteristics (Freidson, 1970). This checklist includes, for example, possession of a body of esoteric or abstract knowledge, reliance on a specialized technical language or vocabulary, and membership in associations that control entry and membership in the occupation through licensing, accreditation, and regulation.

Critics, however, argue that trait theory does not fully explain how and why some occupations come to be defined as professional while others do not. Rather than list a series of traits that define a profession, Terence Johnson (1972) highlights the resources available to different occupational groups. These resources have enabled physicians, psychologists, and lawyers to define themselves as distinct from other groups such as managers, clerical workers, and massage therapists. In focusing on the process of professionalization, critical theorists have noted that at the heart of the struggle to professionalize are relations of power and control. Feminist scholars have recently offered a more nuanced analysis of the ways in which **patriarchy** (a system of male dominance), too, structures the process of securing professional authority and control (Witz, 1991).

Labour Unions and Labour's Agenda

But the struggle to professionalize is not one in which many Canadians will be engaged—it is largely an exclusive one. Greater numbers of people in Canada, and globally, turn to another form of collective action to secure their rights and dignity in the workplace: they look to unionization. Just as campaigns to secure professional control have had a middle-class base, the struggle to unionize in this country has traditionally been one of white men in blue-collar jobs. In the latter part of the twentieth century and into the present time, however, increasing numbers of women, people of colour, white-collar workers, and middle-class employees have joined the ranks of the labour movement.

When most of us think of unions, strikes come to mind. Some of us may view trade unionists as just a bunch of greedy, overpaid workers demanding higher wages and, in the process, disrupting our lives, transportation, communication—even our garbage collection. We may owe this perception to dominant media representations of unions, their members, and their leaders.

The labour movement in this country goes far beyond this narrow and unfair characterization. The basic premise of the organized labour movement is to take collective action through the process of bargaining a contract. This *collective agreement* is the outcome of days, weeks, or even months of negotiations between two parties: worker representatives and company representatives. The contract is a legally binding document, an agreement that has been signed by both the employer and the union. Only if the two parties cannot reach an agreement is there potential for strike action. The actual incidence of strikes in Canada is, in fact, low. In 2001, the estimated work time lost through strikes and lockouts was 0.07 per cent, one-sixth the level of 20 years earlier (Statistics Canada, 2002b: 3). The strike is usually a measure of last resort. The vast majority of contracts that come up for renewal are settled without resorting to strike action. Indeed, some would argue that the leadership of unions acts to contain militancy on the part of its rank-and-file membership.

Workers in the nineteenth century first struggled to secure union representation in an effort to protect themselves against excessively long work days, extremely hazardous work environments, low pay, and blatant favouritism on the job. Critical to the survival of the labour movement in Canada was the passage of the Rand formula at the end of World War II. The Rand formula, named for Supreme Court Justice Ivor Rand, ensured the automatic deduction of union dues by the employer in a unionized workplace.

Today, labour–management conflict arises over a host of issues. Not only are wages an item of dispute, but companies and union representatives also negotiate benefits packages, job security, the implementation of technological change, outsourcing, concessions, and anti-harassment policies. Because of the struggles of union members, Canadian workers in offices, stores, and factories now have the right to refuse unsafe work, the right to participate in company-sponsored pension plans, and, in some cases, access to on-site daycare centres.

The gains of unionized workers, moreover, spill over into the wider society. Both unionized and non-unionized workers now have employment standards, (un)employment insurance, a standard work day of eight hours, a five-day work week, overtime premiums, vacation pay, health benefits, and sick-leave provisions. Unions have been pivotal in lobbying governments to introduce worker-friendly provincial and federal legislation.

Union Membership

In the first half of 2004, union membership in Canada was 4.1 million (of 13.4 million paid employees). This represented an increase from 4 million in the first half of

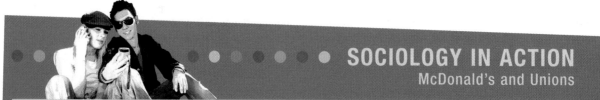

A Quebec trade union has signed a labour contract with a McDonald's fast-food franchisee, the first in North America and only the second in the world.

'We had so many problems, so much repression,' said Jean Lortie, a division president with the Quebec Confederation of National Trade Unions in Montreal. 'But we didn't give up.'

It took more than a year of often bitter negotiations to get a contract with the fast-food outlet in the tiny resort town of Rawdon, in the Laurentians north of Montreal. The process, Mr Lortie said, was so unpleasant and lengthy that by the time the union won only two of the 25 original signatories were still on staff.

The CNTU nearly became the first union in the world to get a labour contract with McDonald's, but a French union signed up a McDonald's restaurant only six weeks ago, said Len Ruel, area director of the Canadian Auto Workers in British Columbia.

The French union had to strike for six months to get a contract. By contrast, the Quebec contract was negotiated through the normal arbitration channels without a work stoppage. 'All parties negotiated in good faith,' said Maureen Kitts, a spokeswoman for McDonald's Restaurants of Canada Ltd in Toronto. She said McDonald's pays fair and equitable wages. Employees often start at the minimum legal wage with merit increases that are based on performance.

Rawdon is the first Canadian McDonald's outlet to sign a labour contract. Several other Canadian outlets have been certified by provincial labour authorities, but were unable to reach a first contract.

Ms Kitts said an outlet in Squamish, BC, was the first to be certified in North America. But Mr Ruel said the company decertified that union before he was able to negotiate a first contract.

Unions have organized other outlets in recent years, notably in Orangeville, Ont., in Montreal, and in St-Hubert, Que.

But Mr Lortie said those outlets were closed or decertified shortly after. Another outlet, in the United States, was bulldozed by the franchisee shortly after it was certified, Mr Ruel said. 'The company does everything it can to stop the union,' he said.

With the first contract, the McDonald's workers in Rawdon will get a base pay of $7 an hour and a raise of 10 cents every six months on the job. 'It's not a very good deal, but it's a start,' Mr Lortie said. 'This is the first time that everybody will get the same wage. There will be no favouritism.'

More important, he said the workers will get seniority rights and layoff protection, a key factor in a resort town where the work is highly seasonal. The company has also agreed to stiffer safety regulations, a contentious issue in a restaurant that fries potatoes in boiling oil.

The labour contract in Rawdon will not apply to other McDonald's outlets because it is owned by an independent franchisee.

The two union leaders said McDonald's fought hard to stop the union coming in. They say the company and the franchisee harassed the union leaders by moving them to midnight shifts, giving them dirty jobs or by neglecting to call them into work.

'They had so many problems, they quit,' Mr Lortie said. 'They were only getting $7 a hour, so it wasn't worth it for them.'

'We had to rebuild the union from scratch after they pushed out the union officers,' he added. 'It was a tough job to implement the new agreement.'

Source: Oliver Bertin, 'Quebec Union's Labour Contract with McDonald's Is Landmark', *Globe and Mail*, 18 Apr. 2002. Reprinted with permission from The Globe and Mail.

2003). Women accounted for nearly all of this increase. In 2006, the rate of union membership among women was 30.1 per cent, for the first time surpassing that of men, which dropped slightly to 29.4 per cent (http://www.statcan.ca/english/studies/75-001/comm/fact-2.htm). In part, growth in female membership reflects the high rate of unionization in the (female-dominated) public service (for example, in Crown corporations, public schools, and hospitals). It is also, in part, a result of recent union organizing in private services (Jackson and Robinson, 2000). In comparison, the unionization rate for men has dropped since the 1960s. This is largely attributable to a shrinking proportion of jobs in traditionally male-dominated and heavily unionized sectors, such as primary/resource, manufacturing, and construction (Jackson and Robinson, 2000).

Union membership also varies with terms of employment. Almost one in three full-time employees belongs to a union, compared to one in four part-time workers. Similarly, close to one in three permanent employees is a union member compared to about one in four non-permanent employees (Statistics Canada, 2002b: 2). We can, furthermore, see variations by age. Employees aged 45–54 (41.6 per cent) are more likely to be unionized than those aged 15–24 (13.3 per cent). Education is also a factor. A higher-than-average unionization rate can be found among men with post-secondary credentials (34.7 per cent) and those with less than a Grade 9 education (34 per cent). For women, the highest rate is for those with a university degree (40 per cent), reflecting unionization in health care and teaching (Statistics Canada, 2002b: 3).

Global comparisons reveal that the rate of union membership in Canada is higher than those in the United States and Japan and lower than those in most Western European nations. The dramatic decline in union membership in the United States has been a particular source of concern. The US unionization rate fell from 30 per cent at the end of the 1960s to less than 15 per cent in the current period (Jackson and Robinson, 2000: 25). This drop can be explained by a variety of forces, not the least of which are the electoral success of anti-union governments and the growth of anti-union employers such as Wal-Mart and Radio Shack. The assault on trade unions has been blatant in the United States.

The Union Advantage

There is absolutely no doubt that unionization benefits workers (see Table 12.4). Collective bargaining has secured for employees advantages in wages, benefits, job security, and extended health plans. This has been called the *union advantage*. The union wage premium in particular is greatest for (traditionally disadvantaged) workers who would otherwise be low-paid. Unionization tends to compress wage and benefit differentials and thereby promote an equalization of wages and working conditions among unionized workforces (Jackson and Robinson, 2000). In 2003, for example, average hourly earnings of unionized workers in Canada were $21.01, while for non-unionized workers the average hourly rate was $16.65. Thus, the union advantage as a percentage of the non-union hourly wage was over 26 per cent. The difference in wage between unionized and non-unionized women was even greater, at 37 per cent. As would be expected, the advantage for union workers was least in the public sector, where most employees are union members. Part-time unionized workers also are in a better position than non-union part-timers; in 2001, the hourly wage figures were $17.31 and $10.60, respectively. In addition, unionized part-timers also tended to work more hours per week than their non-unionized counterparts. Consequently, their average weekly earnings were nearly double—$343.94 compared to $181.65 (Statistics Canada, 2002b: 3).

The advantages of unionization to women are perhaps the most obvious. In 2001, unionized women working full-time received on average 90 per cent of the hourly earnings of their male counterparts, and female part-time workers earned 9 per cent more than men who were in part-time work (Statistics Canada, 2002b: 3). Women in unionized jobs are more than twice as likely to be included in pension plans as are women in non-unionized jobs (Jackson and Robinson, 2000).

According to the 1995 *World Employment Report* of the International Labour Organization (ILO), it is erroneous to believe that unions or good labour standards are the 'fundamental cause of unemployment, and it is important to recognize the positive impacts for society in terms of greater equality and less poverty'; collective bargaining efforts should be regarded as an 'important source of social well-being' (Jackson and Robinson, 2000: 96).

Table 12.4   The Union Advantage, 2003

	Union	Non-Union	Union Advantage	Union Advantage as % of Non-Union
Median hourly wage				
All	$20.00	$14.00	$6.00	42.9%
Men	$21.00	$15.98	$5.02	31.4%
Women	$18.75	$12.02	$6.73	56.0%
Average hourly wage				
All	$21.01	$16.65	$4.36	26.2%
Men	$22.00	$18.69	$3.31	17.7%
Women	$19.94	$14.55	$5.39	37.0%
Age 15–24	$12.66	$9.88	$2.78	28.1%
Public sector	$23.10	$22.09	$1.01	4.6%
Private sector	$18.70	$16.17	$2.53	15.6%
Sales and service occupations	$13.16	$11.28	$1.88	16.7%
Processing and manufacturing occupations	$18.11	$14.76	$3.35	22.7%

Source: Statistics Canada, *Guide to the Labour Force Survey, 2004*, Catalogue no. 71-543, 17 Feb. 2004.

● Conclusion: ● ● ● ● ● ●
Work in the Future,
Our Future as Workers

Workers and unions, of course, have limited powers. While newspaper headlines promote the 'big' collective bargaining gains of the most strongly organized unions, most unionized workers across the country are still struggling to attain basic rights that others managed to secure years, if not decades, ago. Every day, in small workplaces, employees (unionized and non-unionized) negotiate their rights. More often now than in the past, these are women, people of colour, the disabled—not members of the dominant groups in this country.

These struggles have been difficult, and continue to be so, particularly in the context of the current assault on unions. Powerful corporations such as Wal-Mart and McDonald's effectively curb workers' rights to organize by simply closing down stores, mounting strong union decertification campaigns, or stalling when it comes time to bargain a first contract. In Ontario, furthermore, the Harris-led Conservative government curbed the power of the Ontario Labour Relations Board by introducing legislation that removes the board's right to give union certification to workers who have faced (illegal) intimidation by anti-union employers. The power of workers and their movements is being even more severely circumscribed by the aggressiveness of global capitalists, many of whom are openly supported by networks of governments in both developing and developed nations. Whether you work part-time at The Gap, labour a 60-hour week in a steel factory, freelance as a consultant, or find sporadic office employment through a temporary help agency, you are faced with a challenge.

Regardless of theoretical perspective or political agenda, scholars today are debating the nature of the challenge of the transformation of work. Young people entering the labour market for the first time and middle-aged people confronting reconfigured jobs and refashioned workplaces both are part of this transformation. Workers, young and old, must work in order to survive, to nurture families, to participate in life. Given this reality, it is crucial to know the debate, engage in it, and perhaps transform the world of work according to your own vision.

Questions for Critical Thought ● ● ○ ● ● ● ●

1. Think about where you are located in the economy. If you are not currently employed, where do you plan to find work? How does this depart from your parents' and grandparents' work histories? What factors have shaped (or constrained) your work-related aspirations?

2. Think about the work that you perform in the course of an average day. What proportion of this is paid and what unpaid? Do you believe that we should define unpaid domestic activities as 'work' that is of economic worth? If you were asked to calculate the economic worth of unpaid domestic labour, how would you begin? What factors would you take into account?

3. Even though women's workforce participation rate is now almost the same as men's, there are many persisting gender-based inequalities in employment. Identify some of these inequities. What are some of the formal and informal barriers to equality between women and men in the labour market today? How would you confront them?

4. Labour unions have long faced challenges in capitalist societies. Some people would argue that today union leaders and members face new challenges, perhaps more formidable than those of the past. Identify and discuss some of the new challenges that confront the labour movement in this country.

Recommended Readings ● ○ ● ● ●

Gillian Creese, *Contracting Masculinity: Gender, Class, and Race in a White-Collar Union, 1944–1994* (Toronto: Oxford University Press, 1999).

A carefully researched case study of the white-collar office workers' union at BC Hydro, Creese uncovers the negotiation of gender, class, and race in collective bargaining.

Ann Eyerman, *Women in the Office: Transitions in a Global Economy* (Toronto: Sumach, 2000).

In presenting the stories of 12 female office workers in Canada, the author makes a highly accessible critique of new managerial approaches in the context of global competition, corporate restructuring, computer technology, and the rise of contingent work arrangements.

Randy Hodson, *Dignity at Work* (Cambridge: Cambridge University Press, 2001).

Based on an examination of 109 organizational ethnographies, Hodson sensitively highlights the ways in which workers search for dignity and self-worth on the job.

Graham S. Lowe, *The Quality of Work: A People-Centred Agenda* (Toronto: Oxford University Press, 2000).

A refreshing and informative empirical analysis, by one of Canada's experts on the sociology of work, examines the quality of work performed by Canadians today.

Recommended Websites ● ○ ● ○ ●

Canadian Centre for Occupational Health and Safety (CCOHS)

www.ccohs.ca

The CCOHS, based in Hamilton, Ontario, promotes a safe and healthy working environment by providing information and advice about occupational health and safety issues.

Canadian Centre for Policy Alternatives (CCPA)

www.policyalternatives.ca

The CCPA offers an alternative to the message that we have no choice about the policies that affect our lives, by undertaking and promoting research on issues of social and economic justice.

Labour/Le Travail

www.mun.ca/cclh/llt/

Labour/Le Travail is the leading academic journal for labour studies in Canada. In operation since 1976, the journal publishes historical and contemporary articles on all aspects of work in Canada.

No Sweat

www.nosweat.org.uk

No Sweat is a UK-based activist organization that fights sweatshops around the world. It stands for a living wage, safe working conditions, and independent trade unions. No Sweat is an open, broad-based campaign that aligns with anti-capitalist protest movements and the international workers' movement.

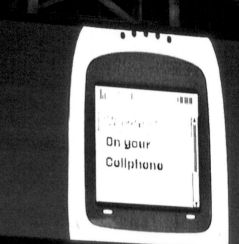

Dundas

SEARS

● ● ● ● ● ● ● ● ● ●

Mass Media and Communication

David Young

Learning Objectives

In this chapter, you will:

▶ learn about different theories sociologists have used to analyze the mass media;

▶ identify various forms of media ownership and critically understand concerns about deepening ownership concentration among media companies;

▶ study the role of the state in relation to media policy and media organizations;

▶ consider how economic and cultural globalization is connected to the mass media;

▶ grasp how media content represents relatively powerless groups in society, such as the working class, women, and ethno-racial minorities;

▶ discover how media content is interpreted by audience members;

▶ become aware of the conflicts that exist over media policy and media content; and

▶ examine how the Internet reflects long-standing issues in the sociology of mass media.

● Introduction ● ● ● ● ● ●

The mass media include newspapers, magazines, recorded music, motion pictures, radio, and television. We are exposed to the mass media frequently in contemporary society. In light of this, a number of questions may come to mind when you think about the mass media. What is the role of the mass media in society? Who has power over what we read, see, or hear in the mass media? What kinds of messages exist in media content, and how do people react to them? What are the social implications of the Internet, which is associated with the 'new media'? Sociology provides the tools to grapple with such questions. Throughout this chapter, you will be introduced to answers developed by media sociologists.

● Sociological ● ● ● ● ● ● Theories of the Media

The classical theorists who have informed sociological research—Karl Marx, Émile Durkheim, and Max Weber—did not write specifically about the mass media. All three men were aware of newspapers, and Marx even spent some time working as a journalist (Ryan and Wentworth, 1999). However, Marx died in 1883 and did not live to see even the emergence of motion pictures. Motion pictures had been in existence for some time when Durkheim and Weber died, in 1917 and 1920 respectively, but radio was only beginning to emerge as a form of mass communication. Consequently, the three thinkers who offered sociologists so much specific guidance in approaching such issues as class and status inequality or religion were not in a position to provide an analysis of the mass media. Nevertheless, at least some of the classical theorists presented ideas that sociologists have applied to the study of mass communication. Four sociological perspectives on communication and media can be identified: symbolic interactionism, structural functionalism, conflict theory, and feminism.

Symbolic Interactionism

The theoretical perspective known as symbolic interactionism was named by Herbert Blumer, and its key elements were further developed by a number of sociologists. This approach focuses on the microsociological issue of interaction among individuals through the use of symbols. Symbols can be verbal (such as the words used in spoken language) or non-verbal (including forms of body language such as a smile, frown, or gesture). All of these symbols carry meaning, which the members of a society come to understand and share through the process of socialization. Without this shared understanding of symbols, interaction among people would not be possible. An aspect of symbolic interactionism known as *social constructionism* suggests that we construct our own social reality through symbols. Reality consists not of something that objectively exists but rather what we subjectively perceive through our interpretation of symbols, and this interpretation in turn shapes our social behaviour. For example, from your interpretation of verbal and non-verbal cues, you may believe that a friend is angry at you. This may not in fact be the case, but it is the reality you have constructed and it will affect how you respond to your friend.

Especially since the 1970s, symbolic interactionism has been used in research on communication and media. Faules and Alexander (1978) identified how symbolic interactionist theory could be employed to study different forms of communication, including mass communication. They indicated that symbolic interactionism can be applied to *interpersonal communication* (face-to-face interaction between two individuals that involves the reciprocal exchange of verbal and non-verbal symbols); *group communication* (face-to-face interaction among several individuals in a context, such as a seminar discussion, that still permits the mutual exchange of verbal and non-verbal cues); *public communication* (sending messages to large groups in a face-to-face setting, as in a lecture, where the participants have a much more limited opportunity for the exchange of verbal and non-verbal symbols); and *mass communication* (which exists through the use of mass media such as newspapers, motion pictures, radio, or television).

Faules and Alexander (1978: 11) noted that mass communication is different from the other forms of communication because it does not involve direct, face-to-face interaction and 'there is no opportunity for immediate mutual exchange of verbal and nonverbal cues between the initiator of a message and the recipients of that message.' However, because much of our interpretation of the world is based on our previous experience with direct and indirect forms of communication, they concluded that 'the media are a prime source of indirect experience and for that reason have impact on the construction of social reality' (1978: 23).

Symbolic interactionism is not one of the principal theories employed by media sociologists. Its microsociological focus is the reason for this. An approach that addresses interaction through symbols can be useful in certain areas of sociology, such as the analysis of socialization, and it can also be useful to scholars who study various forms of face-to-face communication. However, in terms of research on mass communication, symbolic interactionist theory has more limited applicability. It does not allow sociologists to address macrosociological concerns such as the role of media institutions in society.

Structural Functionalism

Structural functionalism is inspired by the ideas of Émile Durkheim, but the theory took shape in the work of later sociologists. As a macrosociological framework, structural functionalism focuses on social order. The order and stability of society is facilitated by consensus (agreement) among its members regarding norms and values. Stability is also facilitated by the interconnected parts of society. According to structural functionalists, the maintenance of society depends on its different parts fulfilling their particular functions. Structural functionalists make this point through an analogy between society and a biological organism. The body of any person or animal is made up of different parts (organs such as the heart or the lungs), and all of these parts must continue to perform their specific functions if the person or animal is to survive. Similarly, social institutions make up the different parts of society, and these institutions must carry out certain functions for the entire society to endure.

Structural functionalism frequently was used in studies of the mass media during the 1950s. Unlike symbolic interactionism, this theoretical approach enabled sociologists to examine the role of media institutions. Building on the work of Lasswell (1948), Wright (1959) argued that media institutions contribute to the maintenance and survival of society by performing four functions: (1) surveillance of the environment, (2) correlation of the parts of society, (3) transmission of the social heritage, and (4) entertainment.

Surveillance of the environment involves the collection and distribution of information about events that occur inside and outside a particular society. This surveillance is provided by news media organizations, and it is functional for society in several ways. The flow of information through the news helps institutions or individuals to organize their activities, and the population can be warned of imminent danger (such as a hurricane or military attack).

Correlation of the parts of society refers to interpretation of information about the environment and prescription for behaviour in response to events. Editorials in the news or commentaries through other media, such

as televised speeches by political leaders, are functional for society because they help people to make sense of what is happening. They are also functional because they aim to integrate society by building consensus. A specific example is the patriotic tone of the American media after the terrorist attacks on 11 September 2001.

Transmission of the social heritage involves communicating information, norms, and values from one generation to another or from the members of a group to new members. Various mass media are functional for society because they contribute to the socialization process and help to ensure that the culture of a society or group will continue across time.

Entertainment involves forms of communication that are mainly intended to provide amusement or diversion. Entertainment is functional for society because it provides relaxation and enables the release of emotional tensions that may generate conflict and threaten social order.

Although structural functionalism offered some important insights, media sociologists had largely abandoned this theoretical approach by the 1970s; it was seen as having several problems, including a conservative orientation. The conservative nature of structural functionalism is evident in the value it places on the order and stability of society. Structural functionalist theory stresses the role of media institutions (and other social institutions) in maintaining society as it is. The theory makes little attempt to question media institutions and their role.

Conflict Theory

Conflict theory is rooted in the work of Karl Marx. Like structural functionalism, it provides a macrosociological framework; however, conflict theory differs from structural functionalism by emphasizing social change rather than social order. Marx theorized that social change occurs through conflict in society. In capitalist society, the conflict is between the bourgeoisie and the proletariat. Members of the *bourgeoisie* (the capitalist class) own the means of production (such as the factories, technology, and capital needed in the production process). Because members of the *proletariat* (the working class) do not own the means of production, they have to sell their labour to capitalists in exchange for a wage so that they have money to live. Marx also recognized the *petite bourgeoisie*, a middle class of farmers and small business people who own the means of production but hire little or no wage labour. However, the focus of his analysis was on the conflict that stemmed from the exploitation of workers by capitalists. Marx expected that the working class eventually would lead a revolution against the capitalist class and capitalism would be replaced by socialism.

Conflict theory has provided the basis for numerous studies of the mass media since the 1960s. In contrast to structural functionalism, this theoretical approach made it possible for sociologists to question the role of media institutions. For instance, conflict theory enabled sociologists to see how media institutions are tied to power and inequality in capitalist society. Marx's recognition of a middle class also led some sociologists to examine the growth of a new middle class made up of managers (including those in media institutions) and professionals (such as journalists). Members of the new middle class work for an annual salary rather than an hourly wage and some of them, as supervisors of the labour of the working class, may be ideologically aligned with capitalists (Wright, 1983).

The growing popularity of conflict theory during the 1960s had much to do with the inability of structural functionalism—with its focus on social order—to address the social conflict that had taken shape between various social institutions (including media institutions) and social movements. In the 1960s, the labour movement was joined by other movements that had emerged to struggle against social inequality—especially the women's movement and the civil rights movement. These movements were aware of the role the media played in oppressing women or racial minorities, and they were aware also of the potential to use media in ways that might help to generate social change. However, because Marxism focuses on the analysis of class relations, it has had difficulty explaining other aspects of social inequality that are connected to or reinforced by the mass media.

Feminism

By offering analysis of inequality between women and men, feminism has made a valuable contribution to sociology. Feminism can be used to understand microsociological issues associated with the lives of women and their experience with inequality, but it also has a strong focus on addressing macrosociological conditions that account for the oppression of women. Especially with regard to the macro level of analysis, *patriarchy* is a key concept in feminism. Patriarchy refers to a society or form of social organization based on male domination. Due to considerable debate among feminists about patriarchy and the origins or nature of women's oppression, a number of feminist theories have emerged. Some of these theories have informed research on the mass media.

Liberal feminism, which is rooted in liberal philosophy, suggests that the inequality between women and men stems from inappropriate ideas that can be corrected through argument, legislation, and socialization. Many liberal feminists have objected to prevalent ideas about 'masculinity' and 'femininity' that affect young boys and girls. For example, while our culture has traditionally regarded certain behaviours and jobs to be 'masculine' (such as being rational or being a doctor), it has regarded others to be 'feminine' (such as being irrational or being a nurse). Consequently, media research based on liberal feminism has included content analysis of how gendered socializing is evident in television programs that children are exposed to. The research has led to calls for legislation that governs the depiction of gender in television programs aimed at children. Although liberal feminism draws attention to the sexist ideas that circulate in society, it does not challenge the capitalist nature of society (Steeves, 1987).

Marxist feminism (also referred to as *socialist* or *materialist feminism*) has attempted to overcome Marxism's failure to address the inequality experienced by women. Marxist feminists contend that the oppression of women stems from connections between two systems that generate inequality—capitalism and patriarchy—both of which must be overcome through political struggles (Steeves, 1987). A great deal of media research based on Marxist feminism has examined media content to show how 'representations reinforce nuclear families and class distinctions that sustain capitalism and women's secondary status' (Steeves, 1987: 113). Fewer Marxist feminist studies have focused on the role of capitalist patriarchal media institutions and their role in the production of this content or the exploitation of female workers.

Radical feminism is less concerned with explaining the origins of women's oppression. It concentrates on developing radical alternatives. Radical feminists seek separation from men as a solution to the problem of male domination. Little media research has been based on radical feminism, but its proposed political solution implies the need for feminist media with separate processes and audiences (Steeves, 1987).

More recently, feminist theories have addressed three themes in relation to the analysis of media and communication. Wackwitz and Rakow (2004) identify these themes as difference, voice, and representation. *Difference* raises several issues, including the notion of differences between women and men. Feminists have shown that patriarchy justifies inequality between women and men by asserting supposedly biological differences—

men being 'naturally' more aggressive than women, for example—even though these differences are actually products of culture and socialization. The theme of difference also refers to differences among women with regard to class, race/ethnicity, sexual preference, or other aspects of identity. Feminists have increasingly examined these elements of difference in order to overcome the deficiencies of earlier feminist theories, which minimized or ignored diversity among women. The second theme identified by Wackwitz and Rakow focuses on exclusion. *Voice* concerns the degree to which women are denied an opportunity to speak in various forms of communication (including interpersonal or group communication) or given a voice only to have their ideas ignored. The third theme considers the portrayal of women in the media. *Representation* draws attention to the way women are depicted in media content and the way this negatively affects them. Wackwitz and Rakow (2004: 9) see these three themes as overlapping because 'systems of difference and exclusion are linked with the process of representation.'

Critical Perspectives on the Media

Conflict theory and feminism have contributed to critical perspectives on the media. Critical perspectives challenge the type of society we have and analyze the media in relation to power, inequality, conflict, and change.

Critical perspectives on the media are often divided into two categories: political economy and cultural studies. Political economy focuses on ownership and control of the media. It examines private corporations and the state in relation to the media as well as the opposition of subordinate groups to the role of powerful media organizations. In contrast, work within cultural studies addresses the ideological aspects of the media. This approach analyzes the ideology embedded in media content, the interpretation of media content by audience members, and efforts to change media representations or disseminate alternative media messages. Adapting the themes that Mosco (1989) associated with political economy and cultural studies, we will now turn to these two critical perspectives.

● Political Economy ● ● ● ● of the Media

While placing a strong emphasis on historical analysis, researchers who specialize in the political economy of media devote particular attention to several issues. The main issues are forms of media ownership; the state and media policy; globalization and the media; and conflict over ownership, policy, and globalization.

Forms of Media Ownership

There are different forms of media ownership. We can distinguish between public and private ownership as well as various types of ownership that are private.

Public ownership—ownership of media by the government—has a long history in Canada. Examples of public media ownership in this country include the National Film Board of Canada (NFB), the Canadian Broadcasting Corporation/Société Radio-Canada (CBC/SRC), and the educational television broadcasters operated by some provincial governments: TV Ontario, Radio-Québec, and the Knowledge Network (which serves British Columbia). The goal of these organizations is to provide a public service by using the media to satisfy social objectives. Such objectives include providing media that are freely available to citizens, using the media for educational purposes, and ensuring a Canadian voice in the media. Media organizations under public ownership are often supported by government funding, but additional funding may come from advertising or user fees (such as memberships). Public ownership of the media in Canada frequently takes the form of a Crown corporation, a business owned by the federal or provincial government but operating at arm's length (independently) from government (Lorimer and Gasher, 2001).

Critical scholars have often expressed support for public ownership of the media, as when Taras (2001: 26) indicated that the CBC/SRC has played a crucial role as one of the 'public squares' where Canadian citizens can meet. However, these scholars are also aware that public ownership is not without its problems. For instance,

■■ Time to Reflect ■■■■■■■■■■■■■■■■■■■■■■■

Compare and contrast symbolic interactionism, structural functionalism, conflict theory, and feminism in relation to an analysis of the mass media.

Raboy (1990) has argued that public broadcasting must be re-imagined so that it goes beyond the federal or provincial levels of jurisdiction and an emphasis on 'national' or 'Canadian' identity.

Private ownership refers to ownership of the media by commercial firms, and it too has a long tradition in Canada. Most of the mass media in Canada, ranging from newspapers to radio and television stations, are under private ownership. The prevalence of private ownership is illustrated by Table 13.1, which presents a list of the leading media organizations in Canada. Only one of these organizations, the CBC/SRC, is a public corporation. The ownership of a private media company may be held by an individual or a small group (such as a family). Alternatively, the ownership may be held by many shareholders through the stock market. The goal of the private media company is 'survival and growth in a marketplace driven by profit' (Lorimer and Gasher, 2001: 223).

Critical researchers argue that private ownership has significant implications for media content. The interests of private media companies mean that media content 'is regarded by their management not as a public service, but as a business cost to be met as inexpensively as possible' (Hackett et al., 1996: 260). For example, the private television network CTV can purchase the rights to broadcast popular American shows like *Desperate Housewives* or *Law & Order* for approximately one-tenth the cost of producing a Canadian series. As Taras (2001: 189) has indicated, this explains why private television broadcasters in Canada 'put as little as possible into Canadian content and squeeze the most out of imported Hollywood productions'. While noting that private media have done little to reflect Canadian culture in their programming, critical scholars have also been concerned about several specific types of private ownership.

Table 13.1   The Leading Media Organizations in Canada, 2005

Organization	Revenues (2005)
BCE	$19,105,000,000
The Thomson Corp.	$10,539,333,000
Quebecor	$10,208,500,000
Rogers Communications	$ 7,482,154,000
CanWest Global Communications	$ 3,072,542,000
Shaw Communications	$ 2,209,810,000
Torstar	$ 1,566,943,000
Lions Gate Entertainment	$ 1,076,824,000
Alliance Atlantis Communications	$ 1,043,400,000
Corus Entertainment	$ 683,069,000
COGECO	$ 675,605,000
CHUM Ltd	$ 628,392,000
Canadian Broadcasting Corp.	$ 546,706,000
Osprey Media	$ 222,525,000
IMAX	$ 175,510,000

Source: Adapted from *Financial Post Business*, FP500 Online 2006 Database, at: <www.canada.com/nationalpost/npb/500/index.html>.

Independent ownership is the most basic and least problematic of these types. It exists when the owners of a media company confine themselves to that one company and are not involved in the ownership of other firms. Their media company usually operates on a small scale. It is often closely associated with a local community and aims to serve that community. This form of ownership means that the newspaper, radio station, or television station in a small town or city might be owned by an entrepreneur who lives in the area. Independent ownership was once quite common in the Canadian media, but it has diminished as large companies have bought small media firms (Lorimer and Gasher, 2001). For example, the Hamilton, Ontario television station CHCH was independently owned for many years, but was acquired by Western International Communications (WIC) in 1990 and became one of several television stations owned by this company. WIC was purchased by CanWest Global Communications in 2000, and CH (as the station is now known) is currently among CanWest Global's many holdings in television.

Such developments bring us to **horizontal integration**, a second form of private ownership. Horizontal integration, also known as chain ownership, exists when one company owns a number of media organizations in different locations that are doing the same type of business. One company may own several newspapers, for example. Critical scholars contend that this form of ownership has negative implications. For instance, if a company owns a chain of newspapers, it could cut costs by using syndicated news stories across the chain and reducing the number of journalists and local stories at each of the newspapers (Hackett and Gruneau, 2000). Therefore, when an independently owned newspaper becomes part of a chain, a number of jobs disappear along with some of the newspaper's local flavour.

Vertical integration is a third form of private ownership. It exists when one company owns media firms or divisions that are part of the overall process linking production, distribution, and exhibition. A good example is provided by the structure of the Canadian company Alliance Atlantis Communications before its different holdings were recently sold. Alliance Atlantis was involved with television production, film and television distribution, and television broadcasting. The company co-produced (with CBS Productions) the television series *CSI: Crime Scene Investigation* and its two spin-offs, and one of its divisions distributed the three shows in all territories outside the United States. Repeat episodes of *CSI* were broadcast through Showcase, which was among the many specialty television channels that Alliance Atlantis owned in Canada. Such vertical integration enables a company to have a guaranteed market for its production activities and a guaranteed supply of content for its exhibition outlets. However, critical researchers have been concerned about the implications of vertical integration. They suggest that this form of ownership can result in content from other sources being shut out (Croteau and Hoynes, 2000).

Cross-ownership exists when one company owns organizations that are associated with different types of media. CTVglobemedia (formerly Bell Globemedia) provides an example. The holdings of this company include the television network CTV; print media (the *Globe and Mail* newspaper and the magazine *Report on Business*); and specialty television channels (such as CTV Newsnet, The Comedy Network, and Report on Business Television). Cross-ownership has certain advantages for a company, including the opportunity to share resources or personnel among its media outlets, but critical researchers argue that it can limit the variety of journalistic opinions or media messages that are presented (Hackett et al., 1996). When one company owns the number of media outlets that CTVglobemedia has, the concern is that the same news stories and television shows will appear across the range of its holdings. These large companies may provide us with lots of media choices but less diversity in media content (Taras, 2001).

Finally, it is necessary to consider **conglomerate ownership**. A conglomerate is a company containing many firms engaged in a variety of (usually) unrelated business activities. This form of ownership may combine different linkages (horizontal and vertical integration and even cross-ownership). There are also different types of conglomerates. A media conglomerate does most of its business in the media. A non-media conglomerate has its foundation in other types of business, but it might also own one or more media organizations (Lorimer and Gasher, 2001). Critical researchers have been concerned about the content of the news media held by both types of conglomerates. In this regard, Hackett and Gruneau (2000: 60–1) identify 'two worrying implications'. First, news media owned by a conglomerate may be required to carry promotional material for other parts of the company. Second, and even more significantly, news stories could be suppressed if they contain negative and damaging information about other aspects of the corporate empire.

The suppression or slanting of news stories might occasionally stem from orders at the top of a conglomerate, but it is more likely to emerge from self-censorship by journalists or directions from editors when journalists present their stories. These news workers realize that corporate executives do not want such stories broadcast or published and act in a way that protects their jobs (Hackett and Gruneau, 2000; Wasko, 2001).

The State and Media Policy

The concept of **the state** is sometimes confused with that of the government. However, for sociologists, the state is actually a much broader term. Cuneo (1990) defines the state in Canada as encompassing various institutions: the federal, provincial, and local levels of government; the administration (including the civil service and regulatory agencies); parliamentary assemblies; the armed forces and police; intelligence agencies, such as the Canadian Security Intelligence Service (CSIS); the legal, judicial, and court systems; prisons, reform institutions, and asylums; Crown corporations; and the institutions associated with public education, public health care, and public media that are under different levels of government.

While the state includes public media, other parts of the state have implications for both public and private media. As prepared by governments and passed by parliamentary assemblies, various acts associated with the legal system set out certain requirements for media organizations. For example, the Broadcasting Act indicates what is expected of organizations that provide public and private radio or television in Canada. The legislation makes it clear that these organizations must present Canadian programming. The latest version of the legislation, the 1991 Broadcasting Act, sets out a broadcasting policy that includes the following clause: 'each broadcasting undertaking shall make maximum use, and in no case less than predominant use, of Canadian creative and other resources in the creation and presentation of programming' (Canada, 1991: 3.1.f). Regulatory agencies are components of the state that have consequences for the media. For instance, historically Canada has had two independent regulators in relation to broadcasting. The Board of Broadcast Governors (BBG) was established in 1958 and replaced in 1968 by what is now referred to as the Canadian Radio-television and Telecommunications Commission (CRTC).

These regulatory state agencies were created to help ensure that media organizations comply with media legislation by setting specific rules for the organizations to follow. For example, in relation to the Broadcasting Act, the requirement that radio and television undertakings must utilize Canadian resources in programming has been reflected in Canadian content regulations. These regulations were established first by the BBG in 1960, and they initially required that at least 45 per cent of television programming be Canadian. The CRTC maintained the regulations for television and established similar regulations for radio in 1970. At first, a minimum of 30 per cent of the music on popular music stations had to be Canadian. Over the years, the CRTC has set various percentages of required Canadian content for different types of radio and television programming, but Canadian-content regulations remain a key aspect of the agency's policy.

Analysis of media policy is often based on a key point in Marxist theories of the state. As Gold et al. (1975: 31) noted, 'Marxist treatments of the state begin with the fundamental observation that the state in capitalist society broadly serves the interests of the capitalist class.' The state in Canada has served the interests of private media companies in a number of ways. For instance, the federal government responded to the cable industry's desire for vertical integration by placing a clause in the 1991 Broadcasting Act that identified cable companies as distributors and programmers. While cable companies distributed television channels on their systems, the clause paved the way for these companies also to own and program television channels (Raboy, 1995). This is now the case, as is illustrated by the ownership of the OMNI stations and Rogers Sportsnet by Rogers Communications. The CRTC's regulatory process has also done much to assist private media companies. According to Mosco (1989: 57), 'this formal regulatory process generally serves the interests of communications companies and large corporate users of communications systems.' For example, since the CRTC has taken 'a permissive attitude to industry mergers' (Mosco, 1989: 212), the agency usually has given regulatory approval to the deepening concentration of ownership that worries critical scholars.

Some critical scholars suggest that the role of the state has been decreasing as a result of neo-liberalism. **Neo-liberalism** is an economic doctrine influential since the late 1970s that is favoured by private companies and has been adopted by many governments around the world. The doctrine of neo-liberalism supports free trade between countries, cuts in social spending, and measures such as deregulation and privatization. Deregulation means that regulatory agencies reduce or even eliminate rules they had previously imposed on organizations. For instance, under its 1998 Commercial Radio Policy, the CRTC reduced restrictions on how many radio stations private companies could own in a single market (Canada, 1998). Privatization, which means that organizations under public ownership are transferred to private ownership, has also been apparent in the Canadian media; during the 1990s, the government of Alberta sold the Access Network, its educational television broadcaster, to the CHUM Group (which rebranded the service as Access: The Education Station).

While some argue that such developments reveal the decreasing role of the state, other critical scholars contend that terms such as deregulation and privatization obscure the complexity of changes in the state. They suggest that the state's role has also been increasing in some ways, and this, too, has assisted private capital (Salter and Salter, 1997). For example, government funding to support the Juno Awards ceremony for the Canadian music industry has deepened. While the Junos received some federal funding during the 1980s, provincial and municipal levels of government have also spent a great deal of money on the ceremony since the 1990s to facilitate moving the Junos to cities such as Vancouver and Hamilton. Financial support from provincial and municipal governments deepened further after the Canadian Academy of Recording Arts and Sciences (CARAS), the organization that administers the Juno Awards, began to encourage competitive bidding among Canadian cities for the rights to host the annual ceremony. Cities with the highest bids have won the opportunity to host the Junos. Increasing government funding for the Juno Awards has benefited the music industry, but it has also benefited host cities and private companies in those cities through economic spin-off effects for hotels and other local businesses as people come to town for the Junos (Young, 2004).

Globalization and the Media

In recent decades, the issue of globalization has been the focus of much analysis by sociologists. **Globalization** involves the flow of goods, services, media, information, and labour between countries around the world. Researchers often examine different but interrelated aspects of globalization. *Economic globalization* concerns worldwide production and financial transactions while *cultural globalization* refers to 'the transmission or diffusion across national borders of various forms of media and the arts' (Crane, 2002: 1).

Several factors are associated with the deepening impact of globalization. Developments in information and communications technologies are certainly among these factors. Computers and telecommunications technologies make possible the instantaneous transfer of data, which has contributed to the formation of a transnational financial system and facilitated the worldwide production undertaken by the multinational corporations that are central to economic globalization. Linkages between satellite and cable technologies have played an important role in cultural globalization by enabling the news media to make us almost immediately aware of important events as they are occurring even half a world away (Nash, 2000).

While technological factors are significant, it is crucial to realize that globalization is also being driven by a complex mixture of economic and political factors. Economic factors include deepening ownership concentration within countries and across national borders as well the international impact of neo-liberalism and free trade between countries. These economic factors are tied to political factors. The latter include the role of the state in assisting private capital, partly through the negotiation of the North American Free Trade Agreement (NAFTA) and similar international treaties. Political factors also include the emergence of the World Trade Organization (WTO), an international institution that enforces trade rules on member countries and has thereby reduced the control of governments over their own economies (Karim, 2002). These various developments have generated a number of issues that concern critical media sociologists.

Cultural Globalization

In relation to cultural globalization, critical researchers are concerned about the historically deepening and worldwide impact of media industries. We can illustrate this through reference to the American motion picture industry. The dominance of the American film industry was established soon after the earliest Hollywood productions at the beginning of the twentieth century. By 1939, Hollywood was already supplying 65 per cent of the films shown in theatres worldwide. This export flow expanded dramatically after World War II, and the United States was providing over 80 per cent of the world's films in the 1990s (Miller et al., 2001). Major importers of Hollywood films include Canada, Japan, the Netherlands, and the United Kingdom. American films generate at least half of the total box-office receipts in all their major markets and sometimes even more than two-thirds of total receipts (Scott, 2004). In Canada, Hollywood films account for over 95 per cent of Canadian box office and video receipts during an average year (Magder and Burston, 2001).

Several factors help to explain the dominance of the American film industry. To begin with, the ownership structure of the industry has played a crucial role. The vertical integration of production, distribution, and exhibition during the early history of the Hollywood studios ensured that the films these studios made were seen in the United States and in many international markets. In Canada and elsewhere, this made it more difficult for domestic films to secure theatrical exhibition (Miller et al., 2001; Pendakur, 1990). Hollywood production companies usually do not own movie theatres any more, but they still have substantial distribution operations around the world. Furthermore, as the Hollywood studios have increasingly come under conglomerate ownership since the 1980s, massive and often non-American multinational firms such as Sony Corporation (which owns Columbia Pictures) have developed strategies to pursue global audiences (Miller et al., 2001).

It is also important to note that the state in various countries has contributed to the global dominance of Hollywood. The film industry in the United States has prospered internationally in part because it has 'a willing servant in the state' (Miller et al., 2001: 24). Under pressure from the Motion Picture Association of America (MPAA), which represents the major film studios, American federal bureaucracies have pushed governments in other countries to satisfy Hollywood's interests (Scott, 2004). In Canada, this has historically resulted in several successful efforts to discourage the federal government from establishing measures to protect the Canadian film industry, including quotas that would place limits on the importation of American films (Magder, 1993).

Especially given the import quotas in other countries, it must be recognized that pressure for free trade aims to further deepen Hollywood's global influence. Ever since the 1940s, American media companies have tried to justify their access to foreign markets on the grounds that there should be a free flow of information rather than quotas or other restrictions (Smythe, 1981). However, the pressure for free trade in culture has mounted since the 1980s due to the influence of neoliberalism and the emergence of the WTO (Miller et al., 2001; Scott, 2004).

GLOBAL ISSUES
The Global Music Industry

Worldwide, the music industry is dominated by a handful of large groups. The 'Big Four' record groups are the Universal Music Group, Sony BMG Music Entertainment, the Warner Music Group, and the EMI Group. These groups are made up of record companies, record labels (various brand names on recordings), and music publishers. Music organizations not held by the Big Four are considered to be independent.

Most of the Big Four are part of massive conglomerates. The Universal Music Group is owned by the French conglomerate Vivendi. Since purchasing Universal from the Canadian company Seagram in 2000, Vivendi has sold most of its interests in Universal Entertainment (which became NBC Universal) while retaining the Universal Music Group. The latter has the largest collection of record labels in the world (including such well-known names as A&M Records and Geffen Records). Sony BMG Music Entertainment was created in 2004 through a merger of the music divisions in two companies. Sony Music is part of the Sony Corporation, a Japanese conglomerate, while BMG is a component of the German conglomerate Bertelsmann.

The merger between Sony Music and the Bertelsmann Music Group (BMG) reduced the Big Five to the current Big Four. The Warner Music Group was once part of the conglomerate AOL/Time Warner, but the music division of the company was purchased in 2004 by a number of investors led by Canadian businessman Edgar Bronfman Jr. Like the Warner Music Group, the EMI Group is not held by a conglomerate (Bishop, 2005). In 2006, the two companies entered talks about joining forces through a merger that would reduce the Big Four to the Big Three.

The Big Four music groups control most of the world music market. The Universal Music Group is in the leading position, with 25.5 per cent of the market in 2004. It was followed by Sony BMG Music Entertainment with 21.5 per cent, the EMI Group with 13.4 per cent, and the Warner Music Group with 11.3 per cent. The independent sector held the remaining 28.4 per cent of the global market (International Federation of the Phonographic Industry, 2005).

As they operate globally, the Big Four make use of various marketing strategies. One of these strategies is *glocalization*. Glocalization involves creating and distributing a product for a global market while making modifications to the product so that it reflects local culture (Nash, 2000). For instance, during the 1990s, Sony Music released albums by Céline Dion and other artists in several slightly different editions that were tailored to different countries or regions. A specific case is the Latin American edition of Dion's 1996 album *Falling Into You*, which featured a Spanish-language version of the song 'All By Myself'.

The global domination of the Big Four and the possibility of further ownership concentration raise several issues of concern. To begin with, the concentration of *ownership* in the music industry is also the concentration of *power* (Bishop, 2005). Fewer and fewer companies get to make decisions about the recorded music heard by people around the world. Many of these decisions are based on generating massive sales from a relatively small number of artists who have enough mainstream appeal to become global superstars. Consequently, the power of the Big Four has implications for the degree of diversity and innovation in music.

In various countries, independent record companies are more willing than the Big Four to take risks on less mainstream music and artists (ibid.). However, these small companies face difficulties stemming from the presence of their multinational competitors. The difficulties are familiar to the Independent Music Publishers and Labels Association (IMPALA), which represents the interests of the independent music sector in Europe. Martin Mills, the chair of IMPALA, argued that 'four big companies can impose their will on retail and media in a

way that 15 did not. In battling each other for space and attention—and leveraging their strength—they intentionally or unintentionally reduce opportunities for smaller players' (Mills, 2006: 8). As a result, Mills noted that a new artist on a small label can easily get squeezed out. He concluded that 'a concentrated market carries dangers to musical diversity, to smaller companies and to music fans' (ibid.).

As a result of these concerns, domination by the Big Four has generated conflicts that are being addressed by regulatory authorities and the courts. Since IMPALA is opposed to any further ownership concentration in the music industry, it challenged the European Commission's 2004 decision to grant regulatory approval to the Sony BMG merger. In 2006, Europe's Court of First Instance ruled that the merger had been allowed on the basis of inadequate evidence about its impact. This gave Sony BMG three options. It could undo the merger, appeal the court's decision, or reapply to the European Commission for approval of the merger (*The Economist*, 2006b). At the time of writing, it appears that Sony BMG is pursuing the last two options (Ferguson and Cendrowicz, 2006). Meanwhile, given that a merger between EMI and Warner might also be rejected, these two companies have put their merger talks on hold until a final decision is made about Sony BMG (Cardew, 2006).

While such mergers in the global music industry have an impact on companies and even fans (at least in terms of the diversity of music available to listeners), we must not forget the impact they can have on workers. It has been suggested that a merger between EMI and Warner would lead to job cuts (ibid.). Clearly, the global music industry raises a number of issues that are of interest to media sociologists.

Economic Globalization

With regard to economic globalization, critical researchers are concerned about the emergence of an *international division of labour*. Sociologists and other scholars have analyzed how multinational corporations, including those with holdings in the media and information industries, have spread their production operations around the world. The standard view of this process suggests that it involves shifting jobs from developed, rich countries (such as the United States) to developing, poor countries (like India). Although the trend is certainly in the direction of

moving jobs to the developing world, Mosco (2005: 52) has pointed to 'an increasingly complex international division of labour involving far more than simply the transfer of service jobs from high- to low-wage nations'.

This is illustrated by the fact that several developed countries, especially Canada and Ireland, have been the recipients of much outsourcing and off-shoring of jobs in the media and information industries. *Outsourcing* occurs when a company shifts a portion of its production to another entity, typically independent local companies in a foreign country. *Off-shoring* exists when a company has one of its own foreign affiliates handle the production. Although developing countries offer cheaper labour and other advantages, multinational corporations maintain some outsourcing or off-shoring in developed countries like Canada because they need certain jobs to be filled by workers with higher levels of skill or education (Mosco, 2005). Due to the value of the dollar and wage rates in these other developed countries, multinationals can still enjoy considerable savings on production costs compared to keeping production in the United States. These factors explain the existence of so-called 'runaway' productions. Hollywood studios have moved a number of film and television productions from Los Angeles to Canadian cities—everything from the *X-Men* movie trilogy to *The X-Files* television series—in order to cut costs while utilizing the expertise of Canadian companies and production crews (Elmer and Gasher, 2005; Magder and Burston, 2001).

We can illustrate some aspects of the international division of labour through the case of Disney. Wasko (2001) has shown that Disney arranges to have some of its film, television, and animation production done in countries such as Canada and Australia. However, where manual labour is involved, as in the production of toys or clothing that feature Disney characters, Disney has most of the work done in less developed countries to take advantage of cheap labour. The products are designed by Disney in the United States, but the actual manufacturing is licensed to independent subcontractors in developing countries. Many of the toys and clothing sold in the Disney Store at your local shopping mall are made 'in Third World countries where workers are paid poverty-level wages and often work in inhumane conditions' (Wasko, 2001: 69).

Conflict Over Ownership, Policy, and Globalization

It is also important to consider the issue of conflict. Capitalist interests in ownership, policy, and globalization have generated conflict between private companies and various subordinate groups. Although the state serves the interests of the capitalist class, Marxist theory suggests that the state makes some concessions to the working class and its allies. Consequently, despite the power of corporate capital and its influence on the state, we must realize that subordinate groups have occasionally won victories through their struggles and resistance.

A Canadian example involves the historical conflict over public sod private ownership of broadcasting in Canada. Broadcasting in this country began during the

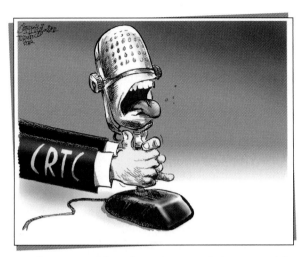

Opponents of Canadian content regulations, especially private broadcasters, claim that these CRTC regulations are an attack on the freedom of broadcasters. Reprinted with permission—Torstar Syndication Services

1920s with private radio stations, but a commission appointed by the federal government (the Royal Commission on Radio Broadcasting) recommended in 1929 that all broadcasting in Canada should be publicly owned and operated by a Crown corporation. Smythe (1981: 165) noted that the period from 1930 to 1936 was marked by 'a struggle between the popular forces in Canada fighting for public service broadcasting and those seeking private profit'.

The 'popular forces' were organized around the Canadian Radio League (CRL), which was headed by two nationalistic young men named Graham Spry and Alan Plaunt. Those who joined with the CRL to call for public broadcasting included trade unions, farm groups, women's organizations, churches, and educational leaders. The advocates of using broadcasting for private profit were led by the Canadian Association of Broadcasters (CAB), a lobbying organization that represented the existing private radio stations in Canada. Supporters of the CAB included the major newspapers (which often owned the stations) and many large corporations or manufacturers that wanted to use private radio for advertising (Raboy, 1990; Smythe, 1981). In the end, the CRL and its allies were successful in their struggle for public broadcasting. The federal government established the Canadian Radio Broadcasting Commission (CRBC) as Canada's first public broadcaster in 1932, and the CRBC paved the way for the emergence of the CBC as a Crown corporation in 1936. However, private broadcasting was allowed to continue and grow in Canada.

The Canadian content regulations for television and radio that were referred to earlier are important aspects of regulatory policy, and they have long provided the basis for conflict. Private broadcasters do not want the regulations; in the pursuit of profit, they are more interested in maximizing audiences and advertising revenues by offering popular American television shows and music. A different position has been taken by Canadian nationalists as well as unions representing actors, musicians, and other workers in Canadian media industries. They contend that Canadian content regulations are necessary to provide

jobs for Canadian artists and ensure that Canadian culture is presented over the Canadian airwaves. In the late 1950s, the BBG's proposal for a minimum percentage of Canadian content on television was opposed by the CAB as well as advertisers (Peers, 1979). However, the proposal was supported by the Canadian Broadcasting League (CBL)—an organization that had been inspired by the CRL—and the Canadian Labour Congress, which represented workers (Raboy, 1990). Similarly, while the CAB

OPEN FOR DISCUSSION
Do We Need CanCon Regulations for Radio?

Canadian content regulations for radio stations in Canada were established in 1970. The regulations are administered by the Canadian Radio-television and Telecommunications Commission (CRTC). Currently, CanCon regulations (as they are often known) stipulate that at least 35 per cent of the music on radio stations featuring popular music must be Canadian. The amount of Canadian content required by the CRTC has varied over time and in accordance with the type of music played by a station. To qualify as Canadian, a piece of music must generally meet at least two of the following four criteria: the music is composed entirely by a Canadian; the lyrics are written entirely by a Canadian; the music or lyrics are performed principally by a Canadian; or the musical selection consists of a live performance that is either recorded wholly in Canada or performed wholly in Canada and broadcast live in Canada.

There has been considerable debate about whether or not we need Canadian content regulations. Opponents of CanCon include private radio broadcasters and some Canadian musicians. Supporters of the regulations include other Canadian musicians, labour unions that represent Canadian musicians, Canadian nationalists, and the owners of Canadian independent record companies. The debate between the opponents and supporters of CanCon has focused on several issues, two of which are outlined below.

The first issue concerns whether or not radio stations should be forced to play Canadian music. Opponents of CanCon, especially owners of private radio stations, contend that CanCon regulations are an attack on the freedom of broadcasters. They

maintain that radio broadcasters should have the right to play whatever music they want and whatever music their listeners want to hear. Supporters of CanCon argue that the owners of private radio stations are making money off of the Canadian airwaves, which are public property and subject to legal requirements under the Broadcasting Act. In exchange for being given the opportunity to use the public airwaves for profit, they point out that it is reasonable for private radio broadcasters to meet some public service obligations by playing music that is Canadian.

The second issue concerns whether or not Canadian artists need CanCon regulations. Opponents of CanCon argue that, if Canadian artists have talent, they will make it on their own without assistance from the CRTC. In their view, radio stations will be happy to play music by Canadian artists as long as their music is good. Supporters of CanCon maintain that Canadian artists will not get on the radio unless they are already well known or unless they are signed to or distributed by one of the multinational conglomerates that dominate the music industry. They contend that developing artists (those who are unsigned or signed to small, independently owned Canadian record companies) will not receive airplay unless there are regulations to force radio stations to give them a chance to be heard.

Now that you have learned about some of the points made on each side of the debate, which side do you agree with? Do we need CanCon regulations for radio or not?

Source: Adapted from Young (2008).

was against the CRTC's notion of having Canadian content regulations for radio, those in favour of such regulations included labour unions.

The efforts of private broadcasters to get around the regulations or get them reduced have provided the basis for further conflict. Conflict has also taken the form of ongoing debate about whether or not these regulations are needed—a debate that is especially fierce in relation to radio and support for Canadian music (Young, 2008).

In recent years, much conflict associated with the media has been connected to globalization. This is most obvious in the protests against economic and cultural globalization that various social movements have held at WTO meetings and at the meetings of other international bodies that focus on economic growth, but conflict over globalization also takes other forms. For instance, in developed countries like the United States, and even in developing countries such as India, trade unions have resisted outsourcing in the media and information industries. Although workers in the developing world appreciate the jobs that outsourcing provides, they are concerned about the low wages and poor working conditions that often come with these jobs. While trade unions in developed countries have resisted the loss of jobs to the Third World, they have also challenged the shifting of work to other developed countries (Mosco, 2005). For example, there has been considerable opposition from labour in the United States to the movement of film and television production to Canada (Magder and Burston, 2001). These 'runaway' productions, many of which are shot in Vancouver, have generated contradictions and conflicts in the Canadian context. A member of the Union of British Columbian Performers (UBCP) made this quite clear: 'All of us are constantly making an effort to woo Hollywood [production companies], but as unions we also have to fight them because they want to exploit' (cited in Coe, 2000: 91).

Conflict is reflected further in the opposition of many countries—including Canada—to the insistence of the United States on a free flow of information. Along with France, Canada led efforts to establish an international agreement upholding the rights of countries to support and promote the diversity of cultural expression (Azzi, 2005). The resulting Convention on Cultural Diversity was drafted through the United Nations Educational, Scientific, and Cultural Organization (UNESCO). In a vote held by UNESCO members during October 2005, 148 countries approved the convention while two countries (including the United States) were against it and four countries abstained from voting. It is hoped that this convention will become an effective counterweight against

pressure from the United States for free trade in culture (Young, 2008).

● Cultural Studies ● ● ● ● of the Media

As noted earlier, while political economy focuses on ownership and control of the media, cultural studies address the ideological aspects of the media. Three key issues in cultural studies need to be discussed. These are representation in mainstream media; interpreting and resisting mainstream media; and opposition through alternative media.

Representation in Mainstream Media

The mainstream media include the newspapers, magazines, radio stations, or television channels that most people are exposed to every day. These means of communication are owned by private companies or by the government. The mainstream media present *texts* (such as newspaper and magazine articles or television shows) that convey certain messages about society and groups in society. Critical media sociologists and other scholars argue that these messages reflect the **dominant ideology**. In other words, the messages express the viewpoints of the capitalist class and other powerful groups. Capitalist, patriarchal, or racist ideologies are some specific forms of the dominant ideology that have been embedded in media texts.

We can investigate aspects of the dominant ideology by considering the representation of social class, gender, and race/ethnicity in the mainstream media. Less powerful groups in society—the working class, women, and racial or ethnic minorities—receive poor representation in media content. This takes the form of *under-representation* (since members of disadvantaged groups are usually not seen in the media as frequently as they actually exist in society) and *misrepresentation* (because members of these groups often are portrayed in ways that are both stereotypical and negative).

Representation of the Working Class
Critical media sociologists and other researchers have been concerned about the representation of social class in the mainstream media. In particular, they have been concerned about the portrayal of the working class and labour unions. The representation of these groups can be illustrated through reference to some North American studies.

Butsch conducted a series of studies on the representation of social classes in American domestic situation comedies. After researching all of the domestic situation comedies that had appeared on American television between 1946 and 1978, Butsch identified the class position of the family in each show through the occupation of the household head (usually the lead male character). The family was considered to be working class if the lead character was a blue-collar worker, clerical worker, retail sales worker, or service worker. The criteria for indicating that the family was middle class included the existence of a professional or salaried manager as the household head. Some comedies fell outside these categories because they featured a self-employed or independently wealthy lead character, and it was not possible to identify the occupation of the household head in a number of shows (Butsch and Glennon, 1983). Once he had categorized the comedies, Butsch examined what they revealed about the representation of social classes.

Butsch demonstrated that there were significant differences in the extent to which social classes were represented in domestic situation comedies. He could not specify the occupation of the household head in 10.1 per cent of the comedies, but he found that 4.8 per cent featured a family that was independently wealthy and 13.2 per cent portrayed a family led by someone who was self-employed. However, his key findings were that 63.5 per cent of domestic situation comedies were about a middle-class family and only 8.4 per cent centred on a working-class family. Butsch noted that these figures were out of line with the existence of both classes in American society; based on census data, 28.7 per cent of actual household heads in the United States were middle class while 65.0 per cent were working class (Butsch and Glennon, 1983). Thus, based on research Butsch conducted in the early 1980s, the middle class was over-represented in domestic situation comedies and the working class was under-represented. Unfortunately, no studies have been done to update these findings.

In his later research, Butsch found sharp differences in the way that social classes were represented in domestic situation comedies. Much of his analysis focused on the portrayal of working-class and middle-class men. Working-class men were generally represented in negative ways; the emphasis was on their 'ineptitude, immaturity, stupidity, lack of good sense, or emotional outburst' (Butsch, 1992: 391). The women in working-class comedies (and sometimes even the children) were portrayed as being much more intelligent and level-headed. In these comedies, the humorous situation typically involved the husband/father. The situation was often one of his own

making, and he was usually helped out of it by his wife (Butsch, 1992). As Butsch (1995) pointed out, this scenario describes various working-class domestic situation comedies and their lead male characters in decades from the 1950s through to the 1980s. Consider *The Honeymooners* (Ralph Kramden), *The Flintstones* (Fred Flintstone), *All in the Family* (Archie Bunker), and *The Simpsons* (Homer Simpson).

In contrast, Butsch found that middle-class men were often represented in positive ways. They were portrayed as being 'intelligent, rational, mature, and responsible' (Butsch, 1992: 391). The women in middle-class families were shown as also having these characteristics in their roles as wives and mothers. In middle-class domestic situation comedies, the humorous situation typically involved one of the children. The parents guided the child through the situation, and they often provided a moral lesson in the process. Examples of these comedies from the 1950s to the 1980s include *Father Knows Best*, *My Three Sons*, *The Brady Bunch*, and *The Cosby Show* (Butsch, 1992). Butsch (1995: 404) argued that the stark differences between the representation of working-class and middle-class men ideologically justify inequality in our class-divided society: 'Blue-collar workers are portrayed as requiring supervision, and managers and professionals as intelligent and mature enough to provide it.'

Representation of Women

Critical media sociologists and feminist researchers have been concerned about gender issues in media content, particularly about the representation of women. Many studies have been done in this area, and on a wide variety of specific topics, but we can illustrate the representation of women in the mainstream media through a few studies of American and Canadian media content.

In a study titled 'Woman with a Gun', Dole (2000) examined the representation of women as law enforcers in American motion pictures that were released during the 1980s and 1990s. Dole (2000: 11) argued that the women in these films had 'types of power culturally coded as masculine'. The women had power because they occupied the position of law enforcer and because they carried a gun (two characteristics socially defined as 'masculine' within our culture). Dole saw the genre of women cop films as emerging in two phases. The earlier films (1987–91), such as *Blue Steel* and *Impulse*, often imitated the physicality and violence of male action films by showing the women using their guns. Because many of these films were commercially unsuccessful, the later films (1991–5) took a softer approach. These films, including *The Silence of the Lambs* and *Copycat*, were more inclined 'to privilege intellectual over physical power' (Dole, 2000: 12). Rather than using their guns, the female law enforcers in the later films relied on their sleuthing skills.

Several other techniques were employed to play down 'the threatening image of Woman with a Gun' (Dole, 2000: 16). These techniques included *domestication* (portraying the female cops as single mothers or at least as women who have 'maternal instincts'), *infantilization* (representing the women as being dependent, vulnerable, helpless, or in need of rescue), and *sexualization* (emphasizing the bodies of the women through the provocative way they are dressed). Finally, those films that focused on intellectual power utilized what Dole called *splitting strategies*. Splitting strategies distributed among multiple characters the power that would otherwise be concentrated in one character. Through the use of splitting strategies, the power of the female law enforcer was reduced. This can be illustrated by *The Silence of the Lambs*. In that film, intellectual power was split between Clarice Starling (Jodie Foster) and Hannibal Lecter (Anthony Hopkins). Although Starling was intelligent, she needed male assistance in the form of Lecter (Dole, 2000). The ideological message was that a woman is incapable of solving the case and catching the killer on her own. Although female cop films gave women more representation than most movies (because they occupied central roles rather than peripheral roles), the stereotypical and patriarchal misrepresentation of women was still quite evident in these films.

It is also important to consider how the news media are connected to the representation of women or issues associated with women, and some Canadian research in this area has focused on news coverage of what is often referred to as the Montreal Massacre. On 6 December 1989, 25-year-old Marc Lépine walked into l'École polytechnique (the School of Engineering) at the University of Montreal with a semi-automatic rifle. He entered a classroom, ordered the men to leave, and accused the women of being 'a bunch of feminists' before shooting six of them to death. Lépine then walked through the hallways of the building, entered other classrooms, and murdered eight more women. He also injured nine women and four men. At the end of his shooting rampage, he killed himself. In a suicide note found on his body, Lépine cited 'political reasons' for the murders: he blamed 'the feminists, who have always ruined my life' (cited in Eglin and Hester, 1999: 256). There was much coverage of the Montreal Massacre in the news media, and some studies have been done on this coverage.

In one study, Hayford (1992) compared newspaper coverage of the Montreal Massacre at the time of the murders to coverage of a similar incident in Chicago during 1966 when eight women were killed by a man named Richard Speck. She found that the killings in Chicago were often interpreted by journalists in individualistic terms as the act of a madman. However, by the time the murders in Montreal occurred 23 years later, the women's movement had experienced some success in raising public awareness about the prevalence of wife-beating, rape, and other acts of violence against women in a patriarchal society. Since this had an impact on at least some journalists, there was media debate about individual versus societal explanations for the murders. Hayford (1992: 209) indicated that 'the question of whether Lépine was no more than a demented individual or a reflection of broader social patterns of male violence against women, a question never raised about Speck, became a central issue in coverage of the Montreal killings.'

In another study, Rosenberg (2003) examined news coverage of the tenth anniversary of the Montreal Massacre. One aspect of her study addressed the 'emblematic' characteristics that the coverage had taken on by this point. She noted that, in order to contest individualistic and psychological explanations for Lépine's actions, many feminists had encouraged interpretation of the Montreal Massacre as an emblem or symbol of violence against women. However, by this time, some feminists had come to see the 'emblematic' interpretation of the Montreal Massacre as problematic due to the growing emphasis within feminism on the issue of difference. These feminists argued that taking the murders of 14 middle-class, white women as emblematic obscured diversity among women in terms of their experiences with violence through other class positions and racial or ethnic backgrounds. However, Rosenberg (2003: 15) found that the 'critiques of emblemization by feminists' were 'largely absent in tenth anniversary coverage'.

Representation of Racial and Ethnic Minorities

We also need to consider the under-representation and misrepresentation of racial and ethnic minorities in the mainstream media. From its beginnings in the 1960s, research on media–minority relations has largely focused on these issues (Mahtani, 2001).

Studies have shown that racial and ethnic minorities have experienced misrepresentation in Canadian mass media. To the extent that they are seen, ethno-racial minorities are portrayed in stereotypical and negative ways. Especially in the news media, this often takes the form of identifying them as social problems; racial and ethnic minorities are depicted as 'having problems or creating problems in need of political attention or costly solutions' (Fleras and Kunz, 2001: 145).

Members of these minorities, particularly immigrants, are presented as social problems in a variety of ways. They are seen to be participating in illegal activities, clashing with police, cheating on welfare, creating difficulties for immigration authorities, and having other undesirable effects (Fleras and Kunz, 2001). Specific groups—blacks, Asians, and Aboriginal people—are often singled out. For instance, Grenier (1994: 313) noted that Aboriginal people are 'portrayed by mass media as strange, as unpredictable threats to social order, and as heavily engaged in emotive and largely deviant forms of conflict.' However, especially since the 9/11 terrorist attacks, Muslims have become the favourite target in media content. The news and entertainment media have depicted Muslims as religious fanatics who have little regard for human life. In the process, an entire group has been demonized for the actions of a few (Fleras and Kunz, 2001). The various portrayals of ethno-racial minorities described above are all based on positioning 'us' (an assumed mainstream audience) against 'them' (the minorities that are seen as posing threats to the majority). As a result, these negative representations may contribute to deepening divisions in society (Mahtani, 2001).

Explaining the Representation

How can we explain the under-representation or misrepresentation of the working class, women, and racial or ethnic minorities in media content? To begin, we must reject the notion that there is a plot or 'conspiracy' by powerful groups against less powerful groups. The circumstances are far more complex than that, and we must return to the concept of the dominant ideology in order to understand this. According to Hall (1980), the dominant ideology is woven into media texts through **encoding**. Messages are constructed within the economic and technical frameworks of media institutions through a complicated production process that involves (among other things) organizational relations or practices and 'meanings and ideas' drawn from the production structure (the media institutions) and 'the wider socio-cultural and political structure' (1980: 129). Therefore, in order to grasp the representation of subordinate groups, we need to consider some of these factors in more depth.

Economic factors associated with media or cultural institutions help to partially account for the representa-tion of subordinate groups in the entertainment media. Butsch (1995) noted that the under-representation of the working class in domestic situation comedies has much to do with the need for producers and broadcasters to develop programs that will attract advertisers by providing a good atmosphere for products. There is a tendency, then, to create shows that feature middle-class characters and occupational groups that can afford to buy the products appearing in the ads. Furthermore, to the limited extent that working-class domestic situation comedies have been made, their persistently negative representation of working-class men exists in part because producers and broadcasters avoid financial risk by relying on formulas that have proven to be successful. Thus, the popularity of *The Honeymooners* in the 1950s spawned *The Flintstones* in the 1960s.

Dole also draws attention to economic factors when addressing the representation of female law enforcers in motion pictures. She explains that 'Hollywood has experimented with various levels of violence, muscularity, and sexualization in women's action films in order to achieve a mix that will produce big profits' (2000: 12). Producers have tried to expand the female audience for types of entertainment that more frequently appeal to a male audience without losing that male audience. This helps to account for the contradictions in films and television dramas that feature female law enforcers.

Finally, economic factors clearly affect the representation of racial and ethnic minorities. The quantity and quality of media representation of minorities is affected by the commercial imperatives of institutions, including the need to attract the largest possible audience (Fleras and Kunz, 2001). For example, the Canadian Academy of Recording Arts and Sciences (CARAS) has attempted to generate the largest possible audience for the telecast of the Juno Awards by getting high-profile musical artists to appear on the ceremony, and this has left few spots for lesser-known artists from minority groups (Young, 2006).

Factors associated with production and ideology also help to explain the problematic representation of subordinate groups in the entertainment media. Members of less powerful groups often do not occupy important positions associated with media production. For example, as an American communications scholar has shown, women have little control over production in the film industry; women comprised only 17 per cent of all directors, executive producers, producers, writers, cinematographers, and editors who worked on the top 250 grossing American films in the United States for the year 2005 (Lauzen, 2006). Such exclusion from the process of media production can have a substantial impact on media content. Butsch (1995) makes this clear in his analysis of domestic situation comedies. He notes that the under-representation of the working class in these comedies, along with the negative representation of working-class men, can partially be explained by the middle-class background of most producers and writers. Middle-class people develop shows based on what is familiar to them and, when they occasionally focus on working-class characters, they rely on the negative stereotypes of the working class that circulate in our culture as part of the dominant system of meanings and ideas.

Some of the same factors also help to explain the representation of subordinate groups in the news media. The need to attract advertising revenues by capturing large numbers of readers or viewers has contributed to the under-representation of the working class and ethno-racial minorities in news stories. For instance, since affluent middle-class audiences are desired by advertisers, the content of the news is designed to attract these audiences by reflecting their interests or concerns (Hackett and Uzelman, 2003). The middle-class, male, white backgrounds of many news personnel also have at least some consequences for how less powerful groups are covered (Mahtani, 2001). Like producers and writers in the entertainment media, the work of journalists is partially shaped by their socio-demographic backgrounds and the dominant meanings and ideas they are exposed to. As Mahtani (2001: 115) has indicated, 'journalists are largely bound by the dominant cultures within which they operate, including embedded societal prejudices, stereotypes, and populist frames of thinking.'

An additional factor unique to the news media is that the routines of gathering news through sources can also affect media representation. When preparing a story, journalists first seek information from *primary sources*. These are the powerful voices of private capital or the state such as corporate representatives, government officials, and the police. Primary sources draw on the dominant ideology to 'define the situation, and establish what the event or issue is essentially about; the terms in which it should be understood' (Knight, 1998: 99). Once the key terms of the story have been established by the primary sources, journalists then get reactions from *second-*

ary sources. These are less powerful individuals such as trade union leaders, spokespeople for women's groups and minority groups, or representatives of oppositional social movements. Secondary sources provide reactions to the event or issue within the boundaries set by the primary sources. Compared to primary sources, 'they speak less often; and they rarely speak as fully and autonomously' (Knight, 1988: 20). As a result, the routines associated with using sources mean that the news is structured more favourably towards the views of the powerful (Knight, 1982). The less powerful receive less representation and, since they are more likely to be paraphrased than quoted, their views may be misrepresented.

Interpreting and Resisting Mainstream Media

In cultural studies, research has gone beyond studying representation in mainstream media to considering interpretation of this representation and resistance to representation. We have seen that the dominant ideology—the perspective of powerful groups—is embedded in media texts through the process of encoding, but it is also important to consider the **decoding** of media content by audience members. As part of his encoding/decoding model, Hall (1980) argued that the dominant ideology is inscribed as the *dominant or preferred meaning* within media content.

Since Hall recognized that audience members may not always adopt this meaning when they interpret media messages, he identified three possible ways of decoding media texts. A *dominant-hegemonic* reading involves taking the preferred meaning while an *oppositional* reading involves resisting a message by interpreting it through an alternative ideological framework. A *negotiated* reading contains a mixture of the dominant-hegemonic and oppositional readings. According to Hall (1980: 137), it reflects 'the dominant definition of events' while refusing to accept every aspect of the definition. Consequently, 'this negotiated version of the dominant ideology is shot through with contradictions' (1980: 137). For example, a worker may accept the argument of government officials (as presented by the news media) that the 'national interest' requires citizens

▆▌ Time to Reflect ▐█ ▐█ ▐█ ▐█ ▐█ ▐█ ▐█ ▐█ ▐█ ▐█ ▐█ █

How are less powerful groups in society represented in the content of the mass media, and why are they represented in these ways?

to make economic sacrifices while opposing the related argument that such sacrifices must be made through legislation imposing wage freezes (Hall, 1980).

Studies have been done on the decoding of media content by relatively powerless or disadvantaged groups, and some of this research has documented the resistance of groups to their representation in media texts or their resistance to other aspects of media messages. In order to examine the decoding positions that Hall identified, Morley (1980) conducted a now-classic study of how groups interpreted the British current affairs television series *Nationwide*. Morley demonstrated that decoding is affected by one's class position. For instance, in relation to a *Nationwide* program that discussed the effects of budget policy on families of different class backgrounds, Morley found that none of the middle-class groups adopted an oppositional reading while working-class groups produced more oppositional and negotiated readings.

Although the research on *Nationwide* is often remembered for analysis of how class position affects interpretation of media texts, Morley (2006) has stressed that his aim was to examine how decoding is also influenced by other types of social position (such as gender, race/ethnicity, and age). These elements of Morley's

study have come through more clearly in a statistical re-analysis of his data conducted by Kim. For example, in relation to age, Kim (2004: 88, 91) found that 'the *younger* working-class viewers are, the more probability they have of producing *dominant* readings . . . . The more youthful viewers' consent to the preferred meanings can be explained by their relatively low-level of political consciousness, which is commonly found among youths in general.'

In another study, Press (1991) discovered differences in the way that working-class and middle-class women interpreted television shows. Her findings indicated that middle-class women tended to respond to television in ways that were gender-specific (connected to patriarchy) while working-class women were more inclined to respond in class-specific terms. Paradoxically, middle-class women accepted 'television's portrayals of independent women and television's stereotypically sexy females' (1991: 138). Press concluded that, for these women, 'television is both a source of feminist resistance to the status quo and, at the same time, a source for the reinforcement of many of the status quo's patriarchal values' (1991: 96). Working-class women resisted the representation of working-class life in television shows, seeing it as unrealistic, but Press (1991: 175) noted that

SOCIOLOGY IN ACTION
Watching Homeless Men Watch *Die Hard*

Fiske and Dawson (1996: 297) wanted to examine 'audiencing', which they defined as 'the process in which audiences selectively produce meanings and pleasures from texts'. They were especially interested in studying how texts associated with the dominant culture were used, through audiencing, by subordinate groups. Fiske and Dawson decided to focus their analysis on how homeless men watched and interpreted television.

The researchers began by getting access to homeless men. They approached the authorities who ran a homeless shelter in an American city. After the researchers convinced the authorities that their work would be done with sensitivity towards the plight of the homeless, they were given permission to conduct their study. Fiske and Dawson then spent time at the shelter (at least twice a week for three months) until the homeless men felt more comfortable with their

presence. Eventually, they started collecting data on how the men made use of a television set and video-cassette recorder in a lounge at the shelter.

Fiske and Dawson tried to make their observations unobtrusively. They just watched television with the homeless men and only talked with those who wanted to talk. The researchers carefully observed the reactions of the men to what was being watched and made notes in private as soon as possible afterwards. By choosing these particular observational strategies, Fiske and Dawson hoped that their presence would not significantly affect the behaviour of the men as they watched television.

The homeless men often borrowed violent action films from the local public library, and one of the films they watched during the study was *Die Hard*. Fiske and Dawson analyzed the reactions of the men to this movie. The main character of the movie is John McClane (Bruce Willis), an off-duty detective who happens to be in the office tower of the Nakatomi Corporation at the time a gang of terrorists invades a Christmas party and takes the company's executives hostage. Although they profess to have political motives, these 'terrorists' turn out to be thieves who want the millions of dollars held in the company's vaults. The plot of the film involves McClane's efforts to kill off the terrorists/thieves one by one as the police unsuccessfully try to contend with the situation from outside the building.

Fiske and Dawson made some interesting observations about the reactions of the homeless men to *Die Hard*. They found the men paid the most attention to 'violence that was directed against the social order' (ibid., 301). For instance, the first scene that captured the interest of the homeless men was the one in which the terrorists/thieves invade the party being held by the corporate executives. The homeless men cheered at the climax of the scene, which showed the thieves killing the head of the Nakatomi Corporation after he refuses to give them a computer code to access the company's vaults.

The men had a similar reaction to another scene. In one part of the movie, the police attempt to retake the building with an armoured vehicle. While hidden and in radio communication with the terrorists, McClane could see the terrorists preparing to fire a rocket that would destroy the vehicle and kill the men in it. McClane begs them not to fire their weapon, but they do it anyway. The homeless men cheered in response. Fiske and Dawson (ibid., 306) note that 'the hero's plea works to position the viewer inside the norms of the dominant social order against the excessive violence of terrorists, but the homeless refused this positioning.' In contrast to the way people are intended to interpret the film, the homeless men were enthusiastic about the attacks on corporate capital and the police.

What explains the reactions of homeless men to *Die Hard*? Their reactions must be understood in terms of their position in society and the reasons for their position. Although the dominant way of thinking about the homeless assumes that these people are to blame for the situation they are in, Fiske and Dawson stress that homelessness is rooted in structural conditions rather than individual failings or inadequacies. This means that homelessness emerges from the structure and conditions of capitalist society.

As they indicate, 'the contemporary conditions of US capitalism . . . have produced and then exacerbated the gap between the privileged and the deprived' (ibid., 301). In the years prior to their study, policies associated with **neo-liberalism** had 'minimized the role of the state in social life and maximized that of capital and the market' (ibid., 302). Millions of jobs had disappeared, many of them at the lower end of the pay scale, and government assistance to the poor was reduced. As a result, poverty increased. Government tax incentives for investment in low-income housing were reduced, also, which meant that average rents doubled and low-income housing decreased. All of these conditions within capitalist society generated an increase in the number of homeless people.

While capitalism has had a negative impact on the homeless, the police have had a parallel impact as agents of social control. As Fiske and Dawson point out, violence 'may be initiated by the social order to control the homeless' (ibid., 303). They note that riot police have been used to clear the homeless from parks in American cities, and the police have also confronted activist homeless groups that organize illegal squats in empty houses.

The experiences of the homeless with capitalism and the police make it possible to understand their reactions to some of the violence in *Die Hard*. Fiske and Dawson conclude that 'certain representations of violence enable subordinated people to articulate symbolically their sense of opposition and hostility to the particular forms of domination that oppress them' (ibid., 304).

it was 'more surprising and disturbing' that these women thought many shows about middle-class life presented 'accurate pictures of reality'.

Some studies have addressed resistance to representation in a different way by examining the efforts of subordinate groups to change their representation through conflicts with cultural organizations. Tator et al. (1998) examined several cases of conflict over racism in the arts. These cases included the opposition of blacks to negative stereotypes in *Show Boat* and the resistance of Asians to the way they were portrayed in *Miss Saigon*. Both musicals were performed on stage in Toronto during the early 1990s, and Tator et al. found a consistent pattern among the events associated with these two cases and most of the others they examined. They identified a five-stage process that is more fully outlined in Table 13.2. After a white-dominated cultural institution stages an event that misrepresents minorities, such as *Show Boat* or *Miss Saigon*, there is resistance from ethno-racial minorities. Once the positions have hardened into two opposing factions, the cultural institution engages in counter-resistance. This is effective, and one of the immediate outcomes is that the resistance of minorities soon disappears (Tator et al., 1998).

Opposition through Alternative Media

While relatively powerless or disadvantaged groups have engaged in resistance to problematic representation and messages in mainstream media, some of these groups have turned to opposition through alternative media. **Alternative media** are forms of communication used by subordinate groups and social movements to present their own messages, which often involve challenging existing conditions in society.

Many types of alternative media have been employed by groups and movements committed to social change, but community broadcasting has historically played a particularly important role in Canada. Beginning in the late 1960s, the terms *alternative* or *community* broadcasting were used to describe a new approach to radio and television that differed from *public* broadcasting—a phrase that had come to be associated with the centralized, hierarchical, and government-owned approach exemplified by the CBC (Raboy, 1990). During the early 1970s, community broadcasting started operating through small radio stations or 'public access' television channels on privately owned cable systems. These new forms of communication strongly emphasized democratic principles. For instance, the community television channels on many cable systems were run by an advisory board of community members (especially in Quebec), and any groups or individuals from the local community could prepare their own programs.

Operated in this fashion, community television enabled social activists and members of marginalized groups to express themselves. However, as Goldberg (1990: 38) noted, community television was 'a collectivist, pluralist, egalitarian concept embedded in a hierarchical, privately controlled, corporate structure'. As private cable companies started to assert their ultimate control over community channels in the late 1970s, the

community advisory boards virtually disappeared (at least in English Canada) and groups committed to social change largely gave up using community television to achieve their goals (Goldberg, 1990). Although community television lost its focus on the disadvantaged and social change, community radio still plays an important role in these respects. For instance, Vancouver Co-operative Radio is a non-commercial station that is owned and run jointly by its members. According to its website (www.coopradio.org), the station is 'a voice for the voiceless that strives to provide a space for under-represented and marginalized communities'.

Other types of alternative media have also been used by oppositional movements in Canada. Carroll and Ratner (1999) investigated the political strategies of three social movement organizations, including Greenpeace and their use of alternative media. Although Greenpeace usually created spectacles that received widespread coverage in the mainstream media, the organization had been involved in the production of magazines and video footage that permitted more control over the presentation of its messages. Carroll and Ratner noted that The Centre, an organization for gay men and lesbians in Vancouver, was even more involved with alternative media. It had established the monthly newspaper *Angles* and the *Coming Out Show* on Vancouver Co-operative Radio. The final organization that Carroll and Ratner examined was End Legislated Poverty (ELP). Committed to mobilizing the poor and fighting various state policies that perpetuate poverty, ELP had engaged in popular education through alternative media directed at the poor and the general public. ELP's alternative media included 'Fighting Poverty Kits' and a newspaper, *The Long Haul*.

Documentaries provide an effective way for progressive social movements to present their messages. For instance, during the summer of 1993, environmental activists filmed their protests against the clear-cutting of trees at Clayoquot Sound in British Columbia by the logging company MacMillan Bloedel. This enabled the activists to document their actions and express their concerns without potentially being misrepresented in the mainstream news media, where they would be limited to the role of secondary sources. Filming a documentary also gave the activists, many of whom were women, an opportunity to record how the state dealt with their opposition. The activists underwent mass arrests by the police as well as mass trials. Some of them even served prison terms. The resulting documentary film, *Fury for the Sound: The Women at Clayoquot*, is often shown on Canadian university campuses. There is a continuing need for such alternative media. As Hack-

Table 13.2   Stages in Conflict between Cultural Institutions and Ethno-racial Minorities over Representation in the Arts

Stage	Key Characteristics
Stage 1: Selection and staging of the event	• A cultural institution decides to produce an event that is problematic because of the way it depicts ethno-racial minorities. • Members of the institution are typically from the white majority, so they often do not see the problematic aspects of the event. • The institution plans, organizes, produces, and markets the event.
Stage 2: Resistance mounted by ethno-racial minorities	• The resistance effort begins as minorities express concerns about how they are portrayed in the cultural event. • Minorities try to generate support for their resistance through pamphlets, the ethnic media, demonstrations, etc.
Stage 3: Development of two distinct factions	• The institution defends its cultural event, deflects criticisms, and rejects alternatives. • The two sides clash over the correctness of their different positions. • The positions become more polarized, and resentment or anger grows.
Stage 4: Counter-resistance by the majority	• The institution fights back with the aim of maintaining the cultural event. • Alliances with other power elites and access to the mainstream media are used to suppress the resistance of minorities.
Stage 5: Immediate outcomes	• The resistance effort led by minorities is crushed and disappears. • The resistance results in little or no change, and the institution is victorious.

Source: Adapted from Tator et al. (1998).

ett et al. (1996: 271) have indicated, 'establishment of alternative media is essential to building popular democratic movements, without which the hope of progressive social transformation is in vain.'

● The Internet: Extending ● ● Political Economy and Cultural Studies

The critical perspectives of political economy and cultural studies have long been utilized by sociologists and other researchers to study so-called 'old media' like newspapers, motion pictures, and television. It is sometimes argued that new approaches are needed to examine the 'new media' of digital communications such as the Internet (an interconnected computer network) and the World Wide Web (interconnected documents accessible through the Internet).

However, it is quite clear that the old theoretical tools can still be very useful for understanding the 'new media'. For instance, despite the futuristic discussion of these media through technological rather than sociological theories, the emphasis that political economy places on historical analysis reminds us that industrial capitalist society has generated similar waves of technological and media change before. Furthermore, since much theoretical discussion of the Internet and other 'new media' returns us to the notion of *technological determinism*—the view that technologies themselves transform the world—it is worth keeping in mind that cultural studies have long challenged this asocial notion and the way its ideology conceals the role of private companies and the state in generating and using these media or technologies (Morley, 2006).

While the Internet has opened up fresh areas of research into media and communications, we must consider what the old perspectives can teach us about the 'new media'. Research on the Internet provides opportunities to extend work in political economy and cultural studies.

The Internet and Political Economy

Through research on the Internet, media sociologists and other scholars have given renewed emphasis to an issue in political economy that was not addressed in our earlier discussion—namely, social inequalities in access to information and communications technologies (ICTs). This issue had been important in political economy up to the late 1980s. Critical scholars investigated how private ownership and control of ICTs helped to 'deepen social class divisions nationally and internationally, as people now divide into those who can afford the technology, services and content—the *information rich*—and those who cannot—the *information poor*' (Mosco, 1989: 80). The research encompassed social class differences in access to such technologies as cable, video-cassette recorders, direct-to-home satellite receivers, and the initial personal computers.

With the further development of personal computers and the explosive growth of the Internet that began in the mid-1990s, scholars in political economy have revived the issue of inequalities in access through research on the **digital divide**. However, there has been much debate among researchers about the meaning of this concept. It is often seen as referring to inequalities in access to computers and/or the Internet, but some academics extend the concept to inequalities in the skills needed to use computers or to assimilate information transmitted through the Internet. Scholars also disagree about the types of inequalities that are the basis for the digital divide. Most sociologists view the digital divide in terms of divisions in access by socio-economic status and social class. Feminists prefer to focus on gender, arguing that the digital divide represents another way in which women have experienced exclusion from equal opportunities with men (Cuneo, 2002). With these different types of inequalities in mind, let us consider some recent data.

The data presented in Figure 13.1 support the view of sociologists that there is an economic and class dimension to the digital divide. The figure shows home computer access by household income quartiles in different countries for the year 2003. In all countries, the highest quartile (the top 25 per cent of households in terms of income) had considerably more access to home computers than the lowest quartile. In Canada, while 91.8 per cent of the highest income group had access, only 54.6 per cent of the lowest group did (Canada, 2005a). Clearly, as a recent study concluded from this

data, 'income is a key factor shaping the digital divide. It determines whether households can afford to purchase computers and access to the Internet as well as other ICTs' (Canada, 2005a: 183).

In relation to gender, the data provided in Figure 13.2 offer some support for the argument of feminists that a digital divide exists between women and men. The figure shows male and female use of computers in 2003 for task-oriented purposes (such as writing or editing text and preparing spreadsheets or statistical analyses). Clear differences by gender were evident in Switzerland, Norway, and Italy. However, the differences were much smaller in Canada as well as in the United States and in Bermuda. Men also had higher rates of computer and Internet access than women in the three European nations while differences in these rates were almost non-existent in the North American countries. Therefore, although some evidence suggests the existence of a digital divide by gender, the evidence is only apparent in certain national contexts (Canada, 2005b).

The Internet can also be understood through other long-standing issues in political economy. Analysis of the Internet must consider the state as well as globalization and private ownership. The state was crucial to the ori-

School pupils in Alexandra Township, Johannesburg, South Africa, learn computer skills. Poverty and lack of resources often hamper the development of technical skills in the developing world. Reuters/Corbis/Mike Hutchings

gins of the Internet. The Internet had its beginnings in the late 1950s when the US Department of Defence established the Advanced Research Projects Agency (ARPA) to ensure that the Soviet Union would not develop military superiority over the United States, especially in relation to computers and communications technologies. ARPA developed a means to interconnect computers in such a way that an attack on one server and one part of the network would not knock out other servers or the rest of the network. That aspect of the Internet is one reason why national governments have found it difficult to regulate or censor information flowing through the network of computers (Cuneo, 2002). Indeed, in 1999, the CRTC announced that it would not attempt to regulate the Internet (Canada, 1999). Therefore, while the Internet began with the state, it has also had implications for regulatory control through the state.

As the Internet has grown, it has joined satellite communications systems and other technologies in contributing to cultural globalization. However, rather than simply being the product of a technological process, the global impact of the Internet is closely tied to private ownership. Like the 'old media', the 'new media' have become associated with deepening ownership concen-

tration. For instance, in 2000, America Online (AOL) took over the global media conglomerate Time Warner to form AOL/Time Warner. This allowed AOL to combine its role in Internet services with Time Warner's involvement in film, television, music, and magazine and book publishing. AOL's objective was to attract advertisers with multimedia deals and promote its own services across a range of media (Taras, 2001).

The Internet and Cultural Studies

Key issues associated with cultural studies also provide a basis for thinking about the Internet and its implications. These issues highlight how the content of the Internet is linked in contradictory ways to mainstream media and alternative media.

Mainstream Media
On the one hand, the Internet represents an extension of mainstream media and the content provided by powerful groups. Mainstream media content and the dominant ideology within this content have spread onto the Internet. Recorded music, motion pictures, and television shows are available for download. The advertising

Figure 13.1   Home Computer Access, Ages 16–65, by Household Income Quartiles, 2003

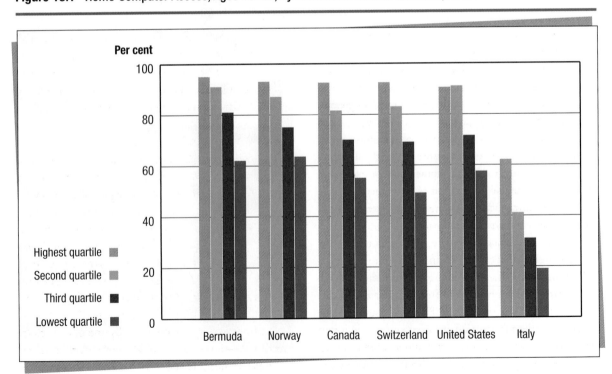

Countries are ranked by the rate of access among those in highest income quartile.
Source: Statistics Canada, 'Learning a Living: First Results of the Adult Literacy and Life Skills Survey', Cat. 89-603, released 11 May 2005, available at <http://www.statcan.ca/english/freepub/89-603-XIE/2005001/pdf/89-603-XWE-part1.pdf>, p. 186.

Figure 13.2   Use of Computers for Task-Oriented Purposes, by Gender, Ages 16–65, 2003

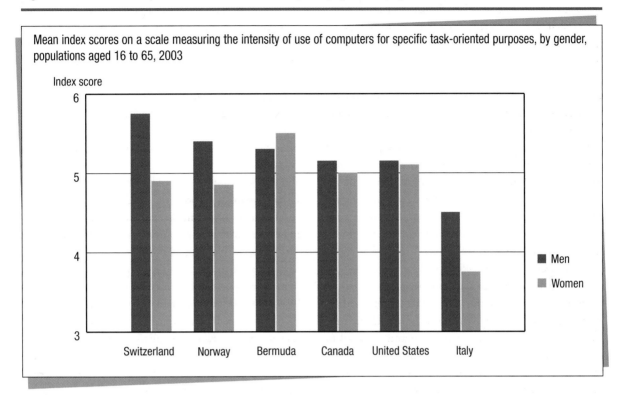

Mean index scores on a scale measuring the intensity of use of computers for specific task-oriented purposes, by gender, populations aged 16 to 65, 2003

Countries are ranked by mean index scores for men.

Source: Statistics Canada, 'Learning a Living: First Results of the Adult Literacy and Life Skills Survey', Cat. 89-603, released 11 May 2005, available at <http://www.statcan.ca/english/freepub/89-603-XIE/2005001/pdf/89-603-XWE-part1.pdf>, p. 186.

that is crucial for supporting many of the mainstream media is appearing with increasing frequency on web-sites. Newspapers and television news channels have websites where they can reproduce news stories. While offering stories that reflect the dominant ideology, the websites maintained by news organizations also have a promotional role; they are a form of advertising that encourages people to view upcoming specials on a news channel or to examine the greater variety of stories offered in the hard-copy edition of a newspaper. Similarly, radio stations, television networks (such as CTV), and specialty channels on cable (including Much Music and Space: The Imagination Station) have established websites where they can promote their programming.

Various companies have set up websites for promoting themselves, their products or services, and their activities. The use of the Internet for such promotion is strikingly evident in the case of Nike, a corporation that has its shoes and other products manufactured in Third World sweatshops—factories employing people to work for long hours and little pay under poor conditions. Nike has received more negative attention than other companies for exploiting workers in developing countries, and

it has attempted to contend with this criticism through its website. The corporation has used its website to provide a 'Frequently Asked Questions' page on wages and labour rights issues and to offer a virtual video tour of Nike factories in Asia (Knight and Greenberg, 2002).

Alternative Media

On the other hand, the Internet can also be seen as a new form of alternative media that subordinate groups use to present their own content and messages. The anti-sweat-shop movement consists of various groups that have drawn on different tactics—including public protests and use of the Internet—to raise awareness about Nike's labour practices. For instance, in their efforts to counter Nike's promotional activities, these groups have used the Internet to distribute accounts of abuse told by Nike factory workers (Knight and Greenberg, 2002).

Another example is provided by the global justice movement—the various social movements that are opposed to neo-liberalism and other aspects of the agenda that multinational corporations have adopted in relation to globalization. Sometimes referred to as the anti-globalization movement, particularly in the mainstream media, these activists have made considerable use of the Internet. For instance, the Independent Media Centre established a website just before the Ministerial Conference of the World Trade Organization in Seattle during 1999. The aim was to provide coverage and analysis that would counter news of the conference offered by the corporate-dominated mainstream media (Downey and Fenton, 2003). Through the website, which was known as Indymedia, journalists broke stories about the brutality of the police in relation to the demonstrators. The website had received over one million hits from individual users by the end of the conference. The success of the website spawned other Indymedia websites around the world. Within a year, there were 24 new Indymedia sites. As of 2005, Indymedia was a network of over 150 websites in 50 countries across six continents (Pickard, 2006).

Although the focus here has been on 'left-wing' social movements, the Internet has also been used by extreme 'right-wing' movements. These include neo-Nazis and other racist groups. The Internet is useful to movements on the political left and right in a number of ways. For instance, through e-mail and websites, members of these groups can communicate with each other and organize protests or other off-line political activities. The Internet may even enhance solidarity among the group members (Downey and Fenton, 2003).

● Conclusion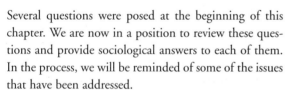

Several questions were posed at the beginning of this chapter. We are now in a position to review these questions and provide sociological answers to each of them. In the process, we will be reminded of some of the issues that have been addressed.

What is the role of the mass media in society? Sociologists provide different answers to this question. Inspired by Durkheim's ideas, structural functionalists suggest that the mass media perform key functions for society by contributing to its order and stability. In contrast, drawing on Marx's work, conflict theorists indicate that the mass media help to sustain the power and inequality that characterize capitalist society. Media institutions and media content, therefore, are a basis for conflict between unequal groups. Feminists also focus on power and inequality by indicating that the mass media are an aspect of patriarchal society. They contend that media institutions and media content contribute to the oppression of women.

Who has power over what we read, see, or hear in the mass media? The critical perspective of political economy holds that much of this power is held by private companies through their ownership and control of media organizations. Ownership by private companies is becoming concentrated—falling into fewer and fewer hands—through horizontal or vertical integration, cross-ownership, and conglomerate ownership. These interrelations raise concerns about the diversity and suppression of media content and its use for promoting specific agendas. Private ownership also raises concerns about the amount of American media content in Canada and other countries, especially in view of globalization. The state in Canada has countered some of these tendencies through public ownership of the media and media regulations. However, since the state generally serves the interests of the capitalist class, these types of measures were implemented only because groups with little power pushed for them or supported them.

What kinds of messages exist in media content, and how do people react to them? According to the critical perspective of cultural studies, media content reflects the dominant ideology in society. Media texts are encoded with capitalist, patriarchal, and racist ideology through a complex mixture of economic and production factors. However, these texts are decoded by audience members in a variety of ways. Dominant, negotiated, and oppositional readings are possible. Oppositional readings point to the issue of resistance to media content. It is clear that some members of subordinate groups object to certain messages or representations in media texts, but they also struggle against their misrepresentation (and even their under-representation) by directly challenging dominant cultural and media institutions. Subordinate groups have gone beyond resisting mainstream media to express their own messages through alternative media.

What are the social implications of the Internet, which is associated with the 'new media'? Inequalities in access to media technologies have long existed in society, and the digital divide indicates that these inequalities are continuing through the Internet. Furthermore, as Taras (2001: 113) has noted, 'the Internet seems more and more to be an instrument that reflects and reinforces the power of the powerful.' This is evident, for instance, in the way it has become tied to deepening ownership concentration as well as to the distribution of mainstream media content and the dominant ideology embedded in this content. However, the Internet clearly presents new opportunities for movements on the left to challenge social inequality and generate social change.

Questions for Critical Thought

1. Consider how symbolic interactionism, structural functionalism, conflict theory, and feminism might be used to study a particular media institution (like a private broadcasting company) or a television program (such as a children's show). Would some of these sociological theories be more useful than others? What might they suggest about the institution or the program?

2. Compare the evening television schedules of the CBC, CTV, and Global by looking at their websites or your local television listings. How much Canadian and American content do you see being scheduled? What differences exist when you compare the CBC's schedule to that of the two private broadcasters? Is there too much American content on Canadian television? Do we need more Canadian content? Why or why not?

3. Find a newspaper article that reports on a regulatory decision the CRTC has made about radio or television. Does the CRTC's decision favour powerful groups or less powerful groups? What do sociological ideas about the state suggest about the reasons for the CRTC's decision? Do you agree with the decision made by the CRTC? Why or why not?

4. Examine the content in some form of alternative media (such as Vancouver Co-operative Radio or an Indymedia website). Identify specific ways in which the content is different from that of the mainstream media.

5. Examine the content of websites that you often visit. In what ways do they involve an extension of mainstream media and the content provided by powerful groups?

Recommended Readings

Augie Fleras and Jean Lock Kunz, *Media and Minorities: Representing Diversity in a Multicultural Canada* (Toronto: Thompson Educational Publishing, 2001).

Fleras and Kunz offer a sociological approach to the representation of minorities in the Canadian media. Their book is especially appropriate for sociology students who want to learn more about these issues in second- or third-year media or race and ethnicity courses.

Naomi Klein, *No Logo: Taking Aim at the Brand Bullies* (New York: Picador, 2000).

In this very readable book, Klein examines several issues associated with brands and logos (such as the Nike Swoosh and the Golden Arches of McDonald's). She discusses the expansion of branding by companies, the role of giant corporations in relation to globalization, and forms of resistance to these developments.

Bohdan Szuchewycz and Jeannette Sloniowski, eds, *Canadian Communications: Issues in Contemporary Media and Culture*, 2nd edn (Toronto: Prentice-Hall, 2002).

Szuchewycz and Sloniowski present a collection of articles on Canadian media and culture that were previously published in magazines or newspapers. This book provides good background for students who want to explore a variety of contentious issues.

Serra Tinic, *On Location: Canada's Television Industry in a Global Market* (Toronto: University of Toronto Press, 2005).

Tinic examines television production in Vancouver, particularly in terms of the tensions that exist between meeting the needs of Hollywood and reflecting culture in Canada. Since her analysis draws on political economy and cultural studies, the book may be of particular interest to students who want to learn more about these two approaches.

Recommended Websites

Adbusters www.adbusters.org

Adbusters is a group of artists, activists, writers, educators, and others who provide anti-corporate criticism on a range of issues. Its website features parodies of corporate ads or logos as well as information about the group's magazine.

Alliance of Canadian Cinema, Television, and Radio Artists (ACTRA) www.actra.ca

ACTRA is a labour union that represents more than 21,000 performers working in the English-language media. Among other things, ACTRA's website includes the collective agreements the union has with various media organizations.

Canadian Broadcasting Corporation/Société Radio-Canada (CBC/SRC) www.cbc.radio-canada.ca

The website for the CBC/SRC will enable you to find out more about Canada's national public broadcaster. The site supplies the broadcaster's annual reports, corporate documents and policies, background on the CBC/SRC, and other information.

Canadian Media Guild (CMG) www.cmg.ca

The CMG is a labour union that represents nearly 6,000 workers who help to create information and entertainment programming for media organizations such as the CBC/SRC. The website for the CMG features the union's policies and newsletters.

• • • • • • • • •

Chapter 14

Religion in Canada

Lori G. Beaman

Learning Objectives

In this chapter, you will:

▶ explore definitions of religion and spirituality,

▶ examine the theory of secularization,

▶ learn about the changing religious demography of Canada and its potential impact,

▶ consider new religious movements and minority religious groups,

▶ examine the concept of secularization,

▶ explore the relationship between law and religion, and

▶ think about the gendered dimensions of religious participation.

Photo: AFP/Getty Images

● Introduction ● ● ● ● ● ● ●

Religion is an important point of identity for many people in Canada. Almost daily we hear or read about an aspect of someone's religious beliefs that bump up against a regulation, law, or policy. Even as this chapter was being written, an Orthodox Jewish family in Winnipeg was fighting to keep an 84-year-old family member on life support against his physicians' orders to remove life support, citing their religious beliefs as the basis for their position (CBC, 2007); he subsequently passed away in June 2008 (CBC, 2008). Eleven-year-old Asmahan (Azzy) Mansour was called off a soccer field in Montreal by a referee who ruled her hijab violated Rule 4 of the International Football Association Board, which states that 'a player must not use equipment or wear anything that is dangerous to himself or any other player (including any kind of jewelry)' (Mennie, 2007). In Saskatchewan, civil servant Orville Nichols refused to marry a same-sex couple, citing his religious beliefs and his conviction that 'God hates homosexuality' as reason for his refusal (*Orville Nichols v. Dept. of Justice*, 2006); Nichols launched a complaint against the Saskatchewan Human Rights Code in March 2005. A Montréal daycare's refusal to accommodate the beliefs of a Muslim couple by serving halal meat to their child has recently come before the Québec Human Rights Commission (Leong, 2007). In Alberta, the Court of Appeal has supported the claim by Hutterites that they be exempt from photo identification on their driver's licenses' (Harding, 2007). No matter how one may feel personally about religion, it matters to a good many people. As social sci-

entists, religion constitutes an important area of study in our pursuit to better understand social life.

Sociologists of religion do not ask questions about the veracity of particular sets of religious beliefs. In other words, we do not care whether god exists or whether Raelians have really had contact with extraterrestrial beings. Rather, our concern is with how human beings act out their religious beliefs and practices, as well how religious beliefs and social institutions intersect. How are certain sets of beliefs legitimized? What is constructed as being a 'religion'? What are the power relations embedded in these processes? In other words, who gets to decide whether a religion is really a religion?

● Marxist Influence ● ● ● ●

Until relatively recently, sociology—as a discipline—did not take the study of religion particularly seriously. There are a number of reasons for this. First, a good number of scholars accepted the popular wisdom that we live in a secular society. However, religion remains an important part of the Canadian social fabric and is likely to continue to do so.

Another reason for the lack of attention to religion within sociology can be explained by the strong Marxist tradition, particularly in Canadian sociology. Marx worried about the power of religion, and in fact stated that 'Religion is the sight of the oppressed creature, the heart of a heartless world' (Marx, as cited in Raines, 2002: 167). While he recognized the ability of religion to offer solace in times of trouble, he worried that the

SOCIOLOGY IN ACTION
Capturing the Complexity of Religious Participation

Despite the fact that participation in organized religion has indeed declined in Canada, the vast majority of Canadians still identify with a faith tradition, however sporadic their participation in the formal rituals of that tradition might be. Moreover, Canadians are finding new and interesting ways of expressing their religious interests that do not necessarily manifest as participation in traditional religious groups. The increasing participation in yoga, for example, might arguably be a 'religious practice'. Think too about the creation of sacred space

through labyrinths in the past five or so years. For example, on 14 September 2005 the Toronto Public Labyrinth opened. While it is adjacent to the Church of the Holy Trinity, it is fully accessible to the public and its creation was supported by the city of Toronto. Many people walk this labyrinth, some of whom are connected to faith communities, some are not. Many such forms of participation in sacred rituals don't fit into traditional measures of religious behaviour, and thus remain undetected in research that measures religious participation.

happiness offered by religion was illusory and that it distracted people from seeking real happiness (which inevitably involved the transformation of economic arrangements and the end of capitalism). Marx concluded that 'the abolition of religion as the illusory happiness of the people is the demand for their real happiness' (Marx, as cited in Raines, 2002: 167). Some sociologists understood this statement as a license to ignore the importance of religion in society, to exclude religion as a variable from research, and to ignore its importance in theoretical work. This hardly reflects the spirit in which Marx wrote (one would think something deemed to be so powerful would need to be studied carefully) and has resulted in a paucity of research about religion and social life.

Moreover, on a substantive note, there have been some significant social movements that have been grounded in a combination of religion and Marxism, most specifically liberation theology, which began in South and Central America in the 1960s and was based on the premise that part of the mission of Christianity is to bring 'justice to the poor and oppressed, particularly through political activism' (Smith, 1991: 12). Its goal was to effect socio-economic change and indeed, it became so sufficiently threatening that it was condemned by the Vatican. Several Latin American Bishops were deposed for their continued fight for social and economic justice based on Marxist principles.

● Religion in Profile ● ● ● ●

What does religion in Canada look like from a demographic perspective? Mainstream Christianity has dominated Canada's historic landscape and, to some extent, continues to do so. Mainstream Christianity includes Roman Catholicism and Protestant groups such as the United Church of Canada and the Anglican Church of Canada. Numbers of affiliates have been approximately equal between Roman Catholics and Protestants. Groups outside of those two broad categories make up a relatively small proportion of the religious picture in Canada, but, as we will see below, that picture is rapidly changing. For the most part Canadians have remained affiliated with the religions of their parents and grandparents, even if they do not actually attend church. Social scientists have realized that while church attendance is a measure of religious commitment or participation, it is *only* one measure and thus offers a fairly limited understanding of religion in Canada.

Table 14.1 Top 10 Religious Denominations, Canada, 2001	Number	%
Roman Catholic	12,793,125	43.2
No religion	4,796,325	16.2
United Church	2,839,125	9.6
Anglican	2,035,495	6.9
Christian, not included elsewhere[1]	780,450	2.6
Baptist	729,475	2.5
Lutheran	606,590	2.0
Muslim	579,640	2.0
Protestant, not included elsewhere[2]	549,205	1.9
Presbyterian	409,830	1.4

[1] Includes persons who report 'Christian', as well as those who report 'Apostolic', 'Born-again Christian', and 'Evangelical'.
[2] Includes persons who report only 'Protestant'.
Source: Statistics Canada. 2003. *2001 Census: analysis series Religions in Canada*, page 20. Catalogue no. 96F0030XIE2001015. Ottawa: Statistics Canada. Available at http://www12.statcan.ca/english/census01/products/analytic/companion/rel/pdf/96F0030XIE2001015.pdf.

Statistically speaking, Canada is still dominated by Christianity. The 2001 Statistics Canada General Survey shows that 80 per cent of Canadians identify as 'Christian'. We are fortunate in Canada that the government has collected data on religious affiliation since the late 1800s, thus allowing us to formulate a longitudinal understanding of religious participation in Canada. These data also show the historical presence of Sikhs, Muslims, Buddhists, and Hindus. Moreover, we know that the Canadian Jewish community has roots that date to the 1700s. Thus, while we hear much about the increasing presence of religious groups who are not Christian, most of these religions have been present since the birth of Canada as a nation.

Reginald Bibby has spent a great deal of time investigating religious participation of Canadians, focusing primarily on Christian-centred behaviours such as church attendance, belief in biblical teachings, and experiences of god's presence. Bibby has found much evidence of both identification and lack of participation amongst Canadians in relation to Christian churches. He argues that Christian churches have and will continue to dominate the religious scene in Canada (Bibby, 1993; 2002; 2006). Bibby is concerned that while there is still a strong identification with Christian churches amongst Canadians, there is much less evidence of actual participation.

The statistical data collected by Statistics Canada and researchers like Bibby provide invaluable resources for important information about religious beliefs and behaviours in Canada. However, we need more information about how Canadians do religion and spirituality. In other words, what do religion and spirituality look like in their daily lives? Do some Canadians have shrines at home? What role do they play in everyday life? What is the nature of religious or spiritual practice at home? Unfortunately, statistical data can give us little information about these sorts of questions. Especially lacking is data that gives us insight into minority religious communities.

Since 9/11, connections between religion and violence that were previously unseen have become more visible. Though this connection might seem recent, the connections have been present throughout history. We need only to examine Canada's history of violence against and violation of its First Nations peoples to uncover a horrifying picture of the intertwining of religion, political goals, and power relations to understand the intersection of religion and violence. If we look beyond Canada, the Christian crusades (the first in 1095) provide another example in which the political and economic desires of kings and princes combined with religious ideology to justify a so-called holy war on Muslims, Jews, Orthodox Christians, and many other groups who fell outside of the then-mainstream definitions of Christian religion. More subtle forms of violence can be identified in the anti-condom messages of some Christian missions in an AIDS-ridden Africa.

Does religion cause violence? The answer to this question is not easy. Certainly religion can provide an ideological justification for violent acts or approaches which do violence to people or their culture in more subtle ways.

When we look at the power of religious ideology we can begin to understand why it is important to have a better sense of the role of religion in the lives of Canadians. Religion can provide a source of comfort, direction, and community for people. It can be both prescriptive, in that it offers people direction on important choices, and explanatory, in that it provides a source of explanation for everyday events. It is often an important influence on how people think about issues like same-sex marriage, abortion, and gender roles. It can influence how and why new Canadians feel welcome and a part of Canadian society or if they feel excluded and marginalized.

The religious demographic in Canada is changing. We are becoming increasingly diverse as a nation, with a stronger presence of religious groups who, while they have always been present in Canada, are becoming a larger percentage of the overall population. For example, between 1981 and 1991 the census data show a 144 per cent increase in the category of 'other non-Christian religions' (Statistics Canada, 1993b). There is growth in Jewish, Muslim, Sikh, Buddhist, and Hindu communities; at the same time there is a decline in attendance and belonging among the Canadian Christian communities. Intersecting with these trends are immigration policies, human rights legislation, and policies linked to the *Canadian Multiculturalism Act*. Religious identity is an important part of what people bring to their roles as employees and employers, their financial choices, their political involvement and decisions, and their conceptualizations of how society should respond to social issues. While religion is, of course, not the only factor in people's decisions, it is nonetheless important to understand the ways in which it informs people in their day-to-day lives.

Thus, as the demographic picture changes, so too does the picture of how Canadians 'do' religion. Statistics Canada (2003) notes:

Immigration is a central feature of Canada's demographic landscape and in 2001, the share of Canadians who were born outside of the country—at 18 per cent—was higher than it had been in 70 years. Among individuals aged 25–54, those who were born in

Canada were less likely than immigrants to have attended religious services in the past year. Indeed, 39 per cent of immigrants who arrived in Canada during the 1990s had attended services on a monthly basis in the previous year while this was the case for 22 per cent of Canadian-born persons. Overall, while places of worship were central to community life in years past, most Canadians today do not have a long-standing attachment to a place of worship. Only 37 per cent of all Canadians attended religious services or meetings at least once in the previous year and had attended the same place of worship for more than five years.

What worship service participation rates by new Canadians means has yet to be closely studied. Places of worship may be playing an important role in the lives of new Canadians, but the parameters of that impact are little-known. So, for example, do religious communities facilitate integration, or are new Canadians somewhat isolated from other parts of Canadian society? Do faith communities play a role in political decisions? What are the generational implications of this involvement?

Peter Beyer, head of the Religion and Immigrant Youth Research Team at the University of Ottawa, situates a sociological understanding of religion in Canada in the context of the global flows of which it is a part. The Immigrant Youth and Religion research team has spent the last four years examining the intersection of religion, youth, and Canadian culture. Participants self-identify as having Islam, Hinduism, or Buddhism as part of their religious background, have at least one immigrant parent, and have been born in Canada or arrived here as an immigrant when they were under the age of 11. Over 200 youth have participated in the study thus far. Preliminary results show that these youth locate their religious or spiritual quests in a complex web of family and cultural reference points. For these youth, spiritual definition is their own prerogative and while they may rely on their parents and extended families to some extent for spiritual or religious information, they take responsibility for their own spiritual and religious journeys. This group of immigrant youth from Toronto, Montréal, and Ottawa were generally highly integrated into Canadian society, feeling connected to Canada as

their country. Certainly they had experienced incidents of discrimination but this was generally explained as a product of individual ignorance rather than a reflection of Canadian society (Beyer, 2006a; 2006b). For these youth, multiculturalism in Canada is a positive ideal which situates Canada as a progressive nation. Here is how one Muslim participant expressed this idea:

Give it a couple of. . .generations for people to get. . . out of the shell of their own culture, to mix with the world. Because I believe what we have in Canada is an opportunity that a lot of the world doesn't have, I mean, don't get me wrong, there's a lot of blood on the hands of everybody who lives in this country. But we have an opportunity for people to start fresh. We have people from all different backgrounds, all over the world. We are a representation to the world. . . . There are certain points into staying and understanding your own culture and appreciating your own culture. But to be able to evolve and to move on with the times. . .we can show the world here how to live amongst people from all different backgrounds (MM26). (Beyer, 2008)

● Definitions of Religion

What do we mean when we use the word religion? Does it include spirituality? And what do we mean by spirituality? Sociologists face an ongoing challenge when they attempt to define religion. Meredith McGuire (2005) very simply categorizes definitions of religion into functional definitions and substantive definitions. In short, functional definitions focus on what religion does for the social group and for the individual. The dominant theme running through most functional definitions is social cohesion—in other words, how religion offers a sense of connectedness to others and to a larger picture. Substantive definitions, on the other hand, examine what religion is and what does not count as religion. Substantive definitions attempt to define religion by examining its core elements, most typically a belief in a higher being, a set of prescribed beliefs and rituals, and so on.

▮▮ Time to Reflect ▮▐▮▐▮▐▮▐▮▐▮▐▮▐▮▐▮▐▮▐▮▐▮▐▮▐▮

Why do you think many Canadians are less tied to religious institutions? What are the potential impacts on micro and macro levels of society?

Émile Durkheim (1965) certainly deserves some of the credit for the shape of functional definitions of religion, but his influence can be seen in substantive understandings as well. Durkheim's preoccupation was with social cohesion, and thus he viewed religion through this lens. For Durkheim, religion contributed to social cohesion in that it was fundamentally a reflection of the society in which it existed and it was, at its core, a social or group phenomenon. He argued that society divided the world into the sacred and the profane, and that the former were the focus of religion. Durkheim's work had some powerful effects on how sociologists of religion define and think about religion. The binary between the sacred and the profane has limited conceptual resonance for some cultures, especially, for example, many aboriginal groups. Moreover, the emphasis on the social aspects of religion as they are highlighted by Durkheim has resulted in a denigration of sacred practices that are not communally oriented. Wiccans, for example, are often sole practitioners, unconnected to a 'faith community' in the traditional Christian sense of the word, or in the sense that Durkheim thought was necessary for religious expression.

A contemporary application of Durkheim's functional ideas is reflected in the research of Robert Bellah and his colleagues (1985) in the United States. They spent considerable time exploring the role of religion in social cohesion, or, *civil religion*. This elusive and amorphous concept emerged in the American context and was most vocally defended as a 'real' phenomenon by Bellah and his colleagues, who argued that it transcended any specific religious tradition and formed an ethical framework which existed apart from any one religion. However, the strong Christian presence in the United States might belie that claim. Perhaps the most important thing to remember about civil religion is its proponents argue that it forms an overarching framework which supports a cohesive society. It is equally important to remember that underlying this notion is the idea that society is based on and functions because of shared values and perspectives, something that is highly contested by many scholars. Much of Bellah's work has focused on understanding how society has departed from those common ideals and the consequences of that, which they identify as being largely negative.

In part, narratives of a cohesive society lost, such as that told by Bellah, return us to debates about the definitions of religion and spirituality. Many people neatly divide the two into religion as 'organized religion' and spirituality as somehow representing something less institutional and more private. This division is arbitrary

at best, and hidden behind this categorization are particularly power sedimentations that create a hierarchy in which 'religion' is privileged as what counts in terms of spiritual belief and practice. The implications of this are profound. Think, for example, about Wiccans, who are often sole practitioners or part of a very loosely organized group with broadly defined rituals and practices. Further, Canada's First Nations peoples are largely excluded from these conceptualizations of religion. It is important that sociologists think carefully about the work such categories do in the preservation of particular hierarchies of what 'counts' as religion.

Substantive definitions focusing on content are equally vulnerable and are often characterized by a reliance on Christianity to form the basis of the determining criteria. There are some important challenges to conventional thinking about definitions of religion that have emerged both within sociology and from other disciplines, such as anthropology. For example, Talal Asad (1993) and Naomi Goldenberg (2006) each call into question the work that definitions of religion do. They argue that the separating out of religion as something distinct from everyday life is a decidedly Christian approach to thinking about spirituality and religion. As Asad states: 'It is preeminently the Christian church that has occupied itself with identifying, cultivating and testing beliefs as a verbalizable inner condition of true religion' (1993: 48).

Naomi Goldenberg (2006: 7) makes a similar argument:

> I think that to be considered legitimately 'religious' at this point in history, one has to be seen as some type of Christian. At present, I believe that every citation of the category of 'religion' is a citation of Christianity. Through a series of discursive, political practices, Christianity has become the standard which other religions imitate whether in conscious harmony that mimics Christian practices or in fruitless rebellion that stresses minor points of difference in text and ritual. Christianity defines the terms by which any institution or set of actions and habit of language is judges to be a 'religion'.

These scholars are making important inroads to the ways in which we conceptualize religion which may eventually impact on how religion is measured.

Other scholars are making related arguments. For example, Linda Woodhead (2007) is especially critical of the dominance of functionalist conceptualizations of religion, especially Durkheimian models which privilege religion over magic, despite the fact that both are related to the sacred or transcendent. We see amongst sociologists a tendency to denigrate or minimize those religious or spiritual behaviours which don't fit into an organized religion patterns after Christianity. Woodhead makes a point similar to that of Goldenberg: 'Religions look remarkably like what Christians think of as religion' (2007: 2).

What might an alternative approach be? How would we think about people's involvement with the sacred if we were able to step outside of Christian thinking about religion? Meredith McGuire (2005) has proposed a methodological strategy for attempting to move outside of the confines of Christianity. She asks us to attempt to bracket assumptions that we hold about religion and to travel with sociological eyes or a sociological imagination, to the 'past as another country'. She uses this strategy in order to present the possibility of thinking in a time when there were 'no tidy boundaries between the sacred and profane' (2005: 3).

Canadian scholar William Closson James (2006) offers a beginning point for the exercise in boundary deconstruction. He argues that, 'as religion in Canada in the twentieth century becomes more highly personal and individual, we should expect it to continue to be characterized more by an eclectic spirituality cobbled together from various sources rather than a monolithic and unitary superordinating system of beliefs' (2006: 288). If we only consider religion that looks a particular way (in the view of the scholars mentioned above, that is religion that looks like Christianity) we will miss a great deal of the richness of Canadian's spiritual lives.

● New Religious ● ● ● ● ● Movements

There are some very practical implications of decisions about what constitutes a religion. Religious groups in many countries receive privileges simply because they are religious. In Canada, for example, there are certain tax exemptions that accompany religions as charitable organizations. Thus the determination of a group's status as a religion is not merely an academic discussion. In many countries religions must register with a central state authority in order to be recognized for some benefits. Moreover, those who are not on official state lists are often persecuted through the harassment of group members, the denial of benefits, and the use of state apparatus such as the criminal justice system to keep groups under close scrutiny. Especially vulnerable are new religious movements (NRMs).

The classic study on new religious movements is *The Making of a Moonie* by Eileen Barker (1984). Barker was intrigued by the increasing frenzy around new religious movements, particularly the talk of 'cults', 'brainwashing' and 'deprogramming' in the late 1970s and early 1980s. As a social scientist, she decided that she would investigate the workings of the Reverend Sun Myung Moon's Unification Church, also known as the Moonies. As it turned out, the mostly young adults who were joining the Unification Church were not brainwashed, deprived of sleep, or malnourished, as the hysterical discourse around their 'conversion' had suggested. Rather, these were simply middle class young adults who were seeking a spiritual or religious experience and a sense of community. Barker's research (1984; 2005; 2007) had profound implications and triggered a debate that continues to this day.

Many scholars have taken up the challenge of studying new religious movements, but debates around these very interesting groups rage on, complete with lawsuits from so-called deprogrammers who disagreed with social scientific findings that new religious movements are not dangerous. Occasional, dramatic events such as the mass suicide by 39 members of Heaven's Gate, led by Hale and Bop in California in 1997, served to fan the flames of the debates. For the most part, events like this are relatively unusual; however, they often shape public perceptions of new religious movements.

Susan Palmer is a Canadian researcher who is internationally known for her research on new religious movements. She has studied a number of religious groups, including the Raelians, the Québec-based UFO cult who claimed several years ago that they had successfully cloned a human being. After 15 years of fieldwork with the Raelians, which involved attending their meetings, countless interviews with members and leaders, and examining video and written materials, Palmer wrote a book about Raelian culture. Her findings described a new religious movement and challenged the stereotypes associated with NRMs. For example, she found that 'Raelians with children make no effort to transmit the message to them, true to the Raelian ethic of individual choice' (Palmer, 2004: 139). Children cannot be baptized until at least age 15; even when they ask to be baptized as Raelian they must pass a test 'to prove that their choice was not due to parental influence or pressure' (Palmer, 2004: 139). As Palmer discovered, the Raelians have sometimes contradictory beliefs and, like any social organization, there are power struggles and tensions. In her response to a journalist who wanted to know whether she had observed coercive or manipulative behaviour among the Raelians, Palmer stated: 'Well, sure, but no more so than in my women's Bulgarian choir or my PTA meetings. In any human organization you'll find people who try to control other people. Often they have to, just to get the job done' (2004: 6).

Unfortunately, new religious movements still suffer from a great deal of stigma. The language of cults and brainwashing used in the news media and in day-to-day conversation undergoes little critical examination of why it is that we are sometimes quick to marginalize such groups. After all, what is the difference between brainwashing and socialization? This is where questions of agency come into play. What we mean by agency is the capacity and ability of a human being to freely make decisions. This sounds simple enough, but ultimately none of us make decisions 'freely' or without constraints. Whether it is the influence of parents, friends, economic constraints, or possibilities, our decisions are shaped by our social world and by social structure. It is often marginal religious groups who are conceptualized as exerting 'undue influence' on its members, simply because the decisions those members make may be different than the choices we might make.

Raelist founder and leader Claude Vorilhon.
© Christopher J. Morris/Corbis

● Theories of ● ● ● ● ●
Religion and Society

Do we live in a secular society? We frequently hear this question as an affirmative statement with little explanation about what it means. To say a society is secular is to say that it is without religion in its public sphere. Secularization is the process by which religion increasingly loses its influence. Whether and how society is secular has occupied a great deal of time and energy among sociologists of religion. The narrative begins like this: once upon a time society was very, very religious—everyone participated in religious activity and religion formed a sacred canopy of meaning over life for the vast majority of people. State and church were one and the same, with no separation between them and no perceived need for a separation. Then along came the Enlightenment, and gradually, science replaced religion (Berger, 1967).

To complicate the story, secularization theory developed some very sophisticated versions. In the midst of it all were contested notions of how religion should be defined. They are important because in order to determine whether religion is on the decline we must first know what religion is. So, if people stop attending church, but take up yoga and engage in rituals such as meditative walks in labyrinths can we say that we live in a more secular world? If we measure secularization as the decline in people's participation in the rituals and practices of organized religion, such as church attendance, marriage, and baptism, then yes, Canada has definitely secularized. But what happens if the population is increasingly made up of a population for whom church attendance is not and has never been a measure of religious participation? How then do we think about secularization? So, while one measure of secularization can be the level of individual participation in religious activities, we can see that this presents some interesting measurement challenges.

Another measurement of secularization exists at the level of institutions. As religion loses its influence, it has less and less presence in social institutions such as law, education, health care, and so on. And, in this process, religion loses its influence as an important social voice. The overt involvement of religion in social institutions, to be sure, is different than it was in other periods in Canadian history. But, the religious voice cannot be discounted entirely. Think, for example, about the religious lobby against the same-sex marriage legislation. The *Reference Re Same-Sex Marriage* case was decided in 2004; the legislation passed and the Civil Marriage Act was approved on 20 July 2005. Groups opposed to the legislation include the Catholic

Civil Rights League, the Convention of Atlantic Baptist Churches, the Christian Heritage Party of Canada, and the Roman Catholic Church of Canada. The Canadian Conference of Catholic Bishops, the Ontario Conference of Catholic Bishops, and the Seventh-Day Adventist Church acted as religious interveners in opposition to the legislation. Moreover, in some provinces access to abortion is severely limited due to the insistence of religious lobby groups. In court, witnesses still swear to tell the truth on the bible. Public institutions close on Christian holidays such as Christmas and Easter. In some measure religious beliefs are so embedded in our social institutions and form part of their histories that it is almost impossible for them to become completely secular or without religious influence.

One of the most important pieces of social scientific research on the idea of secularization in recent years is that of José Casanova (1994), whose work employs a multilevel conceptualization of secularization. Casanova conducted a comparative study of religion using five case studies from two religious traditions (Protestantism and Catholicism) in four countries (Spain, Portugal, Brazil, and the United States). Casanova identified a trend of 'deprivatization' of religion. He argued that, beginning in the 1980s, religions began to reassert their intentions to have a say over contemporary life. Casanova argues that secularization theory is actually made up of three interwoven strands of argument: (1) secularization as religious decline, (2) secularization as differentiation, and (3) secularization as privatization. While Casanova says that the idea that religion is differentiated (there is a secular and sacred sphere) is a possible proposition, it does not follow that religion must be marginalized and privatized. Of course, if we think about world events Casanova's argument seems plausible. Religion is intertwined with many of the major world events we might think about.

The Quiet Revolution

The province of Québec deserves special mention in our consideration of secularization. Its unique cultural position has numerous facets, not least of which is the story of religion in that province. If ever there was a classic story of secularization, Québec seems to tell it. It had what we might consider to be an established church; historically the Roman Catholic Church played an enormous role in the lives of Québec citizens at a personal level as well as institutionally (Simpson, 2000: 276). Schools, hospitals, and much of public life was intertwined with the church. Public officials were Roman Catholic, as were most members of Québec society.

In the late 1960s it seemed that, quite suddenly, the church pews were empty. The Quiet Revolution had happened. How this seemingly sudden shift came about remains a bit of a mystery, but the perception of the church as anti-modern, oppressive, and representative of an establishment with which the people of Québec no longer wished to identify combined to create an impetus to abandon what had been a core part of identity in Québec. David Seljak has argued that the Roman Catholic Church did not give up its place in Québec society; instead, it recreated its public role (1998: 135). Gregory Baum argues that the Quiet Revolution 'initiated a gradual process of secularization' (2000: 151) in Québec. What this means in practice is still unclear. The influence of the Roman Catholic Church in Québec institutions has not been completely eliminated, and the relationship between the Church and the citizens of Québec remains a complex one in the process of negotiation.

In both Québec and elsewhere in Canada we now have what some scholars describe as 'believing without belonging', which means that while many Canadians still cite an affiliation with organized religion at census time, many of them do not have much, or any, contact with the churches to which they say they belong. Given current measures of religious life, it is difficult to determine the parameters of belief. To what extent individuals engage in religious and spiritual activities that are not included in common measures cannot be known. Home-based religious practices, for example, remain largely invisible. Some scholars argue that such 'private' religious behaviours do not really count when thinking about secularization or when measuring religious behaviour. This is a puzzling argument because such thinking would exclude many religious groups who engage in religious practice almost exclusively in the realm of the so-called private. Scholars like Robert Orsi (2003), who argues that even prayer is public, have challenged this public–private dichotomy. The essence of Orsi's argument is that we cannot create a meaningful dichotomy between the public and the private. In other words, you take your 'private' self with you in the realm of the 'public'.

Also discounted by some scholars are 'seekers', or people who may combine a variety of spiritual practices to create a pastiche of spiritual meaning. Thus, someone may engage in yoga, go to the Valentine's Day labyrinth walk at a neighbourhood church, and do a cleansing ritual of her living space to rid it of bad energy. Canada's First Nations present a complex blending of Christianity and Native Spirituality which is difficult to characterize. This blending of traditions remains outside of the focus of study of much of the research on religion in Canada.

Understanding religion in complex ways can give us a rich picture of how people integrate religion and spiritual practices into their daily lives. One of the reasons secularization theory seemed to have so much credibility is the problem of definition. If religion is conceptualized in narrow ways—church attendance, institutional involvement, and so-called other public measures—then without a doubt it has shown a decline of such proportions that it might be reasonable to conclude that it will eventually disappear. But, there are alternative practices that are not measured, and which form an important part of spiritual identity. Moreover, at an institutional level much of Canada's Christian heritage remains embedded in day-to-day practices, as we will discover in the next section.

● Religion and Law ● ● ● ●

One important social institution that mediates the ways in which religious beliefs can be expressed through practice is law. For example, if you are a Sikh and you wish to wear your *kirpan* (ceremonial dagger) to school, you may find yourself, as Gurbaj Multani did, arguing for your right to do so before the courts (*Multani v. Commission scolaire Marguerite-Bourgeoys,* 2006). Law sets important boundaries on religious practices. Law provides a forum to which people can come to affirm their right to engage in certain religious practices. It is especially important for minority religious groups, whose practices are more likely to be called into question than those of majority religious groups.

Sections 2(a) and 15 of the Charter are the core sections dealing with the protection of religious beliefs in Canada:

2. Everyone has the following fundamental freedoms:
   a) freedom of conscience and religion;

15. (1) Every individual is equal before and under the law and has the right to the equal protection and equal benefit of the law without discrimination and, in particular, without discrimination based on race, national or ethnic origin, colour, religion, sex, age or mental or physical disability.

In addition to these sections, two others have an impact on the shape of religion in the public sphere:

27. This Charter shall be interpreted in a manner consistent with the preservation and enhancement of the multicultural heritage of Canadians.

29. Nothing in this Charter abrogates or derogates from any rights or privileges guaranteed by or under the Constitution of Canada in respect of denominational, separate or dissentient schools (93).

The broad considerations mandated in s. 27 mean that the intertwining of ethnic and religious interests must receive some consideration in policy matters.

Contrary to popular belief, mostly imported from the United States and France, both of which establish the separation of church and state in their founding constitutional documents, there is no separation of church and state in Canada. Separation of church and state means that the church has no authority over the state or political decisions. You can see, particularly in the United States, that this is more an ideal than a reality. Keep in mind though, that while Canada does not have a strict separation of church and state it also does not have an established church, or a church that has authority over the state. So where does religion fit in Canada from a socio-legal perspective?

Since the Charter was enacted in 1982 the Supreme Court of Canada has attempted to find a workable definition of religion that can be applied in its considerations of religious freedom. To this end, the Court has attempted to use a comprehensive definition which employs both functional and substantive elements. For example, in the *Syndicat Northcrest v. Amselem* (2004) decision the Court states:

In order to define religious freedom, we must first ask ourselves what we mean by 'religion'. While it is perhaps not possible to define religion precisely, some outer definition is useful since only beliefs, convictions and practices rooted in religion, as opposed to those that are secular, socially based or conscientiously held, are protected by the guarantee of freedom of religion. Defined broadly, religion typically involves a particular and comprehensive system of faith and worship. Religion also tends to involve the belief in a divine, superhuman or controlling power. In essence, religion is about freely and deeply held personal convictions or beliefs connected to an individual's spiritual faith and integrally linked to one's self-definition and spiritual fulfillment, the practices of which allow individuals to foster a connection with the divine or with the subject or object of that spiritual faith.

Trying to define religion is no easy task, as we have already seen. It becomes especially challenging as courts try to distill a very complex concept into a workable definition that acts as a gatekeeper for claims based on religious identity. Thus, courts are faced with the unenviable task of trying to capture a dynamic idea in a definitional box. Orsi's work on lived religion offers important insight into the enormity of the task of definitions and why it might pose especially difficult in law: 'The study of lived religion is not about practice rather than ideas, but about ideas, gestures, imaginings, all as media of engagement with the world. Lived religion cannot be separated from other practices of everyday life, from the ways that humans do other necessary and important things, or from other cultural structures and discourses (legal, political, medical, and so on)' (2003: 1972). In the definition quoted above we see the Court using a substantive understanding of religion in its statement that religion is 'a particular and comprehensive system of faith and worship'. This begs the question of why a religion must be a comprehensive system of faith and worship. We might also argue if that is even a useful way to conceptualize religion, since the religious behaviour of the vast majority of Canadians does not actually seem to fit with this notion of 'comprehensiveness'. Belief in a divine, superhuman, or controlling power poses some similar problems in that some religions do not have what we might call a central authority figure. How is it possible to determine whether a conviction is 'deeply' held? These are the challenges posed by attempts to solidify religious behaviour into manageable definitions for law.

Although the *Charter of Rights and Freedoms* guarantees religious freedom and equality, the guarantees and rights in the Charter are limited by section 1, which provides a balance of sorts between individual rights and interests and those of society more generally. Section 1 states that the rights and freedoms included in the Charter are subject only to 'such reasonable limits prescribed by law as can be demonstrably justified in a free and democratic society'. This limitation means a court can find that rights have been violated, but the offending legislation or policy can remain because it is a reasonable limit on religious freedom by standards of section 1. Take, for example, a Jehovah's Witness parent who wishes to refuse blood transfusions for her child's cancer treatment. A court may force the child to receive transfusions by assuming temporary custody and overriding the wishes of the parent (and the child). While a court may find that such treatment constitutes a violation of the religious freedom provisions of the Charter, it may also find that such a violation is justifiable under Section 1 as representing a societal interest (see Beaman, 2008).

To give this discussion a bit more context, let's consider one case in a bit more detail. As we have discussed the definition of religion and the matching of definitions and actual religious beliefs and practices as they come before the courts, we have questioned whether it is possible to define religion in an inclusive way. The *Multani* case (2006) provides an example of the subtleties of this process. In that case, 'G' (the son) and 'B' (the father) were fully observant Sikhs, or, as the Court described them, orthodox Sikhs. An arrangement was made to accommodate G's wearing of a *kirpan* (an article of faith which resembles a dagger) to school; this agreement specified that it be kept under his clothing, sheathed, and sewn shut. The school commission refused to ratify the agreement; however, the superior court set aside that decision. The court of appeal upheld the school commission and the Supreme Court of Canada allowed the appeal. We might see the carrying of a the kirpan as an issue of safety but, given the extent of the provisions the Multani's made to keep the *kirpan* relatively inaccessible, this is not a viable argument and was not one that the Supreme Court of Canada accepted. We must ask, therefore, why the *kirpan* became an issue to the point that the family was forced to go to the Supreme Court of Canada to be able to exercise their religious beliefs. In part, we can identify the very narrow conceptualization we have of religion and the way it is practiced. Fortunately, the Supreme Court was not so limited in its approach.

The naming and construction of the *kirpan* as a weapon is a discursive practice that relies on a socially constructed set of categories. Manjit Singh (*Multani v. Commission scolaire Marguerite-Bourgeoys* at para 39) comments:

> Rather than go into a detailed explanatory meaning of the kirpan, I would like to talk about another weapon with origins in medieval Europe that has been adopted in Canada and Quebec as a symbol of public authority. I am talking about the mace that lies on a table in front of the speaker of the House of Commons in Ottawa as well as in the National Assembly in Quebec City. According to Webster's dictionary, a mace is 'akin to a staff or club used especially in the Middle Ages for breaking armour' and 'an ornamental staff borne as a symbol of authority before a public official or legislative body.' It is clear from the above wording that a mace is a weapon. In the context of the two legislative chambers, however, it is a symbol of state authority. No one has ever questioned that some day, some member of one of these chambers, in a fit of rage, could use this weapon to attack a fellow member. The point of this discussion is that through mutual consent an historical tradition, this lethal weapon has come to represent the authority of the state.

Singh's insightful commentary points to the constructed nature of religious symbols. James Beckford (2003) employs a moderate social constructionism which acknowledges the culturally and socially situated position of religion as a concept and as a practice. Beckford notes the definition of religion as shifting throughout time, and the link between those shifts and power relations: 'what counts as "really religious" or "truly Christian" are authorized, challenged and replaced over time' (2003: 17).

Religious groups complicate issues around definition because they may disagree among themselves about who counts as a 'real' member of their group. Adherents may challenge others who claim to be members of their group but who don't participate in particular rituals or adhere to specific, beliefs fundamental to their religious worldview. Thus we have some Anglicans, for example, who support same-sex marriage while others are opposed to it. Some Muslims support the use of *sharia* law; others do not, and so on. These tensions can be confusing to those who are outside of the religious group and who might be trying to understand the group's religious identity. Some members of a religious group may claim to speak for all members. However, to perceive that all members of a religious group believe and practise in the same way is misleading at best. Think about the variations of the faith group with which you are most familiar. You will quickly see that religious identity is a complex factor in the consideration of religious belief and practice and its protection.

● Religion and Gender ● ● ●

Why is it important to talk about religion and gender? Because there are some decidedly gendered aspects to religious participation. Women tend to make up the bulk of religious congregations, and some argue that it is women's decisions to stop attending that has been the catalyst in the sharp decline in religious participation, at least among Christians. Gender roles are a definite flashpoint in contemporary conversations about the ways in which religion and society intersect.

A number of scholars, most notably Mary Daly (1985) and Naomi Goldenberg (2006), have argued that religion has been a key institutional site of women's oppression. Women have been excluded from positions of power within church structure; they are instead being relegated to 'domestic' roles within the church. Some of these same debates are emerging in relation to Muslim women. Interpretations over wearing the *hijab* vary; some define it as a cultural rather than a religious symbol, while others see it as a symbol of women's agency or choice, and

still others perceive it as a sign that a woman is oppressed by her religion. Perhaps most important, but sometimes overlooked in this discussion, are the voices of Muslim women themselves. Research reveals the complexity of this issue, but most significantly clearly demonstrates that women's interpretations cannot be excluded from the interpretation of the meaning of a particular practice.

Homa Hoodfar's research (2003) helps us to better understand the complex ways in which women interpret their own choices to wear a *hijab*. For many of the young women Hoodfar interviewed, the choice to wear the *hijab* created a newfound sense of freedom from strict parents. All of a sudden, they were free to engage in activities that their parents had previously forbidden: 'parents seem to be relieved and assured that you are not going to do stupid things, and your community knows that you are acting like a Muslim woman, you are much freer' (2003: 214). Moreover, for some women it was a strategy to generate respect not only among fellow Muslims, but also in the broader society: 'I am telling them to see me otherwise. Do not think of my body, but of me as a person, a colleague, and so on' (Hoodfar, 2003: 221). Many of the women interviewed by Hoodfar were extremely strategic in their choices to wear the *hijab*, weighing the advantages and disadvantages and often concluding that the advantages outweighed the negatives. For some, it also opened opportunities to discuss their Muslim beliefs and to dispel prejudices and misconceptions.

Ultimately, there are a number of strategic choices involved in women's engagement with religion. Some, like Daly (1985), who is a former Roman Catholic nun, argue that religion is so patriarchal that there is no way that women can freely exercise agency within its confines, and that women must therefore abandon traditional religion and create their own spheres for spiritual fulfillment. In part this has been, if not the goal, the effect of some Wiccan groups. Wendy Griffin's (2000) research on pagan groups has documented the approach of Dianic Wiccan groups which is largely separationist and her research on the Circle of the Redwood Moon found that they largely abandoned traditional approaches to religion and spirituality. Naming themselves Dianics after the Roman Goddess Diana, their holy days are largely based on seasonal cycles. They conceptualize the divine as female rather than male, and they situate their spirituality in feminist analysis that includes political activism. They are largely a women-only group and in this way have separated themselves both from the patriarchy of larger society and from traditional religious practices and beliefs.

Some strategies are less radical and call simply for a reshaping or reframing of religious teachings. For example, while evangelical Christians describe gender roles in rather particular ways (wives, for example, are taught to submit to their husbands), the exact ways in which these roles are interpreted is perhaps not as literal as one might think. Listen to Jane, for example, an evangelical Christian woman who, while she says she is a 'submissive' wife, tells the interviewer that all decisions in her marriage are made jointly:

> I have had some discussions with women who have a real difficult time with that—wives submit to your husbands. Now, I don't have difficulty with that at all, because in the next breath it says 'Husbands love your wives as Christ loved the church.' In my mind, we've got the easy end of the job, they've got the hard one. I mean, they've got to love like Christ.

Jane's approach is representative of that of many women who are part of more conservative religious traditions. Women within those groups grow impatient with those who would characterize them as having no choice or agency. While there is a tendency to characterize them negatively by those who are not members, they often see themselves as benefiting from the demands of their religious traditions, which create rules for both men and women.

One of the most heated areas of discussion in relation to such teachings is that of violence against women. The relationship between teachings, such as submission or male headship, and violence against women is rendered even more complex by the valourization of family unity within faith communities (Alkhateeb and Abugideiri, 2007; Nason-Clark and Kroeger, 2004). This often means that women from conservative faith communities—whether Christian, Muslim or Jewish—are often especially hesitant to take action if they are abused by their husbands for fear of disrupting the family unit. Thus such women are 'more likely stay in abusive relationships, more likely to return to abusive relationships after counseling, and tend to be more optimistic that abuse will stop if the abuser has some form of counseling' (Nason-Clark and Fisher-Townsend, 2007; Nason-Clark et al., 2004).

Violence against women within religious communities is made even more complex by the fact that such communities are reluctant to admit the existence of violence within the family, perpetuating what Nason-Clark and Kroeger (2004) have called a 'holy hush' of denial. To further muddy the waters, secular agencies for women are often reluctant to include religious resources in their strategies for helping abused women, thus sometimes excluding a resource that is important to abused women from faith communities.

Gender roles within new religious movements are difficult to generalize because new religious movements are incredibly varied in their teachings. Further, with the exception of a few pioneering scholars like Susan Palmer (2004), there is little research on new religious move-

Bryan F. Peterson/Corbis

ments in Canada. Palmer's research on Raelians, for example, found shifting gender roles during the life course of the group. Pre-1998, for example, gender roles were egalitarian; however, following the founding of 'The Order of Rael's Angels', a special women's caucus within the movement which emphasizes women's 'feminine charisma' and highlights free love, Raelian views shifted to place an emphasis on the so-called unique qualities of women, a move which, observes Palmer, has served to polarize the sexes within the movement (2004: 139).

The intersection of religion and gender often triggers interesting debates. The opposition of some religious groups to same-sex marriage was arguably a reaction to what they perceived to be shifting gender roles. Some groups argued, for example, that marriage was solely the terrain of opposite sex couples, and that it was inherently designed (by god) that way. Heather Shipley (2008: 5) notes that 'Defining marriage as an historically religious institution, while inaccurate, is a common argument promoted by religious interest groups who seek to preserve the heterosexual institution of marriage.' For example, in their factum regarding Bill C-23, *An Act to Modernize the Statutes of Canada in Relation to Benefits and Obligations* in 2000, The Evangelical Fellowship of Canada argued that 'God instituted marriage for the express purposes of companionship, partnership in the task of procreation, for fulfilling a stewardly responsibility for the earth, but fundamentally to mirror the intimate relationship which God desires to have with his people' (2000: 3). At the core of their arguments was a sense that there is a divinely

mandated purpose to marriage. The Supreme Court of Canada rejected this argument and it is now legally possible for same-sex couples to marry in Canada. However, the legislation has allowed for 'the freedom of officials of religious groups who choose not to perform marriages that are not in accordance with their religious beliefs' (2004: 3), preserving a space in which religious voices override basic human rights.

● Conclusions ● ● ● ● ● ●

This chapter has considered the contemporary picture of religion in Canada and explored some of the issues that are of key concern to sociologists of religion. We have seen that the religious demographic of Canada is in an interesting period of flux which may have an important impact on Canadian society. Despite their small numbers, religious minorities in Canada play an important role in defining diversity in Canadian society. It is an exciting time to be a sociologist of religion in Canada in this time of rapid change.

We have already discussed to a great extent the limits of existing social scientific research on religion in Canada. Quantitative measures need to be more comprehensive to reflect Canada's shifting demographic. We need to understand how religious beliefs and practices fit into the day to day lives of Canadians and, most especially, the religious and spiritual practices of those who have arrived in Canada more recently. We need defini-

OPEN FOR DISCUSSION
Polygamy: Do Women Really Choose?

After years of keeping a low profile in BC's lush Creston Valley, the community of Bountiful opened its doors to the public April 21—media and protestors alike—to set some records straight.

A group from the community, calling itself the Women of Bountiful, hosted a press conference at a community centre 10 km away in Creston. Their aim was to show Canada that they are fully aware of their lifestyle choice; they enjoy sharing husbands even though they admit polygamy is illegal in Canada, and they will use Canada's Charter of Rights and Freedoms to argue that plural marriage is covered by their freedom of religion.

'We the women of our community will be silent no more,' said Zelpha Chatwin to the 300 people in attendance. 'I love the fact that my girls and I only have to cook and clean once a week. [Polygamists are] a team of players who care for each other.'

The women also said plural marriages come with various benefits, such as pooling resources and talent, and higher household incomes, reported the *National Post*.

—Meghan Wood

tional and measurement standards that are not based on Christian understandings of religion. In other words, our research needs to extend beyond church attendance and bible belief. Our measures of spiritual practices should take an inclusive turn.

Research on religion in Canada is slowly becoming a priority. Sociology has an important role to play in the study of religion in Canada. No matter which theoretical tradition one uses, it brings tools that are invaluable to research. Ethnographic accounts of religious communities will provide insight that is as important as more detailed survey work. Research into important intersections—like youth and religious practice and belief—is central to predicting the role that religion will play in Canada's future. Key, though, to understanding the role of religion in Canada's future are interdisciplinary approaches that seek to draw on the expertise and insights of various traditions of scholarly thought.

● Questions ● ● ● ● ● ●
for Critical Thought

1. Critically examine your own religious history. Where do you and your family fit in terms of believing and belonging? Are you part of a religious minority or the religious majority?
2. Do we live in a secular Canada? Are there some areas of life that are more or less removed from the influence of religion?
3. How is religion best defined? Explain your decision.
4. Should religion have a say in public policy issues?
5. Why do you think the language of 'cults' and 'brainwashing' persists?
6. The United States and France have a separation of church and state. What does this mean? Can you think of other examples of states that have such a separation? Examples of states that have a merging of church and state, either now or historically?

● Recommended
● Readings ● ● ● ●

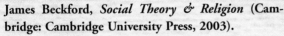

James Beckford, *Social Theory & Religion* (Cambridge: Cambridge University Press, 2003).

James Beckford presents an important examination of religion by developing clear links between social theory and the social scientific study of religion. Relying on moderate social constructionism, his theory focuses on the ways in which religion is a complex and social phenomenon.

Peter Beyer, *Religions in Global Society* (London: Routledge, 2006).

In this book, Peter Beyer analyzes religion as a dimension of the historical processes of globalization, as a means of understanding religion in a contemporary global society. Beyer uses examples ranging from Islam and Hinduism to African traditional religions, resulting in an overview of how religion has developed in a globalized society.

Reginald Bibby, *Restless Gods: The Renaissance of Religion in Canada* (Toronto: Stoddart, 2002).

In this book Bibby develops his idea that religion, especially Christianity, still matters to Canadians. Drawing from survey data, Bibby empirically demonstrates the facets of Canadian religious participation.

Sian Reid, ed., *Between the Worlds: Readings in Contemporary Paganism* (Toronto: CSPI/Women's Press, 2006).

Neopaganism is an important part of the religious mosaic in Canada. This edited collection provides a good overview of neopaganism from both academic and non-academic contributors.

● Recommended ● ● ● ●
Websites

Human Rights Watch http://www.hrw.org

Human Rights Watch is dedicated to protecting the human rights of people around the world.

United Church of Canada, Wonder Café
http://www.wondercafe.ca

This site, hosted by the United Church of Canada, is a place where discussion and exploration of spiritual topics are encouraged.

Canadian Charter of Rights and Freedoms
http://laws.justice.gc.ca/en/charter

This is Canada's declaration of human rights and freedoms.

Chapter 15

Politics and Social Movements

Randle Hart, Peter R. Sinclair, and John Veugelers

Learning Objectives

In this chapter, you will:

▶ discover the value of comparing different societies;

▶ review and evaluate competing perspectives on democratic societies;

▶ consider the global dimensions and implications of many political issues;

▶ grasp why women, the poor, and minority ethnic groups have been poorly represented in political life;

▶ review the theoretical approaches to the study of social movements;

▶ read about key debates within the study of social movements;

▶ see how empirical research is used to test and criticize social movement theories; and

▶ learn how social movements are embedded in national and international (global) politics.

Photo: Getty Images

● Introduction ● ● ● ● ● ●

This chapter is largely about the use of power for political ends. As we will see, power is exercised in the political arena by political parties, elected legislators, and civil servants, among others. In politics, **the state** is the chief actor, using its great power and resources to control and change people's behaviour. Of interest to students of political sociology is the relation between the state and the economy—between political actors, on the one hand, and the largest corporations, dominant social classes, and major economic groupings such as consumers and labour unions, on the other. No less important is the relation between the state and civil society, between political actors and those institutions that make up the everyday lives of ordinary people—families, schools, churches, communities, and so on. In this context, social movements represent the political arm of civil society. This chapter pays particular attention to social movements, how they form, and how they influence both civil society and the state.

● Core Concepts ● ● ● ● ●

Politics and Power

Politics is the process by which individuals and groups act to promote their interests, often in conflict with others. It is intimately connected to social and economic **power**. In all spheres of action, power reflects the extent to which available resources both constrain and enable people's actions (Giddens, 1979). Resources provide the means for action, but they also provide a limit on what action is possible. Following Max Weber (1978 [1908]), one of sociology's outstanding social theorists of the early twentieth century, power is often defined as the ability of a person or group to achieve their objectives, even when opposed. Power typically becomes concentrated in society because some people consistently have greater discretion in controlling what others do (Barnes, 1988). However, in some situations power is more or less equal, as in most friendships.

Thus, power is about the capacity to act in a desired way, and politics is the process of mobilizing these capacities. Politics is most visible when it involves struggle between opposing forces; however, it is also evident in what people do to avoid conflict and maintain their domination. Examples include controlling agendas and the timing of decisions, even how other people define their interests (Lukes, 1974). John Gaventa (1980)

demonstrated the way power was maintained for generations in his investigation of why Appalachian miners remained politically inactive, despite much poverty, from the late nineteenth century until 1975. Apart from brief periods when recessions weakened the position of landowners and mine operators, this local elite wielded effective power. In particular, the poor miners and their families accepted existing conditions because their opponents controlled not only vital resources—jobs, houses, land, stores, access to medical facilities, and even the local electoral process—but also the opinion-forming institutions of the area: schools, churches, and the media.

An excellent example of the difficulty of challenging power-holders is Bent Flyvbjerg's study (1998) of the politics of urban planning in Aalborg, Denmark. Flyvbjerg provides careful documentation of the ill-fated attempt to reduce the use of private cars in the centre of Aalborg and to make conditions more favourable for other forms of transportation. This study investigates the process of winning and losing and how reason is argued and manipulated in the exercise of power. Local business people believed that restrictions on automobiles would reduce their sales. Through the Chamber of Industry, they prevented measures to control cars while supporting aids to buses, bicyclists, and pedestrians. Much of this activity was covert, unnoticed by the general public. In the end, the environment and virtually every citizen lost out when all forms of traffic increased. Yet this study paradoxically shows the practical value of sociology.

Power is often hidden in relationships. For power to be observed, those subject to it must actively resist. However, opposition will be rare if people believe they have no chance of successfully resisting the demands being placed on them; and it will not appear when power-holders enjoy authority, which may be defined as power considered legitimate by those subject to it.

Types of Authority

To hold authority over others is a critical resource in the conduct of politics. Where authority is widely accepted, politics will likely follow peaceful, established patterns, but when it does not exist, intense conflicts are probable sooner or later. In order to understand how authority becomes established, the work of Max Weber, developed almost a century ago, remains important. Weber (1978 [1908]) identified three types of authority according to the grounds on which it was accepted by those subject to it. These types seldom appear in pure form because actual relationships usually involve combinations.

Traditional authority is evident when people obey because that is the way things have always been done. The power-holder enjoys 'the sanctity of immemorial traditions' (Weber, 1978 [1908]: 215) and may expect obedience as long as these established rules are followed. Examples include chiefs and elders who ruled tribal societies by customary practice and acceptance of their rights. Authority of this type is more secure when it is grounded in the belief that it derives from a revered spiritual source. Thus, to oppose one's leader would also be to oppose one's god.

Charismatic authority rests on belief in the exceptional qualities of an individual person, someone of exemplary or heroic character who reveals how life will unfold, perhaps involving new social **values** and patterns of conduct. The person with charisma is thought to be able to resolve problems beyond the capacity of ordinary people and may build a devoted following, sometimes rooted in religious faith, as with the Hebrew prophets, or in secular **ideologies**, as with Mao Zedong and Adolf Hitler. Charismatic leaders are innovative, even revolutionary, but their authority is fragile, being dependent on their personal qualities and the appearance of results.

Rational-legal authority is based on formally established rules, procedures, and expertise in which an individual's acknowledged right to command is limited to his or her official position. Personal characteristics of the office holder and those subject to command are irrelevant to the conduct of business. It is expected that each person will be treated as any other, which gives rise to formal procedures both for appointment to positions and for the treatment of citizens. This form of authority is characteristic of bureaucratic structures, both public and private, where those in higher-ranked positions may command those in lower positions within the limits of their jurisdiction. Thus, the manager who attempts to obtain sexual services from a secretary engages in behaviour that is considered illegitimate in that context. Specialized knowledge or expertise is another modern basis of authority, as when a physician persuades a patient to

SOCIOLOGY IN ACTION
The Impact of Research on Political Practice: The Aalborg Project

Social research can have an effect on what is studied by helping to change the way people conduct their affairs. Bent Flyvbjerg's investigation of Aalborg's transportation system (1998) uncovered how effectively the local business elite was able to bypass formal democratic processes and achieve its objectives over a period of 15 years. However, Flyvbjerg (2001) was also committed to research that would be critical and reflexive. This required placing the results of his research back into the political arena in the hope that improvements might take place—here, in the functioning of democracy. Flyvbjerg therefore presented his results in the mass media and in public meetings. For example, he demonstrated that, contrary to expectations, traffic accidents in the centre of Aalborg increased over the life of the plan without officials apparently noticing, and that 'the increase in accidents was caused by city officials allowing the rationality of the Chamber of Industry and Commerce to slowly, surely, and one-sidedly, influence and undermine the rationality of the Aalborg project' (Flyvbjerg, 2001: 157).

Initially, those whose positions were threatened by his evidence challenged Flyvbjerg by claiming his information was inaccurate, but a determined defence of that evidence was eventually accepted by the alderman responsible for city planning. After that, dialogue developed. Dialogue is understood as a respectful exchange of ideas, a requirement of the democratic process, in contrast with mere rhetoric and polemic, which impede informed judgement.

As the public debate proceeded, the alderman and his officials realized that reports about the research were influencing the public and that the Aalborg plan had to change. They could no longer defend what was demonstrably not working, especially as the project was by this time receiving much international attention. A new plan emerged based on an open democratic process. The city government invited a variety of interest groups to join the planning and implementation processes. The European Union, inspired by Flyvbjerg's research and determination that it should be noticed outside the academy, recognized this new practice by commending Aalborg for its innovative, democratic planning process.

endure unpleasant and undignified procedures that the patient does not fully understand.

Modern states develop bureaucratic structures based on claims to rational-legal authority, though backed by the capacity to draw on the means of force should there be opposition. Of course, bureaucratic officials, in practice, are at times corrupt (which means that some people are treated with special favour in return for unofficial personal payments) or obstructionist. These departures from the rules weaken the legitimacy of the **bureaucracy** and may increase the likelihood of radical opposition to the regime in control of the state.

Although power and politics are dimensions of all **social relationships**, 'politics' in common use refers, in the first instance, to processes of government and regulation within and between modern states. It is this more specific understanding of politics that will be developed in this chapter.

Political institutions are established rules and procedures for the conduct of political affairs, including the government of society. They constitute a network of power relationships. Specialized political institutions were evident in some form in most earlier societies but became more complex in the industrial countries of the modern world, on which we focus here. There is no uniform course of development, but several important trends can be identified: increasing scale of government, growing political intervention in social affairs, the rise of the nation-state, and various forms of bureaucratic administration (Bottomore, 1979), including attempts at organization more inclusive than the state, particularly the United Nations and its component frameworks and sub-groups. We can analyze these networks of power in light of their internal structures and their links to the rest of society. Special interest groups, **social movements**, and political parties connect various segments of

As the institution exercising the state's monopoly over the legitimate use of force, the military has always played an important political role. In some states, questions rightly arise over whose interests the military is protecting. Reuters/Daniel Aguilar

the public to the state, which is the core political frame of contemporary complex societies.

In modern societies, state institutions are both objectives of political struggle and resources in these struggles. In Weber's famous definition, **the state** is 'a human community that (successfully) claims the monopoly of the legitimate use of physical force within a given territory' (1946 [1922]: 78). Residents consider the use of force to be acceptable only when state leaders call on it, and probably only when it is applied according to widely held rules. However, it is common for physical coercion to be deployed within a particular territory without that force being viewed as legitimate by most residents. Tyrants, dictators, and zealots can rule effectively for long periods. Unless we insist that states exist only when rule is legitimate, another definition is called for. Thus, the state may be considered to be that set of procedures and organizations concerned with creating, administering, and enforcing rules or decisions for conduct within a given territory. Here, legitimacy is not assumed.

Pre-industrial states were usually rudimentary in form, for example, extensions of the household of a ruler. They were also small, as reflected in the Greek city-states. **Monarchy** is rule by a single individual who claims legitimacy based on royal lineage. Today's monarchs, as in Britain and the Netherlands, have survived the transition to democratic constitutions, but their powers are only formal, their practice essentially ceremonial.

Modern nation-states certainly vary in scale, but they typically are much more complex, with their legislatures, governments, public bureaucracies, police, judiciary, and military components. Remembering the complexity and scale of these states, it is misleading to assume that 'the state' is coherently unified; in practice, the parts are loosely integrated and often work at cross-purposes. Canada's federal Department of Finance, for example, may wish to reduce taxes at the same time as the Department of Health and Welfare pushes for a better-funded health-care system. The federal structure also creates layers of government with overlapping jurisdictions and potential conflicts.

● Modern State ● ● ● ● ● Institutions

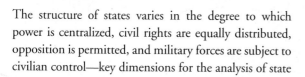

The structure of states varies in the degree to which power is centralized, civil rights are equally distributed, opposition is permitted, and military forces are subject to civilian control—key dimensions for the analysis of state political institutions. The forms of the state are usefully summarized as authoritarian, totalitarian, and liberal-democratic. Since the nineteenth century, the importance of the idea of nationhood to many cultures means that a society within the territorial boundaries of a state is often referred to as a nation-state, even though state and national boundaries rarely coincide perfectly. We shall see that attempts to establish truly national states often have generated severe conflict in the last 50 years.

Authoritarian States

In authoritarian states, public opposition is forbidden and the population as a whole is under great pressure to accept and comply with the expectations of political leaders. At a minimum, authoritarian leaders insist on compliance in all public life and depend on control of military force to maintain their positions if challenged.

Absolutist monarchies, which combine tradition and force to control the population, were common in pre-industrial societies in which the labour of ordinary people supported an elite. Although this type of state became rare in the late twentieth century, one example was the regime of the Shah of Iran prior to that country's Islamic revolution of 1979. Some contemporary states come close to this model. Thus, the Saudi royal family rules Saudi Arabia with an appointed advisory council and imposes a strict *shariah* code of conduct on all residents. There is no parliament and no formal opposition is permitted, but covert opposition and resistance challenge the notion that power really is absolute (e.g., see Ménoret, 2005). In 2005, the introduction of municipal elections (for men only) was the first sign of concession to some form of popular representation.

Military dictatorships have frequently taken power in Asian, African, and Latin American countries following their independence from colonial rule. Usually these seizures are claimed to be temporary measures until corruption or ethnic conflicts can be solved. Nigeria, Haiti, Myanmar, Chile, and Argentina are among many countries that have experienced military rule at least once. Military regimes lack popular legitimacy and may be short-lived. At times, experimental democratic regimes and military dictatorships replace each other in a cyclical pattern.

Totalitarian States

Totalitarianism is more extreme than authoritarianism because it involves intervening in and controlling all aspects of both public and private life. It demands cultural homogeneity in every important respect. Totalitarianism is best considered as a strategy for achieving total domination through a centralized repressive state apparatus. Although no case perfectly fits the concept, Nazi Germany is often considered an example of totalitarianism because the Nazi Party (the National Socialist German Workers' Party) mobilized cultural institutions (mass media, schools, religion) to promote its ideology and tried to eliminate any opposition. Such states usually function in alliance with established classes and corporations, although the rhetoric of their leaders may be populist; for example, they may appeal to the anger of ordinary people, who may be suffering economic pain or political humiliation, by selecting visible minorities as targets for extremist action.

Liberal-Democratic States

Literally, *democracy* means 'rule by the people', but who is to count as 'the people' and how ruling takes place can vary enormously. *Direct democracy*, in which all citizens discuss and vote on all issues of importance to them, can function effectively only in small settings such as utopian communities or the classical Greek city-states. That said, liberal-democratic states are characterized by institutions that allow representation of the views of ordinary citizens through political parties that compete for the power to govern. These states may be *constitutional monarchies*, like Norway and Canada, in which the head of state is a hereditary position, or *republics*, like France and the United States, in which the head of state is elected.

At the heart of democracies are their election practices. These electoral institutions are quite varied. Some create legislatures by electing members from small areas (*constituencies*) within the state. In a sense, such societies (such as the United Kingdom and Canada) conduct a set of mini-elections all at the same time. Other democracies count votes for the whole society and candidates are elected from a party list in proportion to the party's share of the total votes cast. These *proportional representation* systems are found in many countries, including Israel and Italy.

The rapid spread of democracy has been one of the world's great dramas over the last 50 years. As Table 15.1 indicates, democratization proceeded rapidly in the twentieth century. These data are open to challenge because they depend on the Freedom House definitions and procedures for allocating cases, but they do clearly indicate general trends. In 1900, no society qualified as fully democratic because the first democracies of Europe, North America, Australia, and New Zealand restricted voting rights to men. After 1945, many societies emerged from colonial rule, sometimes to continuous democratic politics (like India), and sometimes to unstable democracies with periods of military rule (like Nigeria). In addition, many Latin American states formally established in the nineteenth century did not transform effectively to democratic institutions until the latter part of the twentieth century. Although China continues to try to maintain authoritarian central control in political life while opening the economy to market rules, it has proven exceptionally difficult to restrict individual freedom to the marketplace in socialist societies. After 1989, the spread of democracy accelerated for several years with the dramatic appearance of fledgling democratic political institutions when the Soviet Union and its East European allies collapsed, as indicated above.

● Perspectives ● ● ● ● ● ● on the Democratic State

Sociologists have attempted to explain the politics of the modern state by analyzing the connection between political institutions and the social groups of which society is composed. Sociological theories of the state revolve around the question of whose interests are represented in institutions and actual policies. (See Table 15.2 for summary statements.) Do all these approaches provide part of the answer, or does the evidence fit some better than others?

Old Foes

The Ruling Elite
Until the 1970s, the chief contending perspectives stressed either elite domination or pluralism. The 'ruling elite' approach pointed to a small clique that effectively

▊▊ Time to Reflect ▊▊ ▊▊ ▊▊ ▊▊ ▊▊ ▊▊ ▊▊ ▊▊ ▊▊ ▊▊ ▊▊ ▊▊ ▊▊

Political leaders in the West, particularly in the United States, speak of introducing democracy to formerly authoritarian and totalitarian states. Do you think this is a reasonable or laudable objective? What possible reasons would the liberal-democratic countries have for 'exporting' democracy to other states?

dominated political decisions on all matters that were of central interest to its members. C. Wright Mills argued for the existence of a power elite at the national level in the United States—'those political, economic and military circles which as an intricate set of overlapping cliques share decisions having at least national consequences' (1956: 18). This power elite was not a fixed group whose members, in conspiratorial fashion, made all the decisions; rather, it was composed of people who knew each other, shared an upper-class background, and consulted each other on issues of fundamental importance to society. Other researchers identified elites that effectively controlled decision-making at the local level (Hunter, 1953). Thus, the vision of elite domination encompassed all levels of the state.

Mills believed that the corporate elite was the most powerful segment of the power elite. Closer to Marx's concept of the ruling class is William Domhoff (1990), who believes that the corporate wealthy (about one per cent of the US population) are able to limit government to actions that serve the interests of the capitalist class. Similarly, Wallace Clement (1975) describes at length a ruling class in Canada intimately interconnected at the highest levels of corporate power and between private boardrooms and the national government.

The image of the state implicit in 'ruling elite' theory is one that puts little emphasis on administration.

Instead, it focuses on policy, which is linked to the interests of those who hold key institutional positions. In all cases, this theory agrees that the interests of ordinary people are ignored whenever they might clash with those of the elite. Without explicitly writing about the state, these theorists create a vision of the state as necessarily anti-democratic. The state becomes nothing more than a means of domination, even when policy is couched in formally democratic procedures.

Pluralism and Elite Competition

Mills and his followers wrote partly in criticism of pluralism, advocates of which presented a benign view of American democracy as a forum in which any person or group had a fair chance of being represented. In turn, they themselves were attacked by those identifying a pluralist structure in US politics. Robert Dahl (1961), for example, cautioned that Mills had merely pointed out a group with high potential for control but had failed to demonstrate that this group actually dominated decision-making. Furthermore, Dahl insisted that only issues on which a clear difference of position could be observed in public debate ought to be considered. He also adopted the restrictive view that power is not exercised in situations where people are persuaded by others to adopt their attitudes. Dahl's own research, particularly in the city of New Haven, Connecticut, led him to

Table 15.1	Political Development, States and Colonies, 1900–2000		
	2000	**1950**	**1900**
Democracy[a]	120 (62.5%)	22 (14.3%)	0
Restricted democratic practice[a]	16 (8.3%)	21 (13.6%)	25 (19.2%)
Constitutional monarchy	0	9 (5.8%)	19 (14.6%)
Traditional monarchy	10 (5.2%)	4 (2.6%)	6 (4.6%)
Absolute monarchy	0	2 (1.3%)	5 (3.8%)
Authoritarian regime	39 (20.3%)	10 (6.5%)	0
Totalitarian regime	5 (2.6%)	12 (7.8%)	0
Colonial dependency	0	43 (27.9%)	55 (42.3%)
Protectorate	2 (1.0%)	31 (20.1%)	20 (15.4%)
Total	**192**	**154**	**130**

[a]Freedom House defines democracies as competitive party systems in which 'opposition parties have a legitimate chance of attaining power or participating in power', whereas restricted democratic practices are systems that preclude 'meaningful challenge' to ruling parties.
Source: Freedom House, Democracy's Century report, 1999, at: <www.freedomhouse.org>. Reprinted by permission of Freedom House.

conclude that democracy was alive and well in the America of the 1950s.

The pluralist approach recognizes that modern states all have intermediate organizations between government and the people—namely, parties and interest or lobby groups, which represent those with particular issues to promote in the state. Interest groups attempt to influence parties but rarely offer their own candidates for election because their objectives are limited to particular issues. Pluralists claim that no one interest is able to dominate the state and that democracy is protected by the competition between interests. Political leaders will be swayed by mass opinions because of their desire to win elections.

Political Economy Perspectives

Neo-Marxism

Since the late 1960s, political economy perspectives have focused discussions on the state, which is seen as the core of the political system. For the most part, these modern thinkers abandoned the old Marxist view, associated with Vladimir Ilyich Lenin, that the state was merely the instrument of capital designed to solve periodic problems of accumulation. Although they have disputed the degree to which the state should be seen in

this simplistic way, neo-Marxists usually consider the state to be structured, or even programmed, so that it acts in the long-term interests of capitalists as a class. Consequently, these authors de-emphasize the evidence that workers appear not to be against capitalism, and see reformist labour or social democratic parties as fulfilling a need for capitalism to make concessions in order to maintain legitimacy and continuity. Similar to ruling-elite theory, the liberal-democratic processes are thought to function at a secondary level in the power structure.

Nicos Poulantzas (1978) developed the neo-Marxist perspective most fully, arguing that the state must be relatively autonomous from class conflict in the production process if it is to serve the needs of the dominant class. Here, *autonomy* does not mean independence from class control, but rather that the state is not directly representing dominant class interests. The key role of the state is to attain cohesion by 'individualizing' the workers—that is, by contributing to their sense of **identity** as individuals and as part of a nation rather than as members of a class. Legal and ideological structures resting on claims of equality among citizens conceal from workers the fact that they are engaged in class relations. To achieve this outcome, the state may act to protect certain economic interests of the dominated classes, but it never

Table 15.2	Key Features of Perspectives on Liberal-Democratic States		
	Social Bias of the State	**Basis of Political Power**	**Possibility of Major Change**
Power/Ruling elite	Captive of the elite: leading members of state, military, and especially economic elite	Common socialization process and control of key political resources	Highly unlikely because the mass public lacks effective organization
Pluralism/Elite competition	Neutral arena for debate: wide range of interest groups and public as a whole benefit	Success in persuading electorates in open competition plus interest group mobilization	Normal rotation of parties and effective interest groups; no structural change
Neo-Marxism	Serves the capitalist class and, to a lesser extent, the service class	Control of wealth and, indirectly, of the political elite	Unlikely but occasionally possible through revolutionary class action
Autonomous state	State elite and more powerful interest groups	Control of means of force, taxation, and votes	Possible if balance of resources shifts among key social groups
Feminism	Reflects male values and organizations; state helps maintain patriarchy	Male control of institutional patterns; limited participation by women	Unlikely without radical transformation of gender attitudes

challenges the political power of the dominant class. The state may have to resist certain short-term demands of capitalists (for example, reduced taxes and reduced public spending) to meet the long-term needs of capitalism as a whole (for example, maintaining an appropriately educated labour force). From this perspective, the expansion of public welfare against capitalist opposition is interpreted as a move to shore up the future of capitalism by smoothing over some of the discontent engendered by unemployment, poor health care, and unequal access to education.

The Partially Autonomous State

Theda Skocpol (1979) and Fred Block (1980), among others, put forward another theory of the state. These theorists claim a genuinely independent source of power for state officials based on the resources of the state that these officials control. This position challenges Marxist theory by claiming, first, that the continuation of capitalism is not necessary; second, that other forms of state or institutional action might meet the 'needs' of capitalism; and, third, that much state action is opposed by those very persons for whom it is thought to be essential.

Block's answer to the key question of why state managers should act in the interests of capitalism is that they need capitalists to continue investing, or the state will lose income and political legitimacy. Nevertheless, state intervention often takes a form opposed by capital, because the state is forced to respond to working-class political pressure and because state managers have an interest in expanding their sphere of influence. Depending on the relative flow of power among these groups, state policies can be expected to oscillate. In this model, the state becomes a third effective force, although it is tied to the perpetuation of capitalist interests.

In a more radical version of this thesis, Skocpol argues persuasively that the state should be recognized as a 'structure with a logic and interests of its own not necessarily equivalent to, or fused with the interests of the dominant class in society or the full set of member groups in the polity' (1979: 27). Here, we are directed to the interests of state actors themselves, as well as to the process of policy formation, to explain the policy that is actually produced. Skocpol does acknowledge that the state often protects dominant class interests, but not in all circumstances—in particular, not when such protection would threaten political stability. Hence, according to Skocpol, 'the state's own fundamental interest in maintaining sheer physical order and political peace may lead it—especially in periods of crisis—to enforce concessions to subordinate class demands' (1979: 30). Skocpol charges neo-Marxists with a failure to accord sufficient independence to state and party and with an unjustified insistence that the state must work towards the reproduction of capitalism. Without accepting the idea that politics is a free-for-all competition among equals, this position goes some way towards the pluralist interpretation by recognizing that the capitalist class is not consistently dominant.

Feminist Perspectives

Most theories of the state focus on class issues to the exclusion of **gender** and **ethnicity**. By contrast, feminist theory makes gender a central component in the analysis of politics and the state, as it does for social life generally. Specifically, the **feminist perspective** has brought attention to the state as a contributor to the subordination of women and as an institution permeated by gender inequality. However, there is no single feminist position. Judith Allen (1990), for example, even asserted that feminists have no need for a theory of the state because the concept of the state is too vague and unitary to be applicable to women's political strategies, which must focus on specific local conditions or 'sites'.

Nonetheless, other feminists have considered state theory important. In her influential paper, Mary McIntosh (1978) argues that the state supports a system in which men control women in the household, where they work without pay to maintain capitalism's labour force, and from which they can be drawn as needed to supply cheap labour. Referring mainly to the United Kingdom, McIntosh reviews the ways in which the state indirectly subordinates women by staying out of certain areas such as family life, which are left to the control of men, and through legislation, such as husbands' tax allowance, which privileges employed, married men. In a sense, McIntosh contends, women are hidden in the family or household to serve the needs of men and capitalism.

Jill Quadagno claims, with justification, that the explanation of the development of the welfare state has emphasized class analysis, while ignoring the welfare state's 'organization around gender' (1990: 14). Feminist theorists often claim that welfare programs maintain male dominance insofar as their rules of eligibility favour male breadwinners. Women are more often subject to means tests for social assistance programs, whereas men are more likely to qualify for universal entitlement programs. However, Quadagno notes that some social programs could advance women's interests by reducing their dependence on men. But the development of 'gender-equal policies' requires women to become mobilized as effective political actors. The latter point is effectively supported by Quadagno's analysis of the defeat of the US Family Assistance Plan in 1972. Had it been implemented, this program would have improved the economic position of both women and blacks in the southern states.

Quadagno's view is consistent with the earlier work of Varda Burstyn (1983), a Canadian feminist, who also identifies the state as acting to maintain domination both by capitalism and by men, and with subsequent studies of how state policies often discriminate against women's interests or simply fail to address them (Brodie, 1996). Burstyn explains the gender-biased actions of the state largely by the massive extent to which men occupy higher-level state positions. The most extreme bias in the state's structure is the inadequate representation of women. Most Canadian women achieved federal voting rights only in 1918—in Quebec, not until 1940. The 65 women elected between 1921 and 1984 amount to 0.8 per cent of all elected members of the House of Commons (Brodie, 1985: 2–4). Since then, the situation has improved, with women constituting 20.8 per cent of MPs in 2006 (Cool, 2006), about the same as their share based on elections held since 1997. Still, Sylvia Bashevkin's (1985) generalization that the more powerful the position, the fewer the women remains apt for both party and state. Only one woman has been Prime Minister—Kim Campbell, for several months in 1993, until her Conservative government was defeated.

Does representation matter? While there is no reason to expect women to hold views different from those of men on many issues, it is more likely that the interests of women would be effectively represented if they were present in decision-making positions. Manon Tremblay's analysis of women in Parliament in the mid-1990s (Tremblay, 1998) gives some support to this position (see also Ogmundson, 2005). Although women's issues (women's rights and traditional areas of women's involvement, such as elder care) were marginal in House activities, when discussion did take place women were more involved than men. MPs who were women gave greater importance than did men to women's issues; they were more likely to report interest in these matters and to feel that they should be given priority. Yet differences were moderate. Regardless of whether or not women would be better protected by greater political participation, their absence from positions of power is unacceptable because it seems to rest purely on the ascriptive criterion of gender.

The position of Canadian women in politics is barely intermediate when compared with other societies, as Table 15.3 demonstrates. In the Scandinavian countries and the Netherlands, women fare much better, holding over 39 per cent of electoral seats in 2008, while the United States, with 16.8 per cent, did not rank in the top 50. Rwanda (1), Cuba (3), Argentina (5) and Costa Rica (8), are developing societies that now rank in the top 10 for representation of women in their legislatures. Women also have made substantial advances since the 1980s in holding executive positions. As of December 1990, women headed just six of the United Nation's 159 member states, while in 93 countries women held no ministerial positions (United Nations, 1990: 31). Since then, it has been much more common to find a woman holding the highest office. Thus, between 1990 and 2000, 36 women were elected as heads of state (Lewis, 2002). In European Union countries, women held an average of 24.6 per cent of cabinet positions in 2001, with parity actually achieved in Sweden (FCZB, 2001).

Women are dismantling the bastions of male political dominance, but the process is slow and depends on reorienting attitudes towards gender roles. The **socialization** process must change before this form of discrimination will disappear. Although some men are sensitive to women's issues, male-controlled legislatures in Canada and elsewhere have been slow to act on many matters of importance to women. Can it be purely coincidental that women are primarily responsible for child care prior to school but that the state provides inadequate assistance for mothers who wish to be employed? As of 2006, there was still no national daycare policy; rather, a patchwork of provincial programs and federal payments of $1,200 per child (under six-years-old) to parents to spend as they wish. Yet, daycare facilities do not meet the demand (CBC News, 2006a). Furthermore, child-care workers are unable to earn the professional salaries that would justify the necessary training and commitment. In the labour market generally, part-time workers are disproportionately women and receive inferior job protection. Legislation that would end pay discrimination in the private sector based on gender has been slow to arrive and is difficult to enforce. These are only a few examples of the gender-related problems that remain to be solved in Canada and most other societies.

● Democracy ● ● ● ● ● and Politics in Canada

Party Politics

A **political party** is an organization dedicated to winning political power by controlling government. In liberal democracies, this means winning a general election. Canada is a federation with a complex structure in which the powers of legislation are divided between federal and provincial governments. The organization of parties mirrors this institutional arrangement, and securing as much electoral support as possible within this structure is the key to their success.

At the federal level, only the Liberal and Conservative parties had ever governed by 2008, and the Liberal Party had been dominant. This is evident in Figure 15.1, which shows party support since the 1953 election. Until the 1990s, these two parties competed with each other for control of the state by following a brokerage strategy in which the parties would attempt to appeal to diverse social groups in order to establish a winning combination. Usually, this meant avoiding controversial ideologi-

cal issues and adopting broadly similar positions on major issues. An exception was the 1988 election campaign in which the Progressive Conservatives championed free trade and claimed victory after a bitter struggle.

The Co-operative Commonwealth Federation (CCF) and its successor, the NDP, have taken positions similar to European labour and social democratic parties but have never succeeded in gaining sufficient support in central Canada to become credible as a governing party at the federal level. In Quebec, the CCF/NDP has failed to establish itself. With this weak performance in the most populated provinces, the CCF/NDP has been unable to exceed 20 per cent of the vote after more than 70 years of campaigning, not even in 2008 when the

Table 15.3 Women as Per Cent of Legislatures, Most Recent Election, Regions and Selected Countries, Ranked by Lower House Representation, 2008

	Lower or Combined House	Upper House
Countries		
Rwanda	48.8	34.6
Sweden	47.0	—
Cuba	43.2	—
Finland	41.5	—
Argentina	40.0	38.9
Netherlands	39.3	34.7
Denmark	38.0	—
Costa Rica	36.8	—
Spain	36.3	28.3
Norway	36.1	—
Canada	21.3	34.4
United States of America	16.8	16.0
Regions		
Nordic Countries	41.4	—
Europe - OSCE[a] members including Nordic countries	21.2	20.7
Americas	21.6	20.0
Europe - OSCE members excluding Nordic countries	19.3	18.8
Asia	18.4	16.6
Sub-Saharan Africa	17.2	20.8
Pacific	13.4	31.8
Arab States	9.7	7.0

[a] Organization for Security and Co-operation in Europe

Source: Inter-parliamentary Union: Women in National Parliaments, http://www.ipu.org/iss-e/women.htm, accessed 25 July 2008. Reprinted by permission of the publisher.

Liberal Party fell to its lowest level in the last 60 years.

In the 1990s, important new parties emerged in federal politics. The Bloc Québécois, paradoxically, has represented separatist voters in the national Parliament since 1993, but this party, like the provincial Parti Québécois, is social democratic as well as nationalist. That made it quite different from the other newcomer to federal politics, the Canadian Alliance, which began its existence as the Reform Party. The Alliance was a socially conservative, populist party that emerged from Alberta and spread eastward with decreasing success beyond Manitoba except for pockets of support in Ontario and the Maritimes. The populist dimension was reflected in the party's formal commitment to direct democracy and members' control of the organization, although this was seldom evident in practice, despite sharp attacks on the elitism of established parties. As environmental concerns emerged in the current century, the Green Party in Canada became a significant political force. Having obtained 6.8 per cent of the popular vote in the 2008 federal election, the Greens show particular strength in coastal BC and parts of Ontario, but remain without a seat in parliament. In 2008, the party's popular leader, Elizabeth May, ran second to senior Conservative Peter MacKay in his Nova Scotia riding. The Greens' may yet break through to parliament, although they must somehow overcome the perception that they are a single issue party, especially when the NDP and Liberals have taken up broadly similar environmental concerns.

The Electoral System

Canada's electoral system has several advantages. Citizens may be able to approach their local area's member of Parliament (MP), although it would be impossible for everyone actually to do so. More important, this system usually produces a majority, and thus a stable government. But it clearly makes some people's votes more influential than others, depending on where they live, and often produces a Parliament that does not reflect the wishes of the population as a whole.

Most people vote for the party rather than for the individual candidate. The electoral system, however, provides no assurance that the party receiving the most votes over the whole country will win the election. If two parties have roughly equal total support but one party has voters equally distributed and the other much more concentrated, the party with equal distribution will certainly win.

None of this makes Canada unusual. Rule by minorities occurs because more than two parties contest the elections and the system of competition in constituencies spread across the country means that popular vote does not translate directly into representation in Parliament. Indeed, in three elections (1957, 1962, and 1979), the Progressive Conservatives formed the government after having received fewer votes than the Liberals. Getting more than 40 per cent is usually enough to assure success. For example, in the election of 2000, the Liberal Party translated 40.8 per cent of the votes cast into 57.1 per cent of the seats. The elections of 2004, 2006, and 2008 led to minority governments with no party reaching 40 per cent of the popular vote.

The constituency system often leaves supporters of minority parties with little or no representation. It is especially difficult for new parties to be successful in this system because they have difficulty translating their support into seats and political visibility. Thus, a party that obtains 10 per cent of the votes may not win a single seat unless those votes are concentrated in a few ridings. This discourages participation and makes it difficult for new parties to become established and considered as viable options by the electorate as a whole. Proportional representation is designed to avoid these problems. Had such

This parody of Michelangelo's painting on the Sistine Chapel ceiling in the Vatican, of God animating Adam, shows Prime Minister Harper being brought to life by the all-powerful American deity, Uncle Sam. Monaerik/www.lecornichon.qu.ca

Figure 15.1 Popular Vote (%) by Party, Canadian Federal Elections, 1953–2008

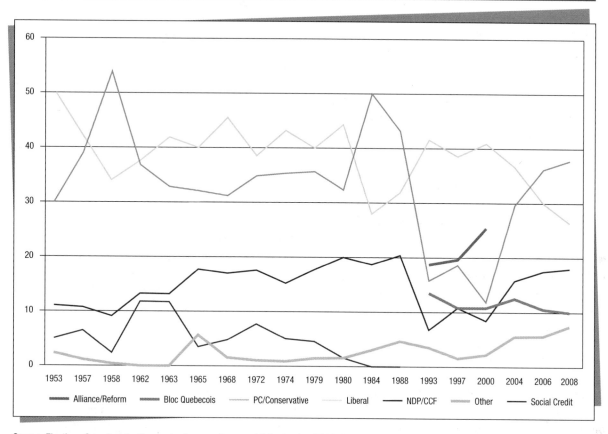

Source: Elections Canada, http://www.elections.ca. Accessed 4 September 2006; 2008 data from *CBC Canada Votes*, http://www.cbc.ca/news/canadavotes/.

a system functioned in Canada with the same voting distributions, the country would have had a minority or coalition government in 2000 and in 12 other elections from 1949 until then. Political compromises would have been necessary, but many societies achieve stable governments with election by proportional representation. Usually, a party must obtain a minimum of 5 per cent of electoral support in order to obtain any seats; this prevents excessive fragmentation of the legislature. Because the party that governs and benefits from the present system would have to support a change, it is extremely unlikely that Canadians will adopt a more representative system in the foreseeable future.

Political Participation

Participation in the political process varies from informal discussion, listening to media reports, and voting to more demanding activities such as attending meetings, assisting with campaigns, contacting politicians in order to influence them, and even running for office. For most

Canadians, political participation is limited to discussion and voting for candidates to the various levels of government. However, it appears that the public is becoming increasingly cynical about politicians; turnout at elections is falling, with federal elections now attracting about 60 per cent of eligible voters.

Sociologists are interested in the social characteristics that may influence participation. However, a great deal of research has demonstrated that there is no necessary link between a person's social background and the party he or she supports. Harold Clarke's team (1991) examined the variables of class, gender, ethnicity, religion, region, community size, and age, and found that they all have some effect on Canadians' voting preferences, but much less than political variables such as prior voting record, concern about immediate issues, and the image of the party leader. Nonetheless, in 2000 the Liberal Party could not have won without the strong support outside Quebec of Catholics (54 per cent) and Canadians of non-European ethnicity (70 per cent) (Gidengil et al., 2001: 28). Region was more critical than it had been in earlier elections, with the Alliance powerful west of Ontario (where Liberals were much weaker) but unable to break through in eastern Canada, where Conservatives and especially Liberals were stronger. Women supported the NDP much more than did men, whereas men were more drawn to the Alliance. Age and language were critical to voting in Quebec, where those under 55 and francophones were more likely to support the Bloc Québécois.

Class is not a defining force in contemporary Canadian politics, but economic issues and beliefs do influence the choices of many voters. Thus, outside Quebec, those who believed in giving increased priority to market forces were more attracted to the Alliance and Conservative parties in 2000, while those with the opposite view favoured Liberals and the NDP; social conservatives preferred the Alliance to the Progressive Conservative Party (Gidengil et al., 2001). In the election of 2004, those doubtful of the fairness of the free market were much more likely to be NDP voters, as were those with certain characteristics of lower social status—minimal education and, especially, those who rented (Gidengil et al., 2006: 9–11).

A crude theory in which voting behaviour inevitably follows from social experience is obviously untenable. A more useful sociological account, influenced by **symbolic interactionist** theory, starts from the assumption that voting is an interpretive action to which people carry assumptions from their prior experience, filtered through their social positions and possibly their previous commitments to a party. Usually they have incomplete information and an incomplete understanding of how the political system operates. Typically, the strongest parties play down social issues and try to emphasize the quality of their leaders (or record in office) to cope with whatever problems exist. To achieve overall victory, care will be taken not to appear too closely linked to the interests of any particular group. In the end, voters make choices that respond only partially to social and cultural factors. Of course, for decades in Quebec, the priority of cultural concerns and the issue of independence have made political life more ideological and socially influenced. Nonetheless, voting does not really determine state policy—it provides legitimization for those who control it.

Figure 15.2 Percentage Distribution of Votes and Seats by Party, Federal Election, 2006

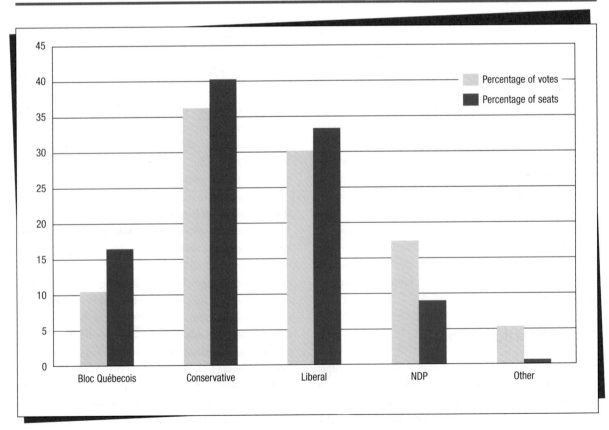

Source: Calculated from Elections Canada data.

Neo-Conservatism and Privatization

After decades of expansion of the welfare state and of standards of living, many countries faced problems of inflation, lower economic growth, and budget deficits in the 1970s and 1980s. Continued demands for better public education and health care were incompatible with pressure to reduce taxes. Many states seemed to be suffering from or on the brink of what some called a 'crisis of legitimation' (Habermas, 1975; Offe, 1984). With welfare state programs under severe stress, political space opened up for more conservative policies. These policies stressed eliminating public deficits by reducing expenditure, stimulating the economy by cutting taxes, and withdrawing the state from the economy by privatizing existing public enterprises and contracting to the private sector for services previously provided by public employees. Sometimes **privatization** sales have been legitimized as contributions to debt reduction. The promotion of 'free' market forces and a smaller state is at the core of this new conservatism, which has found favour with many voters, especially those who would benefit from tax reductions and who have the capacity to purchase services for themselves.

In Canada, this trend has been evident not only in the rise of the Canadian Alliance and now the Conservative Party, but also in practices of various provincial governments, especially Conservatives in Ontario (under Mike Harris) and Alberta (Ralph Klein) and Liberals in British Campbell (Gordon Campbell). However, all levels of government have participated to some degree. For example, the federal government sold Air Canada to the private sector, and shares of Petro-Canada can now be purchased on the stock market. Airport security was subcontracted prior to the terrorist attacks of 11 September 2001. The privatization of basic public goods, such as power and water supply, is proving to be controversial: many people are concerned that prices will rise in the long term once supply is in corporate hands. Thus, the decision to sell Ontario Hydro was reversed ...plement in ... as citizen groups mobilized in opposition.

Certainly among the most critical issues is the reform and increased privatization of health care, which was on the political agenda for some years and subject of several investigations, most recently the Romanow Commission on the Future of Health Care in Canada, which reported in 2002. As of 2003, the federal government insisted that it would use its power to maintain standards across Canada, including universal access. Nevertheless, there have been signs of creeping privatization, especially in Alberta, and considerable dispute between the federal government and the more conservative provincial administrations. Canadians worry about what is happening to their health-care system when they see so many publicized delays in accessing specialist services and when hospital emergency rooms are frequently overflowing. The 2003 SARS outbreak in Toronto again brought such concerns to the forefront as the hospital system appeared close to collapse. Several hospitals had to be diverted from their normal activities, and medical staff were required to function under dangerous and stressful conditions. Some are convinced that privatization or a two-tier system is necessary, while others prefer a reform of the existing system and the injection of the necessary funds to make it work properly. In 2008, the outcome remains unclear but two senior editors of the *Canadian Medical Association Journal* were fired in February 2006, possibly for their pro-medicare opinions, and the Association elected the operator of a private clinic as its head some months later. The federal Minister of Health, Tony Clement, is also on record as favouring private medicine (Canada Health Coalition, 2006; CBC News, 2006b).

Social Movements

Typically, a social movement depends on the actions of non-elite members of society, those people who have relatively little or no control over major economic, symbolic, political, or military resources—in short, over anything scarce that, if controlled, gives one power over others.

People form a social movement when they voluntarily work together to influence the distribution of social goods. A social good is anything that a particular society values. Familiar examples include money, honour, peace, security, citizenship, leisure time, political power, and divine grace. There are probably no universal social goods, because no two societies have exactly the same set of values. Furthermore, social goods vary historically. They emerge and disappear as values change or traditions lose relevance (Walzer, 1983).

Social goods are scarce—that, in part, is why they are valuable—and some individuals or groups get more of them than others. How people make sense of such inequalities depends on **ideologies**, sets of ideas that justify how social goods are distributed. *Dominant ideologies* defend existing inequalities by making them seem right. *Counter-ideologies* challenge the justice of the existing social system, promote alternative values and goals, and present a plan for change. Promoting counter-ideologies is a goal of social movements.

Social movements try to achieve change through the voluntary cooperation of the relatively powerless. These people may contribute financial or other material resources, recruit new members, or spread a counter-ideology. They may also participate in strikes, sit-ins, boycotts, demonstrations, protest marches, violent action, or civil disobedience. The efforts of social movements can be focused on changing attitudes, everyday practices, public opinion, or the policies and procedures of business and government.

Environmental movements, for example, have the basic impacts set forth in Figure 15.3. Social change through collective action involves dynamic and complex processes: social movements affect individuals and political policies, but they are influenced also by them. As Figure 15.3 shows, environmental problems are identified usually by natural scientists. Once a problem of this kind is identified, the environmental movement may choose to address the issue. It may lobby the government or appeal to individuals' sense of moral indignation. In some instances, an environmental organization may choose to run in democratic elections, thus forming a political party with ecological issues as its main concern.

Social movements are easier to understand when compared and contrasted with other phenomena studied by sociologists (Diani, 1992). A *social trend*, for example, is simply a changing pattern of social behaviour, whereas a social movement is a cooperative effort to achieve social change from below. The rising labour market participation of women is a social trend; a group of volunteers who fight for gender equality is a social movement. Certainly, social movements influence some social trends. For instance, feminist movements may encourage the trend for women to enter the paid workforce. However, many social trends—such as changing fashions or unemployment patterns—may be scarcely affected by social movements.

OPEN FOR DISCUSSION
Controversy over Health Care Reform

According to various polls, Canadians consider protection of the health-care system to be a priority for public action. Nevertheless, a national poll in 2001 reported that 56.6 per cent were generally satisfied with the existing system and 81.7 per cent were content with services they had received in the previous five years. The main problems that respondents perceived were poor management, inadequate financing, and staff shortages. A majority believed the Canadian system to be superior to that of the United States and were against privatization of hospitals (Leger Marketing, 2001: 2–6).

Although problems are often recognized, many Canadians resist major changes that might affect universal access, especially a reduction in the services that are currently paid from state treasuries. Canadian health care is not, for the most part, socialized because most health-care professionals work in private practice or for independent hospital boards. About 30 per cent of services are not covered by public medicare. Access to health services could be privatized by eliminating state payments so that patients would have to rely on their own resources or a private insurance plan.

The key issue here is whether or not social inequality would affect availability of health care if public services were reduced and access determined by capacity to pay the market rate for the service. Opponents clearly believe this to be the case and prefer other solutions to existing problems. In 2002, the Romanow Commission investigated alternatives prior to the federal government's announcing its plan of action. Preliminary evidence of public opinion on these options indicates that most prefer system reform with a focus on preventative medicine, but nearly half would be willing to accept more private-sector participation (Decima Research, 2002). By 2002, the most radical plan to date to alter the existing system was put forward by Ralph Klein's government in Alberta, which planned to contract out certain services from public hospitals to private clinics. By 1994–5, Alberta had already moved to allow physicians to bill the state for certain core services and to privately sell additional services to their patients. These plans have been bitterly attacked by those concerned about inequities in the emerging health-care system.

A *pressure group* is an organization that aims to influence large institutions, particularly **the state**. A social movement is one kind of pressure group. However, other pressure groups—known as *interest groups*—represent the concerns of specific sets of people. Prominent interest groups include the Canadian Labour Congress, the Canadian Medical Association, Canadian Manufacturers and Exporters (formerly the Canadian Manufacturers Association), and the Consumers' Association of Canada. Interest groups restrict their membership and rely heavily on a professional staff rather than volunteers. Moreover, lobbying politicians and receiving recognition from government can give them semi-official or even official status. Like social movements, interest groups may use public opinion to put pressure on political or economic elites. But membership in social movements is more open, and their ideologies typically appeal to people from different walks of life.

Since social movements depend on voluntary participation, they are voluntary associations. However, not all *voluntary associations* seek deeper changes in the distribution of social goods. Some provide social or health services; others organize leisure activities or unite the followers of a spiritual doctrine. Examples of voluntary associations are groups that help the homeless, run food banks, offer classes in English as a Second Language (ESL) for immigrants, or mobilize residents for annual cleanups of garbage in the public areas of their neighbourhood. Voluntary associations that only help people to accept or enjoy the existing social system are not social movements.

While social movements try to change the distribution of social goods, political parties try to win and keep political power. In principle, a social movement becomes a political party when it fields candidates in elections. The Green parties in Germany, France, and example, have grown from environmental m these countries. In practice, the differe social movements and political parties hazy. Parties that have grown out of soci often retain features from their past. The sectarian or rely heavily on grassroots su ers. These features foster a strong party identity, b y may discourage outsiders from joining.

Finally, not all groups with non-elite, volunta members who aim to reallocate social goods are necessarily social movements. A counter-movement may have all of the characteristics of a social movement, but with one important difference: a counter-movement arises in response to a social movement. Three conditions must be met for counter-movements to appear:

Figure 15.3 The Impact of Environmental Movements

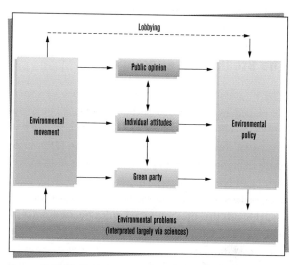

Source: Dieter Rucht, 'The Impact of Environmental Movements in Western Societies', in Marco Giugni et al., eds, *How Social Movements Matter* (Minneapolis: University of Minnesota Press, 1999), 214.

1. A social movement must be seen as successful (or as gaining success).
2. A social movement's goals must be seen as a threat to another group.
3. Allies must be available to support mobilization of the counter-movement.

While some counter-movements (such as the National Rifle Association) wish to defend the status quo against a perceived threat by social movements, others (such as the anti-abortion movement) emerge when a state or government agency has ambiguous policies or is internally divided on a particular social issue (Meyer

the **breakdown** nsus is the basis of social order a e is the major determinant of action. The **resource mobilization approach** assumes that social order is based on competition and conflict and that interests are the fundamental cause of action. The **identity-based approach** and the **political process approach** draw selectively from the other two. Both assume that social order rests on an unsteady resolution of conflict and that culture is the major determinant of action. Table 15.4 summarizes the assumptions that underlie these four perspectives.

The Breakdown Approach

The breakdown approach builds on a view of society developed by the French sociologist Émile Durkheim (1858–1917) and later by the American founder of structural functionalism, Talcott Parsons (1902–79). Both thought that shared norms and values hold society together. The breakdown approach holds that rapid, thorough, or uneven change in society weakens the social bonds that promote social order. Social disintegration, in turn, encourages the formation of groups advocating radical change.

The assumptions of the breakdown approach underlie **relative deprivation theory**, which claims that radi-

The economic image of the Argentine-born Marxist revolutionary Ernesto 'Che' Guevara has been a symbol of struggle for revolutionary movements around the globe, as in this International Labour Day rally, 1 May 2007, in Karachi, Pakistan. The Canadian Press/AP Photo/Shakil Adil

cal social movements result from feelings of fear and frustration. According to James C. Davies (1962), revolutions and rebellions are preceded by two phases. The first phase is characterized by economic and social progress. More and more social goods become available—food becomes more plentiful, for example, or the rights of citizens expand—and expectations rise. But if a sharp reversal follows—if food suddenly becomes scarce and costly, or if authorities ban opposition parties and the free press after a period of liberalization—rising expectations are no longer met. In the second phase, the gap between what people expect and what they actually get grows ever wider. Rebellion results when anxiety and frustration become widespread and intense.

Critics of relative deprivation theory point out that the most frustrated members of society are not the only people who fight for radical change. Revolutions, especially successful ones, are often led and supported by people from the middle and upper classes. Moreover, relative deprivation theory does not provide a convincing link between people's feelings and revolution. Surely the people of Haiti, for instance, have endured many decades of anxiety and frustration under brutal dictatorships. Yet their dissatisfaction has not led to revolution. A great deal must happen before individual grievances will translate into major changes such as the toppling of a political regime.

Like relative deprivation theory, Neil Smelser's **systemic theory** highlights the role of social breakdown in the growth of social movements. But instead of focusing on individuals, as relative deprivation theory does, Smelser looks at society as a whole. He sees society as a set of linked elements that work to maintain stability. Social movements reflect the breakdown of stability, but they do not form unless six conditions are met (Smelser, 1963):

1. *Structural conduciveness.* Social conditions must give people a chance to unite for change. If people remain isolated, they cannot pool their efforts.
2. *Structural strain.* The dominant ideology must be viewed with dissatisfaction or uncertainty.
3. *Growth and spread of a generalized belief.* Potential participants in social movements must share a counter-ideology that binds them together.
4. *A precipitating factor.* This is the straw that breaks the camel's back—some event so serious that people finally decide to fight for change.
5. *Mobilization.* People's readiness for action must have an outlet; they must be able to join a social movement.

SOCIOLOGY IN ACTION
Craig Kielburger and Free The Children

The child shall be protected against all forms of neglect, cruelty and exploitation. He shall not be the subject of traffic, in any form. The child shall not be admitted to employment before an appropriate minimum age; he shall in no case be caused or permitted to engage in any occupation or employment which would prejudice his health or education, or interfere with his physical, mental or moral development.

—From the UN Declaration on
the Rights of the Child

One morning when he was searching for the comics section in his local newspaper, 12-year-old Craig Kielburger of Thornhill, Ontario, came across a photo that stopped him short. Beside it was a headline that read 'Battled child labour, boy, 12, murdered' and an article about Iqbal Masik, a Pakistani boy sold to a carpet factory by his parents at the age of four. Unable to attend school, for many years he had been forced to work as many as 14 hours a day, six days a week. After the Pakistani police finally freed Iqbal, the boy wanted to fight the enslavement of child workers. He joined in demonstrations and spoke with journalists so the public would become aware of the plight of child workers. Then, when Iqbal was 12, he paid the price of speaking out: he was murdered.

This news shocked Kielburger. Even though he had never heard about child labour and did not even know where Pakistan was exactly, he decided to act. With friends and classmates in Thornhill, he formed Free The Children. Their goal was to end the abuse and exploitation of children around the world. The young members of this new group faxed world leaders and organized petitions to end child exploitation. To raise funds for their efforts, they also ran car washes, bake sales, and garage sales. In alerting the world to injustice towards children, they learned more about the conditions under which children who are often abused work long hours without having the chance to play or attend school. They also learned about and decided to fight a related injustice: child prostitution.

At the age of 14, Kielburger made a much-publicized visit to South Asia in search of sweatshops. He joined the police during a raid to free children working in a factory. Free The Children wanted Canada to start putting special labels on imported rugs not made by children. The group also wanted a new law that would make it possible for police in Canada to charge a person who had sex with a child prostitute in another country. Two years after it was founded, Free The Children used funds it had raised to set up a centre for children in Pakistan who had escaped from slavery.

Not everybody was pleased. Kielburger was criticized as too young to tell adults in positions of authority what they should be doing. And a social worker in Brazil asked: 'Why is it that North Americans always think they can save the world?' But Kielburger and Free The Children went on. The organization he started has created more than 100 centres and schools worldwide for freed children who are trying to recover after years of physical and psychological abuse.

Today, Free The Children, headed by Craig and his older brother Marc, is involved in the construction of another 420 schools that will provide education for 40,000 children in poor regions of the world. While Kielburger—who is now 24 years old—has received many awards for leadership, good citizenship, and humanitarian service, on three occasions (in 2002, 2003, and 2004) Free The Children itself has been nominated for the Nobel Peace Prize.

Sources: <peaceheroes.com>; <www.freethechildren.com>.

6. *The response of authorities.* Because the state is so powerful, its response affects a social movement's chances of survival and success.

Smelser's systemic theory improves on relative deprivation theory. It corrects the overemphasis on individuals by specifying group and societal factors involved in the rise of social movements. Moreover, systemic theory recognizes that shared grievances alone will not bind protestors together. For a movement to last, protestors must share a counter-ideology, a set of ideas that gives them guidelines to work together for change. Finally, the theory brings mobilization into the picture. Personal dissatisfaction alone will not form a social movement, no matter how widespread the grievance.

Unfortunately, Smelser's theory does not establish causes and effects, but rests partly on circular reasoning. An example of circular reasoning would be as follows: Suppose you ask someone to explain what caused hail, and the person replies, 'It's frozen rain.' Because hail and frozen rain are the same thing, your respondent's reply is not an explanation, but merely a restatement using different words. Hence, your question has been left unanswered.

Smelser does something similar, though less obviously. On the one hand, he defines social mobilization for action as a response to strain on generalized belief. But he also lists mobilization for action, strain, and generalized belief among the six factors that explain social movements. In this respect, his theory is a restatement of what needs to be explained, not an explanation (Aya, 1990).

Contrary to the assumptions of the breakdown approach, social conflict may be a normal feature of social life. If this is so, then the breakdown of value consensus and stability may not explain the formation of social movements.

Breakdown theory has also been accused of treating social movements as ailments. This charge arose during the 1960s, a time when social movements supported by mainstream members of society were flourishing in Western democracies. Many sociologists welcomed the new movements against war, racism, sexism, pollution, bureaucracy, and the educational system as positive signs of healthy protest against injustice and alienation.

Finally, critics have argued it is misleading to treat social movements as outbursts of uncontainable emotion. Experience suggests that participation in social movements may involve the same kind of calm and rational decision-making found in other areas of life. This interpretation underlies the resource mobilization approach.

The Resource Mobilization Approach

The resource mobilization approach challenges the image of social movements as unusual, impermanent, or disorderly. Instead, it assumes that social movements are quite similar to other organizations. They are managed by leaders whose decisions are no less calculating than anyone else's. Some sociologists go so far as to treat social movement organizers as entrepreneurs who have a 'product' to sell.

Unlike business entrepreneurs, however, social movement entrepreneurs must deal with free-riding—non-cooperation in the attainment of a good that will be available to all members of the community. For movement leaders, the solution is to make their 'product' appealing in the competitive market for potential members' time, energy, and resources. From this perspective, social movement propaganda is a form of marketing that advertises the benefits of joining (Jenkins, 1983).

Proponents of the resource mobilization approach argue that the breakdown approach is wrong in assuming

Table 15.4		Approaches to the Study of Social Movements	
		Primary Cause of Social Action	
		Culture	Interests
Underlying Societal Dynamic	Consensus	• breakdown approach	• undeveloped approach
	Conflict	• identity-based approach • political process approach	• resource mobilization approach

that satisfaction with the social order is the normal state of affairs. Instead, dissatisfaction is built into society. There will always be people with grievances because social goods are unequally distributed. But grievances alone do not make a social movement. What social movements do is lift grievances out of the shadows, giving them ideological form and propelling them into public life.

The resource mobilization approach puts **power** at the centre of analysis. Power is not something one has: one can only be in a position that confers power, for power means having the ability to carry out one's wishes. As the German sociologist Max Weber (1864–1920) put it, power refers to a person's or group's chance of fulfilling their goals even when others would have it otherwise (1978 [1908]: 926).

The source of power is control over resources. Control creates leverage, the ability to get others to do what one wants. What represents a resource in any given situation varies, but three kinds of power stand out. One is *economic power*, which is based on control over the means of material production: land, energy, capital, technology, labour, factories, raw materials, and so forth. Another is *political power*, based on control over the legitimate means of violence: the police and the armed forces. A third is *ideological power*, which is based on control over the means of producing and disseminating **symbols**: schools, churches, newspapers, publishing houses, television and radio, film and advertising companies, and the like. The resource base for each of the three kinds of power differs. Nonetheless, control over any resource allows elites to shape the lives of the powerless.

Social movements must compete against other **social institutions** for the scarce resources necessary to start and operate an organization. The resource mobilization approach therefore searches for the social conditions that affect social movements' control over resources, and focuses on the strategies that translate power into success.

There are two perspectives on resource mobilization: the utilitarian and political conflict perspectives (Ramirez, 1981). While both assume that actors (whether individuals or groups) are rational and seek to maximize self-interest, each addresses somewhat different problems.

The **utilitarian perspective** focuses on how individuals promote their own interests. The free-rider problem is a central concern, in particular the question of how and why selective incentives attract volunteers and cut down on free-riding. Utilitarians study the relationships between social movements and how rewards motivate social movement entrepreneurs.

Critics of the utilitarian perspective have stressed the limited applicability of the free-rider problem. The assumption that social movements attract support only by providing selective incentives may misconstrue people's reasons for joining. Instead, people may join a movement simply because it seems headed for success. Or, they may join because they identify with other members of the social movement and believe the group will benefit if its members work together (Barry, 1978 [1970]). Finally, norms of fairness may override concerns about efficiency. Pressures to conform may lead people to join social movements, irrespective of selective incentives (Elster, 1989). Such considerations are ruled out by an exclusive focus on the free-rider problem. The utilitarian perspective forgets that people are ruled by more than self-interest. Further, it forgets that social movements are groups, so they cannot be explained by individualistic decisions alone.

The **political conflict perspective** focuses on how parts of society (typically, **classes**) promote collective interests. Although not a Marxist approach, it tends to stress issues central to the Marxist tradition: working-class mobilization, class conflict, and revolution. Hence, analysis from this perspective usually tries to explain the origins of class **solidarity**. Studies in the political conflict tradition also search for factors that determine the success and failure of class-based movements, including class alliances, pre-existing social ties that foster communication and group action, and ties with other groups and political authorities.

In recent decades, sociologists who work from the political conflict perspective have reduced an earlier emphasis on class strength and class alliances. Simultaneously, they have lent more attention to the state. Because it is so powerful, the state can tip the balance in favour of one class over another. Thus, domestic and

▮▮ Time to Reflect ▮▮▮▮▮▮▮▮▮▮▮▮▮▮▮▮▮▮▮▮

Do you believe the breakdown approach adequately explains the development of social movements? Are Durkheim's and Parsons's approaches more or less convincing than Smelser's?

international events that affect the state may decide the fate of a revolution.

Culture in Social Movements

The analysis of culture in social movement scholarship came about with the so-called 'cultural turn' in the social sciences in the 1980s. Though social movement scholars did not eschew culture before this, it was often left implicit in their analysis. As we discussed above, resource mobilization theory focuses almost entirely on rational action, and largely ignores culture. Cultural approaches to the study of social movements criticize this view for forgetting that neither the goals of social movements nor the ways they calculate the best means of achieving them is self-evident. Since norms and values are created in and by social movements, proponents of the cultural approach believe that the formation of goals needs to be explained (Nedelmann, 1991). The resource mobilization approach also takes for granted the sense of community that creates collective identity and a willingness to work together. How people define themselves depends very much on whom they identify with—on what community, with its unique norms, values, and ways of feeling. Effective social movements redefine identities by changing or reinforcing people's sense of community, and by providing them with opportunities to work together with a shared sense of purpose.

The New Social Movements

European *new social movement* (NSM) theorists (e.g., Melucci, 1989; Touraine, 1981) propose that structural changes in Western societies have fundamentally altered people's identities and cultures. This gives rise, they argue, to social movements that are distinct from older class-based movements. Where resource mobilization theory explains *how* social movements operate, NSM theories explain *why* social movements occur, *why* they are organized differently from the past, and *why* their grievances appear different from movements earlier in the century. Instead of concerning themselves with the politics of redistribution, NSMs are interested in the politics of cultural recognition; they are concerned less with the redistribution of wealth and status than with securing rights to expressive freedoms, symbolic practices, and/or styles of life. In this sense, the appearance of NSMS may be explained by a value shift (Inglehart, 1990b).

The NSM perspective focuses largely on the relationship between culture and collective identity. It proposes that social movements are cultural laboratories where people try out new forms of **social interaction** (Melucci, 1989). The breakdown and resource mobiliza-

tion approaches define the success of social movements in terms of change in economic or political institutions. The NSM approach defines success differently. To be sure, it does not deny the desirability of change in dominant institutions. However, for NSM activists more important struggles take place in civil society, those areas of social interaction that stand largely outside of the state and the market. In fact, theorists claim that NSMs have come about since the 1960s because state and economic practices have increasingly encroached on people's everyday lives. Slogans such as 'the personal is political' are meant to express how everyday life is pervaded by government and corporate activities, as well as by dominant cultural ideas that create inequality.

According to this approach, civil society offers greater chances for freedom, equality, and *participatory democracy*, a system of decision-making in which all members of a group exercise control over group decisions. Indeed, NSMs are, in part, characterized by institutional arrangements wherein their members try to organize according to the ideals of equal participation. This is what social movements are good at, and striving for other kinds of success risks perverting these ideals (Cohen, 1985).

Framing Theory

At the same time European NSM scholars were criticizing resource mobilization theory, so were some North American researchers, albeit in a different way. Rather than assume that collective action was entirely rational, these scholars were interested in how collective understandings were created, communicated, and used to further a movement's goals. Because they sought to understand the role of cultural meaning in collective action, they looked to the symbolic interactionist tradition for inspiration. The result was **framing theory**, a cultural approach that explains the ways movements create and proselytize their understandings of the world, and how these meanings help form a sense of collective identity and common purpose.

Drawing on Erving Goffman's ideas, these social movement theorists define collective action frames as 'action-oriented sets of beliefs and meanings that inspire and legitimate the activities and campaigns of a social movement organization' (Benford and Snow, 2000: 614). Collective action frames are the communal understandings of a social movement, and these understandings are used to identify and promote grievances.

The process whereby individuals come to adopt the ideology and methods of a particular movement organization is called *frame alignment* (Snow et al., 1986). The alignment of interpretations is a necessary condition for maintaining participation. This is because members can identify with an organization once their cultural understandings are the same as everyone else's in the movement. In other words, collective identity is a product of frame alignment. And, as Gamson suggests, 'any movement that seeks to sustain commitment over a period of time must make the construction of collective identity one of its most central tasks' (Gamson, 1991: 27).

According to framing theory, a social movement must succeed at three core framing tasks in order to mobilize support. First, an organization must articulate *diagnostic* frames that define social problems (or injustices) and their culpable agents. Second, *prognostic* frames must propose solutions to these social problems. Prognostic frames give meaning to specific strategies and are used to persuade potential recruits and members that these actions are the best way to solve or address particular social problems. Third, since agreement with diagnostic and prognostic frames does not necessarily translate into participation, a social movement organization must provide compelling *motivational* frames that convince people to join.

Frame theorists recognize that collective action frames are not simply imposed on members by leaders, but are often changed and agreed on through social interaction and discussion. Though disputes over how to frame something inevitably arises, a minimum level of agreement must be maintained in order for a movement to be viable. There would be little reason to participate in a social movement that could not agree on how to collectively define a social problem or issue.

● The Political ● ● ● ● ● ● Process Approach

While the breakdown, resource mobilization, and cultural approaches have been very useful for understanding social movements, scholars have attempted to create a synthesis. The political process approach is generally attributed to Peter Eisinger's study of movements during the 1960s. Eisinger (1973) argued that collective action depends on the structure of local political opportunities at the institutional and governmental levels. Charles Tilly (1978), an early proponent of this approach, built on this idea by showing how nation-states can manipulate the political terrain to stymie the activities of social movements. Tilly argues that the rise of nation-states gave rise to the national social movements of the early modern era in Europe. New political ideas that helped to create nation-states also generated grievances that led people to act collectively. These national social move-

ments had characteristics that set them apart from previous forms of collective action (see also Tarrow, 1998).

The political process approach assumes that the polity can be characterized by its opportunities and constraints. Opportunities involve almost anything that provides reasons and resources for people to mobilize—so long as the political climate is not so oppressive that people cannot mobilize without fear or great difficulty. Political opportunities may include economic crises, laws ensuring the right to assemble, a history of previous collective action, even accidents that show the need for social change. Constraints include anything within the polity that may act as a barrier to the mobilization and survival of a social movement. Political constraints include a repressive police state, inexperience with collective action, even a lack of communication among social movement participants. Opportunities and constraints go hand in hand: no polity is completely open or completely closed.

The breakdown approach assumes that some form of social or political crisis is needed for people to act collectively. By contrast, the political process approach proposes that collective action is an ongoing social phenomenon. Where the breakdown approach assumes that social movements arise from outside the polity but enter the political terrain when there are reasons to do so, the political process approach believes that social movements have a historical position within the polity and that the frequency of social movement activity changes according to opportunities and constraints (Tilly, 1978).

Fluctuations in the opportunities and constraints that influence the incidence of collective action create a cycle of contention (Tilly, 1978). A rise in the cycle means that social movements have created or met new opportunities and have made room for the rise of other movements. For instance, the rise and decline of collective action by Canadian Aboriginal bands from 1981 to 2000 can be seen in Figure 15.4 (Wilkes, 2001). Protest events among Native groups in Canada rose dramatically between 1989 and 1991, peaking in the 'Indian summer' of 1990. This increase can be attributed to the 78-day armed uprising at Kanesatake (Oka, Quebec) over municipal plans to convert a Mohawk burial ground into a golf course. In support of the Kahnawake, Akwesasne, and Kanesatake, bands across Canada increased their protest activities.

Like the resource mobilization approach, the political process model focuses on institutions. Specifically, this approach looks at mobilizing structures, which include levels of informal and formal organization (McCarthy, 1996). An example of informal organization is a friendship network. When the cycle of contention is at its lowest point—when there are relatively few (or no) active social movement organizations—the network of

Figure 15.4   Number of Protests by First Nations, 1981–2000, Canada

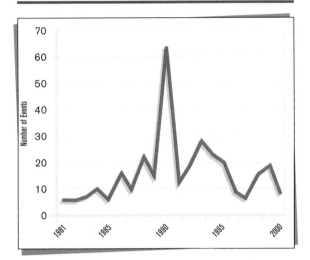

Source: Rima Wilkes, 'Competition or Colonialism? An Analysis of Two Theories of Ethnic Collective Action', PhD thesis (University of Toronto, 2001). Reprinted by permission of the author.

friendships among demobilized movement participants keeps the spirit of collective action alive. These latent networks explain why social movements arise when political opportunities appear and when constraints are eased (Melucci, 1989). Although informal communication alone cannot give rise to a social movement, it can become an important resource for mobilization.

The analysis of formal organization looks at the inner dynamics of social movements. These generally include leadership structures, flows of communication, the entry and exit of members, and the means of identifying, obtaining, and using resources. By studying mobilizing structures, sociologists can understand the institutional processes whereby movements rise, persist, and decline.

The study of social movement organizations also includes inter-organization dynamics, such as movement coalitions. A coalition results when two or more social movement organizations share resources, such as information, in the course of pursuing a common good. Coalitions can be temporary or enduring, and they can bridge different types of movements. Environmental, feminist, gay and lesbian, labour, peace, and anti-poverty organizations in British Columbia, for example, have formed coalitions based on shared understandings of social injustice (Carroll and Ratner, 1996).

Incorporating the insights of framing theory, the political process approach assumes that social movements develop their own cultural understandings of the world. These understandings form the basis for identifying and acting on social grievances, and provide movement partic-

ipants with the resources needed to create activist identities. In this view, collective action frames can be used to identify appropriate forms of protest. For example, Table 15.5 shows the frequency of types of protest among Native bands in Canada between 1981 and 2000. Clearly, road blockades were the most common protest strategy during this period. This may be due to framing processes: the popularity of roadblocks as a tactic may arise from the cultural significance of this form of protest. As more Native groups block roadways to express their grievances, this form of protest becomes more strongly associated with their social movement. Other Native bands then become more likely to adopt the same tactic.

Social movements may also use collective action frames as strategic resources. To mobilize general support for their cause, movements promote their own ideologies in the wider culture. If a social movement's framing of injustice and its solution are accepted in society, then it has created its own political opportunities. If a movement is unsuccessful, however, it risks adding to its own difficulties.

● The Analysis ● ● ● ● ● ● of Social Movements

At one time, sociologists argued that successful movements promote their supporters' interests. Nowadays such explanations are rejected, for they fail to recognize that interests are themselves cultural constructs. Moreover, a movement's supporters often have only a schematic or confused understanding of its ideology. But the compelling question remains: Why do some movements succeed, while others fail?

Unity and Diversity in the Canadian Women's Movement

Social movements need both diversity and unity. In the history of the Canadian women's movement, diversity of membership and experience has helped the movement adapt to a range of situations. Diversity has also encouraged recognition of the many faces of gender inequality. By maintaining a stock of alternative views and ideas, ideological diversity readies the movement for social change. Unity, in turn, gives the movement strength. A one-woman strike, boycott, or sit-in scarcely represents a threat to dominant institutions. But women who are individually powerless gain leverage by acting together. Unified, they can disrupt patriarchal institutions and pressure authorities into finding new solutions.

Table 15.5   Frequency of Types of Protest among Native Bands in Canada, 1981–2000

	Number	Percentage
Road blockade	114	36.08
March/demonstration	86	27.22
Train and boat blockade	19	6.01
Boycott	18	5.70
Occupation of land	17	5.38
Illegal fishing/logging	17	5.38
Occupation of building	11	3.45
Hunger strike	5	1.58
Toll booth	5	1.58
Non-strategic violence	4	1.26
Withdrawal from school	3	0.95
English signs changed	2	0.63
Illegal gambling	2	0.63
Invitation of foreign ambassadors	2	0.63
Eviction of police and non-Natives	2	0.63
Dam diversion	2	0.63
Destruction of property	2	0.63
Other	5	1.58
Total	**316**	**100.00**

Source: Rima Wilkes, 'Competition or Colonialism? An Analysis of Two Theories of Ethnic Collective Action', PhD thesis (University of Toronto, 2001). Reprinted by permission of the author.

Though diversity and unity are both beneficial, they pull social movements in opposite directions. Diversity tends to impede unity and may lead to factionalism. Unity tends to suppress diversity and may stifle flexibility and innovation. As in any complex social arrangement, there can be no either/or choice for social movements: survival and efficacy dictate a balance between diversity and unity. The story of the first and second waves of the Canadian women's movement illustrates this dilemma.

The first wave of **feminism** in Canada began in the late nineteenth century and effectively ended in 1918 when women gained the right to vote in federal elections. During this period, women formed organizations for the protection and education of young single women, such as the Anglican Girls Friendly Society and the Young Women's Christian Association (YWCA). Women's groups also protested against child labour and poor working conditions and pressed for health and welfare reforms.

Feminists of the first wave differed in their religious, class, and ethnic backgrounds. While many were Protes-tant, others were not. Anglo-Saxon women from the middle and upper classes predominated, especially among the leadership, and language divided anglophone and francophone feminists. Moreover, women's organizations had diverse goals. But the battle for women's voting rights unified the movement. One of the earliest women's groups in Canada, the Toronto Women's Literary Club (soon renamed the Women's Suffrage Association), was founded in 1876. By 1916, women had won the right to vote in provincial elections in Alberta, Saskatchewan, and Manitoba. Other provinces soon followed, and Canadian women finally received the federal franchise in 1918.

As with many other social movements, success led to decline. The fight for voting rights had given the women's movement a common goal. When this goal was attained, the movement lost unity and momentum. Certainly, women did not stop pushing for change after winning the right to vote. Some worked within the labour movement; others continued to fight for social reform or female political representation. Yet, after

1918, the Canadian women's movement became fragmented, and four decades would pass before it regained strength (Wilson, 1991).

The second wave of the movement rose out of the peace, student, and civil rights movements of the 1960s. In some cases, organizations advanced the women's cause by branching out. For example, a Toronto organization called the Voice of Women (VOW) was founded in 1960 as a peace group. But the VOW gradually adopted other women's issues, and by 1964 it was promoting the legalization of birth control.

The social movements of the 1960s spurred women in other ways. Women in the student movement came to realize that many male activists were sexist. This drove home the extent of gender inequality and the need to organize apart from men. Through the New Left movement, women discovered that socialism helped make sense of gender inequality. More generally, the cultural upheaval of the 1960s encouraged women to question their position in private and public life.

As a distinct women's movement emerged in the late 1960s and early 1970s, so did internal diversity. Some members were revolutionary Marxists, while others were socialists, liberals, or radical feminists. At times, those who favoured grassroots activism criticized those who worked through high-profile official committees such as the Canadian Advisory Council on the Status of Women. The specific concerns of lesbian, non-white, immigrant, or Native women often were ignored or marginalized by mainstream women's groups. Finally, issues of language and separatism split women's organizations in Quebec from those in the rest of Canada.

Still, the movement found bases for unity. In 1970, a cross-Canada caravan for the repeal of the abortion law attracted much publicity. The caravan collected thousands of petition signatures, showing women what could be achieved through collective action. Other coalitions formed around the issues of daycare, violence against women, labour, and poverty. Women's groups also worked together on International Women's Day celebrations.

To better represent their interests, in 1972 Canadian women formed the National Action Committee on the Status of Women (NAC). The NAC grew and by the late 1980s had become an umbrella organization for over 575 women's groups. At the same time, however, debate over the use of assisted reproductive technologies was growing, too. These technologies include cloning, surrogacy, assisted insemination, *in vitro* fertilization, embryo research, and prenatal diagnosis techniques. During a first round of consultations about these technologies with the federal government (1989–1993), the NAC adopted a position that dissatisfied many of its members. Leaders of the women's organization argued that reproductive technologies were being developed not to meet the needs of ordinary women, but to further the interests of the scientific community and the biotechnology industry. These technologies, claimed the NAC, 'represent the values and priorities of an economically stratified, male-dominated, technocratic science' (NAC, 1990, quoted in Montpetit et al., 2004: 145). Many within the NAC disagreed with this position, which was seen as too simple and out of touch with concerns at the grassroots. Those offended included lesbians and infertile women who wished to bear children.

Between 1993 and 1997, therefore, the NAC adopted a more open approach in reviewing the question. Discussions within the women's organization allowed ample room for the expression of diverse views. Rejecting its earlier stance against science, as a result of this more open process the NAC now argued that assisted reproductive technologies are acceptable when they reduce inequalities between women. This stance resulted from a compromise between different perspectives within the NAC. But policy-makers in Ottawa were puzzled because the translation of this stance into actual public policy was not obvious. Losing influence as a result, thereafter the NAC was pushed to the margins relative to other pressure groups involved in making Canadian policy on assisted reproductive technologies, such as the Canadian Bar Association and the Canadian Medical Association (Montpetit et al., 2004; Scala et al., 2005).

During both its first and second waves, then, the Canadian women's movement has organized around many issues. The diversity of its concerns and perspectives not only reflects the many faces of gender inequality, but also promotes a diffusion of the movement's ideas and its survival in the face of changing social conditions. However, serious internal arguments may exhaust activists. Although factions permit the coexistence of different constituencies, they draw attention and energy away from common interests that unite diverse organizations. When the time for action comes, a movement may lose effectiveness if its factions do not set aside their differences. As with all social movements, the success of the women's movement depends on balancing the trade-offs between diversity and unity (Briskin, 1992).

The Roots of Agrarian Protest in Canada

A study by Canadian sociologist Robert J. Brym (1980) shows why regional differences between farming economies have affected agrarian social movements in Canada. The ideology and popularity of these movements and their links with other social groups all depend on the type of farming found in each region. Brym's study examines regional differences in agrarian protest by comparing farming economies in Alberta, Saskatchewan, and New Brunswick during the Depression years.

During the 1930s, agrarian protest grew rapidly in the Prairie provinces, but not in New Brunswick. Much of this difference can be explained by the degree to which farmers' livelihoods were affected by the market. In the West, farmers concentrated on producing beef or wheat, both for the rest of Canada and for export. Hence, western ranchers and wheat farmers faced similar economic pressures. Eastern Canada set the tariffs on manufactured goods, the rates for railroad freight and bank credit, even the prices of beef and wheat. United by common economic interests, western farmers responded by creating marketing, consumer, and other voluntary associations that stressed co-operation.

In New Brunswick, by contrast, farmers practised mixed agriculture. Their primary productive goal was meeting their economic needs without selling what they produced or buying what they needed—strictly speaking, they were peasants rather than farmers. Since changes in market prices hardly affected them, they had little reason to defend themselves by forming co-operatives. Historical and geographical factors also mattered. While the dominance of shipping and timber interests had hampered the commercialization of agriculture in New Brunswick, the province's poor soil and rugged terrain confined farming to river valleys and the coastline. Finally, New Brunswick farmers not only were more isolated than those in the West, they also had much smaller debts. Farmers in New Brunswick, therefore, were much less likely to form associations. In 1939, for instance, membership in farmers' co-operatives per 1,000 rural residents over 14 years of age was 32 in New Brunswick, compared with 326 in Alberta and 789 in Saskatchewan (Brym, 1980: 346).

Thus, the greater radicalism of western farmers stemmed from high solidarity and a loss of control over their means of production. But the two western provinces diverged in their approach to agrarian protest. Alberta's Social Credit Party was right-wing, while Saskatchewan's CCF (Co-operative Commonwealth Federation, the predecessor of today's New Democratic Party) was left-wing. What accounts for this divergence?

In Alberta, a leftist agrarian party known as the United Farmers of Alberta excluded small-town merchants and others seen as exploiters of farmers. During the difficult Depression years of the 1930s, however, co-operation between farmers and merchants increased when they saw that their economic fortunes were connected—

if farmers did badly, so would local businesses, and vice versa. With the support of right-wing merchants, teachers, professionals, and preachers, the new Social Credit Party spread from Calgary to the small towns of southwestern Alberta. Eventually, Social Credit reached farmers and won their support, too, but the party never lost the right-wing ideology of its urban roots.

In Saskatchewan, on the other hand, the CCF maintained strong ties between farmers and the left-wing urban working class. Of the CCF leadership, 53 per cent were farmers and 17 per cent workers, while of the Social Credit Party 24 per cent were farmers and none were workers (Brym, 1980: 350). Thus, the differing class backgrounds of the farmers' allies helps to explain differences in the ideologies of agrarian movements in Saskatchewan and Alberta.

Brym's study suggests that economic factors affect the formation of social movements, as well as affecting which ideological direction they take. Agricultural producers such as prairie farmers are more likely to protest if there is a downturn in the capitalist economy because their livelihood, unlike that of producers in New Brunswick, depends on the market. Furthermore, the organization of a protest movement is hampered when potential supporters lack pre-existing social ties or work in isolation from other potential supporters. Finally, the alliances of a social movement affect both its ideology and its chances of success.

● Is the Future of ● ● ● ●
Social Movements Global?

The world is going through an accelerated phase of globalization. While this is hardly new, some sociologists claim the level of global interdependence and the scale of global interaction are becoming more complex too. Capital and commodities, information and ideas, people and their cultures are criss-crossing the globe, and these interactions are changing the world's societies.

Many social movements recognize that globalization is changing the political terrain. New opportunities and constraints are appearing that force social movements to adapt their strategies, resources, and ideologies. Recall Charles Tilly's research (1978) on the development of the nation-state in Europe: the rise of new forms of social protest was a product of the rise of nations. Will globalization also give rise to new, global forms of protest?

Some environmental organizations, such as Greenpeace International, Amnesty International, and the Sea

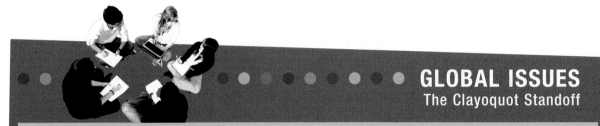

GLOBAL ISSUES
The Clayoquot Standoff

The tourist board markets British Columbia as 'Super, Natural', a Pacific Eden full of lush rainforests and forgotten inlets harbouring killer whales and inexhaustible salmon runs. That wild, virginal image began fading in Clayoquot Sound, on the west coast of Vancouver Island, as loggers and environmentalists battled over the giant cedars and Sitka spruce that have stood on the West Coast since before the time of Columbus.

In the summer of 1993, more than 800 protesters were charged by police after trying to block loggers' attempts to start felling the old-growth stands of Clayoquot Sound. The loggers had the legal right to do so, since the provincial government has decided that 62 per cent of the 270,000 hectare area should be opened up for a timber harvest by forestry giant MacMillan Bloedel Ltd. The rest was to be preserved. The protesters, ranging from teenagers with nose-rings to pensioners in cable-knit sweaters, were carted off in one of the biggest mass arrests in Canadian history. In the courts, some received unexpectedly harsh sentences: up to 60 days in jail and fines as high as $3,000.

But the battle was far from over. Though the environmentalists found themselves on the wrong side of the law, they testified in court that they had the moral high ground. Some used a character in one of Dr Seuss's children's books to illustrate what they viewed as a spiritual quest to save the forests from greedy timber conglomerates: 'I am the Lorax, I speak for the trees.' They settled in outside the Vancouver headquarters of MacMillan Bloedel, where they were to be found most lunch hours, toting billboards in a legal picket. One group planned to take a stump from Clayoquot Sound on a European protest tour in the spring of 1994.

The message of the environmental groups was simple: Forestry companies have been criminally negligent in their stewardship of British Columbia's forestry resource, turning the province into the 'Brazil of the North'. As a result, they do not deserve to be trusted with the logging of Clayoquot Sound, the largest coastal temperate lowland rainforest left in the world. Those in Ireland and Scotland were cut down long ago.

MacMillan Bloedel's response was that the environmentalists simply want to stop logging. Period. Dennis Fitzgerald, a company spokesman, commented, 'I've yet to see them approve of a logging plan anywhere.' To fight back, the forestry industry began doing its own politicking and myth-building. To prove that MacMillan Bloedel is sensitive to the environment, Fitzgerald pointed out that clearcuts no longer stretch over 80 to 100 hectares of forest land, creating eyesores that leave tourists gasping. In the previous five years, the forestry industry reduced clearcuts to between 30 and 40 hectares. MacMillan Bloedel has also stated that it can log in Clayoquot Sound forever, since it will cut at a rate that will give seedlings 80 to 100 years to grow before the chainsaws return.

Ironically, both sides said they want the same thing: sustainable development, the buzzword of the decade. That is easy to overlook, however, given the din of loggers' chainsaws and the TV-savvy theatrics of the environmentalists blocking logging roads.

Source: Adapted from Miro Cernetig, 'The Clayoquot Standoff', *Report on Business* (Jan. 1994), 31–2. Reprinted with permission from The Globe and Mail.

Shepherd Society, as well as a variety of anti-globalization movements, claim to operate in a global polity. These organizations take the globe as their site of struggle while simultaneously operating in specific locations. In other words, these organizations claim to 'think globally but act locally'. Their strategy is clear: concerted efforts in locations throughout the world will alter the negative social and environmental effects of globalization.

The link between globalization and social movements has not gone unnoticed by sociologists. German sociologist Ulrich Beck (1996) claims that globalization creates opportunities for new forms of collective action that operate outside the politics of the nation-state, in the politics of what Beck calls a 'world risk society'. Beck suggests that ordinary people in all societies have been socialized to understand that the modern world is full of human-created hazards. Widely publicized dangers, such as the radioactive cloud that drifted from a nuclear reactor in Chernobyl in Ukraine (at that time part of the Soviet Union) to the rest of Europe in 1986, have forced people to acknowledge that many political issues transcend borders. For Beck, the emerging recognition of global risks marks a new reality for social movements.

Greenpeace International is a good example of a global, or *transnational*, social movement that appears to have adapted to this world risk society. Greenpeace originated in the late 1960s, and its earliest members were environmental activists from Canada and the United States. From the start, this environmental movement was concerned with global issues and it organized protests throughout the world.

Greenpeace has developed its own political opportunities by creating unique forms of global diplomacy (Beck, 1996). It often operates outside the boundaries of the nation-state, such as on the high seas, where individual nations have no legal jurisdiction (Magnusson, 1990). Conscious of the influence of the international media, Greenpeace rallies support by organizing global boycotts that challenge governments and corporations to change their environmental policies and practices. Through these media events, Greenpeace attempts to stir up moral indignation while recognizing that different cultures have various understandings and experiences of global environmental dangers (Eyerman and Jamison, 1989).

Not all sociologists agree that globalization has created a fundamentally new political reality. Leslie Sklair (1994) argues that global politics are very much like national politics, simply on a larger scale. For Sklair, organizations such as Greenpeace International mirror the organizational structures of trans-national corporations. He suggests that the global environmental movement consists of transnational environmental organizations whose professional members make up a global environmental elite. This elite plays an ideological game with the transnational corporate and governmental elite: each side attempts to have its version of the environmental reality accepted as the truth. For Sklair, this is politics as usual.

Sociologists also question whether the rise of supranational organizations, such as the European Union (EU), will bring about new forms of collective action that link activists across national boundaries. Although the EU does constitute a new political terrain, Doug Imig and Sidney Tarrow (2001) have found that collective action in Europe remains strongly rooted within the nation-state. While Europeans have many grievances against the EU, most protest against it is domestic rather than transnational. This may simply indicate that activists have yet to develop new transnational strategies and linkages. Nevertheless, domestic politics remain a viable political arena for voicing concerns about the EU (Imig and Tarrow, 2001).

Today the world is more intricately connected than in the past. A variety of new social issues have arisen as a result, and there are now social movements that attack globalization. Each has to identify guilty institutions and actors, however, and states and corporations remain the best choice because they are largely responsible for the policies and practices that promote globalization.

Generally, two characteristics are needed for a social movement to be truly global. First, a social movement must frame its grievances as global grievances. Many environmental organizations do this. By framing environmental risks as global risks, the environmental movement hopes to demonstrate that environmental degradation affects everyone. Second, to be global a social movement needs to have a worldwide membership and organizational structure. On a global scale, membership and frame alignment probably are supported by communication technologies such as e-mail and the Internet. Alternatively, a global movement can arise through a long-term coalition or network of movement organizations. For example, indigenous peoples across North and South America, Australia, and New Zealand have united against the ongoing effects of colonialism and to ensure that the rights of indigenous populations are recognized.

● Conclusion ● ● ● ● ● ●

Politics in Canada and around the globe is changing quickly as people grapple with major technological, environmental, and social forces impinging on their lives. While long-term effects of such developments as genetic engineering are debated, the critical political questions are: Who is in control? and What will be permitted?

In the early twenty-first century, some forces imply that decentralization and fragmentation are the likely course of societies in the years to come. After all, cultural groups struggle for political autonomy (like Quebec) and others advocate a smaller role for the state in many ways, from privatization to more partnerships with non-state actors. Probably these forces are weaker than the integrating, regionalizing, and even globalizing tendencies associated with high-speed communication, cultural diffusion of tastes and values, an international division of labour, corporate concentration, world-level environmental problems, North–South inequality, and new or more powerful transnational organizations.

Does this globalization mean the eclipse of the state (Strange, 1996)? Probably not within the next 20 years. So far, despite the tendencies mentioned, there is little sign that any global decisions, whether taken in political institutions, such as the United Nations, or by other assemblies, such as inclusive meetings on AIDS or climate change, can be effective if the most powerful states are unwilling to support them.

We live in difficult and dangerous times in which no country is truly isolated from external economic, cultural, and political forces. To that extent, life is internationalized, if not fully globalized. Violent conflicts spill over national borders. Maintaining the civil rights of all people is one of the greatest political challenges that societies face in the early twenty-first century.

Much of this work will be done by social movements. Sociologists seek to explain how and why social movements form, continue, and dissolve. Comparative studies of movements can help to determine whether or not any common features point to a general explanation or whether existing explanations hold for different situations. And historical studies reveal how social movements change over time.

Early forms of collective action were poorly organized and relatively sporadic. Often their grievances were tied to local affairs, and thus their targets were usually local elites. With the rise of nation-states, however, new kinds of social movements appeared. These movements were highly organized and often identified social issues that stemmed from structural conditions such as economic inequality and narrow political representation. They also routinized protest activities: different social movements learned to apply similar methods of protest, such as the mass demonstration. The rise of new social movements in the second half of the twentieth century marks another change. These movements are more concerned with gaining cultural recognition than with the redistribution of social goods. So even though NSMs tend to use traditional forms of protest, they are more concerned with the politics of everyday life than with the traditional politics of governance.

While issues and methods of protest have changed over time, the success of collective action is always linked to the social and political climate. In other words, social and political changes can create opportunities for social movements, or they can create constraints. According to a theory developed by Herbert Kitschelt (1993), present conditions in Canada have created opportunities that may lead to an increase in social movement activity. To understand why, short- and long-term social movement dynamics must be distinguished. Support for social movements usually rises when political parties and interest groups fail to channel citizens' demands. Social movements can then mobilize support, attract resources, and forge alliances among protest groups. However, according to Kitschelt, this surge in social movement activity peaks as resources dwindle, as political parties begin to take up citizens' concerns, and as people's interest in collective mobilization wanes. Social movement activity then falls, only to rise again the next time organizers capitalize on frustration with parties and interest groups. In other words, the short-term pattern of movement activity is cyclical.

The long-term trend, by contrast, is towards an increase in the number of social movements. In the wealthy capitalist democracies, social movement activity has grown steadily since the 1960s. Established parties and politicians have proven increasingly incapable of providing satisfactory solutions to such issues as nuclear power, toxic waste disposal, resource management, abortion rights, pornography, and equal rights. Today, many Canadians share a distrust of established politicians, political parties, and interest groups. The extent of citizen discontent should not be exaggerated, however. Recent federal elections have shown that an established party like the Liberals can still attract much support. Nevertheless, many burning public issues—citizen participation, the environment, and gender, ethnic, and Native rights—often elude both parties and interest groups. The current climate in Canada favours an expansion of social movement activity. Of course, if organizers will actually exploit this situation remains to be seen. The outcome will depend on social movement leaders and on the political establishment's ability to co-opt them.

Questions for Critical Thought

1. What changes have occurred since 1980 in women's participation in the legislatures and cabinets of liberal democracies? Discuss some of the differences you observe. How would you explain these findings?

2. Select a key issue in the province or municipality where you live. Using media sources, try to determine who was able to exercise power. What theory of the state best explains what you observed?

3. Find an ideological statement from a social movement, such as a leaflet, a website, or an interview with a movement representative. What are the movement's ideals? What social goods does it value, disparage, or neglect? How does the statement use emotional appeals to make its message more persuasive? What kinds of people are most and least likely to be persuaded by this statement?

4. All sociological theories make **ontological** assumptions. In other words, theorizing about the social world requires particular assumptions about how it operates. How can empirical research on social movements be used to refute or confirm the ontological assumptions of social movement theories?

Recommended Readings

Douglas E. Baer, ed., *Political Sociology: Canadian Perspectives* (Toronto: Oxford University Press, 2002).
Baer has compiled a valuable collection on topics of both Canadian and international interest.

Louise Chappell and Lisa Hill, eds, *The Politics of Women's Interests: New Comparative Perspectives* (London and New York: Routledge, 2006).
This book provides feminist interpretations of political issues by drawing on experiences in many societies.

Donatella della Porta, et al., *Globalization from Below: Transnational Activists and Protest Networks* (Minneapolis: University of Minnesota Press, 2006).
Challenging the idea that global social movements are merely coalitions of local movements, the authors argue that the global movement against neo-liberalism is a form of collective action that represents important changes in tactics, collective identities, and patterns of organization.

Murray Knuttila and Wendee Kubik, *State Theories: Classical, Global and Feminist Perspectives*, 3rd edn (Halifax: Fernwood, 2000).
A thorough review of theorizing about the state.

Eric R. Wolf, *Peasant Wars of the Twentieth Century* (New York: Harper & Row, 1969).
Peasant rebellion and revolt in Mexico, Russia, China, Vietnam, Algeria, and Cuba are explained in terms of the penetration of capitalism.

Recommended Websites

Assembly of First Nations www.afn.ca
This comprehensive site contains detailed information about social issues pertaining to Canada's First Nations.

Canadian Lesbian & Gay Archives (CLGA) www.clga.ca/archives/
This site provides information that relates to lesbian, gay, bisexual, and transgender movements. Its focus is mostly Canadian, but the archive also provides plenty of information from around the world.

Canada's Parliament www.parl.gc.ca
This government website provides information on the conduct of parliamentary life and on members of the two houses of Parliament.

Canadian Election Study (CES) www.ces-eec.umontreal.ca/surveys.html
The results of investigations into federal elections from 1997 to 2006 may be obtained at this site, from which various academic presentations may be downloaded.

Canadian Race Relations Foundation www.crr.ca
The Canadian Race Relations Foundation's primary goal is to end race- and ethnic-based discrimination in Canada.

Centre for Social Justice www.socialjustice.org
This organization was established in 1997 and is based in Toronto. Its goals are to foster national and international social change through research and advocacy.

Greenpeace Canada www.greenpeace.ca
This site provides information about Greenpeace's past and current campaigns. Peruse the site and try to establish how this organization frames environmental issues.

United Nations www.un.org
The UN provides a vast range of information about its activities, as well as databases and bibliographies.

Women in National Parliaments www.ipu.org/wmn-e/world.htm
The Inter-parliamentary Union's website contains extensive, regularly updated information on women's political participation.

Chapter

●●●●●●●●

Population, Urbanization, and the Environment

William Michelson, Frank Trovato, and G. Keith Warriner

Learning Objectives

In this chapter, you will:

▶ see how the 'population explosion' is a recent phenomenon;

▶ compare the demographic transition histories of industrialized and developing countries;

▶ explore the implications of Malthusian theory of population growth and available resources;

▶ consider the Marxist perspective on overpopulation;

▶ see how the existence and prevalence of cities reflects societal and world conditions;

▶ examine the extent to which cities affect behaviours;

▶ examine global population growth and its relationship to poverty and development; and

▶ critically assess terms such as sustainable development, scarcity, and carrying capacity.

Introduction ● ● ● ● ● ● ●

This chapter deals with the interplay of social phenomena with varying, more material forms of context. Studying demography, urban sociology, and environmental sociology requires locating sociological principles and processes in the real world situations that both impact and are impacted by them.

Moreover, these three topics are related in obvious and not-so-obvious ways. Obviously, the environment is significantly affected by population growth, migration, and the large-scale gathering of people in cities. Equally obviously, **urbanization** affects migration patterns and birth and death rates. More subtly, the environment shapes settlement and migration patterns, ordinary rates of birth and death, and even large-scale demographic crises such as wars, epidemics, and natural disasters.

World Population ● ● ● ●

The current population of the world and its projected future must be understood in the broader context of human history. Ansley Coale (1974) divides population history into two broad segments of time: the first, from the beginning of humanity to around 1750 CE, was a very long era of slow population growth; the second, relatively brief in broad historical terms, is one of explosive gains in human numbers. According to Coale (1974: 17), the estimated average annual growth rate between 8000 BCE and 1 CE was only 0.036 per year. Between 1 CE and 1750, the average rate of growth rose to 0.056 per cent, and from 1750 to 1800 it went up to 0.44 per cent. In modern times, the trajectory of population growth has followed an exponential pattern (1, 2, 4, 8, 16, . . .). Since the early nineteenth century, each successive billion of world population has arrived in considerably less time than the previous one. It took humanity until about 1750 CE to reach a population size of approximately 800 million. The first billion of population occurred in 1804, the second 123 years later in 1927. Only thirty-four years passed before the world witnessed its third billion. The four billion mark was reached in 1974, only 14 years later; another 13 later the earth welcomed its five-billionth person, in 1987 (Birg, 1995: 85; UN Population Division, 1999: 8). In 1999, the globe's population turned 6 billion (see Figure 16.1).

World population growth rates peaked at just over 2.0 per cent during the 1960s and early 1970s. In recent decades the growth rate has been declining to its present level of 1.2 per cent (Population Reference Bureau, 2006). This trend is expected to proceed into the foreseeable future, such that by the year 2050, the growth rate of the world might be as low as 0.5 per cent per year—a rate of growth not seen since the 1920s (Bongaarts and Bulatao, 2000: 20; Eberstad, 1997; Lutz, 1994). This remarkable reduction will come about as a result of anticipated declines in fertility and mortality over the next half-century. The 2006 medium variant projection of the United Nations (a projection that assumes change in fertility and mortality thought to be most likely, given past trends) assumes that the total fertility rate at the world level will decline from 2.55 children per woman in 2005–10 to about 2.02 children per woman in 2045–50. The change in **life expectancy at birth** during this same period is expected to be from 67 years in 2005–10 to 75 years in 2045–50 (UN, 2007). This 'central' scenario projection suggests a population of just over nine billion in 2050 (see Table 16.1).

During this century, population growth will occur unevenly across the major regions of the world. Most of the projected growth will take place in the **developing countries**, especially in the poorest nations, where rates of natural increase remain high. Though fertility has been declining in many developing countries, natural increase is high because of the faster pace of the mortality declines. Although some of the African countries have been hit hard by the HIV/AIDS epidemic and are consequently experiencing either low or negative rates of natural increase (e.g., Botswana, Zimbabwe, Lesotho, South Africa, and Swaziland), Africa's share of the world's population will increase rapidly regardless, and is projected to account for about 22 per cent of the world's population in 2050 (UN, 2007). The growth rate for the **developed** countries is only 0.2 per cent per year; in nations such as Germany, Italy, and Japan, for example, annual rates of natural increase have been close to zero or slightly negative (Population Reference Bureau, 2008).

Some of the anticipated population growth for the world over the next 50 years is unavoidable because of the powerful effects of **population momentum** (Bongaarts and Bulatao, 2000; Lutz, 1994). That is, because of past high fertility and mortality declines, the proportion of the world's population in the reproductive ages (roughly ages 15–49) has been growing and is expected to continue to grow over the next several decades. Even with their much reduced fertility rates, large parental cohorts will be bringing many babies into the world. Even the 'low variant' projection by the United Nations (2007), which assumes substantial declines in fertility, shows a population of about 7.8 billion in 2050. But under this low variant, the population of the world

Figure 16.1 The World Population Explosion

Most of the world's population increase has taken place in the past two centuries. It took hundreds of thousands of years for the human race to reach its 1960 total of about 3 billion people. But in the 40 years that followed, it grew by another 3 billion people, to its present total of over 6 billion.

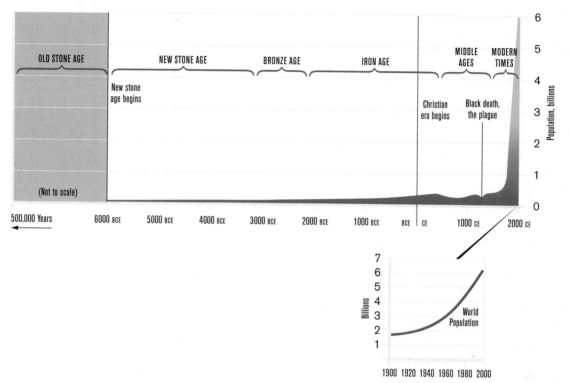

Source: Adapted from Glenn Trewartha, *A Geography of Population: World Patterns* (New York: Wiley, 1969), 29.

Period	Estimated population	Estimated average annual growth rate (%)	Years to add 1 billion
1 million BC–8000 BC	8 million	0.010[1]	
8000 BC–AD 1	300 million	0.036[1]	
AD 1–AD 1750	800 million	0.056[1]	
1804	1 billion	0.400[1]	all of humanity
1927	2 billion	0.540[1]	123
1950	2.5 billion	0.800[1]	—
1960	3 billion	1.7–2.0[2]	33
1974	4 billion	2.0–1.8[2]	14
1987	5 billion	1.8–1.6[2]	13
1999	6 billion	1.6–1.4[2]	12
2013 (projected)	7 billion	1.04[3]	14
2028 (projected)	8 billion	0.90[3]	15
2050 (projected)	9 billion	0.57[3]	22

World Population Growth through Broad Historical Periods and Projections

Note: For the years 2013, 2028, and 2054, the projected populations are based on the UN 2004 revision of World Population Prospects, medium variant (UN, 2006a).
[1]Estimated average population or average rate of growth at the end of the period.
[2]Range of growth rates between specified periods.
[3]Estimated.
Sources: Adapted from Coale (1974); Trewartha (1969); Bongaarts and Bulatao (2000); Population Reference Bureau World Population Data Sheets (various years).

Table 16.1   Estimated and Projected Population of the World, Major Development Groups and Major Areas, 1950, 2007, and 2050 According to Different Projection Variants

| Region | Estimated population (millions) | | Population in 2050 (millions) by Type of Variant | | | |
	1950	2007	Low	Medium	High	Constant
World	**2 535 (100)**	**6 671 (100)**	**7 792 (100)**	**9 191 (100)**	**10 756 (100)**	**11 858 (100.0)**
More developed regions	814 (32.1)	1 223 (18.3)	1 065 (13.7)	1 245 (13.5)	1 451 (13.5)	1 218 (10.3)
Less developed regions	1 722 (67.9)	5 448 (81.7)	6 722 (86.3)	7 946 (86.5)	9 306 (86.5)	10 639 (89.7)
Least developed countries	200	804	1 496	1 742	2 002	2 794
Other LDCs	1 521	4 644	5 232	6 204	7 304	7 845
Africa	224 (8.8)	965 (14.5)	1 718 (22.0)	1 998 (21.7)	2 302 (21.4)	3 251 (27.4)
Asia	1 411 (55.6)	4 030 (60.4)	4 444 (57.0)	5 266 (57.3)	6 189 (57.4)	6 525 (55.0)
Europe	548 (21.6)	731 (11.0)	566 (7.3)	664 (7.2)	777 (7.2)	626 (5.3)
Latin America/Caribbean	168 (6.6)	572 (8.6)	641 (8.2)	769 (8.4)	914 (8.5)	939 (7.9)
Northern America	172 (6.8)	339 (5.1)	382 (4.9)	445 (4.8)	517 (4.8)	460 (3.9)
Oceania	13 (0.5)	34 (0.5)	42 (0.5)	49 (0.5)	56 (0.5)	57 (0.5)

Note: Numbers in parentheses are percentages. The sum of least developed and other less developed countries adds up to the total population for the less developed countries. The sum of the six regions adds up to the overall world total population.

The United Nations considers as 'less developed regions' the regions of Africa, Asia (excluding Japan), Latin America and the Caribbean, as well as Melanesia, Micronesia and Polynesia. The 'more developed' regions comprise Australia/New Zealand, Europe, Northern America, and Japan. The 'least developed' countries consist of 50 countries: Afghanistan, Angola, Bangladesh, Benin, Bhutan, Burkina Faso, Burundi, Cambodia, Cape Verde, Central African Republic, Chad, Comoros, Democratic Republic of the Congo, Djibouti, Equatorial Guinea, Eritrea, Ethiopia, Gambia, Guinea, Guinea-Bissau, Haiti, Kiribati, Lao People's Democratic Republic, Lesotho, Liberia, Madagascar, Malawi, Maldives, Mali, Mauritania, Mozambique, Myanmar, Nepal, Niger, Rwanda, Samoa, Sao Tome and Principe, Senegal, Sierra Leone, Solomon Islands, Somalia, Sudan, Timor-Leste, Togo, Tuvalu, Uganda, United Republic of Tanzania, Vanuatu, Yemen and Zambia.

Source: United Nations Department of Economic and Social Affairs Population Division. 2007. *World Population Prospects. The 2006 Revision.* Highlights. New York: UN (ESA/P/WP.202), 1.

would peak around 2040 and then start a course of decline. The projected 7.8 billion in 2050 under the 'low variant' scenario would be part of a downward trend in world population. Of course, we must recognize that predicting population growth over the long term is an inexact science; the projections depend largely on changes in fertility, which can be a rather unpredictable **variable**. Even small changes in fertility can have dramatic effects on the projected population numbers.

Over the course of this century, all populations in the world will become older as a result of decades of fertility declines worldwide. Countries with more rapid and sustained fertility reductions will experience greater degrees of demographic aging. For example, in 2005, Japan and Italy had the oldest median ages in the world (42.9 and 42.3, respectively). In 2050, the median variant projections for these two countries show their median ages increase to 52.5 and 52.3, respectively (UN, 2006: 31). Italy will see its potential support ratio—the number of persons of working age (15–64) per older person—drop to less than 2 by the year 2050, from its current ratio of about 4. For the Republic of Korea—a society that has also been experiencing rapid fertility declines—the fall in the magnitude of its potential support ratio will be even more dramatic. The United Nations has estimated that Korea's potential support ratio of 7.1 in 2007 will likely decline to 1.5 by 2050 (UN, 2007a). In 2050, it is anticipated that the world will see 16 per cent of its population being over the age of 65. (In 2007, the percentage was 7.5.) Seniors will account for almost 26 per cent of the population in the developed countries, while in the developing regions as a whole, this proportion will rise to almost 15 per cent (Bongaarts and Bulatao, 2000: 23; UN, 2007a).

● Theories of ● ● ● ● ● Population Change

Two influential themes can be identified in the literature regarding the interrelationship of population and resources. The first proposes that curbing population growth is essential for maintaining a healthy balance between human numbers, resources, and the sustainability of the environment; the second characterizes population as a minor or inconsequential factor in such matters. Thomas Malthus and Karl Marx (with Friedrich Engels) are the principal thinkers representing these opposing views. Before examining their ideas, let us review another influential theory of population dynamics: the demographic transition theory.

Demographic Transition Theory

The **demographic transition** theory was first developed on the basis of the experience of Western European countries with respect to their historical pattern of change in birth and death rates in the context of socio-economic modernization. In general terms, the theory can also describe the situation of the developing countries, though the structural conditions underlying changes in vital rates are recognized as being substantially different from the European case (Kirk, 1998; Teitelbaum, 1975). The demographic transition of Western societies entailed three successive stages: (1) a pre-transitional period of high birth and death rates with very low population growth; (2) a transitional phase of high fertility, declining death rates, and explosive growth (which itself may be divided into an early stage and a late stage); and (3) a final stage of low mortality and fertility and low natural increase. By the early 1940s, most European societies had completed their demographic transitions (see Figure 16.2).

Crude birth and death rates in the ancient world probably fluctuated between 35 and 45 per 1,000 population (Coale, 1974: 18). With gradual improvements in agriculture and better standards of living, the death rate declined, though fertility remained high. During the second stage, the excess of births over deaths was responsible for the modern rise of population—the so-called population explosion (McKeown, 1976). With gradual modernization and socio-economic development, during the middle and later years of the nineteenth century, birth rates in Europe began to fall, first in France and then in other countries. In the early 1930s, Western nations had attained their lowest birth rates up to that point in their histories; the death rate was also quite low by historical standards, and a new demographic equilibrium had been reached. In pre-transition times, the low growth rates were the result of humans' lack of control over nature; the end of the demographic transition came from incremental controls over nature—agricultural development, industrialization, **urbanization**, economic growth, and modern science and medicine.

Coale (1969, 1973) undertook an extensive investigation to re-examine the causes of the European fertility transition. Theorists had proposed that in pre-transitional societies, conscious use of family limitation was absent, that economic development and urbanization preceded the onset of fertility declines, and that a drop in mortality always occurred prior to any long-term drop in the birth rate (Davis, 1945; Notestein, 1945; Thompson, 1929, 1944). But some of the empirical evidence uncov-

Figure 16.2   The Classical Demographic Transition Model and Corresponding Conceptual Types of Society

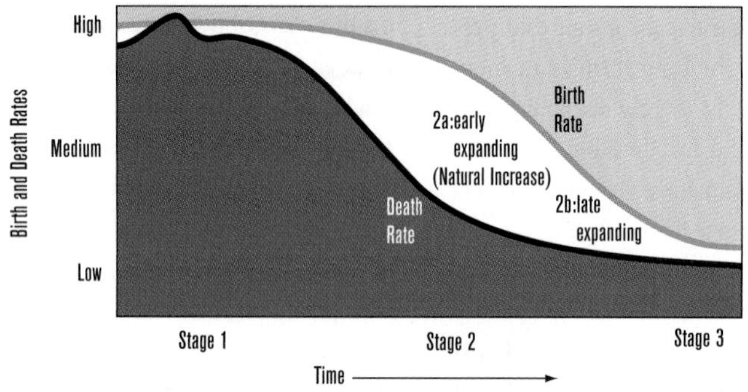

Stage	Fertility	Mortality	Population Growth	Economy
1. Pre-industrial	High, fluctuating	High, fluctuating (low life expectancy)	Static to very low	Primitive or agrarian
2. Early industrial	High	Falling	High, explosive	Mixed
3. Modern urban industrial	Controlled: low to moderate to sub-replacement levels	Low (high life expectancy)	Low to moderate to negative	Urban industrial to post-industrial

Source: Adapted from Glenn Trewartha, *A Geography of Population: World Patterns* (New York: Wiley, 1969), 45, 47.

ered by Coale failed to support some of these propositions. For instance, one important discovery was that economic development is not always a precondition for a society to experience the onset of sustained declines in fertility (though economic development would help speed up the transition). Coale concluded that sustained fertility declines in a society would take place when three preconditions were met: (1) fertility decisions by couples must be within the calculus of conscious choice; that is, cultural and religious norms do not forbid couples to practise family planning, nor do they promote large families; (2) reduced fertility must be viewed by couples as economically advantageous; and (3) effective methods of fertility control must be known and available to couples (Coale, 1969, 1973; Coale and Watkins, 1986).

Having long completed their mortality and fertility transitions, the industrialized countries have gained widespread economic success; their populations enjoy a great deal of social and economic security and well-being. Couples in these societies see little need to have large families. In many developing countries, however, entrenched cultural norms and traditions favour high fertility and parents tend to view children as a source of

security in an insecure environment (Cain, 1983; Caldwell, 1976). Nevertheless, over recent decades much progress has been made in raising the prevalence levels of contraceptive practices. Organized family planning programs have played a major role in this trend (Caldwell et al., 2002). New evidence suggests a growing number of developing nations are now approaching the end of their demographic transitions, and others in the poorer regions of the world (for example, sub-Saharan Africa) have recently begun their fertility transitions (Bulatao, 1998; Bulatao and Casterline, 2001).

Figure 16.3 displays in schematic form the demographic transitions of the West and of the contemporary developing countries, the latter subdivided into 'transitional' and 'delayed transition' societies. Examples of transitional populations are India, Turkey, China, Indonesia, Taiwan, Thailand, Mexico, and countries in Latin America and the Caribbean. Delayed transition societies are found in sub-Saharan Africa, southern Africa, and southwest Asia (for example, Afghanistan, Pakistan, and Bangladesh). In both these cases, mortality reductions have been fairly rapid. In the European historical context, health improvements occurred more

HUMAN DIVERSITY
Youth in the International Labour Market

As the world's population surges past the six-billion mark . . . 700 million young people will enter the labour force in developing countries—more than the entire workforce of the developed world in 1990—the United Nations says.

And as the largest-ever group of young people enters its child-bearing and working years, the number of people over the age of 65 continues to swell as health and longevity improve, according to the UN's annual State of the World Population report. . . .

If jobs can be found or created for the global bulge of one billion people between the ages of 15 and 24—the result of past high fertility—there is a chance to increase human capital so that the dependent young and elderly age groups can be better cared for, the report said.

But without investment in jobs for the young, better education for children, especially girls, and better health care for both young and old, social unrest and instability are inevitable.

'The rapid growth of young and old "new generations" is challenging societies' ability to provide education and health care for the young, and social, medical and financial support for the elderly', the report says. . . .

Some developing nations, particularly in Southern Asia and Northern Africa, could reap an economic windfall in the next couple of decades as the bulge in 15- to 24-year-olds swells the workforce in comparison to dependent age groups, the report says.

To avoid squandering this one-time 'demographic bonus', these countries will have to ensure their young people can find jobs and don't start families too soon.

Stan Bernstein, chief author of the UN report and a research adviser at the UN Population Fund, said developing countries need both private and public, domestic and international investment in their basic social services to ensure they don't miss this 'window of opportunity'.

Global Population Growth by Age Group

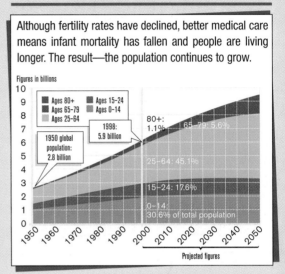

Although fertility rates have declined, better medical care means infant mortality has fallen and people are living longer. The result—the population continues to grow.

Figures in billions

- Ages 80+
- Ages 65–79
- Ages 25–64
- Ages 15–24
- Ages 0–14

1950 global population: 2.8 billion

1998: 5.9 billion

80+: 1.1%   65–79: 5.6%

25–64: 45.1%

15–24: 17.6%

0–14: 30.6% of total population

Projected figures

Source: : United Nations, *State of the World Population Report.*

It is in the interest of wealthier nations and private companies to make this investment, Mr Bernstein said in a phone interview from New York yesterday.

'These countries, if given the opportunity to accelerate their development now, are going to be significant economic, trade and social partners in the future. It's a win-win situation.'

However, with most developed nations steadily reducing the amount of foreign aid they provide, and cutting their own social-service budgets, other sources of investment are needed. . . .

At the other end of the age spectrum, a rapidly growing population over the age of 60—578 million this year—is seeing more years of healthy life, is able to work longer and is moving toward greater independence from grown children. . . .

Source: From Jane Gadd, 'Record Numbers of Youth Will Seek Work: UN', *Globe and Mail*, 2 Sept. 1998. Reprinted with permission from The Globe and Mail.

Figure 16.3 Schematic Representation of
Demographic Transition: Western,
Delayed, and Transitional Models

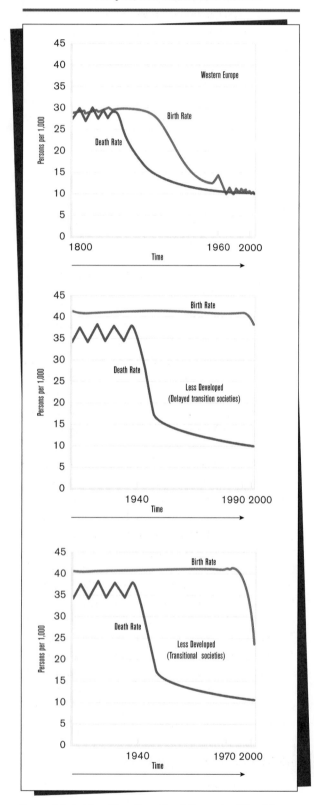

Source: Adapted from Glenn Trewartha, *A Geography of Population: World Patterns* (New York: Wiley, 1969), 45, 46.

gradually in response to incremental socio-economic advancements and economic modernization. In the developing countries, declining death rates have been achieved through family planning, public health programs, and other medical interventions offered by the industrialized countries (Preston, 1986b).

Malthusian Theory

Thomas Malthus (1766–1834) was an ordained Anglican minister and professor of political economy in England. His most famous work, *An Essay on the Principle of Population*, was published in 1798. This important treatise has had a lasting influence on subsequent theorizing about population matters. At the time that Malthus wrote his *Essay*, a number of scholars had already contributed serious thoughts on the question of population and resources. For instance, the Enlightenment theorists Jean-Jacques Rousseau, Marie-Jean-Antoine-Nicolas de Caritat Marquis de Condorcet, and William Godwin viewed population growth as a positive development (Overbeek, 1974). A growing population would help stimulate economic growth, and with further advances in civilization there would be a natural tendency for subsistence to increase faster than population. Malthus reacted strongly to such views; he was less optimistic about humanity's capacity to maintain a sustainable balance between available resources and population growth. He set out to warn humanity about the dangers of unchecked population growth.

Malthus assumed an inherent tendency in humans to increase in numbers beyond the means of subsistence available to them. Mankind, he argued, lives at the brink of subsistence. Population, left unchecked, tends to double once every generation; it thus follows a geometric, or exponential, progression (1, 2, 4, 8, 16, 32, . . .). The food supply, on the other hand, tends to grow arithmetically (1, 2, 4, 6, 8, 10, . . .). Under this scenario, in the long term, population would eventually outstrip food and other essential resources.

As a solution to this problem, Malthus proposed that population could be kept in equilibrium through the activation of two different mechanisms. The first is what he called positive checks (also referred to as vice and misery). These are conditions that raise the death rate and thus serve to reduce population—famine, pestilence, war, and disease. The second, and more desirable, alternative would be widespread exercise of preventive checks (also referred to as moral restraint) to curb population growth—the imposition of the human will to deliberately curtail reproduction through celibacy, postponed marriage, and sexual abstinence. By postponing marriage until people were in an adequate position to maintain a family, individuals and society would gain economically: by working longer before marriage, people would save more of their incomes, thus helping to reduce poverty and raise the overall level of well-being. Malthus considered abortion and contraception to be immoral.

Malthusian theory has provoked strong reactions. One criticism is that Malthus failed to fully appreciate the resilience of humanity when faced with difficult problems. Throughout history, humanity has shown a remarkable ability to solve many of its predicaments. Writers point out that progress in science, technology, and socio-economic well-being has evolved in tandem with explosive population growth and that the agricultural and industrial revolutions arose in response to problems and demands arising from a rapidly growing population (Boserup, 1965, 1981; Fogel and Costa, 1997; Simon, 1995, 1996).

Malthus suggested that population and food supply must be in balance. But exactly what constitutes an 'optimum' population size is difficult, if not impossible, to specify. Perceptions of the 'optimal', in this sense, are highly dependent on available resources to a society, as well as on consumption patterns and the degree of economic activity and production. Consumption and production are closely tied to a society's cultural standards for material comfort and demand for consumer products. As described by Paul Ehrlich and J.P. Holdren (1971), the potential impact of population on the environment is multiplicative. That is, the effect of the population depends partly on its size and growth, but also on a society's level of affluence and technological complexity. In a slow-growing population with strong material expectations, the potential for environmental and resource depletion may be greater than in a fast-growing population with lower levels of material aspirations and technological sophistication. The more developed the society, the higher the expected standard for 'basic' necessities. As material aspirations rise, so do levels of consumption and expenditures by the public. Increased consumer demand for material goods spurs economic activity; greater levels of economic activity heighten the risk of environmental damage because of increased pollution and resource depletion (Ehrlich and Ehrlich, 1970, 1990).

It has been proposed that industrial societies may be facing an inversion of the Malthusian scenario (Woolmington, 1985). In these societies, overpopulation is no longer the threat Malthus advocated. Rather, the seeds of systemic instability in these societies may lie more in their reliance on endless economic growth and consumption.

Rather than population pressing on resources, as was proposed by Malthus, the economy now presses the population to consume—economic growth and stability depend on this. However, in the long term, the spiral of consumption and production may not be sustainable in slow-growing or declining populations (Woolmington, 1985).

Finally, Malthus's insistence on the unacceptability of birth control is inconsistent with his advocacy of curbing rapid population growth. The reality is that people throughout the centuries have always resorted to some means of birth control at one time or another.

The Marxist Perspective on Population

Marxist scholars have refuted the Malthusian principles. They contend that population is a secondary issue to the pernicious problems of widespread economic inequality and poverty. Large families arise from poverty. With Friedrich Engels, Marx advocated the elimination of hunger, poverty, and human suffering through the radical restructuring of society to ensure the equitable distribution of wealth and resources (Marx and Engels, 1970 [1845–6]). As for poor developing nations, their population predicament can be traced to their relative economic deprivation. In response to Malthus's principle that population grows geometrically, it also is the case that scientific and technological solutions tend to progress geometrically. Scientific and technological progress could be used to relieve human suffering.

The Marxist perspective is grounded in the idea that socio-economic inequality is a root cause of human problems and suffering. However, in matters of population control, Marxist skepticism towards the role of population in human problems is now largely ignored (Petersen, 1989). China—a Communist state—has outwardly rejected the Marxist doctrine of population. Chinese officials have recognized that slowing population growth through concerted family planning policies is, in the long term, essential to societal well-being (Bulatao, 1998; Caldwell et al., 2002; Haberland and Measham, 2002). With few exceptions, developing countries now embrace population policies that are consistent with neo-Malthusian principles. Family planning and reproductive health programs are recognized by governments as critical means in their quest to curb population growth.

Contemporary Perspectives on Population

Neo-Malthusian scholars—the contemporary followers of Malthus—believe that the world's population has been growing too fast and that the planet is already close to reaching critical ecological limits. Unlike Malthus, however, neo-Malthusians view contraception and family planning as a key element in population control (Ehrlich and Ehrlich, 1990). The neo-Malthusian perspective inherently implies that the world would be a better and safer place if it contained fewer people. An expanding population in conjunction with excessive consumerism and economic production will lead to the depletion of essential resources and to ecological breakdown in the long term.

Neo-Marxist scholars place less emphasis on the centrality of population as a source of human predicaments. Focusing on population as the root cause of human suffering obscures the reality that the world is divided into wealthy and relatively poor regions and that this divide is widening rather than narrowing. Neo-Marxists alert us to the extreme consumerism of wealthy regions and their overwhelming economic and political influence over less advantaged nations. It is also argued that the **globalization** of capital—seen by many other observers as the key to emulating the 'success story' of the West—often exacerbates, rather than diminishes, socio-economic disparities within and across societies. Investigations by neo-Marxist scholars tend to focus their analyses on regional inequalities in resources and wealth and on the political and economic dependence of developing countries on the developed nations. Some nations enjoy inordinate power and influence over others (Gregory and Piché, 1983; Wimberley, 1990). In this connection, Andre Gunder Frank (1991) has coined the phrase 'the underdevelopment of development' to refer to the overwhelming influence and control the world's major economic powers hold over the developing countries. Development, it is argued, serves mostly the interests of the most powerful nations. Aid received by the poor nations comes at the cost of being in a persistent state of dependence on the providers.

Other writers concerned with the complex interactions of population, environment, and resources take a revisionist stance on such questions. Revisionists are neither neo-Marxists nor neo-Malthusians (Ahlburg, 1998; Cincotta and Engelman, 1997; Clarke, 1996; Evans, 1998; Furedi, 1997; National Research Council, 1986).

Julian Simon (1995, 1996), for instance, has written that population growth historically has been, on balance, beneficial to humankind—people are the 'ultimate resource', Simon contends.

The US National Research Council's report on population, environment, and resources (1986) exemplifies a revisionist perspective. This committee has proclaimed that, in some cases, population may have no discernable relationship to some of the problems often attributed to it. The report also concludes that population's relationship to depletion of exhaustible resources is statistically weak and often exaggerated. Indeed, income growth and excessive consumption are more important factors in this sense: a world with rapid population growth but slow increases in income might experience slower resource depletion than one with a stationary population but rapid increase in income. It was found, also, that reduced rates of population growth would increase the rate of return to labour and help bring down income inequality in a country.

The National Research Council committee also suggested that while rapid population growth is directly related to the growth of large cities in the **Third World**, its role in urban problems is most likely secondary. Ineffective or misguided government policies may play a more important role in the development of urban problems. Moreover, the committee has noted that although it is often assumed in the literature that reducing population growth leads to a reduction in poverty and income inequality, in fact this relationship holds to a certain point only. For instance, if the population of Bangladesh were halved, its status as a poor nation would not change appreciably; it would move from being the second poorest nation in the world to thirteenth poorest (National Research Council, 1986). Many factors beyond rapid population growth are responsible for poverty (Keyfitz, 1993).

● The First Cities ● ● ● ● ●

The emergence of cities in about 3500 BC truly represented something new under the sun. Perhaps the most elementary conception of a city is that it must contain at least some non-agricultural workers. The effect of

▐▌ Time to Reflect ▐▌▐▌▐▌▐▌▐▌▐▌▐▌▐▌▐▌▐▌▐▌

Reflect on your own views regarding the relationship of population to environment and resources. Is your view more consistent with Malthus or Marx? Or is your view perhaps different from that of either of these two thinkers?

cities on the rest of the society was therefore immediate and direct: the rural sector had to grow a surplus of food to feed the urbanites. Creating stable and predictable agricultural surpluses required simultaneous developments throughout the whole of society in technology and social structure in such geographic areas as Mesopotamia and the Indus Valley that could support intensive agriculture (Adams, 1966).

Technological innovations of importance for urbanization included irrigation; bronze metallurgy for plowing and cutting instruments; animal husbandry for use in agriculture; stone mortars; the selective cultivation of rich, non-perishable foods such as grains and dates; wheeled carts and sailing vessels for transport; and building bricks for permanent settlements.

Alongside of technology, social organization evolved, and the division of labour beyond age and sex became a legacy to later cities and societies. One aspect of the enhanced division of labour was *vertical stratification*, differentiation in the degrees of responsibility and power. For instance, it became the responsibility of some individuals to see to it, by providing technological support and controlling delivery, that the farmers produced surpluses for the non-agricultural workers. Another aspect of the division of labour was *horizontal stratification*, different job specializations even at the same level of power and prestige. Full-time soldiers, artists, and producers of consumer goods appeared in the urban settlements, while farmers became ever-more specialized. From the beginning, then, cities had heterogeneous populations with complex, usually coercive relationships with the rest of society. Although the farmers did obtain products and the often dubious benefits of laws and protection, they relinquished some of their food under terms beyond their control.

This relationship between urban and rural people may appear like what we experience currently. However, there have been enormous changes over time in the balance between the two groups, reflecting developments in the central elements of technology and social organization. At first, technology was barely adequate for producing the necessary food surplus; 50 to 90 farmers were needed to produce enough surplus food for one urbanite. Today, a single farmer in a technologically developed country produces food for about nine urbanites.

In the first few thousand years after the appearance of cities, even the largest urban settlements were very small. Archaeological evidence suggests the largest were between 5,000 and 30,000 in population. Their size was limited by the distance over which a labour-intensive transportation technology could bring food from outlying areas, by how far coercion could be extended, and by

the state of sanitation and public health. With refinements in technology and social structure, some ancient cities grew much larger. Athens had about 150,000 residents in 500 BC. At its height, Rome grew to between 250,000 and a million inhabitants.

City-states often dominated vast tributary areas. The size and prosperity of these cities depended on the extent to which people could travel safely to and from these hinterlands. Such dependence on peaceful connections to the outside world has been reflected in the rise and fall of cities throughout history—a relationship reconfirmed by the impacts of violence and epidemics on cities during the current decade. Fostering a climate of violence in the 'outside' world is no recipe for security and prosperity at home!

Although many aspects of urbanization appear to be timeless, the kind of urbanization we know today did not develop until after the Middle Ages.

Paths to Urban Development

The development of industry, based on non-living energy sources such as coal and steam, is commonly given credit for a substantial shift in the population balance from rural to urban. Powered industry reflected societal developments in technology and accentuated the division of labour. The same advances in science and engineering that made possible large-scale factories with machinery also led to innovations in agricultural technology that enabled fewer farm workers to grow food more intensively and on larger holdings.

In technologically advanced societies, therefore, a surplus of agricultural labour became available for newly emerging, specialized city jobs. These workers were *pushed* from the countryside and *pulled* to cities. They became specialists—in housing, food, transportation, financial services, and warehousing distribution, for example—and several specialists were needed to provide services and supplies for every factory worker. This led to a growth in urban population by what is called the *multiplier effect*: population growth several times the number accounted for by factory workers alone.

Technically, observers think of urbanization as the percentage of a nation's population living in settlements of a certain minimum size, usually defined as 5,000 and over. Just two centuries ago, only about three per cent of the world's population lived in settlements of 500 or more inhabitants. A city about the size of the current Vancouver metropolitan area would have been the largest in the world. Today's technologically advanced nations have urbanization levels exceeding 75 per cent.

If you look at the development of urbanization in historical perspective, as in the timeline in Figure 16.4, you can see that it took many thousands of years of human life for the prerequisites for cities to occur and to lead to the establishment of urban settlements in various parts of the world. The ingredients of modern cities have become known only in 'the last few minutes in the day' of the human timeline. Indeed, the predominantly urban society is largely a phenomenon only of the past 60 years of the 50,000 or so years of recorded human history. During this recent time, however, the tempo of technological innovation and societal adaptation has grown phenomenally. Considering that powered industry came about in the eighteenth century, electricity in the nineteenth, and the automobile, telephone, radio, television, airplane, computer, and nuclear power in the twentieth century, it is difficult to predict or imagine what cities and society will be like even in the next decade.

Figure 16.4 Timeline of Significant Events in the Development of Urbanization[a]

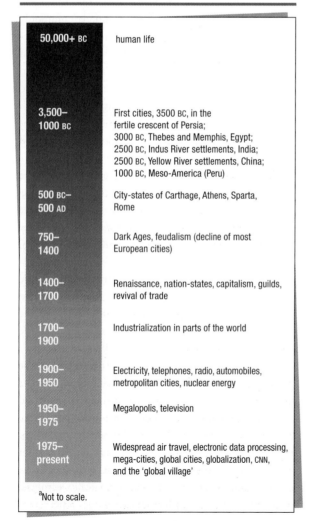

50,000+ BC	human life
3,500–1000 BC	First cities, 3500 BC, in the fertile crescent of Persia; 3000 BC, Thebes and Memphis, Egypt; 2500 BC, Indus River settlements, India; 2500 BC, Yellow River settlements, China; 1000 BC, Meso-America (Peru)
500 BC–500 AD	City-states of Carthage, Athens, Sparta, Rome
750–1400	Dark Ages, feudalism (decline of most European cities)
1400–1700	Renaissance, nation-states, capitalism, guilds, revival of trade
1700–1900	Industrialization in parts of the world
1900–1950	Electricity, telephones, radio, automobiles, metropolitan cities, nuclear energy
1950–1975	Megalopolis, television
1975–present	Widespread air travel, electronic data processing, mega-cities, global cities, globalization, CNN, and the 'global village'

[a]Not to scale.

Canada and the United States belong to a club of industrial nations with reasonably similar, high rates of urbanization. According to the United Nations Population Division (2005), the more developed nations of the world had a mean urbanization percentage of 74.1 in the year 2005, compared to 42.9 for less developed regions. Canada is slightly above this level, with 80.1 per cent urbanization, as is the US with 80.8 per cent as of 2005. Table 16.2 shows that the highly industrialized continents of the Americas, Europe, and Oceania all have mean urbanization levels of over 70 per cent, compared to much lower levels (under 40 percent) for Africa and Asia.

Figure 16.5 shows that urbanization levels in the more and less developed nations have increased in parallel patterns from 1950 to 2005. However, this means that the less developed areas, starting at a very low level of urbanization, have encountered a greater *degree* of change in existing levels of urbanization over these years.

Nonetheless, a concentration on such large land masses obscures differences in levels of industrialization within them. Hence, a focus on national urbanization levels shows that Western Europe has some of the highest levels in the world (for example, Belgium, 98 per cent in 2005; United Kingdom, 90 per cent), while some nations in Eastern Europe have less urbanization (for example, Romania, 56 per cent; Croatia, 59 per cent). Australia and New Zealand are at the 92 and 86 per cent levels, respectively, while the smaller islands in Oceania bring down the regional mean level. Japan has a markedly higher urbanization rate, at 79 per cent, than many other Asian nations that have not as yet achieved the same level of industrialization (World Bank, 2005: Table 3.10).

Table 16.2	Urbanization by Continents, 2005
North America	80.7%
Latin America & Caribbean	77.5%
Europe	71.9%
Oceania	70.5%
Asia	39.7%
Africa	37.9%

Source: United Nations, Department of Economic and Social Affairs, *World Population Prospects: The 2007 Revision Population Data Base*, 2008, at http://esa.un.org/unup. Retrieved 12 August 2008.

Figure 16.5 Urbanization by Development Level, in Five-Year Intervals

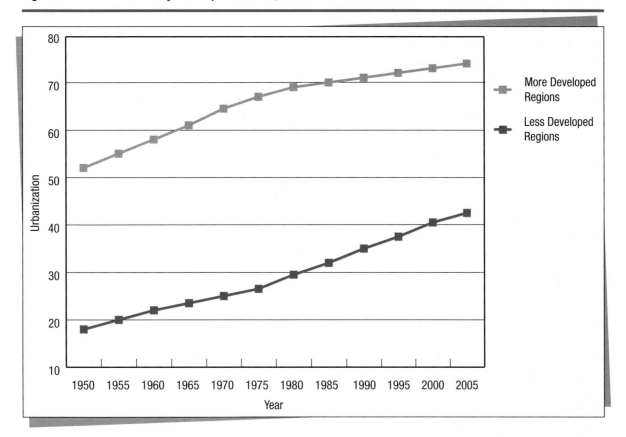

Source: UN (2006c).

Nations with low urbanization rates may nonetheless have very large cities. Indeed, as Table 16.3 indicates, many of the largest cities in the world are found in less developed nations. Knowing the economic and technological contexts in which cities become established is important to understanding their size and distribution within the nation.

The urban population in Western industrial societies is distributed quite evenly among a number of reasonably sized settlements, as capital and technology are diffused. In less developed nations, it is concentrated in the single very large metropolis in the country or in a region. Most of the extremely large cities in the developing world, such as Bombay, Calcutta, and Shanghai, were centres from which foreign imperial powers exported the nation's or region's raw materials for industrial production in the home countries. This system is called *imperialism*. Dogon and Kasarda (1988) suggest that these urban settlements grew to such size as they became obvious destinations for the rural poor, despite the virtual absence of an industrial economic base either in the cities or in the countries at large. Urban populations in such situations typically are underemployed, poor, and predominantly male. When more people reside in a city than would be expected from its economic base, *overurbanization* is said to occur.

When the technology and infrastructure catch up to overurbanized cities that are already large, as a second stage of growth, they become huge. Cities of 10 million or more persons are called **mega-cities**, and the majority of them are in less developed nations. Often their expansion is accompanied by environmental degradations of air, water, hazardous wastes, road accidents, noise, and various social problems such as substandard housing and poor health (Hardoy et al., 2001).

Globalization and Global Cities

Although industrialization is largely held responsible for high rates of urbanization, the recent trend of **globalization**—of corporations expanding their production and sales to many nations of the world, exporting investment capital to take advantage of lower-paid employees in other nations, and exploiting non-traditional markets for the resultant products—has led to added growth and wealth in a few cities. Such cities have witnessed extensive

Table 16.3	The 20 Largest Cities in the World in 2005	
		Population (in millions)
1.	Tokyo	35.2
2.	Mexico City	19.4
3.	New York City	18.7
4.	São Paulo	18.3
5.	Mumbai (Bombay)	18.2
6.	Delhi	15
7.	Shanghai	14.5
8.	Kolkata (Calcutta)	14.3
9.	Jakarta	13.2
10.	Buenos Aires	12.6
12.	Dhaka	12.4
13.	Karachi	11.6
14.	Rio de Janeiro	11.5
15.	Osaka/Kobe	11.3
16.	Al-Qahirah (Cairo)	11.1
17.	Lagos	10.9
18.	Beijing	10.7
19.	Manila	10.7
20.	Moskva (Moscow)	10.7
47.	Toronto	5.3
75.	Montreal	3.6
167.	Vancouver	2.2

Source: Compiled from UN (2006b).

development of corporate organization, finance, telecommunications, and air transportation. These favoured cities, known as **global cities**, manifest high levels of technology. As David Thorns puts it, 'Global cities are now the key sites for the control, coordination, processing and distribution of knowledge that makes them the engines of growth within the present stage of capitalist development' (2002: 54). They are vital centres for the flow of information, direction, and money, and do not have to be on the doorstep of the heavy industries that they indirectly control and co-ordinate. Global cities reflect the presence of interacting financial enterprises through highly concentrated and prominent office buildings (Castells, 1989; Sassen, 1991).

Saskia Sassen (1991) argues that such cities as New York, London, and Tokyo have achieved more prominence than might be projected from their manufacturing base, while large cities based more fully on manufacturing, such as Detroit in the United States and Manchester in England, do not gain global status because they do not need the same degree of white-collar employment right at hand. Toronto is considered a minor global city, and Vancouver is similarly active on the Pacific Rim.

Can globalization be viewed as a modern form of imperialism, in which profits and consumer products flow from around the world to the home country, rather than the traditional imperialism where raw materials were imported for home-country industries and their wage workers? Globalization provides return on capital to corporate investors in the economically advantaged countries, while exporting productive jobs to the developing nations. The process puts large numbers of people in the latter nations into a growing international economic market that increasingly supersedes the social and political policies and actions of sovereign nations. One impact of this free-wheeling commerce is increasing polarization between rich and poor on a global scale.

In Canada, as in the United States, economic factors pull people to cities rather than push them away from rural areas. Figure 16.6 shows that, as of 2006, the majority of people in every Canadian province and territory except Prince Edward Island and Nunavut were city dwellers. Thus, high levels of urbanization are not confined to Ontario and Quebec, with Canada's two largest cities. There is a predominant urban presence in British Columbia, the Prairie provinces, and in most of the Atlantic provinces, too. The relatively large recent growth of Toronto and Vancouver is related to major global factors, while cities such as Winnipeg, Montreal, and Hamilton, though major centres within the Canadian context, lack comparable levels of international roles with which to boost their employment and population. For more detail on Canadian urbanization, see Hiller (2005).

● Urbanism ● ● ● ● ● ●

One of the reasons sociologists are interested in cities is the popular belief that life in cities differs from life in other forms of settlements. Research findings over many years have shown that the issue is subtler than simple urban–rural differences. The path to understanding urbanism is a good example of the convergence of many

Figure 16.6   Urbanization of Canada, by Province and Territory, 2006

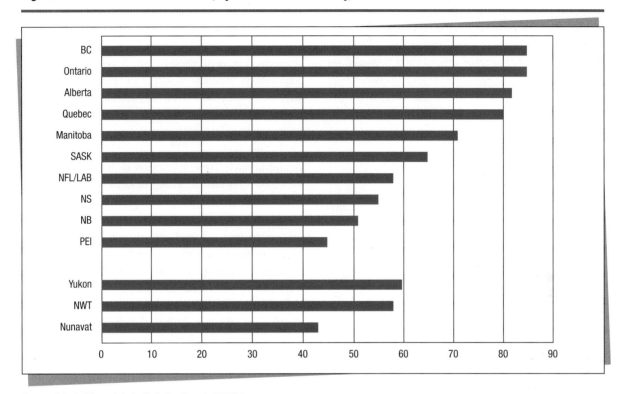

Source: Adapted from data in Statistics Canada (2007a).

different theories and the research that has been done to document them.

Classical Approaches

Early approaches to urbanism seemed to make the assumption that urban contexts cause certain forms of behaviour in a very direct way. This viewpoint is known as *determinism*, since it supposes that a given set of conditions determines behavioural outcomes. Does life in an urban context differ systematically from that in a rural context? Sjoberg (1960) found that job specialization and the complexity of production and marketing that accompanied industrialization required standardization in weights, measures, currencies, pricing, and financial interaction. For the system to work, rational, exact actions became necessary. Classical theorists such as Max Weber, Sir Henry Maine, Ferdinand Tönnies, and Émile Durkheim used different words, but made similar observations that urban life is more likely to involve rational, universalistic, impersonal, and logistically oriented behaviours than had been the case in earlier rural settings. Noting that German urbanites had to pay constant attention to contextual signals—lights, signs, footsteps, whistles, and the like—Georg Simmel (1950a) summa-

rized these observations by saying that the head, rather than the heart, dictates most urban behaviours.

The best-known ideas on urbanism may be attributed to Louis Wirth's 1938 article 'Urbanism as a Way of Life'. Wirth believed that cities have three defining characteristics—large numbers of inhabitants, high densities, and heterogeneous populations—each accounting for important aspects of an urban way of life. Large numbers lead to the impossibility of knowing all persons, and hence to the relative absence of intimacy in most interpersonal relationships. Human relations become segmented into many largely anonymous, superficial, transitory contacts. At the same time, high density fosters human diversification and specialization. Social distance is established to maintain personal space in response to the inescapable presence of close physical contact with diverse persons. Nonetheless, accentuated friction inevitably arises, and formal means of social control, notably uniformed police, assume prominence in cities. Despite, or perhaps because of, such close proximity, complex patterns of segregation take shape. Finally, heterogeneity makes it difficult for individuals to be constricted by rigid social structures, as in rural areas. Urban individuals more often find themselves in varied social settings and groups. Both upward and downward mobility, with the resultant greater feelings of instability and insecurity, are more likely in cities.

Although classical approaches to urbanism never achieved total consensus among sociologists, the classical legacy was sobering. Any societal gains derived from greater division of labour, rationality, and personal freedom seemed counterbalanced by unending suspicion, distrust, and isolation.

Modern Social-Psychological Approaches

Modern social psychologists have been particularly taken by the earlier theoretical themes dealing with urban life as situated in the impersonal presence of great numbers of strangers, some of whom represent annoyance at the least and, more seriously, risk. Lyn Lofland wrote a valuable analysis of how people relate to each other in cities, with the germane title, *A World of Strangers* (1985). In it,

Most of the population growth in the coming years will occur in the poorest countries, where rates of natural increase remain high. Reuters

she stressed that people minimize interpersonal interaction as a way to maximize public order (that is, safety). In more recent work Lofland (1998) delves into how urbanites have a love–hate relationship with public spaces. She suggests that even though people potentially access unparalleled experiences in the congregating spaces of large cities, the public realm has been largely neglected as a result of the ambivalence urbanites have about contact with strangers.

Stanley Milgram (1970: 1462) made a noteworthy contribution to Simmel's notion of impersonal signals bombarding urbanites. Using modern systems analysis, Milgram characterized it as sensory overload: 'City life, as we experience it, constitutes a continuous set of encounters with overload, and of resultant adaptations.' He went on to describe a variety of ways in which urbanites cope with overload. All of them are textbook examples of the *Gesellschaft* side of Tönnies's classical theoretical dichotomy between *Gemeinschaft* and *Gesellschaft*—figuratively, 'heart' *versus* 'head' as describing social interaction in societies.

One common strategy for coping with overload is to tune out what is found to be overburdening: anything from drunks, through poverty, to negative consequences of public- or private-sector policies or practices that benefit only some. Increasing numbers of persons literally live on the streets of Canada. Many citizens have taken active ameliorative roles in food drives, food banks, and night patrols for the homeless, but the context of everyday life for most people involves passively working around difficult situations.

In another coping strategy, urbanites are said to avoid aiding strangers who need help in order to avoid trouble themselves. Much research followed the public shock that resulted when Kitty Genovese was murdered after appealing for help outside the windows of at least 38 onlooking neighbours in a New York City apartment house. The research suggested that the more people there are, the less likely any individual will intervene. People are more likely to intervene if they feel that they are needed in the absence of others.

Urbanites also minimize involvement by taking action to remove themselves from easy contact with strangers. They buy telephone-answering devices or subscribe to voice-mail services, institute scripted menus to provide information, fail to list their telephone numbers (this is certainly the case for ubiquitous cell phones), preview incoming calls, filter visitors through secretaries and assistants, travel by private automobile, and live in segregated (increasingly guarded) buildings and **neighbourhoods**. Ironically, the same people are in greater contact than ever with those they know, through the medium of electronic mail.

People use a range of coping procedures in public places. They pretend not to see each other (for example, on beaches), and tolerate other lifestyles except where these represent clear and present dangers. They follow unspoken but definite rules about how much distance to keep from others for particular purposes, where they sit (for example, on buses or in libraries), and the way they walk (Hall, 1966; Sommer, 1969).

Urbanites, however, are not totally isolated beings. There are public settings where people come to expect to interact with other persons in ways that they don't during most public encounters. Churches, bars, and sporting events, for example, all provide the opportunity for positive interactions among persons with similar interests and objectives. When people want to communicate to others their personal identity, they once relied on clothing in general and uniforms in particular to provide a basis for secure interaction without previous personal acquaintance. In smaller settings, the family name was noteworthy, and it still is in some circles. However, in urban circles in which consumer goods like clothing are rampant and family connections may be obscure, personal credentials (transcripts, credit cards, etc.) and home addresses help complete the introduction, for good and for ill. According to Abu-Lughod (1991: 338), 'the larger neighborhood or even the city can take on an important symbolic and social meaning, serving as a source of identity ("I come from Grosse Pointe").' However, government-issued photo identification has become *de rigueur*. Even people without cars have driver's licenses for personal identification. And, increasingly, this is not sufficient.

The Subcultural Theory of Urban Life

Is it really some aspect of the city that calls for coping behaviours such as those described by Milgram? Albert J. Reiss Jr (1959) found that the anonymous, segmented, and impersonal relations noted by Wirth reflected occupation more than residence. For instance, men living in rural areas with non-farm jobs had daily contact patterns resembling those of their urban counterparts.

In contrast to the deterministic approach of the classical thinkers, other sociologists adopt a *compositional* perspective, according to which behaviour reflects the composition of the population. Herbert Gans (1967), for example, explained suburban behaviour not in terms of the physical nature of the area, but in terms of the social class background and life-cycle characteristics of

the population in the suburb he studied. The nature and extent of their contact with neighbours, their participation in organizations, and their interest in schools all reflected middle-class background and the presence of families with young children, according to Gans. In short, exponents of the compositional approach believe that urban life reflects the most salient features (for example, class, ethnic background or race, religion, age, and sex) of the particular population groups living in particular cities and/or their constituent parts.

In *The Urban Experience* (1976), Claude Fischer attempted to reconcile deterministic and compositional theories and to go beyond them. Fischer argues that Wirth was right in stressing the significance of large numbers of persons in cities. But Fischer does not see the numbers as providing various direct effects; rather, he considers their primary importance as providing the nucleus for various specialized *subcultures* within cities. It is the particular compositions of the various subcultures that influence so-called urban lifestyles.

Fischer calls his approach the *subcultural theory* of urban life. Which subcultures become significant in a given city depends on many macroscopic characteristics of cities: their economic base, sources of migration, climate, and more. Within highly urbanized societies, cities of different sizes and in different locations may be functionally specialized. This does not mean that they are monolithic in terms of their activities or resident populations; but there are distinct tendencies regarding who chooses to live and work there and, hence, which subcultures take root. It is unusual even for a city specializing in industry to have more than 25 per cent of its jobs in manufacturing because of the need for complementary and supportive activities; yet the difference between 25 per cent in manufacturing and 10 per cent spells a big difference in the *critical mass* of a blue-collar subculture. Hamilton, with its huge steel mills, differs substantially in its ways of life from nearby London, an insurance and financial centre; both cities differ from Victoria, with its combination of government jobs, retirees, mild weather, and afternoon tea! However, the largest national cities tend to be diverse economically, with their population size supporting varied subcultures and lifestyles. It takes a Toronto, not a Truro, to supply the critical masses for creating the world's most ethnically diverse city, where the varied ethnic communities enjoy rich, visible cultural lives—some manifestations of which are shared with the city population at large—and where these cultural groups exist side-by-side with youth, yuppie, gay, sports, criminal, and endless other subcultures.

Does Fischer's subcultural theory invalidate the generalizations made by urban social psychologists about such problems as overload, anonymity, and coping adaptations? In subsequent work, Fischer (1982) shows that the personal contact patterns of urbanites are more firmly concentrated in specialized groupings (which in cities means subcultures) than those of people living in smaller communities and rural areas. Similarly, big-city dwellers are likely to trust their closest neighbours, but not urbanites in general.

● Ecology of Cities ● ● ● ●

Examining the city in ecological terms strongly supports such an expectation. We know that most cities comprise distinct parts. The ecological perspective addresses the nature of these parts and what kinds of patterns they form.

Cities, Suburbs, and Metropolitan Areas

While urbanization levels in Canada show that Canadians live predominantly in cities, they do not reveal in what types of settlements or where within them we live. Do most Canadians live in large or small cities, in central cities or suburbs?

A common pattern in technologically advanced societies has been the build-up of population beyond the borders of older cities and into newer municipalities immediately adjacent. These are commonly called *suburbs*, although the word is often applied to areas that simply look newer and less crowded than the centres of the traditional cities. Montreal and Vancouver, for example, have many suburbs, while much of Calgary and Edmonton appear suburban.

Large cities and their suburbs may represent different municipalities, but, in terms of everyday behaviour and economic activity, they form an entity known as a **metropolitan area**. Many people live in one part of a metropolitan area and work in another; there is, for instance, an active interchange between Vancouver and New Westminster.

Statistics Canada defines a *census metropolitan area* (CMA) as an area comprised of one or more large cities (totalling at least 100,000 inhabitants at the previous census) in the centre (the urban core) together with surrounding areas that are economically and socially integrated on a day-to-day basis with the urban core (1992: 29). On the basis of these criteria, some CMAs include a central city with many municipalities extending a considerable distance from the urban core, while others consist of a single municipality. The makeup of a CMA reflects the size of the urban area, its history, and the amount of land suitable for expansion under the control of the central city. Toronto extends as a functional entity almost as far as Hamilton (that is, through Oakville), while the formal city of Saskatoon not only includes nearly all the residents in its vicinity but also controls undeveloped land for future development. There are 33 CMAs in Canada. Although these metropolitan areas take up only a tiny fraction of the land in Canada, in 2006 they were home to approximately 21.5 million of Canada's population of 31.6 million—more than two-thirds of the national population (Statistics Canada,

OPEN FOR DISCUSSION
Individual Identity in a World of Strangers

In response to the unprecedented taking of American civilian lives on 11 September 2001, the issue of individual identity has arisen not only in the United States but in Canada and other nations as well. The fear of strangers has been made a public issue by some political leaders. The public sector has stepped into the void of personal acquaintance to screen persons more thoroughly at fixed locations such as airline check-in counters and border crossings, though photo ID scrutiny has increased in countless other situations. Personal searches of those entering clubs and sporting events have increased.

Do you think that the circumstances of 9/11 and subsequent developments justify proactive public intervention into the largely impersonal world of urban residents? Compare political reactions to the tragic loss of life on 9/11 to the considerably greater morbidity each year in cities from firearm violations and automobile accidents (not least from drunk drivers). How does the fear of strangers alter public reaction to these different situations?

2007a). Canada's urban population is not characterized by dispersal into many small cities and towns across the landscape; it is highly concentrated within metropolitan areas. This is especially true when we realize that nearly 11 million people live in Canada's three largest cities—Toronto, Montreal, and Vancouver.

Many people have an image of the city as an older municipality with a high density and buildings that are large and striking or old and grey. The suburbs are, somehow, something else. This view needs revision. Table 16.4 presents Canadian CMAs with about 300,000 residents or more in order of size in 2006, indicating in the final column the percentage of inhabitants living outside what is currently designated as the central city; this varies from 0 to 76 per cent of CMA population. Within all of these 16 cities, 44.2 per cent of residents are suburbanites by this measure. However, this considerably underestimates the extent of suburban presence in CMAs, as the current central-city boundaries of Toronto, Montreal, Ottawa, Quebec City, Hamilton, and Halifax have recently been expanded to include substantial numbers of suburban municipalities that had grown outside original central-city boundaries; thus, until now, these amalgamated municipalities were considered suburban. It is not an exaggeration to confirm the conclusion drawn from previous analyses that most residents of Canadian (and American) metropolitan areas are suburbanites.

This distribution is essential to an understanding of the pattern of local areas and lifestyles in metropolitan areas. Whereas previously people focused on the central city and spoke in stereotypical terms about the suburbs and suburbanites, now it is essential to recognize that the majority of the urban population live outside of traditional central cities.

Metropolitan Population and Land-Use Patterns

How are people and their subcultures patterned within metropolitan areas? Several theories have been proposed to answer this question.

From studies of Chicago, Ernest Burgess (1925) identified the *concentric ring* land-use and stratification pattern of cities. At the heart of this pattern is the *central business district* (CBD), consisting of the principal private- and public-sector offices, department stores, and hotels. The CBD is serviced by public transit to make it the most accessible place in the city. Burgess assumed that the CBD would be the only major centre in the city, and that it would continue to grow indefinitely.

Because of this growth, the land around the CBD would be held speculatively for future profit. Before upgrading, the *zone in transition* would be used, without maintenance or improvement, for rooming houses, transient hotels, and other impermanent uses. This zone would contain the poorest, newest migrants, the criminal element, and prostitutes—all subcultures requiring short-term affordable housing and, in many cases, anonymity. The more regularized sectors of the population would be distributed in rings around both the CBD and the zone in transition, in proportion to their ability to pay for greater amounts of land increasingly far from these two areas, as well as for the cost and time involved in longer commutes. Thus, working-class communities would be surrounded by the middle class, which in turn would be surrounded by the upper class. In short, according to Burgess, major land uses would claim the city centre through market-mechanism competition, while residential areas would be distributed at varying distances from the CBD according to income.

Another member of the Chicago School of urban sociology, Robert E. Park (1925), labelled as **community** the forms of behaviour thought to arise because 'birds of a feather flock together.' Within a given ring, local communities that were homogeneous by ethnic or religious background would form within boundaries formed by major streets, railways, parks, and the like. Park called these communities *natural areas* because no one rationally planned their location—they were simply a function of land value (thought to lie beyond the control of individuals) and incidental boundaries. According to this view, by the physical proximity of people to one another in the natural area the critical mass of people in subcultures could exercise a strong influence on individual behaviour.

Unfortunately for theorists, the concentric ring pattern is far from universal; it has been demonstrated to exist in few places outside Chicago. Indeed, in many settings outside the United States, the rich occupy the city centres, while the poor are left outside of the benefits of urban infrastructure.

Ironically, it was right in Chicago that another researcher, Homer Hoyt (1939), discovered a rather different pattern. Hoyt's *sectors* resemble pieces of a pie, extending from the centre outward without interruption. Hoyt noted that certain amenities, such as waterfront parks, and eyesores, such as freight railways, extended outward. People of means would try to live within view of the amenities; those of few means would follow the tracks; still others would locate themselves in-between. One side of town would become better than another, if only because it was upwind from centrally located industries.

A third approach is Harris and Ullman's *multiple nuclei theory* (1945), which states that each land use or

Table 16.4 The Size and Suburban Proportion of Canada's Largest Census Metropolitan Areas, 2006

Census Metropolitan Area	Total Population in 2006	Per cent of Population Outside Central City
1. Toronto	5,113,149	51
2. Montreal	3,635,571	55
3. Vancouver	2,116,581	73
4. Ottawa–Gatineau	1,130,761	28
5. Calgary	1,079,310	8
6. Edmonton	1,034,945	29
7. Quebec City	715,515	31
8. Winnipeg	694,668	9
9. Hamilton	692,911	27
10. London	457,720	23
11. Kitchener	451,235	33
12. St Catharines–Niagara	390,317	45
13. Halifax	372,858	0
14. Victoria	330,088	76
15. Oshawa	330,594	57
16. Windsor	323,342	33

Source: Calculated from Statistics Canada, Population and dwelling counts, for Canada, census metropolitan areas, census agglomerations and census subdivisions (municipality), 2006 and 2001 censuses – 100% data, at: <www12.statcan.ca/english/census06/data/popdwell>.

subculture is located according to unique criteria having to do with the proximity of other land uses. Heavy industry, for example, wants to be near railroads and highways, but doesn't need to be as accessible to consumers as do retailing land uses. Head offices draw fine restaurants, banks, and law offices to their vicinity, while universities attract fast-food and coffee chains, copy shops, computer outlets, and bookstores. The result is a city with many diverse centres whose locations are not in a fixed geometric pattern.

A statistical process called *factorial ecology* lets sociologists analyze census statistics for local areas of a given city to determine the patterns shown by such dimen-

sions. Robert Murdie (1969) drew a number of conclusions in his pioneering analysis of Metro Toronto: that family size increased with distance from the centre; that social class segregation was in sectors from the centre outward; and that ethnic groups lived in unique clusters of multiple nuclei. He demonstrated that a single city could show several different patterns, depending on the criterion. No one pattern of land use characterizes all cities.

The Environment and Ecological Scarcity

As the world's population has grown to an unparalleled size and more and more people have gathered in cities, human concern has turned increasingly to the impact on the natural environment.

Issues of ecological scarcity have been of considerable interest to environmental sociologists. Scarcity has to do with problems associated with the overuse of natural resources, leading to their exhaustion, or with their waste or destruction by contamination or misuse. The immense reliance of societies on natural resources and the extent to which this reliance influences social arrangements as well as prospects for social change often go unrecognized. Sociological interest in resource scarcity therefore addresses questions of world population growth, the limits of global carrying capacity, and the relationship between development and scarcity.

Population Growth

There are presently more people living on the Earth than throughout all of human history. As discussed earlier, it took over one million years for the population to reach one billion, around the mid-nineteenth century. In the century and a half since then, the figure has grown to approximately 6.6 billion (in 2006). Some 77 million people are added each year, at a rate of around three people per second. Although the rate of world population increase is slowing, the absolute amount of growth continues to be substantial. By 2050, the world's population will have increased by more than half its size today, to 9.4 billion people (US Bureau of the Census, 2006). These startling statistics explain why world population has been likened to a time bomb threatening to destroy the planet. Population pressure is regarded as one of the most serious environmental threats, contributing to resource exhaustion, destroying species and habitat, causing pollution, and taxing the capacity of agricultural systems. It is a major factor in such diverse ecological disasters as famines in Africa, global warming, acid rain, the garbage crisis, and the spread of disease. While we have not yet arrived at the theoretical limits for food production on the planet, they will be reached by the year 2100, with a projected population of 11.2 billion (World Commission on Environment and Development, 1987: 98–9).

The most serious environmental problems primarily affect the more than five billion people in the developing countries of Africa, Asia, Latin America, and the Caribbean—more than 80 per cent of the global population. The 172 countries classified by the United Nations as the 'less developed regions' (LDRs) account for 99 per cent of global population natural increase—the difference between numbers of births and numbers of deaths. By the end of the first quarter of the twenty-second century, the world's more developed countries (MDCs) will be experiencing negative natural increase, and all of the global population increase will come from the less developed world (UN Department of Economic and Social Affairs, 2006: 5). It is not surprising, then, that environmental scientists and population experts generally agree that the way to avoid reaching the limits of the global carrying capacity is to reduce the birth rates of developing nations.

Sustainable Development

The concept of sustainable development grew out of the perspective that economic development and environmental conservation are compatible goals. First appearing during the 1972 United Nations Conference on the Human Environment in Stockholm, the principle gained widespread support over the three decades that followed while being the focus of various international conferences and reviews, including the 1987 Brundtland Commission and the 1992 and 2002 Earth Summits. Sustainable development calls for the conciliation of several apparently competing ends: environmental integrity; the protection of ecosystems and biodiversity, and the meeting of human needs; and positive economic growth and equitable distribution of the benefits of the environment and resources among social classes and across nations. While the idea of the existence of ecological limits is clearly ingrained in sustainable development, and while there is an insistence on strict resource husbandry, the principle is unabashedly pro-development.

After initial enthusiasm, certain environmentalists have come to regard sustainable development with skepticism. Some see it as no more than a legitimization of development under the guise of environmental stewardship. An extension of this view is that sustainable devel-

opment is an excuse for further incursions by Western nations into the Third World for the sole purpose of profit. In the words of Wolfgang Sachs, 'Capital, bureaucracy and science . . . the venerable trinity of Western Modernization declare themselves indispensable to the new crisis and promise to prevent the worst through better engineering, integrated planning and sophisticated models' (1991: 257). Others claim that the principles of ecology, together with the scientific community, are being co-opted to support the further destruction of nature on the grounds of scientific rationality. While such criticisms are undoubtedly sometimes valid, it is nevertheless the case that the concept of sustainable development has become so widely adopted as a planning goal that it should be considered a new benchmark to thinking on human–environment interactions.

● The Environment ● ● ● ● and Social Theory

Environmental sociology has its theoretical bases in several sociological traditions. Among these is the field of human ecology, a sociological perspective with important ties to the work of Émile Durkheim. More recently, human ecology has been revised for the insights it provides for environmental sociology. Another theoretical topic debated by environmental sociologists concerns whether their field should be seen as constituting a paradigm shift for sociology in general. The division between the order and conflict schools so prevalent elsewhere in sociology is also a characteristic feature of environmental sociology. More generally, there has been broad debate over the relevance of sociology's classical theoretical traditions to the study of environmental issues. Contemporary theoretical approaches include the concept of the risk society, developed by Ulrich Beck. Finally, social constructionism, a perspective found elsewhere in sociology, has developed to become a prominent approach within environmental sociology. In this section, we review these theoretical positions.

Human Ecology

The science of ecology is central to the study of environmental issues; human ecology is the application of the same approach to sociological analyses. Human ecology emerged under the direction of Robert Park and Ernest Burgess at the University of Chicago during the 1920s (Park and Burgess, 1921; Park, Burgess, and McKenzie, 1925; Theodorson, 1961, 1982). Much as the science of ecology studies plant and animal communities, human

Figure 16.7   The World Model from The Limits to Growth

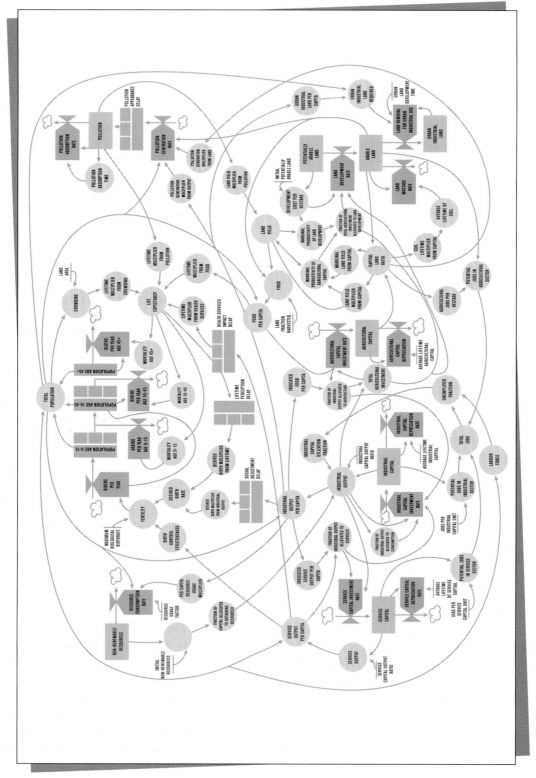

Source: This flow diagram is for the version of the world model published in 1972. The model has been revised to reflect recent data. It is analyzed in Donella Meadows, et al., *Limits to Growth: The 30-Year Update*, Chelsea Green Publishing, White River Junction, VT, 2004.

ecology sought to explain human spatial and temporal organization by concentrating on the dynamic processes of competition and succession that influence human social organization. Park and Burgess and their students concentrated on studying how Chicago's rapidly changing society physically accommodated increases in population and changes in the industrial and cultural organization of the city. Their approach, and that of their successors, was to focus on symbiosis, the dynamic interdependencies that bind people together in communities and lead to particular living arrangements.

In developing the concept of human ecology, Park was greatly influenced by Durkheim's *The Division of Labor in Society* (1964 [1893]). Durkheim addressed the development of social complexity from human population growth and density. As populations grow, the threat to available resources is crucial from a sociological viewpoint because it leads to competition and conflict. Problems of resource scarcity can therefore affect societal organization.

Durkheim's work was appealing to early human ecologists because of their interest in sustenance activities—the routine functions necessary to ensure the survival of a population from generation to generation (Hawley, 1950). Humans have a greater capacity for adapting to resource scarcity than any other organism, an ability labelled competitive co-operation. Adaptive responses include reductions in per capita consumption, increases in production through technology or more intensive resource exploitation, changes to distribution networks, and decreases in competition because of emigration from the community or an increased division of labour (Micklin, 1973; Schnore, 1958). Through such adaptive mechanisms, involving reciprocal cause-and-effect processes between the population and its vital resources, a state of equilibrium is reached. Park and Burgess (1921) postulated that competition and co-operation are the key forms of human exchange by which organized populations seek to maintain equilibrium within a dynamic environment.

Park and Burgess's theory underwent significant revision beginning in the mid-1950s to correct what are commonly regarded as major shortcomings: an overemphasis on the spatial arrangements of populations at the expense of understanding societal–environmental relations, and the neglect of culture and values (Dunlap and Catton, 1979a, 1979b; Hawley, 1981). Moreover, while highly influenced by the conceptual approaches and terminology

of ecology, early human ecologists concentrated on human social organization and patterns and did not include other species or aspects of the natural world in their analyses. They veered away, therefore, from a concern about environmental issues. During the 1950s, the ecological complex (Duncan and Schnore, 1959; Hawley, 1950), which viewed societies as being constituted of four interrelated dimensions—population, organization, environment, and technology (POET)—substantially revised the conceptual basis of human ecology. But even after this reformulation, human ecologists continued to use the concept of environment in socio-cultural, symbolic terms (Dunlap and Catton, 1983; Michelson, 1976).

● The Environment ● ● ● ● and Social Movements

Fascinated by the environmental movement from its inception, environmental sociologists continue to be deeply interested in it. The environmental movement has proven to be among the most successful and enduring social movements of all time; few other recent movements can match it in terms of sustained activity, size of following, and ability to affect the lives of so many people. It has even changed our language, with such terms as NIMBY ('not in my back yard') and 'environmentally-friendly product' entering the vernacular. The first Earth Day, staged 22 April 1970, was impressive, drawing some 20 million people (Dunlap and Gale, 1972), and Earth Day has since grown to become an international annual event—Earth Week, celebrated in 180 countries. Today few people admit to not supporting environmentalism; in fact, most people claim to be environmentalists (Dunlap, 1992). The environmental lobby, institutionalized as a significant player in government decision-making, is further evidence of the movement's impressive success.

The environmental movement has changed significantly over the years, often appearing to share little with its student-activist beginnings. The movement seems less angry today, but at the same time far more meticulous and deliberate in its approaches, often more at home in the corridors of power than on the protest line. The discussion that follows offers a look at the several strands of the contemporary environmental movement.

● Progressive   ● ● ● ● ● ●
Conposition
Conservation

Contemporary environmentalism traces its roots to the **progressive conservation** movement of the late-nineteenth-century United States (Fox, 1985; O'Riordan, 1971). Led by such reformers as Gifford Pinchot and John Muir, the founder of the Sierra Club, progressive conservation was a reaction against the unchecked destruction of nature during this period of freewheeling capitalism. The wanton environmental damage caused by private ownership of resources led to widespread public support for placing limits on the private use of land. Progressive conservation was instrumental in the creation of the national parks system in the United States, the increase of government control over public lands, and the founding of such conservation groups as the Sierra Club and the Audubon Society.

Reflecting a period in which science and technology were revered, progressive conservation sought to formulate and implement 'scientific management' of the environment. Two alternative science-based approaches to environmental management emerged. The preservationists, led by John Muir, advocated setting aside and protecting wilderness so that its natural, aesthetic, recreational, and scientific values could remain undisturbed for the benefit of future generations. Consumptive wildlife users, on the other hand, promoted conservation for utilitarian ends. Led by Pinchot and supported by President Theodore Roosevelt, this group wanted lands to be set aside mainly for recreational needs, but also for logging, mining, and grazing. American conservation policies in the early twentieth century tried to accommodate both sides of the debate through the creation of a liberal policy of greater government control over both private enterprise and public lands.

Mainstream Environmentalism

One legacy of the progressive conservation movement was the legitimation of government involvement in the economy and the environment. The responsibility for maintaining some balance between environmental preservation and economic growth is mainly the province of government planners and politicians. Hence, progressive conservation set the scene for the current relationship between business and government. The main beneficiaries of this policy are the large corporations, which, while gaining controlled access to resources, have paid little in resource rents. Some observers regard the sustainable development movement as a new expression of the principle of consumptive wildlife use. Meanwhile, the voices of the early preservationists, calling for environmental protection on moral, scientific, and aesthetic grounds, have largely gone unheard.

According to Robert Cameron Mitchell, Angela Mertig, and Riley Dunlap (1992), the other legacy of progressive conservation can be seen in the relationship between contemporary mainstream environmentalists and the government. Early preservationists quickly learned that they had to co-operate with the consumptive wildlife users and the Roosevelt administration or they would have little hope of making progress towards environmental protection. By now, environmentalists have become highly skilled at working as partners with government and developers in reaching compromise on environmental decisions. The inevitable result is trade-offs on preferred environmental solutions. Rik Scarce (1990: 15) reports that most environmental organizations admit to having no specific approach or plan for the environment other than saving what they can. Such 'muddling through' has resulted in some checks on development, but also in serious environmental losses. Rarely have the mainstream environmental groups been in a position to claim complete victory in their efforts to stop a development or save an ecosystem.

Contemporary mainstream environmentalism is increasingly in the form of inside lobbying, politicking, and consultation, and relies mainly on its well-organized bureaucracies for success (Mertig et al., 2002). The leaders tend to be highly educated environmental professionals, often having backgrounds in public administration or environmental law and holding permanent, salaried positions. Fundraising and research are essential to successful competition with large corporations over the fate of resources. The individual member is far more likely to write a cheque or the occasional letter to an elected representative than to take part in a sit-in or blockade.

Many mainstream environmentalists argue that it has only been through these increasingly well-organized, well-funded, professional organizations that environmental review and assessment have become a permanent part of economic planning. Critics such as William Devall (1992) have suggested, however, that these same organizations are too accommodating to development interests, their leaders too close to their opposite numbers in business and government and too secure in their professional status. Still others are critical of mainstream environmentalism in general, arguing that it has long suffered from elitism. Various writers have pointed out the middle- or upper-class origins and high educational levels of environmental leaders and members of mainstream environmental organizations

(Humphrey and Buttel, 1982; Morrison and Dunlap, 1986). However, supporters of the environmental movement—if not those actually involved in it—tend to be drawn widely from across the social class spectrum (Mertig and Dunlap, 2001). A related criticism levelled at mainstream environmentalism is that the programs or policies advocated may lead to reductions in resource-based jobs or even in wholesale plant closures because of the high costs of environmental regulation or the protection of a given wilderness area (Schnaiberg, 1975). Such economic events are likely to have the most adverse effects on the working class and the poor.

The New Ecologies

Mainstream environmentalism is one wing of the larger environmental movement, which includes various alternatives. The new ecologies are a range of approaches within environmentalism with a number of common features. First, they are critical of mainstream environmentalism for its failure to address ecological problems by taking into account the systems of dominance in social relations that help to create those problems. Inequality among nations and regions serves to enhance competition for scarce resources and thereby increases environmental harm. The new ecologies argue that central to solving environmental problems is the promotion of social equity and self-determination, which will allow peoples and nations to meet their human needs while maintaining ecological integrity (Gardner and Roseland, 1989).

Another distinguishing feature of the new ecologies, according to Nicholas Freudenberg and Carol Steinsapir (1992), is their devolved character. Hierarchical relations of authority between the membership and leaders, or between the branches of each organization, are rejected as being inconsistent with the prevailing thesis of human equality with nature rather than domination over it. This essentially ecocentric (and preservationist) stance is yet another characteristic of these groups, which tend to be sharply critical of any anthropocentric tendency to 'manage' the environment—an approach mainstream environmentalists seem all too willing to accept.

Finally, the new ecologies tend to outline specific principles for environmental reform consistent with their broad vision of the human–nature relationship, rather than simply muddling through. They are also far less willing than the mainstream to accommodate solutions in the interest of political and economic expediencies. Indeed, some radical arms of the new ecologies movement advocate the use of illegal, even violent, actions in order to win environmental disputes. While these radicals are in the minority, mainstream environmentalists

admit to having been helped by them in reaching compromises more favourable to the environment—they appear reasonable in comparison to the unbending demands and extremism of the radicals (Scarce, 1990).

Thus far, we have enumerated the similarities among the new ecologies. Now we look at three of these movements in order to highlight their differences.

Eco-feminism

Eco-feminism represents the partnership of ecology and feminism. It is founded mainly on mutual opposition to hierarchy and domination. Feminists argue that the subordination of women by men has been achieved through the ability of men to employ conceptual frameworks that place women at a disadvantage. According to Val Plumwood (1992), these include hierarchical frameworks that justify inequality; dualism, which justifies exclusion and separation; and rationality, which justifies logic and control. By advancing these three conceptual preferences, men have succeeded in legitimizing their domination over both women and nature.

The logic of domination holds that by virtue of the distinctiveness of men from nature and of men from women, together with the supposed greater rationality of men, the domination of men over both women and nature is 'reasonable'. In other words, eco-feminists argue that exactly the same male-controlled value system is used to justify both patriarchal human relations and the exploitation of nature.

Feminism and environmentalism connect, then, at the point of recognizing the similarities in the ways men treat women and nature. If one form of domination—of men over women—is wrong, then all forms of domination are wrong, including that of humans over nature. To be a feminist, therefore, compels one to be an environmentalist. Moreover, eco-feminists argue, inasmuch as environmentalists recognize and reject the domination of men over nature, they must also reject the domination of men over women. Therefore, all environmentalists must be feminists (Warren, 1990).

Social Ecology

Social ecology is a body of philosophical thought appealing to many in the contemporary environmental movement who are seeking to understand the interplay between humans and nature. Founder Murray Bookchin articulated this philosophy during nearly five decades until his death in 2006. Bookchin's conception of social ecology advances a holistic world view of the human–nature partnership, one based on community. Bookchin (1989) identifies the dualism and domination informing current human–nature relations as products of human ideology and culture through which society has come to be defined as distinct from and superior to nature. While he acknowledges that culture and technology do distinguish society from nature, Bookchin rejects the idea that they are separate. Rather, society springs from nature, reworking it into the human experience. Society always has a naturalistic dimension, and social ecology is largely involved with attempting to describe how both the connectedness and the divergences between society and nature occur. Appropriate technology, reconstruction of damaged ecosystems, and human creativity will combine with equity and social justice to produce an ecological society in which human culture and nature are mutually supportive and evolve together. Social ecology envisions a society in harmony with nature, combining human-scale sustainable settlement, ecological balance, community self-reliance, and participatory democracy. Social ecology is not the sole advocate of many of these objectives by any means, which are shared by various environmental schools of thought, including the writings of David Suzuki, Eurpoean Greens, and several branches of green political thought. What Bookchin's social ecology, along with these other schools, shows is how deeply philosophical various segments of the environmental movement are while seeking to establish an intellectual foundation for social change and environmental improvement.

Deep Ecology

Deep ecology is among the more intriguing of the new ecologies, as well as the most controversial. The name was coined in 1973 by Norwegian philosopher Arne Naess. Defining contemporary environmentalism as 'shallow' ecology, Naess (1973) argued that its advocacy of social reforms to curb problems of pollution and resource depletion identifies it as concerned mainly with protecting the health and affluence of the developed countries. By contrast, deep ecology is concerned with the root causes of environmental crisis and inspired by the understanding derived through personal experiences as humans in nature. The most distinctive aspect of deep ecology is its biocentric emphasis. Deep ecologists claim to hold all forms of life equally valuable, but at the same time raise non-human life forms beyond the human. Therefore, while deep ecology shares with the other new ecologies the rejection of anthropocentrism, it goes beyond the humanistic, ecocentric ecology of human–nature coexistence. Deep ecologists desire humans to have the least possible effect on the planet and respect ecological integrity above all else (Tokar, 1988).

Deep ecology also places heavy emphasis on self-realization, the extension of the environmentally conscious individual's self beyond his or her personal needs to include the environment as a whole. The idea that human insight and experience are enhanced by contact with nature follows logically from biocentrism.

Deep ecologists believe that an important practical consequence of self-realization is the obligation to strive actively to prevent environmental destruction. The emphasis on direct action has particularly inspired the best-known of the deep ecology groups, Earth First!, which advocates the use of whatever means are necessary to save wilderness areas. Earth First! has garnered much attention—and criticism—for the use of ecological sabotage ('ecotage'), that is, illegal force intended to block actions perceived as harming the environment (Taylor, 1991). 'Monkey wrenching'—disruption by such covert and unlawful means as removing survey stakes, destroying machinery, or spiking trees—is controversial even within Earth First! These tactics stand in sharp contrast with the more widely accepted civil disobedience strategies of other radical environmentalists. Civil disobedience involves public protest for a cause, and while the marches or blockades may result in the protestors' being charged with civil crimes, there is a strong commitment to non-violence.

Grassroots Environmentalism

While the roots of environmentalism date back to the preservationist movement of the nineteenth century, it was the publication of Rachel Carson's *Silent Spring* in 1962 that led to human health risks assuming significance along with conservation and preservation as environmental goals. The current era of environmentalism has increasingly focused on the dangers associated with industrial pollution and the occurrence of pollution sources in residential communities. Recent years have seen the emergence of new grassroots forms of environmentalism with this focus as their mandate.

The Toxic Waste Movement

The toxic waste movement is a branch of environmentalism unlike either the mainstream environmental movement or the new ecologies. On the one hand, the well-funded and organized mainstream environmental organizations, such as the Sierra Club, rely on professional leadership and a skilled staff, along with well-placed connections within the power structure, savvy insight into the political process, and a large public base of followers willing to provide financial support or to lend their voices to back a cause. On the other hand, the new ecologies are far less resourced but are inspired and maintained by the ideology and shared values of the members.

The toxic waste movement reflects few of the tendencies of either of these more general arms of the environmental movement. The movement is, in a sense, all the disputes and protests by myriad groups opposed to perceived environmental threats present in their own communities and neighbourhoods. Diffuse in its focus, the toxic waste movement is associated with all manner of protest against everything from proposed developments, such as a new landfill, factory, or highway, to those affected by pollution caused by an existing industry. What unites the toxic waste movement is a common focus on perceived health threats to the community. The movement is intrinsically grassroots in its composition and approach, constituted typically of groups of formerly uninvolved citizens now struggling in their cause to stop a development or clean up pollution while facing the efficient and well-funded opposition of industry and/or government.

The toxic waste movement may be the fastest-growing branch of environmentalism (Szasz, 1994) and in many ways it is far less distinguishable than the other types of environmentalism. For one thing, there is little in the way of national organizing bodies or even communication among the various local groups. This extreme decentralization means that local protestors have very few resources, outside of their own means, on which to draw in developing their plans of opposition. Mainstream environmental organizations typically employ professional social movement organizers in order to guide their agendas, but local toxic waste protestors rarely have the backgrounds or resources required to mount a well-managed and effective campaign. Valuable skills may be learned as the protest develops, but as these campaigns are often short-lived, such knowledge may not be passed on.

What is characteristic of the toxic waste movement is the high proportion of its members who are women and homemakers, minorities, and those from lower socioeconomic backgrounds (Brown and Masterson-Allen, 1994). Toxic waste activists also tend to be older, politically conservative, and trusting of existing institutions, laws, and regulations. The movement's high composition of women and homemakers is in keeping with its principal focus on preserving human health, especially that of children, in the face of an immediate threat from a nearby development or pollution source. These groups' membership is on average less educated than that found within mainstream environmentalism and the new ecologies, and their protests are more emotional than those of these other groups, which prefer to emphasize rational opposition based on scientific and legal evidence.

Unlike the new ecologies, ideology is not a prominent factor relating either to the formation or to the reasoning of toxic waste groups. Toxic waste activists are motivated by the presence of a nearby environmental threat and are conditioned by their experiences in responding to it. Initially apolitical and inexperienced in the art of protest, these activists have learned lessons at the hands of the authorities and corporations that compel a loss of innocence leading to personal transformations (Aronson, 1993). Along with bringing lifestyle and value changes, such personal reconsideration may also prompt new skepticism about the political process, along with mistrust of the authorities, business, and scientific experts.

Grassroots toxic waste protest is often dismissed as NIMBYism by those who disagree with its ends, and it is true that it often does appear that self-interest is an underlying motivation on which such protests are based. Nevertheless, if the threat is real, why should self-interest depreciate the legitimacy of the group's goal? It is also the case that a general increase within society in concerns over health risk from pollution and development is helping to move the toxic waste movement towards a more formally defined foundation of support and new allegiances. This is seen, for example, in connection with the general movement to supplant NIMBY with NIABY—'not in anyone's back yard'—indicative of the reduced emphasis on self-interest, as well as with LULU ('locally unwanted land uses'), reflective of the greater sensitivity to the broader public interest currently sought in the development of many municipal land-use plans (Freudenburg and Pastor, 1992).

Environmental Justice

Recently, another new grassroots movement, known as the **environmental justice** (EJ) movement, has emerged, with an agenda going beyond the traditional concerns of conservation and preservation common to most environmentalism. The EJ movement has ties to the toxic waste movement, but is also altering the focus of environmentalism generally to include broader concerns with regard to the societal inequities that result from industrial facility-siting and industrial development.

While the environmental movement has long been concerned with the risks to human health from industrial pollution, only recently has that awareness developed over the distributional risks associated with these effects. Various US studies have documented the inequitable distribution of environmental hazard (Bryant and Mohai, 1992; Bullard, 1990; Hofrichter, 1993), showing that, for the most part, people of low income and racial minorities are disproportionately being affected by poor environmental quality resulting from exposure to industrial pollution, workplace pollution, and contaminated water and lands. A similar finding for low-income people and the likelihood of exposure to contamination risk was found in a comparison of pollution sites across Toronto,

Hamilton, and Niagara Falls, Ontario (Nabalamba, 2001), and lower socio-economic status has often been found to be a prevalent condition within Canada's worst-polluted neighbourhoods.

Various explanations revolve around the processes that result in the inequitable distribution of environmental burdens. One position reflects economic or market dynamics, suggesting that 'sound' business decisions and the need to reduce costs may be grounds for locating potentially polluting industrial facilities (Kriesel et al., 1996; Oakes, 1996). It points to economic efficiency within the marketplace as the central criterion that guides what results as the unfair distribution of environmental risks to the poor. Industry's desire to minimize costs specifically associated with land or property values is seen as a major contributing factor to the disproportionate exposure to environmental pollutants. The suggestion is that this unequal risk occurs because cost-efficient industrial areas with low property values also are likely to be near areas with low residential property values or affordable housing and, therefore, a concentration of low-income populations.

Another rationale given for why the poor face greater pollution risk is the 'path of least resistance' argument (Higgins, 1994; Hofrichter, 1993). This suggests that low-income and minority communities end up with a disproportionate share of disposal and polluting industrial facilities and poor environmental quality in general because they have less political clout than the more affluent communities.

Finally, a more contentious explanation cites 'environmental racism' among private industry and government decision-makers as being behind the disparities found in the uneven distribution of polluting industrial facilities (Bryant and Mohai, 1992; Bullard, 1994). This position draws largely on interpretations of evidence from the United States that show race to be a major factor in who is likely to be exposed to pollution risk. Hence, it is concluded that when race stands out as being significantly associated with the location of new disposal and polluting industrial facilities, it is racism that is influencing the decision-making process

● Conclusion

The history of the human population can be subdivided into two broad stages: a very long period of slow growth, from the beginning of humankind to about 1750, followed by a relatively recent phase of explosive growth. As a legacy of the population explosion that took place in the modern era and that continues in many develop-ing countries, the world faces challenges heretofore unforeseen in the history of humanity.

Three demographic trends seem inevitable over the course of this new century: the population of the world will become older; the developing countries will grow much more than the developed countries; and there will be intense pressure on highly industrialized countries to accommodate an even larger share of immigrants from developing countries than they do currently. The implications of this eventuality will be far-reaching: with increased immigration, the highly industrialized receiving nations will become even more racially and ethnically heterogeneous. Given its relatively long history of immigration and its multicultural orientation, Canada seems well positioned to deal with this reality. For the countries that are relatively new immigrant-receiving societies in Western Europe (many of which until recently were sending nations), the adjustment process to this emerging reality poses difficult challenges. Their conceptions of nationhood may need to be modified in view of the changing racial and ethnic composition of their societies.

Cities are not immutable structures with predictably deterministic effects on human beings. They are a part of societies and of social changes, and are a reflection of people's conscious actions. Cities may be large and complex, but—for good or for ill—they are subject to human agency and organization. In many respects, cities mirror on an impressive scale the interacting agendas of individuals, groups, cultures, and nations. As in other areas of sociological inquiry, analysis and research help clarify what goes on around us and provide a basis for shaping contexts and structures in useful ways. It remains for everyone to benefit from such knowledge by taking conscious steps for the common good.

Either societies will change to achieve environmental integrity, or they will be changed by environmental contamination and resource depletion. Social change on behalf of the environment is therefore one of the most pressing global issues.

If sociology can be said to make one substantial contribution to the understanding of ecological crisis, it is the recognition that environmental problems are social products. This understanding goes beyond descriptions of how individuals or firms contribute to environmental degradation, and the solutions suggested involve more than promoting more environmentally responsible behaviours or technologies. While such approaches may help deal with an immediate situation, they ultimately do more harm than good by deflecting attention from the real roots of environmental problems and the discovery of long-term solutions. In short, social systems must change in order that global disaster may be averted. What this chapter has illustrated, as dramatically as any in the book, is the remarkable, inescapable relationship between finite human individuals, their enduring, collectively created environment, and their often taken-for-granted natural environment. Sociologists must never forget that human systems and the environments in which they are nested all disappear in the end, but they have different life trajectories and all influence one another. All living things are also dying things whose survival and decline are inextricably connected on Planet Earth. Humans, despite their grand achievements—of which cities rank among the grandest—cannot escape this fact.

● Questions ● ● ● ● ● ●
for Critical Thought

1. Describe how populations change. What are the demographic components of change?

2. What is atypical about the current stage of the demographic history of the world? Describe the relationship of demographic transition to the history and projected future of the human population. Are there any certainties about the future population of the world?

3. Assess the theories of Malthus and Marx on current population and its relationship to issues concerning resources and the environment. Discuss how contemporary perspectives on population relate to the Malthusian and Marxist theories of population.

4. Environmental sociologists argue that ecological problems are social problems; that is, they exist because of the nature of social arrangements and social organization. Discuss this idea by selecting one or more environmental problems and suggesting how they might have been avoided or reduced if alternative social arrangements had existed.

5. The concept of sustainable development is central to much economic planning, but its critics often argue that it is used mainly as a rationale for allowing more economic growth at the expense of the environment. Can economic growth and environmental quality coexist? Is sustainable development the answer?

● Recommended ● ● ● ● ●
Readings

Frank Trovato, *Canada's Population in a Global Context: An Introduction to Social Demography* (Toronto: Oxford University Press, 2008).

This introduction to social demography—its concepts, measures, and theories—focuses on both Canada and the international demographic scene.

Lyn H. Lofland, *The Public Realm: Exploring the City's Quintessential Social Territory* (New York: Aldine de Gruyter, 1998).

Lyn Lofland is one of the leading students of urbanism. In this book, she examines in a thorough and engaging way how people adapt to urban spaces.

Mathis Wackernagel and William Rees, *Our Ecological Footprint: Reducing Human Impact on the Earth* (Gabriola Island, BC: New Catalyst, 1996).

This book introduces the metaphor of the ecological footprint, a term used to refer to the productive land needed in order to sustain different lifestyles.

● Recommended ● ● ● ●
Websites

Earth Day Network Ecological Footprint Quiz
http://www.earthday.net/footprint/index.html

A number of websites allow the online calculation of your ecological footprint, that is, the amount of productive land needed to sustain an individual's lifestyle. This one from the Earth Day organization calculates your ecological footprint based on information you provide on your consumption, housing, and travel patterns.

United Nations Population Division
www.unpopulation.org

The *United Nations Demographic Yearbook* contains a wealth of demographic information by country. Another key product from the United Nations is the *Human Development Report*.

Chapter

Globalization and Social Change

Satoshi Ikeda

Learning Objectives

In this chapter, you will:

▶ study how globalization happened as a historical process;

▶ examine corporate domination under globalization;

▶ examine your involvement in globalization as both a victim and a culprit;

▶ examine negative consequences of globalization on nature, society, and economy; and

▶ learn about the emerging alternatives to corporate domination.

● Introduction ● ● ● ● ● ●

Economic globalization is a result of globalized corporate activities, and the degree of our dependence on these corporations has increased enormously in recent years. Consider the following: corporations provide employment opportunities, goods and services, and investment venues. In order to sell their goods and services, the corporation uses advertisement. Branding is a key component to successful advertisement, and through branding the corporation influences our value system and manipulates and creates personal identity. In this sense, the corporation creates culture. People all over the world come under the influence of consumer culture at a young age. As children reach school-age, corporate logos (such as Nike and Gap) become important attributes for social stratification. Representation of social status through consumption relies heavily upon corporate brands and logos. The corporation defines our aspiration, leads our life, and tells us who we are. Corporate power is also apparent in media and politics. Corporate sponsorship is the major source of revenue for mass media corporations including cyber media, and corporate associations have huge influence on policy decisions. Also, corporate greed for short-term financial gain led to a global financial crisis in 2008 that is developing into a global economic recession/depression.

As the term 'global village' aptly expresses, globalization is a process of spreading the awareness that societies are connected and share a common fate. For example, global warming is just one of the issues that stimulate our imagination of connectedness and that stir our passion to take action. Our economy is heavily dependent on fossil fuel, and our lifestyle and growing economy contribute to greenhouse gas emissions, which are the primary cause of global warming. Corporations do not take the environment into consideration unless the law requires them to do so. Furthermore, economists encourage continued growth regardless of ecological consequences. As a result, the majority of people remain ignorant of the ecological impact of their consumption. The existing political and economic system deprives the majority of the population the right to participate in important political and economic decision-making. While the economy is globalized, there is not a global government or the global civil society to check the global corporation. A democratic society gives its citizens sovereign rights and holds the elected officials accountable under the constitution. How can we, as Canadians, create a global civil society before we destroy our eco-system irretrievably?

The emergence of the global economy challenges the conventional understanding of our society and our existence as the political, economic, and social beings. This chapter provides information on the historical process of globalization and also challenges readers to investigate their involvement in globalization both as victims and culprits. It calls for personal reflection of their roles in global corporate domination and asks what we as individuals can do to change the existing system, and how we can overcome isolation in the marketplace by reclaiming the society. First we will review how globalization came about and its historical characteristics. Then we will discuss the changes in our society, particularly how corporate domination influences our sense of who we are and how we relate to each other and with the environment. Lastly, we will investigate the emerging social movements that strive to create better futures for the majority of humanity.

● The World-System Perspective ● ● ●

The **world-system perspective** offers a way of thinking about society that is different from conventional sociology (Wallerstein, 2004). First, this perspective challenges the separation of social science from political science (the study of the state, or the institution of governance including parliament, cabinet, judiciary, and influential groups), economics (the study of the market), sociology (the study of the society), and anthropology (the study of non-European people in the beginning, people in general later). As the phenomenon of globalization shows, economic, political, and social elements are integral and cannot be compartmentalized into disciplinary boxes. The story of globalization needs to be told by incorporating various aspects of our social reality, including economical, political, and ecological impacts.

Secondly, this perspective understands the world economy to be a historical system that covers all countries and peoples, as opposed to seeing the world economy as a collection of national economies. Even before the formation of a global economy, the world-system researchers insisted that the trajectory of one country could not be explained without placing it in a global and historical framework.

Thirdly, the world-system perspective proposes a zonal structure of 'core–semiperiphery–periphery' as a device to understand the unequal relations among the countries. The world-economy does not give 'peripheral' countries much opportunity to develop, grow, or accumulate resources. Periphery implies the marginalized position in the world-economy, and the peripheral countries are the poorer countries, often referred to as developing countries or the Global South. In this chapter we will use the term 'periphery' to refer to these countries instead of 'developing', because they are not developing along the prescribed development paths. They are constrained by the world-systemic relationality with the core, and their 'development' has been 'dependent development' (Frank, 1978). The 'core' countries are the richer countries, often referred to as developed countries or the Global North. They include the West European countries, the United States, Canada, Australia, New Zealand, and Japan. These countries continue to gain from the world-system's division of labour. There is also an in-between category to be considered: semiperiphery. The examples of the semiperipheral countries in the post-World War II period include Korea and Taiwan. These countries succeeded in elevating their status out of the ranks of the peripheral countries, but they could not change their subordinate relations with the core. When we use the term core or periphery, we are referring to the unequal relations among the countries in the capitalist world-system.

Lastly, the world-system perspective insists on relational understanding as opposed to individualistic understanding. Be it personal, social, or national, we tend to identify these 'units' based on their intrinsic or internal characteristics. The world-system perspective sees an individual, a society, or a nation as a relational being with other individuals, societies, and nations. In a capitalist society, the result of competition is accepted based on the assumption that everyone has equal opportunity. In reality, not everyone, or every company, that enters into competition has the same footing. The chance of success depends on one's relation with others.

● Historical Process ● ● ●
of Globalization

Prior to the 1980s, a Canadian company would have produced goods to be sold mainly in Canada and to be exported to the US and Europe. The Canadian economy was closely linked with the US economy through trade and finance but economic interaction among the countries became increasingly transborder and global beginning in the 1980s. A manufacturer of footwear, for example, compares the cost and benefit of operating in a diverse array of countries before deciding where its plant will be located. In order to maximize profit, the company will consider worldwide distribution of the products, rather than being limited to a single country market. Recently, Canadian companies, such as lululemon athletica and Roots, which began their operations in Canada, have expanded the scope of their operations globally. Investment decisions also became global as financial markets in many countries were opened. Although this globalization process seemingly took place in the 1980s, it began much earlier.

Nineteenth-Century Structure of Accumulation and Its Limitations

In the nineteenth century the world was composed of imperialist countries, such as the United Kingdom, France, Russia, and the US, and their official and unofficial (nominally independent) colonies in Asia, Africa, and Latin America. Industrial factory production became the key for capitalist activities. The champion of industrialization was the UK with cotton manufacturing as its leading industry. The production and sales of cotton involved a division of labour that spanned the entire world. Raw cotton produced in the American South by the slaves was exported to UK cotton factories. The factory workers attended machines that ginned (removed the seeds), spun raw cotton into yarn, and wove yarn into cloth. The wages paid to the workers in general were quite low and their small income prevented the growth of the domestic market within the UK. This made it necessary for the cotton industry to find markets overseas; the market they found existed in wealthy Asian countries, such as India and China. Before industrialization, Europe was relatively poor compared to Asia (Frank, 1998). Europeans imported Asian products such as cotton, silk, tea, sugar, and porcelain, but Asians did not find much use for European goods, such as woolen textiles. Europeans settled this trade deficit by shipping silver, which came from Spanish America. Outflow of silver from Europe limited the expansion of the European economies because the silver

▌▌ Time to Reflect ▌▐▌▐▌▐▌▐▌▐▌▐▌▐▌▐▌▐▌▐▌▐▌▐▌▐▌▐▌▐

Does the world-system perspective and the notion of 'periphery' alter your previous assumptions about different countries and their rate of success or failure in the market economy?

was the key monetary medium. The British colonization of India in the seventeenth century enabled the British to collect taxes that complemented silver exports, but the British trade deficit continued until they started exporting manufactured cotton. Cotton exports to India increased throughout the nineteenth century, and transformed the country from the producer of fine hand-woven cotton cloths to the exporter of raw cotton and importer of factory-made British cotton cloths.

This inter-continental division of labour and cross-oceanic distribution network was the key characteristic of the nineteenth century structure of accumulation, but it suffered from three major limitations (Ikeda, 2002). The first was the limit of place and people that could be colonized. Once all the territories and peoples beyond Europe were colonized, intense competition among the imperial powers ensued. The US became an independent country in the late eighteenth century after colonial settlers gained power against the UK. American industrialization was accompanied by westward expansion of the Union through commercial deals and warfare. Japan was the only non-European country that emerged as an imperialist country after escaping the fate of colonization. The US forced Japan to open for trade in the middle of the nineteenth century. After military unification and state-led industrialization, Japan emerged as an imperialist power in East Asia.

These imperialist countries competed for raw material and markets. The American Civil War, in a sense, was an inter-imperialist war between the British and the industrialists in the American North. For the expansion of cotton industry, the industrialists in the northern states needed raw cotton from the southern states that had been exported to the UK; the victory of the Union force allowed the industrialists in the American North to secure raw cotton from the South. The race for the colonies for raw material and market intensified toward the end of the nineteenth century into the twentieth century. When the entire extra-European world was colonized, the competition turned into inter-imperialist military confrontation that ended in two world wars in the twentieth century.

The second contradiction involved the exploitation of the workers in the imperial homelands. From the coal mines to cotton factories, working conditions were horrible and wages were low throughout Europe. Karl Marx and Friedrich Engels analyzed the contradiction of capitalism and identified that workers' class struggle would lead to a communist revolution to end capitalist exploitation (Marx and Engels 1998). Marx and Engels gave direction to the working class movement, and the workers in Europe struggled to obtain the right to participate in the political system, to unionize, and to strike against the factory owners. The ruling capitalist class responded to workers movements with 'carrots' (participation in political system through expanded franchise for working class males) and 'sticks' (anti-union legislations). As predicted by Marx, the capitalist system experienced the cycles of economic boom and bust, and the depth of recession increased toward the end of the nineteenth century, encouraging worker's movement for socialism.

The third limitation came from the rising resistance of the colonized people against the politico-military and economic subordination. As colonial rule expanded to cover the entire extra-European world and the colonial exploitation of the resources and peoples deepened, the resistance to colonialism spread and intensified. There existed resistance at the time of initial colonization, but it was stopped with force. As colonial rule deepened, however, the existing socio-economic arrangement was disrupted because the colonies were transformed to serve the interest of the imperial homeland. For example, heavy taxation made it necessary for the colonized people to engage in cash-earning activities. Small land-holdings by peasants were replaced by large-scale plantations, creating a situation in which a few landowners benefited from colonial export activities while the mass of landless peasants had to earn meager cash income as hired workers. Resentment toward the colonial master and his local compradors mounted as a result. The emancipation rhetoric of Marxism influenced the leaders of anti-colonial movements, and these movements often resorted to violent action, thus increasing the cost of maintaining colonial rule for the imperialist countries.

Three Twentieth-Century Revolutions

The limitations of the nineteenth century structure of accumulation continued into the first half of the twentieth century, leading to three revolutions (Ikeda, 2002). The first revolution was the socialist revolution in Russia. The Russian state was challenged by the widespread strike during the Russo–Japan war (1905) and World War I (1914–1919) due to massive mobilization of national resources that left the general population in misery. The socialists succeeded in taking control of the state in 1917, and after repression of the opposition, the USSR (Union of Soviet Socialist Republics) was established in 1922. The birth of a socialist state gave momentum to working class movements all over the world, but it was in the US where the capitalist solution for workers' demand for improved living conditions was prepared. Henry Ford, in the 1910s, guaranteed a one-dollar-a-day wage; this wage was sufficient to support a family with single income and would allow the worker to purchase the very product he produced. This idea was later conceptualized by the researchers of the French Regulation School as Fordism, or the Fordist regime of accumulation (Aglietta, 1979; Lipietz, 1987). By giving workers a good wage, the workers' zeal for socialist revolution was replaced by the desire to work within capitalism. Furthermore, rising wages allowed capitalist enterprises to sell their products within the US. The expansion of territories in the US from its independence provided rising consumer and investment demand in the nineteenth century, but the spread of the Fordist wages created the domestic market for the emerging heavy and chemical industries.

Another problem of capitalism was the deepening crisis that accompanied violent business cycles. John Maynard Keynes (1936) criticized the prevailing liberal economists who insisted on no government intervention in the market. Keynes introduced the idea of financial regulation and government intervention in order to alleviate the negative impact of economic recession using government spending and controlling the interest rate. During the 1930s, when the world economy suffered from the Great Depression, Franklin Roosevelt introduced the New Deal as a policy to use government spending to assist the unemployed, together with the regulation of finance and business activities. The new roles of the government—active intervention in business and finance, together with the use of government spending to alleviate recession—was exactly what Keynes believed would correct the problems of nineteenth-century liberal capitalism. Together with Fordism, which challenged exploitative low wages, economic management of the Keynesian policies modified the nineteenth-century liberal economics. The Fordist-Keynesian revolution gave a new life to capitalism (Aglietta, 1979).

This Keynesian-Fordist revolution solved one of the key limitations of imperialism—the reliance on colonial markets. By creating an expanding domestic market, the US corporations had less need to sell abroad as compared to other imperialist countries. This Keynesian-Fordist structure of accumulation, however, still required colonies for resources. The US secured resources through direct rule or the establishment of puppet regimes, as in Latin America and the Philippines, and the demand for equal access to colonies held by other imperialist countries, such as Japan. Gallagher and Robinson (1953) characterized this US-style imperialism as 'the imperialism of free enterprise' (see also Arrighi, 1994); this feature of US imperialism continues today. The Keynesian-Fordist structure of accumulation was adopted by other imperialist powers only after their empires were dismantled. After World War II, the USSR and other imperialist countries, except for the US, were left in ruins and the US-led reconstruction of the post-World War II order dismantled the trade barriers erected around the empires. While imperialists were busy battling against one another in two World Wars, the colonial resistance movement escalated into a colonial independence movement.

After the Second World War, the devastation of imperial homelands made it difficult for the imperialist countries to continue a physical rule over their colonies, and many Asian colonies gained independence as a result. The exception to this was Vietnam. After France, the former colonial ruler left, the US continued military intervention for fear of communist expansion. The Vietnamese people finally became independent in 1975, after the US pulled out in 1973 and the US-propped South Vietnam was defeated by North Vietnam. Most African countries also achieved independence in the 1950s after winning battles against imperialist powers. Colonial empires such as the UK, France, Germany, and Japan were dismantled and the US accepted the Philippines' independence. With the revolution of colonial independence, the age of colonial empires came to an end.

National Economic Development, 1950s–1970s

The three revolutions of the twentieth century created a structure of accumulation based on national economic development, beginning in the 1950s and lasting to the 1970s. The former imperialist countries, including Germany and Japan, received US aid under the American anti-communist policies, in order to recover from the devastation of World War II. They undertook national economic development policies that followed the Keynesian-Fordist model. Domestic industries and companies were promoted with protection against imports, government subsidies, and restriction on international financial flows (to take-over domestic companies). The working class movements turned into strong socialist movements at the end of the Second World War but these movements were repressed with police force. The workers were incorporated into the national development project with rising wages and improved living standards, and company unions that were cooperative to business replaced the militant unions that demanded socialist revolution. On the other hand, the East European countries that were 'emancipated' by the USSR toward the end of World War II established socialist governments and launched a socialist national development project. (For an overview of national economic development, see McMichael, 2004).

During the Cold War—the confrontation that existed without direct military confrontation between the US and USSR—capitalists and socialists competed for national economic development. On the west end of the socialist block, West Germany rebuilt its economy and military with US funds to shield the Eastern block. In China the People's Liberation Army, led by Mao Zedong, unified the country in 1947 by pushing the US-backed Chiang Kai-shek and his Kuomintang army to Taiwan; the People's Republic of China was born in 1948. The Korean peninsula was divided into the USSR-occupied north and the USA-occupied south. The socialist regime established in the north—the People's Democratic Republic of Korea (or North Korea)—invaded the south—the Republic of Korea (South Korea)—in 1950. After three-year war, North Korea was pushed back to the original demarcation line. The US attempted to contain communism to the east-end of socialist block (USSR, China, PDRK) by supporting economic development in the anti-communist regimes of Japan, South Korea, and Taiwan.

National economic development in the post-World War II period was supported by the liberal international economic order that promoted international trade. The framework for international economic management was negotiated among the allied countries (US, UK, France, Russia, etc.) that fought against the axis powers (Germany, Japan, and Italy). The resulting international economic framework was the **Bretton Woods System**, named after the town where the conference was held in 1944. This system is based on four pillars (Gowan, 1999; Helleiner, 1994). The first pillar was the dollar-gold standard with a fixed exchange rate for the international currency exchange arrangement. Until then, each country pegged the currency value to gold under the gold standard system. Imbalance in trade was settled by the physical shipment of gold, but gold was serving as the basis of domestic money supply, and a country running a trade deficit was unwilling to send gold abroad because a decline in gold stock would mean a reduction in currency circulating in the economy, which in turn would bring on economic slowdown. To avoid this situation, countries devalued their currency until it became impossible to maintain the gold standard system. Without a stable system of currency exchange, it became difficult to settle international trade. This was one of the reasons why inter-imperialist war broke out. At the Bretton Woods conference, the US proposed a system of pegging currencies to the US dollar (a fixed exchange rate) and pegging the US dollar to gold ($35 for one ounce of gold) with a promise that US would give up gold for dollars upon request. Despite opposition from the UK, who sent Keynes to the conference with the idea of international joint management of currency value, the dollar-gold standard system was adopted. The US obtained the seigniorage—the right to print money and spend abroad—because they could run a trade deficit (imports exceeding exports) as long as the surplus country is willing to accept the US dollar for settlement.

The second pillar of the Bretton Woods System was the **International Monetary Fund** (IMF). The member countries contributed to the fund with their currencies and US dollars (or gold). When a country faced a balance of payments problem (like the country's foreign currency reserve was insufficient to cover payment obligation to other countries), the Fund provided short-term relief money. The Fund expanded its member contribution to create more liquidity (money to lubricate international trade). But, the IMF is not a democratic institution. Member countries have the voting power depending on their contribution to the fund, and the US maintains the largest share that gives them vetoing power.

The third pillar of the Bretton Woods System was the **General Agreement on Tariffs and Trade** (GATT). This is a multilateral agreement to promote free trade through tariff reduction and the elimination of non-tariff barriers (such as quantitative restriction and the laws that give advantage to domestic players).

The fourth pillar was the International Bank for Reconstruction and Development (IBRD) that later became the **World Bank**. (The International Development Association joined the World Bank in 1960.) This bank supplied funds for European reconstruction in early years, but since then the bank has funded development projects in the newly independent countries, together with the regional development banks such as the African Development Bank. Like the IMF, the World Bank is not a democratic institution even though it is placed in the United Nations framework. The director of the World Bank is nominated by the US and all of the directors so far have been Americans (the director of the IMF was chosen from the European countries). The development projects funded by the World Bank were mainly for infrastructure development (construction of roads, ports, dams, and power plants) in the peripheral countries so that they could continue exporting the primary commodities just like they did in the colonial period.

The US enjoyed economic advantage after World War II because of the war devastation in Europe and Japan. This advantage, however, eroded as the West European countries promoted domestic industry under a tariff union called the European Economic Community (established in 1958; later developed into European Union), and Japan with industrial protection/promotion policies. The US war in Vietnam caused a mushrooming US trade deficit and the demand by the creditor countries (France, in particular) to demand gold for US dollar. President Richard Nixon unilaterally declared the end of gold-dollar convertibility in 1971. The pressure on the fixed exchange rate system continued as West European currencies and the Japanese yen gained strength against the US dollar. The fixed exchange was abandoned in 1973, and since then the value of the major currencies is determined in the foreign exchange market. The first pillar of the Bretton Woods System was abandoned in the early 1970s.

The US achieved a great social transformation in the 1960s (Gilbert, 1989). The civil rights movement from 1950s to the 1960s and the feminist movement in the 1960s raised the status of disenfranchised ethnic Americans and women. The Great Society policy of Democratic President Lyndon B. Johnson included numerous welfare state provisions including civil rights, war on poverty, education, health, culture, consumer protection, etc. Unintended consequences of the policy, however, included rising wages that squeezed corporate profitability, particularly in the labour-intensive manufacturing sectors. American corporations started closing operations in the US and either moved their operations to cheap-labour countries such as Taiwan and Korea or became contractors who purchased manufactured goods from companies already working in cheap-labour countries. The Johnson government also raised taxes to finance welfare programs and the Vietnam War, and this made the US an unattractive place for business. Furthermore, twin deficits—the government budget and the trade deficit—weakened the US dollar and resulted in inflation. These problems eroded the US economy; Richard Nixon succeeded Johnson in 1971, and implemented drastic measures to counter these problems including price control, discontinuation of dollar-gold convertibility, and the end of the Vietnam War. These policies, however, were ineffective to stop the rise of rival countries such as West Germany and Japan. However, the fundamental shift that eventually led to globalization came from an unexpected place, the Middle East.

After the proclamation of the State of Israel in 1948, Israel fought repeated wars with the neighbouring Arab countries. The Fourth Arab–Israel War, also known as Yom Kippur War, in 1973, triggered the imposition of an oil embargo, as punishment for their support of Israel, by the oil-producing Arabic countries. The oil-producing countries formed the Organization of Petroleum Exporting Countries (OPEC) in 1965 to negotiate better deals with the major oil companies (from the US, the UK, and Holland), but their power was restricted until 1973 when Saudi Arabia—the largest crude oil exporter in the world—restricted oil export to the pro-Israel core countries (the US, West European countries, and Japan). The embargo forced some of the oil importing countries to stop supporting Israel, but the most important impact was the tidal effect of a tripling of oil prices, which was known as the 1973 Oil Shock, on the world economy.

A restricted oil supply caused a global energy shortage. The world economy entered a recession; energy prices increased and triggered a sudden increase in production and transportation costs. Many countries experienced 'stagflation', a mix of stagnation and inflation. Most seriously affected were the people in the oil-importing peripheral countries, such as Bangladesh, that faced difficulty in exporting goods to the core countries in the middle of recession while their energy bill skyrocketed. Among core countries, Japan came out of stagflation first because of its less-energy dependent economy and the strength of exports (especially small-size energy efficient automobiles). The oil-exporting countries, on the other hand, enjoyed a sudden increase in revenue from petroleum export, and this money played a critical role in both the Third World debt problem in the 1980s and the eventual arrival of globalization. Oil money was deposited in US-dollar bank accounts in Europe that were out of US regulatory control. The banks loaned the money to the Third World countries such as South Korea, Brazil, and Mexico, to finance their industrialization projects in the form of short-term loans that would be renewed on the condition that the interest was paid. It was easy for the borrowing countries to keep up with their payment obligations as long as the interest rate was kept low. Low interest rates, however, did not last long.

Until the 1970s, the economists in the core countries were dominated by Keynesians who believed in the effectiveness of government intervention to regulate the economy. The principle was that, through the manipulation of interest rate and government expenditure, it was possible to achieve full employment. But the stagflation that plagued the US and other economies beginning in 1973 discredited the effectiveness of Keynesian policy. The cause of the inflation was the increase in oil prices (supply side), and this was not in the Keynesian model. In the middle of defunct Keynesianism, there emerged the Chicago School, led by Milton Freedman, who insisted on a small government and minimalist policy intervention, an economic prescription called neo-liberalism.

They were called Monetarists because their major policy instrument was the control of money supply to combat inflation. The objective of US economic policy changed in late 1970s from full-employment to inflation control, and the Federal Reserve Board (the American version of the central bank) raised the interest rate from 6 per cent in 1978 to 13 per cent in 1980. The result was a recession in the early 1980s, which occurred in conjunction with the impact of another oil price hike in 1979.

The unexpected consequence of this policy change was the Third World debt problem. The countries that borrowed Eurodollar to finance their development projects were counting on the export of the products to pay back the loans. This expectation was dashed by the 1979 Oil Shock that was triggered by the Iranian Revolution, which had ousted the US-friendly Shah's regime and disrupted oil exports from Iran. The economies of the world again entered into recession between 1980 and 1982. The borrowing countries faced a serious problem; they could not earn income because of recession but their payment obligation mushroomed because of interest hikes. The situation was bleak for many borrowing countries. Mexico announced in 1982 that it would not be able to pay the interest on time, and the Third World debt crisis ensued. This was the beginning of the end of the national development project for the peripheral countries and the beginning of globalization based on neo-liberal policy. (For a more detailed discussion of the transition from national economic development to globalization, see Gowan, 1999; Harvey, 2006; and McMichael, 2004.

Neo-liberalism and Globalization, 1980s–1990s

The accumulated debt of the Third World countries became a serious issue in the 1980s (see Fig. 17.1). The blame was placed on the borrowers, and economists rarely mentioned the responsibility of the lender. When the debtor countries became unable to pay interest, the US government reformulated the IMF and World Bank into debt collectors and enforcers of neo-liberal policies. The original loans were issued by US and European private banks. In order to help the banks that faced a potential default (borrowers become bankrupt), the US government ordered the IMF and World Bank to 'rescue' these private banks by buying up the bad loans from them. The borrower was prohibited to default, not like consumer debt that is usually cleared in the event of default with a penalty of low credit rating. The IMF/World Bank offered the structural adjustment loans (the shorter term loans by the IMF and the project-

base, long-term loans by the World Bank) to the debtor country to pay back the original loans. This rescued the private banks, but the debtor countries were forced to pay back the new structural adjustment loans over many years. The condition attached to the structural adjustment loan was that the debtor country had to accept the **Structural Adjustment Programs** (SAPs) that were supposed to 'rehabilitate' the debtor country. (For an analysis of this process, see McMichael, 2004.)

The SAPs followed the prescription of neo-liberalism as the foundation of economic management. The countries that accepted the Structural Adjustment Programs had to devalue their exchange rate, allegedly to promote export, so that the country could earn foreign exchange to pay back the loans. They had to raise interest rates to attract foreign capital inflow; privatize government enterprises to promote efficiency by ending government monopoly; eliminate subsidies, including food subsidies, so that the price signal would work properly; cut back government spending so that the government could save money to repay debt; eliminate regulations on corporate activities to attract foreign corporations; and liberalize financial sectors to attract foreign investment. These measures were not designed to help economic development of the debtor country. Instead, their objectives were to make the debtor country earn foreign exchange and to generate government surplus so that the debt would be paid at any cost. The debt collectors did not care what happened after they got their money. The SAPs brought economic devastation and social degradation to the peripheral countries. Currency devaluation meant an increase in import prices that caused input price increases for the industry and rising consumer prices for the household. Moreover it did not increase income from exports because other indebted countries also devalued currencies. The debt collector told every indebted country to export more, which created an oversupply of primary commodities.

The end result was the deterioration of the terms of trade for the peripheral countries. Interest rate increases did not attract foreign investment to expand production in the periphery. Instead, higher interest rates choked the domestic economic activities; it became difficult to borrow money to sustain business. Privatization of government enterprises was supposed to increase government revenues and reduce government spending to support corporations. The net impact of the privatization was the take-over of the privatized companies by the foreign corporations at a bargain price because of the devalued currency. Instead of correcting market distortion by eliminating monopolies, privatization allowed

Figure 17.1 Peripheral Debt by Regions (Billions, Current USD)

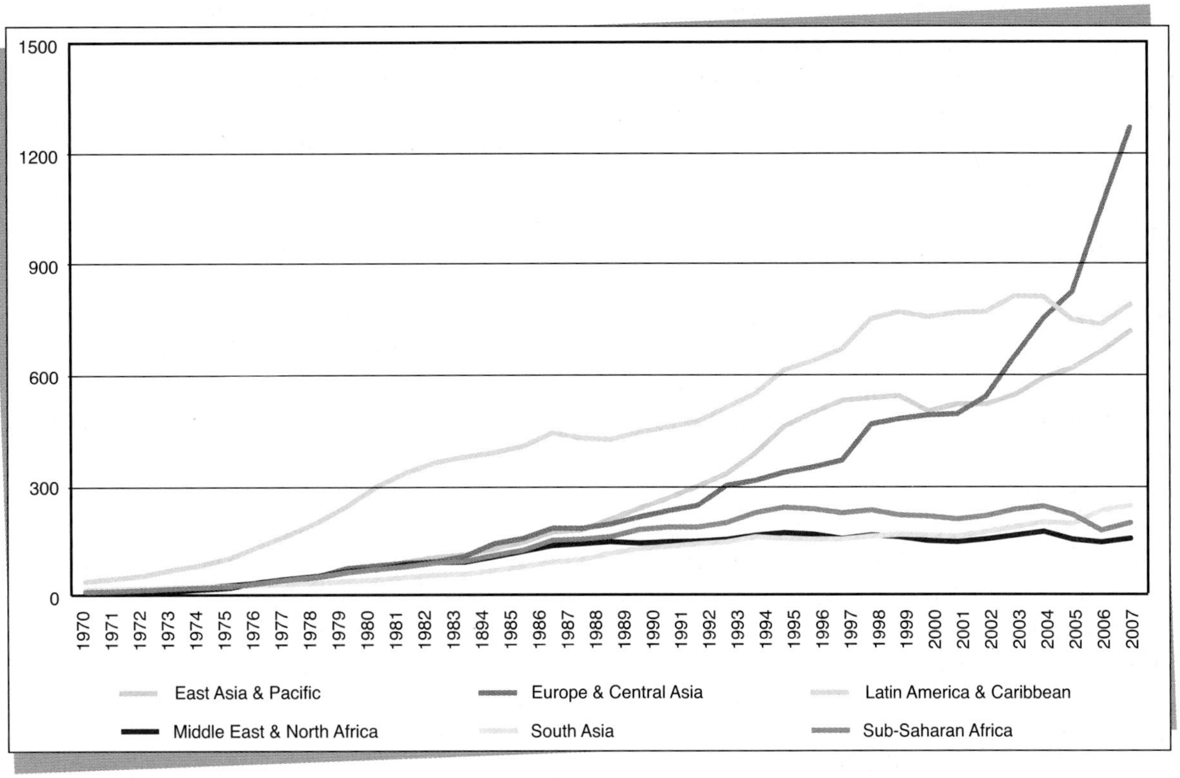

Source: World Bank, World Development Indicators (electronic resource)

Note: Europe and Central Asia is composed mainly of the former socialist countries.

Interpretation: The peripheral debt increased in the 1980s and 1990s. After the fall of communism in 1989/1990, the former socialist countries became the major borrowers, particularly in the 2000s, followed by East Asia & Pacific and South Asia. The total debt is stagnant in the 2000s for Latin America & Caribbean, Sub-Saharan Africa, and Middle East & North Africa.

the giant foreign company to continue exploiting monopolies. Elimination of subsidies, particularly food subsidies, resulted in food riots because the general population faced the sudden loss of purchasing power as a result of rising food prices. A reduction in government spending was done at the cost of education and health, a blow to the weakest strata of the country. Deregulation led to a harsher exploitation of nature and humans because corporations, particularly the foreign corporations, became free from working condition regulations and environmental protection laws. Financial sector liberalization usually led to the wholesale takeover of banks and leading corporations in the peripheral countries. The global corporations, including banks from the core countries, enjoyed the newly-opened peripheral country economies and pillaged anything of value at discount price. (For the impact of SAPs on the peripheral economy, see Elwood [2001] and McMichael [2004]). The aspiration of these countries to develop their domestic economy after gaining independence in 1940s and

1950s were replaced by the nightmares of neo-liberal globalization in the 1980s.

The application of the neo-liberal policy was not limited to peripheral countries. Prime Minster Margaret Thatcher introduced neo-liberal policy to the UK in 1979 and President Ronald Reagan did the same in the US in 1981. Their policies marked a departure from both the Keynesian intervention policy and the Fordist incorporation of the workers into the capital accumulation process. It was a return to the nineteenth century liberalist position of small government (at least on paper), no market intervention, and labour union busting. The twist was that the government did not reduce its size, used protectionist measures rampantly to protect domestic corporation while imposing free trade onto the weaker countries, and used the term 'free market' to justify the existing market that was plagued by the monopolistic domination of a few gigantic sellers and buyers. Reagan's policy was filled with contradictions and misconceptions, and its origin was the decline of the US

Economics is a social science that analyzes the market (as opposed to the state and society). The predominant economics framework is neoclassical economics, which uses mathematical models to derive policy recommendation. Economic models start from the assumption that complicated realities can be reduced to simple mathematical equations that can be manipulated to derive relations between policy instrument and policy objective. The most important assumption for the neoclassical economist is perfect competition. In order to have perfect competition, there have to be numerous suppliers and numerous buyers who have all information regarding the product and market. This makes it impossible for any single player to set the price and make profit over the cost of capital. The buyers are assumed to know exactly how much they want at what price, based on a clear idea of their 'preference'. Also, sellers are assumed to have the same knowledge of production technology, market condition, etc. Another important assumption they make is 'zero adjustment cost', meaning that capital invested in one sector can be moved to the other sector without any cost, and workers can be shifted to other sector without retraining or reeducation.

With these assumptions, economists derive conclusions that the 'free' market achieves the best resource allocation. 'Free' means that there is no intervention or interference by the government and that there are no big players that block free competition. The real world is far from what economists assume. Our economy is dominated by a few giant corporations, and competition is, at best, oligopolistic (competition among a few sellers). These corporations withhold information from each other and from the consumer so that they can out-compete rival companies and sell their products.

In addition to 'free market' doctrine, the economist insists that 'free trade' is beneficial to all countries. Again, economists make numerous assumptions to derive this conclusion. The famous 'theory of comparative advantage' by David Ricardo says that a country can gain from trade even if its technology is inferior to other countries as long as the degree of inferiority is different between sectors. The country should specialize in a sector with comparative advantage, or the sector with less inferiority in comparison with other sectors. When this theory is applied to the trade between a peripheral and a core country, the conclusion is clear that the peripheral country should specialize in the production of primary commodities and import industrial goods because the peripheral country does not have comparative advantage in industries. Moreover, the 'theory of factor endowment' claims that even if the two countries have the same technology, there exist gains from trade. According to this theory, the core country should specialize in capital-intensive goods and the periphery country in labour-intensive goods. These trade theories keep the peripheral country in traditional sectors without the possibility of dynamic economic development because the theories assume no change in technology.

Another unrealistic assumption made by the economists is the absence of externality. Externality is the benefit and cost that are not compensated with monetary transaction. For example, your neighbour may play piano. If you like the music, then you may be receiving a benefit from your neighbour without paying money. This is an example of positive externality. If you do not like the music, then your neighbour is inflicting negative externality on you, unless he or she pays you money to compensate your annoyance. Corporate activities are based on positive externality for which the corporation does not pay, and on negative externality that the corporation inflicts upon the society and environment without compensation. For example, roads and port facilities are prepared with taxpayer's money, and corporations do not pay the cost of construction when they use them (they may pay a fee, but it is not enough to build the entire facility). This is an example of public goods, and without public goods, corporate activities would become too costly. On the other hand, the corporation may inflict negative externality. When a company does not compensate for pollution, it is externalizing the cost. When a company clear cuts forest and sells the lumber, the price does not include the cost of ecological restoration. The economist usually assumes away externality and does not include the cost of eliminating negative externality such as ecological devastation or environmental destruction.

Ironically, when critics point out the unrealistic assumptions made in economic models, the economist insists that their model is not wrong; it is the reality that is wrong. Instead of abandoning dysfunctional models, the economist elevates their theory into theology. Economics is the only social science acknowledged by the Nobel Prize as 'scientific' because they use mathematical models and statistical inferences. This gives economists authority to dismiss other social sciences such as sociology and political science as not scientific enough. Economists dismiss those who challenge the theology of 'free market' and 'free trade' as unenlightened and unworthy. From a sociological point of view, it is necessary to criticize the conclusions derived from the neoclassical economic model as science in disguise because these conclusions neglect the very subject of social science—the real world.

economy in the 1970s. The US suffered from international humiliation throughout the 1970s, beginning with the admission of the weak dollar as a result of the cancellation of US-dollar convertibility in 1971 and the fixed exchange rate system in 1973. Saudi Arabia's oil embargo against the US in 1973 was the first defiance by the Third World country that escaped US retaliation. Next, the US lost the Vietnam War in 1975. In 1978, the USSR deployed their military in Afghanistan to support the socialist government, which created the impression of rising Soviet power (and, conversely, weakening US power); in 1979 the US lost the Shah of Iran after the Islamic Revolution. Americans were held hostage in the US embassy in Teheran for more than a year, beginning in November 1979, which furthered the impression of declining US power. Against this background, Ronald Reagan introduced the 'strong' US policy.

In order to restore the image of the 'strong' US, Reagan undertook the largest military expansion in peacetime. The USSR had difficulty catching up with US military build-up because the Soviet people demanded a higher standard of living and the protracted Afghan war had drained the country's resources. The US Marine Corps invaded Panama to arrest President Manuel Noriega for drug charges. They then invaded Granada to displace a government that opposed to IMF/World Bank policies. Successful overseas engagements boosted military morale, which had declined after the defeat in Vietnam, just as the British 'emancipation' of Falkland Island/Islas Malvinas did for the British military. Reagan also pushed the Strategic Defense Initiative, known as Star Wars, and promoted the development of new military technology in order to gain advantage over the USSR. Military spending was, and still is, an important part of the US economy; it stimulates the economy, and it spills into non-military areas to create advantages for

corporations, and overseas military engagements secure new markets and resources.

Reagan also wanted to make the US dollar 'stronger'. This idea was based on the misperception that anything 'strong' is good. A strong US dollar meant that US exports would cost more in the overseas market, and US corporations would move their operation overseas to take advantage of devalued currencies abroad. However, this policy made it easy for the Japanese and Europeans to export industrial goods to the US, further eroding the US corporate competitiveness. In order to protect their corporate interests, the US government resorted to protectionism; they imposed local content requirements on automobiles and employed retaliatory tariffs on goods imported from Europe and Japan. As a result, the European and Japanese companies started establishing operations in the US, which served to accelerate the globalization of corporate activities. With protectionist policies, the US succeeded in intimidating Canadian businesses until the business interest group pushed the Canadian government to sign the Free Trade Agreement (FTA) (McBride and Shields, 1997; McBride, 2001). The FTA gave numerous advantages to the US, including the access to Canadian natural resources, while the agreement failed to support the Canadian softwood lumber exports to the United States. As well, the Canadian economy deepened its dependency on the US economy as the volume of exports to the US increased. While some Canadian companies have been able to expand their investments to the US, many Canadian corporations have been purchased by Americans. Even though neo-liberalism was argued against protectionism, the US used protectionist threats and retaliation to open foreign markets for US corporations and investors.

Reagan's external economic policy changed markedly in 1985. The government was suffering as a result of expanded military expenditures and tax cuts for the rich, as well as because of the trade deficit, which resulted from a strong US dollar. At the 1985 G5 meeting, attended by the US, the UK, France, Germany, and Japan, the US pushed others to appreciate their currencies, or in other words, to devalue the US dollar. This measure was expected to reduce the US trade deficit according to the neoclassical trade model. It did not. Instead, the consumers continued to buy imports, just at higher prices. Meanwhile, the US export market did not increase; American products did not attract European and Japanese consumers. While Japan enjoyed a strong currency and a great deal of international financial and industrial success, the future of the US economy seemed bleak. In 1987 the US financial market, together with other financial markets, suffered from a significant drop in stock prices.

The US was not the only core nation experiencing difficulties. Many European countries experienced stagnation in the 1990s, partly because of the fall of communism and because of the formation of European Union. The Reagan administration's massive military growth applied pressure on the USSR, while its war in Afghanistan drained its resources. A mass exodus from the east to the west stripped the legitimacy of the socialist states, and lead to the end of the socialist regimes in 1989 and 1990. The fall of communism, however, created an unexpected burden for the West European states because of the inflow of people. West Germany absorbed East Germany and there was a substantial cost involved in accepting unemployed and unemployable East Germans. On the other hand, neo-liberalism was imposed on the European countries through the formation of the European Union. In order to create a common currency and a single market for labour, capital, and products, the member countries had to maintain balanced budgets and the balance of external payments.

Self-imposed, austere measures ended Keynesian policy in Europe. Even though many European countries maintained high levels of taxation and welfare spending, the incorporation into a single European economy ended the focus on national development for the European countries (Hermann, 2007). The Japanese economy was transformed to accept neo-liberal globalization after Japan went through a protracted recession in the 1990s that followed the economic 'bubble' in the late-1980s. Speculation in real estate and corporate stocks inflated the book value of the Japanese assets, but policy mismanagement led to a sudden end of the bubble economy. The structural reform introduced under US pressure in the late 1990s opened the Japanese market to US and other foreign corporations. The Japanese corporations globalized their operations while the majority of the population experienced stagnant or declining living standards (Ikeda, 2004). Aside from the US, China is a 'winner' in globalization, and it deserves a special consideration.

GLOBAL ISSUES
China and Globalization

The majority of the peripheral population is suffering from economic polarization, social dislocation, and ecological degradation under neo-liberal globalization, while only a small number of peripheral countries take advantage of the opportunity presented by globalization. Among them, China stands out as a truly exceptional country.

Since its birth as a communist country in 1948, led by the Chinese Communist Party (CCP), the country went through an experiment with collective production, stagnation, the Cultural Revolution, and high-level power struggle followed by economic disarray. In 1978 the CCP brought back pragmatist Deng Xiaoping, an important figure during the independence war who was purged during the Cultural Revolution. Deng initiated economic reforms; he introduced the market system, ended collective farming, distributed land among farmers for cultivation under state contracts, and created the Export Processing Zones (EPZ). In an EPZ corporations can import inputs and export outputs without paying tariffs (tax imposed on goods imported or exported). The East Asian economies such as Taiwan and Korea succeeded in industrial development starting with the EPZ. Foreign manufacturers flocked to the EPZs in China, attracted by the docile and literate workers ready to work at low wages (Chen, 1994).

Successful Chinese development in the 1980s came from the labour-intensive manufacturing exports and agriculture. The state-owned enterprises in the capital-intensive industries, on the other hand, were suffering from inefficiency. The government invited the foreign companies to establish joint ventures with the Chinese counterpart while maintaining the majority control of the ventures and negotiated with multiple foreign companies to obtain the best and most out of the foreigners. The capital-intensive sectors acquired foreign technology with latest production facilities, and with relatively low wages, the Chinese became competitive in many industry sectors in the 1990s. China has recorded high growth rates since 1979, and the coastal regions plus the Beijing areas became the growth centers (Lu, 1999).

How could China 'succeed' under globalization? China did not share the fate of the many peripheral countries and China did not need to obey the IMF and World Bank. This is because China did not become a debtor country even though it borrowed development finance from the World Bank, and export-oriented industrialization generated foreign exchange earnings. China received official development assistance from Japan and other core countries, but the most important form of foreign capital was the Foreign Direct Investment (FDI). The FDI was introduced through joint ventures so that China could introduce advanced foreign technology with capital, together with access to the core market. Chinese partners were required to have at least 51 per cent of the shares of the joint venture so that China maintained control and foreign companies complied with the Chinese strategy because they wanted to secure access to the growing Chinese market when the world economy was stagnating (Studwell, 2002).

What were the key factors that separated China from those peripheral countries that were structurally adjusted by the IMF and World Bank? Firstly, the most important difference is that China is a strong state that could negotiate the terms of international economic engagement with the core states and the IMF/World Bank. The CCP maintained coherent and unified state that could not be corrupted by foreign influence. The second factor is the growth potential. The consumer markets in core countries are saturated with goods, and mature economies do not grow at a high rate. In contrast, the Chinese market had a potential for continued growth at high rate, being pulled by huge investment demand for infrastructure and consumer demand for home appliances, cars, houses, etc. The third factor is the low labor costs. The communist revolution prepared the Chinese workers to become one of the most literate, efficient, docile, and low-wage workers in the world.

It is possible that China is offering a different path for peripheral development, a path that is better than what is available under the capitalist world-system (Arrighi, 2007). On the other hand, it is possible to predict that China will join the core countries and establish exploitative relationships with the peripheral countries. The Chinese resource policy to secure oil and minerals in Africa may provide a better condition for the African countries. But their entrance into the resource procurement competition will deepen the environmental contradiction of globalization. China aspires to join the ranks of the developed countries, but the earth's carrying capacity is already exhausted many times over with the consumption in the core countries. Instead of providing higher living standards for the entire population, China will likely become a stratified society with a few rich and the majority poor. The contradiction between the reality of polarized society and the egalitarian communist ideology may split China into hyper-capitalist regions and the backward communist regions. It is necessary to remember that China, in the end, is not offering an alternative path out of globalization.

Social Consequences of Globalization

How can we understand the social transformation accompanying globalization? Karl Polanyi (2001) used the term the 'Great Transformation' to describe the socio-economic transformation that occurred under liberalism in the nineteenth century. He argued that the 'self-regulating market' was eroding society, and that the economy became 'disembedded' from the society. In other words, the economy subjected society to profit-making activities. Society counter-acted this trend through the 'self-protection of society' in the form of socialist movements, fascism, and Keynesian interventions. This observation can also be applied to analyze the transformation under neo-liberal globalization. Neo-liberalism is a process of eliminating government intervention and leaving the society and nature to 'free' corporate activities. What are the emerging counter-movements to globalization? When examining social changes under globalization, it is useful to investigate our involvement in globalization using the viewpoint of 'victim' and 'culprit'. This viewpoint allows us to understand globalization as a personal issue, and to use our personal experiences to judge globalization.

Commodification of Everything and the Creation of Wants

Under globalization, consumers in core countries have increased their dependency on corporations for their supply of everyday items. We purchase food, clothes, cell phones, automobiles, furniture, construction materials, vacations, education, elderly care, drugs, and more. Is there anything you produce for your own consumption? You may have a home garden to grow vegetables and you may cook your dinner once in a while, but the proportion of do-it-yourself activities is quite low for the average Canadian. A near total reliance on corporations for our material existence is the result of the long historical development of capitalism. Prior to capitalism, the majority of the population lived in rural communities that were generally self-sufficient. The rural people produced vegetable, fruits, cattle, fish, and raw material for the urban dwellers who, in turn, specialized in arts, crafts, and administration. Capitalist development from the sixteenth century changed this situation, and now we rely almost completely on the goods and services supplied by others. World-system researchers call this process the 'commodification of everything' (Wallerstein, 1995).

Technological advancement expanded both the scale and the scope of commodification. New products are now developed and released at a fast pace, and corporations invent and promote new wants and needs to sell these products. Laptop computers and cell phones are relatively new commodities. Portable personal music devices have became smaller in size and larger in storage capacity, changing from the 'boom box' to the 'walkman', and from the 'Discman' to the 'iPod'. The pharmaceutical industry now claims to have cures for many heretofore-untreatable ailments such as erectile dysfunction and baldness, and they have designed an assortment of chemicals to treat depression, anxiety, and tension. These new products satisfy our new wants and needs, but these very wants and needs are cultivated through advertisements and media. Ultimately, corporations attempt to create addictions

among consumers because a docile addict is the best customer. This has affected our culture significantly under globalization. For example, from a young age youth are trained to want Disney products. This obsession with branded goods grows into an addiction, and youth may graduate from Disney to designer clothes, accessories, and cosmetics. The consumer is ultimately transformed into the passive receptacle of values and cultural practices represented by brand names and logos. (For the analysis of corporate branding and the rule logos of our culture, see Klein, 2000. For the critical analysis of corporations, see Bakan, 2004.) Do you think you have benefited from goods and services supplied by the corporation?

Corporate Domination

Today the corporation dominates our lives (Khor, 2001). A corporation is a legal entity with transferable shares, perpetual succession capacity, and limited liability. Joint stock companies were an early invention to share the risk associated with business ventures. When the business failed, stockowners would be responsible only to the extent of their investment. In order to raise profit, the corporation tries to minimize cost, often at the expense of people and nature. For a more detailed analysis of the corporation and corporate domination, see Bakan (2004). Also, the film based on Bakan's book—*The Corporation*—is an excellent visual critique of the corporation.

For income earning activities we are directly or indirectly dependent on the corporation. In order to earn an income we have to find jobs, and often it is global corporations that offer well-paying jobs. We are also dependent on the corporation for investment. Many parents can no longer rely on their children to take care of them in their old age and it is necessary to prepare for retirement by saving money and investing wisely. The financial instruments available to Canadians include corporate stocks and bonds, government bonds (from municipal, provincial, federal, and even the World Bank issued bonds), and bank deposits; the gains from these investments depend on corporate health. Even government bonds depend on corporate health because the government's tax revenue comes from employment and business income. We are dependent on the corporation for our income, for the goods and services we consume, and for investment opportunities.

Corporate Alienation

Deepening corporate reliance has transformed society in such a way that the traditional social ties were severed and replaced by market relations. Corporations promote individual rather than communal consumption. For example, in the early twentieth century the Ford Motor Company bought the company that ran the street car system in Detroit and dismantled it. This left the public with no other choice but to purchase individualized transportation, i.e. an automobile. Individualized consumption exists hand-in-hand with materialism. Corporations tell us what we must have, what we must eat, and what we must aspire to own to indicate our social status. Since money is the medium which purchases goods and services, individualized consumption and materialism leads to money-centrism. How much do you 'buy' into money-centrism?

Karl Marx (1977) pointed out that alienation was one of the key features of capitalism. Workers are alienated from the means of production because they do not own the means of production in the workplace, such as plants, equipment, and tools. They are also alienated from the products themselves because they cannot appreciate what they are creating. Globalization also deepened alienation through consumption. Consumers in core countries are often unaware of the effect their consumption has in peripheral countries, not only for those who make the products, and the conditions they work under, but also in terms of the cost to the environment. Your clothing and shoes may be made by underage workers in a sweatshop; the vegetables and fruits you buy at the supermarket may be picked in pesticide-, herbicide-, and fungicide-infested fields by pregnant women and nursing mothers who as a result experience high risks of birth deformity and infant maldevelopment; and the products you buy may be contributing to environmental degradation. Globalized corporate activities create distance between the consumers and the place and people involved in the production process. As consumers become alienated from the producers, they become increasingly distanced from nature. This alienation of nature is promoted by the corporate practice of seeing nature as a 'free' commodity. Moreover, corporations promote wasteful lifestyles through model changes and built-in obsolescence. For example, a laptop computer sold ten years ago is not able to use the latest software. Mounting wastes from our continuous consumption pollutes the environment, and leads to our further environmental alienation. (For negative impacts of globalization, see Barndt, ed., 1999; Barndt, 2002; and the essays in Mander and Goldsmith, 1996.)

Corporate Activities and Global Inequality

In the process of economic globalization the rich get richer and the poor suffer. Throughout the 1980s and 1990s, many peripheral countries experienced a decline in per capita income. It was the US that was the winner under globalization. When we compare the per capita income as a percentage of US per capita income, almost all peripheral countries experienced a decline between 1980 and 2000. Even most core countries, other than the US, went through a significant decline in the 1990s. When inequality is measured on a per capita basis, the US is the only country that gained in the 1990s, and the rest of the world declined relatively. The end result of this transformation was the domination of the periphery in terms of global population and the shrinking of the semiperiphery and core populations (see Figure 17.2).

In addition to international inequality, income gaps between the rich and the poor widened within countries (Chossudovsky, 2004). Many peripheral countries experienced 'enclosure', a process where farmers were pushed away from the land. For example, as a result of late-twentieth-century enclosure, Brazil became the biggest soybean exporter in the world. The average Brazilian soybean farm is huge in size and its operation is highly industrialized with the use of genetically modified seeds, chemical fertilizers and herbicides, huge tractors, and the latest storage and transportation facilities; global corporations such as Cargill often manage the operations. In the process of expanding soybean operations, farmers were pushed out from the fertile land south of the Amazon and were forced into the rain forest, where they cut down trees to open farmland (Barbosa, 1996; Wolford, 2008). When consumers in the Global North enjoy hamburgers at fast-food restaurants, they contribute to the destruction of the Amazon rain forest, because Brazilian soybeans are exported to feed cattle in Central America that, in turn, become the hamburgers in North America. Similar developments occurred in many countries. Mexican peasants had access to communal land under the *ejido* system, but the system was abolished under the North American Free Trade Agreement (NAFTA). The concentration of land in the hands of a few ensued. Uprisings in Chiapas, Mexico, in 1994, represented an opposition against globalization from the grassroots (Saavedra, 2005). Likewise, the IMF and World Bank told many indebted countries to eliminate protection of food production for the domestic market and promote agricultural exports to earn foreign exchange. As a result, huge tracts of land were enclosed for global corporate operations. Only a small percentage of the population gained, as a result, while the majority of people experienced hardship (Farshad, 2000). Global corporate activities deepened the income gap between the rich and the poor both within and among countries.

Figure 17.2 Zonal Structure by Population Shares

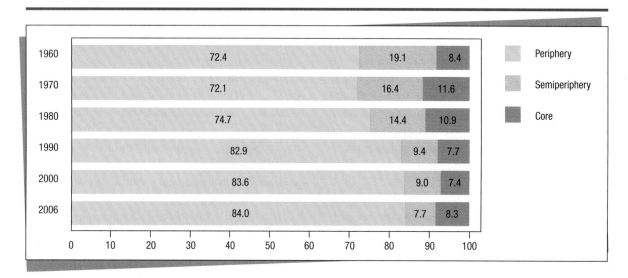

Data Source: World Bank, World Development Indicators (electronic resource).

Note: 209 countries are classified into core, semiperiphery, and periphery, and the population of the countries in each zone is tabulated to derive the world population shares of the each zone. To derive a country's zonal position, its per capita income is divided by the US per capita income. Those countries whose relative per capita income is less that 19.9% of the US per capita income are designated as the peripheral country, those with 20% to 69.9% are designated as the semiperiphery, and those with 70% or above are designated as the core. In this derivation, GDP (Gross Domestic Product) per capita was used as the proxy of per capita income because Gross National Income data are not available for all countries all the time. When the GDP per capita figure is missing, an estimated figure was applied based on the educated guess from the historical trend, or from other countries with similar economic situation. A similar adjustment was made for missing population data.

Interpretation: This figure shows that the population share of the periphery increased markedly between 1980 and 1990 (8.2% increase) while the share of the semiperiphery and the core declined. Between 1990 and 2000, the same trend continued but the changes in the population percentage was not significant. Globalization was a process of subordinating the peripheral and semiperipheral countries as shown by the declining share of the semiperiphery and the rising share of periphery. Also, economic globalization from the 1980s lowered the per capita income for most countries relative to the US, supporting the interpretation that globalization was a process where the US defeated those that challenged US economic domination.

● Limits of Globalization

In order to examine the current situation and the future of globalization, let us examine the emerging processes that came from the limits of the current system. There are at least four limits to be considered: the ecology-resource limit, the social limit, the politico-military limit, and the limit of neo-liberal economy. The expanding global economy is pushing the limit of ecology and resources as exemplified by global warming. The Kyoto Protocol for the reduction of greenhouse gas emissions, which was negotiated in the 1990s, was never implemented by the largest polluters such as the US and Canada. Another example is deforestation in peripheral countries. Facing the pressure to increase exports, many countries harvest trees for consumption in the core countries and clear forests for cultivating export crops. Forest clearing also accelerates the pace of species extinction.

The second limitation takes the form of widening and deepening social crisis, as unequal distribution of income destabilizes societies in peripheral countries. Those who have financial resources are able to migrate into a core country, leaving poor families trapped in a country whose government is often corrupt and concerned only with meeting demands made by the IMF and World Bank and pleasing global corporations.

Directly related to this is the rising global phenomenon of ethno-nationalism. After the East Asian financial crises in 1997, ethnic tension increased in Thailand, Indonesia, and the Philippines. Economic difficulties in the core countries invited the rise of fundamentalism, and fascism gained popularity in former East Germany, where unemployment was high. In France, anti-Muslim sentiment rose after the 2005 riots. These can be seen as examples of ethno-nationalism of the majority against the ethnic/racial minority in the core countries. In the United States, the September 11th terrorist attacks were followed by a widespread racist/ethno-centrist attack on those who appear to be from the Middle East or South

American cultural influence extends across the globe. This photograph was taken in an open-air market in Kabul, Afghanistan. Even in countries where America is not favoured, an impressive array of US-brand running shoes are ready for sale. Steve McCurry/Magnum Photos

Asia. Economic difficulties experienced by the lower strata of the American society promoted Christian fundamentalism from the 1980s, as reflected in the growing popularity of TV evangelism and the spread of new sects.

The third limitation involves politico-military control of the periphery. The capitalist world-system has been a system of accumulation based on the core-periphery zonal structure. Economic globalization dashed the hopes of peripheral countries to succeed by improving the living standard through national economic development. Countries that had succeeded in development up to the 1990s (such as Korea, Thailand, and Malaysia) were pushed back into the subordinate peripheral position after global financial speculators defeated them in the East Asian financial crises in 1997 (Singh, 1999). It appears that the coalition of core countries is succeeding in controlling the peripheral countries using the debt-leveraged management administered by the IMF and World Bank. But would it be possible to continue suppressing the civil unrest in the Global South?

In the fall of 2008, the American housing market crisis triggered a worldwide financial crisis. Many financial institutions in the core countries faced bankruptcy and some were saved through partial nationalization or with the infusion of public money. This financial crisis may

lead to a prolonged recession/depression and the end of neo-liberal globalization. Or have we reached the limit of neo-liberal economy? While the wealthy (corporate executives and investors) may be saved by the government, the cost of adjustment will be born by the poor, just like what happened to the peripheral countries under the SAPs. The corporate economy is in crisis and the public economy (government sector activities) will expand. Instead of trying to restore the failed corporate economy, however, this crisis may be inviting us to create better futures that are ecologically sustainable, socially just (with less unequal income distribution), and economically stable.

● Emerging ● ● ● ● ● ● Post-Global Alternatives

People living in the core countries are dependent on global corporations, and without them, we could not live the lifestyles to which we have become accustomed. When the global economy faces limitations, it will be the poor people who have to deal with the problem first, and the people in the Global North will continue enjoying privileged lifestyles. Despite this material and cultural entrapment of the corporate-dominated society, the awareness of the impending crisis is spreading, prompting people to take action against the governments that refuse to employ measures to stop global warming, against the corporations that violate human rights and pollute the environment, and against global powers such as the US, G8, the IMF/World Bank, and WTO. Some movements intend to make corporations behave responsibly, and some attempt to change the government. These movements are based on the idea that the corporation and government can be reformed to make the future sustainable. Capitalism went through a major reform in the early twentieth century in the form of Keynesian-Fordist revolution, but it was reversed in the process of economic globalization. Deepening crisis under globalization calls for either another reform of capitalism or the creation of post-capitalist society. There already exist various movements that are opening up the possibility for better futures. Let us discuss some of them.

Social Economy and Social Enterprises

The capitalist system, with profit-driven corporations, achieved remarkable material growth, but it also created problems such as financial crisis, unemployment, income inequality, social tensions, and social problems such as alienation, materialism, and money-centrism that led to an erosion of society's commitment to collective goals. Social economy is 'a grass-roots entrepreneurial, not-for-profit sector, based on democratic values that seeks to enhance the social, economic, and environmental conditions of communities, often with a focus on their disadvantaged members' (Human Resources and Social Development Canada, n.d.). Social economy has a long history in Quebec where the provincial government has been keen on promoting rural communities by promoting diverse agricultural and manufacturing products. There are estimated 6,200 social economy enterprises with total 65,000 employees and annual sales exceeding $4 billion in the province (HRSDC, n.d.).

Social enterprises set themselves apart from the capitalist corporation in many ways. The objective of a social enterprise is to provide essential goods and services to the community. In order to make the operation viable, they have to maintain good financial standing; however, the operation is never for profit and they are based within the communities they serve. Important decisions are made locally, unlike global corporations where key decisions (such as factory closures) are decided in a boardroom halfway across the globe. The face-to-face contact between the producer and the consumer promotes mutual appreciation and trust for the goods, in stark contrast to the corporate supplied goods that the consumers do not know (and often do not want to know) how they were made by whom. Moreover, those who are engaging in social enterprises derive satisfaction from their contribution to the well-being of the customers and the community, rather than from how much money they made. Also, social enterprises take better care of the environment because they have to live with the local environment; they strive to avoid exploiting and polluting other people's backyard. The interest for social economy is increasing as an alternative way of organizing our economic activities that overcome corporate alienation.

Local Sustainable Agriculture

Ecologically sustainable agriculture takes care of the watershed; eliminates the use of chemicals such as pesticides, herbicides, fungicides, and fertilizers; and avoids soil erosion/deterioration from over-grazing or single-crop cultivation. The emerging sustainable practices are characterized by direct sales to the consumer through farmers' markets, on-site sales, and the Community Supported Agriculture (CSA). The CSA connects the organic/natural farmers and urban customers through a contract. Its participants pay money to the farmers in early spring, and the farmers deliver fresh groceries weekly in summer and fall. The farmers can schedule planting based on the contracts without taking the risk of selling to the large distributors at the price under cost. In the case of bad weather, the producer and the consumer share the cost. These direct sales eliminate middle-men and bring the producer and consumer closer together. This creates a new form of community across rural–urban boundaries, and local production and consumption eliminates the long distance transportation which contributes to greenhouse gas emissions. The CSA idea, which originated in Japan, is now spreading throughout other core countries.

World Social Forum

Davos, Switzerland, is the site of the annual meetings of the World Economic Forum. The heads of the core states, CEOs of powerful global corporations, and noted economists gather to discuss how to achieve economic growth. This organization became the forum for pro-globalization advocates, although the issues discussed are of great social concern. The solutions sought are usually from the perspective of economics, which makes the

▬▬ Time to Reflect ▮█ ▮█ ▮█ ▮█ ▮█ ▮█ ▮█ ▮█ ▮█ ▮█ ▮█ ▮

Do you think that social enterprise, sustainable agriculture, or the World Social Forum will have lasting global impacts? Do you feel one reform will have a greater impact than the others?

forum a tool for those who support globalization. Activists against globalization held the first World Social Forum (WSF) in Porto Alegre, Brazil, in January of 2001 (at the same time of the World Economic Forum). The participants of the forum included anti-globalization and alter-globalization activists such as labour union activists, community development activists, environmentalists, and human rights activists. Since then the WSF has had annual conferences every year (except for 2008), and the number of participants, countries represented, and social movements involved has steadily expanded. Regional forums such as the European Social Forum were also held to create networks of anti-globalization and alter-globalization activists. The expansion of the WSF activities indicates that economic globalization has created social problems all over the world, and that it has stimulated the imagination and practice for post-global futures. The WSF exchanges information and discusses common problems, but it does not attempt to create a unified political action. Participants recognize the importance of local diversity and local initiative for the creation of alternative futures in order to overcome the ills of economic globalization, such as ecological unsustainability, social injustice, and economic polarization.

Does the World Social Forum represent the emergence of a global civil society? In a democratic society, the citizens have the right to govern, usually through the control of elected government officials. The constitution is a contract between the citizens and the government. Through economic globalization the citizens of various countries are integrated into a single division of labour that is controlled primarily by the powerful global corporations. However, there is no global government that represents all peoples of the world, and the people's rights are limited by the boundaries of their states. The closest representation of a world government is the United Nations, but the veto power given to the permanent members of the UN security council (the US, UK, France, Russia, and China) makes it undemocratic and the supra-state agencies such as the IMF, World Bank, and WTO erode the sovereignty of peripheral countries. As globalization faces its limits, the contradiction of the capitalist system deepens and encourages more people to participate in the

WSF in order to achieve economically egalitarian, socially just, and ecologically sustainable global futures.

● Conclusion

Globalization is a historical process that reversed the three 'revolutions' of the twentieth century—the socialist revolution, the Keynesian-Fordist revolution, and colonial independence. As corporations all over the world were emancipated from the constraint of national regulations, people and the environment became subjected to corporate profit-making. Workers in the core countries that became the middle class consumers were integrated into the system as investors and enjoy the goods supplied by corporations at low costs. The majority of the humanity that lives in the periphery suffered when the national development project came to an end, save a few who benefited from their connection to the global financial market and the global corporation. The global financial crisis from 2008 will bring down the living standard of the middle class people in the core countries and leave them with financial uncertainty and/or disaster. Also, the ecological, social, and politico-military limitations of globalization are deepening. There are emerging social movements that call for a new direction. From a long-historical perspective, we can identify the contemporary period as a time of another great transformation. The outcome of this transformation is not clear because it depends on the awareness and actions of the people. The most obvious direction is the restoration of the failed neo-liberal path. Even though the financial crisis will wreck the lives of the majority, and even though global warming may cause disaster, the rich will continue to enjoy the bulk of the global wealth at the expense of the poor. Bleak prospects in the periphery may encourage ethno-nationalism to negotiate a better deal with the corporation, or to attempt attacks on the rich and powerful. Another direction may prepare an economy embedded in society, or an economy driven by social concerns and not by profit. What will be your choice? Will you continue enjoying your material privilege? Or, would you become a concerned global citizen who would challenge the corporate domination?

● Questions ● ● ● ● ● ● ●
for Critical Thought

1. How do you benefit from economic globalization? How are you a victim of economic globalization?
2. What is the role the corporation plays for your daily life and future aspirations? How will the 2008 financial crisis affect your future aspiration?
3. Do you think you are a victim or culprit of corporate domination? Discuss how the corporation dominates our society. How is it possible to reduce corporate domination?
4. Examine how your consumption may adversely affect the global environment.
5. Summarize the negative impacts of economic globalization on our society and environment. How could they be changed so that we can create a sustainable future?

● Recommended ● ● ● ● ●
Readings

Joel Bakan, *The Corporation: The Pathological Pursuit of Profit and Power* (New York: Free Press, 2004).
Bakan's starkly honest look at 'the most influential institution of our time' highlights the extent to which the corporation has influenced nearly every aspect of society.

Wayne Ellwood, *No-Nonsense Guide to Globalization* (Toronto: Between the Lines, 2001).
Ellwood's book is a clear and concise overview of the problems inherent within the world system, including the debt trap, the acceleration of neo-liberalism and the free trade model, competition for energy resources, and the links between the war on terror, the arms trade, and privatization.

Philip McMichael, *Development and Social Change: A Global Perspective*, 3rd edn (Thousand Oaks: Pine Forge Press, 2004).
McMichael's book uses case studies and current examples to help students understand how globalization has become part of public discourse while encouraging them to think about their individual roles in social change.

● Recommended ● ● ● ● ●
Websites

World Economic Forum www.weforum.org
The World Economic Forum serves as the promoter of free trade through an annual forum and other activities. They express concerns over social issues, but their basic stance is one of support for the neo-liberal position.

International Labor Organization http://www-old.itcilo.org/actrav/actrav-english/telearn/global/ilo/default.htm
This website offers a critical assessment of globalization from the viewpoint of labour and workers.

Human Resources and Social Development Canada www.hrsdc.gc.ca/en/cs/comm/sd/social_economy.shtml
Social economy is an alternative form of organizing economic activities, with a focus on the provision of social services rather than on profit-making. The Canadian government recognizes the importance of this growing sector.

Canadian Social Entrepreneur's Network www.csen.ca/
Social entrepreneurs are those who undertake social enterprise. This online network shares information on ideas and examples of social enterprises.

● Glossary ● ● ● ● ● ● ●

Accountability   The expectation that public education, like other state-provided services, has clearly defined objectives that members of the public can identify and assess how well and how cost effectively they are being met.

Aesthetics   A system of rules for the appreciation of the beautiful.

Age composition   The distribution of the population with respect to age (and usually also sex); typically displayed graphically as a population pyramid.

Agents of socialization   Those groups in a child's environment that have the greatest impact on his or her socialization.

Alienation   A concept derived from Marx's analysis of the position of workers under capitalism, referring to the separation of workers from the products of their labour, from the control of the work process, from owners, managers, and other workers, and even from themselves.

Allopathic medicine   Conventional medicine that treats by opposing something, whether germs, bacteria, cells, organs, or other pathology.

Altercasting   The counterpart of impression management. In impression management actors self-cast, whereas in altercasting actors force on others identities that are in the altercaster's interests.

Alternative media   Types of communication that have been used by subordinate groups and social movements to present their own messages, which often involve challenging existing conditions in society. Examples include community radio, documentary films, and the Internet.

Anticipatory socialization   Explicit or implicit learning, in preparation for a future role; in Merton's definition, the acquisition of values and orientations found in statuses and groups in which one is not yet engaged but that one is likely to enter.

Authority   Power considered legitimate by those subject to it.

Baby boom   The dramatic rise in the birth rate in Canada following World War II and lasting until well into the 1960s.

Baby bust   The continuing decline in fertility following the end of the baby boom in the industrialized world.

Behavioural school   An approach within organizational theory that developed out of human relations theory and a psychological conception of human needs.

Beliefs   Any statement or part of a statement that describes an aspect of collective reality. Beliefs are ideas and explanations of what is commonly accepted as the truth. Beliefs may also be normative, saying what ought—or ought not—to be done.

Bilateral descent pattern   A system under which a married couple is considered part of both the female's and the male's kin groups.

Biological determinism   The view that nature dominates nurture.

Bourgeoisie   Owners of the means of production; the merchant (economically dominant) or ruling class.

Breakdown approach   An approach to social movements that assumes rapid, thorough, or uneven change in social institutions weakens social bonds and encourages the formation of groups advocating radical change.

Bretton Woods System   The international economic order in the post-WWII period based on the dollar-gold convertibility, fixed exchange rates, the GATT, the IMF, and the World Bank; the objective was the promotion of international trade and capitalist development.

Bride price   Money, property, or labour provided by the groom or his family to a bride's family for permission to marry the bride.

Brownfields   Large tracts of urban land, usually central, whose original uses have become outdated by changes in production and/or transportation technology.

Built environment   Tangible settings, such as buildings, streets, and other, often urban, settings constructed by humans for their repeated use.

Bureaucracy   A type of formal organization, found in government and private industry, and in capitalist and socialist societies alike, that has the following six characteristics: a division of labour; a hierarchy of positions; a formal system of rules; a separation of the person from the office; hiring and promotion based on technical merit; and the protection of careers. Administrative efficiency is achieved by depersonalized treatment and mass processing of cases, as dictated by regulations and filed information.

Capital-intensive production   All production involves both labour and capital, but the proportions of the two used can vary considerably across different goods and services. In dollar terms, the inputs of capital into the production of aluminum are enormous (plant, equipment, electricity, bauxite) but the labour inputs are modest—a capital-intensive industry. In contrast, hairdressers use negligible amounts of capital equipment (a chair, sink and water, scissors, a mirror, some chemicals). The bulk of the cost of that activity is labour—a labour-intensive industry.

Capitalism   An economic system characterized by a relationship of unequal economic exchange between capitalists (employers) and workers. Because they do not own the means of production, workers must sell their labour to employers in exchange for a wage or salary. Capitalism is a market-based system driven by the pursuit of profit for personal gain.

Carrying capacity   The ability of the earth to provide the resources to sustain all of humankind.

Census   A complete count of the population at one point in time, usually taken by a country every 5 or 10 years. The census is distinguished from the vital statistics system, a continuous registration system of births, deaths, marriages, and divorces.

Census family   The Statistics Canada definition of the family used in the census, which usually includes married or long-term cohabiting couples, with or without never-married children, as well as single parents living with never-married children.

Census metropolitan areas (CMAs)   Statistics Canada term for large urban agglomerations of 100,000 or more people, sometimes consisting of more than one political jurisdiction or municipality, interconnected in relatively close proximity by systems of roadways. Today in Canada there are 33 CMAs.

Ceremonial theories Building on the later work of Durkheim, a series of theories that stress the unifying function of rituals, holidays, and sporting events in society for the maintenance of social cohesion and community.

Charismatic authority Power considered legitimate because those subject to it believe in the exceptional qualities of an individual person, who appears exemplary or heroic and able to solve what others cannot.

Charter groups Canadians of British and French origin are known as charter groups because they have a special status entrenched in the Canadian constitution and have effectively determined the dominant cultural characteristics of Canada. Each of these groups has special rights and privileges, especially in terms of the language of the legislature, of the courts, and of education.

Claims-making The social constructionist process by which groups assert grievances about the troublesome character of people or their behaviour.

Class Inequality among groups of people based on the distribution of material resources and social capital.

Coherence Interrelationships that link parts to make a whole.

Collective conscience; collective consciousness Durkheim's term for the collective intellectual property of a culture; something that we can all share in and contribute to but that no one person can know or possess. The cognitive-moral system of shared symbols, beliefs, and sentiments of a social group. Individuals think and feel what they learn and internalize as members of a collective. The content of the conscience collective is determined by the structural organization of the society in question.

Collective effervescence The experience of psychological excitement and empowerment that often happens to individuals caught up in large crowd activities such as political rallies, sporting events, or rock concerts.

Common-sense knowledge Facts of life accepted without being fully researched and understood.

Community Tangible interpersonal contact patterns.

Compensators Things that are provided in place of some real but unattainable goal or object, for example, the religious promise of life after death in lieu of actual immortality in one's present existence.

Concept An abstract idea that cannot be tested directly. Concepts can refer to anything, but in social research they usually refer to characteristics of individuals, groups, or artifacts, or to social processes. Some common sociological concepts include religiosity (strength of religious conviction), social class, and alienation.

Conflict theory A theoretical paradigm linked to the work of Marx and Weber that emphasizes conflict and change as the regular and permanent features of society, because society is made up of various groups that wield varying amounts of power. Conflict theorists often stress the importance of status, economic inequality, and political power.

Conglomerate ownership A form of ownership in which one company has many firms that engage in a variety of often unrelated business activities. It may combine *horizontal integration*, *vertical integration*, and even *cross-ownership*.

Control theory A category of explanation that maintains that people engage in deviant behaviour when the various controls that might be expected to prohibit them from doing so are weak or absent.

Cross-ownership A form of ownership in which one company owns organizations associated with different types of media. For instance, a company might own a newspaper and a television network.

CRTC The Canadian Radio-television and Telecommunications Commission, which governs the broadcasting as well as the telecommunications business in Canada, setting the rules for operation based on principles of scarcity, public resource, and national importance.

Cults Religious groups, usually very small, that have either been newly created or imported into a society from a quite different culture.

Cultural capital A term coined by Pierre Bourdieu for the cultural and linguistic competence, such as prestigious knowledge, tastes, preferences, and educational expertise and credentials, that individuals possess and that influence the likelihood of their educational and occupational success.

Cultural diffusion The process whereby the beliefs and customary behaviours of one society spread to, and are adopted within, another society.

Cultural support theory A category of explanation that argues people become and remain deviant because the cultural environments in which they find themselves teach deviance and define such behaviour as appropriate.

Culture At its broadest, the sum total of the human-produced environment (the objects, artifacts, ideas, beliefs, and values that make up the symbolic and learned aspects of human society) as separate from the natural environment; more often refers to norms, values, beliefs, ideas, and meanings; an assumption that different societies are distinguished by their shared beliefs and customary behaviours; the products and services delivered by a number of industries—theatre, music, film, publishing, and so on.

Decoding The process of interpreting or 'reading' media content. It may involve a dominant-hegemonic reading, an oppositional reading, or a negotiated reading. See *Encoding*; *Encoding and decoding*.

Deep ecology Term coined by Norwegian philosopher Arne Naess referring to a philosophical approach to environmentalism calling for fundamental social change in contrast to the more reformist orientation of mainstream environmentalism, referred to by Naess as 'shallow ecology'. Deep ecology has been criticized for its biocentric emphasis claiming nature to be separate from and superior to human society, and used by some environmental organizations to justify any means, even illegal, for addressing environmental problems.

Demographic components equation A method of estimating population size by adding births, subtracting deaths, and adding net migration occurring in an interval of time, then adding the result to the population at the beginning of the interval; also knows as a balancing equation.

Demographic transition The process by which a country moves from high birth and death rates to low birth and death rates. The shift in fertility rates is often referred to as the fertility transition, while the complementary change in death rates is referred to as the mortality transition. The epidemiological transition theory is a complementary theory to demographic transition theory.

Developed countries The most industrialized countries of the world. According to the United Nations, these are the countries in Europe and in North America, as well as Australia, New Zealand, and Japan.

Developing countries All the countries not in the developed world. A subdivision of developing countries is the least developed countries, defined by the United Nations as countries with average annual incomes of less than $9,000 (US). See also *Third World*.

Deviance People, behaviours, and conditions subject to social control.

Digital divide Inequalities in access to computers and/or the Internet; also used to describe inequalities in the skills needed to use computers or information transmitted through the Internet. Inequalities associated with social class, gender, national origin, and other characteristics are seen as the basis for the digital divide.

Discourse A way of talking about and conceptualizing an issue, presented through ideas, concepts, and vocabulary that recur in texts.

Discrimination An action whereby a person is treated differently (usually, unfairly) because of his or her membership in a particular group or category.

Disease, illness, and sickness Distinguished from one another in the sociology of health, illness, and medicine. *Disease* is the disorder that is diagnosed by the physician. *Illness* is the personal experience of the person who acknowledges that he or she does not feel well. *Sickness* is the social action taken by a person as a result of illness or disease.

Doctrine of emergence A key ontological principle in the social realist perspective: new properties or realities are created by the combination of elements.

Dominant ideology The ideas and viewpoints held by the capitalist class or other powerful groups in society. Specific forms of the dominant ideology include capitalist, patriarchal, and racist ideology.

Double standard Expecting or requiring different behaviour from women than men, and from boys than girls.

Dowry Money or property provided by a bride's family upon her marriage, to help obtain a suitable husband and to be used by her new household (or sometimes to support her in case of divorce or widowhood).

Ecology In the context of urban studies, the internal makeup, patterning, and dynamics of cities. See also *Human ecology*.

Edge city Highly concentrated business, commercial, and high-technology centre on lower-cost land on the fringe of an urban area.

Education The process by which human beings learn and develop capacities through understanding of their social and natural environments, which takes place in both formal and informal settings.

Encoding The process of embedding ideology in media content. Encoding emerges through the complex interplay of economic and technical conditions associated with a media institution, the organizational relations and practices of the institution, and the ideology existing within the institution and the wider society. See also *Decoding*; *Encoding and decoding*.

Encoding and decoding The embedding and subsequent interpretation of cues, meanings, and codes in cultural productions.

Environmental justice The branch of environmentalism that focuses on the inequitable distribution of environmental risks affecting the poor and racial minorities.

Epistemology A branch of philosophy concerned with the nature of knowledge, how it is obtained, and the means for establishing its validity.

Essence; essentialism; essential nature The idea that a 'true' or core reality lies behind appearances, which makes something what it is and which, once identified, can establish its 'truth'. In the study of sexual and gender identities, for example, many challenge the idea that there is an essence of 'femaleness' (something all women share/are) or 'maleness' that sets females and males apart from each other.

Ethnic group People sharing a common ethnic identity who are potentially capable of organizing and acting on their ethnic interests.

Ethnicity Sets of social distinctions by which groups differentiate themselves from one another on the basis of presumed biological ties. Members of such groups have a sense of themselves as a common 'people' separate and distinct from others.

Ethnocentric bias The tendency to think that the beliefs, values, and customs of one's own culture are universal (that is, that they can be applied to others).

Ethnomethodology A type of qualitative research founded by Harold Garfinkel that analyzes the methods people use in relation to one another to make sense of social life and conceptual order at the everyday level.

Exploitation At the heart of Marxist sociology, the situation under capitalism in which the bourgeoisie takes advantage of the proletariat. Class-based exploitation occurs when the bourgeoisie appropriates the labour effort of the proletariat to create its own material advantage.

Extended family Several generations and/or married siblings and their children sharing a residence and co-operating economically.

Face The positive presentation of self projected by an individual.

False consciousness Condition in which the working class does not recognize its exploitation and oppression under capitalism.

Feminism A theoretical paradigm, as well as a social movement, that focuses on causes and consequences of inequality between men and women, especially patriarchy and sexism.

Finance capital In contrast to physical capital, instruments that can be used to purchase physical capital—bank loans, equity (voting shares in a company), fixed interest bonds, and so on; the monetary expression of physical capital.

First Nations 'Indians' in Canadian law; together with Métis and Inuit, they constitute Canada's Aboriginal peoples.

Flexible specialization Another component of the new flexible approach to management; involves multi-skilling, job rotation, the organization of workers into teams, and concentrated yet decentralized decision-making power within work organizations.

Formal organization A deliberately formed social group in which people, resources, and technologies are consciously co-ordinated through formalized roles, statuses, and relationships to achieve a division of labour intended to attain a specific set of objectives.

Forms of association An approach to sociology founded by German scholar Georg Simmel that focuses on identifiable generic patterns to discover how people interact with each other in groups; distinct from the content of associations, which vary much more widely.

Functionalism A theoretical approach stressing order, consensus, social stability, and the positive functions of certain levels of inequality in social life, with a major emphasis on shared values and norms and on the importance of community.

Gender Socially recognized distinctions of masculinity and femininity.

Gender stereotyping Beliefs about differences in the natural capabilities and attributes of women and men.

General Agreement on Tariff and Trade (GATT) This is a multi-lateral treaty to reduce tariff and non-tariff barriers to trade. In order to implement free trade, the World Trade Organization (WTO) was formed as a regulatory agency of the GATT in 1993.

Generalized other In Mead's theory, the 'internalized audience' with which we, as 'minded selves', dialogue or converse during the reflective prelude to action. It represents the acquired collective attitudes and sentiments of our society or group.

Global cities Cities favoured under globalization that are at high levels of technology, finance, and international transportation, serving as the focal points for multinational corporations but not for local manufacturing.

Globalization The flow of goods, services, media, information, and labour between countries around the world; different but interrelated aspects include economic globalization and cultural globalization. Worldwide control and co-ordination by large private-sector interests not constrained by local or national boundaries.

Globalization of work The relocation of production and consumption beyond national borders to various parts of the globe done in the interest of increasing profits by decreasing labour costs and maximizing employer control of the overall work process.

Hawthorne effect The finding that when people know they are subjects of an important experiment and receive a large amount of special attention, they tend to behave the way they think the researchers expect them to.

Health Defined by the World Health Organization (WHO, 2003) as a 'state of complete physical, mental, and social well-being'.

Hermaphroditism A term no longer used in the social sciences (but still used in the natural sciences in sexual differentiation) to refer to individuals born with 'ambiguous' genitalia.

Heteronormativity The assumption that heterosexuality is a universal norm, therefore making homosexuality invisible or 'abnormal'.

Heterosexism A set of overt and covert social practices in both the public and private spheres that privileges heterosexuality over other sexual orientations.

Hidden curriculum The understandings that students develop as a result of the institutional requirements and day-to-day realities they encounter in their schooling; typically refers to norms, such as competition, individualism, and obedience, as well as to a sense of one's place in school and social hierarchies.

Historical-comparative theory An approach that stresses how societies evolve, temporally and over large areas of geography, in particular ways based on the specific history of the unit (city, region, or nation) under consideration.

Homophobia A term coined by George Weinberg, in 1972, to refer to the psychological fear of homosexuality; tends to neglect the wider structural sources of the homosexual taboo.

Homosexual Someone who has sex with or is attracted to a person of the same sex.

Horizontal integration A form of ownership in which one company owns a number of media organizations in different locations that are doing the same type of business; also known as 'chain ownership'; e.g., a company might own several radio stations across Canada.

Hot money Liquid assets that can be turned into cash quickly and with negligible cost. They can, consequently, be moved between investment locations—including countries—rapidly and easily.

Household People who share a dwelling, whether or not they are related by blood, adoption, or marriage.

Human capital The notion that education, skills development, and other learning processes are investments that enhance our capacities. Human capital theory builds on this notion.

Human ecology The science of ecology, as applied to sociological analyses. See also *Ecology*.

Human exemptionalism paradigm (HEP) The term used by Catton and Dunlap in arguing that the competing theoretical perspectives in sociology, including functionalism, conflict theory, and symbolic interactionism, all share a world view based on anthropocentrism.

Human relations school An approach within organizational theory that focuses on relationships within informal groups and assumes that happy group relationships produce job satisfaction, which, in turn, produces high productivity.

Hypermasculinities An excessive emphasis on practices associated with being male in any culture.

Hypotheses Testable statements composed of at least two variables and how they are related.

Identity How we see ourselves and how others see us. How we view ourselves is a product of our history and of our interpretation of others' reactions to us. How others view us is termed 'placement' and is other people's reactions to our projections of ourselves, which is termed 'announcement'.

Identity-based approach An approach to social movements that assumes dominant interpretations of reality preserve class, gender, racial, and other inequalities. The central task of social movements is to challenge and reformulate the dominant culture by reshaping identities.

Ideology A system of beliefs, ideas, and norms, reflecting the interests and experiences of a group, class, or subculture, that legitimizes or justifies the existing unequal distribution of power and privilege; ways of seeing and of understanding the world and its actors. Ideologies function by making the social appear natural or functional rather than constructed for partisan interests and advantage.

Illness See *Disease, illness, and sickness*.

Impression management Goffman's term for the 'dramatic moves' individuals make in trying to advance 'definitions of the situation' favourable to their interests and self-image. It is achieved by carefully manipulating the elements of appearance, manner, and setting.

Informal economy A wide range of legal and illegal economic activities that are not officially reported to the government.

Informal organization Complex personal and informal networks that develop among people within a bureaucracy who interact on the job.

Institutional completeness A measure of the degree to which a community offers a range of services to its members.

Institutional discrimination Discrimination built into how an institution is structured or how it operates.

International Monetary Fund (IMF) The IMF was established as a part of the Bretton Woods System to supply short term relief funds to the member country that are suffering from the shortage of foreign exchange to settle the balance of payments. The function of the fund was altered in the late 1970s as an enforcer of neoliberal policies on those countries that borrowed the structural adjustment loans.

Interpretive theory An approach that pays close attention to the cultural meanings held by actors, derived from socialization in the group, which is seen as the key to understanding human behaviour and patterns of action.

Intersexed (bodies) Infants born with genetic, hormonal, and anatomical configurations that do not coincide with normative anatomical sexual difference (male/female).

Labour power Marx argued that labour is work and labour power is the capacity to work. The only real power that the proletariat has under capitalism is the power to choose whether to work.

Labour process theory A neo-Marxist approach to organizations and the conduct of work that focuses on the alienation of the worker and on power relationships between capitalists and workers.

Level of analysis Refers to the scale and size of population being looked at in a work of empirical research. Large-scale historical trends and data about large populations of people (macro), organizational processes (meso), or small groups (micro) are the most common levels of analysis, though any one study may bridge or move between these three levels as necessary.

Life expectancy at birth The average number of years left to live for a newborn in a given period. Life expectancy is distinct from life span, which is the oldest age humans can attain.

Lifelong learning The ongoing expectations for people to acquire new knowledge and capacities through learning that occurs in various levels and kinds of formal education as well as in other learning contexts; associated with increasing emphasis on the new economy and the continuing transitions that individuals undergo throughout their lives.

Lifeworld A concept in phenomenology referring to the lived, intersubjective experiences of people sharing a way of life. It is characterized by taken-for-granted assumptions about their constructed social reality.

Looking-glass self In Cooley's symbolic interactionist approach, the idea that self-concept is based on a person's perceptions of the opinions that others hold about him or her.

Macro See *Micro; macro*.

Macrosociology The study of social institutions and large social groups; the study of the processes that depict societies as a whole and of the social structural aspects of a given society.

Marxism Based on the work of Karl Marx, the historical materialist school of thought that posits a structural explanation for historical change, namely, that the economic base of society determines change in all other realms.

Mass-society theory An argument that holds that modern life creates isolated, disoriented individuals who are easily manipulated by the media and extremist politicians.

Master status A status characteristic that overrides other status characteristics. When a person is assigned a label of 'deviant' (for example, 'murderer', 'drug addict', 'cheater'), that label is usually read by others as signifying the most essential aspects of the individual's character.

Matrifocal A family life system focused around the women, who earn most of the money and hold the family together (often in the absence of a male breadwinner).

Matrilineal descent The tracing of relationships and inheritance through the female line.

Means of production Wealth-generating property such as land, factories, and machinery.

Medicalization The tendency for more and more of life to be defined as relevant to medical diagnosis and treatment.

Mega-cities Cities of 10 million or more residents.

Melting-pot policies Policies that are most notable for their failure to recognize difference among communities and ethnic/racial groups, derived from American liberal individualistic ideology that assumes that immigrants should discard all of the traditions and distinctions they brought to the United States with them, such as their ethnic language or national identity, and become nothing but 'Americans'.

Metropolitan area With respect to everyday behaviour and economic activity, the unified entity formed on a de facto basis by a large city and its suburbs. See also *Census metropolitan areas*.

Micro; macro Used analytically to distinguish small-scale, face-to-face interaction settings (*micro*) from institutional arrangements such as the economy or state and from large-scale collective processes like revolutions and religious movements (*macro*).

Microsociology The analysis of small groups and of the face-to-face interactions that occur within these groups in the everyday.

Middle-range theory Developed by American sociologist Robert Merton, theories of the middle range consider levels of analysis above the micro and somewhat below the whole society in order to develop manageable theories that can be tested. Theories of suicide, theories regarding the relationship between Protestantism and capitalism, and theories of revolutions are examples of such middle-range theories.

Mind In Mead's theory, a 'social emergent' created through symbolic interaction, consisting of the ability to think, to carry on an internal conversation. Mind is made possible through the internalization of language.

Mode of production   Marx's concept referring to the economic structure of society, consisting of the forces and relations of production; the 'base' that conditions the 'superstructure' of politics, law, religion, art, and so on.

Modified extended family   Several generations who live near each other and maintain close social and economic contact.

Monarchy   Rule by a single individual who claims legitimacy based on royal lineage.

Morbidity rate   The sickness rate per a specified number of people over a specified period of time.

Mortality rate   The death rate per a specified number of people over a specified period of time.

Multiculturalism   In Canada, a government policy to promote tolerance among cultural groups and to assist ethnic groups in preserving the values and traditions that are important to them; multiculturalism became official policy in 1971, following the report of the Royal Commission on Bilingualism and Biculturalism.

Multinational corporations   Companies that have significant production facilities in more than one national jurisdiction; those detached from any particular country, with loyalty to no country, are sometimes labelled 'transnational corporations'.

Multivariate theory   A theoretical approach that stresses how society can be understood as being made up of certain 'variables' that interact with each other, producing results that can be measured in order to develop a theory of society. Durkheim's analysis of the various 'variables' of religion and marital status that help predict suicide rates is probably the most influential early version of multivariate theory.

Naturalistic attitude   Schütz's term for the common-sense mindset of people inhabiting a lifeworld. It is grounded in an intersubjective agreement that their world is as it appears to the members of a group or community—that is, a collective suspension of doubt that permits a taken-for-granted practicality.

Negotiation   A discussion intended to produce an agreement.

Neighbourhood   A recognizable physical area within a city, with or without formal boundaries.

Neo-liberalism   An economic doctrine that supports free trade between countries, cuts in social spending, and measures such as deregulation or privatization.

New economy   A term used to highlight the shift in emphasis from industrial production within specific industries, firms, and nations to economic activities driven by information and high-level technologies, global competition, and international networks, and knowledge-based advancement.

New environmental paradigm (NEP)   The term used by Catton and Dunlap in arguing that environmental sociology constitutes a paradigm shift within general sociology based on the understanding that human societies cannot be separate and distinct from nature.

Nominalism   An ontological position that insists that only flesh-and-blood individuals are real and have the capacity to act; collective terms like 'the state' or 'economy' are mere verbal expressions and consist only of aggregated individual actions.

Non-standard work   Jobs that are characterized by an increasingly tenuous or precarious relationship between employer and employee, including part-time employment, temporary employment, contract work, multiple job-holding, and self-employment; also termed 'contingent work' and 'casual work'.

Norms   The rules and expectations of appropriate behaviour under various social circumstances. Norms create social consequences that have the effect of regulating appearance and behaviour.

Nuclear family   A husband, wife, and their children, sharing a common residence and co-operating economically.

Numerical flexibility   Part of a new general managerial approach that rests on flexibility in employment; involves shrinking or eliminating the core workforce (in continuous, full-time positions) and replacing them with workers in non-standard employment.

Objective   Something completely unaffected by the characteristics of the person or instrument observing it. 'Objective' observations were used in the past to establish the truth of scientific theories until it became clear that completely objective observations are impossible.

Ontology   Inquiry that deals with the fundamental nature of things—of reality or existence—and that specifies the essential properties or characteristics of phenomena.

Operationalization   The translation of abstract theories and concepts into observable hypotheses and variables. Once abstract ideas are operationalized, we can test them in a study.

Organization   A group of people participating in a division of labour that is co-ordinated by communication and leadership to achieve a common goal or goals; includes both spontaneous and formal organizations.

Paradigm   A set of assumptions used to view society and people's behaviour. A paradigm serves as a model for which questions sociologists should ask and how they should interpret the answers.

Parties   Voluntary associations that organize for the collective pursuit of interests such as political parties or lobbying groups; common in Weberian scholarship.

Patriarchy   A society or family system in which men have more authority than women.

Patrilineal descent   The tracing of relationships and inheritance through the male line.

Pedagogy   Processes associated with the organization and practice of teaching; more generally, various kinds of interactions (and how these are understood and organized) in teaching/learning situations.

Political conflict perspective   A resource mobilization approach that focuses on how groups (typically classes) promote collective interests.

Political institutions   Established rules and procedures for the conduct of political affairs.

Political movements   Social movements that challenge established state policies and practices in order to bring about social and political changes.

Political party   An organization dedicated to winning political power by controlling government.

Political process approach   An approach that assumes that political constraints and opportunities influence the rise and fall of social movements, as well as their institutional organization.

Politics   The process in which individuals and groups act to promote their interests, often in conflict with others.

Polyandry   The practice of being legally married to more than one husband at a time.

Polygamy   The practice of being legally married to more than one spouse at a time.

Polygyny   The practice of being legally married to more than one wife at a time.

Population momentum   The tendency for population to keep growing even when the fertility rate drops to just the replacement level of 2.1 children per woman, as a consequence of a high proportion of persons in the child-bearing ages.

Power   In Marxist sociology, a social relationship that has a material base. Those who own the means of production have the power to exploit workers through the appropriation of their labour efforts. In Weberian sociology, power is more broadly defined and can reflect an individual's or group's capacity to exert their will over others.

Prejudice   An attitude by which individuals are prejudged on the basis of stereotyped characteristics assumed to be common to all members of the individual's group.

Primary socialization   The most intense socialization, which occurs from birth to adolescence and which takes place in or is strongly influenced by the family.

Privatization   The movement away from a completely universally available and state-funded medical system to one that includes profit-making components.

Progressive conservation   The movement originating in the nineteenth century that sought to check environmental destruction caused by unbridled economic growth and that resulted in the founding of such modern environmental organizations as the Audubon Society and the Sierra Club.

Proletariat   People who sell their labour power to capitalists in return for a wage; the working class.

Protestant ethic thesis   Weber's argument that aspects of the Protestant religion originally imbued people with a sense of dedication to their work that helped to lay the foundations for capitalism.

PYLL   'Potential years of life lost'; refers to premature mortality, taking into account the average age of death from a particular cause.

Queer   A once derogatory term reclaimed by the LGBT (lesbian, gay, bisexual, transgendered) community to galvanize and help forge a public collective identity and to take apart and blur sexual boundaries. The term is used to stress the inessential, fluid, and multiple-sited forms of sexual identity.

Race   A group that is defined on the basis of perceived physical differences, such as skin colour.

Race to the bottom   The outcome produced by competitive tax-cutting motivated by the desire to attract (and keep) investors.

Racialization   Sets of social processes and practices whereby social relations among people are structured according to visible physical difference among peoples, to the advantage of those in the visible majority and the disadvantage of those who are visible minorities.

Racism   A belief that groups that differ in physical appearance also differ in personality characteristics, intelligence, honesty, reliability, law abidingness, and so on. Racism also implies a belief that these differences make one group superior to another.

Rationalization   In Weber's view, the movement away from mystical and religious interpretations of the world to the development of human thought and belief based on the systematic accumulation of evidence; associated with the emergence of impersonal authority.

Rational-legal authority   Power considered legitimate because those subject to it believe commands are based on formally established rules, procedures, and certified expertise.

Reductionism   An analytical strategy that explains wholes or totalities by reducing them to the aggregated properties of their constituent parts; for example, attempts to explain social facts in strict psychological terms (behaviourism) or as the consequence of underlying biological factors (sociobiology).

Relative deprivation theory   A breakdown approach that claims radical social movements result from people's subjective feelings of fear and frustration.

Relativism   The idea that there is no single, unchangeable truth about anything; all things are either true or false only relative to particular standards. Many sociologists who do not view sociology as a science take their stance persuaded by relativism.

Reliability   The consistency of a measure, indicator, or study. Note that reliability is different from validity and does not refer to the accuracy of a measure or study.

Resocialization   The process of learning new roles in response to changes in life circumstances.

Resource mobilization approach   An approach that assumes social movements are quite similar to other organizations.

Risk society   A theory of the new modernity that argues that perception of risk is modernity's defining feature, creating uncertainty and compelling individuals to seek new strategic allegiances.

Rites of passage   Rituals performed by all cultures to mark major transitions in life; these rites usually display a three-part structure: a symbolically marked departure from an old identity or phase of life, a symbolically marked period of innocent non-involvement, and a symbolic incorporation into the rights and responsibilities of a new identity or phase of life.

Role expectations   The expected characteristics and social behaviours of an individual in a particular position in society.

Role-making   The continual improvising and revising of our actions as others' reactions to them change and are imputed.

Roles   The specific duties and obligations expected of one who occupies a specific status.

Role-taking   The construction in our mind of what others mean by their actions.

Sample   The group of people or objects drawn from the whole population that will be studied. In quantitative research, a great deal of time and effort is devoted to the selection of truly random samples, while in qualitative research, samples are often selected based on the theoretical importance of the people or objects.

Schooling   Processes that take place within formal educational institutions.

Scientific management   A managerial method developed in the early twentieth century by F.W. Taylor that rests on breaking up work processes into their smallest constituent parts in an effort to maximize efficiency in productivity, resulting in the separation of mental from manual labour and in the deskilling of workers; assumes that workers are motivated by economic rewards alone and that specialists know more than workers about how a task can most effectively be performed; also known as Taylorism.

Secondary socialization   The ongoing lifelong process of socialization, based on the accumulated learning of childhood and adolescence.

Sects   Religious groups, still usually relatively small, that come into being as a result of a disagreement between the members of an established church.

Secularization   The social process resulting in the declining presence and influence of religious beliefs, practices, symbols, and institutions.

Self   In Mead's theory, an emergent entity with a capacity to be both a subject and an object, as reflected upon in one's own mind. In Goffman's dramaturgical theory, the self is a more shifting 'dramatic effect', a staged product of the scenes one performs in.

Serial monogamy   A pattern of marriage, divorce, and remarriage, resulting in having more than one spouse over a lifetime, but only one at a time.

Service economy   The economic sector in which most Canadians currently are employed. In comparison to primary industry (the extraction of natural resources) and manufacturing (processing raw materials into usable goods and services), the service economy is based on the provision of services rather than a tangible product, ranging widely from advertising and retailing to entertaining to generating and distributing information. Also called the 'tertiary sector'.

Sex   The biological differences between females and males, determined at conception.

Sex ratio; primary sex ratio; secondary sex ratio   The number of males in relation to the number of females in a population. The primary sex ratio is the sex ratio at birth, typically in the range of about 105 baby boys per 100 baby girls. The secondary sex ratio is the sex ratio beyond infancy.

Sexual harassment   Unwanted attention linked to the gender of the person receiving that attention.

Sexuality   The ways in which we experience and express ourselves as sexual beings.

Sexual orientation   An individual's sexual preference(s), which could include partners of the opposite sex, same sex, both sexes, or neither.

Sexual scripting   An approach that argues that socio-cultural processes are fundamental in determining what is perceived as sexual and how individuals should behave sexually.

Sickness   See *Disease, illness, and sickness*.

Situated identity   According to symbolic interactionist theory, social life is in a constant process of change, imposing changes in, and new forms of, identity announcement and identity placement. A particular announcement–placement identity at any point in time is referred to as a situated identity.

Situated transaction   A process of social interaction that lasts as long as the individuals find themselves in each other's company. As applied to the study of deviance, the concept of the situated transaction helps us to understand how deviant acts are social and not just individual products.

Social capital   A concept widely thought to have been developed by American sociologist James Coleman in 1988, but discussed by Pierre Bourdieu in a similar way in the early 1980s; reflects the power that is derived from ties to social networks.

Social constructionism   The sociological theory that argues that social problems and issues are less objective conditions than they are collective social definitions based on how they are framed and interpreted.

Social control   The various and myriad ways in which members of social groups express their disapproval of people and behaviours. These include name-calling, ridicule, ostracism, incarceration, and even killing.

Social environment   The people and relationships that surround us.

Social facts   Patterns of social life and forces external to the individual that shape behaviour (e.g., religion, age distribution, ethnicity, rates of suicide, crime, or divorce); drawing causal connections between these larger social facts becomes a main sociological tool to explain behaviour, rather than individual or psychological explanations.

Social group   A number of individuals, defined by formal or informal criteria of membership, who share a feeling of unity or are bound together in stable patterns of interaction; two or more individuals who have a specific common identity and who interact in a reciprocal social relationship.

Social institution   A stable, well-acknowledged pattern of social relationships that endures over time, including the family, the economy, education, politics, religion, the mass media, medicine, and science and technology. Social institutions are the result of an enduring set of ideas about how to accomplish various goals generally recognized as important in a society.

Social interaction   The process by which people act and react in relationships with others.

Social movement   The co-ordinated, voluntary action of non-elites (those people with no control over major resources) for the manifest purpose of changing the distribution of social goods.

Social networks   Based on kinship, friendship, or economic ties, these may include social transactions (shared recreation, communication, gift exchanges, mutual assistance) and shared tastes and values.

Social realism   The ontological position that collective terms—such as 'patriarchy', the 'economy', 'the church'—correspond to real emergent entities, to structures that exert causal influence on individual lives.

Social relationships   Interactions of people in a society. Because people share culture and a sense of collective existence, these interactions will to some extent be recurrent and predictable.

Social reproduction   A range of unpaid activities that help to reproduce workforces daily and over generations; typically, though not exclusively, performed by women in the family household.

Social revolution   A rapid, fundamental transformation of a society's state and class structures, often accomplished through violent means.

Social structure   Patterns of behaviour or social relationships developed and accepted through time in a given group, organization, or society.

Social support   The various ways people support each other through interactions.

Socialization   The process by which people learn to become members of society. See also *primary socialization*; *secondary socialization*.

Society   The largest collection of social relationships in which people live their lives; some very encompassing international relationships among nations (such as the European Common Market or the North American Free Trade Agreement), but these cover only a narrow range of types of activities (for example, economic relationships) compared to societies.

Sociological imagination   A term coined by American sociologist C Wright Mills that calls on sociologists and on all people to attempt to fit so-called individual circumstances (private troubles) appropriately within their social and historical context, thus moving them to the level of public issues.

Sociology   The systematic study of social behaviours in human societies.

Socio-technical systems theory   An approach within organizational theory that holds that the social and technological aspects of an organization should be developed simultaneously. It also focuses on semi-autonomous work groups rather than on individual workers.

Solidarity   The quality of an integrated and well-functioning society that is brought into harmony through an adaptive cultural foundation.

'Sound economic policies'   As understood by a number of international economic organizations, these usually imply assurance that government budgets are not in deficit, a dominant role for the private sector in the provision of most goods and services, and policies of openness to trade. See also *Neo-liberalism*.

Spontaneous organization   An organization that arises quickly to meet a single goal then disbands when that goal is achieved or perceived to be beyond reach, or when the organization becomes absorbed by a formal organization.

State   Institutions associated with governing over a specific territory as well as establishing and enforcing rules within that territory. The state in a number of countries (including Canada) also is involved with providing various public services. Procedures and organizations concerned with creating, administering, and enforcing rules or decisions for conduct within a given territory.

Status   A socially defined position that a person holds in a given social group or organization, to which are attached certain rights, duties, and obligations; a relational term, as each status exists only through its relation to one or more other statuses filled by other people.

Status degradation ceremony   The rituals by which formal transition is made from non-deviant to deviant status. Examples include the criminal trial and the psychiatric hearing.

Status groups   Organized groups comprising people who have similar social status situations. These groups organize to maintain or expand their social privileges by excluding outsiders from their ranks and by trying to gain status recognition from other groups.

Strain theory   A category of explanation that seeks to understand how deviant behaviour results as people attempt to solve problems that the social structure presents to them.

Stratification   The hierarchical patterns of inequality found in social life, in terms of gender, economic well-being, status, and political power.

Structural Adjustment Programs (SAPs)   SAPs are loans advanced to the peripheral countries in order to secure their payment of interest and principle with the objective of securing foreign exchange earnings.

Structural analysis or approach   An approach within organizational theory in the Weberian tradition; focuses on the structural characteristics of organizations and their effect on the people within them; in the context of urban studies, the analysis of the functions cities perform, the size and shape of their governments, and who has what bearing on decisions and outcomes involving cities.

Structural discrimination   See *Institutional discrimination*.

Structural functionalism   A theoretical paradigm that emphasizes the way each part of a society functions to fulfill the needs of society as a whole.

Structure   The 'concrete' elements of society that are embodied and enacted by things and people, in opposition to the cultural elements of society.

Subculture   A subset of cultural traits of the larger society that also includes distinctive values, beliefs, norms, style of dress, and behaviour.

Supply-side theory   The notion that a product available in a society is determined as much by how it is being supplied as by the demand for the product; the state of religion can be viewed through supply-side theory as a product like any other.

Sustainable development   The principle that economic growth and environmental conservation are compatible goals.

Symbolic ethnicity   Ethnicity that has become purely a matter of personal identification and that has little or no impact upon how people live their lives or relate to one another.

Symbolic interactionism   An intellectual tradition in sociology akin to interpretive theory, founded in the early twentieth-century work of Charles Horton Cooley and George Herbert Mead, although the term itself was not coined until years later by Herbert Blumer. Symbolic interactionism emphasizes the importance of understanding the meanings of social action, and uses ethnographic methods to discover these meanings for individuals in an effort to explain human conduct.

Symbols   The heart of cultural systems, for with them we construct thoughts, ideas, and other ways of representing reality to others and to ourselves; gestures, artifacts, or uses of language that represent something else.

Systemic discrimination   Discrimination that is built into the fabric of Canadian life, as in the case of institutional self-segregation.

Systemic theory   A breakdown approach, advanced by Neil Smelser, that views society as a set of interrelated elements that work together to maintain stability.

Systems theory   An approach within organizational theory that sees organizations as open systems and that views organizations and their goals as shaped by the interests of their participants and their environments.

Taboo   Behaviour that is prohibited, such as incest and sexual relations with specific categories of kin; from the Tongan word meaning 'sacred' or 'inviolable'.

Technology   The practical things we as humans make and use, and the knowledge we require to build, maintain, and enhance them.

Terrorism   Physical violence directed against civilians, without regard for who will suffer, in order to promote political objectives.

Theory   An integrated set of concepts and statements that specify relations of ordered dependence and causal connection between phenomena. At the most general level, theories are perspectives, or ways of seeing, that conceptualize and highlight certain patterns and relations among complex realities. Theories are not tested directly. They may also be simple or complex: the more complex a theory, the more difficult it is to operationalize and test it.

Third World   Poor countries; an element of a classification in which the First World was made up of Western Europe, North America, Australia, and New Zealand, the Second World of the various Communist countries (the Soviet Union, the numerous Soviet satellites, and China), and the Third World of poorer countries in Asia, Africa, and Latin America. See also *Developing countries*.

Totalitarianism   Form of the state that involves intervening in and controlling all aspects of life both public and private.

Traditional authority   Power considered legitimate because those subject to it believe that is the way things have always been done.

Transitions   The pathways that people follow from family life, into and out of education, and into various jobs or other social situations throughout their life course.

Unemployment rate   People are considered to be unemployed only if they do not have a job and are actively looking for a job. The unemployment rate is the number of people who meet those two conditions divided by the labour force (which includes both the employed and unemployed) expressed as a percentage. Those who do not have a job and are not looking for one are considered to be not in the labour force.

Urbanism   Behaviour patterns associated with cities.

Urbanization   The nature, extent, and distribution of cities in the larger society or nation.

Urban renewal   A general term for improving buildings and land use; can include redevelopment, rehabilitation, or both.

Utilitarian perspective   A resource mobilization approach that focuses on how individuals promote self-interest.

Validity   The accuracy of a measure, indicator, or study; many different dimensions to validity can be established through formal tests, logic, or depth of understanding.

Values   Shared ideas about how something is ranked in terms of its relative social desirability, worth, or goodness; what a group or society views as right and wrong, good and bad, desirable and undesirable.

Variable   The operational or observable equivalent of concepts. Many concepts require more than one variable for proper operationalization. The key characteristic of variables is that there must be a range of different values that can be observed.

Verstehen   Popularized by Max Weber, the German word for 'understanding' emphasizes the need to understand the cultural meanings actors carry (in Weber's context, the meanings associated with Calvinist religious values) to develop an adequate explanation of their behaviour.

Vertical integration   A form of ownership in which one company owns firms or divisions that are part of the overall process; in media production firms would be integrated by linking production, distribution, and exhibition, e.g., a company that owns a movie studio, a movie distributor, and movie theatres.

Vertical mosaic   A view of Canadian society as constituting an ethnically divided stratification system, with the charter groups at the top, Native people at the bottom, and other ethnic immigrant groups fitting in depending on their entrance status; from John Porter's *The Vertical Mosaic* (1965).

World Bank   The World Bank was established as a part of the Bretton Woods System to supply reconstruction funds to the war-devastated European countries and Japan. The function of the Bank was altered in the late 1970s as an enforcer of neoliberal policies on those countries that borrowed the structural adjustment loans.

World-system perspective   A perspective that suggests a historical understanding of social transformation by looking at inter-connectedness of the countries and by overcoming the disciplinary boundaries among social sciences.

● References ● ● ● ● ● ●

Abercrombie, Nicholas, Stephen Hill, and Bryan S. Turner. 2006. *The Penguin Dictionary of Sociology*, 5th edn. Toronto: Penguin.

Abrahams, Roger D. 2006 [1964]. *Deep Down in the Jungle: Black American Folklore from the Streets of Philadelphia*. New York: Aldine de Gruyter.

Abu-Laban, Baha, and Daiva Stasiulis. 1992. 'Ethnic Pluralism under Siege: Popular and Partisan Opposition to Multiculturalism', *Canadian Public Policy* 27, 4: 365–86.

Abu-Lughod, Janet L. 1991. *Changing Cities: Urban Sociology*. New York: HarperCollins.

Acker, Joan. 1980. 'Women and Stratification: A Review of Recent Literature', *Contemporary Sociology* 9: 25–34.

———. 1988. 'Class, Gender, and the Relations of Distribution', *Signs* 13: 473–97.

———. 1990. 'Hierarchies, Jobs, and Bodies: A Theory of Gendered Organizations', *Gender and Society* 4: 139–58.

———. 2000. 'Rewriting Class, Race, and Gender: Problems in Feminist Rethinking', in Myra Marx Ferree, Judith Lorber, and Beth Hess, eds, *Revisioning Gender*. New York: AltaMira, 44–69.

Acker, Sandra. 1999. *The Realities of Teachers' Work: Never a Dull Moment*. London: Cassell.

Adamic, L., and Eytan Adar. 2005. 'How to Search a Social Network', *Social Networks* 27: 187–203.

Adams, Robert M. 1966. *The Evolution of Urban Society*. Chicago: Aldine.

Adams, Tracey L. 1998. 'Combining Gender, Class, and Race: Structuring Relations in the Ontario Dental Profession', *Gender and Society* 12: 578–97.

———. 2000. *A Dentist and a Gentleman: Gender and the Rise of Dentistry in Ontario*. Toronto: University of Toronto Press.

Adler, Patricia A., and Peter Adler. 1995. 'Dynamics of Inclusion and Exclusion in Preadolescent Cliques', *Social Psychology Quarterly* 58, 3: 145–62.

——— and ———. 2006. 'The Deviance Society', *Deviant Behavior* 27: 129–48.

Aglietta, Michel. 1979. *A Theory of Economic Regulation: The US Experience*. London: Verso.

Agnew, Robert. 1985. 'A Revised Strain Theory of Delinquency', *Social Forces* 64, 1: 151–67.

———. 2006. 'General Strain Theory: Current Status and Directions', in F.T. Cullen, J.P. Wright, and K.R. Blevins, eds, *Taking Stock: The Status of Criminological Theory*. New Brunswick, NJ: Transaction.

——— and Lisa Broidy. 1997. 'Gender and Crime: A General Strain Theory Perspective', *Journal of Research in Crime and Delinquency* 34: 275–306.

Agocs, Carol, and Monica Boyd. 1993. 'The Canadian Ethnic Mosaic Recast for the 90s', in James Curtis, Edward Grabb, and Neil Guppy, eds, *Social Inequality in Canada: Patterns, Problems, Policies*, 2nd edn. Scarborough, Ont.: Prentice-Hall Canada, 330–52.

Ahlburg, Dennis A. 1998. 'Julian Simon and the Population Growth Debate', *Population and Development Review* 24: 317–27.

Akers, R. L., and G.F. Jensen. 2006. 'Empirical Status of Social Learning Theory: Past, Present, and Future', in F.T. Cullen, J.P. Wright, and K.R. Blevins, eds, *Taking Stock: The Status of Criminological Theory, Vol. 15: Advances in Criminological Theory*. Piscataway NJ: Transaction Publishing.

Albanese, Patrizia. 2006. 'Small Town, Big Benefits: The Ripple Effect of $7/day Child Care', *Canadian Review of Sociology and Anthropology* 43, 2: 125–40.

Albas, Dan, and Cheryl Albas. 2003. 'Aces and Bombers: The Postexam Impression Management Strategies of Students', in Ramón S. Guerra and Robert Lee Maril, eds, *A Social World: Classic and Contemporary Sociological Readings*, 3rd edn. Boston: Pearson Custom Publishing, 27–36.

Albury, Rebecca M. 1999. *The Politics of Reproduction*. Sydney, Australia: Allen & Unwin.

Alden, H.L., and K.F. Parker. 2005. 'Gender Role Ideology, Homophobia and Hate Crime: Linking Attitudes to Macro-Level Anti-Gay and Lesbian Hate Crimes', *Deviant Behavior* 26 (4): 321–343.

Alford, Robert. 1998. *The Craft of Inquiry: Theories, Methods, Evidence*. New York: Oxford University Press.

Ali, Jennifer, and Edward Grabb. 1998. 'Ethnic Origin, Class Origin and Educational Attainment in Canada: Further Evidence on the Mosaic Thesis', *Journal of Canadian Studies* 33: 3–21.

Alkhateeb, M.B., and S.E. Abugideiri. 2007. *Change From Within: Diverse Perspectives on Domestic Violence in Muslim Communities*. Great Falls, VA: Peaceful Families Project.

Alksnis, Christine, Serge Desmarais and James Curtis. 2008. 'Workforce Segregation and the Gender Wage Gap: Is "Women's" Work Valued as Highly as "Men's"?', *Journal of Applied Social Psychology* 38 (6): 1416–1441.

Allahar, Anton. 1994. 'More Than an Oxymoron: The Social Construction of Primordial Attachment', *Canadian Ethnic Studies* 16, 3: 15–63.

———. 1995. *Sociology and the Periphery: Theories and Issues*, 2nd edn. Toronto: Garamond.

——— and James E. Côté. 1998. *Richer and Poorer: The Structure of Inequality in Canada*. Toronto: Lorimer.

Allcorn, Seth. 1997. 'Parallel Virtual Organizations: Managing and Working in the Virtual Workplace', *Administration and Society* 29: 412–39.

Allen, Judith. 1990. 'Do We Need a Theory of the State?', in Sophie Watson, ed., *Playing the State: Australian Feminist Interventions*. London: Verso, 21–37.

Allen, Mary, and Chantal Vaillancourt. 2004. *Class of 2000: Profile of Post-Secondary Graduates and Student Debt*. Ottawa: Statistics Canada.

Altman, Dennis. 1986. *AIDS in the Mind of America*. New York: Doubleday-Anchor.

Alwin, Duane. 1990. 'Historical Changes in Parental Orientations to Children', in Patricia Adler and Peter Adler, eds, *Sociological Studies of Child Development*, vol. 3. Greenwich, Conn.: JAI, 65–86.

Amato, Paul. 2004. 'Parenting through Family Transitions', *Social Policy Journal of New Zealand* 23 (Dec.): 31–44.

Andersen, Robert, and Anthony Heath. 2002. 'Class Matters: The Persisting Effects of Contextual Social Class on Individual Voting in Britain, 1964–97', *European Sociological Review* 18: 125–38.

Andres Bellamy, Lesley. 1993. 'Life Trajectories, Action, and Negotiating the Transition from High School', in Paul Anisef and Paul Axelrod, eds, *Transitions: Schooling and Employment in Canada*. Toronto: Thompson Educational, 136–57.

Anisef, Paul, Paul Axelrod, Etta Baichman-Anisef, Carl James, and Anton Turritin. 2000. *Opportunity and Uncertainty: Life Course Experiences of the Class of '73*. Toronto: University of Toronto Press.

Apple, Michael W. 1997. 'What Postmodernists Forget: Cultural Capital and Official Knowledge', in A.H. Halsey, Hugh Lauder, Phillip Brown, and Amy Stuart Wells, eds, *Education: Culture, Economy, and Society*. New York: Oxford University Press, 595–604.

Appleton, Lynn M. 1995. 'Rethinking Medicalization: Alcoholism and Anomalies', in Joel Best, ed., *Images of Issues: Typifying Contemporary Social Problems*, 2nd edn. New York: Aldine de Gruyter, 59–80.

Arat-Koç, Sedef. 1990. 'Importing Housewives: Non-citizen Domestic Workers and the Crisis of the Domestic Sphere in Canada', in Meg Luxton, Harriet Rosenberg, and Sedef Arat-Koç, eds, *Through the Kitchen Window: The Politics of Home and Family*, 2nd edn. Toronto: Garamond, 81–103.

Archibald, W. Peter. 1976. 'Face-to-Face: The Alienating Effects of Class, Status and Power Divisions', *American Sociological Review* 41: 819–37.

———. 1978. *Social Psychology as Political Economy*. Toronto: McGraw-Hill Ryerson.

Armstrong, Pat, and Hugh Armstrong. 1994. *The Double Ghetto: Canadian Women and Their Segregated Work*. Toronto: McClelland & Stewart.

Aronson, Hal. 1993. 'Becoming an Environmental Activist: The Process of Transformation from Everyday Life into Making History in the Hazardous Waste Movement', *Journal of Political and Military Sociology* 1: 63–80.

Arrighi, Giovanni. 1994. *The Long Twentieth Century: Money, Power, and the Origins of Our Time*. London & New York: Verso.

———. 2007. *Adam Smith in Beijing*. London & New York: Verso.

Artis, Julie, and Eliza Pavalko. 2003. 'Explaining the Decline in Women's Household Labor: Individual Change and Cohort Differences', *Journal of Marriage and Family* 65: 746–761.

Asad, T. 1993. *Genealogies of Region: Discipline and Reasons of Power in Christianity and Islam*. Baltimore: The Johns Hopkins University Press.

Asbridge, M., R.E. Mann, and R. Flam-Zalcman. 2004. 'The Criminalization of Impaired Driving in Canada: Assessing the Deterrent Impact of Canada's First Per Se Law', *Journal of Studies in Alcohol* 65, 4: 450–9.

Atwood, Margaret. 1994 [1968]. *The Edible Woman*. Toronto: McClelland & Stewart.

AuCoin, Kathy. 2005. 'Children and Youth as Victims of Violent Crime', *Juristat* 25, 1. Ottawa: Statistics Canada Catalogue no. 85–022–XIE.

Aya, Rod. 1990. *Rethinking Revolutions and Collective Violence: Studies on Concept, Theory, and Method*. Amsterdam: Het Spinhuis.

Azzi, Stephen. 2005. 'Negotiating Cultural Space in the Global Economy: The United States, UNESCO, and the Convention on Cultural Diversity', *International Journal* 60, 3: 765–84.

Baer, Doug. 2004. 'Educational Credentials and the Changing Occupational Structure.' in James Curtis, Edward Grabb, and Neil Guppy, eds, *Social Inequality in Canada: Patterns, Problems, and Policies*, 4th edn. Toronto: Pearson Prentice-Hall, 115–30.

Bafoil, François. 1998. 'Weber critique de Marx: Elements d'une interpretation de la crise des systèmes bureaucratiques communistes', *L'Année sociologique* 48: 385–415.

Baines, Carol T., Patricia M. Evans, and Sheila Neysmith, eds. 1998. *Women's Caring: Feminist Perspectives on Social Welfare*, 2nd edn. Toronto: Oxford University Press.

Baird, P. 1997. 'Individual Interests, Societal Interests, and Reproductive Technologies', *Perspectives in Biology and Medicine* 40, 3: 440–52.

Baird, Vanessa. 2001. *The No-Nonsense Guide to Sexual Diversity*. Toronto: Between the Lines.

Bakan, Abigail, and Daiva K. Stasiulis. 1994. 'Foreign Domestic Worker Policy in Canada and the Social Boundaries of Modern Citizenship', *Science and Society* 58, 1: 7–33.

Bakan, Joel. 2004. The Corporation: *The Pathological Pursuit of Profit and Power*. New York: Free Press.

Baker, Maureen. 1995. *Canadian Family Policies: Cross-national Comparisons*. Toronto: University of Toronto Press.

———. 2001. *Families, Labour and Love: Family Diversity in a Changing World*. Vancouver: University of British Columbia Press.

———. 2005. 'Medically Assisted Conception: Revolutionizing Family or Perpetuating a Nuclear and Gendered Model?', *Journal of Comparative Family Studies* 36, 4: 521–43.

———. 2006. *Restructuring Family Policies: Divergences and Convergences*. Toronto: University of Toronto Press.

———. 2007. *Choices and Constraints in Family Life*. Toronto: Oxford University Press.

——— and David Tippin. 1999. *Poverty, Social Assistance and the Employability of Mothers: Restructuring Welfare States*. Toronto: University of Toronto Press.

Baker, P.M. 1991. 'Socialization after Death: The Might of the Living Dead', in B.B. Hess and E.W. Markson, eds, *Growing Old in America*. New Brunswick, NJ: Transaction, 539–51.

Bales, Robert F. 1950. *Interaction Process Analysis: A Method for the Study of Small Groups*. Chicago: University of Chicago Press.

Bandura, Albert. 1973. *Aggression: A Social Learning Analysis*. Englewood Cliffs, NJ: Prentice-Hall.

Banton, Michael. 1987. *Racial Theories*. Cambridge: Cambridge University Press.

Barbosa, Luiz C. 1996. 'The People of the Forest against International Capital: Systemic and Anti-Systemic Forces in the Battle for the Preservation of the Brazilian Amazon Rainforest', *Sociological Perspective* 39 (2): 317–31.

Bardasi, Elena, and Janet Gornick. 2008. 'Working for less? Women's part-time wage penalties across countries', *Feminist Economics* 14 (1): 37–72.

Barker, E. 1984. *The Making of a Moonie: Choice or Brainwashing?* Oxford: Blackwell Publishers.

———. 2005. 'New Religions and Cults in Europe', in Lindsay Jones, ed., *The Encyclopedia of Religion*, Lindsay Jones, ed., New York: The Free Press.

———. 2007. 'How do modern European societies deal with new religious movements?', in Peter Meusburger, Michael Welker, and Edgar Wunder, eds, *Knowledge & Space: Clashes of Knowledge*. Heidelberg: Springer.

Barker, John. 2003. 'Dowry', in James J. Ponzetti, ed., *International Encyclopedia of Marriage and Family*, 2nd edn. New York: Thomson Gale, 495–6.

Barndt, Deborah, ed. 1999. *Women Working the NAFTA Food Chain: Women, Food & Globalization*. Toronto: Second Story Press.

———. 2002. *Tangled Routes: Women, Work, and Globalization on the Tomato Trail*. Aurora, Ont.: Garamond Press.

Barnes, Barry. 1988. *The Nature of Power*. Cambridge: Polity.

Baron, S.W. 2003. 'Self Control, Social Consequences, and Criminal Behavior: Street Youth and the General Theory of Crime', *Journal of Research in Crime and Delinquency* 40: 403–425.

Barron, Martin, and Michael Kimmel. 2000. 'Sexual Violence in Three Pornographic Media: Towards a Sociological Explanation', *Journal of Sex Research* 37, 2: 161–8.

Barry, Brian. 1978 [1970]. *Sociologists, Economists and Democracy*. Chicago: University of Chicago Press.

Bartsch, Robert, Theresa Burnett, Tommye Diller, and Elizabeth Rankin-Williams. 2000. 'Gender Representation in Television Commercials: Updating an Update', *Sex Roles* 43: 735–43.

Bashevkin, Sylvia. 1985. *Toeing the Lines: Women and Party Politics in English Canada*. Toronto: University of Toronto Press.

Basran, Gurcharn, and B. Singh Bolaria. 2003. *The Sikhs in Canada: Migration, Race, Class and Gender*. New Delhi: Oxford University Press.

Baum, G. 2000. 'Catholicism and Secularization in Québec', in D. Lyon and M. Van Die, eds, *Rethinking Church, State, and Modernity: Canada between Europe and America*. Toronto: University of Toronto Press, 149–65.

Baumrind, Diana. 1971. 'Current Patterns of Parental Authority', *Developmental Psychology Monographs* 4: 1–107.

Beaman, L.G. 2008. *Defining Harm: Religious Freedom and the Limits of the Law*. Vancouver: UBC Press.

Beaujot, Roderic. 2000. *Earning and Caring in Canadian Families*. Peterborough, Ont.: Broadview.

Beck, Ulrich. 1996. 'World Risk Society as Cosmopolitan Society? Ecological Questions in a Framework of Manufactured Uncertainties', *Theory, Culture, and Society* 13, 4: 1–32.

Becker, Howard. 1952. 'Social Class Variations in the Teacher–Student Relationship', *Journal of Educational Sociology* 25: 451–65.

———. 1963. *Outsiders: Studies in the Sociology of Deviance*. New York: Free Press.

———. 1982. *Art Worlds*. Berkeley: University of California Press.

Beckford, J. 2003. *Social Theory & Religion*. Cambridge: Cambridge University Press.

Beck-Gernsheim, Elisabeth. 2002. *Reinventing the Family: In Search of New Lifestyles*. Cambridge: Polity.

Bell, Daniel. 1973. *The Coming of Post-industrial Society*. New York: Basic Books.

Bell, Shannon. 1994. *Reading, Writing and Rewriting the Prostitute Body*. Bloomington: Indiana University Press.

Bellah, R.N., R. Madsen, W.M. Sullivan, A. Swidler, and S.M. Tipton. 1985. *Habits of the Heart: Individualism and Commitment in American Life*. Berkeley: University of California Press.

Belsky, Jay. 1985. 'Exploring Individual Differences in Marital Change across the Transition to Parenthood: The Role of Violated Expectations', *Journal of Marriage and the Family* 47: 1037–44.

Benford, Robert D., and David A. Snow. 2000. 'Framing Processes and Social Movements: An Overview and Assessment', *Annual Review of Sociology* 26: 611–39.

Benkert, Holly. 2002. 'Liberating Insights from a Cross-Cultural Sexuality Study about Women', *American Behavioral Scientist* 45, 8: 1197–1207.

Berger, P. 1967. *The Sacred Canopy: Elements of a Sociological Theory of Religion*. Garden City, NY: Doubleday.

Berger, Peter L., and Brigitte Berger. 1975. *Sociology: A Biographical Approach*, 2nd edn. New York: Basic Books.

——— and Thomas Luckmann. 1966. *The Social Construction of Reality: Treatise in the Sociology of Knowledge*. Garden City, NY: Anchor.

Bernburg, J.G., M.D. Krohn, and C.J. Rivera. 2006. 'Official Labeling, Criminal Embeddedness, and Subsequent Delinquency: A Longitudinal Test of Labeling Theory', *Journal of Research in Crime and Delinquency* 43, 1: 67–88.

Bernstein, Basil. 1977. 'Class and Pedagogies: Visible and Invisible', in Jerome Karabel and A.H. Halsey, eds, *Power and Ideology in Education*. New York: Oxford University Press, 511–34.

Best, Joel. 2001. *Damned Lies and Statistics: Untangling Numbers from Media, Politicians and Activists*. Berkeley: University of California Press.

Beyer, P. 2006a. *Religions in Global Society*. London: Routledge.

Beyer, P. 2006b. 'Religion Among Immigrant Youth in Canada: Research Project', Department of Classics and Religious Studies, University of Ottawa. Available at http://aix1.uottawa.ca/~pbeyer/immyouth.pdf.

Beyer, Peter. 2008. 'From Far and Wide: Canadian Religious and Cultural Diversity in Global/Local Context', in L.G. Beaman and P. Beyer, eds, *Religion and Diversity in Canada*. Leiden: Brill Academic Press.

Bezanson, Kate. 2006. *Gender, the State, and Social Reproduction: Household Insecurity in Neo-Liberal Times*. Toronto: University of Toronto Press.

Bezanson, Kate, and Ellen Carter. 2006. *Public Policy and Social Reproduction: Gendering Social Capital*. Ottawa: Status of Women Canada.

Bianchi, Suzanne M., Melissa A. Milkie, Liana C. Sayer, and John P. Robinson. 2000. 'Is anyone doing the housework? Trends in the gender division of household labor', *Social Forces* 79 (1): 191–228.

Bibby, Reginald. 1993. *Unknown Gods: The Ongoing Story of Religion in Canada*. Toronto: Stoddart.

———. 2001. *Canada's Teens: Today, Yesterday and Tomorrow*. Toronto: Stoddart.

———. 2002. *Restless Gods: The Renaissance of Religion in Canada*. Toronto: Stoddart.

———. 2004. 'Section 2–Dating, Sexuality and Cohabitation', *The Future of Families Project: A Survey of Canadian Hopes and Dreams*. Ottawa: Vanier Institute of the Family, 11–24.

———. 2006. *The Boomer Factor: What Canada's Most Famous Generation Is Leaving Behind*. Toronto: Bastion Books.

Bielby, William, and James Baron. 1984. 'Men and Women at Work: Sex Segregation and Statistical Discrimination', *American Journal of Sociology* 91: 759–99.

Bies, Robert J., and Thomas M. Tripp. 1996. 'Beyond Distrust: "Getting Even" and the Need for Revenge', in Roderick M. Kramer and Tom R. Tyler, eds, *Trust in Organizations: Frontiers of Theory and Research*. Thousand Oaks, Calif.: Sage, 246–60.

Birg, Herwig. 1995. *World Population Projections for the 21st Century: Theoretical Interpretations and Quantitative Simulations*. Frankfurt: Campus Verlag; New York: St Martin's.

Bittman, Michael, and Jocelyn Pixley. 1997. *The Double Life of the Family: Myth, Hope and Experience*. Sydney, Australia: Allen & Unwin.

Bittman, Michael, James Mahmud Rice, and Judy Wajcman. 2004. 'Appliances and Their Impact: The Ownership of Domestic Technology and Time Spent on Household Work', *British Journal Of Sociology* 55 (3): 401–422.

Blackledge, David, and Barry Hunt. 1985. *Sociological Interpretations of Education*. London: Routledge.

Bliss, Michael. 1991. *Plague: A Story of Smallpox in Montreal*. Toronto: HarperCollins.

———. 1992. *Banting: A Biography*, 2nd edn. Toronto: University of Toronto Press.

Block, Fred. 1980. 'Beyond Relative Autonomy: State Managers as Historical Subjects', in Ralph Miliband and John Saville, eds, *The Socialist Register, 1980*. London: Merlin, 227–40.

Blum, William. 2004. *Killing Hope: U.S. Military and C.I.A. Interventions since World War II*, Updated Edition. Monroe, Maine: Common Courage Press.

Blumer, Herbert. 1969. *Symbolic Interactionism: Perspective and Method*. Englewood Cliffs, NJ: Prentice-Hall and Berkeley: University of California Press.

Bohm, Robert M. 1997. *A Primer on Crime and Delinquency*. Belmont, Calif.: Wadsworth.

Bolaria, B. Singh, and Peter Li. 1988. *Racial Oppression in Canada*, 2nd edn. Toronto: Garamond.

Bongaarts, John, and Rodolfo Bulatao, eds. 2000. *Beyond Six Billion: Forecasting the World's Population*. Washington: National Academy Press.

Bookchin, Murray. 1989. *Remaking Society*. Montreal: Black Rose.

Booth, Alan, and John N. Edwards. 1990. 'Transmission of Marital and Family Quality over the Generations: The Effect of Parental Divorce and Unhappiness', *Journal of Divorce* 13: 41–58.

Boritch, Helen. 1997. *Fallen Women: Women, Crime and Criminal Justice in Canada*. Toronto: Nelson.

Boserup, Ester. 1965. *The Conditions of Agricultural Growth: The Economics of Agrarian Change under Population Pressure*. Chicago: Aldine.

———. 1981. *Population and Technological Change: A Study of Long-Term Trends*. Chicago: University of Chicago Press.

Bostock, L. 2002. '"God, She's Gonna Report Me": The Ethics of Child Protection in Poverty Research', *Children and Society* 16, 4: 273–83.

Boston Women's Health Collective. 1971. *Our Bodies, Our Selves*. Toronto: New Hogtown Press.

Bottomore, Tom. 1979. *Political Sociology*. London: Hutchinson University Press.

Bourdieu, Pierre. 1997a. 'The Forms of Capital', trans. Richard Nice, in A.H. Halsey, Hugh Lauder, Phillip Brown, and Amy Stuart Wells, eds, *Education: Culture, Economy, and Society*. Oxford: Oxford University Press, 46–58.

——— and Jean-Claude Passeron. 1979. *The Inheritors: French Students and Their Relations to Culture*, trans. Richard Nice. Chicago: University of Chicago Press.

Bowlby, Jeffrey, and Kathryn McMullen. 2002. *At a Crossroads: First Results for the 18- to 20-Year-Old Cohort of the Youth in Transition Survey*. Ottawa: Human Resources Development Canada.

Bowles, Samuel, and Herbert Gintis. 1976. *Schooling in Capitalist America: Education Reform and the Contradictions of Economic Life*. New York: Basic Books.

Boyd, Monica. 1992. 'Gender, Visible Minority, and Immigrant Earnings Inequality: Reassessing an Employment Equity Premise', in Vic Satzewich, ed., *Deconstructing a Nation: Immigration, Multiculturalism and Racism in '90s Canada*. Halifax: Fernwood, 279–321.

———. 1999. 'Integrating Gender, Language and Visible Minority Groups', in Shiva S. Halli and Leo Driedger, eds, *Immigrant Canada: Demographic, Economic and Social Challenges*. Toronto: University of Toronto Press, 282–306.

Bozeman, Barry, and Hal G. Rainey. 1998. 'Organizational Rules and the "Bureaucratic Personality"', *American Journal of Political Science* 42: 163–89.

Bradbury, Bettina. 1993. *Working Families: Age, Gender, and Daily Survival in Industrializing Montreal*. Toronto: McClelland & Stewart.

———. 2005. 'Social, Economic, and Cultural Origins of Contemporary Families', in M. Baker, ed., *Families: Changing Trends in Canada*, 5th edn. Toronto: McGraw-Hill Ryerson, 71–98.

Braithewaite, John. 1979. *Inequality, Crime and Public Policy*. London: Routledge & Kegan Paul.

Braverman, Harry. 1974. *Labor and Monopoly Capital: The Degradation of Work in the Twentieth Century*. New York: Monthly Review Press.

Briskin, Linda. 1992. 'Socialist Feminism: From the Standpoint of Practice', in M. Patricia Connelly and Pat Armstrong, eds, *Feminism in Action: Studies in Political Economy*. Toronto: Canadian Scholars' Press, 267–93.

Brodie, Janine. *Women and Canadian Public Policy*. Toronto: Harcourt Brace.

Bromley, David G., and Anson D. Shupe Jr. 1981. *Strange Gods: The Great American Cult Scare*. Boston: Beacon.

Brook, Barbara. 1999. *Feminist Perspectives on the Body*. London: Longman.

Brooks, Bradley, Jennifer Jarman, and Robert Blackburn. 2003. 'Occupational Gender Segregation in Canada, 1981–1996: Overall, Vertical and Horizontal Segregation', *Canadian Review of Sociology and Anthropology* 40 (2): 197–213.

Brower, Ralph S., and Mitchel Y. Abolafia. 1997. 'Bureaucratic Politics: The View from Below', *Journal of Public Administration Research and Theory* 7: 305–31.

Brown, Louise. 2002. 'Two-Tier Grade Schooling Feared', *Toronto Star*, 31 May, A1, A26.

Brown, Phil, and Susan Masterson-Allen. 1994. 'The Toxic Waste Movement: A New Type of Activism', *Society and Natural Resources* 7, 3: 269–87.

Brown, Rupert. 1995. *Prejudice: Its Social Psychology*. Oxford: Blackwell.

Brownmiller, Susan. 1975. *Against Our Will: Men, Women and Rape*. New York: Simon & Schuster.

Bryant, Bunyon, and Paul Mohai, eds. 1992. *Race and the Incidence of Environmental Hazard: A Time for Discourse*. Boulder, Colo.: Westview.

Bryant, Heather. 1990. *The Infertility Dilemma: Reproductive Technologies and Prevention*. Ottawa: Canadian Advisory Council on the Status of Women, Feb.

Brym, Robert J. 1980. 'Regional Social Structure and Agrarian Radicalism in Canada: Alberta, Saskatchewan and New Brunswick', in Alexander Himelfarb and C. James Richardson, eds, *People, Power and Process: A Reader*. Toronto: McGraw-Hill Ryerson, 344–53.

——— and Bonnie Fox. 1989. *From Culture to Power: The Sociology of English Canada*. Toronto: Oxford University Press.

Brzozowski, J.A., A. Taylor-Butts, and S. Johnson. 2006. 'Victimization and Offending among the Aboriginal Population in Canada', *Juristat* 26, 3.

Bulatao, Rodolfo. 1998. *The Value of Family Planning Programs in Developing Countries*. Santa Monica, Calif.: Rand.

——— and John Casterline, eds. 2001. 'Global Fertility Transition', *Population and Development Review* 27 (suppl.).

Bullard, Robert. 1990. *Dumping in Dixie: Race, Class and Environmental Quality*. Boulder, Colo.: Westview.

Bullock, Cathy Ferrand, and Jason Culbert. 2002. 'Coverage of Domestic Violence Fatalities by Newspapers in Washington State', *Journal of Interpersonal Violence* 17: 475–99.

Burgess, Ernest. 1925. 'The Growth of the City: An Introduction to a Research Project', in Robert E. Park, Ernest Burgess, and R. McKenzie, eds, *The City*. Chicago: University of Chicago Press, 47–62.

Burstyn, Varda. 1983. 'Masculine Domination and the State', in Ralph Miliband and John Saville, eds, *The Socialist Register, 1983*. London: Merlin, 45–89.

Burt, Ronald S., and Marc Knez. 1996. 'Trust and Third-Party Gossip', in Roderick M. Kramer and Tom R. Tyler, eds, *Trust in Organizations: Frontiers of Theory and Research*. Thousand Oaks, Calif.: Sage, 68–89.

Bush, Diane Mitsch, and Roberta G. Simmons. 1981. 'Socialization Processes over the Life Course', in Morris Rosenberg and Ralph Turner, eds, *Social Psychology: Sociological Perspectives*. New York: Basic Books, 133–64.

Bussière, Patrick, Fernando Cartwright, Robert Crocker, Xin Ma, Jillian Oderkirk, and Yanhong Zhang. 2001. *Measuring Up: The Performance of Canada's Youth in Reading, Mathematics and Science*. Ottawa: Statistics Canada.

———, ———, and Tamara Knighton. 2004. *Measuring Up: Canadian Results of the OECD PISA Study: The Performance of Canada's Youth in Mathematics, Reading, Science and Problem Solving, 2003. First Findings for Canadians Aged 15*. Ottawa: Minister of Industry.

Butler, Judith. 1990. 'Performative Acts and Gender Constitution: An Essay in Phenomenology and Feminist Theory', in Sue-Ellen Case, ed., *Performing Feminisms: Feminist Critical Theory and Theatre*. Baltimore: Johns Hopkins University Press.

———. 1992. 'Contingent Foundations: Feminism and the Question of "Postmodernism"', in Judith Butler and Joan W. Scott, eds, *Feminists Theorize the Political*. New York: Routledge, 3–21.

———. 1999. 'Bodily Inscriptions, Performative Subversions', Janet Price and Margaret Shildrick, eds, *Feminist Theory and the Body: A Reader*. New York: Routledge.

Butlin, George, and Jillian Oderkirk. 1996. *Educational Attainment: A Key to Autonomy and Authority in the Workplace*. Ottawa: Statistics Canada.

Butsch, Richard. 1992. 'Class and Gender in Four Decades of Television Situation Comedy: Plus ça Change . . .', *Critical Studies in Mass Communication* 9: 387–99.

———. 1995. 'Ralph, Fred, Archie and Homer: Why Television Keeps Recreating the White Male Working-Class Buffoon', in Gail Dines and Jean M. Humez, eds, *Gender, Race and Class in Media: A Text-Reader*. Thousand Oaks, Calif.: Sage, 403–12.

——— and Lynda M. Glennon. 1983. 'Social Class: Frequency Trends in Domestic Situation Comedy, 1946–1978', *Journal of Broadcasting* 27, 1: 77–81.

Butters, Jennifer, and Patricia Erickson. 2002. 'Addictions as Deviant Behaviour: Normalizing the Pleasures of Intoxication', in Lori G. Beaman, ed., *New Perspectives on Deviance: The Construction of Deviance in Everyday Life*. Toronto: Prentice-Hall Allyn and Bacon, 67–84.

Cain, Mead. 1983. 'Fertility as an Adjustment to Risk', *Population and Development Review* 9: 688–702.

Cairney, John. 1999. 'Socio-economic Status and Self-Rated Health among Older Canadians', *Canadian Journal on Aging* 19: 456–77.

Calavita, K., and H.N. Pontell. 1991. '"Other People's Money" Revisited: Collective Embezzlement in the Savings and Loan Insurance Industries', *Social Problems* 38, 1: 94–112.

Caldwell, John C. 1976. 'Toward a Restatement of Demographic Transition Theory', *Population and Development Review* 2: 321–66.

———, James F. Phillips, and Barkat-e-Khuda, eds. 2002. 'Family Planning Programs in the Twenty-First Century', *Studies in Family Planning* 33, 1 (special issue).

Calliste, Agnes. 1993. 'Sleeping Car Porters in Canada: An Ethnically Submerged Split Labour Market', in Graham S.

Lowe and Harvey Krahn, eds, *Work in Canada: Readings in the Sociology of Work and Industry*. Scarborough, Ont.: Nelson, 139–53.

Calvert, Barbara, and Warren R. Stanton. 1992. 'Perceptions of Parenthood: Similarities and Differences between 15-Year-Old Girls and Boys', *Adolescence* 27: 315–28.

Campey, John. 2002. 'Immigrant Children in Our Classrooms: Beyond ESL', *Education Canada* 42, 3: 44–7.

Canada. 1991. Broadcasting Act. *Statutes of Canada* 1991, c. 11.

Canada. Canadian Radio-television and Telecommunications Commission. 1998. Commercial Radio Policy. Broadcasting Public Notice 1998-41, 30 April 1998. Ottawa: CRTC.

Canada. Statistics Canada and Organisation for Economic Co-operation and Development. 2005a. *Learning a Living: First Results of the Adult Literacy and Life Skills Survey*. Ottawa and Paris: Minister of Industry, Canada and Organization for Economic Co-operation and Development.

Canada. Statistics Canada. 2005b. *Literacy and Digital Technologies: Linkages and Outcomes*. Ottawa: Minister of Industry.

Canada Health Coalition. 2006. 'Health Minister Clement Must Divest or Resign', Press release, 20 June. At: <www.healthcoalition.ca/2tierTony.html>.

Canadian Centre on Substance Abuse. 2005. *Canadian Addictions Survey: Detailed Report*. Ottawa: Health Canada

Canadian Health Services Research Foundation. 2002. *Myth: For-Profit Ownership of Facilities Would Lead to Better Health Care*. Ottawa: Canadian Health Services Research Foundation.

Canadian Institute of Child Health. N.d. Available at www.cich.ca.

Canadian Multiculturalism Act, R.S., 1985, c. 24 (4th Supp.). Available at http://www.pch.gc.ca/progs/multi/policy/act_e.cfm, accessed December 3, 2007.

Carley, Kathleen. 1989. 'The Value of Cognitive Foundations for Dynamic Social Theory', *Journal of Mathematical Sociology* 14, 2/3: 171–208.

———. 1991. 'A Theory of Group Stability', *American Sociological Review* 56: 331–54.

Carr, Deborah. 2004. 'Gender, Preloss Marital Dependence and Older Adults' Adjustment to Widowhood', *Journal of Marriage and Family* 66 (1): 220–235.

Carre, Dominique, and Sylvie Craipeau. 1996. 'Entre delocalisation et mobilité: analyse des strategies entrepreneuriales de teletravail', *Technologies de l'information et société* 8: 333–54.

Carroll, William K. 1987. 'Which Women Are More Proletarianized Than Men?', *Canadian Review of Sociology and Anthropology* 24: 465–95.

——— and Robert S. Ratner. 1996. 'Master Framing and Cross-movement Networking in Contemporary Social Movements', *Sociological Quarterly* 37: 601–25.

——— and ———. 1999. 'Media Strategies and Political Projects: A Comparative Study of Social Movements', *Canadian Journal of Sociology* 24, 1: 1–34.

Carson, Rachel. 1962. *Silent Spring*. Boston: Houghton Mifflin.

Casanova, J. 1994. *Public Religions in the Modern World*. Chicago: University of Chicago Press.

Castells, Manuel. 1989. *The Informational City: Information Technology, Economic Restructuring, and the Urban-Regional Process*. Cambridge, Mass.: MIT Press.

CBC News. 2006a. 'Day Care in Canada'. At: <cbc.ca/news/printablestory.jsp>.

———. 2006b. 'Canadian Medical Association Journal Fires 2 Editors'. At: <www.cbc.ca/health/story>.

———. 2007. 'Family argues taking 84-year-old off life support is against their faith'. Available at http://www.cbc.ca/canada/story/2007/12/12/court-life-support.html.

———. 2008. 'Winnipeg man at centre of end-of-life controversy dies'. Available at http://www.cbc.ca/health/story/2008/06/25/golubchuk.html.

Chandler, Bill. 1994. *The Value of Household Work in Canada, 1992*. Ottawa: Statistics Canada.

Chappell, Neena L., and Nina L. Colwill. 1981. 'Medical Schools as Agents of Professional Socialization', *Canadian Review of Sociology and Anthropology* 18, 1: 67–79.

Chase-Dunn, Christopher K. 1989. *Global Formation: Structures of the World-Economy*. Cambridge, Mass: B. Blackwell.

Chasteen, Amy L. 2001. 'Constructing Rape: Feminism, Change, and Women's Everyday Understandings of Sexual Assault', *Sociological Spectrum* 21: 101–39.

Chen, Xiangming. 1994. 'The Changing Roles of Free Economic Zones in Development: A Comparative Analysis of Capitalist and Socialist Cases in East Asia', *Studies in Comparative International Development* 29 (3): 3–25.

Chilton, R. 2004. 'Regional Variations in Lethal and Non-lethal Assaults', *Homicide Studies* 8 (1): 40–56.

Chippendale, Nigel. 2002. *Access to Post-secondary Education in Canada: Facts and Gaps: Conference Report*. Ottawa: Canadian Policy Research Networks for the Canadian Millennium Scholarship Foundation. At: <www.cprn.ca/en/doc.cfm?doc=59>.

Chodorow, Nancy. 1989. *Feminism and Psychoanalytic Theory*. New Haven: Yale University Press.

———. 1990. 'What is the Relationship Between Psychoanalytic Feminism and the Psychoanalytic Psychology of Women?', in Deborah Rhode, ed., *Theoretical Perspectives on Sex Differences*. New Haven: Yale University Press.

Chossudovsky, Michel. 2004. *The Globalization of Poverty and the New World Order*. Montreal: Global Research Publishers.

Chung, Lucy. 2004. 'Low-Paid Workers: How Many Live in Low-Income Families?', *Perspectives on Labour and Income* (Oct): 5–14.

Cincotta, Richard P., and Roberta Engelman. 1997. *Economics and Rapid Change: The Influence of Population Growth*. Washington: Population Action International.

Clark, S.D. 1995. *State and Status: The Rise of the State and Aristocratic Power in Western Europe*. Montreal: McGill-Queen's University Press.

Clark, Terry, and Seymour Martin Lipset. 1991. 'Are Social Classes Dying?', *International Sociology* 6: 397–410.

Clark, Warren. 2000. 'Education', *Canadian Social Trends* (Winter): 3–7.

Clarke, Harold D., Jane Jensen, Lawrence Leduc, and Jon H. Pammett. 1991. *Absent Mandate: The Politics of Discontent in Canada*, 2nd edn. Toronto: Gage.

Clarke, John I. 1996. 'The Impact of Population Change on Environment: An Overview', in Bernardo Colombo, Paul Demeny, and Max F. Perutz, eds, *Resources and Population:*

Natural, Institutional, and Demographic Dimensions of Development. Oxford: Clarendon, 244–68.

Clarke, Juanne N. 2000. *Health, Illness, and Medicine in Canada*, 3rd edn. Toronto: Oxford University Press.

———— and G. Van Amerom. 2008. 'The Differences between Parents and People with Aspergers', *Social Work in Health Care*.

———— and G. Van Amerom. 2008. 'Asperger's syndrome: Differences between parents' understanding and those diagnosed', *Social Work in Health Care* 46 (3): 85–106.

Cleland, John. 1996. 'Population Growth in the 21st Century: Cause for Crisis or Celebration?', *Tropical Medicine and International Health* 1, 1: 15–26.

Clement, Wallace. 1975. *The Canadian Corporate Elite*. Toronto: McClelland & Stewart.

———— and John Myles. 1994. *Relations of Ruling: Class and Gender in Postindustrial Societies*. Montreal: McGill-Queen's University Press.

Clevedon, Gordon, and Michael Krashinsky. 2001. *Our Children's Future: Child Care Policy in Canada*. Toronto: University of Toronto Press.

Cloward, Richard A., and Lloyd E. Ohlin. 1960. *Delinquency and Opportunity: A Theory of Delinquent Gangs*. New York: Free Press.

Coale, Ansley J. 1969. 'The Decline of Fertility in Europe from the French Revolution to World War II', in S.J. Berhman, Leslie Corsa, and Ronald Freedman, eds, *Fertility and Family Planning: A World View*. Ann Arbor: University of Michigan Press, 3–24.

————. 1973. 'The Demographic Transition Reconsidered', in International Union for the Study of Population, *Proceedings of the International Population Conference*, vol. 1. Liège, Belgium, 53–72.

————. 1974. 'The History of the Human Population', *Scientific American* (special issue): 15–25.

———— and Susan Cotts Watkins, eds. 1986. *The Decline of Fertility in Europe: The Revised Proceedings of a Conference on the Princeton European Fertility Project*. Princeton, NJ: Princeton University Press.

Coats, Patricia B., and Steven Overman. 1992. 'Childhood Play Experiences of Women in Traditional and Nontraditional Professions', *Sex Roles* 26, 7/8: 261–71.

Cockburn, Cynthia. 1983. *Brothers: Male Dominance and Technological Change*. London: Pluto.

Cockett, Monica, and John Tripp. 1994. *The Exeter Family Study: Family Breakdown and Its Impact on Children*. Exeter, UK: University of Exeter Press.

Coe, Neil M. 2000. 'On Location: American Capital and the Local Labour Market in the Vancouver Film Industry', *International Journal of Urban and Regional Research* 24, 1: 79–94.

Cohen, Albert K. 1966. *Deviance and Control*. Englewood Cliffs, NJ: Prentice-Hall.

Cohen, J.L., and J.H. Davis. 1973. 'Effects of Audience Status, Evaluation, and Time of Action on Performance with Hidden-Word Problems', *Journal of Personality and Social Psychology* 27: 74–85.

Cohen, Jean L. 1985. 'Strategy or Identity: New Theoretical Paradigms and Contemporary Social Movements', *Social Research* 53: 663–716.

Collier, Gary, Henry L. Minton, and Graham Reynolds. 1991. *Currents of Thought in American Social Psychology*. New York: Oxford University Press.

Collins, Randall. 1975. *Conflict Sociology: Toward an Explanatory Science*. New York: Academic Press.

————. 1979. *The Credential Society: An Historical Sociology of Education and Stratification*. New York: Academic Press.

————. 2004. *Interaction Ritual Chains*. Princeton, NJ: Princeton University Press.

Comack, E., V. Chopyk, and L. Wood. 2000. *Mean Streets: The Social Location, Gender Dynamic and Patterns of Violent Crime in Winnipeg*. Ottawa: Canadian Centre for Policy Alternatives.

Comninel, George C. 1987. *Rethinking the French Revolution: Marxism and the Revisionist Challenge*. New York: Verso.

Condry, John, and Sandra Condry. 1976. 'Sex Differences: A Study of the Eye of the Beholder', *Child Development* 47: 812–819.

Conley, James. 2004. 'Working-Class Formation in Twentieth-Century Canada', in James Curtis, Edward Grabb, and Neil Guppy, eds, *Social Inequality in Canada: Patterns, Problems, and Policies*. Toronto: Pearson Prentice-Hall, 38–54.

Connell, Erin, and Alan Hunt. 2006. 'Sexual Ideology and Sexual Physiology in the Discourses of Sex Advice Literature', *Canadian Journal of Human Sexuality* 15, 1: 23–45.

Conrad, Peter, and Joseph Schneider. 1980. *Deviance and Medicalization: From Badness to Sickness*. St Louis: Mosby.

Constant, David, Lee Sproull, and Sara Kiesler. 1996. 'The Kindness of Strangers: The Usefulness of Electronic Weak Ties for Technical Advice', *Organization Science* 7, 2: 119–35.

Cook, J. 2001. 'Practical Guide to Medical Education', *Pharmaceutical Marketing* 6: 14–22.

Cool, Julie. 2006. 'Women in Parliament', Library of Parliament, Government of Canada. At: <www.parl.gc.ca/information/library/PRBpubs/prb0562-e.htm>.

Cooley, Charles Horton. 1902. *Human Nature and Social Order*. New York: Scribner.

————. 1962 [1909]. *Social Organization: A Study of the Larger Mind*. Glencoe, Ill.: Free Press.

Council of Ministers of Education, Canada. 1996. *Enhancing the Role of Teachers in a Changing World*. Report in response to the International Survey in Preparation for the Forty-Fifth Session of the International Conference on Education. Toronto: Council of Ministers of Education, Canada.

————. 2001. *The Development of Education in Canada: Report of Canada*. Toronto: Council of Ministers of Education, Canada.

Coverman, Shelly. 1983. 'Gender, Domestic Labour Time and Wage Inequality', *American Sociological Review* 48: 623–37.

Crane, Diana. 2002. 'Culture and Globalization: Theoretical Models and Emerging Trends', in Diana Crane, Nobuko Kawashima, and Kenichi Kawasaki, eds, *Global Culture: Media, Arts, Policy, and Globalization*. New York: Routledge, 1–25.

Crockett, Lisa, Mike Losoff, and Anne C. Petersen. 1984. 'Perceptions of the Peer Group and Friendship in Early Adolescence', *Journal of Early Adolescence* 4, 2: 155–81.

Crompton, Susan. 2000. 'Health', *Canadian Social Trends* 59: 12–17.

Crossley, Michelle L. 2002. 'The Perils of Health Promotion and the "Barebacking" Backlash', *Health* 6, 1: 47–68.

Croteau, David, and William Hoynes. 2000. *Media/Society: Industries, Images, and Audiences*, 2nd edn. Thousand Oaks, Calif.: Pine Forge.

Crozier, M. 1964. *The Bureaucratic Phenomenon*. Chicago: University of Chicago Press.

Cuneo, Carl. 1985. 'Have Women Become More Proletarianized Than Men?', *Canadian Review of Sociology and Anthropology* 22: 465–95.

———. 1990. *Pay Equity: The Labour-Feminist Challenge*. Toronto: Oxford University Press.

———. 2002. 'Globalized and Localized Digital Divides along the Information Highway: A Fragile Synthesis across Bridges, Ramps, Cloverleaves, and Ladders', 33rd Annual Sorokin Lecture, University of Saskatchewan. 31 Jan.

Cunningham, Mick. 2001. 'The Influence of Parental Attitudes and Behaviors on Children's Attitudes toward Gender and Household Labor in Early Adulthood', *Journal of Marriage and the Family* 63, 1: 111–23.

Curra, John. 2000. *The Relativity of Deviance*. Thousand Oaks, Calif.: Sage.

Currie, Dawn. 1988. 'Starvation amidst Abundance: Female Adolescents and Anorexia', in B. Singh Bolaria and Harley D. Dickinson, eds, *Sociology of Health Care in Canada*. Toronto: Harcourt Brace Jovanovich, 198–215.

Curtis, James, Edward Grabb, Thomas Perks, and Tina Chui. 2004. 'Public Involvement, Civic Engagement, and Social Inequality', in James Curtis, Edward Grabb, and Neil Guppy, eds, *Social Inequality in Canada: Patterns, Problems, and Policies*, 4th edn. Toronto: Pearson Prentice-Hall, 431–49.

Daenzer, Patricia, 1993. *Regulating Class Privilege: Immigrant Servants in Canada, 1940s–1990*. Toronto: Canadian Scholars' Press.

Dahl, Robert. 1961. *Who Governs? Democracy and Power in an American City*. New Haven: Yale University Press.

Daly, M. 1985. *Beyond God the Father: Toward a Philosophy of Women's Liberation*. Boston: Beacon Press.

Darder, Antonia, Marta Baltodano, and Rodolfo D. Torres, eds. 2003. *The Critical Pedagogy Reader*. New York: Routledge Falmer.

Das, Mallika. 2000. 'Men and Women in Indian Magazine Advertisements: A Preliminary Report', *Sex Roles* 43: 699–717.

Das Gupta, Tania. 1996. *Racism and Paid Work*. Toronto: Garamond.

Davey, Ian E. 1978. 'The Rhythm of Work and the Rhythm of School', in Neil McDonald and Alf Chaiton, eds, *Egerton Ryerson and His Times*. Toronto: Macmillan, 221–53.

Davidson, Kenneth, and Linda Hoffman. 1986. 'Sexual Fantasies and Sexual Satisfaction: An Empirical Analysis of Erotic Thought', *Journal of Sex Research* 22, 2: 184–205.

Davies, James C. 1962. 'Toward a Theory of Revolution', *American Sociological Review* 27: 5–19.

Davies, Lorraine, and Patricia Jane Carrier. 1999. 'The Importance of Power Relations for the Division of Household Labour', *Canadian Journal of Sociology* 24, 1: 35–51.

Davies, Lorraine, and Donna McAlpine. 1998. 'The Significance of Family, Work, and Power Relations for Mothers' Mental Health', *Canadian Journal of Sociology* 23: 368–88.

Davies, Scott. 2004. 'Stubborn Disparities: Explaining Class Inequalities in Schooling', in James Curtis, Edward Grabb, and Neil Guppy, eds, *Social Inequality in Canada: Patterns, Problems, and Policies*, 4th edn. Toronto: Pearson Prentice-Hall, 173–86.

Davis, Charles R. 1996. 'The Administrative Rational Model and Public Organization Theory', *Administration and Society* 28: 39–60.

Davis, Kingsley. 1937. 'The Sociology of Prostitution', *American Sociological Review* 2, 5: 744–55.

———. 1945. 'The World Demographic Transition', *Annals of American Academy of Political and Social Sciences* 237: 1–11.

——— and Wilbert E. Moore. 1945. 'Some Principles of Stratification', *American Sociological Review* 10: 242–9.

Dawe, Alan. 1970. 'Two Sociologies', *British Journal of Sociology* 21: 207–18.

Day, R. 2000. *Multiculturalism and the History of Canadian Diversity*. Toronto: University of Toronto Press.

Day, S., and G. Brodsky. 1996. 'The Duty to Accommodate: Who Will Benefit?', *Canadian Bar Review* 75: 433–73.

DeAnna, Mori, Shelly Chaiken, and Patricia Pliner. 1987. '"Eating Lightly" and the Self-Presentationof Femininity', *Journal of Personality and Social Psychology* 53: 693–702.

Deaux, Kay, and Brenda Major. 2004. 'A Social-Psychological Model of Gender', in Michael Kimmel, with Amy Aronson, eds, *The Gendered Society Reader*, 2nd ed. New York: Oxford University Press.

DeLamater, John, and Janet Shibley Hyde. 1998. 'Essentialism vs. Social Constructionism in the Study of Human Sexuality', *Journal of Sex Research* 35 (1): 10–18.

de la Torre, Isabel. 1997. 'La formacion y las organizaciones. Los acuerdos nacionales de formacion continua', *Revista Espanola de Investigaciones Sociologicas* 77–8 (Jan.–June): 15–33.

Dei, George J. Sefa. 1996. *Anti-racism Education: Theory and Practice*. Halifax: Fernwood.

———, Irma Marcia James, Leeno Luke Karumanchery, Sonia James-Wilson, and Jasmin Zine. 2000. *Removing the Margins: The Challenges and Possibilities of Inclusive Schooling*. Toronto: Canadian Scholars' Press.

DeKeseredy, Walter. 2005. 'Patterns of Family Violence', in M. Baker, ed., *Families: Changing Trends in Canada*, 5th edn. Toronto: McGraw-Hill Ryerson, 229–57.

Dellinger, Kirsten. 2002. 'Wearing Gender and Sexuality "On Your Sleeve": Dress Norms and the Importance of Occupational and Organizational Culture at Work', *Gender Issues* 20, 1: 3–25.

Dery, David. 1998. '"Papereality" and Learning in Bureaucratic Organizations', *Administration and Society* 29: 677–89.

Desjardins, Richard, Scott Murray, Yvan Clermont, and Patrick Werquin. 2005. *Learning a Living: First Results of the Adult Literacy and Life Skills Survey*. Ottawa and Paris: Statistics Canada and OECD.

Deutschmann, Linda. 2007. *Deviance and Social Control*, 4th edn. Toronto: Thomson Nelson.

Devall, William B. 1992. 'Deep Ecology and Radical Environmentalism', in Riley Dunlap and Angela G. Mertig, eds, *American Environmentalism*. Philadelphia: Taylor and Francis, 51–62.

Devereaux, P.J., et al. 2002. 'A Systematic Review and Meta-analysis of Studies Comparing Mortality Rates of Private For-Profit and Private Not-for-Profit Hospitals', *Canadian Medical Association Journal* 166: 1399–1406.

Dhalla, Irfan A., et al. 2002. 'Characteristics of First-Year Students in Canadian Medical Schools', *Canadian Medical Association Journal* 166: 1029–35.

Diani, Mario. 1992. 'The Concept of Social Movement', *Sociological Review* 40: 1–25.

Dias, K. 2003. 'The Ana Sanctuary: Women's Pro-anorexia Narratives in Cyberspace', *Journal of International Women's Studies* 4, 2: 31–45.

Di Martino, Vittorio. 1996. 'Télétravail: à la recherche des règles d'or', *Technologies de l'information et société* 8: 355–71.

Dobash, R. Emerson, Russell P. Dobash, Margo Wilson, and Martin Daly. 1992. 'The Myth of Sexual Symmetry in Marital Violence', *Social Problems* 39: 71–91.

Dogon, Mattei, and John Kasarda, eds. 1988. *The Metropolis Era*. Beverly Hills, Calif.: Sage.

Doherty, Gillian, Martha Friendly, and Mab Oloman. 1998. *Women's Support, Women's Work: Child Care in an Era of Deficit Reduction, Devolution, Downsizing and Deregulation*. Ottawa: Status of Women Canada.

Dole, Carol M. 2000. 'Woman with a Gun: Cinematic Law Enforcers on the Gender Frontier', in Murray Pomerance and John Sakeris, eds, *Bang Bang, Shoot Shoot! Essays on Guns and Popular Culture*, 2nd edn. Needham Heights, Mass.: Pearson Education, 11–21.

Domhoff, G. William, ed. 1990. *The Power Elite and the State: How Policy Is Made in America*. Hawthorne, NY: Aldine de Gruyter.

Dooley, Martin. 1995. 'Lone-Mother Families and Social Assistance Policy in Canada', in Martin Dooley, Ross Finnie, Shelley A. Phipps, and Nancy Naylor, eds, *Family Matters: New Policies for Divorce, Lone Mothers, and Child Poverty*. Toronto: C.D. Howe Institute, 35–104.

Doucet, Andrea. 2006. *Do Men Mother? Fathering, Care, and Domestic Responsibility*. Toronto: University of Toronto Press.

Downes, D., and P. Rock. 2003. *Understanding Deviance*, 4th edn. Toronto: Oxford University Press.

Downey, John, and Natalie Fenton. 2003. 'New Media, Counter Publicity and the Public Sphere', *New Media & Society* 5, 2: 185–202.

Doyal, Lesley. 1995. *What Makes Women Sick: Gender and the Political Economy of Health*. New Brunswick, NJ: Rutgers University Press.

Dreeben, Robert. 1968. *On What Is Learned in School*. Reading, Mass.: Addison-Wesley.

Driedger, Leo. 1996. *Multi-ethnic Canada: Identities and Inequalities*. Toronto: Oxford University Press.

Du Bois, W.E.B. 1899. *The Philadelphia Negro: A Social Study*. New York: Lippincott.

———. 1903. *Souls of Black Folk*. New York: Penguin Books.

———. 1935. *Black Reconstruction in America, 1860–1880*. New York: Atheneum.

Duffy, Ann, Dan Glenday, and Norene Pupo. 1997. *Good Jobs, Bad Jobs, No Jobs: The Transformation of Work in the 21st Century*. Toronto: Harcourt Brace.

DuMont, Janice. 2003. 'Charging and Sentencing in Sexual Assault Cases: An Exploratory Examination', *Canadian Journal of Women and the Law* 15, 2: 305–30.

Duncan, Otis Dudley. and Leo F. Schnore. 1959. 'Cultural, Behavioral and Ecological Perspectives in the Study of Social Organization', *American Journal of Sociology* 65: 132–45.

Dunlap, Riley. 1992. 'Trends in Public Opinion toward Environmental Issues: 1965–1990', in Riley Dunlap and Angela G. Mertig, eds, *American Environmentalism*. Philadelphia: Taylor and Francis, 89–116.

——— and William Catton Jr. 1979a. 'Environmental Sociology', *Annual Review of Sociology* 5: 243–73.

——— and ———. 1979b. 'Environmental Sociology: A Framework for Analysis', in Timothy O'Riordan and R.C. d'Arge, eds, *Progress in Resource Management and Environmental Planning*, vol. 1. Chichester, UK: Wiley, 57–85.

——— and ———. 1983. 'What Environmental Sociologists Have in Common (Whether Concerned with "Built" or "Natural" Environments)', *Sociological Inquiry* 53, 2/3: 113–15.

——— and Richard P. Gale. 1972. 'Politics and Ecology: A Political Profile of Student Eco-activists', *Youth and Society* 3: 379–97.

Dunn, Judy. 1986. 'Growing Up in a Family World: Issues in the Study of Social Development in Young Children', in Martin Richards and Paul Light, eds, *Children of Social Worlds: Development in a Social Context*. Cambridge: Polity, 98–115.

Durkheim, Émile. 1964 [1893]. *The Division of Labor in Society*, trans. George Simpson. New York: Free Press.

———. 1958, 1964 [1895]. *The Rules of Sociological Method*, trans. S. Solovay and John Mueller. New York: Free Press.

———. 1951 [1897]. *Suicide: A Study in Sociology*, trans. John A. Spaulding and George Simpson. New York: Free Press.

———. 1966 [1897]. *Suicide*. Glecoe Ill.: Free Press.

———. 1995 [1912]. *The Elementary Forms of Religious Life*, trans. Karen E. Fields. New York: Free Press.

———. 1956 [1922]. *Education and Society*, trans. Sherwood W. Fox. Glencoe, Ill.: Free Press.

———. 1965. *The Elementary Forms of the Religious Life*. New York: The Free Press.

Dworkin, Andrea. 1981. *Pornography: Men Possessing Women*. New York: Perigee.

Eaves, Elizabeth. 2002. *Bare: On Women, Dancing, Sex and Power*. New York: Knopf.

Ebaugh, Helen. 1988. *Becoming an Ex: The Process of Role Exit*. Chicago: University of Chicago Press.

Eberstadt, Nicholas. 1997. 'World Population Implosion?', *The Public Interest* 129: 3–20.

Edin, Kathryn, and Maria J. Kefalas. 2005. *Promises I Can Keep: Why Poor Women Put Motherhood before Marriage*. Berkeley: University of California Press.

Edwards, Richard. 1979. *Contested Terrain: The Transformation of the Workplace in the Twentieth Century*. New York: Basic Books.

Eglin, Peter, and Stephen Hester. 1999. "'You're All a Bunch of Feminists': Categorization and the Politics of Terror in the Montreal Massacre', *Human Studies* 22: 253–72.

Ehrenreich, Barbara. 2001. *Nickel and Dimed: On (Not) Getting By in America*. New York: Henry Holt.

Ehrlich, Paul R. and Anne H. Ehrlich. 1970. *Population, Resources, Environment: Issues in Human Ecology*. San Francisco: Freeman.

———— and ————. 1990. *The Population Explosion*. London: Hutchinson.

———— and J.P. Holdren. 1971. 'The Impact of Population Growth', *Science* 171: 1212–17.

Eichler, Margrit. 1996. 'The Impact of New Reproductive and Genetic Technologies on Families', in Maureen Baker, ed., *Families: Changing Trends in Canada*, 3rd edn. Toronto: McGraw-Hill Ryerson, 104–18.

————. 1997. *Family Shifts: Families, Policies, and Gender Equality*. Toronto: Oxford University Press.

————. 2005. 'Biases in Family Literature', in Maureen Baker, ed., *Families: Changing Trends in Canada*, 5th edn. Toronto: McGraw-Hill Ryerson, 121–42.

Eisenberg, David M., et al. 1998. 'Trends in Alternative Medicine Use in the United States, 1990–1997: Results of a Follow-up National Survey', *Journal of the American Medical Association* 280: 1569–75.

Eisinger, Peter K. 1973. 'The Conditions of Protest Behaviour in American Cities', *American Political Science Review* 67: 11–28.

Elliott, J., and M. Richards. 1991. 'Parental Divorce and the Life Chances of Children', *Family Law* 481–4.

Elmer, Greg, and Mike Gasher, eds. 2005. *Contracting Out Hollywood: Runaway Productions and Foreign Location Shooting*. Lanham, Md: Rowman and Littlefield.

Elster, Jon. 1989. *The Cement of Society: A Study of Social Order*. Cambridge: Cambridge University Press.

Ellwood, Wayne. 2001. *No-Nonsense Guide to Globalization*. Toronto: Between the Lines.

Emery, Robert. 1994. 'Psychological Research on Children, Parents, and Divorce', in Robert Emery, ed., *Renegotiating Family Relationships: Divorce, Child Custody, and Mediation*. New York: Guildford, 194–217.

Engels, Friedrick. 1972. *Origin of the Family, Private Property, and the State*. New York: Pathfinder Press.

————. 1994 [1845]. *The Condition of the Working Class in England*, trans. W.O. Henderson and W.H. Chaloner. Stanford, Calif.: Stanford University Press.

————. 1942 [1884]. *The Origin of the Family, Private Property and the State*. New York: International Publishers.

————. 1990 [1884]. *The Origin of the Family, Private Property and the State*, vol. 26 of *Karl Marx and Frederick Engels Collected Works*. New York: International Publishers.

England, Paula. 1982. 'The Failure of Human Capital Theory to Explain Occupational Sex Segregation', *Journal of Human Resources* 17: 358–70.

————, George Farkas, Barbara Kilbourne, and Thomas Dou. 1988. 'Explaining Occupational Sex Segregation and Wages: Findings from a Model with Fixed Effects', *American Sociological Review* 53: 544–58.

Ennett, Susan T., and Karl E. Bauman. 1996. 'Adolescent Social Networks: School, Demographic, and Longitudinal Considerations', *Journal of Adolescent Research* 11: 194–215.

Entwisle, Doris, and Leslie Hayduk. 1988. 'Lasting Effects of Elementary School', *Sociology of Education* 61: 147–59.

Epstein, Debbie, Jannette Elwood, Valerie Hey, and Janet Maw. 1997. *Failing Boys? Issues in Gender and Achievement*. Buckingham, UK: Open University Press.

Erikson, Erik. 1982. *The Life Cycle Completed: A Review*. New York: Norton.

Erikson, Kai T. 1966. *Wayward Puritans: A Study in the Sociology of Deviance*. New York: Wiley.

Ermann, M. David, and Richard J. Lundman. 1996. 'Corporate and Governmental Deviance: Origins, Patterns, and Reactions', in M. David Ermann and Richard J. Lundman, eds, *Corporate and Governmental Deviance: Problems of Organizational Behavior in Contemporary Society*. New York: Oxford University Press, 3–44.

Estes, Carroll L. 1999. 'The New Political Economy of Aging: Introduction and Critique', in Meredith Minkler and Carroll L. Estes, eds, *Critical Gerontology: Perspectives from Political and Moral Economy*. Amityville, NY: Baywood, 17–35.

Evans, L.T. 1998. *Feeding the Ten Billion: Plants and Population Growth*. Cambridge: Cambridge University Press.

Eyerman, Ron, and Andrew Jamison. 1989. 'Environmental Knowledge as an Organizational Weapon: The Case of Greenpeace', *Social Science Information* 28, 1: 99–119.

Fagot, B.I. 1986. 'Beyond the Reinforcement Principle: Another Step Towards Understanding Sex Role Development', *Developmental Psychology* 21: 1097–1104.

Farshad, Araghi. 2000. 'The Great Global Enclosure of Our Times: Peasants and the Agrarian Question at the End of the Twentieth Century', in Fred Magdoff, John Bellamy Foster, and Frederick H. Buttel, eds, *Hungry for Profit: The Agribusiness Threat to Farmers, Food, and Environment*. New York: Monthly Review Press.

Faules, Don F., and Dennis C. Alexander. 1978. *Communication and Social Behaviour: A Symbolic Interaction Perspective*. Reading, Mass.: Addison-Wesley.

Featherstone, Liza. 2004. *Selling Women Short: The Landmark Battle for Workers' Rights at Wal-Mart*. New York: Basic Books.

Feld, Scott L. 1982. 'Social Structural Determinants of Similarity among Associates', *American Sociological Review* 47: 797–801.

Filion, Normand. 1998. 'The Management of Self-Discipline: Social Norms and Cultural Surveillance', paper presented at the annual meeting of the International Sociological Association.

Fineman, Martha A. 1995. *The Neutered Mother, the Sexual Family, and Other Twentieth Century Tragedies*. New York: Routledge.

Fischer, Claude S. 1976. *The Urban Experience*. New York: Harcourt Brace Jovanovich.

————. 1982. *To Dwell Among Friends: Personal Networks in Town and City*. Chicago: University of Chicago Press.

Fleras, Augie, and Jean Leonard Elliott. 1996. *Unequal Relations: An Introduction to Race, Ethnic and Aboriginal Dynamics in Canada*. Toronto: Prentice-Hall.

————— and Jean Lock Kunz. 2001. *Media and Minorities: Representing Diversity in a Multicultural Canada*. Toronto: Thompson Educational Publishing.

Flyvbjerg, Bent. 1998. *Rationality and Power: Democracy in Practice*. Chicago: University of Chicago Press.

Fogel, Robert W., and Dora L. Costa. 1997. 'A Theory of Technophysio Evolution, with Some Implications for Forecasting Population, Health Care Costs, and Pension Costs', *Demography* 34: 49–66.

Ford, Clellan, and Frank Beach. 1951. *Patterns of Sexual Behavior*. New York: Harper & Row.

Ford, J., N. Nassar, E. Sullivan, G. Chambers, and P. Lancaster. 2003. *Reproductive Health Indicators, Australia, 2002*. Sydney: Australian Institute of Health and Welfare.

Foucault, Michel. 1990. *The History of Sexuality: An Introduction*. New York: Vintage Books.

Fox, Bonnie, ed. 1980. *Hidden in the Household: Women's Domestic Labour under Capitalism*. Toronto: Women's Press.

—————. 1989. 'The Feminist Challenge: A Reconsideration of Social Inequality and Economic Development', in Robert J. Brym with Bonnie J. Fox, *From Culture to Power: The Sociology of English Canada*. Toronto: Oxford University Press, 120–67.

—————, ed. 2001a. *Family Patterns, Gender Relations*, 2nd edn. Toronto: Oxford University Press.

————— and John Fox. 1986. 'Women in the Labour Market, 1931–1981: Exclusion and Competition', *Canadian Review of Sociology and Anthropology* 23: 1–21.

————— and —————. 1987. 'Occupational Gender Segregation of the Canadian Labour Force, 1931–1981', *Canadian Review of Sociology and Anthropology* 24: 374–97.

————— and Pamela Sugiman. 1999. 'Flexible Work, Flexible Workers: The Restructuring of Clerical Work in a Large Telecommunications Company', *Studies in Political Economy* 60: 59–84.

Fox, James Alan, and Jack Levin. 2001. *The Will to Kill: Making Sense of Senseless Murder*. Boston: Allyn and Bacon.

Fox, Stephen. 1985. *The American Conservation Movement: John Muir and His Legacy*. Madison: University of Wisconsin Press.

Frank, Andre Gunder. 1978. *Dependent Accumulation and Underdevelopment*. London: McMillan.

—————. 1991. 'The Underdevelopment of Development', *Scandinavian Journal of Development Alternatives* 10, 3: 5–72.

—————. 1998. *ReOrient: Global Economy in the Asian Age*. Berkeley, Calif: University of California Press.Fraser, Nancy. 1997. 'After the Family Wage: A Post-industrial Thought Experiment', in Nancy Fraser, *Justice Interruptus: Critical Reflections on the 'Postsocialist' Condition*. New York: Routledge, 41–66.

————— and Linda Nicholson. 1990. 'Social Criticism without Philosophy: An Encounter between Feminism and Postmodernism', in Linda Nicholson, ed., *Feminism/Postmodernism*. London: Routledge, 19–38.

Frauen Computer Zentrum Berlin (FCZB). 2001. 'Canadian Opinion on Climate Change', *European Database: Women in Environics International (2000)*. Available at www.taiga.net/nce/Environics_climate_eFlash.pdf.

Frederick, Judith, and Jason Hamel. 1998. 'Canadian Attitudes to Divorce', *Canadian Social Trends* 48: 6–11.

Freidson, Eliot. 1970. *The Profession of Medicine: A Study in the Sociology of Applied Knowledge*. New York: Harper & Row.

Freire, Paulo. 1970. *Pedagogy of the Oppressed*, trans. Myra Bergman Ramos. New York: Herder and Herder.

Frenette, Marc, and Simon Coulombe. 2007. 'Has Higher Education Among Young Women Substantially Reduced the Gender Gap in Employment and Earnings?', *Analytical Studies Branch Research Paper Series*. Cat. no. 11F0019MIE2007301. Ottawa: Statistics Canada. Available at http://www.statcan.ca/english/research/11F0019MIE/11F0019MIE2007301.pdf.

Freud, Sigmund. 1974 [1923]. *The Ego and the Id*, trans. James Strachey. London: Hogarth.

—————. 1973 [1938]. *An Outline of Psychoanalysis*, trans. James Strachey. London: Hogarth.

Freudenberg, Nicholas, and Carol Steinsapir. 1992. 'Not in Our Backyards: The Grassroots Environmental Movement', in Riley Dunlap and Angela G. Mertig, eds, *American Environmentalism*. Philadelphia: Taylor and Francis, 27–38.

Freudenburg, William, and Susan Pastor. 1992. 'NIMBYs and LULUs: Stalking the Syndromes', *Journal of Social Issues* 48, 4: 39–61.

Friendly, Martha. 2001. 'Child Care and Canadian Federalism in the 1990's: Canary in a Coal Mine', in Gordon Cleveland and Michael Krashinsky, eds, *Our Children's Future: Child Care Policy in Canada*. Toronto: University of Toronto Press.

Fuller, Colleen. 1998. *Caring for Profit: How Corporations Are Taking Over Canada's Health Care System*. Vancouver: New Star.

Furedi, Frank. 1997. *Population and Development: A Critical Introduction*. New York: St Martin's.

Furnham, Adrian, and L. Gasson. 1998. 'Sex Differences in Parental Estimates of Their Children's Intelligence', *Sex Roles* 38: 151–162.

Gagnon, J., and W. Simon. 1986. 'Sexual Scripts: Performance and Change', *Archives of Sexual Behavior* 15: 98–104.

Gaines, Donna. 1991. *Teenage Wasteland: Suburbia's Dead End Kids*. New York: Pantheon Books.

Galabuzi, Grace-Edward. 2006. *Canada's Economic Apartheid: The Social Exclusion of Racialized Groups in the New Century*. Toronto: Canadian Scholars' Press.

Gallagher, John, and Ronald Robinson. 1953. 'The Imperialism of Free Trade', *The Economic History Review*, Second series 6 (1): 1–5.

Gamson, William. 1991. 'Commitment and Agency in Social Movements', *Sociological Forum* 6: 27–50.

Gannagé, Charlene. 1986. *Double Day, Double Bind: Women Garment Workers*. Toronto: Women's Press.

Gannon, M., K. Mihorean, K. Beatie, A. Taylor-Butts, and R. Kong. 2005. *Criminal Justice Indicators, 2005*. Ottawa: Canadian Centre for Justice Statistics, Statistics Canada.

Gans, Herbert J. 1967. *The Levittowners: Ways of Life and Politics in a New Suburban Community*. New York: Pantheon.

Gardner, Julia, and Mark Roseland. 1989. 'Thinking Globally: The Role of Social Equity in Sustainable Development', *Alternatives* 16, 3: 26–35.

Garfinkel, Harold. 1956. 'Conditions of Successful Status Degradation Ceremonies', *American Journal of Sociology* 61: 420–4.

———. 1967. *Studies in Ethnomethodology*. Englewood Cliffs, NJ: Prentice-Hall.

Garriguet, Didier. 2005. 'Early Sexual Intercourse', *Health Reports* 16, 3: 9–19. Statistics Canada Catalogue no. 82-003-XPE.

Gaskell, Jane. 1993. 'Feminism and Its Impact on Educational Scholarship in Canada', in Leonard L. Stewin and Stewart J.H. McCann, eds, *Contemporary Educational Issues: The Canadian Mosaic*, 2nd edn. Toronto: Copp Clark Pitman, 145–60.

Gaventa, John. 1980. *Power and Powerlessness: Quiescence and Rebellion in an Appalachian Valley*. Urbana: University of Illinois Press.

Gergen, Kenneth. 2001. 'From Mind to Relationship: The Emerging Challenge', *Education Canada* 41, 1: 8–11.

Giddens, Anthony. 1971. *Capitalism and Modern Social Theory: An Analysis of the Writings of Marx, Durkheim, and Max Weber*. Cambridge: Cambridge University Press.

———. 1979. *Selected Problems of Social Theory*. London: Macmillan.

———. 2000. *Introduction to Sociology*, 3rd edn. New York: Norton.

Gidengil, Elisabeth, Andre Blais, Joanna Everitt, Patrick Fournier, and Neil Nevitte. 2006. 'Back to the Future? Making Sense of the 2004 Canadian Election Outside Quebec', *Canadian Journal of Political Science* 39: 1–25.

———, ———, Richard Nadeau, and Neil Nevitte. 2001. 'Making Sense of the Vote: The 2000 Canadian Election', paper presented at the annual meeting of the Association for Canadian Studies in the United States.

Gidney, R.D. 1999. *From Hope to Harris: The Reshaping of Ontario's Schools*. Toronto: University of Toronto Press.

Gilbert, Neil. 1989. *The Enabling State: Modern Welfare Capitalism in America*. New York: Oxford University Press.

———. 1997. 'Advocacy Research and Social Policy', *Crime and Justice* 22: 101–48.

Gilligan, Carol. 1982. *In a Different Voice: Psychoanalytic Theory and Women's Development*. Cambridge, Mass.: Harvard University Press.

Giroux, Henri. 1997. *Pedagogy and the Politics of Hope: Theory, Culture, and Schooling: A Critical Reader*. Boulder, Colo.: Westview.

Glass, Jennifer, and Tetsushi Fujimoto. 1994. 'Housework, Paid Work and Depression Among Husbands and Wives', *Journal of Health and Social Behaviour* 35 (2): 179–191.

Glassner, Barry. 1999. *The Culture of Fear: Why Americans Are Afraid of the Wrong Things*. New York: Basic Books.

Glenmary Research Center. 2002. 'Religious Congregations and Membership: 2000'. At: <www.glenmary.org/grc/RCMS_2000/release.htm>.

Glenn, Evelyn Nakano. 2000. 'The Social Construction and Institutionalization of Gender and Race: An Integrative Framework', in Myra Marx Feree, Judith Lorber, and Beth B. Hess, eds, *Revisioning Gender*. New York: AltaMira, 3–43.

~~fman~~, Erving. 1959. *The Presentation of Self in Everyday ~~Life~~*. Garden City, NY: Doubleday-Anchor.

———. 1961a. *Asylums: Essays on the Social Situation of Mental Patients and Other Inmates*. New York: Doubleday.

———. 1961b. *Encounters: Two Studies in the Sociology of Interaction*. Indianapolis: Bobbs Merrill.

———. 1967. *Interaction Ritual: Essays on Face to Face Behavior*. Garden City, NY: Anchor.

———. 1971. *Relations in Public: Microstudies of the Public Order*. New York: Basic Books.

Gold, David A., Clarence Y.H. Lo, and Erik Olin Wright. 1975. 'Recent Developments in Marxist Theories of the Capitalist State', *Monthly Review* 27: 29–43.

Goldberg, David Theo. 1993. *Racist Culture: Philosophy and the Politics of Meaning*. Oxford: Blackwell.

Goldberg, Kim. 1990. *The Barefoot Channel: Community Television as a Tool for Social Change*. Vancouver: New Star Books.

Goldenberg, N. 2006. 'What's God Got to Do With It? A Call for Problematizing Basic Terms in the Feminist Analysis of Religion'. Paper presented at the biannual meetings of the Britain and Ireland School of Feminist Theology in Edinburgh in July.

Goldenberg, Sheldon. 1992. *Thinking Methodologically*. New York: HarperCollins.

Goldthorpe, J.E. 1987. *Family Life in Western Societies: A Historical Sociology of Family Relationships in Britain and North America*. Cambridge: Cambridge University Press.

Goldthorpe, J.H., David Lockwood, Frank Bechhofer, and Jennifer Platt. 1969. *The Affluent Worker in the Class Structure*. Cambridge: Cambridge University Press.

Gonzales, Alicia, and Gary Rolison. 2004. 'Social Oppression and Attitudes toward Sexual Practices', *Journal of Black Studies* 35, 6: 715–29.

Goode, William J. 1960. 'A Theory of Role Strain', *American Sociological Review* 25: 483–96.

Gordon, Robert M., and Jacquelyn Nelson. 2000. 'Crime, Ethnicity, and Immigration', in Robert A. Silverman, James J. Teevan, and Vincent F. Sacco, eds, *Crime in Canadian Society*, 6th edn. Toronto: Harcourt Brace.

Gorz, Andre. 1999. *Reclaiming Work: Beyond the Wage-Based Society*, trans. Chris Turner. Cambridge: Polity.

Gottfredson, M.R. 2006. 'Feminist Theories of Crime', in F.T. Cullen, J.P. Wright, and K.R. Blevins, eds, *Taking Stock: The Status of Criminological Theory, Vol. 15: Advances in Criminological Theory*. Piscataway NJ: Transaction Publishing.

——— and Travis Hirschi. 1990. *A General Theory of Crime*. Stanford, Calif.: Stanford University Press.

GPI Atlantic. n.d. 'The Economic Value of Housework and Child Care'. At: <www.gpiatlantic.org/ab_housework.shtml>.

Grabb, Edward G. 2007. *Theories of Social Inequality*, 5th edn. Toronto: Thomson Nelson.

Graham, Hilary. 1984. *Women, Health and the Family*. Brighton, UK: Wheatsheaf.

Gramsci, Antonio. 1992. *Prison Notebooks*, vol. 1, trans. Joseph A. Buttigieg and Antonio Callari. New York: Columbia University Press.

Granovetter, Mark S. 1974. *Getting a Job: A Study of Contacts and Careers*. Cambridge, Mass.: Harvard University Press.

Gray, Gary, and Neil Guppy. 2003. *Successful Surveys: Research Methods and Practice*, 3rd edn. Toronto: Thomson Nelson.

Grbich, Carolyn. 1992. 'Societal Response to Familial Role Change in Australia: Marginalisation or Social Change', *Journal of Comparative Family Studies* 23, 1: 79–94.

Greer, Germaine. 1984. *Sex and Destiny: The Politics of Human Fertility*. London: Martin Secker & Warburg.

Gregory, J.W., and V. Piché. 1983. 'Inequality and Mortality: Demographic Hypotheses Regarding Advanced and Peripheral Capitalism', *International Journal of Health Services* 13: 89–106.

Grenier, Marc. 1994. 'Native Indians in the English-Canadian Press: The Case of the "Oka Crisis"', *Media, Culture & Society* 16: 313–36.

Griffin, W. 2000. 'The Embodied Goddess: Feminist Witchcraft and Female Divinity', S.C. Monahan, W.A. Mirola, and M.O. Emerson, eds, *Sociology of Religion: A Reader*. New York: Prentice Hall/Penguin Putnam.

Grimes, Michael D. 1991. *Class in Twentieth-Century American Sociology: An Analysis of Theories and Measurement Strategies*. New York: Praeger.

Grosjean, Michele, and Michele Lacoste. 1998. 'L'oral et l'écrit dans les communications de travail ou les illusions du "tout ecrit"', *Sociologie du travail* 40: 439–61.

Gross, Edward, and Gregory P. Stone. 1981. 'Embarrassment and the Analysis of Role Requirements', *American Journal of Sociology* 70: 1–15.

Guernsey, Judith Read, Ron Dewar, Swarna Weerasinghe, Susan Kirkland, and Paul J. Veugelers. 2000. 'Incidence of Cancer in Sydney and Cape Breton County, Nova Scotia 1979–1997', *Canadian Journal of Public Health* 91: 285–92.

Guppy, Neil, and Scott Davies. 1998. *Education in Canada: Recent Trends and Future Challenges*. Ottawa: Statistics Canada.

Gusfield, Joseph R. 1963. *Symbolic Crusade: Status Politics and the American Temperance Movement*. Urbana: University of Illinois Press.

———. 1981. *The Culture of Public Problems: Drinking-Driving and the Symbolic Order*. Chicago: University of Chicago Press.

———. 1989. 'Constructing the Ownership of Social Problems: Fun and Profit in the Welfare State', *Social Problems* 36: 431–41.

Haberland, Nicole, and Diana Measham, eds. 2002. *Responding to Cairo: Case Studies of Changing Practice in Reproductive Health and Family Planning*. New York: Population Council.

Habermas, Jürgen. 1975. *Legitimation Crisis*, trans. Thomas McCarthy. Boston: Beacon.

Hackett, Robert A. 1992. 'The Depiction of Labour and Business on National Television News', in Marc Grenier, ed., *Critical Studies of Canadian Mass Media*. Markham, Ont.: Butterworths, 59–82.

——— and Richard Gruneau. 2000. *The Missing News: Filters and Blind Spots in Canada's Press*. Aurora, Ont.: Garamond.

——— and Scott Uzelman. 2003. 'Tracing Corporate Influences on Press Content: A Summary of Recent NewsWatch Canada Research', *Journalism Studies* 4, 3: 331–46.

Hagan, John, and Ruth D. Peterson, eds. 1995. *Crime and Inequality*. Stanford, Calif.: Stanford University Press.

Hall, Edward T. 1966. *The Hidden Dimension*. Garden City, NY: Doubleday.

Hall, Emmett. 1964–5. *Report of the Royal Commission on Health Services*. Ottawa: Queen's Printer.

Hall, Stuart. 1980. 'Encoding/Decoding', in Stuart Hall, Dorothy Hobson, Andrew Lowe, and Paul Willis, eds, *Culture, Media, Language: Working Papers in Cultural Studies, 1972–79*. London: Hutchinson, 128–38.

Hamdad, Malika. 2003. *Valuing Households' Unpaid Work in Canada, 1992 an 1998: Trends and Sources of Change*. Ottawa: Statistics Canada.

Hamilton, Richard F. 1996. *The Social Misconstruction of Reality: Validity and Verification in the Scholarly Community*. New Haven, Conn.: Yale University Press.

Hampton, Mary, Bonnie Jeffery, Barb McWatters, and Pamela Smith. 2005. 'Influence of Teens' Disapproval and Peer Behaviour on Their Initiation of Sexual Intercourse', *Canadian Journal of Human Sexuality* 14, 3/4: 105–21.

Handel, Gerald, ed. 1988. *Childhood Socialization*. New York: Aldine de Gruyter.

Harding, K. 2007. 'Hutterites Win Right to Photoless Driver's License', *The Globe and Mail*, 18 May; accessed 6 February, 2008.

Hardoy, Jorge E., Diana Mitlin, and David Satterthwaite. 2001. *Environmental Problems in an Urbanizing World*. London: Earthscan.

Harris, Chauncy, and Edward L. Ullman. 1945. 'The Nature of Cities', *Annals of the American Academy of Political and Social Science* 242: 7–17.

Harris, Judith. 1998. *The Nurture Assumption*. New York: Free Press

Hartmann, Heidi. 1981. 'The Unhappy Marriage of Marxism and Feminism: Towards a More Progressive Union', in Lydia Sargent, ed., *The Unhappy Marriage of Marxism and Feminism: A Debate on Class and Patriarchy*. London: Pluto, 2–41.

Harvey, David. 1989. *The Condition of Postmodernity: An Enquiry into the Origins of Cultural Change*. New York: Routledge.

———. 2006. *Spaces of Global Capitalism*. London and New York: Verso.

Hathaway, A.D. 2004. 'Cannabis Users' Informal Rules for Managing Stigma and Risk', *Deviant Behavior* 25, 6: 559–77.

Hawley, Amos A. 1950. *Human Ecology: A Theory of Community Structure*. New York: Ronald Press.

———. 1981. *Urban Society*, 2nd edn. New York: Wiley.

Hawley, Willis, and Frederick M. Wirt. 1968. *The Search for Community Power*. Scarborough, Ont.: Prentice-Hall.

Hayford, Alison. 1992. 'From Chicago 1966 to Montreal 1989: Notes on New(s) Paradigms of Women as Victims', in Marc Grenier, ed., *Critical Studies of Canadian Mass Media*. Markham, Ont.: Butterworths, 201–12.

Health Canada. 2002. *A Report on Mental Illness in Canada*. Ottawa: Health Canada.

Hearn, Jeff, and Wendy Parkin. 1987. *'Sex' and 'Work': The Power and Paradox of Organizational Sexuality*. New York: St Martin's.

Heimer, Robert. 2002. *Social Problems: An Introduction to Critical Constructionism*. New York: Oxford University Press.

Helleiner, Eric. 1994. *State and the Reemergence of Global Finance: From Bretton Woods to the 1990s*. Ithaca, NY: Cornell University Press.

Henry, Frances, and Effie Ginzberg. 1985. *Who Gets the Work: A Test of Racial Discrimination in Employment*. Toronto: Urban Alliance on Race Relations and Social Planning Directorate.

——— and Carol Tator. 2005. *The Colour of Democracy: Racism in Canadian Society*, 3rd edn. Toronto: Thomson Nelson.

Hermann, Christoph. 2007. 'Neoliberalism in the European Union', *Studies in Political Economy* 79: 61–89.

Herodotus. 1996. *Histories*. Hertfordshire: Wordsworth.

Hickman, B. 1988. 'Men Wise Up to Bald Truth', *Australian*, 21 May, 4.

Hier, Sean P. 2002. 'Raves, Risks and the Ecstasy Panic: A Case Study in the Subversive Nature of Moral Regulation', *Canadian Journal of Sociology* 27: 33–52.

Higgins, Robert R. 1994. 'Race, Pollution and the Mastery of Nature', *Environmental Ethics* 16: 251–64.

Hilberg, Raul. 1996. 'The Nazi Holocaust: Using Bureaucracies, Overcoming Psychological Barriers to Genocide', in M. David Ermann and Richard J. Lundman, eds, *Corporate and Governmental Deviance: Problems of Organizational Behavior in Contemporary Society*. New York: Oxford University Press, 158–79.

Hilgartner, Stephen, and Charles Bosk. 1988. 'The Rise and Fall of Social Problems: A Public Arenas Model', *American Journal of Sociology* 94: 53–78.

Hiller, Harry. 2005. *Urban Canada: Sociological Perspectives*. Toronto: Oxford University Press.

Hirschi, Travis. 1969. *Causes of Delinquency*. Berkeley: University of California Press.

Hochschild, Arlie. 1983. *The Managed Heart: Commercialization of Human Feeling*. Berkeley: University of California Press.

———. 1989. *The Second Shift: Working Parents and the Revolution at Home*. New York: Viking.

———. 1997. *The Time Bind: When Work Becomes Home and Home Becomes Work*. New York: Metropolitan Books.

———. 2001. 'The Third Shift', in Bonnie J. Fox, ed., *Family Patterns, Gender Relations*, 2nd edn. Toronto: Oxford University Press, 338–51.

——— and Anne Machung. 1989. *The Second Shift: Working Parents and the Revolution at Home*. New York: Viking.

Hodson, Randy. 2001. *Dignity at Work*. Cambridge: Cambridge University Press.

Hofrichter, Richard, ed. 1993. *Toxic Struggles: The Theory and Practice of Environmental Justice*. Philadelphia: New Society.

Holmes, Malcolm D., and Judith A. Antell. 2001. 'The Social Construction of American Indian Drinking: Perceptions of American Indian and White Officials', *Sociological Quarterly* 42: 151–73.

Hoodfar, H., S.A. Sajida, and S. McDonough. 2003. *The Muslim Veil in North America: Issues and Debates*. Toronto: Women's Press.

hooks, bell. *Outlaw Culture*. New York: Routledge.

Hope, Steven, Chris Power, and Bryan Rodgers. 1998. 'The Relationship between Parental Separation in Childhood and Problem Drinking in Adulthood', *Addiction* 93, 4: 505–14.

Hopkins, T.K., and Immanuel Wallerstein, eds. 1980. *Processes of the World-System*. Beverly Hills, Calif.: Sage Publications.

———, et al. 1982. *World-System Analysis: Theory and Methodology*. Beverly Hills: Sage Publications.

Hou, Feng, and T.R. Balakrishnan. 1999. 'The Economic Integration of Visible Minorities in Contemporary Canadian Society', in James Curtis, Edward Grabb, and Neil Guppy, eds, *Social Inequality in Canada: Patterns, Problems, and Policies*, 3rd edn. Scarborough, Ont.: Prentice-Hall Canada, 214–43.

——— and John Myles. 2007. 'The Changing Role of Education in the Marriage Market: Assortative Marriage in Canada and the United States Since the 1970s'. *Analytical Studies Branch Research Paper Series*, No. 299. Ottawa: Statistics Canada.

Hoyt, Homer. 1939. *The Structure and Growth of Residential Neighborhoods in American Cities*. Washington: Federal Housing Administration.

Hughes, Diane, and Deborah Johnson. 2001. 'Correlates in Children's Experiences of Parents' Racial Socialization Behaviors', *Journal of Marriage and Family* 63: 981–96.

Hughes, Karen. 1999. *Gender and Self-Employment in Canada: Assessing Trends and Policy Implications*. Ottawa: Canadian Policy Research Networks.

Hull, Jeremy. 2005. *Post-Secondary Education and Labour Market Outcomes, Canada 2001*. Ottawa: Minister of Indian Affairs and Northern Development.

Human Resources Development Canada (HRDC). 2002. *Knowledge Matters: Skills and Learning for Canadians*. Hull, Que.: HRDC.

——— and Statistics Canada. 1998. *High School May Not Be Enough: An Analysis of Results from the School Leavers Follow-up Survey 1995*. Ottawa: Minister of Public Works and Government Services Canada.

Humphrey, Craig R., and Frederick R. Buttel. 1982. *Environment, Energy and Society*. Belmont, Calif.: Wadsworth.

Humphreys, Laud. 1970. *Tearoom Trade: Impersonal Sex in Public Places*. Chicago: Aldine.

Humphries, Karin H., and Eddy van Doorslaer. 2000. 'Income-Related Health Inequality in Canada', *Social Science and Medicine* 50: 663–71.

Hunter, Alfred A. 1981. *Class Tells: On Social Inequality in Canada*. Toronto: Butterworths.

——— and Jean McKenzie Leiper. 1993. 'On Formal Education, Skills and Earnings: The Role of Educational Certificates in Earnings Determination', *Canadian Journal of Sociology* 18: 21–42.

Hunter, Floyd. 1953. *Community Power Structure: A Study of Decision Makers*. Chapel Hill: University of North Carolina Press.

Hurrelmann, Klaus, ed. 1989. *The Social World of Adolescents*. Berlin: Walter de Gruyter.

Ihinger-Tallman, Marilyn, and David Levinson (revised by J.M. White). 2003. 'Definition of Marriage', in J. Ponzetti Jr, ed., *International Encyclopedia of Marriage and Family*, 2nd edn. New York: Macmillan Reference and Thomson Gale.

Ikeda, Satoshi. 2002. '20th Century Anti-Systemic Historical Processes and US Hegemony: Free Trade Imperialism, National Economic Development, and Free Enterprise Imperialism', in Ramon Grosfoguel and Ana Margarita Cervantes-Rodriguez, eds, *The Modern/Colonial/*

Capitalist World-System in the Twentieth Century. Westport, Conn.: Praeger.

———. 2004. 'Japan and the Changing Regime of Accumulation: A World-System Study of Japan's Trajectory from Miracle to Debacle', *Journal of World-Systems Research* 10 (2): 362–94.

Illich, Ivan. 1976. *Limits to Medicine*. Toronto: McClelland & Stewart.

Imershein, Allen W., and Carroll L. Estes. 1996. 'From Health Services to Medical Markets: The Commodity Transformation of Medical Production and the Non-profit Sector', *International Journal of Health Services* 26: 221–38.

Imig, Doug, and Sidney Tarrow. 2001. 'Mapping the Europeanization of Contention: Evidence from a Quantitative Data Analysis', in Imig and Tarrow, eds, *Contentious Europeans: Protest and Politics in an Emerging Polity*. New York: Rowman and Littlefield, 27–49.

Inglehart, Ronald. 1977. *The Silent Revolution: Changing Values and Political Styles among Western Publics*. Princeton, NJ: Princeton University Press.

———. 1990b. 'Values, Ideology, and Cognitive Mobilization in New Social Movements', in R.J. Dalton and M. Kuechler, eds, *Challenging the Political Order*. New York: Oxford University Press, 23–42.

Irvine, Janice. 2003. '"The Sociologist as Voyeur": Social Theory and Sexual Research, 1910–1978', *Qualitative Sociology* 26, 4: 429–56.

Isajiw, Wsevolod. 1999. *Understanding Diversity: Ethnicity and Race in the Canadian Context*. Toronto: Thompson Educational Publishing.

Jablin, Frederic M. 1984. 'Assimilating New Members in Organizations', in R.N. Bostrom, ed., *Communication Yearbook*. Newbury Park, Calif.: Sage, 594–626.

Jackson, Andrew, and David Robinson. 2000. *Falling Behind: The State of Working Canada, 2000*. Ottawa: Canadian Centre for Policy Alternatives.

James, Daniel Lee, and Elizabeth A. Craft. 2002. 'Protecting One's Self from a Stigmatized Disease . . . Once One Has It', *Deviant Behavior* 23: 267–99.

James, W.C. 2006. 'Dimorphs and Cobblers: Ways of Being Religious in Canada', in L.G. Beaman, ed., *Religion and Canadian Society: Traditions, Transitions and Innovations*. Toronto: Scholar's Press.

Jameson, Frederic. 1998. *The Cultural Turn*. London & New York: Verso.

Jamieson, Lynn. 1998. *Intimacy: Personal Relationships in Modern Societies*. Cambridge: Polity.

Janis, Irving Lester. 1982. *Groupthink: Psychological Studies of Policy Decisions and Fiascoes*, 2nd edn. Boston: Houghton Mifflin.

Jenkins, J. Craig. 1983. 'Resource Mobilization Theory and the Study of Social Movements', *Annual Review of Sociology* 9: 527–53.

Jenkins, Philip. 1994. *Using Murder: The Social Construction of Serial Homicide*. New York: Aldine de Gruyter.

Jette, Allan M., Sybil L. Crawford, and Sharon L. Tennstedt. 1996. 'Toward Understanding Ethnic Differences in Late-Life Disability', *Research on Aging* 18: 292–309.

Johnson, Carol. 2002. 'Heteronormative Citizenship and the Politics of Passing', *Sexualities* 5, 3: 317–36.

Johnson, Holly. 1996. *Dangerous Domains: Violence against Women in Canada*. Toronto: Nelson.

———. 2005. 'Assessing the Prevalence of Violence against Women in Canada', *Statistical Journal of the United Nations ECE* 22: 225–38.

Johnson, Terence. 1972. *Professions and Power*. London: Macmillan, 1972.

Junger, Marianne, Peter van der Heijden, and Carl Keane. 2001. 'Interrelated Harms: Examining the Association between Victimization, Accidents and Criminal Behaviour', *Injury Control and Safety Promotion* 8, 1: 13–28.

Kachur, Jerrold L., and Trevor W. Harrison. 1999. 'Introduction: Public Education, Globalization, and Democracy: Whither Alberta?', in Harrison and Kachur, eds, *Contested Classrooms: Education, Globalization, and Democracy in Alberta*. Edmonton: University of Alberta Press and Parkland Institute, xiii–xxxv.

Kanungo, Shivraj. 1998. 'An Empirical Study of Organizational Culture and Network-Based Computer Use', *Computers in Human Behavior* 14, 1: 79–91.

Karim, Karim H. 2002. 'Globalization, Communication, and Diaspora', in Paul Attallah and Leslie Regan Shade, eds, *Mediascapes: New Patterns in Canadian Communication*. Scarborough, Ont.: Thomson Nelson, 272–94.

Karmis, Demetrios. 2004. 'Pluralism and National Identity(ies) in Contemporary Quebec: Conceptual Clarifications, Typology, and Discourse Analysis', in Alain-G. Gagnon, ed., *Quebec: State and Society*. Peterborough, Ont.: Broadview, 69–96.

Kasper, Anne S., and Susan J. Ferguson, eds. 2000. *Breast Cancer: Society Shapes an Epidemic*. New York: St Martin's.

Kawachi, Ichiro, Bruce P. Kennedy, Vanita Gupta, and Deborah Prothrow-Stith. 1999. 'Women's Status and the Health of Women and Men: A View from the States', *Social Science and Medicine* 48: 21–32.

Kay, Robin, and Liesel Knaack. 2008. 'A formative analysis of individual differences in the effectiveness of learning objects in secondary school', *Computers & Education* 51 (3): 1304–1320.

Kemp, Alice. 1994. *Women's Work: Degraded and Devalued*. Englewood Cliffs, NJ: Prentice Hall.

Kenway, Jane, and Helen Modra. 1992. 'Feminist Pedagogy and Emancipatory Possibilities', in Carmen Luke and Jennifer Gore, eds, *Feminisms and Critical Pedagogy*. London: Routledge, 138–66.

———, Sue Willis, Jack Blackmore, and Leonnie Rennie. 1998. *Answering Back: Girls, Boys, and Feminism in Schools*. New York: Routledge.

Kessler, S. 1998. *Lessons from the Intersexed*. New Brunswick, NJ: Rutgers University Press.

Keyfitz, Nathan. 1993. 'Are There Ecological Limits to Population?', *Proceedings of the National Academy of Sciences* 90: 6895–9.

Keynes, John Maynard. 1936. *The General Theory of Employment, Interest and Money*. Cambridge, Mass: Macmillan Cambridge University Pres.

Khor, Martin. 2001. *When Corporations Rule the World*, 2nd ed. San Francisco: Berrett-Koehler Publishers.

Kiernan, Kathleen. 1997. *The Legacy of Parental Divorce: Social, Economic, and Demographic Experiences in Adulthood*. London: Centre for Analysis of Social Exclusion.

Killingsworth, B. 2007. '"Drinking Stories" from a Playgroup: Alcohol in the Lives of Middle-Class Mothers in Australia', *Ethnography* 7, 3: 357–84.

Kim, Sujeong. 2004. 'Rereading David Morley's The "Nationwide" Audience', *Cultural Studies* 18, 1: 84–108.

King, Samantha. 2006. *Pink Ribbons, Inc.* Minneapolis: University of Minnesota Press.

Kinney, David. 1993. 'From Nerds to Normals: The Recovery of Identity among Adolescents from Middle School to High School', *Sociology of Education* 66: 21–40.

Kinsey, Alfred, Wardell Pomeroy, and Clyde Martin. 1948. *Sexual Behavior in the Human Male*. Philadelphia: W.B. Saunders.

———, ———, ———, and Paul Gebhard. 1953. *Sexual Behavior in the Human Female*. Philadelphia: W.B. Saunders.

Kirk, Dudley. 1998. 'Demographic Transition Theory', *Population Studies* 50: 361–87.

Kitschelt, Herbert. 1993. 'Social Movements, Political Parties, and Democratic Theory', *Annals of the American Academy of Political and Social Science* 528 (July): 13–29.

Klein, David M., and James M. White. 1996. *Family Theories: An Introduction*. Thousand Oaks, Calif.: Sage.

Klein, Naomi. 2000. *No Logo: Taking Aim at the Brand Bullies*. Toronto: Knopf Canada.

Knight, Graham. 1982. 'News and Ideology', *Canadian Journal of Communication* 8, 4: 15–41.

———. 1988. 'Stratified News: Media, Sources, and the Politics of Representation', in Peter A. Bruck, ed., *A Proxy for Knowledge: The News Media as Agents in Arms Control and Verification*. Ottawa: Carleton International Proceedings, 15–24.

———. 1998. 'Hegemony, the Press and Business Discourse: News Coverage of Strike-Breaker Reform in Quebec and Ontario', *Studies in Political Economy* 55: 93–125.

——— and Josh Greenberg. 2002. 'Promotionalism and Subpolitics: Nike and Its Labor Critics', *Management Communication Quarterly* 15, 4: 541–70.

Knight, Rolf. 1996. *Indians at Work: An Informal History of Native Labour in British Columbia, 1858–1930*. Vancouver: New Star.

Knighton, Tamara, and Sheba Mirza. 2002. 'Postsecondary Participation: The Effects of Parents' Education and Household Income', *Education Quarterly Review* 8, 3: 25–31.

Kong, Rebecca, Holly Johnson, Sara Beattie, and Andrea Cardillo. 2003. 'Sexual Offences in Canada', *Juristat* 23, 6. Ottawa: Statistics Canada Catalogue no. 85–002–XIE.

Kortenhaus, Carole, and Jack Demarest. 1993. 'Gender Stereotyping in Children's Literature: An Update', *Sex Roles* 28, 3/4: 219–33.

Krahn, Harvey J., Graham S. Lowe, and Karen D. Hughes. 2007. *Work, Industry, and Canadian Society*, 5th edn. Toronto: Thomson Nelson.

Krane, Julia. 2003. *What's Mother Got to Do With It? Protecting Children from Sexual Abuse*. Toronto: University of Toronto Press.

Kriesel, Warren, Terrence J. Centner, and Andrew Keeler. 1996. 'Neighborhood Exposure to Toxic Releases: Are There Racial Inequities?', *Growth and Change* 27: 479–99.

Kwong, Jeff C., Irfan A. Dhalla, David L. Streiner, Ralph E. Baddour, Andrea E. Waddell, and Ian L. Johnson. 2002. 'Effects of Rising Tuition Fees on Medical School Class Composition and Financial Outlook', *Canadian Medical Association Journal* 166: 1023–8.743

Kymlicka, Will. 1998. 'The Theory and Practice of Canadian Multiculturalism', *Canadian Federation of the Social Sciences and Humanities* 23 (Nov.): 1–10. At: <www.fedcan.ca/english/fromold/breakfast-kymlicka1198.cfm>.

Landy, Sarah, and Kwok Kwan Tam. 1996. 'Yes, Parenting Does Make a Difference to the Development of Children in Canada', in Statistics Canada, *Growing Up in Canada*. Ottawa: Human Resources Development Canada and Statistics Canada, 103–11.

Langlois, S., and P. Morrison. 2002. 'Suicide Deaths and Suicide Attempts', *Health Reports* 13, 2: 9–22.

Lasswell, Harold D. 1948. 'The Structure and Function of Communication in Society', in Lyman Bryson, ed., *The Communication of Ideas: A Series of Addresses*. New York: Cooper Square, 37–51.

Laufer, William S., and Freda Adler. 1994. *The Legacy of Anomie Theory: Advances in Criminological Theory*. New Brunswick, NJ: Transaction.

Lauzen, Martha M. 2006. *The Celluloid Ceiling: Behind-the-Scenes Employment of Women in the Top 250 Films of 2005*. At: <www.moviesbywomen.com/marthalauzenphd/stats2005.html>.

Lawr, Douglas, and Robert Gidney, eds. 1973. *Educating Canadians: A Documentary History of Public Education*. Toronto: Van Nostrand Reinhold.

LeBlanc, J. Clarence. 1994. *Educating Canadians for the New Economy*. Working paper prepared for the Canadian Institute for Research on Regional Development. Moncton, NB.

Lemert, Edwin. 1951. *Social Pathology: A Systematic Approach to the Theory of Sociopathic Behavior*. New York: McGraw-Hill.

Leong, M. 2007. 'Non-Halal Meat; Latest "Reasonable Accommodation" Quarrel in Québec', *National Post*, 5 April; accessed 6 February, 2008.

Lesnick, Alice. 2005. 'On the Job: Performing Gender and Inequality at Work, Home and School', *Journal of Education and Work* 18 (2): 187–200.

Lévesque, Stéphane. 1999. 'Rethinking Citizenship and Citizenship Education: A Canadian Perspective for the 21st Century', paper presented at the Citizenship Research Network Symposium, Fourth International Metropolis Conference, Georgetown University, Washington, DC.

Levin, Benjamin, and J. Anthony Riffel. 1997. *Schools and the Changing World: Struggling Toward the Future*. London: Falmer.

Levitt, Cyril. 1994. 'Is Canada a Racist Country?', in Sally F. Zerker, ed., *Change and Impact: Essays in Canadian Social Sciences*. Jerusalem: Magnes Press, Hebrew University, 304–16.

Lewicki, Roy J., and Barbara Benedict Bunker. 1996. 'Developing and Maintaining Trust in Work Relationships', in Roderick M. Kramer and Tom R. Tyler, eds, *Trust in*

Organizations: Frontiers of Theory and Research. Thousand Oaks, Calif.: Sage, 114–39.

Lewis, Jone Johnson. 2002. 'Women Prime Ministers and Presidents: Twentieth Century', *Women's History Guide*. At: <womenshistory.about.com/library/weekly/aa010128a.htm>.

Li, Peter. 1988. *Ethnic Inequality in a Class Society*. Toronto: Thompson Educational Publishing.

———, ed. 1999. *Race and Ethnic Relations in Canada*, 2nd edn. Toronto: Oxford University Press.

———. 2003. *Destination Canada: Immigration Debates and Issues*. Toronto: Oxford University Press.

Lian, Jason Z., and Ralph Matthews. 1998. 'Does the Vertical Mosaic Still Exist? Ethnicity and Income in Canada, 1991', *Canadian Review of Sociology and Anthropology* 35, 4: 461–81.

Lieberson, Stanley. 2000. *A Matter of Taste: How Names, Fashions, and Culture Change*. New Haven: Yale University Press.

Liebow, Elliot. 1993. *Tell Them Who I Am: The Lives of Homeless Women*. New York: Free Press.

Lin, Zhengxi, Janice Yates, and Garnett Picot. 1999. *Rising Self-employment in the Midst of High Unemployment: An Empirical Analysis of Recent Developments in Canada*. Ottawa: Statistics Canada.

Linton, Ralph. 1936. *The Study of Man: An Introduction*. New York: Appleton-Century-Crofts.

Liodakis, Nikolaos. 1998 'The Activities of Hellenic-Canadian Secular Organizations in the Context of Canadian Multiculturalism', *Études Helléniques/Hellenic Studies* 6, 1: 37–58.

———. 2002. 'The Vertical Mosaic Within: Class, Gender and Nativity within Ethnicity', Ph.D. dissertation, McMaster University.

——— and Victor Satzewich. 2003. 'From Solution to Problem: Multiculturalism and "Race Relations" as New Social Problems', in Wayne Antony and Les Samuelson, eds, *Power and Resistance: Critical Thinking about Canadian Social Issues*, 3rd edn. Halifax: Fernwood, 145–68.

Lipietz, Alain. 1987. *Mirages and Miracles: The Crisis of Global Fordism*. London: Verso.

Lipman, Ellen L., David R. Offord, and Martin D. Dooley. 1996. 'What Do We Know about Children from Single-Parent Families? Questions and Answers from the National Longitudinal Survey on Children', in *Growing Up in Canada*. Ottawa: Human Resources Development Canada, 83–91.

Little, Don. 1995. 'Earnings and Labour Force Status of 1990 Graduates', *Education Quarterly Review* 2, 3: 10–20.

Livingston, Jessica. 2004. 'Murder in Juarez: Gender, Sexual Violence, and the Global Assembly Line', *Frontiers* 25, 1: 59–76.

Lofland, Lyn H. 1985. *A World of Strangers: Order and Action in Urban Public Space*. Prospect Heights, Ill.: Waveland.

———. 1998. *The Public Realm: Exploring the City's Quintessential Social Territory*. New York: Aldine de Gruyter.

Looker, E. Dianne, and Graham S. Lowe. 2001. *Post-secondary Access and Student Financial Aid in Canada: Current Knowledge and Research Gaps*. Ottawa: Canadian Policy Research Networks. At: <www.cprn.ca/en/doc.cfm?doc=192>.

Lorimer, Rowland, and Mike Gasher. 2001. *Mass Communication in Canada*, 4th edn. Toronto: Oxford University Press.

Loseke, Donileen R. 2003. *Thinking about Social Problems: An Introduction to Constructionist Perspectives*. New York: Aldine de Gruyter.

Losh-Hesselbart, Susan. 1987. 'Development of Gender Roles', in Marvin B. Sussman and Suzanne K. Steinmetz, eds, *Handbook of Marriage and the Family*. New York: Plenum, 535–63.

Lowe, Graham S. 1987. *Women in the Administrative Revolution: The Feminization of Clerical Work*. Toronto: University of Toronto Press.

———. 2000. *The Quality of Work: A People-Centred Agenda*. Toronto: Oxford University Press.

Lu, Aiguo. 1999. *China and the Global Economy since 1840*. New York: Palgrave Macmillan.

Luckenbill, David F. 1977. 'Criminal Homicide as a Situational Transaction', *Social Problems* 25: 176–86.

Luffman, Jacqueline. 2006. 'Core-Age Labour Force', *Perspectives On Labour and Income* 7 (9): 5–11.

Lukes, Steven. 1974. *Power: A Radical View*. London: Macmillan.

Lutz, Wolfgang, ed. 1994. *The Future Population of the World: What Can We Assume Today?* London: Earthscan.

Luxton, Meg. 1980. *More Than a Labour of Love*. Toronto: Women's Press.

———. 2001. 'Family Coping Strategies: Balancing Paid Employment and Domestic Labour', in Bonnie Fox, ed., *Family Patterns, Gender Relations*, 2nd edn. Toronto: Oxford University Press, 318–37.

——— and June Corman. 2001. *Getting By in Hard Times: Gendered Labour at Home and on the Job*. Toronto: University of Toronto Press.

Lynch, Kathleen. 1989. *The Hidden Curriculum: Reproduction in Education, A Reappraisal*. London: Falmer.

Lyon, David and Marguerite Van Die. 2000. *Rethinking Church, State, and Modernity: Canada Between Europe and America*. Toronto: University of Toronto Press.

McBride, Stephen. 2001. *Paradigm Shift: Globalization and the Canadian State*. Halifax: Fernwood Publishing.

McBride, Stephen, and John Shields. 1997. *Dismantling a Nation: The Transition to Corporate Rule in Canada*, 2nd ed. Halifax: Fernwood Publishing.

McCarthy, John D. 1996. 'Constraints and Opportunities in Adopting, Adapting, and Inventing', in Doug McAdam, John McCarthy, and Mayer Zald, eds, *Comparative Perspectives on Social Movements*. New York: Cambridge University Press, 141–51.

McCary, James Leslie. 1967. *Human Sexuality: A Contemporary Marriage Manual*. Toronto: D. Van Nostrand.

Maccoby, Eleanor. 1992. 'Trends in the Study of Socialization: Is There a Lewinian Heritage?', *Journal of Social Issues* 48, 2: 171–86.

——— and Carole Jacklin. 1974. *The Psychology of Sex Differences*. Stanford, Calif.: Stanford University Press.

McDaniel, Susan. 1988. 'Women's Roles, Reproduction and the New Reproductive Technologies: A New Stork Rising', in Nancy Mandell and Ann Duffy, eds, *Reconstructing the Canadian Family*. Toronto: Butterworths, 175–206.

MacDonald, Martha, Shelley Phipps, and Lynn Lethbridge. 2005. 'Taking Its Toll: The Influence of Paid and Unpaid Work on Women's Well-Being', *Feminist Economics* 11 (1): 63–94.

MacDowell, Laurel Sefton, and Ian Radforth, eds. 1992. *Canadian Working Class History: Selected Readings*. Toronto: Canadian Scholars' Press.

Macek, S. 2006. *Urban Nightmares*. Minneapolis: University of Minnesota Press.

McGuire, M. 2005. 'Rethinking Sociology's Sacred/Profane Dichotomy: Historically Contested Boundaries in Western Christianity'. Paper presented at SISR/ISSR, Zagreb.

McIntosh, Mary. 1978. 'The State and the Oppression of Women', in Annette Kuhn and Ann Marie Wolpe, eds, *Feminism and Materialism*. London: Routledge & Kegan Paul, 254–89.

McKee, Alan. 2007. 'The Relationship Between Attitudes Towards Women, Consumption of Pornography, and Other Demographic Variables in a Survey of 1,023 Consumers of Pornography", *International Journal of Sexual Health* 19 (1): 31–45.

McKenzie, Michael. 2007. 'Science and Engineering PhDs: A Canadian Portrait', *Analysis in Brief—Analytical* Paper. Ottawa: Statistics Canada.

McKeown, Thomas. 1976. *The Modern Rise of Population*. London: Edward Arnold.

Mackie, Marlene. 1987. *Constructing Women and Men: Gender Socialization*. Toronto: Holt, Rinehart and Winston.

———. 1991. *Gender Relations in Canada: Further Explorations*. Toronto: Butterworths.

MacKinnon, Catherine. 1989. *Toward a Feminist Theory of the State*. Cambridge: Harvard University Press.

MacKinnon, Mark, and Keith Lacey. 2001. 'Bleak House', *Globe and Mail*, 18 Aug., F1.

McLaren, Angus. 1990. *Our Own Master Race: Eugenics in Canada, 1885–1945*. Toronto: McClelland & Stewart.

McLaren, Peter. 1998. *Life in Schools: An Introduction to Critical Pedagogy in the Foundations of Education*, 3rd edn. New York: Longman.

McMichael, Philip. 2004. *Development and Social Change: A Global Perspective*, Third Edition. Thousand Oaks: Pine Forge Press.

MacMillan, Harriet L., Angus B. MacMillan, David R. Offord, and Jennifer L. Dingle. 1996. 'Aboriginal Health', *Canadian Medical Association Journal* 155: 1569–78.

Magder, Ted. 1993. *Canada's Hollywood: The Canadian State and Feature Films*. Toronto: University of Toronto Press.

——— and Jonathan Burston. 2001. 'Whose Hollywood? Changing Forms and Relations Inside the North American Entertainment Economy', in Vincent Mosco and Dan Schiller, eds, *Continental Order? Integrating North America for Cybercapitalism*. Lanham, Md: Rowman and Littlefield, 207–34.

Magnusson, Warren. 1990. 'Critical Social Movements: Decentring the State', in Alain G. Gagnon and James Bickerton, eds, *Canadian Politics: An Introduction*. Peterborough, Ont.: Broadview, 525–41.

Mahtani, Minelle. 2001. 'Representing Minorities: Canadian Media and Minority Identities', *Canadian Ethnic Studies* 33, 3: 99–133.

Malenfant, Romaine, Andrée Larue, and Michel Vézina. 2007. 'Intermittent Work and Well-Being: One Foot in the Door, One Foot Out', *Current Sociology* 55 (6): 814–835.

Malthus, Thomas R. 1970 [1798]. *An Essay on the Principle of Population*. Harmondsworth, UK: Penguin.

Mander, Jerry, and Edward Goldsmith. 1997. *The Case against the Global Economy and for a Turn toward the Local*. San Francisco: Sierra Club Books.

Mankoff, Milton. 1971. 'Societal Reaction and Career Deviance: A Critical Analysis', *Sociological Quarterly* 12: 204–18.

Manzer, Jenny. 2001. 'Clinical Guidelines Ignore Gender Differences', *Medical Post* 37, 13: 2, 65.

Mao, Y., J. Hu, A.M. Ugnat, and K. White. 2000. 'Non-Hodgkin's Lymphoma and Occupational Exposure to Chemicals in Canada', *Annals of Oncology* 11, suppl. 1: 69–73.

Maquiladora Solidarity Network. 2000. 'Child Labour and the Rights of Youth'. At: <www.maquilasolidarity.org/resources/child/issuesheet.htm>.

Marcil-Gratton, Nicole. 1998. *Growing Up with Mom and Dad? The Intricate Family Life Courses of Canadian Children*. Ottawa: Statistics Canada.

Marcus, Sheron. 2005. 'Queer Theory for Everyone: A Review Essay', *Signs* 31, 1: 191–218.

Markin, K.M. 2005. 'Still Crazy after All These Years: The Enduring Defamatory Power of Mental Disorder', *Law and Psychology Review* 29: 155–85.

Marmot, Michael G., Geffrey Rose, Martin Shipley, and P.J. Hamilton. 1978. 'Employment Grade and Coronary Heart Disease in British Civil Servants', *Journal of Epidemiological Community Health* 32: 244–9.

———, George Davey Smith, Stephen Stansfeld, Chandra Patel, Fiona North, Jenny Head, Ian White, Eric Brunner, and Amanda Feeney. 1991. 'Health Inequalities among British Civil Servants: The Whitehall II Study', *Lancet* 337: 1387–93.

Marshall, Katherine. 1998. 'Stay-at-Home Dads', *Perspectives on Labour and Income* 10, 1: 9–15.

———. 2006. 'Converging Gender Roles', *Perspectives (Statistics Canada)*. 7 (7): 5–17.

———. 2008. 'Father's Use of Paid Parental Leave', *Perspectives on Labour and Income* 9 (6): 5–14.

Marshall, Sheree. 1995. 'Ethnic Socialization of African American Children: Implications for Parenting, Identity Development, and Achievement', *Journal of Youth and Adolescence* 24: 377–96.

Martin, Carol Lynn, and Diane Ruble. 2004. 'Children's Search for Gender Cues: Cognitive Perspectives on Gender and Development', *Current Directions in Psychological Science* 13 (2): 67.

Marx, Karl. 1967 [1867]. *Capital: A Critique of Political Economy*. New York: International Publishers.

———. 1976 [1867]. *Capital*, vol. 1. Harmondsworth, UK: Penguin.

———. 1887. *Capital: A Critical Analysis of Capitalist Production*, ed. Friedrich Engels. London: Lowry and Company.

———. 1964. *The Economic and Philosophical Manuscripts of 1844*, ed. Dirk J. Struik, trans. Martin Milligan. New York: International Publishers.

———. 1977. *Capital: A Critique of Political Economy*. New York: Vintage Books.

——— and Friedrich Engels. 1970 [1845–6]. *The German Ideology*, Part I, with Selections from Parts 2 and 3, trans. C.J. Arthur. New York: International Publishers.

—— and ——. 1948 [1848]. *Manifesto of the Communist Party*. New York: International Publishers.

—— and ——. 1983 [1848]. 'Manifesto of the Communist Party', in Eugene Kamenka, ed., *The Portable Karl Marx*. New York: Penguin, 197–324.

Marx, Karl, and Friedrich Engels. 1998. *The Communist Manifest: A Modern Edition*. London, New York: Verso.

Maslovski, Mikhail. 1996. 'Max Weber's Concept of Patrimonialism and the Soviet System', *Sociological Review* 44: 294–308.

Matza, D., and Gresham Sykes. 1957. 'Techniques of Neutralization: A Theory of Delinquency', *American Sociological Review* 5: 1–12.References 747

Maxim, Paul S., and Paul C. Whitehead. 1998. *Explaining Crime*, 4th edn. Newton, Mass.: Butterworth-Heinemann.

Mead, George Herbert. 1934. *Mind, Self, and Society from the Standpoint of a Social Behaviorist*. Chicago: University of Chicago Press.

Mead, Margaret. 1935. *Sex and Temperament in Three Primitive Societies*. New York: Dell.

Meleis, Afaf Ibrahim, and Teri G. Lindgren. 2002. 'Man Works From Sun to Sun, but Woman's Work is Never Done: Insights on Research and Policy', *Health Care for Women International* 23: 742–753.

Melucci, Alerbero. 1989. *Nomads of the Present: Social Movements and Individual Needs in Contemporary Society*. Philadelphia: Temple University Press.

Mennie, J. 2007. 'Other Soccer Teams Show Support', *The Montréal Gazette*, 27 February, accessed 6 February 2008.

Ménoret, Pascal. 2005. *The Saudi Enigma: A History*, trans. P. Camiller. London: Zed.

Mertig, Angela, and Riley Dunlap. 2001. 'Environmentalism, New Social Movement and the New Class: A Crossnational Investigation', *Rural Sociology* 66, 1: 113–36.

——, ——, and Denton Morrison. 2002. 'The Environmental Movement in the United States', in Riley Dunlap and William Michelson, eds, *Handbook of Environmental Sociology*. Westport, Conn.: Greenwood, 448–81.

Merton, Robert K. 1938. 'Social Structure and Anomie', *American Sociological Review* 3: 672–82.

——. 1949, 1957. *Social Theory and Social Structure*. Glencoe, Ill./New York: Free Press.

Meyer, David, and Suzanne Staggenborg. 1996. 'Movements, Countermovements and the Structure of Political Opportunity', *American Journal of Sociology* 101: 1628–60.

Meyerson, Debra, Karl E. Weick, and Roderick M. Kramer. 1996. 'Swift Trust and Temporary Groups', in Roderick M. Kramer and Tom R. Tyler, eds, *Trust in Organizations: Frontiers of Theory and Research*. Thousand Oaks, Calif.: Sage, 166–95.

Michelson, William. 1976. *Man and His Urban Environment: A Sociological Approach*. Reading, Mass.: Addison-Wesley.

——. 1983. *From Sun to Sun: Daily Obligations and Community Structure in the Lives of Employed Women and Their Families*. Totowa, NJ: Rowman and Allanheld.

Micklin, Michael, ed. 1973. *Population, Environment and Social Organization: Current Issues in Human Ecology*. Hinsdale, Ill.: Dryden.

Mihorean, K. 2005. 'Trends in Self-Reported Spousal Violence', in K. AuCoin, ed., *Family Violence in Canada: A Statistical Profile*. Ottawa: Canadian Centre for Justice Statistics, Statistics Canada.

Miles, Robert, and Malcolm Brown. 2003. *Racism*, 2nd edn. London: Routledge.

—— and Rudy Torres. 1996. 'Does "Race" Matter? Transatlantic Perspectives on Racism after "Race Relations"', in V. Amit-Talai and C. Knowles, eds, *Re-situating Identities: The Politics of Race, Ethnicity and Culture*. Peterborough, Ont.: Broadview, 24–46.

Milgram, Stanley. 1970. 'The Experience of Living in Cities', *Science* 167: 1461–8.

Milkman, Ruth. 1987. *Gender at Work: The Dynamics of Job Segregation by Sex during World War II*. Chicago: University of Illinois Press.

Miller, Gale, and James A. Holstein. 1993. *Constructionist Controversies: Issues in Social Problems Theory*. New York: Aldine de Gruyter.

Miller, Toby, Nitin Govil, John McMurria, and Richard Maxwell. 2001. *Global Hollywood*. London: British Film Institute.

Millett, Kate. 1969, 1970. *Sexual Politics*. New York: Doubleday; Avon.

Mills, C. Wright. 1956. *The Power Elite*. New York: Oxford University Press.

——. 1959. *The Sociological Imagination*. New York: Oxford University Press.

Miranda, Dave, and Michael Claes. 2004. 'Rap Music Genres and Deviant Behaviors in French-Canadian Adolescents', *Journal of Youth and Adolescence* 33, 2: 113–22.

Mitchell, Robert Cameron, Angela G. Mertig, and Riley E. Dunlap. 1992. 'Twenty Years of Environmental Mobilization: Trends among National Environmental Organizations', in Dunlap and Mertig, eds, *American Environmentalism*. Philadelphia: Taylor and Francis, 11–26.

Mondschein, E.R., K.E. Adolph, and C.S. Tamis-LeMonda. 2000. 'Gender Bias in Mothers' Expectations about Infant Crawling', *Journal of Experimental Child Psychology* 77: 304–16.

Montpetit, Eric, Francesca Scala, and Isabelle Fortier. 2004. 'The Paradox of Deliberative Democracy: The National Action Committee on the Status of Women and Canada's Policy on Reproductive Technology', *Policy Sciences* 37: 137–57.

Moodie, Susannah. 1995 [1852]. *Roughing It in the Bush*. Toronto: McClelland & Stewart.

Moodley, Kogila. 1983. 'Canadian Multiculturalism as Ideology', *Ethnic and Racial Studies* 6, 3: 320–31.

Morland, Iain. 2005. '"The Glans Opens Like a Book": Writing and Reading the Intersexed Body', *Continuum: Journal of Media and Cultural Studies* 19, 3: 335–48.

Morley, David. 1980. *The 'Nationwide' Audience*. London: British Film Institute.

——. 2006. 'Unanswered Questions in Audience Research', *Communication Review* 9: 101–21.

Morrison, Denton, and Riley E. Dunlap. 1986. 'Environmentalism and Elitism: A Conceptual and Empirical Analysis', *Environmental Management* 10: 581–9.

Morton, Desmond. 1998. *Working People: An Illustrated History of the Canadian Labour Movement*, 4th edn. Montreal: McGill-Queen's University Press.

Mosco, Vincent. 1989. *The Pay-per Society: Computers and Communication in the Information Age*. Toronto: Garamond.

———. 2005. 'Here Today, Outsourced Tomorrow: Knowledge Workers in the Global Economy', *Javnost—The Public* 12, 2: 39–55.

Moss, Kathleen. 2004. 'Kids Witnessing Violence', *Canadian Social Trends* no. 73 (Summer): 12–16.

Moynihan, Ray, Iona Heath, and David Henry. 2002. 'Selling Sickness: The Pharmaceutical Industry and Disease Mongering', *British Medical Journal* 324: 886–91.

Multani v. Commission scolaire Marguerite-Bourgeoys. 2006. SCC 6, 1 S.C.R. 256.

Muncie, John, and Margaret Weatherell. 1995. 'Family Policy and Political Discourse', in John Muncie, Margaret Weatherell, Rudi Dallos, and Allan Cochrane, eds, *Understanding the Family*. London: Sage, 39–80.

Munro, Marcella. 1997. 'Ontario's "Days of Action" and Strategic Choices for the Left in Canada', *Studies in Political Economy* 53: 125–40.

Murdie, Robert. 1969. *Factorial Ecology of Metropolitan Toronto*. Department of Geography Research Paper 116. Chicago: University of Chicago.

Murphy, Elizabeth. 2000. 'Risk, Responsibility and Rhetoric in Infant Feeding', *Journal of Contemporary Ethnography* 29: 291–325.

———. 2007. *Childhood* 14, 1: 105–27. At: <search1.scholarsportal.info/ids70/view_record.php?id=2&recnum=3&SID=dd5cc57671b4400ab13563fc5427839d>.

Mustard, Cameron A., Shelley Derkson, Jean-Marie Berthelot, Michael Wolfson, and Leslie L. Roos. 1997. 'Age-Specific Education and Income Gradients in Morbidity and Mortality in a Canadian Province', *Social Science and Medicine* 45: 383–97.

Mustard, Fraser. 1999. 'Health Care and Social Cohesion', in Daniel Drache and Terry Sullivan, eds, *Market Limits in Health Reform: Public Success, Private Failure*. London: Routledge, 329–50.

Myles, John. 1989. *Old Age in the Welfare State: The Political Economy of Public Pensions*, rev. edn. Lawrence: University Press of Kansas.

Nabalamba, Alice. 2001. 'Locating Risk: A Multivariate Analysis of the Spatial and Socio-demographic Characteristics of Pollution', Ph.D. dissertation, University of Waterloo.

Naess, Arne. 1973. 'The Shallow and the Deep, Long Range Ecology Movement', *Inquiry* 16: 95–100.

Nakhaie, M. Reza, ed. 1999. *Debates on Social Inequality: Class, Gender and Ethnicity in Canada*. Toronto: Harcourt Canada.

———. 2000. 'Ownership and Management Position of Canadian Ethnic Groups in 1973 and 1989', in Madeline A. Kalbach and Warren Kalbach, eds, *Perspectives on Ethnicity in Canada*. Toronto: Harcourt Canada.

———, Robert A. Silverman, and Teresa C. LaGrange. 2000. 'An Examination of Gender, Ethnicity, Class and Delinquency', *Canadian Journal of Sociology* 25: 35–59.

Nanda, Serena, and Richard L. Warms. 2004. *Cultural Anthropology*, 8th edn. Belmont, Calif.: Wadsworth/Thomson Learning.

Nash, Kate. 2000. *Contemporary Political Sociology: Globalization, Politics, and Power*. Oxford: Blackwell.

Nason-Clark, N., and B. Fisher-Townsend. 2007. 'Women, Gender and Feminism in the Sociology of Religion: Theory, Research and Social Action', in Tony Blasi, ed., *American Sociology of Religion: Histories*. Leiden, Holland: Brill Press, 203–21.

Nason-Clark, N., and C. Clark Kroeger. 2004. *Refuge from Abuse: Hope and Healing for Abused Christian Women*. Downers Grove, IL: InterVarsity Press.

Nason-Clark, N., B. Fisher-Townsend, and L. Ruff. 2004. 'When Terror Strikes at Home: The Interface Between Religion and Domestic Violence', *Journal for the Scientific Study of Religion* 43(3): 303–10.

National Council of Welfare. 2001–2. *The Cost of Poverty*. Ottawa: National Council of Welfare.

———. 2002. *Poverty Profile 1999*. Ottawa: Minister of Public Works and Government Services.

National Longitudinal Survey of Children and Youth (NLSCY). 1996. *Growing Up in Canada*. Ottawa: Human Resources Development Canada and Statistics Canada.

National Research Council, Committee on Population and Working Group on Population Growth and Economic Development. 1986. *Population Growth and Economic Development: Policy Questions*. Washington: National Academy Press.

Navarro, Véase Vicente. 1975. 'The Industrialization of Fetishism or the Fetishism of Industrialization: A Critique of Ivan Illich', *Social Science and Medicine* 9: 351–63.

Nedelmann, Birgitta. 1991. 'Review of *Ideology and the New Social Movements*, by Alan Scott', *Contemporary Sociology* 20: 374–5.

Nelson, Adie, and Barrie W. Robinson. 2002. *Gender in Canada*, 2nd edn. Toronto: Pearson Educational.

Nelson, Fiona. 1999. 'Maternal Identities, Maternal Practices and the Culture(s) of Motherhood', paper presented at the annual meeting of the Canadian Sociology and Anthropology Association, Lennoxville, Que., 8 June.

Nett, Emily. 1981. 'Canadian Families in Social-Historical Perspective', *Canadian Journal of Sociology* 6, 3: 239–60.

Netting, S. Nancy, and Matthew Burnett. 2004. 'Twenty Years of Student Sexual Behaviour: Subcultural Adaptations to a Changing Health Environment', *Adolescence* 39, 153: 19–38.

Newbold, K. Bruce. 1998. 'Problems in Search of Solutions: Health and Canadian Aboriginals', *Journal of Community Health* 23, 1: 59–73.

Nicholson, Linda, and Steven Seidman, eds. 1995. *Introduction to Social Postmodernism: Beyond Identity Politics*. Cambridge: Cambridge University Press.

Nielsen, Tracy. 2007. 'Streets, Strangers, and Solidarity', in John J. Macionis, Nijole V. Benokraitis, and Bruce Ravelli, eds, *Seeing Ourselves: Classic, Contemporary, and Cross-Cultural Readings in Sociology*, 2nd Canadian edn. Toronto: Pearson/Prentice-Hall, 173–87.

Nisbet, Robert A. 1959. 'The Decline and Fall of Social Class', *Pacific Sociological Review* 2: 11–17.

Nobles, Melissa. 2000. *Shades of Citizenship: Race and the Census in Modern Politics*. Stanford, Calif.: Stanford University Press.

Nordenmark, Mikael. 2004. 'Does Gender Ideology Explain Differences Between Countries Regarding the Involvement of Women and of Men in Paid and Unpaid Work?', *International Journal of Social Welfare* 13 (3): 233–243.

Notestein, Frank. 1945. 'Population: The Long View', in Theodore W. Schultz, ed., *Food for the World*. Chicago: University of Chicago Press, 36–57.

Nylund, D. 2004. 'When in Rome: Heterosexism, Homophobia, and Sports Talk Radio', *Journal of Sport and Social Issues* 28 (2): 136–168.

Oakes, J.M. 1996. 'A Longitudinal Analysis of Environmental Equity in Communities with Hazardous Waste Facilities', *Social Science Research* 25: 125–48.

O'Brien, Mary. 1981. *The Politics of Reproduction*. Boston: Routledge & Kegan Paul.

Occhionero, Marisa Ferrari. 1996. 'Rethinking Public Space and Power', *International Review of Sociology* 6 (n.s.): 453–64.

O'Connor, Julia S., Ann Shola Orloff, and Sheila Shaver. 1999. *States, Markets, Families: Gender Liberalism and Social Policy in Australia, Canada, Great Britain and the United States*. Cambridge: Cambridge University Press.

Offe, Claus. 1984. *Contradictions of the Welfare State*. Cambridge, Mass.: MIT Press.

Offer, Daniel, Eric Ostrov, Kenneth Howard, and Robert Atkinson. 1988. *The Teenage World: Adolescents' Self-Image in Ten Countries*. New York: Plenum.

Ogmundson, Richard. 1991. 'Perspective on the Class and Ethnic Origins of Canadian Elites: A Methodological Critique of the Porter/Clement/Olsen Tradition', *Canadian Journal of Sociology* 15, 2: 165–77.

———. 1993. 'At the Top of the Mosaic: Doubts about the Data', *American Review of Canadian Studies* (Autumn): 373–86.

———. 2005. 'Does it Matter If Women, Minorities and Gays Govern? New Data Concerning an Old Question', *Canadian Journal of Sociology* 30: 315–19.

——— and J. McLaughlin. 1992. 'Trends in the Ethnic Origins of Canadian Elites: The Decline of the Brits?', *Canadian Review of Sociology and Anthropology* 29, 2: 227–42.

O'Leary, K. Daniel, J. Barling, Ilena Arias, Alan Rosenbaum, J. Malone, and A. Tyree. 1989. 'Prevalence and Stability of Physical Aggression between Spouses: A Longitudinal Analysis', *Journal of Consulting and Clinical Psychology* 57: 263–8.

Organization for Economic Co-operation and Development (OECD). 2001. *OECD Economic Outlook* 70 (Dec.). Paris: OECD.

———. 2006. *Education at a Glance: OECD Indicators 2006*. Paris: OECD.

O'Riordan, T. 1971. 'The Third American Environmental Conservation Movement: New Implications for Public Policy', *Journal of American Studies* 5: 155–71.

Ornstein, Michael. 1981. 'The Occupational Mobility of Men in Ontario', *Canadian Review of Sociology and Anthropology* 18, 2: 181–215.

———. 1983. *Accounting for Gender Differentials in Job Income in Canada: Results from a 1981 Survey*. Ottawa: Minister of Supply and Services.

Orsi, R. 2003. 'Is the Study of Lived Religion Irrelevant to the World We Live in?', *Journal for the Scientific Study of Religion* 42(2): 169.

Orville Nichols v. Department of Justice, Government of Saskatchewan, 25 October 2006.

Osberg, Lars. 1992. 'Canada's Economic Performance: Inequality, Poverty, and Growth', in Robert C. Allen and Gideon Rosenbluth, eds, *False Promises: The Failure of Conservative Economics*. Vancouver: New Star, 39–52.

Osborne, Ken. 1999. *Education: A Guide to the Canadian School Debate: Or, Who Wants What and Why?* Toronto: Penguin.

Overbeek, Johannes. 1974. *History of Population Theories*. Rotterdam: Rotterdam University Press.

Pacione, Michael. 1997. 'Local Exchange Trading Systems as a Response to the Globalisation of Capitalism', *Urban Studies* 34 (8): 1179–1199.

Pais, José Machado. 2000. 'Transitions and Youth Cultures: Forms and Performances', *International Social Science Journal* 52: 219–33.

Pakulski, Jan, and Malcolm Walters. 1996. *The Death of Class*. London: Sage.

Paletta, Anna. 1992. 'Today's Extended Families', *Canadian Social Trends* (Winter): 26–8.

Palmer, S. 2004. *Aliens Adored: Rael's UFO Religion*. New Brunswick, NJ: Rutgers University Press.

Palys, T. 1986. 'Testing the Common Wisdom: The Social Content of Video Pornography', *Canadian Psychology* 27: 22–35.

Palys, T., and J. Lowman. 2000. 'Protecting Research Participant Confidentiality: Toward a Research Participant Shield Law', *Canadian Journal of Law and Society* 21, 1: 163–85.

Pampel, Fred C. 1998. *Aging, Social Inequality, and Public Policy*. Thousand Oaks, Calif.: Pine Forge.

Pandey, Sanjay K., and Stuart I. Bretschneider. 1997. 'The Impact of Red Tape's Administrative Delay on Public Organizations' Interest in New Information Technologies', *Journal of Public Administration Research and Theory* 7: 113–30.

Park, Kristin. 2002. 'Stigma Management among the Voluntarily Childless', *Sociological Perspectives* 45, 1: 21–45.

Park, Robert E. 1925. 'The City: Suggestions for the Investigation of Human Behavior in the Urban Environment', in Park et al. (1925: 1–46).

——— and Ernest Burgess. 1921. *Introduction to the Science of Sociology*. Chicago: University of Chicago Press.

———, ———, and Roderick D. McKenzie, eds. 1925. *The City*. Chicago: University of Chicago Press.

Parsons, Talcott. 1949. *Essays in Sociological Theory*. New York: Free Press.

———. 1951. *The Social System*. Glencoe, Ill.: Free Press.

———. 1955. *Family, Socialization and Interaction Process*. New York: Free Press.

————. 1959. 'The School Class as a Social System: Some of Its Functions in American Society', *Harvard Educational Review* 29: 297–318.

———— and Robert F. Bales. 1955. *Family Socialization and Interaction Process*. New York: Free Press.

Pearce, Frank, and Laureen Snider, eds. 1995. *Corporate Crime: Contemporary Debates*. Toronto: University of Toronto Press.

Peers, Frank W. 1979. *The Public Eye: Television and the Politics of Canadian Broadcasting, 1952–1968*. Toronto: University of Toronto Press.

Pendakur, Manjunath. 1990. *Canadian Dreams and American Control: The Political Economy of the Canadian Film Industry*. Detroit: Wayne State University Press.

Penha-Lopes, Vania. 2006. '"To Cook, Sew, to Be a Man": The Socialization for Competence and Black Men's Involvement in Housework', *Sex Roles* 54, 3/4: 261–74.

Petersen, William. 1989. 'Marxism and the Population Question: Theory and Practice', *Population and Development Review* 14 (suppl.): 77–101.

Peterson, Richard A. 1994. 'Culture Studies through the Production Perspective: Progress and Prospects', in Diana Crane, ed., *The Sociology of Culture: Emerging Theoretical Perspectives*. Oxford: Blackwell, 163–89.

Pfohl, Stephen J. 1977. 'The Discovery of Child Abuse', *Social Problems* 24: 310–23.

Pfuhl, Erdwin H., and Stuart Henry. 1993. *The Deviance Process*, 3rd edn. New York: Aldine de Gruyter.

Pickard, Victor W. 2006. 'Assessing the Radical Democracy of Indymedia: Discursive, Technical, and Institutional Constructions', *Critical Studies in Media Communication* 23, 1: 19–38.

Picot, Garnett, and John Myles. 1995. *Social Transfers, Changing Family Structure, and Low Income among Children*. Ottawa: Statistics Canada.

Piliavin, Erving, and S. Briar. 1964. 'Police Encounters with Juveniles', *American Journal of Sociology* 70: 206–14.

Plumwood, Val. 1992. 'Feminism and Ecofeminism: Beyond the Dualistic Assumptions of Women, Men and Nature', *Ecologist* 22, 1: 8–13.

Polanyi, Karl. 2001. *The Great Transformation: The Political and Economic Origins of Our Time*. Boston: Beacon Press.

Pomerleau, Andrée, Daniel Bolduc, Gerard Malcuit, and Louise Cossess. 1990. 'Pink or Blue: Environmental Gender Stereotypes in the First Two Years of Life', *Sex Roles* 22: 359–67.

Population Reference Bureau (PRB). 2008. *World Population Data Sheet for 2006*. Washington: PRB.

Porter, John. 1965. *The Vertical Mosaic: An Analysis of Social Class and Power in Canada*. Toronto: University of Toronto Press.

Potuchek, Jean L. 1997. *Who Supports the Family: Gender and Breadwinning in Dual-Earner Marriages*. Stanford, Calif.: Stanford University Press.

Poulantzas, Nicos. 1975. *Classes in Contemporary Capitalism*, trans. David Fernbach. London: New Left Books.

————. 1978. *State, Power, Socialism*, trans. Patrick Camiller. London: New Left Books.

Pratt, T.C., and T.W. Godsey. 2003. 'Social Support, Inequality, and Homicide: A Cross-National Test of an Integrated Theoretical Model', *Criminology* 41 (3): 611–644.

Press, Andrea L. 1991. *Women Watching Television: Gender, Class, and Generation in the American Television Experience*. Philadelphia: University of Pennsylvania Press.

Preston, Samuel H. 1986b. 'Mortality and Development Revisited', *United Nations Population Bulletin* 18: 34–40.

Pringle, Rosemary. 1988. *Secretaries Talk: Sexuality, Power and Work*. London: Verso.

Prus, Robert. 1987. 'Generic Social Processes: Maximizing Conceptual Development in Ethnographic Research', *Journal of Contemporary Ethnography* 16: 250–93.

Pryor, Jan, and Bryan Rodgers. 2001. *Children in Changing Families: Life after Parental Separation*. Oxford: Blackwell.

Putney, Norella, and Vern Bengtson. 2003. 'Socialization and the Family Revisited', in Richard Settersten, ed., *Invitation to the Life Course*. Amityville, NY: Baywood, 165–94.

Quadagno, Jill. 1990. 'Race, Class, and Gender in the US Welfare State', *American Sociological Review* 55: 25–7.

Raboy, Marc. 1990. *Missed Opportunities: The Story of Canada's Broadcasting Policy*. Montreal: McGill-Queen's University Press.

————. 1995. 'The Role of Public Consultation in Shaping the Canadian Broadcasting System', *Canadian Journal of Political Science* 28, 3: 455–77.

Raines, J.C. 2002. *Marx on Religion*. Philadelphia: Temple University Press.

Ram, Bali. 1990. *New Trends in the Family: Demographic Facts and Figures*. Ottawa: Minister of Supply and Services Canada.

Ramirez, Francisco O. 1981. 'Comparative Social Movements', *International Journal of Comparative Sociology* 22: 3–21.

Ramsay, Patricia. 1999. *Making Friends in School: Promoting Peer Relationships in Early Childhood*. New York: Teachers College Press, Columbia University.

Ranson, Gillian. 2005. 'Paid and Unpaid Work: How do Families Divide Their Time?', in Maureen Baker, ed., *Families: Changing Trends in Canada*, 5th edn. Toronto: McGraw-Hill Ryerson, 99–120.

Reid, S., ed. 2006. *Between the Worlds: Readings in Contemporary Paganism*. Toronto: CSPI/Women's Press.

Reinarman, Craig. 1996. 'The Social Construction of an Alcohol Problem', in Gary W. Potter and Victor E. Kappeler, eds, *Constructing Crime: Perspectives on Making News and Social Problems*. Prospect Heights, Ill.: Waveland, 193–220.

Reiss, Albert J., Jr. 1959. 'Rural–Urban and Status Differences in Interpersonal Contacts', *American Journal of Sociology* 65: 182–95.

Reiter, Ester. 1991. *Making Fast Food: From the Frying Pan into the Fire*. Montreal: McGill-Queen's University Press.

————. 1996. *Making Fast Food: From the Frying Pan into the Fryer*, 2nd edn. Montreal: McGill-Queen's University Press.

Rich, Adrienne. 1976. *Of Women Born: Motherhood as Experience and Institution*. New York: W.W. Norton.

Rifkin, Jeremy. 1995. *The End of Work: The Decline of the Global Labour Force and the Dawn of the Post-market Era*. New York: Putnam.

Rinehart, James. 2001, 2006. *The Tyranny of Work: Alienation and the Labour Process*, 5th edn. Toronto: Thomson Nelson.

————, Christopher Huxley, and David Robertson. 1994. 'Worker Commitment and Labour–Management Relations under Lean Production at CAMI', *Industrial Relations* 49: 750–75.

Roberts, Barbara. 1988. *Whence They Came: Deportation from Canada, 1900–1935*. Ottawa: Ottawa University Press.

Robertson, Ann. 2001. 'Biotechnology, Political Rationality and Discourses on Health Risk', *Health* 5: 293–310.

Robertson, David, James Rinehart, Chris Huxley, Jeff Wareham, Herman Rosenfeld, A. McGough, and Steven Benedict. 1993. *The CAMI Report: Lean Production in a Unionized Auto Plant*. North York, Ont.: CAW Research, 1993.

Robinson, Tracy L. 2001. 'White Mothers of Non-White Children', *Journal of Humanistic Counseling, Education and Development* 40, 2: 171–85.

Rosen, Bernard C. 1956. 'The Achievement Syndrome: A Psychocultural Dimension of Social Stratification', *American Sociological Review* 21: 203–11.

———. 1959. 'Race, Ethnicity, and the Achievement Syndrome', *American Sociological Review* 24: 47–60.

Rosenberg, Sharon. 2003. 'Neither Forgotten nor Fully Remembered: Tracing an Ambivalent Public Memory on the 10th Anniversary of the Montreal Massacre', *Feminist Theory* 4, 1: 5–27.

Rosenthal, Carolyn J. 1985. 'Kinkeeping in the Familial Division of Labour', *Journal of Marriage and the Family* 47: 965–74.

Ross, David P., and Paul Roberts. 1999. *Income and Child Well-Being: A New Perspective on the Poverty Debate*. Ottawa: Canadian Council on Social Development.

———, Katherine J. Scott, and Peter J. Smith. 2000. *The Canadian Fact Book on Poverty 2000*. Ottawa: Canadian Council on Social Development.

Rossi, Alice. 1984. 'Gender and Parenthood', *American Sociological Review* 49: 1–18.

Rotermann, Michelle. 2001. 'Wired Young Canadians', *Canadian Social Trends* (Winter): 4–8.

Roy, Francine. 2006. 'From She to She: Changing Patterns of Women in the Canadian Labour Force', *Canadian Economic Observer* (June): 1–9.

Royal Commission on Aboriginal Peoples. 1996. *Report of the Royal Commission on Aboriginal Peoples*, vol. 3: *Gathering Strength*. Ottawa: RCAP.

Royal Commission on Equality in Employment. 1984. *Report*. Ottawa: Supply and Services Canada.

Royal Commission on the Status of Women. 1970. *Report on the Royal Commission on the Status of Women*. Ottawa: Information Canada.

Ruble, Diane N., and Carol Lynn Martin. 1998. 'Gender Development', in William Damon, ed., *Handbook of Child Psychology*, 5th edn. New York: Wiley, 933–1016.

Ryan, John, and William M. Wentworth. 1999. *Media and Society: The Production of Culture in the Mass Media*. Needham Heights, Mass.: Allyn and Bacon.

Saavedra, Marco Estrada. 2005. 'The "Armed Community in Rebellion": Neo-Zapatismo in the Tojolab'al Candas, Chiapas (1986–96)', *Journal of Peasant Studies* 32 (3–4): 528–554.

Sacco, Vincent F. 1992. 'An Introduction to the Study of Deviance and Control', in Sacco, ed., *Deviance: Conform-ity and Control in Canadian Society*. Scarborough, Ont.: Prentice-Hall, 1–48.

———. 2005. *When Crime Waves*. Thousand Oaks, Calif.: Sage.

——— and L.W. Kennedy. 2008. *The Criminal Event*, 4th ed. Toronto: Thomson Publishing.

Sachs, Wolfgang. 1991. 'Environment and Development: The Story of a Dangerous Liaison', *Ecologist* 21: 252–7.

Sadker, M.P., and Sadker D.M. 1991. *Teachers, Schools and Society*. New York: McGraw-Hill.

Sadovnik, Alan R., ed. 1995. *Knowledge and Pedagogy: The Sociology of Basil Bernstein*. Norwood, NJ: Ablex.

Salazar, Lilia P., Shirin M. Schuldermann, Eduard H. Schuldermann, and Cam-Loi Huynh. 2001. 'Canadian Filipino Adolescents Report on Parental Socialization for School Involvement', *Canadian Ethnic Studies* 33, 2: 52–76.

Salter, Liora, and Rick Salter. 1997. 'The New Infrastructure', *Studies in Political Economy* 53: 67–102.

Sassen, Saskia. 1991. *The Global City: New York, London, Tokyo*. Princeton, NJ: Princeton University Press.

Sasson, Theodore. 1995. *Crime Talk: How Citizens Construct a Social Problem*. Hawthorne, NY: Aldine de Gruyter.

Satzewich, Vic. 1991. *Racism and the Incorporation of Foreign Labour: Farm Labour Migration to Canada since 1945*. London: Routledge.

———, ed. 1998. *Racism and Social Inequality in Canada*. Toronto: Thompson Educational Publishing.

———. 1999. 'The Political Economy of Race and Ethnicity', in Li (1999: 311–46).

——— and Nikolaos Liodakis. 2007. *'Race' and Ethnicity in Canada: A Critical Introduction*. Toronto: Oxford University Press.

——— and Terry Wotherspoon. 1993. *First Nations: Race, Class and Gender Relations*. Scarborough, Ont.: Nelson.

Savoie, J. 2007. *Youth Self-Reported Delinquency, 2006*. Ottawa: Statistics Canada.

Scala, Francesca, Eric Montpetit, and Isabelle Fortier. 2005. 'The NAC's Organizational Practices and the Politics of Assisted Reproductive Technologies in Canada', *Canadian Journal of Political Science* 38, 3: 581–604.

Scarce, Rik. 1990. *Eco-warriors: Understanding the Radical Environmental Movement*. Chicago: Noble.

Schecter, Tanya. 1998. *Race, Class, Women and the State: The Case of Domestic Labour*. Montreal: Black Rose.

Schissel, Bernard, and Terry Wotherspoon. 2003. *The Legacy of School for Aboriginal People: Education, Oppression, and Emancipation*. Toronto: Oxford University Press.

Schnaiberg, Allan. 1975. 'Social Synthesis of the Societal-Environmental Dialectic: The Role of Distributional Impacts', *Social Science Quarterly* 56: 5–20.

Schnore, Leo F. 1958. 'Social Morphology and Human Ecology', *American Journal of Sociology* 63: 620–34.

Scott, Allen J. 2004. 'Hollywood and the World: The Geography of Motion-Picture Distribution and Marketing', *Review of International Political Economy* 11, 1: 33–61.

Scott, Marvin B., and Stanford M. Lyman. 1968. 'Accounts', *American Sociological Review* 33: 46–64.

Sears, Alan. 2003. *Retooling the Mind Factory: Education in a Lean State*. Aurora, Ont.: Garamond.

Seiber, Timothy, and Andrew Gordon. 1981. *Children and Their Organizations*. Boston: G.K. Hall.

Seljak, D. 1998. 'Resisting the "No Man's Land" of Private Religion: The Catholic Church and Public Politics in Québec', in D. Lyon and M. Van Die, eds, *Rethinking Church, State, and Modernity: Canada Between Europe and America*. Toronto: University of Toronto Press.

Seltzer, Judith, and Debra Kalmuss. 1988. 'Socialization and Stress Explanations for Spouse Abuse', *Social Forces* 67: 473–91.

Sennett, Richard. 1998. *The Corrosion of Character: The Personal Consequences of Work in the New Capitalism*. New York: Norton.

Settersten, Richard. 2003 'Socialization and the Life Course: New Frontiers in Theory and Research', in Settersten, ed., *Invitation to the Life Course*. Amityville, NY: Baywood, 39–40.

Sev'er, Aysan. 2002. *Fleeing the House of Horrors: Women Who Have Left Abusive Partners*. Toronto: University of Toronto Press.

Shelton, Beth Anne, and Juanita Firestone. 1989. 'Household Labor Time and the Gender Gap in Earnings', *Gender and Society* 3, 1: 105–12.

Shipley, H.E. 2008. 'Accommodating Sexuality? Religion, Sexual Orientation and Law in Canada'. Concordia University Graduate Conference Accommodating Religion? Community, Discourse, Definitions, 7 February.

Shively, JoEllen. 1992. 'Cowboys and Indians: Perceptions of Western Films among American Indians and Anglos', *American Sociological Review* 57: 725–34.

Siegel, M. 2005. *False Alarm: The Truth about the Epidemic of Fear*. New York: Wiley.

Silva, Elizabeth B., and Carol Smart, eds. 1999. *The New Family?* London: Sage.

Simmel, Georg. 1950a. 'The Metropolis and Mental Life', in Simmel (1950b: 400–27).

———. 1950b. *The Sociology of Georg Simmel*, trans. Kurt Wolff. New York: Free Press.

Simmons, Alan. 1998. 'Racism and Immigration Policy', in Satzewich (1998).

Simon, Julian, ed. 1995. *The State of Humanity*. Cambridge, Mass.: Blackwell.

———. 1996. *The Ultimate Resource 2*. Princeton, NJ: Princeton University Press.

Simon, William, and John Gagnon. 2003. 'Sexual Scripts: Origins, Influences and Changes', *Qualitative Sociology* 26, 4: 491–7.

Simpson, J.H. 2000. 'The Politics of the Body in Canada and the United States', in d. Lyon and M. Van Die, eds, *Rethinking Church, State and Modernity: Canada Between Europe and America*. Toronto: University of Toronto Press.

Singer, Dorothy, and Jerome Singer. 2001. *Handbook of Children and the Media*. Thousand Oaks, Calif.: Sage.

Singh, Kavaljit. 1999. *The Globalisation of Finance: A Citizen's Guide*. London & New York: Zed Books.

Sjoberg, Gideon. 1960. *The Preindustrial City: Past and Present*. New York: Free Press.

Sklair, Leslie. 1994. 'Global Sociology and Global Environmental Change', in Redclift and Benton (1994: 205–27).

Skocpol, Theda. 1979. *States and Social Revolutions: A Comparative Analysis of France, Russia, and China*. Cambridge: Cambridge University Press.

Smelser, Neil J. 1963. *Theory of Collective Behavior*. New York: Free Press.

Smith, Adam. 1976 [1776]. *An Inquiry into the Nature and Causes of the Wealth of Nations*, ed. W.B. Todd. Oxford: Oxford University Press.

Smith, C. 1991. *The Emergence of Liberation Theology: Radical Religion and Social Movement Theory*. Chicago: University of Chicago Press.

Smith, Dorothy. 1987. *The Everyday World as Problematic: A Feminist Sociology*. Boston: Northeastern University Press.

———. 1999. *Writing the Social: Critique, Theory, and Investigations*. Toronto: University of Toronto Press.

Smith, Philip. 2001. *Cultural Theory: An Introduction*. Oxford: Blackwell.

Smith, Raymond T. 1996. *The Matrifocal Family: Power, Pluralism and Politics*. New York: Routledge.

Smyth, Bruce, ed. 2004. *Parent–Child Contact and Post-Separation Parenting Arrangements*. Research Report #9. Melbourne: Australian Institute of Family Studies.

Smythe, Dallas. W. 1981. *Dependency Road: Communications, Capitalism, Consciousness, and Canada*. Norwood, NJ: Ablex.

Snow, David A., and Leon Anderson. 1993. *Down on Their Luck: A Study of Homeless Street People*. Berkeley: University of California Press.

———, E. Burke Rochford Jr, Steven K. Worden, and Robert D. Benford. 1986. 'Frame Alignment Processes, Micromobilization, and Movement Participation', *American Sociological Review* 51: 464–81.

Snowdon, Frank. 1983. *Before Color Prejudice: The Ancient View of Blacks*. Cambridge, Mass.: Harvard University Press.

Sommer, Robert. 1969. *Personal Space: The Behavioral Basis of Design*. Toronto: Prentice-Hall.

Sontag, Susan. 1978. *Illness as Metaphor*. New York: Farrar, Straus & Giroux.

Spector, Malcolm, and John I. Kitsuse. 1977. *Constructing Social Problems*. Menlo Park, Calif.: Cummings.

Spitzer, Steven. 1975. 'Toward a Marxian Theory of Deviance', *Social Problems* 22: 638–51.

Spreitzer, G.M., and S. Sonenshein. 2004. 'Toward the Construct Definition of Positive Deviance', *American Behavioral Scientist* 47, 6: 828–47.

Sprinkle, Annie. 1991. *Post Porn Modernism*. Amsterdam: Torch Books.

Statistics Canada. 1973. *Education in Canada 1973*. Ottawa: Statistics Canada.

———. 1992. *Census Metropolitan Areas and Census Agglomerations: Population and Dwelling Counts*. Ottawa: Statistics Canada.

———. 1993b. '1991 Census of Canada Highlights: Religion', *The Daily*, 1 June.

———. 1998a. *Characteristics of Dual-Earner Families 1996*. Ottawa: Statistics Canada.

———. 1998b. '1996 Census: Education, Mobility and Migration', *The Daily*, 14 Apr.

———. 2000. *Women in Canada, 2000: A Gender-based Statistical Report*. Ottawa: Minister of Industry.

———. 2001a. *Canada Year Book 2001*. Ottawa: Statistics Canada.

———. 2002b. *Perspectives on Labour and Income: Fact-Sheet on Unionization*. Ottawa: Statistics Canada.

———. 2003. '2003 General Social Survey on Social Engagement, Cycle 17: An Overview of Findings'. Catalogue number 89-598-XIE. Ottawa: Statistics Canada.

———. 2004a. 'Education at a Glance', *Education Quarterly Review* 9, 4: 53–8.

———. 2005. *Census of Population* (Table 9.1). Available at http://www.statcan.gc.ca/pub/63-224-x/2007000/5006463-eng.htm, accessed 24 November 2008.

———. 2005a. 'Back to School . . . by the Numbers', Statistics Canada Media Advisory, 29 Aug. At: www42.statcan.ca/smr08/smr08_009_e.htm.

———. 2005b. 'University degrees, diplomas and certificates awarded', *The Daily*, January 18. Ottawa: Statistics Canada. Available at http://www.statcan.ca/Daily/English/050118/d050118b.htm.

———. 2005c. 'Early Sexual Intercourse, Condom Use and Sexually Transmitted Diseases', *The Daily*, 3 May.

———. 2005d. 'Children and Youth as Victims of Violent Crime', *The Daily*, 20 Apr.

———. 2005f. *Income in Canada*. Catalogue no. 75-202-XIE. Ottawa: Minister of Industry.

———. 2006a. 'Television Viewing', *The Daily*, 31 Mar.

———. 2006b. 'Canadian Internet Use Survey', *The Daily*, 15 Aug.

———. 2006c. 'General Social Survey: Paid and Unpaid Work', *The Daily*, 19 July.

———. 2006d. 'Study: Changing Patterns of Women in the Canadian Labour Force', *The Daily*, 15 June.

———. 2006e. *Education in Canada: School Attendance and Levels of Schooling*. Ottawa: Statistics Canada Catalogue no. 97F0017XCB2001001.

———. 2006f. 'National Longitudinal Survey of Children and Youth: Early Reading Ability and Later Literacy Skills 1994/1995 to 2004/2005', *The Daily*, 5 Dec.

———. 2006g. *Canada Year Book*. Ottawa: Statistics Canada.

———. 2006k. *The Canadian Labour Market at a Glance, 2005*. Ottawa: Statistics Canada, Labour Statistics Division.

———. 2007a. *Population and Dwelling Counts, for Canada, Provinces, and Territories by the Statistical Area Classification, 2006 and 2001 Censuses—100% Data*. At: <www12.statcan.ca/english/census06/data/popdwell>.

———. 2007b. Employment and Immigration. At: <www41.statcan.ca/2007/30000/ceb30000_000_e.htm>.

———. 2007c. Employment and Immigration. At: <www41.statcan.ca/2007/50000/ceb50000_000_e.htm>.

———. 2007d. *Women in Canada: Work Chapter Updates, 2006*. Cat. no. 89F0133XIE. Ottawa: Statistics Canada.

——— and Council of Ministers of Education Canada (CMEC). 2000. *Education Indicators in Canada: Report of the Pan-Canadian Education Indicators Program 1999*. At: <www.cmec.ca/stats/pceip/1999/Indicatorsite/index.html>.

———. 2008. *Labour Force Survey, monthly* statistics. Tables 282-0087 and 282-0089. Ottawa: Statistics Canada. Available at http://www40.statcan.ca/l01/cst01/labr66a.htm.

———. 2008b. 'Income of Canadians', *The Daily*, May 5. Available at http://www.statcan.ca/Daily/English/080505/d080505a.htm.

Steeves, H. Leslie. 1987. 'Feminist Theories and Media Studies', *Critical Studies in Mass Communication* 4, 2: 95–135.

Steffensmeier, Renee. 1982. 'A Role Model of the Transition to Parenthood', *Journal of Marriage and the Family* 44: 319–34.

Stern, Nicholas. 2002. 'Keynote Address: A Strategy for Development', in Boris Pleskovic and Stern, eds, *Annual World Bank Conference on Development Economics 2001/2002*. Washington and New York: World Bank and Oxford University Press, 11–35.

Stevens, Daphne, Gary Kiger, and Pamela J. Riley. 2001. 'Working Hard and Hardly Working: Domestic Labor and Marital Satisfaction Among Dual-Earner Couples', *Journal of Marriage and Family* 63: 514–526.

Stevenson, Kathryn. 1999. 'Family Characteristics of Problem Kids', *Canadian Social Trends* 55 (Winter): 2–6.

Stewart, M.W. 2002. *Ordinary Violence: Everyday Assaults against Women*. Westport Conn.: Bergin and Garvey.

Stokes, Randall, and John P. Hewitt. 1976. 'Aligning Actions', *American Sociological Review* 1: 838–49.

Stone, Gregory P. 1981. 'Appearance and the Self: A Slightly Revised Version', in Stone and Harvey A. Farberman, eds, *Social Psychology through Symbolic Interaction*. New York: Wiley, 187–202.

Storey, Robert. 2002. 'From Capitalism to Socialism', unpublished paper, McMaster University, Hamilton, Ont.

Strange, Susan. 1996. *The Retreat of the State*. Cambridge: Cambridge University Press.

Strauss, Murray A., and Richard J. Gelles. 1990. *Physical Violence in American Families: Risk Factors and Adaptations to Violence in 8,145 Families*. New Brunswick, NJ: Transaction.

Street, Debra, and Ingrid Connidis. 2001. 'Creeping Selectivity in Canadian Women's Pensions', in Jay Ginn, Street, and Sara Arber, eds, *Women, Work and Pensions: International Issues and Prospects*. Buckingham, UK: Open University Press, 158–78.

Studwell, Joe. 2002. *The China Dream: The Quest for the Last Great Untapped Market on Earth*. New York: Atlantic Monthly Press.

Sugiman, Pamela. 1994. *Labour's Dilemma: The Gender Politics of Auto Workers in Canada, 1937–1979*. Toronto: University of Toronto Press.

———. 2001. 'Privilege and Oppression: The Configuration of Race, Gender, and Class in Southern Ontario Auto Plants, 1939 to 1949', *Labour/Le Travail* 47 (Spring): 83–113.

Supreme Court of Canada. 2004. *Reference Re Same-Sex Marriage*, 3 S.C.R. 698, 2004 SCC 79.

Sutherland, Edwin. 1947. *Principles of Criminology*, 4th edn. Chicago: Lippincott.

Syndicat Northcrest v. Amselem, 2004 SCC 47, [2004] 2 S.C.R. 551.

Synnott, Anthony, and David Howes. 1996. 'Canada's Visible Minorities: Identity and Representation', in V. Amit-Talai and C. Knowles, eds, *Re-situating Identities: The Politics of Race, Ethnicity and Culture*. Peterborough, Ont.: Broadview.

Szasz, Andrew. 1994. *Ecopopulism: Toxic Waste and the Movement for Environmental Justice*. Minneapolis: University of Minneapolis Press.

Tannenbaum, Frank. 1938. *Crime and the Community*. Boston: Ginn.

Tanner, Julian. 2001. *Teenage Troubles: Youth and Deviance in Canada*, 2nd edn. Toronto: Nelson.

Tannock, Stuart. 2001. *Youth at Work: The Unionized Fast-Food and Grocery Workplace*. Philadelphia: Temple University Press.

Tapscott, Don. 1998. *Growing Up Digital: The Rise of the Net Generation*. New York: McGraw-Hill.

Taras, David. 2001. *Power and Betrayal in the Canadian Media*, updated edn. Peterborough, Ont.: Broadview.

Tardy, Rebecca. 2000. 'But I Am a Good Mom: The Social Construction of Motherhood through Health-Care Conversations', *Journal of Contemporary Ethnography* 29: 433–73.

Tarrow, Sidney. 1988. 'National Politics and Collective Action: Recent Theory and Research in Western Europe and the United States', *Annual Review of Sociology* 14: 421–40.

———. 1998. *Power in Movements: Social Movements and Contentious Politics*, 2nd edn. New York: Cambridge University Press.

Tator, Carol, Frances Henry, and Winston Mattis. 1998. *Challenging Racism in the Arts: Case Studies of Controversy and Conflict*. Toronto: University of Toronto Press.

Taylor, Bron. 1991. 'The Religion and Politics of Earth First!', *Ecologist* 21: 258–66.

Teitelbaum, Michael S. 1975. 'Relevance of Demographic Transition Theory for Developing Countries', *Science* 2 (May): 420–5.

Ten Bos, Réné. 1997. 'Essai: Business Ethics and Bauman Ethics', *Organization Studies* 18: 997–1014.

Theodorson, George A. 1961. *Studies in Human Ecology*. New York: Harper and Row.

———. 1982. *Urban Patterns: Studies in Human Ecology*. University Park: University of Pennsylvania Press.

Thomas, Derrick. 2001. 'Evolving Family Living Arrangements of Canada's Immigrants', *Canadian Social Trends* (Summer): 16–22.

Thomas, Eleanor. 2006. *Readiness to Learn at School among Five-year-old Children in Canada*. Ottawa: Statistics Canada Catalogue no. 89–599–MIE no. 004.

Thompson, Warren S. 1929. 'Population', *American Journal of Sociology* 34: 959–75.

———. 1944. *Plenty of People*. Lancaster, Penn.: Jacques Cattel.

Thomson, Elizabeth, Sara McLanahan, and Roberta Curtin. 1992. 'Family Structure, Gender and Parental Socialization', *Journal of Marriage and the Family* 54: 368–78.

Thorne, Barry. 1982. 'Feminist Rethinking of the Family: An Overview', in Thorne with Marilyn Yalom, eds, *Rethinking the Family: Some Feminist Questions*. New York: Longman, 1–24.

———. 1990. 'Girls and Boys Together…But Mostly Apart: Gender Arrangements in Elementary School', in M. Kimmel and M. Messner, eds, *Men's Lives*, 3rd ed. Boston: Allyn and Bacon.

Thorns, David C. 2002. *The Transformation of Cities: Urban Theory and Urban Life*. New York: Palgrave Macmillan.

Tilleczek, K.C., and D.W. Hine. 2006. 'The Meaning of Smoking as Health and Social Risk and Adolescence', *Journal of Adolescence* 29, 2: 273–87.

Tilly, Charles. 1978. *From Mobilization to Revolution*. Reading, Mass.: Addison-Wesley.

———. 1998. *Durable Inequality*. Berkeley: University of California Press.

Titchkosky, Tanta. 2001. 'Disability: A Rose by Any Other Name? "People-First" Language in Canadian Society', *Canadian Review of Sociology and Anthropology* 38, 2: 125–40.

Tittle, C.R., W.J. Villemez, and D.A. Smith. 1978. 'The Myth of Social Class and Criminality: An Empirical Assessment of the Empirical Evidence', *American Sociological Review* 43: 643–56.

Tocqueville, Alexis de. 1945 [1835, 1840]. *Democracy in America*. New York: Vintage.

Tokar, Brian. 1988. 'Exploring the New Ecologies', *Alternatives* 15, 4: 31–43.

Tönnies, Ferdinand. 1957 [1887]. *Community and Society (Gemeinschaft und Gesellschaft)*. New York: Harper and Row.

Torres, Carlos Alberto. 1998. *Democracy, Education, and Multiculturalism: Dilemmas of Citizenship in a Global World*. Lanham, Md: Rowman and Littlefield.

Touraine, Alain. 1981. *The Voice and the Eye: An Analysis of Social Movements*. Cambridge: Cambridge University Press.

Tremblay, Manon. 1998. 'Do Female MPs Substantively Represent Women? A Study of Legislative Behaviour in Canada's 35th Parliament', *Canadian Journal of Political Science* 31: 435–65.

Tremblay, Richard E., Bernard Boulerice, Philip Harden, Pierre McDuff, Daniel Perusse, Robert Pihl, and Mark Zoccolillo. 1996. 'Do Children in Canada Become More Aggressive as They Approach Adolescence?', in Statistics Canada (1996b: 127–38).

Troyer, Ronald, and Gerald Markle. 1983. *Cigarettes: The Battle over Smoking*. New Brunswick, NJ: Rutgers University Press.

Tuggle, Justin L., and Malcolm D. Holmes. 1997. 'Blowing Smoke: Status Politics and the Shasta County Smoking Ban', *Deviant Behavior* 18: 77–93.

Turk, Austin T. 1976. 'Law as a Weapon in Social Conflict', *Social Problems* 23: 276–92.

Turner, Bryan S. 1988. *Status*. Minneapolis: University of Minnesota Press.

Turner, R. Jay, and William R. Avison. 2003. 'Status Variations in Stress Exposure: Implications for the Interpretation of Research on Race, Socioeconomic Status and Gender', *Journal of Health and Social Behaviour* 44, 4: 488–505.

Turner, Ralph. 1962. 'Role-Taking: Process versus Conformity', in Arnold Rose, ed., *Human Behavior and Social Processes*. Boston: Houghton Mifflin, 20–40.

United Nations. 1990. *The World's Women: Trends and Statistics*. New York: UN.

———. 1999. *The World at Six Billion*. New York: UN Dept. of Economic and Social Affairs, Population Division.

———. 2000a. *The World's Women. Trends and Statistics*. New York: UN.

———. 2006a. *World Population Prospects—The 2004 Revision. Volume III: Analytical Report*. New York: UN Dept. of Economic and Social Affairs, Population Division.

———. 2006b. *Urban Agglomerations 2005*. New York: UN Dept. of Economic and Social Affairs, Population Division. At: <www.un.org/esa/population/WUP2005/2005WUP_agglo.htm>.

———. 2006c. *World Urbanization Prospects: The 2005 Revision*. At: <esa.un.org/unup>.

United Nations Department of Economic and Social Affairs Population Division. 2007. *World Population Prospects. The 2006 Revision. Highlights*. New York: UN.

———. 2007a. *World Population Ageing 2007*. New York: UN.

United States, Bureau of Census. 2006. *International Data Base, 2006*. At: <www.census.gov/ipc/www/idbnew.html>.

Urmetzer, Peter, and Neil Guppy. 1999. 'Changing Income Inequality in Canada', in James Curtis, Edward Grabb, and Guppy, eds, *Social Inequality in Canada: Patterns, Problems, and Policies*. Toronto: Pearson Prentice-Hall, 75–84.

Ursel, Jane. 1992. *Private Lives, Public Policy: 100 Years of State Intervention in the Family*. Toronto: Women's Press.

Vanier Institute of the Family. 2004. *Profiling Canadian Families III*. Ottawa.

Veenstra, Gerry. 2001. 'Social Capital and Health', *Canadian Journal of Policy Research* 2: 1672–81.

Vold, George B., Thomas J. Bernard, and Jeffrey B. Snipes. 2002. *Theoretical Criminology*, 5th edn. New York: Oxford University Press.

Vorst, Jesse, et al., eds. 1991. *Race, Class, Gender: Bonds and Barriers*. Toronto: Garamond.

Vosko, Leah. 2000. *Temporary Work: The Gendered Rise of a Precarious Employment Relationship*. Toronto: University of Toronto Press.

———. 2003. 'Gender Differentiation and the Standard/Non-Standard Employment Distinction in Canada, 1945 to the Present', in Danielle Juteau, ed., *Patterns and Processes of Social Differentiation: The Construction of Gender, Age, 'Race/Ethnicity' and Locality*. Toronto: University of Toronto Press.

Wackwitz, Laura A., and Lana F. Rakow. 2004. 'Feminist Communication Theory: An Introduction', in Rakow and Wackwitz, eds, *Feminist Communication Theory: Selections in Context*. Thousand Oaks, Calif.: Sage, 1–10.

Wagley, Charles, and Marvin Harris. 1959. *Minorities in the New World*. New York: Columbia University Press.

Wagner, David. 1997. *The New Temperance: The American Obsession with Sin and Vice*. Boulder, Colo.: Westview.

Waksler, Frances. 1991. *Studying the Social Worlds of Children: Sociological Readings*. London: Falmer.

Walkom, Thomas. 1997. 'The Harris Government: Restoration or Revolution?', in Graham White, ed., *The Government and Politics of Ontario*, 5th edn. Toronto: University of Toronto Press, 402–17.

Wall, Sarah. 2008. 'Of heads and hearts: Women in doctoral education at a Canadian University', *Women's Studies International Forum* 31 (3): 219–228.

Waller, Willard. 1965 [1932]. *The Sociology of Teaching*. New York: Wiley.

Wallerstein, Immanuel. 1995. *Historical Capitalism with Capitalist Civilization*. London: Verso.

———. 2004. *World-System Analysis: An Introduction*. Durham and London: Duke University Press.

Walzer, Michael. 1983. *Spheres of Justice: A Defense of Pluralism and Equality*. New York: Basic Books.

Waring, Marilyn. 1996. *Three Masquerades: Essays on Equality, Work and Human Rights*. Toronto: University of Toronto Press.

Warren, Karen. 1990. 'The Power and Promise of Ecological Feminism', *Environmental Ethics* 12, 2: 125–46.

Waters, Lea, and Kathleen Moore. 2002. 'Predicting Self-esteem During Unemployment: The Effect of Gender, Financial Deprivation, Alternate Roles, and Social Support', *Journal of Employment Counseling* 39 (4): 171–199.

Watson, James. 2006. *Golden Arches East: McDonald's in East Asia*, Second Edition. Palo Alto, Calif.: Stanford University Press.

Weber, Max. 1958 [1904]. *The Protestant Ethic and the Spirit of Capitalism*, trans. Talcott Parsons. New York: Scribner.

———. 1978 [1908]. *Economy and Society*, trans. Ephraim Fischoff, eds Guenther Roth and Claus Wittich. Berkeley: University of California Press.

———. 1946 [1922]. *From Max Weber: Essays in Sociology*, trans. and ed. H.H. Gerth and C. Wright Mills. New York: Oxford University Press.

———. 1958 [1922]. *Essays in Sociology*, trans. H.H. Gerth and C. Wright Mills. New York: Oxford University Press.

Weeks, Jeffrey. 1993. *Sexuality*. London: Routledge.

———, Catherine Donovan, and Brian Heaphy. 1998. 'Everyday Experiments: Narratives of Non-heterosexual Relationships', in Elizabeth B. Silva and Carol Smart, eds, *The New Family?* London: Sage, 83–99.

Weinberg, E., and P. Deutschberger. 1963. 'Some Dimensions of Altercasting', *Sociometry* 26: 545–66.

Weiner, Gaby. 1994. *Feminisms in Education: An Introduction*. Buckingham, UK: Open University Press.

Weinfeld, Morton. 1988. 'Ethnic and Race Relations', in James Curtis and Lorne Tepperman, eds, *Understanding Canadian Society*. Toronto: McGraw-Hill Ryerson, 587–616.

Weis, David. 1998. 'Conclusion: The State of Sexual Theory', *Journal of Sex Research* 35, 1: 100–14.

Weitz, Rose, ed. 2002. *The Politics of Women's Bodies: Sexuality, Appearance and Behaviour*, 2nd edn. Oxford: Oxford University Press.

Welsh, Sandy. 1999. 'Gender and Sexual Harassment', *Annual Review of Sociology* 25, 1: 169–90.

Wepman, Dennis, Ronald B. Newman, and Murray B. Binderman. 1976. *The Life: The Lore and Folk Poetry of the Black Hustler*. Philadelphia: University of Pennsylvania Press.

Wertham, Frederic. 1954. *Seduction of the Innocent*. New York: Rinehart.

West, G. Page, III, and G. Dale Meyer. 1997. 'Communicated Knowledge as a Learning Foundation', *International Journal of Organizational Analysis* 5: 25–58.

Whitaker, Reginald. 1993. 'From the Quebec Cauldron to the Canadian Cauldron', in Alain-G. Gagnon, ed., *Quebec: State and Society*, 2nd edn. Toronto: Nelson Canada.

White, David Manning. 1950. 'The "Gatekeeper": A Case Study in the Selection of News', *Journalism Quarterly* 27: 383–90.

Whyte, William Foote. 1943. *Street Corner Society: The Social Structure of an Italian Slum*. Chicago: University of Chicago Press.

Wilkes, Rima. 2001. 'Competition or Colonialism? An Analysis of Two Theories of Ethnic Collective Action', Ph.D. dissertation, University of Toronto.

Williams, Christine, Patti Giuffre, and Kirsten Dellinger. 1999. 'Sexuality in the Workplace: Organizational Control, Sexual Harassment and the Pursuit of Pleasure', *Annual Review of Sociology* 25, 1: 73–93.

Williams, David R., and Chiquita Collins. 1995. 'U.S. Socioeconomic and Racial Differences in Health: Patterns and Explanations', *Annual Review of Sociology* 21: 349–86.

Williams, F.P., and M.D. McShane. 2004. *Criminological Theory*, 4th ed. Upper Saddle River, NJ: Prentice-Hall.

Willis, Paul. 1977. *Learning to Labour: How Working Class Kids Get Working Class Jobs*. Farnborough, UK: Saxon House.

Wilson, Susannah J. 1991. *Women, Families, and Work*, 3rd edn. Toronto: McGraw-Hill Ryerson.

Wimberley, Dale W. 1990. 'Investment Dependence and Alternative Explanations of Third World Mortality', *American Sociological Review* 55: 75–91.

Wirth, Louis. 1938. 'Urbanism as a Way of Life', *American Journal of Sociology* 44: 1–24.

Witz, Anne. 1992. *Professions and Patriarchy*. London: Routledge.

Wolfe, David A., and Meric S. Gertler. 2001. 'The New Economy: An Overview', discussion paper produced for the Social Sciences and Humanities Research Council of Canada.

Wolfgang, Marvin, and Franco Ferracuti. 1967. *The Subculture of Violence: Towards an Integrated Theory in Criminology*. Beverly Hills, Calif.: Sage.

Wolford, Wendy. 2008. 'Environmental Justice and the Construction of Scale in Brazilian Agriculture', *Society and Natural Resources* 21 (7): 641–55.

Wollstonecraft, Mary. 1986 [1792]. *Vindication of the Rights of Women*. Middlesex, UK: Penguin.

Woodhead, Linda. 2007. 'Religion as Normative, Spirituality as Fuzzy: Questioning some Deep Assumptions in the Sociology of Religion', paper presented at SISR/ISSR, Zagreb.

Woodiwiss, M. 2005. *Gangster Capitalism*. New York: Caroll and Graff.

Woods, James, with Jay Lucas. 1993. *The Corporate Closet: The Professional Lives of Gay Men in America*. New York: Free Press.

Woods, Peter. 1979. *The Divided School*. London: Routledge & Kegan Paul.

Woolmington, Eric. 1985. 'Small May Be Inevitable', *Australian Geographical Studies* 23: 195–207.

World Bank. 2005. *World Development Indicators*. Washington: World Bank.

World Commission on Environment and Development. 1987. *Our Common Future*. New York: Oxford University Press.

World Health Organization (WHO). 2003. 'WHO Definition of Health'. At: <www.who.int/about/definition/en/>.

———. 2008. 'Sexual Health'. Available at http://www.who.int/topics/sexual_health/en/.

Wortley, Scott. 1999. 'A Northern Taboo: Research on Race, Crime and Criminal Justice in Canada', *Canadian Journal of Criminology* 41: 261–74.

Wotherspoon, Terry. 2004. *The Sociology of Education in Canada: Critical Perspectives*, 2nd edn. Toronto: Oxford University Press.

Wright, Charles R. 1959. *Mass Communication: A Sociological Perspective*. New York: Random House.

Wright, Erik Olin. 1983. *Class, Crisis and the State*. London: Verso.

———. 1985. *Classes*. London: Verso.

———. 1997. *Class Counts: Comparative Studies in Class Analysis*. Cambridge: Cambridge University Press.

———. 1999. 'Foundations of Class Analysis: A Marxist Perspective', paper presented at the annual meeting of the American Sociological Association.

Wrong, Dennis. 1961. 'The Oversocialized Concept of Man in Modern Sociology', *American Sociological Review* 26: 183–93.

Young, David. 2004. 'The Promotional State and Canada's Juno Awards', *Popular Music* 23, 3: 271–89.

———. 2006. 'Ethno-racial Minorities and the Juno Awards', *Canadian Journal of Sociology* 31, 2: 183–210.

———. 2008 'Why Canadian Content Regulations Are Needed to Support Canadian Music', in Charlene Elliott and Joshua Greenberg, eds, *Communications in Question: Canadian Perspectives on Controversial Issues in Communication Studies*. Scarborough, Ont.: Thomson Nelson.

Zang, Xiaowei. 1998. 'Elite Transformation and Recruitment in Post-Mao China', *Journal of Political and Military Sociology* 26, 1: 39–57.

Zawilski, Valerie, and Cynthia Levine-Rasky. 2005. *Inequality in Canada: A Reader on the Intersection of Gender, Race, and Class*. Don Mills, Ont.: Oxford University Press Canada.

Zola, Irving Kenneth. 1972. 'Medicine as an Institution of Social Control', *Sociological Review* 20: 487–504.

Zucker, Lynne G., Michael R. Darby, Marilynn B. Brewer, and Yusheng Peng. 1996. 'Collaboration Structure and Information Dilemmas in Biotechnology', in Roderick M. Kramer and Tom R. Tyler, eds, *Trust in Organizations: Frontiers of Theory and Research*. Thousand Oaks, Calif.: Sage, 90–113.

● Contributors ● ● ● ● ●

Patrizia Albanese, Associate Professor in the Department of Sociology, Ryerson University, is a recognized expert on families and childhood; she is also the co-director of the Centre for Children, Youth, and Families at Ryerson. Some of her current research involves a large survey and follow-up interviews with youth in military families, with a focus on risk and resiliency related to health problems brought on by parental transfers and placements. Recent publications include two chapters on Canadian families, a journal article (*Canadian Review of Sociology*), and two book chapters on child care in Quebec, and *Mothers of the Nation: Women, Family and Nationalism in 20th Century Europe* (U of T Press).

Cheryl Albas is part-time associate professor at the University of Manitoba. She has a continuing interest in higher education as it relates to university student life, where she is researching study types. Another area of interest is families and how the physical structure of households influences family interaction. In addition, she is involved in a long-term study of non-tenured faculty and the dynamics of knowledge production in university-based professional education. Her publications have appeared in *Handbook of Symbolic Interactionism* and the *Canadian Review of Sociology and Anthropology*.

Daniel Albas is professor of sociology at the University of Manitoba. His areas of interest include social psychology and non-verbal communication. He is currently studying university student study types and issues relative to academic integrity. His published works have appeared in a wide variety of national and international journals, including *Journal of Cross-Cultural Psychology*, *Sociological Quarterly*, *Symbolic Interaction*, and the *Canadian Review of Sociology and Anthropology*, and in *Handbook of Symbolic Interactionism*.

Bruce Arai is associate professor of sociology at Wilfrid Laurier University. His research interests are in the areas of economic sociology, environmental sociology, and the sociology of education. Recent publications have appeared in *Education Policy Analysis Archives*, the *Canadian Journal of Education*, the *Canadian Review of Sociology and Anthropology*, and *Organization and Environment*.

Maureen Baker is professor of sociology at the University of Auckland in New Zealand. From 1984 to 1990, she worked as a senior researcher in Ottawa for the Canadian Parliament specializing in policy issues relating to families, women, and children. Professor Baker is the author or editor of 13 books and over 60 articles on family trends, aging, adolescent women, cross-national family policies, women and work, and comparative restructuring. Her most recent books are *Families: Changing Trends in Canada, 6th edition* (in press); *Choices and Constraints in Family Life* (2007); and *Restructuring Family Policies: Convergences and Divergences* (2006). In 2008, she was named a Fellow of the New Zealand Academy of the Humanities.

Shyon Baumann is assistant professor of sociology at the University of Toronto at Mississauga. He works in the areas of the sociology of art, culture, and the media. His current projects include an analysis of the intersection of racial and gender stereotypes in advertising. His most recent publications are 'The Moral Underpinnings of Beauty: A Meaning-based Explanation for Light and Dark Complexions in Advertising' (2008); 'Democracy vs. Distinction: A Study of Omnivorousness in Gourmet Food Writing' (with Josee Johnston, 2007); 'A General Theory of Artistic Legitimation: How Art Worlds are Like Social Movements' (2007); and *Hollywood Highbrow: From Entertainment to Art* (2007).

Lori Beaman is Associate Professor, Department of Classics and Religious Studies, University of Ottawa and Canada Research Chair in the Contextualization of Religion in a Diverse Canada. Her work examines the ways in which we define religion, how these definitions are translated into interpretations of religious freedom, and the global implications of various definitions of religious freedom. Recent books include *Shared Beliefs, Different Lives: Women's Identities in Evangelical Context* (1999) and *Defining Harm: Religious Freedom and the Limits of the Law* (2008). Edited volumes include *Religion and Canadian Society: Traditions, Transitions and Innovations* (2006); *Religion, Globalization and Culture* (2007), edited with Peter Beyer; and with Beverly Matthews, *Gender in Canada* (2007).

Juanne Nancarrow Clarke, a medical sociologist at Wilfrid Laurier University, is the author of *Health, Illness and Medicine in Canada* (4th edn, 2004). One of her areas of research interest is the social construction of illness in the mass print media. Her current studies concern mass print media presentations of diseases such as cancer, heart disease, and AIDS, and their portrayal in magazines and newspapers directed to audiences that differ in gender, social class, ethnicity, and age. After her daughter Lauren was diagnosed with leukemia in 1995, Clarke researched parents whose children have cancer and has written a book, with her daughter, called *Finding Strength: A Mother and Daughter's Story of Childhood Cancer* (1999).

Randle Hart recently completed his PhD in the Department of Sociology at the University of Toronto. His co-authored articles on aging, immigration, cohabitation and marriage, and health have appeared in the *Journal of Marriage and the Family*, the *Journal of Family Issues*, *Social Biology, Research on Aging*, and the *International Journal of Sociology*. He is currently teaching at Southern Utah University.

Satoshi Ikeda is Professor, Department of Sociology and Anthropology, Concordia University, and Canada Research Chair in Political Sociology of Global Futures. He examines socially and ecologically sustainable alternatives to the current global economy and politics dominated by the USA and global corporations—research intended to contribute to our understanding of the problems with current globalization and how we could work toward socially and ecologically sustainable futures. He is completing work on an SSHRC Standard Research Grant for his project titled 'Trajectories of 150 Countries under Neoliberal Globalization' (2004–2008) and has recently authored or co-authored chapters in several recent books.

Nikolaos Liodakis is Assistant Professor, Department of Sociology, Wilfrid Laurier University. He is interested in quantitative analyses of class, gender, and nativity earnings differentials within selected ethnic and 'visible' groups in Canada, using Canadian census data. His research calls for a more integrationist examination of social inequality in Canada, the re-conceptualization of 'race'/ethnicity, and a more critical analysis of their interconnections with class and gender. He also examines the differential educational attainment of class and gender groups within foreign-born and native-born members of ethnic and racialized groups. Dr Liodakis has co-authored, with Dr Vic Satzewich of McMaster University, *'Race' and Ethnicity in Canada: A Critical Introduction*.

Neil McLaughlin is Associate Professor, Department of Sociology, McMaster University. The author of many refereed journal articles and one co-authored book, Professor McLaughlin's major research interests fall into four broad categories. One stream is concerned with developing a sociological theory and empirical research agenda on what has often been called the 'public intellectual'. Second, he has an interest in studying intellectual 'reputations'. Third, drawing from the sociology of science and culture as well as from classical and contemporary sociological theories, he is studying the sociology of creativity and its relationship to marginality. Finally, he is researching the sociology of sociology itself, in historical/comparative context.

Julie Ann McMullin is associate professor in the Department of Sociology at the University of Western Ontario. Her research explores how class, age, gender, ethnicity, and race structure inequality in paid work and families. She is also the author of *Understanding Inequality: Class, Age, Gender, Ethnicity, and Race in Canada* (2003). Recent publications include 'Generational Affinities and Discourses of Difference: A Case Study of Highly Skilled Information Technology Workers' (with Duerden, C. and Jovic, E.) (2007) and 'Ageing, Disability, and Workplace Accommodations' (2006).

William Michelson, Professor Emeritus, is former S.D. Clark Professor of Sociology at the University of Toronto. His long-standing research interests focus on how people's everyday contexts, such as housing and urban infrastructure, bear on their lives and life chances. His publications include *Man and His Urban Environment: A Sociological Approach* (2nd edn, 1976), *Environmental Choice, Human Behavior, and Residential Satisfaction* (1977), *From Sun to Sun: Daily Obligations and Community Structure in the Lives of Employed Women* (1985), and the *Handbook of Environmental Sociology* (2002, co-edited by Riley Dunlap), and *Time Use: Expanding Explanation in the Social Sciences* (2006). In 1994, he was elected to the Royal Society of Canada.

Antony Puddephatt is Assistant Professor, Department of Sociology, Lakehead University. His recent articles include 'George Herbert Mead's Sociology of Scientific Knowledge' (forthcoming); 'Incorporating Ritual into Greedy Institution Theory: The Case of Devotion in Organized Chess' (2007), and 'Special: An Interview with Kathy Charmaz: On Constructing Grounded Theory' (2006). His co-edited book, with William Shaffir and Steven Kleinknecht, *Ethnographies Revisited: The Stories Behind the Stories*, is in preparation.

Vincent Sacco is professor in and former chair of the Department of Sociology, Queen's University. Before coming to Queen's, he was a member of the faculty of the School of Criminology at Simon Fraser University. His research interests relate to the causes of criminal victimization and media images of crime and deviance. His recent publications include several co-authored books, such as *Crime Victims in Context* (1998), and *Advances in Criminological Theory* (2001), as well as several articles in the *International Journal of Law and Psychiatry* and *Criminologie*.

Peter R. Sinclair is University Research Professor at Memorial University of Newfoundland. His current research is in global commodity systems and local restructuring, information technology occupations, timber dependency in rural Alabama and western Newfoundland, and interdisciplinary ecosystems theory. He is author of *From Traps to Draggers: Domestic Commodity Production in Northwest Newfoundland, 1850–1982* (1985) and *State Intervention and the Newfoundland Fisheries* (1987), as well as co-author of many books, including *When the Fish Are Gone: Ecological Disaster and Fishers of Northwest Newfoundland* (1997).

Pamela Sugiman is Professor in the Department of Sociology at Ryerson University. Her research is largely in gender studies, women's history in Canada, the history of Japanese Canadians, oral history, memory, labour, work, and racialization. She is the author of *Labour's Dilemma: The Gender Politics of Auto Workers in Southern Ontario, 1939-79* (1994). Her research has led to many published articles in journals such as *The Canadian Journal of Sociology, Canadian Ethnic Studies, Atlantis, Studies in Political Economy, Labour Le Travail, Histoire Sociale/ Social History, Oral History,* and *The Journal of American Ethnic History*. From 2007–08, she served as President of the Canadian Sociological Association (CSA).

Lorne Tepperman, professor of sociology at the University of Toronto, applies sociology to the study of families, social problems, and deviance—and has recently been applying sociology to problem gambling (where the three topics of interest converge). His books on family include *Lives of Their Own: The Individualization of Adult Women's Lives* (1993), *Next of Kin: An International Reader on Changing Families* (1993), *The Futures of the Family* (1995), and *Close Relations: An Introduction to the Sociology of Families* (2000, 2004, 2007). His most recent book

on families is *Betting Their Lives: The Close Relations of Problem Gamblers* (2009). He has received the Outstanding Contributions Award from the Canadian Sociology Association for his research contributions to sociology, and has served as CSA President and as Director of the Health Studies Program, University of Toronto.

Frank Trovato is professor of sociology at the University of Alberta, where he teaches introductory and advanced courses in demography and population studies. His research topics span diverse aspects of demography and sociology: fertility, nuptiality, internal migration, immigrant health and mortality, sex and marital status differentials in mortality, and the social demography of racial, immigrant, and ethnic groups. Professor Trovato also reviews extensively for journals in the areas of population and general sociology, has served on the editorial boards of *Social Forces* and *Sociological Perspectives*, and is a former editor of *Canadian Studies in Population*. Two recent works are *Canada's Population in a Global Context: An Introduction to Social Demography* (2008); and, with N.M. Lalu, 'From Divergence to Convergence: The Sex Differential in Life Expectancy in Canada' (2007).

John Veugelers is associate professor in the Department of Sociology at the University of Toronto. His previous research has focused on immigration politics and right-wing extremism in Canada and Europe, with recent articles appearing in *Current Sociology, Sociological Quarterly*, and the *Canadian Review of Sociology and Anthropology*. Under a project funded by the Social Sciences and Humanities Research Council of Canada, he is currently studying the politics of French repatriates from colonial North Africa. He was the recipient of an Outstanding Teaching Award from the University of Toronto in 2001. He continues to study right-wing politics in Western Europe, especially France and Italy.

G. Keith Warriner is associate professor and chair of the Department of Sociology, University of Waterloo. Dr Warriner's major research interests concern natural resources and environmental sociology, as well as research methods and statistics. His studies have examined energy conservation, the west coast commercial fishing industry, adaptation to change by Ontario tobacco farmers, public participation in environmental decision-making, and grassroots environmental protest. His recent publications have investigated issues of environmental justice, urban dispersion and the housing preferences of city-dwellers, and bias contained in the measurement of socio-economic status by surveys.

Sue Wilson teaches in the School of Nutrition and is the associate dean of the Faculty of Community Services at Ryerson University. Her research interests include women's work, women's health, women at mid-life, students with dependent care responsibilities, the long-term effects of job loss, and breast cancer and spirituality. She has published several textbooks, including *Women, Work and Families* (4th edn, 1996), and several co-authored introductory and family sociology texts. Her most recent publication is *Connection, Compromise, and Control: Canadian Women Discuss Midlife* (2008), co-authored with York University sociologists Nancy Mandell and Ann Duffy.

Terry Wotherspoon is professor of sociology and head of the Department of Sociology at the University of Saskatchewan, where he has worked since 1986. As well as several years of teaching experience at elementary, secondary, and post-secondary levels, he has engaged in research and published widely on issues related to education, social policy, indigenous peoples, and social inequality in Canada. Among his many publications, he is co-author or co-editor of *First Nations: Race, Class and Gender Relations* (1993), *Multicultural Education in a Changing Global Economy: Canada and the Netherlands* (1995), and *The Legacy of School for Aboriginal People: Education, Oppression, and Emancipation* (2003). He currently serves as Chair of the Board of Governors of the Prairie Metropolis Centre, and is Managing Editor of the *Canadian Review of Sociology*.

David Young is Assistant Professor, Department of Sociology, McMaster University. He teaches courses in mass media and popular culture and has mainly published in these areas. Some recent publications include 'Ethno-racial Minorities and the Juno Awards', (2005), 'The CBC and the Juno Awards' (2005), and 'The Promotional State and Canada's Juno Awards' (2004).

● Index ● ● ● ●